Reginald R. Sharpe

London and the kingdom

a history derived mainly from the archives at Guildhall in the custody of the

corporation of the city of London

Reginald R. Sharpe

London and the kingdom

a history derived mainly from the archives at Guildhall in the custody of the corporation of the city of London

ISBN/EAN: 9783742855640

Manufactured in Europe, USA, Canada, Australia, Japa

Cover: Foto ©ninafisch / pixelio.de

Manufactured and distributed by brebook publishing software (www.brebook.com)

Reginald R. Sharpe

London and the kingdom

CONTENTS.

CHAPTER XXXV.

Accession of George I.—The Old Pretender.—Impeachment of Ministers.—Tory re-action.—End of Jacobite Rebellion.—The King's Picture and Statue.—The Septennial Act.—Trial of the Earl of Oxford.—Disputed Elections.—The right of the City to discharge law costs incurred in Elections over the Chamber, questioned.—Paying "Scot" defined.—An Alderman insulted by the Military.—The South Sea Company.—Supremacy of Walpole.—Fears of another Jacobite rising.—The Election Act, 11 George I, c. 18.—Death of the King. Page 1

CHAPTER XXXVI.

Accession of George II.—Walpole and the Queen.—Dissenters and the Corporation and Test Acts.—Walpole's Excise Bill.—Unpopularity of Billers, Mayor.—Disputes with Spain.—Jenkin's ear.—The Spanish Convention.—"Leonidas" Glover.—War with Spain declared.—Capture of Porto Bello.—George Heathcote.—The Aldermanic Veto again.—Resignation of Walpole.—War declared with France.—The Young Pretender.—"Black Friday."—The Victory of Culloden.—City Address.—Treaty of Aix-la-Chapelle.—The Newcastle Administration.—The National Militia Bill.—A tax on Plate.—The loss of Minorca.—Newcastle succeeded by Pitt.—Execution of Byng.—Civic honours for Pitt and Legge.—Coalition of Pitt and Newcastle.—Conquest of Canada.   *Page 31*

CHAPTER XXXVII.

Accession of George III.—The fall of Pitt.—Alderman Beckford.—Unpopularity of Bute.—The King and Queen at the Guildhall.—John Wilkes.—War with Spain.—The Peace of Paris.—Resignation of Bute.—Wilkes and the "North Briton."—No. 45 burnt at the Royal Exchange.—Conduct of the Lord Mayor.—Wilkes's "Essay on Woman."—Wilkes Expelled the House.—Is outlawed.—Pitt created Earl of Chatham, proposes to bring in an East India Bill.—Wilkes's letters to the Duke of Grafton, is elected M.P. for Middlesex.—Committed to the King's Bench.—Sentence pronounced.—Wilkes elected Alderman.—Again expelled the House.—Is thrice elected for Middlesex and thrice rejected.—Colonel Luttrell usurps his Seat.—Remonstrance of the Livery.—The City and Lord Holland.—Beckford's second Mayoralty.—Another remonstrance of the Livery.—The remonstrance approved by "Junius."—Condemned by the Goldsmiths, Weavers and Grocers.—The King hesitates to receive it as being "entirely new."—Consults Lord North.—Consents to receive it on the Throne.—The remonstrance condemned by Parliament.—Beckford entertains the Opposition at the Mansion House.—Wilkes regains his liberty.—City address to the King.—Beckford's famous Speech.—Chatham's approval.—Vote of thanks to Chatham.—Beckford's death.   *Page 66*

CHAPTER XXXVIII.

Brass Crosby, Mayor.—The legality of Press Warrants.—The Freedom of the Press.—The Messenger of the

House of Commons arrested in the City.—His recognizance ordered to be expunged.—Crosby and Oliver before the House.—Committed to the Tower.—Chatham's opinion as to the conduct of the civic magistrates.—Bitter feeling against the Ministry.—Crosby and Oliver regain their liberty.—Another remonstrance of the Livery.—Received on the Throne—Wilkes and Bull, Sheriffs.—Wilkes and Junius join forces.—Parson Horne.—Nash elected Mayor.—Refuses to summon a Common Hall.—Sawbridge and Short Parliaments.—Townshend elected Mayor.—Riot at the Guildhall.—Address of the Livery in favour of Short Parliaments.—Wilkes declines to attend its presentation.—Claims his seat in the House.—The Recorder's opinion touching the rights of the Livery in Common Hall.—Plumbe's case.—Alderman Bull elected M.P. for the City.—England and America.—The Quebec Bill.—Wilkes elected Mayor.—Takes his seat as Member for Middlesex. Page 106

CHAPTER XXXIX.

Wilkes and his brother Aldermen.—Chatham and the City deprecate England's policy towards America.—The King notifies his intention of receiving no more Addresses of the Livery on the Throne.—Wilkes and the Lord Chamberlain.—New York appeals to London.—An Address of the Livery not received.—Address of the Common Council received in usual manner.—Address of the Livery to the Electors of Great Britain.—Ex-Sheriff Sayre committed to the Tower.—Expenses of Wilkes's Mayoralty.—Wilkes and the Chamberlainship.—Doctor Richard Price.—The Declaration of Independence.—The City and Press Warrants.—Alliance between France and America.—

The Death of Chatham.—His Funeral.—His Monument in the Guildhall. *Page 146*

CHAPTER XL.

Court Martial of Admiral Keppel.—The Freedom of the City conferred on Keppel.—Spain declares war.—Economical Reform.—Committees of Association.—Dunning's Motion.—The City accepts a Form of Association.—Sir George Savile's Act.—The Gordon Riots.—The City's petition for repeal of Savile's Act.—Dispute between Civic and Military Authorities.—Wilkes attacks the Lord Mayor in a violent speech in the House.—The City's claim for damages arising out of the Riots.—A New Parliament.—Alderman Bull and the Livery.—Another remonstrance of the Livery not received.—The fall of North's Ministry.—The City's congratulations to the King.—The first step taken towards Parliamentary Reform.—Alderman Harley.—The younger Pitt.—Rodney's Victory.—The relief of Gibraltar.—The Peace of Paris. *Page 172*

CHAPTER XLI.

Fox's East India Bill.—Pitt and the Coalition.—The City and Pitt.—Pitt's East India Bill.—The Reform Bill.—The City and the Shop Tax.—The Convention with France.—The City and the Slave trade.—Pitt's Regency Bill.—Thanksgiving service at St. Paul's for the King's recovery.—Pitt's Excise Bill for duty on tobacco.—The Military Guard of the Bank of England.—The French Revolution.—France declares war.—The Battle of the first of June.—Riots in the City.—Great scarcity of wheat.—Standard wheaten bread.—Assault on the King.—Negotiations for Peace.—Pitt's Loyalty Loan.—Foreign subsidies.—Suspension *of cash payments by Bank of England.—Another remonstrance of the Livery not received.—The Mutiny at the Nore.—Duncan's victory off Camperdown.—Pitt mobbed in the City.—Military associations in the City.—The Battle of the Nile.—Pitt's Income Tax Bill.—Royal review of City volunteers.—Capture of the Dutch fleet.—French overtures for peace declined.—The Livery protest against the prolongation of the war.—The Act of Union.—Bread riots in the City.—Conduct of Harvey Combe, Mayor.—Pitt resigns.—Battle of Copenhagen.—Peace of Amiens.* Page 204

CHAPTER XLII.

Resumption of hostilities.—Pitt recommends the fortifying of London.—Renewal of the Income Tax.—Nelson takes offence at the City.—Addington gives place to Pitt.—Volunteer review at Blackheath.—Pitt's Additional Force Bill.—The City claims to be treated in a separate Bill.—Artillery practice in Finsbury Fields.—The French camp at Boulogne.—Disgrace of Lord Melville.—The Battle of Trafalgar.—Nelson's funeral.—His monument in the Guildhall.—Death of Pitt.—The Ministry of all the Talents.—The fall of the Ministry.—The Duke of Portland.—The Berlin Decree.—The Peninsular War.—The Convention of Cintra.—The Scandal of the Duke of York.—The Walcheren Expedition.—The King's Jubilee.—The City urges an enquiry into the cause of recent failures.—Another remonstrance of the Livery not received.—The City opposes Wellington's annuity.—Sir Francis Burdett committed to the Tower.—Riots in the City.—Petition of the Livery to Parliament.—Petition dismissed.—Another Petition.—Ordered to lie on the table.—The King seriously ill.—The Regency Bill.—The Freedom of the City declined by the Prince

Regent.—An address of the Livery to the Regent not received.—Assassination of Spencer Perceval.—Battle of Salamanca.—The Shannon and the Chesapeake.— Treaty of Paris.—The Freedom of the City conferred on Wellington.—The City and the Slave trade.—The Battle of Waterloo. Page 251

CHAPTER XLIII.

The City opposes renewal of Income Tax.—Agricultural depression.—The First Corn Law.—Another address of the Livery not received.—Vagrants in the City.— The Spa Fields Riot.—Matthew Wood, Mayor.—City address to Regent on state of affairs.—Outrage on the Regent.—The City urges Parliamentary Reform.— The trial of Hone.—Parliamentary Elections.—The Manchester Massacre or "Peterloo."—The Six Acts.— Tumultuous proceedings in Common Hall.—Conduct of Sheriff Parkins.—Accession of George IV.—Addresses of sympathy to Queen Caroline.—The Queen's trial.—Matthew Wood at Brandenburgh House.— The Queen presents her portrait to the City.—The Queen attends at St. Paul's.—The City urges the dismissal of the King's Ministers.—The Queen's death.— Disgraceful scene at her funeral.—Riots at Knightsbridge.—Sheriff Waithman assaulted.—The City and the Holy Alliance.—Wild speculation followed by great distress. Page 292

CHAPTER XLIV.

The Repeal of Corporation and Test Acts.—The Catholic Emancipation Bill.—Accession of William IV.—The King's visit to the City postponed for fear of riot.— Resolutions respecting Reform.—Introduction of the first Reform Bill.—The Bill approved by the City.—

The Bill withdrawn and Parliament dissolved.—The Bill re-introduced.—Passes the Commons, rejected by the Lords.—City address and King's reply.—Political Unions formed.—Sir John Key re-elected Mayor.—The Freedom of the City voted to lords Grey and Althorp.—Resignation of the Ministry.—The City expresses dissatisfaction.—The Ministry recalled.—The Reform Bill passed.—The rights of the Livery saved.—Grand Entertainment at the Guildhall.—A retrospect.—The Enfranchisement of Jews.—The City's public spirit.—The abolition of Coal and Wine Dues.—The City and the Port of London. Page 326

CHAPTER XXXV.

Like her predecessor on the throne, Queen Anne died on a Sunday. A proclamation was immediately drawn up by the lords spiritual and temporal, assisted by the members of the Privy Council and the lord mayor, aldermen and citizens of London, announcing the accession of Prince George, the Elector of Hanover, and that same afternoon he was duly proclaimed at Temple Bar and elsewhere. The proclamation does not appear on this occasion to have borne the signature of the lord mayor or any of the aldermen.[1] *George I proclaimed king, 1 Aug., 1714.*

Some weeks elapsed before George arrived in England. Meanwhile the Common Council prepared an address which the lords justices, who held the reins of government until the king's arrival, transmitted to his majesty. The address was graciously received, and the king, who knew little or no English, sent word by the lords justices that the City might count upon his support. Both the Common Council and the Court of Aldermen were desirous of presenting addresses to the king in person soon after his arrival.[2] *City addresses to the new king.*

The 20th September being the day fixed for the king's passage through the city to St. James's Palace great preparations were made to give him a befitting reception. It was decided to adopt the same measures *The reception of George I by the City, 20 Sept., 1714.*

---

[1] Journal 56, fo. 130b; Repertory 118, fo. 357.
[2] Journal 56, fos. 132b, 150; Repertory 118, fo. 363.

as those taken for the reception of William III in 1697, after the conclusion of the Peace of Ryswick but with this exception, viz., that members of the Common Council should take the place in the procession of those who had either served or fined for sheriff.[1] The earl marshal, however, ruled that the common councilmen of London should neither ride nor march in the procession. The court thereupon appealed to the lords justices, but the result is not recorded.[2] On the day appointed the mayor and aldermen took up their station at the court-house on St. Margaret's Hill in Southwark. Cushions from the Bridge House were borrowed for the occasion, and the open space before the court-house was fenced with rail to prevent crowding.[3] His lordship was provided with a new crimson velvet gown, the city marshal's men with new liveries, and the city trumpeters with new cloaks.[4] The conduits ran with claret furnished by order of the Court of Aldermen. The erection of balcony stands was discouraged for fear of accidents, and for the same reason the firing of guns or *padreros* under the piazza of the Royal Exchange was forbidden.[5] At St. Margaret's Hill the king was welcomed by the Recorder, who read a congratulatory address on behalf of the citizens, after which the procession moved on towards the city, the Recorder taking up his position immediately in front of the mayor,[6] who rode bareheaded with the city sword in his hand.

[1] Journal 56, fos. 133-134b.
[2] Journal 56, fo. 150; Repertory 118, fo. 394.
[3] Repertory 118, fos. 389-391.   [4] *Id.*, fos. 368, 369, 384.
[5] Repertory 118, fos. 377, 381.
[6] This "indulgence" was granted by the lords justices, but was not to be drawn into precedent.—*Id.*, fo. 395.

Three days later (23 Sept.) the whole of the Common Council proceeded to St. James' to present their congratulations to the king on his safe arrival, and to assure him of their loyalty.[1] This assurance was opportune, for the country was being flooded with pamphlets advocating the claim of Prince James Edward, better known as the Pretender, to the throne, and a reward had been offered for the capture of the prince should he attempt to set foot in any of his majesty's dominions.[2] When Humphreys entered on his mayoralty in the following October he made himself especially active in putting a stop to the spread of seditious literature in the city, and for his services in this respect was heartily thanked by Secretary Townsend.[3]

Precautions against the Pretender.

On the 20th October the king was crowned,[4] and on the 29th, according to custom, he attended the lord mayor's banquet. The lord mayor was called upon to contribute the sum of £300, and each of the sheriffs the sum of £150 towards defraying the cost of the entertainment. The rest of the expenses were paid out of the Chamber.[5] So pleased was the king with the entertainment that he conferred a baronetcy upon the lord mayor. He also bestowed the sum of £1,000 for the relief of poor debtors.[6]

The king attends the lord mayor's banquet, 29 Oct., 1714.

By the end of the year all immediate danger appeared to have passed away, and Thursday, the

Thanksgiving service at St. Paul's, 20 Jan., 1715.

---

[1] Journal 56, fo. 150b.
[2] Proclamation dated 15 Sept., 1714.—*Id.* fo. 135b.
[3] Repertory 119, fo. 8.
[4] The City put in its customary claims, and the masters and wardens of the principal livery companies were appointed to assist the lord mayor in his duties.—Repertory 118, fos. 382–383.
[5] Journal 56, fos. 151b, 161b, 181b. [6] Maitland, i, 517.

20th January, 1715, was appointed to be kept as a day of solemn thanksgiving for the king's peaceful accession.[1] Once more the majestic but gloomy walls of St. Paul's contained a brilliant assembly of worshippers. King George attended the service accompanied by the royal family, and there, too, were the mayor, aldermen and sheriffs of the city seated in their accustomed places in the lower gallery on the south side of the altar, their wives and ladies being accommodated in the opposite gallery.[2]

<small>General Election, 1715.</small>

In the meanwhile the statutory period of six months—during which the parliament existing at the time of the demise of the crown was to continue to sit—had elapsed, and the last parliament of Queen Anne had been dissolved (13 Jan.), a new one being summoned to meet in March. Riots such as had occurred at previous elections were strongly deprecated by royal proclamation (11 Jan.), and a reward of £500 was offered for the discovery of the printer or publisher of a paper intituled "English advice to the freeholders of England," which had been freely circulated for the purpose of advocating the Pretender's claims.[3] The elections, which were hotly contested, resulted in the Whigs—the party already in power—obtaining a large majority. The City returned two aldermen, viz.: Sir John Ward, who had sat in the parliament of 1708 in the Tory interest, and Sir Thomas Scawen;[4] and two commoners, viz.: Robert Heysham and Peter Godfrey, of whom little

---

[1] Proclamation dated 6 Dec., 1714.—Journal 56, fo. 139b.

[2] Repertory 119, fos. 79–81.   [3] Journal 56, fo. 147b.

[4] Both aldermen had been knighted by George soon after his landing.—Maitland, i, 517.

is known. As delegates of the City, they were to carry out the City's instructions given to them under twenty-one heads. They were more particularly to cause an enquiry to be made as to the manner in which the Peace of Utrecht had been brought about.[1]

Similar instructions were drawn up by electors in other parts of the country, and so well were they carried out that as soon as the Houses met preparations were made to impeach Harley, Bolingbroke and the Duke of Ormond, for the part they had taken in the secret agreements made with the French during the negotiations for peace. Bolingbroke and Ormond immediately took fright and fled to France, where the former entered the service of the Pretender as secretary of state. Oxford, who alone stayed at home and faced the storm, was forthwith committed to the Tower. Impeachment of late Ministers, March, 1715.

Such high-handed proceedings on the part of the triumphant Whigs led to a Tory re-action. In spite of all precautions[2] riots broke out in the city on the 28th May, when the king's birthday was being kept with bonfires and illuminations. The next day (29 May), being the anniversary of the restoration of Charles II, there were more bonfires, and those who refused to light up their houses had their windows broken. A patrol of life guards was insulted and made to join in the cry "High Church and Ormond!" A print of King William III was publicly burnt in Smithfield, and the mob carried everything before them until stopt in Cheapside by ward constables and dispersed.[3] Tory re-action.

---

[1] Maitland, i, 518.   [2] Journal 56, fo. 164.
[3] Rapin's Hist. of England (continuation by Tindal), v, 424, 425.

Jacobite Conspiracy, July, 1715.

The Jacobites took advantage of the general disaffection that prevailed to push forward the conspiracy which had been set on foot at the close of the last reign. Ormond had up to the moment of his flight been busily engaged in organising it in England, while Bolingbroke had been no less busy in endeavouring to obtain the assistance of France. On the 20th July the king announced to the new parliament that he had received information of a projected invasion by the Pretender, which was abetted and encouraged by disaffected persons in this country.[1] Three days later (23 July) a similar announcement was made to the lord mayor by letter from secretary Townshend.

The City's loyal address.

Notwithstanding the recent riots to which the aggressive policy of the whigs had given rise, the respectable citizen remained true Hanoverian and staunch supporter of the established church. The municipal body were proud of the part they had taken in bringing about the "glorious" Revolution, and in later years took occasion more than once to remind George the Third that the House of Hanover owed its accession to the crown of England in no small measure to the citizens of London. As soon as the secretary's letter was communicated to the Common Council, they immediately drew up a loyal address, in which they assured the king that they entertained the utmost abhorrence and detestation of all who encouraged either openly or secretly the hopes of the Pretender, and promised their adherence to his majesty's person and government against the

---

[1] Journal House of Commons, xviii, 232.

Pretender and all other enemies to the king at home and abroad.[1]

An Act known in those days as the Proclamation Act, but better known at the present day as the Riot Act, investing magistrates with the power of compelling any number of persons exceeding twelve to disperse on pain of being held guilty of felony without benefit of clergy was passed (20 July, 1715),[2] whilst another Act authorising the appointment of commissioners for tendering the oaths of allegiance and supremacy, as well as the abjuration oath to all suspected persons, was passed a month later (20 Aug).[3] Pursuant to this last Act, commissioners were afterwards (5 Dec.) appointed for the purpose of administering the oaths in each city ward. The names of recusants were to be returned to the next quarter sessions and there enrolled.[4] Nor were the municipal authorities idle. The anniversary of the king's coronation (20 Oct.) was to have been celebrated in the city by a solemn procession with "effigies of several persons," and money had been collected for the purpose of defraying expenses. The mayor, however, hearing of this, issued a precept to the effect that although the promoters of the scheme might well have intended thereby to show their affection to his majesty's person and government "yet at this time, when the nation is

Precautionary measures.

[1] Journal 56, fos. 194b–195.

[2] Stat. 1 Geo., i, c. 5. Journal House of Commons, xviii, 232.

[3] Stat. 1 Geo., i, c. 13. "An Act for the further security of his majesty's person and government . . . and for extinguishing the hopes of the pretended Prince of Wales . . . ." *Id.*, xviii, 279.

[4] Repertory 120, fos. 50–70. Rolls of quarter sessions of this period containing the signatures of those who had not previously subscribed to the oaths are preserved at the Guildhall.

"alarmed by a rebellion, it is not thought convenient to be permitted, lest under that pretence many disaffected persons might gather together and raise tumults to the endangering of the public peace." The constables were accordingly instructed to prevent any meeting for the purpose, and to prevent all bonfires and illuminations.[1]

End of Jacobite rebellion, Feb., 1716.

These precautionary measures were taken not a whit too soon. The Earl of Mar, who had undertaken the organization of an insurrection in Scotland in favour of the Pretender, had already made himself complete master of that country as far as the Forth. He was, however, soon afterwards (13 Nov.) defeated by the Earl of Argyle at Sheriffmuir near Stirling, and although the Pretender himself appeared in Scotland before the close of the year, not another blow was struck, and in the following February (1716) Prince James stole back to France, leaving his army to shift for itself.

City address. 11 May, 1716.

The rebellion being thus put down, the Common Council unanimously resolved (11 May, 1716) to present another address to the king, in which after offering their congratulations upon the failure of the rebels to depose and murder his majesty, and to subvert the Church and State, they declared their resolution (1) as friends to monarchy to promote true zeal and loyalty towards his majesty's person, (2) as members of the Church of England to act up to its principles by submitting to the powers that be, and (3) by all possible means to prevent discord and support the Protestant succession. To this the king returned

[1] Repertory 119, fo. 386. Journal 56, fo. 203.

a gracious answer, and expressed his conviction that the example set by the City would have a good effect upon the nation.¹

The Council at the same time resolved to set up a statue of the king at the Royal Exchange as well as his picture in the Guildhall. The royal assent having been asked and obtained, Sir Godfrey Kneller was sent for to paint the portrait. Considerable delay took place in the execution of the work,² but the picture was at last completed and is still believed to grace the walls of the members' reading room at the Guildhall, although in 1779 it was reported to be so much decayed and torn as to be incapable of repair.³ The statue, if ever set up at the Royal Exchange, probably shared the fate of other statues erected there, and was destroyed in the fire of 1838.

The king's statue and picture.

Thursday, the 7th June (1716), was ordered by royal proclamation (8 May) to be kept as a day of public thanksgiving for the suppression of the rebellion. A sermon was preached at St. Paul's on the occasion. The members of the livery companies were desired to attend in their best gowns and hoods, at nine o'clock in the morning; this early hour being probably fixed so as not unduly to interfere with the business of the day.⁴

Thanksgiving service at St. Paul's, 7 June, 1716.

One of the immediate effects of the rebellion was the repeal of the Triennial Act (passed Dec., 1694), limiting the duration of parliament to three years. According to the provisions of this Act a new

The Septennial Act, April, 1716.

---
¹ Journal 56, fos. 217, 217b, 218b.
² *Id.*, fos. 217b, 218b, 270b. Journal 57, fo. 3b.
³ Journal 67, fo. 267.   ⁴ Journal 56, fos. 216b, 218.

parliament would have to be elected in 1718. The Whigs were afraid, however, to face the country and risk the return of a Jacobite majority. The ministers therefore proposed and parliament agreed that the existing parliament should continue for a term of seven instead of three years—a somewhat arbitrary proceeding on their part and only to be justified by the exigency of the time. The Septennial Act[1] was only intended as a temporary measure, but it has been found to work so well that it continues to this day to regulate the duration of parliaments, notwithstanding repeated efforts made by the City in general and by Alderman Sawbridge in particular to get it repealed.

The King and the Prince of Wales.

A few weeks later, parliament was prorogued (26 June, 1716) and the king paid a visit—often repeated during his reign—to his beloved Hanover, leaving his son, the Prince of Wales, as guardian of the realm and his lieutenant. Between father and son there was never any love lost, there was a sort of hereditary family quarrel, which in this case was brought to a climax in November of the following year over the christening of a babe. The court became split up into two distinct parts. The prince was ordered to quit St. James's and those who paid court to the prince and princess were for ever banished from the king's presence.[2]

Trial of the Earl of Oxford, June, 1717.

After remaining a prisoner in the Tower for nearly two years, the Earl of Oxford was at length, at his own request, brought to trial. The 13th June

---

[1] Stat. 1, Geo. i, c. 38.

[2] Rapin, History of England (contd. by Tindal) iv, 550.

(1717) was originally fixed as the day on which he was to appear at Westminster Hall, but this was afterwards changed to the 24th by desire of the House of Commons, who wished to put off the trial as long as possible. The lord mayor and sheriffs being directed by the House of Lords to take precautions for guarding the city's gates and preventing an unnecessary concourse of people resorting to Westminster, it was resolved to place double watch in the ward of Farringdon Without during the trial "as was done in the tryal of my Lord Winton and the like cases."[1] Fortunately for the earl, a dispute arose between the two houses on a question of procedure. The Commons were glad of the opportunity of backing out and declined to appear as his accusers, and the Lords thereupon ordered his discharge.[2]

For many years past the Corporation Act of 1661, had not been strictly enforced in the city. Such negligence laid the citizens open to pains and penalties. It was therefore deemed advisable towards the end of the next year (1718) to address the king on the subject and a petition was drawn up by the Court of Aldermen setting forth the apprehension of the petitioners of being "disquieted in the execution of "their offices by pretence of not subscribing a declara-"tion against the Solemn League and Covenant at "the time of their admission into their respective offices" according to the Statute. Such subscription they submitted had been generally disused, and the

<small>Act for quieting and establishing corporations (5 Geo. i, c. 6) 1718.</small>

---

[1] Repertory 121, fos. 250, 265, George Seton, the 5th Earl of Winton, had joined the rising of 1715. He was taken at Preston, and being brought to trial was condemned to death. He managed, however, to make his escape from the Tower and fled to France.

[2] Rapin iv, 541-545.

Act in that particular, disregarded. Nevertheless, the petitioners had behaved themselves in their offices with all duty and affection to his majesty and the government. They humbly prayed therefore that His Majesty would take such order as should effectually quiet their minds and enable them " to " proceed with cheerfulness in the execution of their " respective duties."[1] This petition was received very graciously by the king, who looked upon it as a mark of the City's trust and confidence in him. " I " shall be glad"—he said—"not only for your sakes, " but my own, if any defects which may touch the " rights of my good subjects are discovered in my " time, since that will furnish me with means of " giving you and all my people an indisputable " proof of my tenderness for their privileges, and " how unwilling I shall ever be to take advantage " of their mistakes."[2] His Majesty's assurance thus given was quickly followed by the passing of an Act for the purpose of relieving the City of London and other boroughs of any disabilities for their neglect in subscribing the prescribed declaration.[3]

<small>Disputed election in Tower Ward, 1717-1719.</small>

The reign of George I was marked not only with repeated disputes between the Court of Aldermen and the Common Council, but also with disputes over different municipal elections, until in 1725 matters were to a certain extent accommodated by the passing of the Election Act, 11 George I, c. 18. It had been the custom of the City, whenever the ruling of an alderman at a wardmote had been disputed, to defend the alderman's action when brought before a court of

---

[1] Repertory 123, fo. 17. [2] *Id.*, 123, fo. 19.
[3] Journal House of Commons, xix, 47.

law at the City's expense. The legality of this proceeding was now questioned. In December, 1717, when the annual elections for the Common Council came on, there had been a disputed election in Tower Ward, and the ruling of Alderman Sir Charles Peers had been called in question by Peter Bolton and Edward Bridgen, two unsuccessful candidates. The dispute engaged the attention of the Common Council and the law courts for a whole twelve-month, the expenses of the aldermen being defrayed by the City. In February, 1719, it reached the House of Lords, but before the matter came on for hearing a compromise was effected, the City agreeing to pay taxed costs.

The reason for this sudden change of attitude on the part of the City is doubtless to be found in a resolution of the House of Lords (17 Feb., 1719) to appoint a committee to examine and report what sums of money the City had expended out of its own chamber on this and similar causes, and what jurisdiction the Common Council exercised over elections of its members. The committee was authorized to carry its investigations as far back as they deemed proper, and to send for persons, papers and records. On the 17th April the committee made its report to the House. The Town Clerk and the City Chamberlain had attended the committee with the necessary warrants and minutes of proceedings, and it had been found that a sum of £2,827 10s. had been paid out of the City's cash for carrying on causes and suits at law relating to the elections of Aldermen and Common Councilmen since the 8th November, 1711.[1] As regards the claim of the Common Council to hear

---

[1] Journal House of Lords, xxi, 72, 145-147.

and determine matters in connection with elections of its own members, the committee found that it was based upon a resolution of the Court of the 9th January, 1641,[1] which resolution had been disclaimed (with many others) by Act of Common Council of 1683.[2]

Resolution of the House thereon.

The report having been read, the House passed a resolution to the effect that in maintaining suits at law between citizen and citizen in cases of disputed elections, the Common Council had "abused their "trust, and been guilty of great partiality, and of a "gross mismanagement of the city treasure, and a "violation of the freedom of elections in the city."

A protest entered.

So scathing an indictment against the City was not allowed to pass unchallenged. Sixteen peers entered a vigorous protest on the several grounds : (1) that no evidence had been taken on oath, and that without such evidence they conceived that so heavy a censure ought not to be passed on any individual, much less on so important a body as the Common Council of the city, which had done good service on pressing occasions; (2) that the Common Council had not had due notice given them; (3) that the resolution of the House might be construed as prejudging matters which might come before the House judicially; and lastly (4) that had the Common Council been heard they might have shown that the money had been expended in defence of their ancient rights and privileges, and in order to prevent any encroachment thereon.[3] That the dissentient Lords

---

[1] A mistake for 19th Jan., 1641-2. See Journal 40, fo. 16.
[2] Journal 50, fo. 32b.
[3] Journal House of Lords, xxi, 148, 149.

had reason on their side there can be little doubt. Nevertheless, some writers [1] whilst setting out in full the committee's report, as well as the returns made by the Chamberlain of money expended by the City on election suits, and the resolution of the House thereon, have entirely ignored the fact that a solemn protest was made against such resolution, and the reasons which urged the dissentients to make such protest.

In the meantime another disputed election had taken place. This time it concerned an alderman. The mayor had reported the case to the Court of Aldermen the day that the Lords appointed their committee to investigate the City's law costs. The case was shortly this. On the 9th January a wardmote had been held at Cordwainers' Hall, for the purpose of electing an alderman for the ward of Bread Street, in the place of Sir Richard Hoare, deceased. The show of hands for the respective candidates—Robert Baylis and Richard Brocas, both of them members of the Grocers' Company—had been so equal that the mayor had been unable to declare which had the majority. A poll had therefore been demanded, the result being declared by the mayor to be in favour of Brocas, and thereupon a scrutiny had taken place, with the same result.[2] The whole question turned upon the qualification of certain voters. Did they or did they not pay Scot, and in what did "paying Scot" consist? The matter having been argued before the Court of Aldermen by counsel on behalf of each candidate, the Court

What is "paying Scot?"

---

[1] See Maitland i, 521-525; Noorthouck, 312.
[2] Repertory 123, fos. 210-215.

came to the conclusion that paying Scot was "a general contribution to *all* public taxes," and at the same time declared Baylis to be duly elected.[1] The Common Council then attempted to interfere, but the Court of Aldermen would brook no invasion of their rights,[2] and although litigation continued well into the next year (1720) Baylis retained his seat in the Court.

An insult offered to an alderman on Lord Mayor's Day, 29 Oct., 1720.

On Lord Mayor's day (29 Oct.) 1720, an incident occurred worthy of a passing notice. From particulars laid before the Court of Aldermen (10 Jan., 1721) by a committee appointed to investigate the matter,[3] it appears that when the members of the Court of Aldermen were riding in their coaches towards the Three Cranes on the banks of the river, thence to attend the new lord mayor (Sir John Fryer) in his barge to Westminster, a certain ensign in the Second Regiment of the Guards—Thomas Hockenhull or Hocknell by name—who was in charge of a detachment of soldiers on their way to the Tower, thought fit to break through the aldermen's procession, and to bring Sir John Ward's coach to a sudden standstill, his horses being struck over the head by the soldiers' muskets. The affront was too serious to be passed over, and Sir John reported the matter to Secretary Craggs, who forwarded the alderman's letter to the Secretary at War, and at the same time expressed regret that such an incident should have happened.[4] Later on the officer himself appeared before the Court

---

[1] Repertory 123, fos. 223, 242.
[2] Journal 57, fo. 22b; Repertory 123, fo. 401.
[3] Repertory 125, fos. 149-156.
[4] Letter from Secretary Craggs to Alderman Ward "at his house upon Lambeth Hill," 8 Nov., 1720. Repertory 125, fo. 151.

of Aldermen bearing a letter from Sir George Treby to Alderman Ward to the effect that the officer had already received a reprimand, and would (he hoped) make a suitable apology. A written apology was read to the Court of Aldermen in which Hockenhull pleaded ignorance as to whose coach it was that had been stopped, and endeavoured to throw the blame on two of his soldiers, who he declared to be "a little in liquor." The officer being called in offered to make submission and to beg pardon, but the Court was not in the humour to accept his apology, and so the matter rested until the following January (1721), when upon Sir George Treby's intercession and Hockenhull's submission the Court agreed to pass the matter over. The Secretary at War was at the same time desired "that for the future the route for the Guards marching "to and from the Tower may be as usual through "Watling Street, and not through the high streets of "this city."

Sir John Fryer had been elected mayor at one of the most critical times in the history either of London or the kingdom, for his election took place just at the time of the bursting of the great South Sea bubble. The South Sea Company had been formed in 1711 by Harley, with the view of carrying on such trade with Spanish America as Spain might be willing to allow in the treaty which was then expected. When the Treaty of Utrecht was concluded Spain was found to have conceded the right of trading with America, but only to a limited extent. Nevertheless the idea got abroad that the company was possessed of a very valuable monopoly, and that the trade with Spanish America would enrich all who took part in it.

The South Sea Company, 1711-1720.

Accordingly the shares of the company were eagerly bought, and in a few years the institution began to rival the Bank of England itself. Early in 1720, when a scheme was propounded for lessening the National Debt, the company was in a position to outbid the Bank in buying up government annuities, and holders of such annuities were found only too ready to exchange them for shares in the company. The company next invited the public to subscribe new capital, and upwards of £5,000,000 were subscribed in an incredibly short space of time. The wildest speculation prevailed. Bogus companies sprang up in all directions, and no matter how ridiculous the purpose might be for which they were avowedly started, they always found subscribers. Men of all ranks, ages, and professions, nay ! women also flocked to Threadneedle Street (where stood the South Sea House) or to Change Alley, and the very streets were blocked with desks and clerks, and converted into counting-houses. The whole nation suddenly became stock-jobbers. Swift, writing of the ruin worked by the mad speculation of the day, thus characterises Change Alley, the centre of all the mischief :

> "There is a gulf where thousands fell
> Here all the bold adventurers came,
> A narrow sound, though deep as hell ;
> '*Change Alley* is the dreadful name."

The South Sea Company continued to maintain its pre-eminent position, and the value of its shares continued to rise until, in August, a £100 share was worth £1,000.

At last it brought about its own ruin in a way little anticipated. In an evil hour the directors commenced proceedings against the unlicensed, and therefore illegal, companies which had interfered with the great company's more legitimate business. The result was disastrous. One fraud after another was exposed. The nation suddenly recovered its senses. A panic arose as bubble after bubble burst. By the end of September, South Sea stock had fallen from £1,000 to £150, and at last, after an abortive effort to obtain assistance from the Bank of England, this biggest bubble of all collapsed, bringing thousands to beggary. Even the Bank of England itself experienced difficulty in maintaining its credit during the panic, and was compelled once more to resort to strategem. Payments were made in silver, and chiefly to persons who were in league with the bank, and who no sooner received their money than they brought it back. The money had of course to be re-counted, and by this means time was gained, and time at such a crisis, and to such an institution, meant literally money. On Michaelmas day the Bank according to the custom prevailing was closed, and when it opened again, the public alarm had subsided.[1]

A few—a very few—of those who had speculated in South Sea stock kept their heads, and got out before the bubble burst. Among these was Thomas Guy, the founder of Guy's Hospital, at that time carrying on business as a bookseller at the corner of Lombard Street and Cornhill—the "lucky corner." He made a large fortune by buying stock at a low price and selling before the crash came, and right

Thomas Guy and his hospital.

---

[1] Macleod, "Rise and Progress of Banking in England," ii, 55.

good use did he make of his money, for at his death he endowed the hospital called by his name with a sum exceeding £200,000.

<small>Parliamentary enquiry, Jan., 1721.</small>

As is not unusual in such cases, there was a universal endeavour to fasten the guilt upon others than the rash speculators themselves. An outcry was raised, not only against the directors of the company, but also against the ministry. Nothing would suffice but a Parliamentary enquiry into the affairs of the company. This was granted, and early in the following year the Lords commenced an open investigation, whilst the Commons appointed a committee of secrecy. The Lords had scarcely entered upon their investigation before it was discovered that the secretary of the company had made his escape to the continent. Thereupon the Commons gave orders for all ports to be watched in order to prevent the directors of the company following his example. Any director holding office under Government was dismissed. Two members of the House, who were also directors, were expelled the House and taken into custody. These were Jacob Sawbridge, the grandfather of Alderman John Sawbridge, of whom we shall hear more later on, and Sir Theodore Janssen, the father of Stephen Theodore Janssen who, after serving the City in Parliament and in the Mayoralty chair, became the City's Chamberlain. Other directors were also taken into custody and their papers seized.

<small>The Sword-blade Company.</small>

Jacob Sawbridge was a member of the firm of Turner, Caswall and Company, commonly known as the Sword-blade Company, carrying on business as goldsmiths in Birchin Lane. Sir George Caswall, one of the partners, was member for Leominster, and was serving as Sheriff the year of the South Sea Bubble. His firm had acted as cashiers of the South Sea Company, and like many similar firms of goldsmiths, had advanced large sums upon the company's stock. The committee of secrecy appointed by the House of Commons soon discovered that Sir George had been guilty of tampering with the firm's books in order to shield Charles Stanhope. For this he was expelled the House and committed to the Tower, whilst his firm was made to surrender its illgotten gains to the extent of a quarter of a million sterling.[1]

All the directors were forced to send in inventories of their respective estates to the Parliamentary Committee. These were confiscated for the benefit of their dupes, their owners being allowed some small portion of their former wealth to keep them from starvation. Peculation and dishonesty were not confined to the city. Peers of the realm and cabinet ministers were charged with receiving large bribes either in money or stock. The Earl of Sunderland, first commissioner of the Treasury, was reported by the committee of investigation to have received £50,000 stock without any consideration whatsoever, and although the House of Commons refused to find him guilty,[2] the Earl felt compelled to give up his post. Craggs, who was Secretary of State, and Aislabie, the Chancellor of the Exchequer, not to mention others, were convicted by the House of receiving similar bribes.[3] Craggs died of an attack of small-pox, pending the enquiry, but he left a large

Parliament and the South Sea Company.

---

[1] Journal House of Commons, xix, 476.   [2] *Id.*, xix, 482.
[3] *Id* , xix, 472-473, 532.

estate, and this was confiscated for the relief of sufferers. Aislabie was expelled the House, and committed to the Tower. Among the directors who were thus made to feel the heavy hand of Parliament was Edward Gibbon, grandfather of the great historian of the "Decline and Fall of the Roman Empire." Out of an estate of £60,000, Parliament allowed him to retain no more than £10,000. That the action of Parliament towards the directors was afterwards condemned by the historian as arbitrary and unjust, and only to be excused by the most imperious necessity, need not therefore cause surprise.[1]

The action of Parliament upheld by the City.

The city fathers, on the other hand, upheld the action of Parliament, and urged it to take further measures to alleviate the prevalent distress by presenting to the House the following petition (3 April)[2] :—

"Your peticōners think it their duty most humbly "to represent to this Honoble House the present state "of the City of London (so considerable a part of the "kingdom) now filled with numberless objects of "grief and compassion (the sad effects of the mis-"managem^{ts} avarice and fatal contrivances of the late "Directors of the South Sea Company, their aiders, "abettors and confederates in the destruccōn of their "country.)

"Nor is it the case of this great city alone your "peticōners lament, but the general decay of trade "manufactures and of public creditt, whereof this "Honoble House have been alwaies so extreamly

---

[1] Gibbon, Miscellaneous Works, i, 16–18.
[2] Journal 57, fo. 85. Journal House of Commons, xix, 502.

"tender, as also of the honour of the British name "and nacõn.

"Your peticõners beg leave to return their most "humble thanks to this Hono^ble House for the great "pains they have taken to releive the unhappy "sufferers by compelling the offenders to make resti- "tucõn as likewise for their continued applicacõn to "lay open this whole scene of guilt, notwithstanding "the industrious artificers of such sharers in the "common plunder as have endeavoured to obstruct "the deteccõn of fraud and corrupcõn, and your "peticõners doubt not but the same fortitude, impar- "tiality and public spirit wherewith this Hono^ble House "have hitherto acted will still animate them in pursuit "of those truly great and noble ends.

"We are too sensible"—the petitioners went on to say—"of the load of public debts not to wish that "all proper methods may be taken to lessen them, "and it is an infinite concern to us that the paiment "of a great summe towards them (which was expected "from the success of the late scheme) is now rendered "extreamly difficult, if not impracticable, and yet is a "cloud hanging over the heads of the present unfor- "tunate Proprietors of the South Sea Company, and "a great damp to public credit.

"We will not presume," they said in conclusion, "to mention in what manner releif may be given in this "arduous affair, but humbly submit it to the serious "consideracõn of this Hono^ble House."

This petition was followed by others in the same strain from different parts of the country, and conduced to the passing of a Bill which, besides appropriating the sum of £2,000,000 out of the private property of the directors for the relief of sufferers, remitted a sum of £7,000,000 due by the Company to the Government, and made an equitable division of the remainder of the Company's capital among the proprietors.[1]

Supremacy of Walpole.

These measures were greatly, if not exclusively, due to Walpole, the great financier of the day, and one of the few who had not allowed themselves to become involved in the affairs of the South Sea Company. The recent disclosures led to his becoming first lord of the treasury, and chancellor of the exchequer, with his brother-in-law Townshend as secretary of state. In March, 1722, the first septennial Parliament came to an end, and again the Whigs were returned by an overwhelming majority.[2] Walpole thus found himself absolute master of the field, and this position he continued to maintain for twenty years.

Jacobite Conspiracy, 1722.

In the meanwhile the birth of an heir[3] to the Pretender (1721) had raised the hopes of the Jacobites, who were only waiting for a fitting opportunity to renew their attack upon the House of Hanover. The confusion which followed the bursting of the South Sea Bubble seemed to afford them the opportunity they desired. Again the aid of France was invoked. Not only did the Regent refuse assistance, however, but he informed the English minister in Paris of the conspiracy that was on foot. Thus it was that on the 8th May (1722) Townshend informed the Lord

---

[1] Rapin v. 645.—Journal House of Lords, xxi, 584.

[2] Only one of the old members (viz., Peter Godfrey) was returned for the City, the remaining seats being gained by Francis Child, of the banking firm, who in the next Parliament sat for Middlesex, Richard Lockwood and John Barnard, who afterwards became Lord Mayor and one of Walpole's strongest opponents.

[3] Charles Edward Stuart, better known as the young Pretender.

Mayor (Sir William Stewart) by letter[1] that the king had the best of grounds for believing that another plot was being prepared in favour of the Pretender, but that as the plot was unsupported by any foreign power, and the king had been forewarned, there would be little to fear. At the same time the king looked to the mayor and his fellow magistrates to secure the city.

The letter being the next day brought to the notice of the Court of Aldermen, that body prepared a loyal address to the king and presented it to him the same evening.[2] In acknowledging the address the king assured the deputation that his interests and the interests of the City were inseparable, that he would do all in his power to maintain public credit and protect the City's privileges and estate as well as uphold the religion, laws and liberties of the kingdom. An order was issued the same day by the Privy Council for putting into execution the laws against papists, reputed papists and non-jurors, as well as against riots and tumults.[3] In addition to this the Habeas Corpus Act was suspended for a whole year, the longest time on record, and throughout the summer troops were kept encamped ready for any emergency. Some of the chief conspirators in England, among them being Atterbury, Bishop of Rochester, were placed under arrest. Had not the conspiracy been timely discovered and precautions taken the whole kingdom "and particularly the City

City address to the king, 9 May, 1722.

---

[1] Repertory 126, fo. 344.

[2] *Id.*, fos. 344–352. The address as well as the king's reply are set out by Maitland (i, 531–532).

[3] Repertory 126, fo. 355.

of London"—as George told the new parliament when, after frequent prorogations, it met in October—might have become involved in blood and confusion.[1] As matters turned out, the conspiracy proved a complete failure.

<small>Bill for regulating elections in the city, Jan., 1725.</small>

Whilst Walpole continued to pursue his policy of peace and increased in influence year by year, the City found itself constantly involved in disputed elections. At one time it was an election of an alderman, at another a member of the Common Council, at another an election of a sheriff. At length matters arrived at such a pitch that a petition from the citizens at large was presented to the House of Commons (16 Dec., 1724)[2] setting forth that, at elections by the liverymen of the city, numbers of people voted who had no right to vote; that at wardmote elections non-freemen claimed the right to vote on the ground that they contributed to the charges of their respective wards, refusing at the same time to qualify as voters by taking up the freedom of the city because they would thereby restrict their right of testamentary disposition of their estate;[3] that the Court of Aldermen had decided (as we have just seen) that payment of scot was a general contribution to all the public taxes and charges upon the city and inhabitants thereof—a decision which had not met with the favour of the Common Council, and that thus fresh causes of dissension between these two bodies had recently arisen. The petitioners prayed

---

[1] Journal House of Commons, xx, 11.
[2] Journal House of Commons, xx, 363.
[3] By the custom of the City a freeman disposing by will of his personal estate was obliged to leave his wife one-third of that estate, and to his children, if any, another third.

therefore "the relief of the House for preserving the "liberties and peace and quieting the minds of the "citizens and for punishing all intruders upon their "rights and privileges, and settling their elections "upon a just and lasting foundation." In answer to this prayer the House gave leave for the introduction of a Bill "for regulating elections within the City "of London, and for preserving the peace, good order "and government of the said City."

After the Bill had been brought in (27 Jan., 1725), two petitions were laid before the House; one purporting to come from "the major part of the Aldermen of the city," the other from the Common Council.[1] The former, which was in favour of the Bill, had been previously submitted to the Court of Aldermen; but upon the question being proposed that the petition should be the petition of the Court, the lord mayor (Sir George Merttins) declined to put the question on the ground that it would not be consistent with his honour to let his name be inserted in that petition, when already a petition had been presented to parliament in the name of the Lord Mayor, Aldermen and Commons in Common Council assembled.[2] The aldermen's petition drew attention more particularly to a clause in the Bill touching the right of passing Acts or By-laws by the Common Council. It declared that the right of the aldermen to veto such proceedings had never been questioned until the time of the civil war, and not afterwards until quite recently; it further stated that the aldermen had lately (20 Feb., 1724), by their recorder, proposed to

Bill supported by majority of Aldermen.

---

[1] Journal House of Commons, xx, 383, 387, 389.
[2] Repertory 129, fo. 123.

the Common Council a settlement of all disputes by reference either to the judges of the High Court or the parliament; but the offer had been declined.[1]

<small>Bill opposed by Common Council.</small>

The petition of the Common Council was against the Bill as being destructive to many of the rights and privileges which they and their fellow citizens enjoyed by ancient charters.[2] The Bill passed its second reading on the 6th of February, after which both parties were heard by counsel. When the Bill was before the committee, several petitions against it were presented from Livery Companies of the city. On the 19th March it was read a third time and passed the Commons.[3] In the passage of the Bill through the Lower House it had been strenuously opposed by three out of the four members for the city, viz: Francis Child, Richard Lockwood and John Barnard. For their services in this respect the Common Council passed (22 March) them a formal vote of thanks. The Court at the same time prepared to oppose the Bill in the Lords.[4]

<small>Election Act, 11 Geo. i, c, 18, 1725.</small>

When the Bill was carried up to the Lords, petitions from "the major part of the aldermen" and from the Common Council were again presented, as well as another petition subscribed by certain freemen who objected to parts of the Bill.[5] The passage of the Bill through the Upper House was nevertheless expeditious; on the 1st April it was read a second time and committed, and on the 13th, it

---

[1] Repertory 128, fos. 149-150, 204. Journal 57, fo. 110.
[2] Journal 57, fos. 119b. 120.
[3] Journal House of Commons, xx, 403, 426, 462.
[4] Journal 57, fos. 121, 121b.
[5] Journal House of Lords, xxii, 472, 474, 483. Journal 57, fo. 121. Repertory 129, fo. 218.

was passed with some amendments, but not without a protest being formally entered by dissentient lords.[1] On the 20th the Bill received the royal assent.

There are three clauses in the Act of special interest. First, the clause (No. ix), which prescribes the nature of the charges embraced in the term "payment of scot;" secondly, the clause (No. xv), which confirms to the Aldermen of the city their right to negative Acts of the Common Council;[2] and thirdly, the clause (No. xvii) abolishing the custom of the City restraining citizens and freemen from disposing of the whole of their personal estates by will.

Just when the reign of George I was drawing to an unexpected close, it seemed as if England was on the point of becoming involved in a European War. The emperor and the king of Spain had laid aside their quarrels and become united in a confederacy against France and England. Unless Gibraltar were ceded by England, another invasion of the Pretender might be shortly expected. The citizens were highly incensed at the thought of their trade being periodically put in jeopardy by Jacobite risings, and they hastened to assure the king once more of their

Death of George I, 11 June, 1727.

---

[1] Journal House of Lords, xxii, 499, 500. During the debate in committee, a proposal had been made to ask the opinion of the judges whether the Bill repealed any of the privileges, customs, or liberties of the City restored to them or preserved by the Act passed in 2 William and Mary for reversing the judgment on the *Quo Warranto* and for restoring the City its ancient rights and privileges. The proposal was negatived; but 16 lords entered a formal protest against rejecting it, whilst 25 lords protested against passing the Bill.

[2] This clause was repealed by Stat. 19, Geo. ii, c. 8. On the 24 April, 1746, the Common Council passed a general vote of thanks to the lord mayor and Aldermen who had assisted in bringing about the repeal of a clause which had been "productive of great jealousies and discontents and might, if continued, have proved subversive of the rights and liberties of the citizens of London."—Journal 59, fo. 29b.

determination to sacrifice their lives and fortunes in defence of the constitution both in church and state against all enemies whatsoever.[1] Thanks to the pacific tendencies of Walpole and the diplomatic skill of Townshend, hostilities were averted, and George was able to set out for his customary visit to Hanover, where he had been in the habit of spending a portion of each year. Before his journey was completed, however, he was seized with apoplexy and died in his coach, near Osnabrück (11 June).

[1] Journal 57, fo. 149b.

CHAPTER XXXVI.

On the 15th June, 1727, the Court of Aldermen were informed by Sir John Eyles, the lord mayor, that he had received an order of council dated from Leicester House (the residence of the Prince of Wales) for his lordship and the Court to attend at eleven o'clock the next morning at Temple Bar for the purpose of proclaiming King George II. The Court thereupon agreed to be present, and instructed the lord mayor to see that they were allowed to follow in the procession immediately after the lords of the council.[1] Proclamation having been duly made the mayor and aldermen, accompanied by the Recorder, waited upon the king with an address, and afterwards proceeded to pay their compliments to the queen.[2] Another address had been drawn up by a joint committee of aldermen and common councilmen on behalf of the Common Council. But when it was submitted for approval the aldermen insisted upon exercising their right of veto—recently confirmed by parliamentary authority—and as they and the commons failed to agree on the several clauses of the address it had to be abandoned altogether. The mayor was asked to summon another court, "in pursuance to common usage and ancient right," to consider another address,

King George II proclaimed, 15 June, 1727.

[1] Repertory 131, fo. 285. [2] *Id.*, fos. 287, 289-291.

but after consultation with the aldermen he declined to accede to the request.¹

The king's coronation, 11 Oct., 1727.

The coronation did not take place until October. The ceremony was one of far greater splendour than that of George I, such pageants being "as pleasing to the son as they were irksome to the father."² The City put in its customary claims, which were duly allowed. The manner in which these claims were made, as set out in a report made to the Court of Aldermen by the city Remembrancer, whose duty it was to make them, was shortly this. Having first obtained the names of the masters of the twelve superior companies, he put in two claims—written on parchment, and stamped with a treble sixpenny stamp—for the usual services in attendance upon the king and queen. The claims being allowed, he obtained certificates to that effect, and on presenting them at the lord great chamberlain's office he received warrants to the master of the king's jewel office for two gold cups, each weighing 21 ozs. One of these, the king's cup, he conveyed to the lord mayor; the other, the queen's cup, he left until after the ceremony, "for note"—says he—"they were not nor are "they used to be carryed down to Westminster Hall to "be made use of on that solemnity." The coronation

---

¹ Journal 57, fos. 154b-155b; Repertory 131, fos. 345-348. For the next two years the Common Council became practically powerless, the lord mayor for the time being summoning a court only when he thought fit. In 1728 the council only met four times, viz., twice in February and twice in May, after which no court was held until June, 1729. It was then thought high time to re-enact the old Act of Common Council *temp.* Richard II, when Brembre was mayor, compelling the mayor for the time being, to summon a Common Council once a quarter at least, and a Bill for that purpose was brought in and passed.—*Id.*, fos. 166b, 174b, 176, 177b, 182, 188b, 197b, 198, 201.

² Hervey, Memoirs, i, 88.

over, the Remembrancer applied for and received from the Clerk of the Crown a copy of the judgments on the several claims.¹

According to custom the king attended the first lord mayor's banquet after his accession. He was accompanied by the queen, the royal family, the great officers of state, and a large number of the nobility.² The entertainment was signalised by what appears to have been a barefaced attempt at extortion on the part of the king's own cup-bearer who made a claim on the City for a silver cup (or its value) by way of fee. The matter having been brought to the notice of the Court of Aldermen, the Town Clerk was instructed to search the city's Records for precedents, and upon his reporting that he had failed to find one the claim was dismissed.³ The new king, like his father, ordered £1,000 to be paid to the sheriff for the relief of insolvent debtors.⁴

The lord mayor's banquet, 28 Oct., 1727.

The day that the king was invited to the lord mayor's banquet the Common Council resolved to set up his statue at the Royal Exchange.⁵ Eventually they commissioned Charles Jervas, an Irish painter and pupil of Kneller, to paint portraits both of the king and queen for the Guildhall. Jervas had been originally apprenticed to a frame maker, and this may account for the anxiety he displayed to put the portraits into better frames than was usual. To do this he asked for and obtained the consent of the

Portraits of king and queen.

---

¹ Repertory 132, fos. 40–57.
² Journal 57, fo. 162. An account of the entertainment, its cost, etc., is given by Maitland, i, 541–543.
³ Repertory 132, fos. 10, 16.   ⁴ *Id.*, fo. 9.
⁵ Journal 57, fo. 162.

Court of Aldermen.¹ The pictures now hang in the members' reading room at the Guildhall.²

Walpole and the queen.

For a short time after the king's accession it appeared as if Walpole's ascendancy was to be suddenly cut short. The minister was fortunate, however, in winning over the queen to his interests, and her influence, combined with his own masterful tact, turned the scale in his favour, and he was allowed to remain at the head of affairs. Before long he succeeded in gaining the entire confidence of the king himself, but during the lifetime of the queen it was chiefly to her that the minister turned in times of difficulty. She was a woman of considerable ability, and thoroughly appreciated Walpole, and together they were able to avoid many political pitfalls and to persistently carry out that policy of peace which characterised the whole of this reign.

Dissenters and the Corporation and Test Acts, 1730.

Thus it was that in 1730, when the government was placed in an unpleasant dilemma over an attempt that was being made by Dissenters throughout the country to obtain the repeal of the Corporation and Test Acts Walpole took counsel with the queen, and these two laid a plan with Hoadley, Bishop of Salisbury, for getting the Dissenters to postpone bringing their petition before parliament. The plan as we learn from Lord Hervey,³ who had every means of making himself acquainted with the inner workings of the Court of George II, was this. Hoadley, in whom the Dissenters placed much confidence as an

---

¹ Repertory 132, fo. 381.

² Another portrait of Queen Caroline, by the same artist, is preserved in the National Portrait Gallery, having been transferred thither from the British Museum in 1879.

³ Memoirs, vol. i, c. vii.

avowed advocate of ecclesiastical as well as civil liberty, was to do all he could to persuade them to postpone, at least for a short time, their petition to parliament, whilst Walpole was to see that the committee of London Dissenters, which was to be chosen to confer with government, should comprise none but creatures of his own. The scheme succeeded entirely. The Dissenters were hoodwinked. The packed committee went through the form of an interview with the ministers, and in due course reported to the general assembly of Dissenters that the time was inopportune for petitioning parliament. The general body agreed, and the ministry was thus saved.

Although it was chiefly as a financier that the great minister, under whom England enjoyed an unexampled period of peace and prosperity, excelled, it was a financial reform that nearly brought him to ruin three years later. This was his famous Excise Bill. In a hasty desire to curry favour with the landowners by reducing the Land Tax Walpole proposed to establish a new system of levying duties on tobacco and wine. The tax itself was not new, but only the manner of levying it. Hitherto the duty on wine and tobacco had been payable on importation. The new proposal was that these commodities should be allowed to lie in bonded warehouses duty free until taken out for home consumption, when their sale was to be restricted to shops licensed for the purpose. In other words the customs' duties on these commodities were to be changed into excise duties, a form of taxation especially hateful in those days, as seeming to infringe the rights of the subject by giving revenue officers the right of entering and searching houses at any hour without

The City and Walpole's Excise Bill, 1733.

further warrant. The City and the country were up in arms, and the city members of parliament were instructed to oppose the Bill for reasons set out in writing and delivered into their hands.[1]

Walpole delayed bringing in the Bill as long as he could in hopes that the clamour against it— "epidemic madness," as Hervey called it—might subside. Neither London nor the kingdom, however, would listen to reason, and the universal cry was *No slavery—no excise—no wooden shoes!*[2] When the Bill was at last introduced (14 March) it met with violent opposition, and more particularly from two of the city members, viz., Sir John Barnard and Micaiah Perry. During the debate the doors of the House were besieged by such a noisy crowd that Walpole in an unguarded moment characterised the mob as "sturdy beggars." This at once brought Barnard to his feet, and although there was at first a disposition not to hear him, as he had already spoken to the Bill, the House was prevailed upon to give him a second hearing, owing to his position as a representative of "the greatest and richest city in Europe," and a city greatly interested in the issues of the debate. Barnard thereupon took Walpole severely to task for the expression he had let drop. "The "honourable gentleman," said he, "talks of sturdy "beggars; I do not know what sort of people may "be now at the door, because I have not lately been "out of the House, but I believe they are the same "sort of people that were there when I came last into "the House, and then I can assure you that I saw

---

[1] Journal 57, fos. 274-274b.   [2] Hervey, Memoirs, i, 176-179.

"none but such as deserve the name of sturdy beggars "as little as the honourable gentleman himself, or any "gentleman whatever." Sturdy beggars or not (he declared in conclusion) they could not legally be prevented from coming down to the House. After some further debate Walpole gained the day, and on the 4th April the Bill was read a first time.[1]

Before the Bill came on for its second reading a copy of it had been laid before the Common Council (9 April), and a petition had thereupon been drawn up and presented to the House asking that the City might be heard by counsel against the Bill.[2] After long debate the prayer of the petition was refused, but only by a bare majority of seventeen.[3] By this time the clamour had become so great, even the army showing signs of disaffection, that Walpole, true to his principle of expediency, the key-note of his policy, resolved to purchase peace by concession. He postponed the further consideration of the Bill (11 April) for a period of two months, and afterwards withdrew it altogether. On leaving the House the day that the motion for postponement was carried the minister was mobbed. The affair was little more than an "accidental scuffle," but it was studiously represented to parliament as "a deep-laid scheme for assassination." Resolutions were passed condemning in strong terms all actors and abettors of the outrage, and the city members were especially directed to

---

[1] Parl. Hist., viii, 1281–1307; Maitland, i, 558, 559.

[2] Journal 57, fos. 278b–280. On quitting office the lord mayor (John Barber) received the special thanks of the Commom Council for having afforded them this opportunity of preserving the trade and liberty of the citizens.—*Id.*, fo. 298.

[3] Journal House of Commons, xxii, 108, 109, 112, 113.

carry copies to the lord mayor for publication within his jurisdiction—the City being considered as the real author of all the mischief.[1]

<small>Mayoralty of Sir William Billers, 1733-1734.</small>

The defeat of the Bill was received with extravagant joy, and in 1734 it was proposed to celebrate its anniversary in the city with bonfires. For this purpose subscriptions were invited through the medium of the press. The mayor, Sir William Billers, on learning this consulted the Court of Aldermen as to what was best to be done under the circumstances, and by their advice he issued his precept for a special watch to be kept, and for the arrest of all persons attempting to make bonfires or to create disorder.[2] Notwithstanding this precaution a riot broke out, and Billers not only had his windows broken, on account of his obnoxious precept, but was himself pelted with dirt and stones, whilst patrolling the streets in company with the Swordbearer. Insult was added to injury by the newspapers of the day holding him up as having himself been the real cause of all the disorder. The Court of Aldermen, on the other hand, accorded him a hearty vote of thanks for the courage he had displayed.[3] On going out of office Billers again became an object of attack, the mob pelting him with all kinds of filth and endeavouring to smash his coach. The Court of Aldermen were so indignant at this outrage that they offered a reward of £50 for every offender brought to justice.[4]

[1] Hervey, Memoirs, i, 200-202.
[2] Repertory 138, fos. 243-246. See also the *Daily Courant*, cited in the *Gentleman's Magazine*, iv, 208.
[3] Repertory 138, fo. 252.   [4] Repertory 139, fo. 2.

In 1734 the princess royal was married to the Prince of Orange, and two years later the Prince of Wales married the Princess Augusta of Saxe-Gotha. On both occasions the City presented congratulatory addresses.[1] Lord Hervey, the king's vice-chamberlain, was hightly indignant at the first address because of the reference it made to King William III. But if the City sinned in this respect it sinned in good company, for Oxford University and other corporate bodies made similar allusions. "The "city of London," wrote Hervey,[2] "the University of "Oxford, and several other disaffected towns and "incorporated bodies took the opportunity of the "princess royal's marriage to say the most im- "pertinent things to the king, under the pretence of "complimental addresses, that ironical zeal and "couched satire could put together. The tenor of "them all was to express their satisfaction in this "match from remembering how much this country "was indebted to a prince who bore the title of "Orange, declaring their gratitude to his memory, "and intimating as plainly as they dared, how much "they wished this man might follow the example of "his great ancestor, and one time or other *depose his* "*father-in-law* in the same manner that King William "had deposed his." Happily the king took a more sensible view of the address, and vouchsafed a gracious reply. So far from being offended at the City's allusion to William of Orange he was pleased. "It is a "great pleasure to me," he said, "to see this great

Royal marriages, 1734 and 1736.

---

[1] Repertory 138, fo. 228; Journal 57, fos. 318-319; Repertory 140, fo. 254; Journal 57, fos. 375-377.

[2] Memoirs, i, 317.

"metropolis remember with so much gratitude the "deliverance of these kingdoms from popery and "slavery by my great predecessor King William."[1] Soon after the marriage of the Prince of Wales he was presented with the Freedom of the City in a gold box, having previously been admitted a member of the Saddlers' Company.[2]

<small>Disputes between England and Spain in the West Indies.</small>

For nearly twenty years England had enjoyed uninterrupted peace at home and abroad. The last action in which an English force had been engaged had taken place in the summer of 1718, when Admiral Byng defeated a Spanish fleet off Cape Passaro. Since then trade had been flourishing, and the city merchant had been busily sending cargoes of English merchandise across the sea to the West Indies, paying little regard to the restrictions imposed on them by the provisions of the Treaty of Utrecht.[3]

<small>Jenkin's ear, 1738.</small>

Spain on the other hand insisted upon the right of search, and their coastguards had often seized English vessels suspected of smuggling, and were sometimes reported as having brutally ill-used their crews.[4] Matters were fast tending to an open rupture when the episode of Jenkin's ear roused an intense desire for war both in the city and the country generally. The story is well known. Jenkin was master of a small trading vessel which seven years before had been

---

[1] Journal 57, fo. 319b; Repertory 138, fo. 237.

[2] Repertory 141, fos. 48, 60, 69, 75.

[3] By an article of this treaty England obtained the right of sending yearly to Panama one ship of 600 tons, and no more, for the purpose of trading with the Spanish colonists. This restriction was evaded by putting a fresh cargo on board under cover of the night to take the place of that which had been discharged the previous day.

[4] Hervey, Memoirs, ii, 484, 485.

overhauled by a Spanish guarda-costa. Irritated at finding nothing contraband on board the Spanish commander is said to have cut off one of Jenkin's ears, bidding him carry it to the king. Jenkin took advantage of the prevalent feeling against Spain to exhibit his ear wrapt in cotton wool, and when asked as to his feelings at the time of the outrage declared that he had commended his soul to God and his cause to his country. This clap-trap story—it is shrewdly suspected that Jenkin lost his ear in the pillory—had the desired effect. Popular indignation was roused, and the nation clamoured for war.

To all this Walpole turned a deaf ear, and instead of proclaiming war opened negotiations for peace. A Convention with Spain was agreed to, but as it left the question as to right of search still unsettled, great opposition was displayed, both in and out of parliament, to its ratification. The minister was in the greatest straits. His best friend and supporter, the queen, had recently died, and the king, freed from the peaceful influence of his wife, as well as the City, were urging war. It was not often that the Londoners called for war, they were too interested in commercial pursuits not to appreciate to the full the blessings of peace. But on this occasion the City felt bound to make a strong representation to parliament as to "the fatal "consequences of leaving the freedom of navigation "any longer in suspense and uncertainty." They had too much reason to fear (they said) that if the right claimed by Spain of searching British ships at sea were admitted in any degree "the trade of his majesty's "subjects to America will become so precarious as to "depend in a great measure upon the indulgence and

The City and the Spanish Convention, 1739.

"justice of the Spaniards, of both which they have "given us for some years past such specimens as we "humbly think this nation can have no cause to be "satisfied with."[1] The citizens were probably right, although they were held up to much ridicule for venturing to give advice upon affairs of state. During the debate on the convention, lists of the members of the Common Council, with their respective trades or companies, were scattered abroad, and to these lists were appended texts from scripture to the effect that however useful such men might be in a city "they shall not be sought for in public council."[2]

"Leonidas" Glover.

One citizen in particular distinguished himself by advocating war in a poem of greater length than merit. This was Richard Glover,[3] known as "Leonidas" Glover (from another poem he wrote bearing that title), author of "London, or the Progress of Com-"merce," in which he reminds the citizens of their former prowess at Newbury, and asks—

> "Shall we be now more timid, when behold,
> The blackening storm now gathers round our heads
> And England's angry genius sounds to arms?"

Besides being an "eminent Hamburgh merchant" and a writer of verse, Glover took an active part in city elections, and was a strong upholder of the rights of the livery. On Michaelmas-day, when Sir George Champion, who sat for Aylesbury, was put in nomination for the mayoralty and rejected chiefly, if not

---

[1] Journal 58, fo. 122; Journal House of Commons, xxiii, 248.

[2] Ecclesiasticus, c. xxxviii, v. 33.

[3] Horace Walpole, who always showed intense dislike to anyone who had opposed his father, Sir Robert, describes Glover as "the greatest coxcomb and the greatest oaf that ever met in blank verse or prose."—Walpole to Mann, 3 March, 1742; Letters, i, 136.

wholly, on account of his having voted for the Convention,[1] Glover was asked to move a vote of thanks to the city members, for having opposed the Convention. This he did in a spirited speech, in which he referred to Champion's chance of election to the mayoralty as being in all probability for ever lost, a prediction which proved true.[2]

Although the Convention was carried, it became apparent that either war must be declared or Walpole resign. The minister's love of power overcame his convictions, and he allowed himself to be dragged into a war which he felt at the time to be unjustifiable and forboding of evil. The declaration of war which was made in October was welcomed with peals of bells from London churches. "They ring their bells now," said he, "before long they will be wringing their hands." When the outgoing mayor received instructions from the Duke of Newcastle to assist at the proclamation of war according to custom, he demurred on the ground that the town clerk had been unable to find a precedent for the Court of Aldermen attending a proclamation of war; but upon the Duke referring him to what had taken place when war was declared in 1718 against Spain, the objection was withdrawn. A question next arose as to the place the civic authorities should occupy in the procession, and the Remembrancer was instructed to make enquiries on

War declared with Spain, 19 Oct., 1739.

---

[1] According to Maitland (i, 599) Champion was the senior alderman below the chair. This was not the case. There were two senior to him, but these, as well as Champion, were set aside by the livery, who returned Sir John Salter and Sir Robert Godschall to the Court of Aldermen. The Court selected the first named.—Common Hall Book, No. 7, fo. 277.

[2] Maitland, i, 600.

the point both at the secretary's office and the Heralds' College. The information gathered by him proving unsatisfactory, the Court of Aldermen took it upon themselves to decide that the civic party should fall in immediately after Garter King-at-Arms. This order, however, was not carried out, for the Horse Guards thrust themselves into the procession in front of the municipal officers.[1]

Capture of Porto Bello, Nov., 1739.

At the outset of the war fortune favoured British arms, and in November, Admiral Vernon succeeded in surprising and capturing the town of Porto Bello, situate on the Isthmus of Darien (Panama). The City was delighted and presented the king with the usual congratulatory address.[2] Such a feat the citizens declared would not only serve to show that the maritime power of the country, although allowed to lie dormant so long, was still capable of vindicating the honour of the crown, but also gave promise of future successes, and they assured the king that he might depend upon them to contribute towards the support of a war so necessary for the protection of their long injured trade.

"Admiral Hosier's Ghost."

As for Vernon, he became a popular idol with the citizens, who continued to look upon his single success whilst they turned a blind eye to his many subsequent failures. Not only was he presented with the Freedom of the City in a gold box, but his birthday was for some years kept with general rejoicing.[3] His capture of Porto Bello was made the subject of a poem by Glover—his one readable ballad—under the

---

[1] Repertory 143, fos. 469-472. [2] Journal 58, fos. 167-168b.
[3] Walpole to Mann, 12 Nov., 1741. —Letters, i, 89.

title of "Admiral Hosier's Ghost," in which Vernon's good fortune is compared with the ill-luck which attended Hosier's expedition to the West Indies in 1726, when, doomed to inaction by orders from home, that gallant officer saw the greater part of his men swept off by disease, and he himself died subsequently of a broken heart.[1]

When Michaelmas-day again came round Glover was again to the fore. It was customary for the livery to hold a preliminary meeting either at the London Tavern or some company's hall before they met in Common Hall. On this occasion the meeting was held in Vintners' Hall, and Glover took the chair. The business of the day having been opened by a speech from the chairman, in which he referred to the rejection of Sir George Champion the previous year, and exhorted them to choose a mayor for the year ensuing who would be agreeable to the majority of the citizens, the livery proceeded to choose Sir Robert Godschall and George Heathcote, although they were not the senior aldermen below the chair.[2] There names were accordingly submitted to the full body of the livery assembled in Common Hall on Michaelmas-day and were accepted.[3] It now became the duty of the Court of Aldermen to select one of these two to be mayor for the year ensuing. Godschall was the senior, and Heathcote particularly desired not to be chosen on the plea of ill health, and because he had so recently served sheriff. Nevertheless the choice of the aldermen was declared to be for Heathcote, although he repeated his request

Heathcote discharged Mayor by Common Council, Oct., 1740.

---

[1] The poem is preserved among the Percy Reliques, ii, 397.
[2] Maitland, i, 608.   [3] Common Hall Book, No. 7, fo. 284b.

not to serve. A Common Council was thereupon summoned to consider the matter, and it was eventually resolved that Heathcote should be discharged without fine.¹

Humphrey Parsons re-elected Mayor, Oct., 1740.

This necessitated the summoning another Common Hall, and another accordingly met on the 14th October. A preliminary meeting of the livery took place, as before, at Vintners' Hall, and again Glover was in the chair. The action of the Court of Aldermen in thus passing over Godschall merely because the livery had refused to nominate Champion, was strongly condemned by the chairman, who no less strongly eulogised the action of Heathcote for refusing to serve—a refusal which emanated, according to the speaker, not from ill health, but from a determination not to fill the place of the rejected Godschall.² When the election came on in Common Hall the livery returned Godschall for the third time, and with him Humphrey Parsons who had served mayor ten years before. Again Godschall was passed over by the Court of Aldermen, and Parsons was called to the mayoralty chair for the second time, although by the bare majority of one vote.³

The Common Council were desirous (22 Oct.) of passing a vote of thanks to Parsons for again accepting a laborious and expensive office, "*and thereby endeavouring in some measure to restore the peace and tranquility of this city which has been greatly disturbed by a late extraordinary and unusual proceeding.*" A

---

¹ Repertory 144, fos. 389, 400. Journal 58, fo. 182b.
² Maitland, i, 610.
³ Common Hall Book, No. 7, fo. 285. Repertory 144, fo. 406.

long debate arose, some of the aldermen present insisting upon their right of a negative voice in the matter; and upon the question being put to them, the words in *italics* were vetoed by twelve aldermen to one.¹ Those aldermen who had previously voted for Godschall and a large number of the Common Council had already got up and left the Court.²

In 1741 a general election took place. Parsons, who had sat in the last two Parliaments with Sir John Barnard, had, in the meantime, died during his mayoralty, and had been succeeded in the civic chair by Daniel Lambert.³ Barnard retained his seat, and with him were returned the new mayor, and Aldermen Godschall and Heathcote. The ministry still retained a majority in the House, but it was not always to be depended upon. *A general election, 1741.*

Early in the following year two petitions were laid before Parliament complaining of the manner in which the trade of the country was being ruined owing to insufficiency of convoys. One petition—drafted by Glover—was from merchants of the city, and was presented to Parliament by Godschall,⁴ who had at last succeeded in becoming mayor; and the other was from the Common Council of the city, and was presented by the sheriffs.⁵ Both petitions were referred to a committee of the whole House, with Godschall in the chair, and in due course the House *City petitions to parliament, Jan., 1742.*

---

¹ Journal 58, fos. 190–191. ² Maitland, i, 611.
³ He had for some reason been sworn into office before Lord Cornwallis, the Constable of the Tower, with the same ceremony as if sworn before the Barons of the Exchequer; and it was expressly provided that the city's rights and privileges were not to be prejudiced thereby.—Repertory 145, fo. 151. Common Hall Book No. 7, fo. 288.
⁴ Walpole to Mann, 22 Jan., 1742.—Letters, i, 117.
⁵ Journal 58, fo. 222b.

instructed the lord mayor and Sir John Barnard to prepare a Bill for the better protecting and securing the trade and navigation of the kingdom in time of war.[1]

Death of Godschall, mayor, June, 1742.

A Bill was accordingly prepared, which passed rapidly through the Commons but was thrown out by the Lords.[2] This was almost the last parliamentary business on which Godschall was engaged, for he died during his mayoralty in the following June.

Resignation of Walpole. 17 Feb., 1742.

Whilst these petitions were under consideration the ministry suffered a defeat over an election petition, and Walpole resigned (17 Feb.). With the great "corrupter" removed the City hoped for great things. The Common Council had, previously (10 Feb.) made a "representation" to the city members urging them to promote a Place Bill and a Pension Bill, as well as the repeal of the Septennial Act, and so secure the constitution "against all future attempts either of "open or secret corruption or of any undue influence "whatsoever."[3]

The City and the new ministry.

After some difficulty a new ministry was formed in which Carteret soon became the leading man. The City continued to look for the execution of the long-wished-for reforms, but looked in vain. It was the old story. Men who when out of office breathed the spirit of patriotism and virtue were anything but virtuous and patriotic in office. Again were the city members urged by another "representation" to press forward certain measures and not to vote supplies until the government showed some signs of moving in the

[1] Journal House of Commons, xxiv, 49, 111.

[2] Journal House of Commons, xxiv, 231. Journal House of Lords, xxvi, 138.

[3] Journal 58, fo. 225b. Maitland, i, 624.

direction required.[1] The example of the City was followed in other places, and copies of the "representation" were freely circulated in all parts of the country. The newspapers of the day, whilst lamenting the condition into which the country had fallen through "the iniquitous administration of the late corrupter," expressed their confidence that the example set by London—"the source and fountain head of all our wealth and trade"—would continue to have, as it had already had, its proper influence both within and without doors.[2]

When Carteret came into power, Europe was distracted with the war of the Austrian succession, and before long England was drawn into the vortex. Whilst France embraced the cause of the Elector of Bavaria, England supported Maria Theresa. In June, 1743, the French army was defeated at Dettingen, when, for the last time, a king of England appeared in the field of battle at the head of his men, and bore himself right royally. Louis retaliated by promising assistance to Charles Edward Stuart, known in history as the Young Pretender, who meditated an invasion of England to claim the crown. *France and the Young Pretender, 1743.*

Information of the project having been communicated to Parliament (15 Feb., 1744), both Houses concurred in an address of loyalty to the king, promising him their utmost support, and the next day the Common Council voted a similar address.[3] The deputation which waited upon his majesty with the City's address met with a gracious reception, and the *War declared against France, 29 March, 1744.*

---

[1] Journal 58, fos. 254-256. Maitland, i, 628.
[2] Extract from *Common Sense* cited by Maitland (i, 630).
[3] Journal House of Commons, xxiv, 568. Journal 58, fo. 307b.

king conferred the honour of knighthood upon the mayor (Robert Westley), the recorder (Simon Urling), two aldermen, (viz., Daniel Lambert and Robert Willimot), and the two sheriffs, Robert Ladbroke and William Calvert,[1] the latter of whom had succeeded to Godschall's seat in Parliament as one of the members for the city. Before the end of the month the lord mayor was informed by letter from the Privy Council that extensive preparations were being made at Dunkirk, in concert with disaffected persons in this country, for an invasion, and it behoved his lordship to put into operation the Acts against papists and non-jurors.[2] The aspect of affairs began to look black indeed. "If they still attempt the invasion," wrote Walpole to his friend, "it must be a bloody war."[3] The danger that seemed so imminent passed away owing to a violent storm which destroyed the French transports, and England was thus again saved from foreign invasion by the difficulties of the channel passage.[4] Nevertheless on the 29th March, war was declared against France.[5]

The Pretender in Scotland, 1745.

Though bitterly disappointed at the failure of this expedition the prince did not lose courage, but resolved in the following year (1745) to cross over to Scotland unsupported by France, and to trust to the loyalty of his friends there. Landing in the western highlands with a mere handful of followers he gradually drew to his side a small force, and on the 19th August set up his standard in Glenfinnan. On the 4th September

---

[1] Maitland, i, 633. [2] Repertory 148, fo 165.
[3] Walpole to Mann, 1 March.—Letters i, 292.
[4] The same to the same, 5 March.—*Id*. i, 294.
[5] Repertory 148, fo. 230.

the Duke of Newcastle (brother of Pelham, who had recently succeeded Carteret in the premiership) informed the lord mayor by letter of the Pretender having set up his standard and of his then being on his way to Perth or Edinburgh. The king was assured, he said, that the mayor would do his utmost to preserve the peace and the security of the city.[1] Both the Common Council and the Court of Aldermen presented addresses to the king in testimony of their loyalty to the constitution of Church and State, and both bodies in return received assurances of royal favour and promises of protection for their trade and commerce.[2] The London merchant and trader had been the greatest gainers by the Revolution and the policy of peace pursued by Walpole. It would have been base ingratitude, if nothing else, had the City acted otherwise at this important crisis. Dr. Gardiner points out that it was much the same in Scotland, and that the traders there, having profited by the Union, were to a man staunch Hanoverians.

On the 17th September the prince entered Edinburgh and took up his quarters at Holyrood House. A few days later he succeeded in defeating an English force under Sir John Cope at Preston Pans, and thus encouraged he prepared to cross the border and to appeal to England for support. The news caused a run upon the Bank of England, and had it not been for the praiseworthy promptitude of the leading London merchants who met and passed a formal resolution pledging themselves to support the

The Pretender's march to Derby.

[1] Journal 58, fo. 377b.
[2] Journal 58, fos. 378, 383; Repertory 149, fos. 398, 399.

credit of the bank's notes, its doors would probably have been closed.¹

The Pretender enters Derby, 4 Dec., 1745.

Again fortune favoured England. The prince delayed his march so long, collecting money and organising his forces, that time was gained for putting London into a state of defence. A camp was formed at Finchley² to intercept the rebels, and subscription lists were opened in London and the country for the soldiers who were to be engaged in the coming winter campaign. The Common Council voted £1,000 to the fund,³ but England as a whole was strangely apathetic. Carteret, the late prime minister, who had, on the death of his mother recently, become Viscount Carteret and Earl Granville, refused to subscribe anything to the fund, and a similar indifference to the country's danger was displayed by others of the aristocracy.⁴ By Wednesday, the 4th December, the Pretender had succeeded in evading the English forces sent to oppose him under the command of Wade and the Duke of Cumberland and had entered Derby, where he seized all the money he could lay his hands on, including the subscriptions that had been raised to oppose him.⁵

"Black Friday," 6 Dec., 1745.

The news of the rebels being within 150 miles of the capital reached London on Friday, the

¹ Francis, "History of Bank of England," i, 162.

² Hogarth's famous picture of the "March to Finchley" is preserved in the Foundling Hospital.

³ Journal 59, fo. 16b.

⁴ "I had this morning a subscription book brought me for our parish. Lord Granville had refused to subscribe. This is in the style of his friend, Lord Bath, who has absented himself whenever any act of authority was to be executed against the rebels."—Walpole to Mann, 22 Nov., 1745; Letters, i, 404-405.

⁵ Walpole to Mann, 9 Dec., 1745; *Id.*, i, 409.

6th December—"Black Friday," as it came to be called. The Duke of Newcastle immediately wrote off to the lord mayor informing him of the fact of the Pretender's forces having already reached Derby "in their way, as they give out, towards London." The Duke of Cumberland, the letter went on to say, was making every effort to intercept the rebels at Northampton, and part of his cavalry would be there that night and the rest the next day, when the foot soldiers were also expected. The mayor was desired to take immediate steps, in the meantime, for the defence of the city, in case the duke failed to place himself between the rebels and London. The letter having been communicated to a special Court of Aldermen on Saturday it was resolved to issue precepts for returns to be made by the following Monday of the number of coach and saddle horses found in each ward. The trained bands were to take up their quarters in the Royal Exchange, whilst a portion of Bridewell Hospital was to serve as a guard-room for the night guard appointed by the commissioners of lieutenancy. The two city marshals were to be instructed to visit the night watches in the several wards and to see that the constables did their duty.[1] All was excitement and activity. The king prepared to go to the camp at Finchley to take command of the guards. The weavers of London offered to supply him with 1,000 men, whilst the lawyers formed themselves into a little army under the command of Chief Justice Willes, and offered to serve as a body-guard to the royal family during the king's absence.[2] Another

---

[1] Repertory 150, fos. 40–47.
[2] Walpole to Mann, 9 Dec.; Letters, i, 410.

run was made upon the Bank of England, which again had to resort to strategem (as in 1720) in order to avert bankruptcy. Instead of refusing payment the Bank employed agents for the express purpose of presenting notes which, in order to gain time, were cashed in sixpences; "and as those who came first "were entitled to priority the agents went out at one "door with the specie they had received and brought "it back by another, so that the *bonâ fide* holders of "notes could never get near enough to present them."[1]

The Pretender withdraws from Derby.

Fortunately the crisis was soon over, the Pretender had scarcely reached Derby before he reluctantly accepted the advice of his commanders and ordered a retreat. Under the circumstances it was perhaps the best thing to do. The English armies were gradually closing in upon him, this country had shown no disposition to rise in his favour, and the Duke of Cumberland was, as we have seen, hastening towards Northampton to bar his passage to the capital.

The Freedom of the City for Duke of Cumberland, 23 Jan., 1746.

The citizens were not slow to realise how much they owed to the duke for their protection, and on the 23rd January (1746) the Common Council resolved to present him with the Freedom of the City in a gold box, both for his "magnanimous" behaviour against the rebels, as well as for his vigilant care in protecting the city "in a late time of imminent danger."[2]

Victory of Culloden, 16 April, 1746

Some time elapsed before the duke was able to receive the freedom, for as soon as he was aware that

---

[1] Francis, "History of Bank of England," i, 161.
[2] Journal 59, fo. 15.

the rebels were in retreat, he hurried off in pursuit. After defeating General Hawley at Falkirk (17 Jan., 1746) the rebels retired towards Inverness, but in April they were brought to bay by the duke at Culloden Moor and utterly defeated. The duke was a man of violent passions, and his victory was marked with so much wanton cruelty and bloodshed, that he acquired the name of the Butcher. This name he never lost, and when it came to his taking up the Freedom of the City, some one was bold enough to suggest the propriety of his becoming a member of the Butchers' Company.[1]

Cruel as the duke's conduct had been, it had the effect of crushing the rebellion. London and the kingdom could once more breathe freely, and the citizens could follow their commercial pursuits without fear of further abortive attempts being made to restore the crown to the Stuarts. Instead of blaming the duke for his drastic measures, they applauded him and formally thanked the king for giving him the command, "Permit us, Sir"—they said, addressing his majesty—"to return our most unfeigned thanks ". . . . for the appointment of his royal highness "the duke to this important service, whose conduct "and bravery (so early conspicuous) have by the "blessing of the Almighty produced this our happy "deliverance: a glory reserved for one of your "illustrious family, endowed with those princely "qualities which render him amiable to those under "his command, and formidable to his enemies." They, at the same time assured his majesty that it

City address to the king, 3 May, 1746.

---

[1] Walpole to Mann, 1 Aug., 1746.—Letters, ii, 43. The Freedom of the City was conferred on the 6 Aug. Journal 59, fo. 44.

would be always their firm resolution, no less than their indispensable duty "to oppose every attempt of the common disturbers of the peace of Europe" against the rights of his crown.¹

The general election, 1747. One effect of the rebellion was to strengthen the hands of the government. The subscription lists that had been opened during the crisis were the means of displaying to the world who were Jacobites and who were not, and when the general election came on in the summer of 1747 it went hard with those who entertained Jacobite proclivities. Barnard and Calvert retained their seats for the city, but Slingsby Bethell and Stephen Theodore Janssen were returned in place of Lambert and Heathcote. "Both "Westminster and Middlesex have elected court "candidates," wrote Walpole to his friend,² "and the "city of London is taking the same step, the first "time of many years that the two latter have been "whig; but the non-subscribing at the time of the "rebellion, has been most successfully played off upon "the Jacobites."

Treaty of Aix-la-Chapelle, Oct., 1748. The rebellion had also a considerable effect upon the war on the continent, for the Austrians, deprived of English succour, lost nearly the whole of their possessions in the Netherlands to France. The French, however, were unsuccessful in Italy, whilst at sea the English navy attacked their colonial possessions, and captured the island of Cape Breton. All parties being ready to come to terms, a peace was at length concluded (Oct., 1748) at Aix-la-

---

¹ Journal 59, fo. 33.
² Walpole to Mann, 3 July, 1747. Letters, ii, 92.

Chapelle on the general principle of restitution of all conquests.¹

From the time when Henry Pelham succeeded Carteret (Nov., 1744) as Prime Minister, the strife of parties was lulled by the simple expedient of admitting into office any man capable of rendering himself dangerous to the government. Pelham's administration thus became distinguished as the Broad-bottomed Administration. Upon his death in March, 1754, the era of tranquillity passed away. He was succeeded in the Premiership by his brother the Duke of Newcastle. Already there was danger of war with France, as well as opposition at home, but with the assistance of Charles Fox, Newcastle contrived to get through the year. Before another twelvemonth had elapsed, however, England was again threatened with a French invasion.² *The Newcastle administration, 1754-1756.*

On the 11th November (1755) the lords of the council wrote to Slingsby Bethell, who had just entered upon his mayoralty, instructing him to call out the whole of the City's militia for immediate service. The letter was laid before a special Court of Aldermen on Saturday, the 15th, when it was resolved to summon the Commissioners of Lieutenancy to meet that afternoon, and a special court of Common Council for the following Tuesday.³ The Common Council having assembled on the day named the Lord Mayor communicated to them the contents of the letter he *The National Militia Bill, 1756.*

---

¹ The peace was not proclaimed in the City until the 2 Feb., 1749. Repertory 153, fo. 138.

² "I need not protest to you, I believe that I am serious, and that an invasion before Christmas will certainly be attempted." Walpole to Chute, 20 Oct., 1755. Letters, ii, 477.

³ Repertory 160, fos. 3-5.

had received. A motion was thereupon made for applying to Parliament for a more effectual National Militia Bill, but a debate arose, and the matter was adjourned for further consideration. On the 25th the debate was resumed, but upon being put to the vote the motion was lost. Nevertheless, a Bill for better ordering the militia of the country was introduced into Parliament the following spring and passed (10 May, 1756), but the City's militia was exempted from the Bill.[1]

Importation of foreign mercenaries.

Newcastle was not the man to conduct a great war. A fresh election had taken place soon after his appointment as first lord of the treasury, and the result had given the ministry a handsome majority. Nevertheless, so helpless was he that he could devise no better plan for saving the country from invasion than by importing Hessian and Hanoverian mercenaries. Worse than this, his proposal was adopted, although Pitt left a sick bed on purpose to go down to the House and solemnly protest against such a course.[2]

A tax on plate opposed by the City.

A proposal, made by the chancellor of the exchequer, Sir George Lyttelton, to impose a tax upon plate, for the purpose of raising supplies, was reasonable enough, but it met with opposition not only from Pitt but also from the City,[3] partly on account of the existing inland duties being already sufficiently heavy and partly because this particular tax would teach servants to become informers. At the same time the citizens avowed themselves ready to hazard their lives

---

[1] Journal 61, fos. 23b–24, 25, 57; Journal House of Commons, xxvii, 523, 600. The City was in the habit of claiming that its militia should be dealt with by a separate Bill to the rest of the kingdom.

[2] Walpole, "Memoirs of the last ten years of the reign of George the Second," ii, 30, 31; Journal House of Commons, xxvii, 539.

[3] Journal 61, fos. 49b–52; Walpole, Memoirs, ii, 24–28.

and their fortunes in support of the king and the Protestant succession.¹

The threatened invasion was only a trick played by the French king to draw off attention from the real object of attack—the capture of Minorca. Owing to dilatoriness on the part of the ministry Byng was despatched too late to save the island. This loss excited the utmost indignation. The cry was loud against the government, but louder still against Byng, who was accused of rank cowardice, if not treachery. Newcastle was content to make a scapegoat of the admiral, and ordered him home under arrest to await trial. The feeling of disgust which prevailed in the city at Byng having withdrawn to Gibraltar without hazarding a brush with the enemy manifested itself by the display of a placard at the Royal Exchange advertising *Three kingdoms to be let*.² Whilst Byng awaited his trial, popular clamour, throughout the country rose to such a pitch that at last war was declared (17 May, 1756). In August the citizens again assured the king of their readiness to shed their last drop of blood and contribute all that might be necessary for the defence of the kingdom and colonies, but they none the less expressed an eager hope that Byng and those who were responsible for losses in America should be brought to punishment.³

The loss of Minorca, 1756.

The recent failures and the general weakness and incapacity of Newcastle irritated the country to such a degree that the ministry became frightened, and in

A "representation" to city members, Oct., 1756.

---

¹ Journal 61, fo. 55b.
² Walpole, "Memoirs of George the Second," ii, 68.
³ Journal 61, fos. 80b–81b.

October (1756) Fox, who for the last year had undertaken the duties of the leadership in the House of Commons, resigned. At this juncture the Common Council again drew up a "representation" for the guidance of the city's representatives in parliament.[1] First and foremost they were to insist upon a strict and impartial parliamentary enquiry into the causes of the recent disasters at Minorca and in North America, which had rendered the British name contemptible; and in the next place they were to seize the earliest opportunity of urging the necessity of establishing a constitutional militia and of ridding the country of those foreign mercenaries, whose numbers had been constantly increasing, whose support had become an intolerable expense, and who claimed to be above the law of the land. They were to vote for no supplies until this were done. They were further instructed to endeavour to limit the number of placemen and pensioners, which of late had so remarkably increased; to restore at a proper season triennial parliaments, as being the only means of obtaining a free representative of the people; to keep an eye on the proper application of public money; and finally to see that the country did not become involved in continental affairs so as to threaten its independence.

<small>Newcastle succeeded by Pitt, Nov., 1756.</small>

This representation was not without its effect. In November Newcastle resigned, and Pitt, although nominally only secretary of state under the Duke of Devonshire, became virtually prime minister. He had not been many weeks in office before he gratified the City by sending the Hanoverian and Hessian troops

[1] Journal 61, fos. 114-115b.

out of the country, as well as by passing a Bill for re-organising the national militia.

Just as the year was drawing to a close Byng was brought to trial. Owing to a comparatively recent change that had been made in the articles of war the court found itself compelled to bring in a verdict of guilty without any imputation on the personal courage of the admiral.[1] The extent of his criminality was that he had failed to do all that might have been done to save Minorca. Pitt, who was no favourite with the king, was courageous enough to plead for a royal pardon, but the king turned a deaf ear. The country deemed itself betrayed, and called for a victim. The timorous Newcastle had long promised a deputation of citizens that Byng should be speedily brought to justice. "Oh! indeed he shall be tried immediately, he shall be hanged directly."[2] The trial had taken place, and although the court that tried him had shown an unmistakable desire to treat him with leniency, the City began to show signs of impatience and clamoured for his death. Papers bearing the words "Shoot Byng, or take care of your king" are even said to have appeared posted up in the Royal Exchange.[3] The citizens had their wish. The sentence was carried out, and Byng was shot on the quarter-deck of the "Monarque" at Portsmouth (14 March, 1757). *Execution of Admiral Byng, 14 March, 1757.*

Soon after this Pitt was dismissed. His dismissal was the signal for a general ebullition in his favour. The Common Council presented both him and Legge *Civic honours for Pitt and Legge, 24 May, 1757.*

---

[1] Walpole, Memoirs, ii, 121-124.
[2] *Id.* ii, 70.   [3] Walpole to Mann, 3 March, 1757; Letters, iii, 64-66.

(who had served under him as chancellor of the exchequer) with the Freedom of the City and gold boxes, in testimony of their conduct during their "honourable tho' short administration." The City declared its appreciation of the noble efforts of these ministers "to stem the general torrent of corruption "and revive by their example the almost extinguished "love of virtue and our country," their zeal in promoting a full and impartial enquiry into the real causes of the late disasters in America and the Mediterranean, and lastly their efforts to support the glory and independence of Great Britain, the true interests of the crown and the rights and liberties of the subject.[1] The example thus set by the city of London was followed by other corporations in such quick succession that for some weeks, as Lady Hervey wittily remarked, "it rained gold boxes."

Coalition of Pitt and Newcastle, June, 1757.

The king tried to get Newcastle, with his subservient band of supporters, to accept office again, but the duke could not make up his mind whether to resume office or not, and for nearly three months the country was without any ministry at all. At last a compromise was arranged in June between Pitt and Newcastle,[2] whereby the former undertook all affairs of state, leaving to Newcastle the business of patronage, such as his soul loved. Pitt threw himself heartily into the war, determined to raise the national spirit. His task, however, was a difficult one, owing to the incompetency of those he found in command. Thus, for instance, an attempt to take Rochefort failed

---

[1] Journal 61, fos. 156, 158–158b.
[2] Walpole, Memoirs, ii, 224; Walpole to Mann, 20 June, 1757; Letters, iii, 83.

through dissension between Admiral Hawke and General Mordaunt. The Common Council were on the point of considering the advisability of addressing the king on the subject, when the mayor informed them that one of the clerks of the Privy Council had waited on him at the Mansion House to inform him that directions had already been given for an enquiry into the cause of the recent miscarriage; and so the matter was allowed to drop.[1]

Thanks to Pitt's military reforms and to the confidence he inspired, the remainder of the reign was marked by a series of successes culminating in the conquest of Canada. In the summer of 1759 the French again threatened an invasion, but it caused no alarm. A new spirit had been breathed into the nation and animated both services. The City resolved to open a subscription list at the Guildhall for encouraging the enlistment of recruits, and to contribute £1,000 towards the fund. By way of further encouragement the Freedom of the City was offered gratuitously to every soldier who should produce to the chamberlain a testimonial of his good behaviour during his term of service, and who should wish to be admitted to the privilege of exercising a trade within the city and liberties. A committee was appointed to make the necessary arrangements for carrying out the enlistments, and Pitt was desired to lay these resolutions before his majesty as an humble testimony of the City's zeal and affection for king and government.[2] The king commissioned Pitt to thank the City on his behalf, and to express the satisfaction

Subscriptions for bounties, 1759-1760.

[1] Journal 61, fo. 186.　　[2] Journal 62, fos. 32b-34.

he felt at this signal proof of the City's resolution to support the war.¹ The money raised between August, 1759, and June, 1760, amounted to a little over £7,000, which was distributed in bounties to 1,235 men, enlisted for the term of the war with France, at five guineas a head. The livery companies subscribed to the fund : the Grocers' contributing 500 guineas, the Goldsmiths' and the Fishmongers' respectively £500, the Clothworkers' £300, and other companies lesser sums. The names of Pitt himself and of Legge also appear as having each subscribed £100.²

<small>City address in conquest of Canada, 16 Oct., 1760.</small>

But of all the achievements abroad at this time none caused so much joy as the capture of Quebec (Sept., 1759). The City once more embraced the opportunity of presenting a congratulatory address to the king, at the same time expressing deep regret at the loss of so gallant an officer as Wolfe.³ A year later it again offered its congratulations on the complete conquest of Canada,⁴ promising to assist in the preservation of that valuable acquisition, and "to prosecute the various and extensive services" of the just and necessary war. Pitt was delighted with the address. "The address of the city of London," he wrote to Grenville, " will speak for itself, and I believe " you will think that it speaks loud enough to be heard " at Paris. . . . How it was heard at Kensington " you need not be told, as the address is big with *a* " *million in every line*. Were it able to produce an " advantageous peace it would be most happy ; next " to that, such generous and warm assurances of

---

¹ Journal 62, fo. 35.   ² *Id.*, fos. 113–116.
³ Journal 62, fos. 37–38.   ⁴ *Id.*, fos. 140, 158b.

"supporting the war cannot but give the highest "satisfaction to government."¹ Within ten days of listening to the address the king died (25 Oct.).

On the last day of the month the first stone was laid of Blackfriars Bridge. The bridge was originally known as Pitt Bridge, and bore an inscription in Latin and English testifying the City's affection for the great statesman who had done so much to restore the ancient reputation of the British empire,² whilst the approach to the bridge was for some years known as Chatham Place.

The City's admiration for Pitt.

---

[1] Pitt to Grenville, 18 Oct., 1760.—Grenville Correspondence, i, 355.

[2] Journal 62, fos. 161-161b. A lead plate, bearing the inscription in English, is preserved in the Guildhall Museum.

CHAPTER XXXVII.

The accession of George III, 1760.

On the 26th October George III was proclaimed king in the city in the presence of the mayor and aldermen.[1] The usual addresses were presented by the Courts of Aldermen and Common Council, special reference being made by the latter body to the "bloody and expensive war" in which the country was then engaged. They expressed a hope that the new king would continue to carry on the war as prudently and successfully as it had been carried on hitherto, until an end should be put to it by a firm and honourable peace. The king in reply echoed this wish of the citizens, and promised to look after their "liberties, commerce and happiness."[2]

The fall of Pitt, 1761.

George had not long been seated on the throne before he began to display unmistakable signs of a determination to follow the precepts instilled into his young mind by his mother, the Princess of Wales, and to "be a king" in fact as well as in name. The six months that elapsed before Parliament was dissolved[3] were marked with no great changes, although

---

[1] Repertory 164, fos. 367–369.

[2] Repertory 164, fos. 370, 379; Journal 62, fos. 159, 162. This address of the Common Council, as well as similar addresses from 1760 downwards, will be found in a volume printed by order of the Corporation in 1865.

[3] Parliament was dissolved 20 March (1761), and a new Parliament summoned for May. Of the old city members three out of the four were again returned; but the place of Barnard, now getting advanced in years, was taken by Thomas Harley, a brother of the Earl of Oxford.

indications were not wanting of what was likely to take place. With the dissolution (20 March, 1761), however, important changes were made in the ministry, and it became clear that the king was resolved to rule by ministers of his own choosing. Bute, the particular friend and adviser of the Princess of Wales, was appointed one of the secretaries of state. His admission into the ministry could not mean otherwise than sooner or later the dismissal of Pitt, for on the great question of the day—the war with France—they were in direct antagonism; and so it turned out. Pitt would gladly have made peace[1] had not the honour of the country demanded a declaration of war with Spain as well as with France owing to a secret clause in the Family Compact which had come to his knowledge. The ministry refused to declare war, and in the following October Pitt and his brother-in-law, Earl Temple, resigned. In consideration of his great services a peerage in her own right was conferred on Pitt's wife, whilst a pension of £3,000 a year, for three lives, was bestowed on himself.

Pitt's resignation, and more especially his acceptance of a pension, gave rise to so many slanderous rumours and brought upon him so much obloquy that he found it necessary to write to his friend, alderman Beckford, explaining the exact position of affairs:[2] "A difference of opinion with regard to measures to be "taken against Spain, of the highest importance to "the honour of the crown, and to the most essential

His letter to Alderman Beckford, 15 Oct., 1761.

---

[1] When, speaking on the address, Alderman Beckford proposed to push the war with more vigour than formerly, Pitt is recorded as having fired up and to have asked his friend what new piece of extravagance he wished for?—Walpole, "Memoirs of the reign of George III," i, 24.

[2] Chatham Correspondence, ii, 158.

"national interests, and this founded on what Spain
"had already done, not on what that court may further
"intend to do, was the cause of my resigning the
"seals. Lord Temple and I submitted in writing,
"and signed by us, our most humble sentiments to
"his majesty; which being over-ruled by the united
"opinion of all the rest of the king's servants I
"resigned the seals on Monday, the 5th of the month
"(October), in order not to remain responsible for
"measures which I was no longer allowed to guide."
In the same dignified strain he tells his friend of the
honours bestowed on him by his sovereign, the
acceptance of which had set malicious tongues
wagging. "Most gracious marks of his majesty's
"approbation of my services followed my resignation.
"They are unmerited and unsolicited; and I shall
"ever be proud to have received them from the best
"of sovereigns."

The City's vote of thanks to Pitt, 22 Oct., 1761.

The letter was written on the 15th October (1761), and a few days later (22 Oct.) the Common Council passed a vote of thanks to Pitt by a large majority—109 votes to 15—acknowledging his many great and eminent services, and testifying the City's gratitude not only for having roused "the ancient spirit" of the nation from the pusillanimous state into which it had fallen, but also for his having greatly extended the sphere of trade and commerce. In conclusion the Court expressed its sorrow at "the "national loss of so able, so faithful a minister at "this critical conjuncture."[1] Pitt was highly gratified at this recognition of his services, and in his acknowledgment of the vote paid the following tribute to the

Journal 62, fos. 298, 299.

City's loyalty and zeal:—" It will ever be remembered "to the glory of the city of London that through "the whole course of this arduous war that great "seat of commerce has generously set the illustrious "example of steady zeal for the dignity of the crown "and of unshaken firmness and magnanimity."[1] This was no mean praise coming from such a man.

On lord mayor's day the king (following the usual custom of the sovereign attending the first lord mayor's banquet after his accession) came into the city and was entertained at the Guildhall, together with the queen. Pitt also was a guest. He and Temple drove down together in a carriage and pair, and were received with even greater acclamation than the king himself. The entertainment was given in the most costly style, the tables being loaded with "all the "delicacies which the season could furnish or expense "procure."[2] It was, however, unfortunately marred by a violent display of party feeling. Whilst Pitt was received everywhere with cheers and clapping of hands, his rival, Bute, was hooted and pelted, and would, it was thought, have come off still worse had he not taken the precaution of surrounding his carriage with a strong body of "butchers and bruisers." Beckford was believed to have been at the bottom of the mischief. It was by his directions that the Guildhall was packed with Pitt's supporters, and he led the *claque* on the arrival of the ex-minister.[3]

The king and queen at the Guildhall, 9 Nov., 1761.

---

[1] Journal 62, fo. 302.

[2] A schedule of the different "services" at the various tables and particulars of the cost (£6,898 5s. 4d.) of the entertainment are entered on record.—Journal 62, fos. 337-340b.

[3] Walpole, "Memoirs of reign of George III," i, 89, 90; Walpole to Mann.—Letters, iii, 459.

Pitt, on the other hand, was blamed for lending himself to such an ostentatious display, which could not appear otherwise than disrespectful to the king. Indeed he afterwards owned that he had done wrong.

<small>A statue of the king for the Exchange, and pictures of king and queen for the Guildhall.</small>

Ten days later (18 Nov.) the Common Council resolved to erect a statue of the king in the Royal Exchange, and to have pictures painted of the king and queen for the Guildhall.[1] Their pictures, by Ramsay, now adorn the walls of the Guildhall Art Gallery.

<small>Instructions to City members, 22 Oct., 1761.</small>

The events which immediately followed Pitt's resignation enhanced his reputation for political foresight, and Bute, who became prime minister, found himself compelled, as indeed Pitt had predicted, to declare war against Spain (Jan., 1762). Until this was done the City was determined to leave him no peace. The Common Council, as was its wont, drew up instructions for the city members as to the policy they were to pursue in the coming parliament.[2] They were in the first place to use their best endeavours to obtain the repeal of a recent Act for the relief of insolvent debtors, and in the next to keep a sharp eye on "the distribution of the national treasure," but above all they were to oppose any attempt made by government to give up recently acquired possessions, more especially in North America, and they were to vote any supplies that might be necessary for carrying on the war with vigour. The "present happy extinction of parties," the nation's zeal and affection for their "native king," and the increase of commerce were proofs (the

---

[1] Journal 62, fo. 303.   [2] *Id.*, fos. 298b–299.

Council declared) of the ability of the country to carry on the war. Finally the city members were to vote such supplies as were necessary to place the king above the menaces of foreign interference, whilst supporting such measures as would conduce to a safe and honourable peace.[1]

The new ministry soon found themselves in direct opposition not only to the city members but to one who was destined ere long to prove a veritable thorn in their side. John Wilkes, a man of shamelessly immoral character, but of undeniable talent, had for the second time been returned for Aylesbury. His expensive debaucheries had reduced him to the direst possible straits, and he had taken to a political career as a possible means of getting himself out of his pecuniary difficulties. He had at the outset declared himself a staunch supporter of Pitt, and to Pitt he had more than once looked for some crumb of patronage to alleviate his distress. As soon as Parliament met Wilkes seized the opportunity of the debate on the address to pass some censures on the king's speech, or rather the speech of the king's minister, although he affected to be ignorant as to which minister he ought to attribute it. He declared that although the country was nominally at peace with Spain it was in reality in a state of war, and that the nation was being kept in the dark by the ministers, who refused all information. Beckford joined in the debate, urging the right of the country to "demand

John Wilkes, M.P. for Aylesbury, 1761.

[1] Horace Walpole was indignant at the Common Council presuming to speak on behalf of the City of London, and to "usurp the right of making peace and war." At the same time he could not shut his eyes to the fact that the City held the purse-strings, and that without its assistance supplies would run short.—Walpole to Conway, 26 Oct., 1761. The same to Horace Mann, 14 Nov.—Letters, iii, 457, 459.

peace, sword in hand," and offering to second Wilkes in moving for the Spanish papers.¹

Declaration of war with Spain, Jan., 1762.

In January (1762) war was declared, and all the papers relative to the rupture with Spain were laid before Parliament. No sooner was this done than Wilkes wrote a pamphlet entitled "Observations on "the Papers relative to the Rupture with Spain," in which he vindicated the policy of Pitt and exposed the folly of the existing ministry in having let slip the best opportunity that ever offered of crushing Spain beyond recovery. This was his first political essay, and at once stamped Wilkes as a political as well as literary writer of no mean order.²

City address on capture of Martinico, etc., 6 April, 1762.

The success of the war exceeded expectation. One expedition reduced Cuba, another Manila, whilst Spanish commerce was swept from the sea. The surrender of the island of St. Lucia and the capture of Martinico drew forth a congratulatory address to the king from the City, and once more the citizens were assured of his majesty's desire to promote their commercial interests.³ The credit of the war was due to Pitt for having foreseen the struggle, and for the preparations he had made accordingly.

The Peace of Paris, 10 Feb., 1763.

All this time the thoughts of Bute were fixedly directed towards peace, and on the 10th February, 1763, the Peace of Paris was signed and an end put to the Seven Years' War.⁴ The peace was distasteful to the City as well as to the nation at large. The Court of Aldermen, it is true, congratulated the king on

---

¹ Walpole, Memoirs, i, 91-93.
² Almon, "Correspondence of Wilkes," i, 65, 66.
³ Journal 62, fos. 330b, 334b.   ⁴ Repertory 167, fo. 184.

having "happily concluded a very just and expensive "war by a necessary and advantageous peace,"[1] but the Common Council said nothing. When the peace came to be debated in the House of Commons it met with strong opposition from Pitt, who spoke against it for more than three hours, although he was at the time so ill that he had to be carried down to the House. By practising a wholesale system of bribery the government managed, nevertheless, to obtain so large a majority that the Princess of Wales exclaimed in great exultation "Now my son is really king."

The triumph of the king and his favourite were destined to be short-lived. An important feature of the budget for the year was a proposal to impose a tax upon cider. The proposal at once met with the most determined opposition, not only from the cider counties but also from the city of London, where anything in the nature of excise was looked upon with horror. The Common Council raised a strong protest against any such extension of excise duties at a time when there was every prospect of a continuation of peace.[2] The Bill eventually passed, but the unpopularity of Bute increased to such an extent that he got sick of office and retired (8 April). *Resignation of Bute, 8 April, 1763.*

A few days later (23 April) Parliament was prorogued, the king in his speech alluding to the late peace as alike honourable to the crown and beneficial to the people.[3] This gave occasion to Wilkes to make a violent attack in the next number of his *Wilkes and the North Briton.*

---

[1] Repertory 167, fos. 280, 286, 291.
[2] Journal 62, fos. 72–73b, 75–76, 87b–88b, 131–131b, 134–134b.
[3] Journal House of Commons, xxix, 666.

paper, called, in allusion to Bute, the *North Briton.* Fourty-four numbers had appeared at the time of Bute's resignation, and although each number had contained matter more or less libellous no notice had been taken of them. No. 45 was destined to become famous, for although it was not a whit worse than any of its predecessors its prosecution was immediately ordered by Grenville, who had succeeded to the head of affairs. On the last day of April Wilkes was arrested on a general warrant (*i.e.,* a warrant in which no individual is specified by name) and lodged in the Tower, whilst his house was ransacked and papers seized. These harsh and illegal proceedings excited popular feeling and raised Wilkes to the rank of a political martyr. Crowds flocked daily to visit him in his confinement, among them being the leaders of the opposition, Temple and Grafton. Early in May his arrest was pronounced illegal by Pratt, Chief Justice of the Common Pleas, and he was discharged.

No. 45 of North Briton. burnt at Royal Exchange, 3 Dec., 1763.

As soon as Parliament met, which was not until November (1763), Wilkes complained of the breach of privilege in the seizure of himself and his papers. He got no sympathy, however, in that quarter, although he shortly afterwards succeeded in obtaining damages to the extent of £1,000 against the under-secretary of state in a court of law.[1] So far from sympathising with Wilkes the House ordered No. 45 of the *North Briton* to be burnt by the common hangman at the Royal Exchange as a false, scandalous, and malicious libel.[2] Saturday, the 3rd December, was the day appointed for carrying out

[1] Walpole, Memoirs, i, 332.
[2] Journal House of Commons, xxix, 668, 685.

the order, but when the sheriffs attended for the purpose and the executioner began to perform his duty a riot ensued, the magistrates were mobbed, and the paper rescued from the flames. The Lords thereupon summoned the sheriffs to give an account of their conduct. One of the sheriffs, Thomas Harley, a brother of the Earl of Oxford, being a member of the House of Commons, the permission of that House had to be asked before his attendance could be enforced. It was left to Harley to do as he liked; he might attend the Lords "if he thought fit."[1] Harley did think fit, and on the Tuesday following (6 Dec.) attended with his brother sheriff and Osmond Cooke, the city marshal. Being called upon to give an account of what had taken place the previous Saturday, Harley informed the House to the following effect, viz.: that the sheriffs had met at the Guildhall at half-past twelve o'clock, and thence proceeded to Cornhill to carry out the order of Parliament; they there met the city marshal, who expressed a fear that the order could not be carried out without military assistance; that, nevertheless, he was determined, in spite of all opposition, to carry out the order if possible; that he tried to get to the place in his chariot, but could not, and so went on foot; that on arrival at the place where the fuel was prepared he found the wood so wet that it could not take fire, "but he read the "order, and gave the paper with his own hands into "the hands of the executioner, who held it on the "lighted torch, which he held in his hand, till it was "burnt, and that he saw it burnt pursuant to the "order." On his return—he went on to say—the

[1] Journal House of Commons, xxix, 690.

window of his carriage was broken, and he had to take refuge in the Mansion House,[1] where he found the mayor (William Bridgen, who had recently succeeded Beckford) doing business as usual.

The mayor's conduct condemned.

That the mayor should have shown such sympathy with the mob as not to lend assistance to the sheriffs in putting down the disturbance roused the anger of the Duke of Bedford, who broke forth against Bridgen and the City. "Such behaviour," he said, "in any "smaller town would have forfeited their franchises. "The Common Council had long been setting them-"selves up against the Parliament, and last year had "taken on them to advise the king to refuse his assent "to a law that had passed through both Houses. He "hoped their lordships would resent this insult and "disrespect to their orders."[2]

Votes of thanks to the sheriffs.

Harley's statement having been corroborated by the evidence of other witnesses the Lords were content to ignore the mayor's conduct rather than enter upon a serious quarrel with the City, and both Houses concurred in passing votes of thanks to the sheriffs.[3] It was otherwise with the Common Council. They upheld the conduct of the mayor and condemned that of the sheriffs; a motion to pass a vote of thanks to the latter being lost by the casting vote of the mayor, who gave as his reason for so doing that he looked upon the motion as prejudging Wilkes's case.[4]

[1] Journal House of Lords, xxx, 437.
[2] Walpole, Memoirs, i, 331; see also Grenville Papers, ii, 235.
[3] Journal House of Lords, xxx, 438; Journal House of Commons, xxix, 698.
[4] Journal 63, fo. 146b; Grenville Papers, ii, 237.

In the meantime Lord Sandwich, a former friend of Wilkes and his associate in the debauchery carried on by the so-called monks of Medmenham, had produced before the House of Lords a copy of an obscene parody on Pope's *Essay on Man*, which Wilkes had written for the delectation of his intimate friends, but never intended to publish. With much difficulty, and not without some treachery, Sandwich had managed to obtain a copy of this infamous production, and he was now base enough to produce it in evidence against his recent boon companion, and to demand his punishment. The House condemned the poem as a blasphemous libel, but the treachery and hypocrisy displayed by Sandwich, whose own vices were notorious, raised a storm of public indignation, and when the *Beggar's Opera* was shortly afterwards being performed at Covent Garden, and Macheath exclaimed, in the words put into his mouth by Gay, "*That Jemmy Twitcher should peach me, I own surprises me,*" the audience were quick to apply the words to the treacherous earl, who was ever afterwards known as *Jemmy Twitcher*.[1]

Lord Sandwich and Wilkes's Essay on Woman.

In January of the next year (1764) Wilkes ought to have appeared before the House of Commons to answer for his conduct in relation to publishing No. 45 of the *North Briton*. He had, however, fled to France after receiving a wound in a duel, and was unable to travel, so at least the medical certificates which he forwarded to the Speaker alleged, and so we feel bound to believe, although the House of Commons evidently entertained some doubts as to the serious nature of his wound. The matter was

Wilkes expelled the House, 19 Jan., 1764.

---

[1] Walpole, Memoirs, i, 309-314.

debated in his absence, and in the end a resolution was passed expelling him the House (19 Jan.).¹

<small>Sentence of outlawry on Wilkes, 1 Nov., 1764.</small>

A month later (21 Feb.) Wilkes was found guilty in the King's Bench of being the author of the offensive *North Briton* and of the *Essay on Woman*, and as he failed to appear sentence of outlawry was pronounced against him in the following November.² The same day that judgment was pronounced in the King's Bench the Common Council passed a vote of thanks to the city members for their endeavours to obtain a Parliamentary declaration as to the illegality of general warrants, whilst it voted Pratt the Freedom of the City, and invited him to sit for his portrait. The chief justice acknowledged the compliment paid him by the City—"the most respectable body in the kingdom after the two Houses of Parliament"³ as he termed it,—and his portrait, painted by Sir Joshua Reynolds, and formerly bearing a Latin inscription ascribed to Dr. Johnson, now hangs in the Guildhall Art Gallery. The vote of thanks to the city members well nigh cost the City dear; for when application was shortly afterwards made to Parliament for pecuniary assistance to help the City to discharge the debt on Blackfriars Bridge—a debt which had been augmented by the destruction by fire of a temporary bridge that had been erected—a member rose and abused the Common Council for its late behaviour, declaring that the City was entitled to no favour.⁴

<small>Chatham and the East India Company, 1766.</small>

Having quarrelled in turn with Grenville and Rockingham, the king found himself compelled in

---

¹ Journal House of Commons, xxix, 723.
² Walpole, Memoirs, i, 385, ii, 35.
³ Journal 63, fos. 166–167, 171. ⁴ Walpole, Memoirs, i, 391.

July, 1766, to resort again to the "Great Commoner" whom he created Earl of Chatham and made Prime Minister with the office of Lord Privy Seal. His acceptance of a peerage produced a general burst of indignation. According to Horace Walpole—who never misses an opportunity of girding at the City in return for its treatment of his father—"the city and the mob" (convertible terms in his estimation), were angry, because in his new position, Pitt would have less opportunity of "doing jobs" for them than when he was in the House of Commons.[1] But however this may be, the state of the Prime Minister's health had before the end of the year rendered him incapable of "doing jobs" for the City or anybody else, and he left the control of affairs in the hands of the Duke of Grafton and Charles Townshend. Before withdrawing, however, he intimated his intention to the House of bringing in a bill for regulating the East India Company's affairs. Strange to say, the City failed to grasp the full portent of such a bill, or to see any danger to themselves in this meditated attack upon the chartered rights of others. Later on, when Fox introduced his East India Bill, the City was wider awake. The motion for carrying out Chatham's plan was not only made by a city alderman, viz., Beckford,[2] but the Common Council offered (June, 1767) Townshend, a supporter of the motion, the Freedom of the City, in recognition of "his well-" tempered zeal in support of the undoubted legislative

---

[1] Walpole to Mann, 1 Aug., 1766. Letters, v, 8. "The city of London"—he writes elsewhere—"had intended to celebrate Mr. Pitt's return to employment, and lamps for an illumination had been placed round the Monument. But no sooner did they hear of his new dignity, than the festival was counter-ordered." Memoirs, ii, 359.

[2] Walpole. Memoirs, ii, 394.

"authority of the king and parliament of Great
"Britain over all parts of his majesty's dominions."[1]

Wilkes and the Duke of Grafton.

In November of this year (1766), Wilkes, who had slipt over to England in the hope of obtaining the king's pardon, wrote a very submissive letter to Grafton asking for his mediation. The minister coldly referred him to Chatham, a proceeding which so galled Wilkes that he hurried back to the continent for fear of being laid by the heels, and a year later published what purported to be a second letter to the Duke of Grafton expressing the greatest disappointment at his Grace's answer, and inveighing in the strongest possible terms against Chatham as being an apostate to the cause of liberty.[2]

Wilkes elected M.P. for Middlesex, 1768.

When the general election came on in March, 1768, Wilkes again appeared on the scene, and had the boldness, notwithstanding his outlawry, to offer himself a candidate for the City. Every day he appeared on the hustings, and displayed great activity in canvassing for votes, but it was of no avail.

Not in the least dismayed, this irrepressible demagogue rallied his forces and declared himself a candidate for the county of Middlesex. There he was more successful. The election was very riotous; the streets and highways leading to Brentford were in the hands of the mob, who would allow no one to pass without a blue cockade in his hat inscribed with the name of Wilkes, and the number 45. "It was not "safe to pass through Piccadilly; and every family

[1] Journal 64, fos. 142b, 204. Before the freedom could be conferred, Townshend had died (4 Sept.).

[2] The letter is dated from Paris, 12 Dec., 1767. Almon's Life of Wilkes, iii, 184.

"was forced to put out lights; the windows of un-"illuminated" houses were demolished. The coach "glasses of such as did not huzza for *Wilkes* and "*liberty* were broken, and many chariots and coaches "were spoiled by the mob scratching them with the "favourite 45." This was the description of the scene by an eye-witness. In the city matters were no better. The windows of the Mansion House were smashed, Harley, the mayor, being known to be no favourite of Wilkes. The trained bands were called out, but proved insufficient to cope with the multitude, but at length peace was restored with the aid of a military force from the Tower.¹ The result of the poll was that Sir William Beauchamp Porter, who had represented the county for over 20 years was turned out, and Wilkes elected in his place.

Determined to take the bull by the horns Wilkes now voluntarily surrendered himself to the King's Bench and demanded to have the former judgments against him reversed on technical grounds. It was decided, however, that nothing could be done in this direction until he was in legal custody by process of outlawry. A writ of *capias utlegatum* was accordingly taken out, but for some time the sheriffs' officers hesitated to execute it, so popular had he become, and the mayor had to discharge some of them for neglect of duty. At length he was taken into custody and committed to the King's Bench prison (27 April). When he left the Court the mob stopt his coach on Westminster Bridge, took out the horses, and themselves drew him as far as Cornhill. They insisted

Committed to the King's Bench, 27 April, 1768.

---

¹ Walpole. Memoirs, iii, 186-188. Walpole to Mann, 31 March, 1768. Letters, v, 91-93. The City offered a reward of £50 for the capture and conviction of the ringleaders. Journal 64, fos. 247b, 248.

that he should not go to prison, but were at last, persuaded to disperse, and Wilkes quietly made his way to the King's Bench Prison and there surrendered himself.¹

The king's letter to Lord North, 25 April, 1768.

Throughout the whole business the prosecution had shown a great want of resolution and decision, everyone trying to throw the *onus* upon the shoulders of someone else. The same indecision manifested itself in the Cabinet as to whether or not Wilkes should be allowed to take his seat. It was otherwise with the king, however. He had fully made up his mind that Wilkes ought to be expelled the House. Two days before Wilkes's committal he wrote to Lord North: "I think it highly proper to apprise "you that the expulsion of Mr. Wilkes appears to be "very essential, and must be effected; and that I "make no doubt, when you lay this affair with your "usual precision before the meeting of the gentlemen "of the House of Commons this evening, it will meet "with the required unanimity and vigour. . . . "If there is any man capable of forgetting his "criminal writings I think his speech in the Court of "King's Bench on Wednesday last reason enough for "to go as far as possible to expel him; for he declared "'Number 45' a paper that the author ought to *glory* "*in,* and the blasphemous poem a mere *ludicrous pro-* "*duction*." ²

Riots at the King's Bench Prison.

So long as Wilkes remained in the King's Bench, the neighbourhood was a constant scene of rioting,

---

¹ Walpole to Mann, 23 April, 1768.—Letters, v, 98; Walpole, Memoirs, iii, 199.

² The king to Lord North, 25 April, 1768.—"Correspondence of George III with Lord North" (W. Bodham Donne), i, 2.

and on Tuesday, the 10th May, when the new Parliament met, the mob threatened to release him by force and carry him triumphantly to Westminster. His outlawry had been argued by his friend Glynn on the previous Saturday, but Lord Mansfield had postponed giving judgment until the next term, and Wilkes had thus been prevented taking his seat. Hence the display of feeling on the part of the mob, which at length became so violent that the Riot Act was read, the military fired, and a young man was shot. This roused their indignation the more, and there was more bloodshed; but at last peace was restored.[1]

The conduct of Harley—the aristocratic lord mayor—during the disturbance was so much approved that a motion was made in the House of Lords two days after Parliament had assembled to petition the king to confer some mark of royal favour upon him, but the motion was lost. The House, however, instructed the chancellor to convey to Harley a vote of thanks on their behalf for his efforts to preserve the peace of the city.[2] *The Lords pass a vote of thanks to the mayor, 12 May, 1768.*

On the 8th June Wilkes again appeared in Westminster Hall, when he succeeded in getting his outlawry reversed. Ten days later, however, he was condemned to pay a fine of £500 and to suffer imprisonment for ten months for having written the offensive number of the *North Briton*, and to pay another fine of similar amount and to suffer a further term of twelve months imprisonment for his *Essay on Woman*. As if this were not punishment enough he *Sentence pronounced against Wilkes, 18 June, 1768.*

---

[1] Walpole to Mann, 6 June, 1768.—Letters, v, 101; Walpole, Memoirs, iii, 204-205.

[2] Journal House of Lords, xxxii, 152.

was ordered to find security for his good behaviour for seven years, himself being bound in £1,000 and two sureties in £500 each. Still Wilkes had something to thank his judges for. They had spared him the pillory.[1]

<small>Wilkes elected alderman, Jan., 1769.</small>

Notwithstanding his imprisonment Wilkes was as irrepressible as ever, and he nearly succeeded in setting both Houses by the ears over the hard usage he had received. His colleague in the representation of Middlesex having died, he nominated his friend and counsel, Glynn, for the vacant seat, and got him in. Early in the following year (1769) he contrived to get himself returned alderman of the Ward of Farringdon Without, the rival candidate being forced to retire from the poll for fear of raising disturbances in the ward—"even the constables in the city were almost to a man devoted to Wilkes."[2] The Court of Aldermen, however, refused to admit him, and ordered another election.[3] This time he was returned unopposed. Still the Court hesitated to admit him until they had been furnished with copies of the proceedings against him in the King's Bench, and at length resolved to take the opinion of counsel upon the following questions, viz.: (1) whether the election of Wilkes was a valid election; (2) whether he was entitled by law to be admitted by the court by virtue or in pursuance of that election.[4]

<small>Opinions of counsel.</small>

The case as settled by the Court of Aldermen and submitted to counsel is set out *in extenso* in

---

[1] Walpole to Mann, 22 June, 1768.—Letters, v, 110; Walpole, Memoirs, iii, 228, 229.

[2] Walpole, Memoirs, iii, 297.

[3] Repertory 173, fos. 91-94, 114, 115.

[4] Repertory 173, fos. 140-142, 153-155.

the minutes of the court held on the 25th April,[1] when the opinions of the several counsel were read. The attorney and solicitor general as well as Yorke, Glynn, and Leigh gave it as their opinion, that the judgments pronounced against Wilkes did not render him by law incapable of being elected an alderman of the city, and that he might be admitted into office, but they expressed a doubt whether the Court of Aldermen could be forced to admit him. On the other hand, the Recorder and the Common Sergeant as well as Fletcher Norton (who gave a separate opinion) declared Wilkes's election, in their opinion, to be invalid. Had it been valid, the Recorder and Common Sergeant believed there was no other objection to his being admitted except the impossibility of his attending the Court of Aldermen for the purpose; but Norton was of opinion that the crimes of which Wilkes had been convicted were a sufficient justification for the court to refuse to admit him, over and above his incapacity at the present time to attend to the duties of the office.[2] Under the circumstances it was deemed best to keep the aldermanry open until Wilkes regained his liberty.

In the meanwhile Wilkes had appealed to both Houses against the sentence passed on him. He demanded to be heard at the Bar of the House of Lords in defence of his writings, but this was denied him, and the writs of error which he had brought were argued by his counsel, Glynn and Davenport. This was on the 16th January (1769). On the 27th, the day that he was returned unopposed as Alderman of the ward of Farringdon Without, he was brought

Wilkes again expelled the House, 3 Feb., 1769.

---

[1] Repertory 173, fos. 264-314. [2] *Id.*, fos. 315-318.

before the Commons, but nothing urged either by himself or his counsel could move them in his favour and on the 3rd February, they for the second time voted his expulsion.¹

Elected the second time for Middlesex, 16 Feb., 1769.

No sooner had the House passed this resolution than Wilkes announced his intention of again standing for Middlesex, and on the 16th February, he was again returned without any opposition. On this occasion he was proposed by two members of parliament who were shortly to become his brother aldermen, viz., Townshend and Sawbridge. Again the House declared his election void, and himself to be incapable of sitting in the existing parliament.²

Returned the third time, 16 March, 1769.

Not a whit abashed Wilkes again offered himself as a candidate, his only opponent being Charles Dingley. Upon the day of the election (16 March), Dingley, who had on a previous occasion come to blows with Reynolds, Wilkes's election agent, and had come off second best, received such rough handling that he was obliged to retire and leave the field to Wilkes, who was returned unopposed. The election was for the third time declared void, and a fresh writ issued.³

Returned the fourth time, 12 April, 1769.

The struggle began to be very serious. Whilst loyal addresses poured in from various parts of the country, the City held aloof, and the conduct of Samuel Turner, the lord mayor, who was a zealous Wilkite received a distinct mark of approval from the

---

¹ Journal House of Commons, xxxii, 178. Walpole, Memoirs, iii, 292, 298, 313-319, 324-325, 327.

² Journal House of Commons, xxxii, 228, 229.

³ Annual Register, xii, 80, 82.

Common Council.¹ In the meantime a number of rich and influential men—among whom were Horne the vicar of Brentford, who loved to mix himself up in political and municipal matters, Townshend, Sawbridge, Oliver and others—had formed themselves into a society for the purpose of helping Wilkes to pay his fines and other liabilities and of supporting him and his cause. The society came to be known as the Supporters of the Bill of Rights.² The freeholders of Middlesex met at Mile End, and unanimously resolved in spite of all opposition to stand by the representative of their choice; whilst a procession of merchants and tradesmen on their way to St. James's with a loyal address was roughly treated by the mob and broken up.³ It required a man of some courage to oppose Wilkes at the forthcoming election, and he was found in Colonel Luttrell, an Irishman, whose father was a devoted adherent of Lord Bute. So desperate, however, did Luttrell's case appear that his life was specially insured for the occasion.⁴ Two other candidates stood, but the election really lay between Wilkes and Luttrell, the first being nominated by Townshend, and the latter by Stephen Fox, Lord Holland's son. The polling took place on the 12th April, when Wilkes was for the fourth time returned by an overwhelming majority. A huge crowd immediately

---

¹ Journal 64, fo. 341b. Several wards met and drew up instructions to the Common Council not to allow of an address to the king, "as calculated to countenance the unconstitutional measures of the present administration, rather than to express duty and affection to the best of kings."—Annual Register, xii, 88.

² Annual Register, xii, 75. Walpole, Memoirs, iii, 339.

³ Annual Register, xii, 82, 84.

⁴ Walpole, Memoirs, iii, 353.

made its way to the King's Bench Prison with colours flying and bands playing, to congratulate him upon his success. When the result of the election was reported to the House, they not only rejected Wilkes, but declared Luttrell to be elected, and ordered the return to be amended accordingly.[1]

<small>Remonstrance of the livery, 24 June, 1769.</small> Such a proceeding on the part of parliament raised a grave constitutional question, and caused great commotion in the city. If it lay with parliament of its own mere motion, and without the authority of an Act, to deprive electors of their right of choosing their own representatives, the livery of London would suffer with the rest of the kingdom. The matter was warmly taken up by *Junius*, who strenuously condemned this usurpation by parliament.[2] The mayor was asked to summon a Common Hall "for the purpose of taking the sense of the livery of "London on the measures proper to be pursued by "them in the present alarming situation of public "affairs." Turner declined to act in the matter on his own responsibility, and referred the petition to the Common Council who told him not to accede to the request (5 May).[3] Thus thrown on their own resources the livery resolved at their ordinary meeting on the following Midsummer Day when Townshend and Sawbridge were chosen sheriffs, to

---

[1] Journal House of Commons, xxxii, 386, 387.

[2] "The arbitrary appointment of Mr. Luttrell"—he wrote to the Duke of Grafton (8 July)—"invades the foundation of the laws themselves, as it manifestly transfers the right of legislation from those whom the people have chosen to those whom they have rejected. With a succession of such appointments, we may soon see a House of Commons collected in the choice of which the other towns and counties of England will have as little share as the devoted county of Middlesex."— Letters of Junius (Woodfall), i, 509.

[3] Journal 64, fo. 344b.

petition the king himself against the arbitrary action of the government. A petition to this effect had been drawn up by some of the livery previous to the meeting of the Common Hall. It purported to come from "the lord mayor, commonalty and livery of the city of London," but upon the lord mayor objecting to this, the title was changed to "the "humble petition of the livery of the city of London "in Common Hall assembled." The petitioners did not mince words. The king's ministers were charged with peculation, and with illegally issuing general warrants. They had violently seized persons and papers, and after defeating and insulting the law on various occasions, had wrested from the people, the last sacred right they had left, viz., "the right of "election, by the unprecedented seating a candidate "notoriously set up and chosen by themselves." Deprived of all hope of parliamentary redress, the petitioners turned to the king, reminding him that it was for the purpose of redress alone, and for such occasions as the present, that so great and extensive powers had been entrusted to the crown.[1]

Among the ministers whom the livery charged with peculation was Lord Holland, to whom they had made special reference (although not actually mentioning his name) as "a public defaulter of unaccounted millions." Stung to the quick at this imputation, Lord Holland wrote a letter to the lord mayor (9 July), complaining of the aspersion and referring him for the falsehood of the accusation

Lord Holland's letter to the mayor, 9 July, 1769

---

[1] Common Hall Book, No. 8, fos. 146b–147b. The petition is printed in a small volume of "city petitions, addresses and remonstrances," (1778), preserved in the Guildhall Library.

to Beckford, whom he had satisfied (he said) as to the injustice of it.¹ Turner contented himself with a curt reply that he was not answerable for the contents of the petition. There was no love lost between Lord Holland and the citizens. According to the words put into his mouth by Gray, the poet, he would gladly have seen it reduced by fire and sword :—

> " Purg'd by the sword, and purified by fire,
> Then had we seen proud London's hated walls :
> Owls would have hooted in St. Peter's choir,
> And foxes stunk and litter'd in St. Paul's."

Beckford elected mayor for the second time, 10 Oct., 1769.

The address had been ordered to be presented by the lord mayor, the sheriffs, and three of the city's members, but months passed by and no reply was vouchsafed. The livery got impatient. Their attack on the ministry was strengthened by the re-appearance of Chatham,² after a prolonged illness, whilst their own position received material support by Beckford consenting for the second time to occupy the mayoralty chair. "I cannot resist the importunate request of my fellow citizens"—he wrote from his house in Soho Square, the 12th October,³—" their desires have over-
" come resolutions that I once thought were fixed and
" determined. The feeble efforts of a worn out
" man to serve them can never answer their sanguine
" expectations. I will do my best, and will sacrifice
" ease and retirement, the chief comfort of old age,
" to their wishes. I *do* accept the office of lord

---

¹ Beckford denied this—Walpole, Memoirs, iii. 380.

² "That the moment of his [Chatham's] appearance, *i.e.*, so immediately after the petition of the livery of London set on foot and presented by his friend Alderman Beckford, has a hostile look, cannot be doubted."—Walpole to Mann, 19 July, 1769. Letters, v, 177.

³ Common Hall Book, No. 8, fo. 148b.

"mayor. I shall hope for the assistance of your
"Lordship and my brethren the Court of Aldermen.
"The advantage and good effects of their advice
"were experienced on many occasions in my late
"mayoralty." Their position would have been still
more strengthened, had similar petitions been sent
in from other parts of the country, but London's
example was not in this case followed.[1]

On the day that the result of the poll was declared (10 Oct.) in favour of Beckford as mayor for the ensuing year the livery passed several resolutions. The first was that the out-going lord mayor (Turner) should be asked if he had received any answer to the recent petition. Secondly that he should be called upon to produce Lord Holland's letter. They in the next place publicly named Lord Holland as the paymaster to whom they had referred in their petition as "a public defaulter of unaccounted millions," and insisted upon a parliamentary enquiry into his accounts. Should he be found such a defaulter as they alleged, it was the duty of the city's representatives in Parliament to move for his impeachment. These resolutions they ordered to be placed on record, as part of the proceedings in relation to the election of a mayor, and a copy of them was to be sent to each of the city's members.[2] *Resolutions of the livery, 10 Oct., 1769.*

Here matters were allowed to rest until the following March (1770), when the livery sought the assistance of the Common Council to get Beckford to *Another address of the livery, 6 March, 1770.*

---

[1] "London, for the first time in its life, has not dictated to England. Essex and Hertfordshire have refused to petition; Wiltshire and Worcester say they will petition, and Yorkshire probably will."—Walpole to Mann, 19 July, 1769. Letters, v, 177

[2] Common Hall Book, No. 8, fo. 149.

summon a Common Hall for the purpose of taking further measures to secure their rights and privileges.[1] Why they did not make a direct application to the mayor himself, as was the usual practice, is not clear. The Court, after some hesitation, acceded to their request, and a Common Hall was summoned accordingly. Another address, remonstrance and petition was thereupon drawn up (6 March).[2] "A bolder declaration, both against king and Parliament"—Walpole writes to his friend[3]—was never seen. The majority of the Court of Aldermen would have formally disavowed it, but Beckford, who presided, refused to allow a motion to that effect to be moved until the City's Records had been searched with the view of determining the several powers of the Courts of Aldermen and Common Council, and of the livery in Common Hall assembled.[4] After referring to their former petition remaining still unanswered, the petitioners proceeded to inveigh against Parliament and the ministry for having deprived the people of their just rights. The majority in the House (they said) had "done a deed more ruinous in its "consequences than the levying of ship-money by "Charles the First or the dispensing power assumed "by James the Second." They told the king to his face that the House of Commons as then constituted did not only fail to represent the people, but it was "corruptly subservient" to his own ministers, and they called upon his majesty on that account to dissolve

[1] Journal 65, fos. 62b–63b.
[2] Common Hall Book, No. 8, fos. 152–153.
[3] Walpole to Mann, 15 March, 1770.—Letters, v, 229.
[4] Repertory 174, fos. 155, 156.

the Parliament and dismiss those ministers who had advised him badly.

This language was bold, but it conveyed no more than the truth. Its truthfulness, no less than its boldness, attracted *Junius*, who thus wrote approvingly of the attitude taken up by London: "The city of London "hath given an example which, I doubt not, will be "followed by the whole kingdom. The noble spirit of "the metropolis is the life-blood of the state, collected "at the heart; from that point it circulates, with health "and vigour, through every artery of the constitution. ". . . The city of London have expressed their "sentiments with freedom and firmness; they have "spoken truth boldly; and in whatever light their "remonstrance may be represented by courtiers, I "defy the most subtle lawyer in this country to point "out a single instance in which they have exceeded "the truth. Even that assertion, which we are told "is most offensive to Parliament, in the theory of the "English constitution is strictly true. If any part of "the representative body be not chosen by the people "that part vitiates the whole."[1] Adopting the words of the remonstrance, he declared that the principle on which the Middlesex election had been determined was more pernicious in its effects than either the levying of ship-money by Charles I or the suspending power claimed by his son.

The remonstrance approved by Junius.

On the other hand several of the livery companies themselves, viz.: the Goldsmiths, the Weavers, and the Grocers, had declared the remonstrance to be indecent and disrespectful, and forbade the members

Condemned by Goldsmiths, Weavers and Grocers.

---

[1] Junius to the printer of the *Public Advertiser*, 19 March, 1770.—Letters of Junius (Woodfall), ii, 115.

of their respective liveries to attend any Common Hall in future (except for purposes of election) without express leave of their Courts of Assistants. The authority of the mayor and aldermen over the livery companies was thus openly defied. On learning of these resolutions Beckford summoned a Common Hall to meet on the 12th April to consider what course to take, but his precept was ignored by the recalcitrant companies. Such disobedience was hitherto unheard of, and the matter was reported to the livery committee, appointed the 28th September, 1769.[1] This committee was afterwards united with a committee of the Common Council, and after due consideration the question of the rights of the livery was submitted to counsel.[2] The result will be seen in the next chapter.

The king hesitates to receive the address.

Unlike the former address, this was invested with a corporate character by being ordered to be presented by the lord mayor, the city members, the Court of Aldermen, the sheriffs and the Common Council. In due course the sheriffs attended (6 March), to learn when the king would be pleased to receive the address. They were told they had come at an improper time, and must deliver their message on a court day. By treating them in this manner the king hoped to hear no more of the matter; it was— he told Lord Weymouth—the most likely means of putting an end to "this stuff." He desired, however, that the opinion of Lord Mansfield should be taken as to whether the sheriffs could claim to be received

[1] Common Hall Book, No. 8, fo. 154.
[2] Journal 65, fos. 118b, 125.

"as on occasions that they addressed the crown."[1] On the following day the sheriffs again presented themselves. After the levée was over they were admitted to the closet, but not before some questions had been asked as to the nature of the address to be presented. Sheriff Townshend having made his formal request the king replied that as the case was "entirely new" he would take time to consider it, and would send an answer by one of his principal secretaries of state. The question to be decided was whether the address ought to be treated as coming from the citizens of London in their corporate capacity or as only proceeding from a comparatively small body of them, viz., the livery. If the former, it would, in accordance with custom, be received by the king on the throne; if the latter, the king would receive it at a levée or in any other manner he might think fit. In order, therefore, to discover the precise nature of the address the king directed Lord Weymouth to make the necessary enquiries. Lord Weymouth accordingly wrote (8 March) to the sheriffs asking in what manner the address was authenticated and what was the nature of the assembly by which it had been adopted as it appeared to be "entirely new."[2] Instead of answering the letter the sheriffs the next day (9 March) again put in an appearance at St. James's, accompanied by the Remembrancer. Being asked whether they came "with a fresh message or with a message?" they answered "with a message." The secretaries of state then appeared, and Lord

---

[1] The king to Lord Weymouth, 6 March, 1770.—Jesse, Memoirs of George III, i, 490–491.

[2] Lord Weymouth to the sheriffs of London, 8 March, 1770.—Cal. Home Office Papers (1770–1772), p. 20.

Weymouth asked the sheriffs if they had received his letter, and whether they came in consequence of it or on any fresh business? They replied that they had received his letter and had come in consequence of it. The following dialogue is recorded as having then taken place:—

Lord Weymouth: "Would it not be more proper "to send an answer in writing through me?"

The Sheriffs: "We act ministerially. As sheriffs "of London we have a right to an audience, and cannot "communicate to any other person than the king the "subject of our message."

Lord Weymouth: "I do not dispute your right to "an audience, but would it not be better and more "accurate to give your message to me in writing?"

The Sheriffs: "We know the value and conse-"quence of the citizen's right to apply immediately to "the king, and not to a third person, and we do not "mean that any of their rights and privileges should be "betrayed by our means."

<small>Sheriff Townshend's speech to the king, 9 March, 1770.</small>

At last the king consented to see them, and Sheriff Townshend then addressed his majesty in the following terms:—

"When we had last the honour to appear before "your majesty, your majesty was graciously pleased to "promise an answer by one of your majesty's principal "secretaries of state; but we had yesterday questions "proposed to us by Lord Weymouth. In answer to "which we beg leave humbly to inform your majesty "that the application we make to your majesty we "make as sheriffs of the city of London by the "direction of the livery in Common Hall legally

" assembled. The address, remonstrance and petition
" to be presented to your majesty, by their chief
" magistrate, is the act of the citizens of London in
" their greatest court, and is ordered by them to be
" properly authenticated as their act." [1]

To this the king vouchsafed no further reply than that he would take time to consider the matter. The next day (10 March) he wrote to Lord North: " The " more I reflect on the present remonstrance from the " livery the more I am desirous it should receive an " answer, otherwise this bone of contention will never " end; I therefore am thoroughly of opinion that, as " the sheriffs (though falsely) have insinuated that it is " properly authenticated, that the least inconvenience " will be receiving them on the throne." [2] All that the minister could do to help the king out of his difficulty was to instance cases where only " a certain number" were allowed to attend, but the king was not satisfied, and expressed himself as being still of opinion that under the circumstances he had better receive the address on the throne.[3]

The king consults Lord North.

Accordingly it was decided to receive it in that manner on Wednesday, the 14th.[4] Having listened with composure, distasteful as the address was, the king read an answer in which, after declaring his readiness ever to listen to the complaints of his

The king's reply, 14 March, 1770.

---

[1] Gentleman's Magazine, xl, 111-112.

[2] The editor of the correspondence between the king and Lord North gives the date of this letter as the 20th March—a mistake, probably, for the 10th—as the remonstrance was presented on the 14th.—Correspondence, i, 20.

[3] The King to Lord North, 11 March, 1770.—Correspondence, i, 17-18.

[4] Lord Weymouth to the sheriffs, 12 March, 1770.—Gentleman's Magazine, xl, 112.

subjects, he expressed concern at finding that any of them had been so misled as to offer an address at once disrespectful to himself, injurious to Parliament and irreconcilable with the principles of the constitution.[1]

Parliament and the remonstrance, 15-19 March, 1770.

The next day (15 March) the House of Commons resolved to pray the king that he would be pleased to lay the remonstrance and his answer before the House. The king at once gave his consent, but the ministry betrayed the greatest timidity. "The fright at court continues"—wrote Calcraft to Chatham (17 March)—"and they are "not only puzzled, but undetermined what to do "with the remonstrance, now it is got to parliament. "The only resolution taken is to be most temperate "and avoid either expulsion or commitment seeing "the lord mayor and sheriffs court it." Again "the "ministers dread a resolution of the Common Hall "against the advisers of the strong words in his "majesty's answer."[2] After long debate the House contented themselves (19 March) with passing a resolution to the effect that the document was an "unwarrantable and dangerous petition" as well as a gross abuse of the right of petitioning the king.[3]

Entertainment at Mansion House, 22 March, 1770.

In the meantime Beckford, who with the two sheriffs, Townshend and Sawbridge, and with Alderman Trecothick avowed their share in the remonstrance, had issued invitations to a banquet at the Mansion House to "a very numerous though a select number of persons" of both houses of parliament. He had previously taken the precaution of sounding Lord

---

[1] Common Hall Book, No. 8, fo. 153b.
[2] Chatham correspondence, iii, 429, 430.
[3] Journal House of Commons, xxxii, 810.

Rockingham, and in doing so had used the good offices of his friend Lord Chatham. The entertainment would afford a good opportunity (thought the mayor), for obtaining some guarantee of the future policy of the Opposition whenever they should come into power, and he and Horne had devised a plan for getting the guests to sign a formal document committing them definitely to certain reforms. Such a document Horne afterwards declared himself to have actually drawn up " in terms so cautious and precise as to leave no " room for future quibble and evasion."[1] This device becoming known, Chatham wrote to say that in the opinion of himself, Lord Rockingham and Lord Temple, " no new matters should be opened or agitated at or after the convivium "[2] which was fixed for Thursday, the 22nd March,—the eve of the day on which both Houses were to present an address to the king touching the remonstrance. The entertainment was one of the most magnificent ever given by a private individual. The members were escorted to the city by the livery of London on horseback through the crowded streets. Those who failed to illuminate their houses ran the risk of having their windows broken.[3] Chatham was prevented from attending by an attack of his old enemy the gout.[4] Magnificent as was the entertainment from a social point of view, from a political it was money thrown away.

[1] Horne to Junius, 31 July, 1771. Letters of Junius, ii, 298, 299.
[2] Chatham to Beckford, 10 March, 1770.—Chatham correspondence, iii, 431, note.
[3] Annual Register, xiii, 82, 83. Walpole to Mann, 23 March, 1770. Letters, v, 232. Walpole, Memoirs, iv, 115.
[4] " A real or political fit of the gout."—Walpole.

Wilkes regains his liberty, 17 April, 1770.

Wilkes's term of imprisonment was now fast drawing to a close. His release was looked forward to by his friends with great joy, by his enemies with no little fear and concern. In November last (1769), his spirits and the spirits of his party had been raised by a jury awarding him no less a sum than £4,000 by way of damages in his long protracted action against Lord Halifax,[1] by whose orders his papers had been seized. Nevertheless his second fine of £500 remained yet unpaid.[2] On the 17th April (1770) Wilkes regained his liberty, and in order to prevent disturbance slipped away into the country, to the house of his friend Reynolds, for a few days. On his return he was immediately sworn in as alderman of the ward of Farringdon Without (24 April).[3] At the outset of his new career Wilkes behaved with the greatest propriety. "I don't know "whether Wilkes is subdued by his imprisonment"— wrote Walpole to his friend—" or waits for the rising "of parliament, to take the field; or whether his "dignity of alderman has dulled him into prudence "and the love of feasting; but hitherto he has done "nothing but go to city-banquets and sermons, and "sit at Guildhall as a sober magistrate."[4]

A remonstrance by Common Council, 14 May, 1770.

On the 14th May, he was nominated a member of the committee appointed by the Common Council to draw up another humble address, remonstrance and petition to the king, "touching the violated right "of election, and the applications of the livery of "London, and his majesty's answer thereupon." An

---

[1] Walpole, Memoirs, iii, 395. Annual Register, xii, 150.
[2] Annual Register, xiii, 80. [3] Repertory 174, fo. 184.
[4] Walpole to Mann, 6 May, 1770. Letters, v, 235.

address was accordingly drawn up—"much less hot than the former"—calling upon the king to dissolve parliament and dismiss his ministers.[1] It was adopted by the Common Council by a large majority (viz. 98 votes to 46). At first the king was disposed not to receive it at all. "I suppose this is another "remonstrance" he wrote to North, after telling the sheriffs to call again "if so I think it ought not to have any answer."[2] After seeing a draft of it, however, he changed his mind. He acknowledged that it was less offensive than he had been given to understand, but he thought "the whole performance" required no more than "a short dry answer."[3]

In the ordinary course the presentation would have been made by the Recorder on behalf of the citizens. Eyre, however, refused to attend on this occason,[4] so that the address may possibly have been read by the lord mayor himself. The king's reply was even briefer than usual. He would (he said) have been wanting to the public and to himself had he not expressed dissatisfaction at the former address. He declared his sentiments to be unchanged, and he declined to use his prerogative in a manner which might be dangerous to the constitution of the kingdom.[5]

The king's reply, 23 May, 1770.

---

[1] Journal 65, fos. 80–82. Walpole to Mann, 24 May, 1770, Letters, v, 238. It is supposed that Chatham had a hand in drawing it up. It is certain, at least, that he approved of it, and that he and Beckford were intimate friends at the time.—Walpole, Memoirs of reign of George III, iv, 153.

[2] The king to Lord North, 14 May, 1770.—Correspondence, i, 26.

[3] The same to the same, 19 May, 1770.—Correspondence, i, 27.

[4] An order was thereupon made that the services of Eyre as a standing counsel for the city should in future be dispensed with. Two years later his connection with the city was severed and his conduct rewarded by his being created one of the barons of the exchequer.—Journal 65, fos. 117b, 121; Repertory 176, fo. 458.

[5] Journal 65, fo. 83.

Beckford's memorable speech.

It was now that Beckford made that memorable speech with which his name will ever be associated (although claimed by Horne Tooke as his composition), and which was afterwards inscribed, by order of the Common Council, upon the pediment of his statue erected in the Guildhall.[1] Deeming the king's answer unsatisfactory the mayor, to the surprise of all present, and contrary to all form and precedent, again stept forward, and, addressing the king, besought his majesty to allow him—the mayor of the king's loyal city of London—to express on behalf of his fellow citizens their sorrow at having incurred his majesty's displeasure. He assured the king that there were no subjects "more faithful, more dutiful, or more affectionate" than the citizens, and he denounced the man who should attempt to alienate the king's affection from his subjects in general, and from the city of London in particular, as an enemy to the king and constitution. Even Walpole allowed that the speech was "wondrous loyal and respectful," if a trifle disconcerting. The king was so much taken by surprise that he hesitated whether to stay or withdraw. He decided on the former, and remained until Beckford had finished, when he immediately got up and retired without a word. Chatham was immensely pleased at the spirit displayed by Beckford on this occasion, and wrote to tell him so: "The *spirit* "*of Old England* spoke that never-to-be-forgotten "day." His letter concludes with the following enthusiastic passage: "Adieu, then for the present "(to call you by the most honourable of titles) *true*

---

[1] Journal 65, fo. 92. Horne Tooke was accustomed to exclaim "that he could not be deemed a vain man, as he had obtained statues for others, but never for himself!"—Stephen, Memoirs of Horne Tooke, i, 151, 157.

"*Lord Mayor of London;* that is, *first* magistrate of "the *first* city of the world! I mean to tell you only "a plain truth when I say your lordship's mayoralty "will be revered till the constitution is destroyed and "forgotten."[1] Beckford, in his reply, justified his conduct. "What I spoke in the king's presence was "uttered in the language of truth, and with that "humility and submission which become a subject "speaking to his lawful king: at least I endeavoured "to behave properly and decently; but I am inclined "to believe that I was mistaken, for the language of "the court is that my deportment was impudent, in-"solent and unprecedented. God forgive them all!"[2]

When the matter came to be reported to the Common Council (25 May) two aldermen, viz., Rossiter and Harley, objected to Beckford having made a speech to the king without instructions from the Common Council, whilst Wilkes and the two sheriffs, Townshend and Sawbridge, upheld his conduct. The Court then desired Beckford to state what he had said to his majesty. Thereupon the speech was produced and read, and this being done a formal vote of thanks was passed to the mayor for having presented the remonstrance, and "for his vindicating at the foot of the throne the "loyalty and affection of the citizens of London."[3]

Vote of thanks to Beckford for his speech, 25 May.

The same motive which prompted Beckford's action in March last on the occasion of his magnificent entertainment to the Opposition had in the

Vote of thanks to Chatham, 14 May, 1770.

---

[1] Chatham to the Lord Mayor, 25 May, 1770.—Chatham Correspondence, iii, 462.

[2] Beckford to Chatham, 25 May, 1770.—Chatham Correspondence, iii, 463.

[3] Journal 65, fos. 83-84; Gentleman's Magazine, vol. xl. (where the date of the Common Council is given as the 28 May).

meanwhile incited the Common Council to a similar indiscretion. On the 14th May—the day that the last remonstrance was prepared— the Court passed a vote of thanks to Chatham for the zeal he had shown in support of the rights of election and petition, as well as for his " declaration that his endeavours shall " hereafter be used that Parliaments may be restored to "their original purity by shortening their duration and "introducing a more full and equal representation."[1] Here the wish was distinctly father to the thought. Chatham had made no such declaration. The vote was nothing more or less than an attempt to "fix" Chatham to a definite policy of reform just as Beckford had previously tried to fix Rockingham and his party. Chatham was not to be thus caught, and in his acknowledgment of the vote he declared that as to any assurance he was supposed to have given that he was in favour of shorter Parliaments there had been some misapprehension. With all deference to the sentiments of the City he felt bound to say that he could not recommend triennial Parliaments as a remedy for venality in elections. He would not, however, oppose any measure for their introduction if the country showed itself unmistakably in favour of them.[2]

---

[1] Journal 65, fo. 82b.

[2] Journal 65, fos. 82b, 94. A year later he held more decided views as to the advantage of short Parliaments. Writing to Earl Temple on the 17th April, 1771, he remarks: "Allow a speculator in a great chair to add that a plan for more equal representation by additional knights of the shire seems highly seasonable, and to shorten the duration of Parliaments not less so. If your lordship should approve, could Lord Lyttleton's caution be brought to take these ideas, we should take possession of strong ground, let who will decline to follow us. One line of men, I am assured, will zealously support, and a respectable weight of law, *si quid novisti rectius istis candidus imperti.*" This extract was read at a Common Council held the 13th April, 1780, and was ordered to be entered on the Journal of the Court.—Chatham Correspondence, iv, 155, note.—Journal 68, fo. 52.

On the 30th May, Beckford again appeared at court at the head of a deputation from the city to present a formal address of congratulation from the Common Council on the birth of another princess. The address had been passed unanimously by the Council, although Wilkes declared it was no time for such compliments. The deputation met with some little opposition on its way to St. James's, the gates at Temple Bar being suddenly closed by the mob before the whole of the civic party had passed through, and they were not admitted into the presence chamber, until the lord mayor had promised not to repeat his former offence of making a speech.[1] The next day Beckford laid the first stone of the new gaol of Newgate.[2] This was his last appearance in public. He had recently caught a chill whilst at Fonthill, and this had been aggravated by his hasty return to town in order to attend to his mayoralty duties, and the excitement consequent thereto. For some years past he had not enjoyed good health, and age began to tell upon him. Even his first mayoralty in 1762-3, he entered upon with reluctance, and the day before his election had gone so far as to petition the Court of Aldermen to be discharged from his aldermanry on the score of ill-health.[3] He was, as we have seen, still more reluctant to undertake a second year of office, and only consented to do so after pressing solicitation. On the 12th June, he was so ill from rheumatic fever that he was unable to attend a Court of Aldermen, and on the 21st he died.[4]

The last days of Beckford.

[1] Annual Register, xiii, 111.
[2] Annual Register, xiii, 112.   [3] Repertory 166, fo. 358.
[4] Repertory 174, fo. 276. Annual Register, xiii, 119.

CHAPTER XXXVIII.

<small>Barlow Trecothick mayor, June-Sept., 1770.</small>

Upon Beckford's decease Trecothick was elected mayor for the remainder of the year. It was no easy matter for the successor of one of the wealthiest and most hospitable of mayors to avoid invidious comparison, and at the close of his short term of office Trecothick was satirised by Wilkes for not maintaining the City's reputation for hospitality.[1] Trecothick was also out of favour with Wilkes for having officially backed press warrants, the legality of which was much disputed at the time. The mayor, however, justified his conduct in this respect to the livery when they met at Michaelmas, and his speech was very favourably received.[2] Wilkes on the other hand was so strenuously opposed to press warrants that he went so far as to release a man who had been pressed for the navy, although he had been taken by virtue of a warrant from the Lords of the Admiralty, backed by Trecothick.[3]

<small>Brass Crosby elected mayor, 29 Sept., 1770.</small>

When Michaelmas arrived, the livery refused to re-elect Trecothick—as indeed Wilkes had foretold. Bankes was again passed over, and Brass Crosby chosen mayor for the ensuing year. In character he was scarcely less spirited and patriotic than Beckford,

---

[1] See *Annals of the Mayoralty of the Right Hon. Barlow Trecothick, Esq.*, ascribed to Wilkes, printed in Stephens's Memoirs of John Horne Tooke, i, 191, note.

[2] Annual Register, xiii, 161, 162.   [3] *Id.*, xiii, 157.

and he was made to suffer in consequence. Very early in his mayoralty (21 Nov.) it fell to his lot to carry up another address and remonstrance to the king for the dissolution of parliament, and to listen to a curt refusal.[1]

In consequence of Wilkes's opposition to pressing for the king's service, a system then constantly practised owing to the necessities of the time, the new mayor, one of his most steady adherents, consulted Lord Chatham on the legality of press warrants. Chatham advised him to take the opinion of counsel on the matter, and this he accordingly did, with the result that whilst he was advised that press warrants, however objectionable, were legal, the lord mayor could not legally be compelled to sign them. At the same time counsel left it to the mayor's consideration "whether for the peace of the "city, and preservation of the subject, he would not "conform to the practice of most of his predecessors "on such occasions." This decision being deemed unsatisfactory, the City preferred to bestow premiums on voluntary recruits, and the same course was taken by other towns.[2]

Opinion touching press warrants.

It is, however, for the conspicuous part he took in the struggle for the liberty of the press that Brass Crosby is best remembered. Great jealousy had always existed in parliament as to reports of debates held there, and the Commons had comparatively of

The freedom of reporting parliamentary debates, 1771.

---

[1] Journal 65, fos. 140 *seq.* The king was very angry at having to receive more of this "stuff." "The idea of a fresh address, remonstrance and petition is so extremely absurd, and considering the time I may add puerile, that it deserves contempt."—The king to Lord North, 15 Nov., 1770.—Correspondence, i, 39.

[2] Walpole, Memoirs, iv, 196, 197.

recent date (28 Feb., 1729) passed a resolution to the effect that it was an indignity, and a breach of privilege, for anyone " to give in written or printed newspapers" any account of the proceedings of the house.[1] Notwithstanding this resolution, reports of debates continued to appear in the public press, but always with an affectation of secrecy.

The arrest of Wheble and Miller, 15 March, 1771. A scheme was now set on foot by Wilkes for embroiling the House of Commons with the City. At his instigation certain printers in the city commenced to publish the debates without any attempt at disguise, printing the name of each speaker in full. Such a proceeding had always been deemed a distinct breach of privilege. Some members of the House speedily took offence, and the printers were ordered to attend. As they refused to obey the summons, they were ordered into custody. This was precisely what Wilkes had aimed at. On the 15th March, a printer named John Wheble was apprehended by virtue of a proclamation, and was carried before Wilkes, the sitting alderman, who immediately discharged him, after binding him over to prosecute the man who had taken him, for illegal arrest. The same evening a messenger of the House of Commons attempted to arrest Miller, the printer of the *Evening Post*, under warrant of the Speaker; but the messenger himself was taken into custody on a charge of assaulting a freeman of the city, and carried before the lord mayor and aldermen Wilkes and Oliver. These magistrates declared the warrant to be illegal, not having been backed by a magistrate of the city, and released Miller. They at the same time bound over

[1] Journal House of Commons, xxi, **238**.

the messenger of the House of Commons to appear to answer a charge of assaulting a citizen of London.[1]

The king was furious at the authority of parliament being thus openly defied by the civic magistrates, and wrote to Lord North (17 March) to say that unless Crosby and Oliver were not committed forthwith to the Tower by the House of Commons its authority would be annihilated;—"You know "very well I was averse to meddling with the "printers, but now there is no retracting, the honour "of the Commons must be supported."[2] *The king's letter to Lord North, 17 March, 1771.*

The House was no less indignant at being flouted by the City, than the king, and not only called upon Crosby and Oliver, who were members,[3] to answer for their conduct from their places, but sent for the clerk of the Justice Room at the Mansion House and ordered him in their presence to expunge the entry of the recognizance by which their messenger had been bound over to appear at the next Quarter Sessions to answer for his assault on Miller.[4] *His recognizance expunged by order of the House, 20 March, 1771.*

In the meantime Crosby, who was suffering from a severe attack of gout, had attended in his place (19 March). Early in the morning handbills were distributed in the city informing the inhabitants that it was the intention of the mayor to attend Parliament that afternoon—"even though he should be obliged *Crosby and Oliver before the House, 19 March, 1771.*

---

[1] Walpole, Memoirs, iv, 278, 287-289.

[2] Correspondence, i, 64.

[3] Crosby sat for Honiton, whilst Oliver had succeeded Beckford as one of the members for the city. Wilkes was also summoned to attend, but not as a member. He therefore disobeyed the summons, informing the Speaker by letter that when admitted to his seat for Middlesex he would attend, but not before.—Gentleman's Magazine, xli, 140 ; Annual Register, xiv, 188.

[4] Journal House of Commons, xxxiii, 275.

to be carried in a litter"—to uphold their rights and privileges, and calling upon them to escort him home on his return from Westminster. Here is a description of what took place taken from a contemporary newspaper;[1] "At two o'clock in the afternoon the right "hon. the lord mayor set out from the Mansion House "in a coach to attend the House of Commons, in pur-"suance of a summons, to answer for his conduct on "Friday last. His lordship appeared very feeble and "infirm, but in good spirits. Mr. Alderman Oliver and "his lordship's chaplain, Mr. Evans, were in the same "coach. A prodigious crowd of the better sort were "at the Mansion House and in the streets near it, "who testified their approbation by repeated huzzas, "which were continued quite from the Mansion House "to the House of Commons. On his arrival there one "universal shout was heard for near three minutes; "and the people during the whole passage to the "House called out to the lord mayor as the *people's* "*friend, the guardian of the city's rights and the nation's* "*liberties.*" Walpole minimises the display, and tells his friend that although thousands of handbills were dispersed to invite the mob to escort the mayor, not a hundred attended.[2] Having taken his seat in the House Crosby justified his conduct by the oath that he had taken on entering upon his mayoralty to preserve the liberties of the citizens, and desired to be heard by counsel.[3] Before his examination had proceeded far he was taken so seriously ill that he had to ask leave to go home. This was accorded, and

---

[1] Annual Register, xiv, 83.
[2] Walpole to Mann, 22 March.—Letters, v, 286.
[3] Journal House of Commons, xxxiii, 269.

"about five o'clock his lordship returned home, "attended by a great number of people; and the "populace took the horses out of the carriage at "St. Paul's, and drew the coach to the Mansion "House." The enquiry stood adjourned until Friday (22 March). In the meantime, leave having been given to him to appear by counsel, albeit with certain reservations, a committee was appointed to employ such counsel on his behalf as they should think fit, with power to draw on the Chamber to the extent of £500.[1] When Friday came the Speaker informed the House that he had received a letter from the lord mayor to the effect that he (Crosby) was so ill that he could not leave home, but that he would attend in his place as soon as his health permitted. Another adjournment was therefore made until the following Monday (25 March), and Oliver's defence was appointed for the same day.[2]

By Monday the lord mayor had sufficiently recovered to attend the House. At two o'clock in the afternoon he again set out in his coach accompanied, as before, by Oliver. Crowds again escorted them to Westminster, and the approaches to the House were so densely thronged that the Speaker gave orders to have them cleared. Even Walpole acknowledges this.[3] After the orders of the day for their attendance had been read Crosby explained how it was that no

Crosby and Oliver again before the House, 25 March, 1771.

---

[1] Journal House of Commons, xxxiii, 275; Journal 65, fo. 210.

[2] Journal House of Commons, xxxiii, 279, 280.

[3] "Last night, when I went to bed at half-an-hour after twelve, I had just been told that all the avenues to the House were blockaded, and had beaten back the peace-officers who had been summoned, for it was *toute autre chose* yesterday when the lord mayor went to the House from what it had been the first day." Walpole to Mann, 26 March, 1771.—Letters, v, 291.

counsel appeared on his behalf. In the first place the restrictions that the House had placed upon the appearance of counsel—viz., that they should only be heard upon such points as did not controvert the privileges of the House—was such as to prevent counsel speaking on many points material to his defence; and secondly the counsel whom he could depend upon, and whom he wished to employ, were on circuit. He therefore made his own defence. It was now ten o'clock at night, and the exertion he had undergone had rendered him so weak that he again had to ask leave to withdraw, promising to abide by the judgment of the House. On his return to the city he met with another ovation, his coach being drawn by the people all the way to the Mansion House.[1]

Crosby adjudged guilty of breach of privilege.

After Crosby's withdrawal the debate was continued. It was moved that the lord mayor's discharging of Miller out of custody, and his having held the messenger of the House to bail, was a breach of privilege. To this was moved the previous question, but after long debate it was rejected and the original motion passed, order being given for the lord mayor to attend on the following Wednesday, if his health permitted.[2]

Oliver committed to the Tower, 25 March, 1771.

Notwithstanding the lateness of the hour, the House called upon Oliver. The alderman, however, did not detain them long. He declined to call witnesses or to say anything in his defence, beyond asserting that he had acted according to his duty, oath, and conscience. Again there was a long debate

---

[1] Annual Register, xiv, 84; Gentleman's Magazine, xli, 141.
[2] Journal House of Commons, xxxiii, 283–285.

lasting until three o'clock in the morning, when the House resolved to send him to the Tower. The division was a small one, many members having already gone home in disgust. Oliver was allowed to go to his house in Fenchurch Street for a few hours before being removed to the Tower by the sergeant-at-arms.[1]

Speech of Alderman Townshend.

During the debate, Alderman Townshend appeared in the House looking very pale, having risen from a sick-bed—"his hair lank, and his face swathed "with linen, having had his jaw laid open for an "inflammation"—and after commenting severely upon the arbitrary action of the House in erasing a record entered in the lord mayor's book, proceeded to twit the government with its obsequiousness to female caprice and boldly declared their arbitrary measures to be due to the baneful influence of the Princess Dowager of Wales.[2] Such a declaration was not only in bad taste, but contrary to Parliamentary usage. Nevertheless it was placidly listened to and only received a tardy and weak denial from Lord North— a sign that the House felt the insecurity of its position.

"A table" to be provided for Oliver at City's expense, 26 March, 1771.

On Tuesday (26 March) a Common Council sat, summoned by Trecothick, who had been appointed (12 March), to act as *locum tenens* of the lord mayor during his "absence or illness." After transacting several matters of business, the court

---

[1] Journal House of Commons, xxxiii, 285, 286. Walpole to Mann, 26 March, 1771, Letters, v, 291. Calcraft to Chatham, 26 March; Barré to the same, 26 March, Chatham Correspondence, iv, 125-127, 131–133. Walpole, Memoirs of reign of George III, iv, 299, 300.

[2] Barré to Chatham, 26 March.—Chatham Correspondence, iv, 134. Gentleman's Magazine, xli, 170. Walpole, Memoirs, iv, 300, 301.

resolved unanimously "that during the confinement "of Mr. Alderman Oliver in the Tower of London "a table be provided for him at the expense of "this city, under the direction and management "of the committee appointed at the last court to "assist the lord mayor and the Aldermen Wilkes "and Oliver in their defence on the charge brought "against them by the House of Commons." [1]

Chatham's opinion on Oliver's committal.

The committal of Oliver was only one of a series of blunders of which Parliament had been guilty since the arrest of the printers. The position of affairs was clearly defined in letters written by Chatham at the time. "The state of the business seems to "me clearly this: the discharge of Miller, taken "under the Speaker's warrant, I think contrary to "the established jurisdiction of the House, with "regard to printers of their proceedings and debates; "but I hold also as fully, that in a conflict of "jurisdiction, the lord mayor and city magistrates, "acting under an oath of office and their charter, "cannot be proceeded against criminally by the "House, without the highest injustice and op-"pression." Again:—"the House becomes flagrantly "unjust and tyrannical, the moment it proceeds "criminally against magistrates standing for a juris-"diction they are bound to maintain, in a conflict of "respectable rights." He goes on to say that "nothing "appears to me more distinct, than declaring their "right to jurisdiction, with regard to printers of their "proceedings and debates, and punishing their mem-"ber, and in him his constituents, for what he has

[1] Journal 65, fos. 212–212b.

"done in discharge of his oath and conscience as a
"magistrate."[1]

This view was also strenuously supported by Junius,[2] who was emphatic that "as magistrates," Crosby and Oliver "had nothing to regard but the "obligation of their oaths, and the execution of the "laws. If they were convinced that the Speaker's "warrant was not a legal authority to the messenger, "it necessarily followed that, when he was charged "upon oath with a breach of the peace, they *must* "hold him to bail. They had no option."

The opinion of Junius.

On Wednesday (27 March), Crosby again attended in his place, as directed, to hear the decision of the House in his case. He was accompanied as before by an "amazing number of people" anxious to learn the issue; "guards, both horse and "foot, were ordered to be in readiness, in case any "tumult should arise. The city was all in motion; "and by its acclamations testified its satisfaction with "his conduct." Although he arrived at the House early in the afternoon, it was past eight o'clock in evening before the House was ready to take his business into consideration. Meanwhile the approaches to the House were in the hands of the mob who threatened many of the members with violence. Lord North, in particular, was made the object of a violent attack. His coach was demolished and he himself narrowly escaped being killed. Others, and among them Charles Fox, who had made himself especially obnoxious to the citizens by speaking of

Crosby again attends the House, 27 March, 1771.

---

[1] Chatham to Calcraft, 26 March, 1771; The same to Barré. 26 March.—*Chatham Correspondence*, iv, 129-130, 136-137.

[2] *Letters of Junius*, iii, 376.

Oliver as an "assassin of the constitution," were also insulted, but not so outrageously.¹ The justices confessed to the House their inability to read the Riot Act, and declared that the constables were powerless. The sheriffs of London—William Baker and Richard Martin—being members of the House,² were thereupon desired to go themselves and endeavour to disperse the crowd,³ and at their intervention peace was at length restored.

Is committed to the Tower.

The House being now prepared to proceed with the chief business of the day, a motion was made for committing the lord mayor to the custody of the sergeant-at-arms, instead of sending him to the gloomier quarters of the Tower, on account of his ill-health. Crosby, however, at once desired that no such favour might be shown him; he was quite prepared, he said, to join his honourable friend in the Tower. An amendment was accordingly moved that he should be committed to the Tower, and this was carried by 202 votes to 39.⁴ It was now past midnight. Crosby returned to the Mansion House for a short rest, and at four o'clock in the morning sent for a hackney coach and drove to the Tower.

Letter of Alderman Oliver from the Tower, 29 March, 1771.

A few hours later the Common Council resolved to furnish him with a "table" at the City's expense, as they had previously done for Oliver. Both

---

¹ Annual Register, xiv, 85. Gentleman's Magazine, xli, 141. Calcraft to Chatham, 28 March, 1771.—Chatham Correspondence, iv, 138-140. Walpole to Mann, 30 March.—Letters, v, 292. Walpole Memoirs, iv, 292.

² Baker sat for Plympton Earls, co. Devon, and Martin for Gatton, co. Surrey.

³ Journal House of Commons, xxxiii, 289.

⁴ *Id., ibid.*

prisoners acknowledged with gratitude the favour thus shown to them by their fellow-citizens, and both promised solemnly to continue their efforts to maintain the rights and privileges of the City, but the lord mayor declined the offer to furnish his table during his incarceration, as he did not wish to put the City to any additional expense on his account.[1] Oliver's letter contained some very caustic remarks upon the attitude of the government towards the City. "The last ten years have afforded the city "of London, in particular, every instance of neglect, "unkindness, insult and injury; their petitions have "been rejected, slighted, ridiculed; their property un- "justly conveyed to others; their charters violated;[2] "their laws contemned; their magistrates imprisoned. "The power that consumes us has the plainest and "most odious marks of despotism, abject abroad and "insolent at home. Whether our rights will in the "end be peaceably re-established or whether this "violence will be pursued is more than I can "certainly declare, but this I will venture to say for "myself that they must either change their laws or "the magistrates, for my adherence to my duty shall "be invariably the same, regardless of consequences."[3]

The temper of the populace at witnessing "the "new and extraordinary spectacle of the lord mayor "of the city of London and one of its principal magis- "trates being committed prisoners to the Tower," vented itself in a very characteristic manner. On

Supporters of the government beheaded in effigy, April, 1771.

---

[1] Journal 65, fos. 213, 214, 214b.

[2] Referring to Bills in Parliament for embanking the Thames for the purpose of building Adelphi Terrace, which was deemed to encroach upon the City's rights of conservancy.—Walpole, Memoirs, iv, 173.

[3] Journal 65, fo. 214b.

the 1st April a great mob proceeded to Tower Hill following a hearse and two carts, in which were figures representing the princess dowager, Lord Bute, the Speaker, and both the Foxes. The figures were beheaded by a chimney sweeper, after mock prayers, and then burnt. A like ceremony took place a few days later with figures of Lord Halifax, Lord Barrington, Alderman Harley, Colonel Luttrell, nicknamed "the usurper" Lord Sandwich, otherwise known as "Jemmy Twitcher," Colonel Onslow, who had been made so furious because a newspaper had called him "Cocking George," and De Grey, the attorney-general. Their supposed dying speeches were, to the intense amusement of the multitude, hawked about the streets.[1]

The contest won.

Wilkes, who had been no less an offender (if offence there was) in holding the Speaker's warrant to be illegal, got off scot free. Three times was he summoned to the bar of the House to answer for his conduct, and three times he refused to obey unless the House would acknowledge him as member for Middlesex. Ministers preferred to leave him unmolested, resorting even to a subterfuge in order to allow him to escape. It is true that, like Lord Shaftesbury in the reign of Charles II, he had removed for safety from his house in Westminster to lodgings in the city, but few can doubt his readiness, if need be, to share the fate of his brother aldermen in so good a cause. In the words of *Junius*, he was already a "wounded soldier" in the cause of liberty, and could point to "real prosecutions, real penalties, real

[1] Walpole, Memoirs, iv, 307; The *Middlesex Journal*, 2 April, 1771; The *London Chronicle*, 2–6 April.

imprisonment,"[1] and he deserves at least a part of the reward of the victory thus gained for the freedom of the press.

More than one attempt was made by the committee appointed for the defence of Crosby and Oliver to obtain their release on writs of Habeas Corpus, but in vain. They remained therefore in confinement, receiving a constant succession of friends and supporters, including Edmund Burke and the Dukes of Manchester and Portland, until set free by the prorogation of Parliament on the 8th May. The Common Council had, in anticipation of that event, resolved (3 May) to go in procession in their gowns, accompanied by the city officers to escort them from the Tower to the Mansion House.[2] As Crosby and Oliver emerged from the Tower gate they were welcomed with a salute of twenty-one guns by the Artillery Company, and carried, amid universal shouts of joy, to the Mansion House, from the balcony of which they bowed their acknowledgments. In the evening the city was illuminated. *Crosby and Oliver regain their liberty, 8 May, 1771.*

Even after their release the Common Council remained dissatisfied, and determined to take counsel's opinion as to the possibility of testing the legality of the action of Parliament. Counsel having given an adverse opinion it was resolved to let the matter rest until the meeting of the livery on Midsummer-day.[3] As soon as the livery were informed how matters stood they drew up another address and remonstrance calling upon the king to dissolve *Another address and remonstrance of the livery, 24 June, 1771.*

---

[1] Junius to the *Public Advertiser*, 13 Aug., 1771; Woodfall, Letters of Junius, ii, 307.

[2] Journal 65, fo. 222.   [3] *Id.*, fo. 226.

Parliament. This time it was their intention to attend the presentation of the address in a body, clad in their livery gowns.[1] The king, however, objected to receiving so large a number, and the lord mayor was informed that only the number "allowed by law" would be permitted to attend.[2] The livery had to give way, and the address was presented in the manner prescribed by the king. The answer they got was short and sharp; the king contenting himself with expressing his concern that a part of his subjects should have been so misled and deluded as to renew a request with which he had repeatedly declared that he could not comply.[3]

Election of Wilkes and Bull, sheriffs, 3 July, 1771.

The more important business transacted at this Common Hall was the election of sheriffs for the ensuing year. Wilkes had declared his intention of standing, and had asked Oliver—at that time a prisoner in the Tower—if he intended doing the same, regardless of the claims of senior aldermen. Oliver hesitated as to the course he should pursue, but finally wrote to Wilkes (11 April, 1771) expressing a determination not to serve with him, inasmuch as their political aims were not identical. Wilkes little relished this rebuff, and took exception to the propriety of Oliver's reply; as for himself, he said, "I am ready to serve the office of sheriff with you, "sir, or any other gentleman given me by the livery "as a colleague, should they think proper to elect "me."[4] The election was watched with great interest

---

[1] Common Hall Book, No. 8, fo. 165.
[2] Walpole, Memoirs, iv, 328. The number "allowed by law" ppears to have been ten.
[3] Common Hall Book, No. 8, fo. 167.
[4] The *London Chronicle*, 13-16 April, 1771.

by the king, who was afraid that Wilkes might succeed in getting elected, although supported only by "a small, though desperate," part of the livery, and he wrote to Lord North expressing a hope that no effort might be wanting to secure the election of Plumbe and Kirkman, the two senior aldermen who had not served.[1] He was doomed to disappointment. The livery declared for Wilkes and Frederick Bull, a creature of Wilkes, and a poll was demanded. This lasted several days, and on the 3rd July the result showed a large majority in their favour, and they were declared duly elected. Oliver came out at the bottom of the poll.[2]

The activity of court interference in this election was revealed by an unhappy *contretemps*. A letter which "Jack" Robinson, Lord North's secretary, had sent to Benjamin Smith, a partner of Alderman Nash, an "opulent grocer" of Cannon Street, urging him to "push the poll" with as many friends as possible, was carried by mistake to another Smith, of Budge Row, a Wilkite, who immediately published it with an affidavit as to its authenticity. The result was, as might be expected, the greater discomfiture of the ministerial candidates.[3]

Walpole was no less struck with the irrepressibility of Wilkes's character than annoyed at his being elected to an office which would bring him into close contact with the king;—" Wilkes is another Phœnix revived " from his own ashes. He was sunk—it was over with " him; but the ministers too precipitately hurrying to

---

[1] The king to Lord North, 26 June, 1771.—Correspondence, i, 76.

[2] Common Hall Book, No. 8, fos. 161, 161b.

[3] Walpole, Memoirs, iv, 328. The letter will be found printed in Woodfall's Letters of Junius, ii, 252, 253, note.

"bury him alive, blew up the embers, and he is again "as formidable as ever; and what will seem worse he "must go into the very closet whenever the city sends "him there with a message. . . . Wilkes in prison "is chosen member of Parliament and then alderman "of London. His colleagues betray him, desert him, "expose him, and he becomes sheriff of London."[1] Walpole's fears as to Wilkes's personal demeanour in office were goundless. As an alderman of the city he might have made himself sufficiently obnoxious at court had he so pleased, but he knew himself to be no *persona grata* to the king, and on that account was careful to keep out of his sight. That he knew how to behave on occasion is shown by his conduct during his mayoralty, when he surprised everybody, the king included, by his agreeable manner.

Wilkes and the shrievalty. Although determined to act with propriety in his personal relationships, Wilkes was no less determined to make himself as obnoxious to the king and his ministers as he well could in his official capacity as sheriff. "I will skirmish with the great almost every day in some way or other," he wrote to *Junius*. Again, with reference to the House of Lords, he informs his friend that "the sheriff means the attack."[2] A few days previous to his entering upon his duties he and his colleague, Bull, made a bid for popularity by a spirited act. The presence of the military at executions had been resented the previous year, and now in a short letter addressed to the livery they announced their determination to follow the example

---

[1] Walpole to Mann, 6 July, 1771.—Letters, v, 313.

[2] Wilkes to Junius, 12 Sept. and 17 Oct., 1771.—Woodfall, Letters of Junius, i, 299, 323.

set by their predecessors in office and not to allow soldiers to attend: "We are determined to follow so "meritorious an example, and as that melancholy "part of our office will commence in a very few days "we take this opportunity of declaring that as the "constitution has entrusted us with the whole power "of the county, we will not, during our sheriffalty, "suffer any part of the army to interfere or even to "attend, as on many former occasions, on the pretence "of aiding or assisting the civil magistrate. . . . "The magistrate, with the assistance of those in his "jurisdiction, is by experience known to be strong "enough to enforce all legal commands, without the "aid of a standing army." *Junius* thought this letter "very proper and well drawn."[1]

Another proceeding on the part of Wilkes failed however to meet with like approval. The 25th October being the anniversary of the king's accession, there was to be a thanksgiving service at St. Paul's which the sheriffs in the ordinary course of their duties would be expected to attend. Wilkes took it into his head that he would prefer not to go "in "a ginger-bread chariot to yawn through a dull "sermon." He accordingly prepared a letter to the lord mayor, asking that he might be allowed to sit at Old Bailey instead of taking part in what he called a "vain parade" on the anniversary of the accession of a prince, whose government was so unpopular. Before sending this missive he submitted it to *Junius*.[2] The latter thought it "more spirited than judicious,"

---

[1] Woodfall, Letters of Junius, i, 322.

[2] Wilkes to Junius, 17 Oct., 1771. Woodfall, Letters of Junius, i, 323-325.

and suggested that it was impolitic, to say the least, for "a grave sheriff" to mark his entrance into office with a direct outrage to the king, for outrage it was. He advises his friend to "consider the matter coolly," but in case Wilkes persisted, he sent him a more temperate form of letter.[1] The advice thus given was followed, and Wilkes abandoned his intention.

<small>Letter of Junius to Wilkes, 21 Aug., 1771.</small>

Wilkes had thus advanced another step in civic life, in spite of an unfortunate habit he had of quarrelling with his best friends. He had disgusted, or had himself thrown over, Horne, Sawbridge, Townshend and Oliver, all of whom were members with him of the society known as the Supporters of the Bill of Rights, and all had contributed towards relieving him of his pecuniary difficulties. Townshend and Horne had recently joined forces "to wrest the city out of Wilkes's hands," and Horne had done his best in a quiet way to prevent Wilkes being returned as sheriff, although he denied taking any part in the election.[2] He even ridiculed the idea in a letter to Wilkes (10 July), commencing "Give you joy, Sir,[3] the parson of "Brentford is at length defeated. He no longer rules "with an absolute sway over the city of London."[4] Wilkes was now to receive support from a quarter least expected. Hitherto, the redoubtable *Junius*

---

[1] Junius to Wilkes, 21 Oct., 1771.—Letters of Junius, i, 325-328.

[2] Horne to Junius, 13 July, 1771. *Id.*, ii, 259.

[3] A hit at Wilkes's connection with the city. It was usual at one time for the chamberlain thus to address a recipient of the honorary freedom of the city. The expression went out of use, but was revived by Wilkes when he became chamberlain.

[4] Horne to Wilkes, 10 July.—Stephens, Memoirs of John Horne Tooke, i, 310.

had treated Wilkes with little more than contempt.[1] He was now to become one of his warmest supporters. It was not that *Junius* entertained any great respect for Wilkes; it was enough that Wilkes was opposed to the ministry, and that he promised to be "a thorn in the king's side."[2] On the 21st August, about noon, Wilkes received a mysterious letter,[3] the writer of which proved to be *Junius* himself. After assuring Wilkes of his willingness to support him so long as he (Wilkes) depended only upon public favour and made common cause with the people, *Junius* comes to the real purport of his letter. He was especially anxious that Sawbridge should be chosen mayor at the coming election on Michaelmas day, and he uses all his art of persuasion upon Wilkes to get him to support Sawbridge's candidature. He repudiates all idea of self-interest in wishing to see Sawbridge in the mayoralty chair in place of Crosby, who was reported to be seeking a second year of office. "By all that's honourable I mean nothing but the cause"—his letter concluded—"and I may defy your keenest penetration "to assign a satisfactory reason why *Junius*, whoever "he be, should have a personal interest in giving "the mayoralty to Mr. Sawbridge, rather than to "Mr. Crosby."

The letter was very flattering, and Wilkes was pleased. "I am satisfied that *Junius* now means me

The reply of Wilkes, 12 Sept., 1771.

---

[1] "Mr. Wilkes, if not persecuted, will soon be forgotten."—Junius to the Duke of Grafton, 24 April, 1769. Woodfall, Letters of Junius, i, 478.

[2] Junius to Horne, 24 July, 1771. *Id.*, ii, 267.

[3] The letter was placed in Wilkes's hand by a chairman, who said he brought it from a gentleman he had met in the Strand. *Id.*, i, 263, note.

well,"—he wrote in reply (12 Sept.)—"and I wish to merit more than his regard, his friendship," but with his usual independence he declined to desert Brass Crosby, to whom he had promised his support before the arrival of *Junius's* letter. He was even prepared to do a little juggling in order to support Crosby's re-election. "To make Crosby mayor, it is "necessary to return to the Court of Aldermen "another man so obnoxious that it is impossible "for them to elect him. Bridgen I take to be "this man. While he presided in the city, he "treated them with insolence, was exceedingly rude "and scurrilous to them personally, starved them "at the few entertainments he gave, and pocketed "the city cash.[1]" Even if Bridgen were re-elected by any chance, Crosby would probably be appointed his *locum tenens* (Wilkes proceeded to point out), and so in any event all would be well. As for Sawbridge, little good could come of a reconciliation, "I allow "him honest, but think he has more mulishness than "understanding, more understanding than candour." Sawbridge moreover had already declared, that if he were chosen mayor at the next election he would pay fine rather than serve, "because Townshend ought to be mayor"—a declaration which Wilkes characterises as bordering on insanity.[2]

The correspondence thus commenced in so warm and friendly a manner was continued for several

---

[1] It is strange to find Wilkes giving this character of a mayor, who had shown him great partiality at the time that No. 45 of the *North Briton* was ordered to be burnt at the Royal Exchange—and who in other respects displayed a distinct democratic tendency. Can it be possible that Wilkes was hood-winking *Junius*, and that he would have been equally pleased to have seen either Bridgen or Crosby in the mayoralty chair?

[2] Wilkes to Junius, 12 Sept., 1771.—Woodfall, i, 297-304.

months. Finding himself unable to prevail upon Wilkes to become reconciled with Sawbridge, *Junius* contented himself with warning him at all hazards not to allow a "ministerial alderman" to be elected into the mayoralty chair, and begging that if after a fair canvas of the livery it was found that Bridgen had no chance of being returned, he would give up the point at once, and let Sawbridge be returned with Crosby—"a more likely way, in *my* judgment, to make Crosby lord mayor." [1]

When the election came on, Bridgen was not even nominated. The choice of the livery was declared to have fallen on Sawbridge and Crosby. Thereupon a poll was demanded on behalf of Bankes, Nash, Hallifax and Townshend. Whilst the poll was proceeding *Junius* issued an impassioned address to the livery calling upon them to set aside Nash—to whom he refers as the senior alderman below the chair, which Nash was not [2]—and to return Crosby and Sawbridge, men who were ready to execute the extraordinary as well as the ordinary duties of the mayoralty, who would grant Common Halls whenever necessary, carry up remonstrances to the king, and not be afraid to face the House of Commons or to suffer imprisonment. Of Nash's private character he declared he knew nothing, but as a public man he knew him to have done everything in his power to destroy the freedom of popular election in the city, and to have distinguished himself by thwarting the livery. He concludes his address

The election of Nash, Mayor, 8 Oct., 1771.

---

[1] Junius to Wilkes, 18 Sept., 1771.—Woodfall, i, 307–308.

[2] Both Sir Henry Bankes and Richard Peers were senior to Nash, and both were nominated at the election.—Common Hall Book, No. 8, fo. 166.

by apologising for his passionate language.—" The "subject comes home to us all. It is the language of "my heart."[1] The efforts of *Junius* were of little avail. On the 8th October, the result of the poll was declared, and Nash and Sawbridge being returned (the former by a large majority), the Court of Aldermen selected Nash to be mayor for the ensuing year. The "ministerial candidate" had got in. During the election Wilkes and his brother aldermen, Townshend and Sawbridge, were frequently at loggerheads, whilst Nash was so grievously assaulted on his way to the Guildhall that his life was in danger.[2]

Gifts of plate to Crosby, Wilkes and Oliver.

Upon Crosby's quitting office the Common Council passed him a vote of thanks for the courage he had displayed in refusing to back press warrants, and for his conduct in respect of the arrest of Miller. Early in the following year he was voted a silver cup of the value of £200, whilst Wilkes and Oliver were presented with other cups each of the value of £100. A proposal that a piece of plate of the value of £400 should be provided at the City's expense and inscribed in honour of these champions of the City's liberties, to form a part of the City's plate, was not adopted.[3]

Nash refuses to summon a Common Hall, Feb., 1772.

Nash had not long been mayor before he came into collision both with the livery and the Common Council. When a requisition was made to him in February, 1772, to summon a Common Hall for the purpose of instructing the city members to support Sawbridge in one of his many attempts to obtain triennial parliaments, he refused to do so on the

---

[1] Woodfall, Letters of Junius, ii, 338-344.
[2] Walpole, Memoirs, iv, 346.
[3] Journal 65, fos. 250, 253. Common Hall Book, No. 8, fo. 165.

ground that by an order of the livery of Midsummer-day last, the question of the rights of the livery was about to be decided in a court of law, informations having been laid against those companies who had refused to obey the mayor's precept.[1] He thought that in the meantime it would be well to suspend the exercise of his prerogative, more especially as most matters of importance connected with the city could be settled by the Common Council, which he professed himself always ready to call when necessity required. Not satisfied with his reply the livery held an informal meeting at the Half Moon Tavern in Cheapside, and persuaded a number of members of the Common Council to make a written application to the mayor to summon a court on the 18th February, for the purpose of considering the request of the livery. The mayor agreed to summon a court but declined to allow the application of the livery to be placed on the paper of business. A Common Council was eventually summoned for the 20th, when the several applications of the livery and of the members of the court having been read, a motion was made that the Common Council should give instructions to the city members to support Sawbridge's bill. This motion being lost, another was made and carried, desiring the lord mayor to summon a Common Hall for the same purpose. Thereupon Nash addressed the court in these words:—" I am " very sorry this question has been put, I cannot " grant your request for the reasons given in my " former answer to the livery to which I refer you." After passing a resolution that such members of the

---

[1] Common Hall Book, No. 8, fos. 162-163.

court as were also members of parliament, should be requested to support every measure tending to shorten the duration of parliaments, the court proceeded to consider whether it should not on its own responsibility issue precepts for a Common Hall. It was at length decided to leave this question to a committee.[1] *Junius* was very disgusted at Nash's conduct. "What an abandoned prostituted idiot is your lord mayor,"—is the choice expression he makes use of to Woodfall, his printer. Again, "the shameful "mismanagement which brought him into office, gave "me the first and unconquerable disgust."[2] In the following May the committee just mentioned recommended that counsel's opinion should be taken on the matter referred to them, but by this time Sawbridge's motion had been rejected, and all immediate necessity for an extraordinary Common Hall had passed away.[3] When Nash quitted office, this refusal of his to summon a Common Hall was remembered against him, and the customary vote of thanks was denied him.[4]

Instructions of livery to city members, re short parliaments, 24 June, 1772. Matters remained as they were until Midsummer-day, when the livery took the opportunity of a meeting of Common Hall to draw up instructions to the city members to support Sawbridge and short parliaments. The terms of the address were scarcely such as a member of Parliament of the present day would tolerate from his constituents :—"When we made "choice of you, sirs, to transact our business in

---

[1] Journal 65, fos. 278b–280b.
[2] Woodfall, Letters of Junius, i, 250.
[3] Journal 65, fos. 289b, 290. Journal House of Commons, xxxiii, 553. Walpole, Journal of reign of George III, i, 26, 42.
[4] Journal 65, fo. 311.

"Parliament we considered all of you to be possessed
"of fortune sufficient to render you independent;
"but such is the depravity of the present age that
"the more wealthy seem the easiest to be corrupted.
"Altho' some of you may have approved yourselves
"worthy of the confidence reposed in you, yet others,
"we are sorry to be obliged to observe, have been
"deficient in their duty. It becomes necessary,
"therefore, that we should exercise our indisputable
"right of instructing you, our representatives." All
the oppression under which the country had suffered
for the last thirteen years were due (they said) to
long parliaments. As for the existing House they
had not a good word to say. What (they asked) was
to be thought of a House "which, devoid of all
"decency, could force the poor timid servant of a
"corporation to erase a judicial record—an House
"that could even punish two members of its own
"body in a most arbitrary manner for acting with
"integrity in a judicial capacity, nay! for adhering
"to their charters and their oaths, and virtuously
"administering justice!" Experience had taught them
that what had been intended as a bulwark of their
liberties had become a mere engine of oppression.
A worthy alderman of the city (they declared in
conclusion) had realised the danger of septennial
parliaments, and had more than once endeavoured
to shorten their duration, but unfortunately he
had not received the support he deserved. As
Sawbridge would no doubt renew his motion in the
coming winter they insisted that each member should
"afford him all possible support in order to restore
"us to our antient right of annually electing our

"representatives in Parliament."[1] Brave words, these! but all to little purpose. The Septennial Act outlived this and many another effort to obtain its repeal, and remains in force to this day.

<small>Townshend elected mayor, 24 Oct., 1772.</small>

The election of a mayor to succeed Nash was keenly contested. Bankes, Hallifax and Shakespeare were the senior aldermen below the chair, but these were set aside by the livery in favour of Wilkes and Townshend. A poll was demanded, and the business of taking the poll lasted until the 8th October. The king was in a great state of excitement, and was kept posted up by Lord North with each day's proceedings. "I trust by your account of this day's poll," he wrote to the minister (3 Oct.),[2] "that there can be no doubt "that it will end favourably; the mob being less quiet "this day is a proof that to [sic] riot, not numbers, the "*patriots* alone can draw advantage." Again on the 5th October, when the voice of the city was evidently in favour of Wilkes, he writes: "The unpromising "appearance of this day's poll does not in the least "surprise me, knowing that Wilkes is not bound by "any tyes, therefore would poll non-freemen rather "than lose the election." He fancied that if Wilkes failed to get returned as one of the two to be submitted to the Court of Aldermen for selection he would not be allowed to stand again,[3] but here the king was in error. His hopes were damped by Wilkes being returned at the head of the poll, followed closely by Townshend, their respective votes being 2,301 and 2,278.[4] Although Townshend and Wilkes were at the

---

[1] These instructions were not entered on record until the following Midsummer-day (1773).—Common Hall Book, No. 8, fos. 176b, 177.

[2] Correspondence, i, 110.   [3] *Ibid.*

[4] Common Hall Book, No. 8, fo. 171b.

time personal enemies, yet many of Wilkes's friends were induced to give Townshend their second votes, in order to prevent a "court candidate" being successful. This at least is Horace Walpole's account, who declares that Townshend "disdained to canvass or even to attend the election," and that without the assistance of Wilkes's supporters he would have had "scarce any votes." On the other hand we must remember that, intense as was the personal animosity at this time between Townshend and Wilkes, both of them had one and the same political object in view, viz., the overthrow of the government, and Townshend must have added considerably to his popularity in the city by his recent refusal to pay his land tax on the plea that the Parliament which had ordained it was no true Parliament owing to the exclusion of Wilkes and intrusion of Luttrell.[1] The king's only remaining hope was that the result of the poll might be upset by a scrutiny demanded on behalf of Hallifax and Shakespeare. "I hope the scrutiny will be conducted with great exactness," he again writes to Lord North (6 Oct.), at the same time expressing a doubt as to whether such a thing was to be expected from Oliver and Watkin Lewes, who had succeeded Wilkes and Bull in the shrievalty. If these did their duty he felt sure it would go hard with Wilkes, whose "little regard to true votes" would soon be exposed, and "do him great injury, even among his admirers."[2]

[1] Townshend even allowed his goods to be seized rather than pay the tax, and then brought an action for trespass. The case had come on for hearing in June last, when Lord Mansfield, finding that counsel for the plaintiff wanted the court to retry the judgment of the House of Commons touching the case of the Middlesex election, stopt the case, and ordered the jury to find for the defendant.—Walpole, "Journal of the reign of George III," i, 124-126.
[2] Correspondence, i, 112.

Again the king was doomed to disappointment. The scrutiny, according to the Minutes of the Proceedings of the Common Hall preserved at the Guildhall, continued until the 24th day of the month, when the votes for each candidate were declared to be exactly the same as before, and Wilkes and Townshend being returned to the Court of Aldermen for their selection of one, that body chose Townshend to be mayor for the ensuing year. According to Walpole[1] the scrutiny was not proceeded with, and Wilkes was certain of being elected (Townshend being expected to withdraw in his favour) had not alderman and sheriff Oliver, his former friend, brought about his defeat by hastily collecting a Court of Aldermen before the Wilkite aldermen could take their seats, and getting Townshend named lord mayor. Such a proceeding on the part of Oliver is scarcely probable, if, indeed possible, and receives no corroboration from the City's record of what took place.[2]

Riot at the Guildhall on lord mayor's day, 9 Nov., 1772.

On lord mayor's day the partisans of Wilkes, smarting at their defeat, raised a riot at night outside the Guildhall, where a ball was being held. The assistance of the Artillery Company had to be called in, and they remained on duty all night. The new lord mayor, who was somewhat hot-headed, "pro- "posed to sally out with drawn swords and fall on "the mob," but was restrained. He, however, caused some of the rioters to be seized and committed to Newgate, and declared that he would bring home the riot to Wilkes. The whole city was now, and had been for some time, so split up into factions that even

---

[1] Journal of the reign of George III, i, 164.
[2] Common Hall Book, No. 8, fo. 171b.

a vote of thanks to the Artillery Company for striving to keep order was with difficulty passed.[1] "A head-strong, self-willed spirit has sunk the City into nothing," wrote Chatham at the beginning of the year.[2] The government could afford to look upon Wilkes's disappointment and the unpopularity of Townshend with complacency, the real damage was to the nation, which, to use the words of Walpole, "saw those who would have gone farthest to stem the encroachments of the crown divided and warring each other."[3]

Resolution of Court of Aldermen re short parliaments, 16 Feb., 1773.

Following in the steps of Sawbridge, his brother alderman and colleague during his shrievalty, Townshend introduced a motion before the Court of Aldermen on the 16th February (1773) to the effect "that a frequent appeal to the constituent part of the people by short parliaments is their undoubted right and the only means by which they can enjoy or maintain their right of a real representation."[4] Wilkes was the only alderman who raised any objection to the motion. He would willingly have given his vote against it, if only to spite Townshend, but he dared not do so. The motion was therefore carried unanimously.[5]

Another remonstrance of the livery, 11 March, 1773.

Three weeks later (11 March) a special Common Hall was summoned for the purpose of drawing up another remonstrance to the king, and of pledging the livery and the city members to use their utmost

---

[1] Journal 65, fo. 311b.
[2] Chatham to Shelburne, 10 Jan., 1772.—Chatham Correspondence, iv, 187.
[3] "Journal of the reign of George III," i, 164, 165.
[4] Repertory 177, fo. 164.
[5] Walpole, Journal, i, 184, 185.

endeavours to obtain shorter parliaments. This new remonstrance—a "flagrant piece of impertinence," as the king styled it in a letter to Lord North (13 March)[1] —was said to have been the work of Wilkes, who drafted it in such terms that his enemy the lord mayor "would be undone at St. James's if he presented it, "and stoned by the people if he did not."[2] It was resolved that the remonstrance should be presented by the mayor, the city members, the aldermen, the sheriffs and ten of the livery in their gowns, attended by the Recorder and city officers.[3] Wilkes showed considerable shrewdness in declining to attend, excusing himself on the ground that he knew himself to be personally disliked by the king. He would, he said, willingly have attended had he been sheriff, but now that he was only an alderman there was no reason for him to thrust himself where he was not wanted. "I am not used to go into any gentleman's house who does not wish to see me."[4] Even the livery seemed to shrink from having a hand in presenting so disreputable an address, for only eight of them attended at St. James's.

The king's reply, 26 March.

The document was presented to the king on Friday, the 26th March. It was (presumably) received on the throne, although the Common Council do not appear to have been present to give it a corporate character. A copy of it had previously reached the king's hands, and he had made up his mind, as he told Lord North,[5] that a "dry answer, rather bordering on contempt than

---

[1] Correspondence, i, 125. [2] Walpole, Journal, i, 188, 189.
[3] Common Hall Book, No. 8, fo. 175b.
[4] Walpole, Journal, i, 192.
[5] The king to Lord North, 13 March, 1773.—Correspondence, i, 125.

anger," was the most suitable reply to make to a representation at once "the most violent, insolent and licentious ever presented." The answer he actually returned was more than "dry," and the deputation was dismissed with his majesty declaring that their petition was so void of foundation, and withal so disrespectful, that "I am convinced you do not yourselves seriously imagine it can be complied with."[1]

A month later an opportunity was afforded Wilkes of again claiming his seat in Parliament. War with France seemed imminent, and a call of the House[2] was moved for the 26th April. The sheriffs of London[3] thereupon sent a summons to Wilkes (*not* Luttrell) as member for Middlesex, and informed the Speaker of what they had done. Wilkes also wrote a bold letter to the Speaker asserting his right. On the day of the call Wilkes went to the crown office and demanded his writ, which was refused him by the deputy-clerk. Thence he proceeded to Westminster, attended by his friends and supporters. The guards were held in readiness, but there was no disturbance. Glynn—recently appointed Recorder of London—moved that Wilkes should be heard at the bar of the House as to his complaint against the deputy-clerk, and the motion was seconded by Sawbridge. The House was in no mood, however, to meet one who had so often worsted them, and the motion was rejected by 227 votes to 124.[4]

Wilkes again claims his seat, 26 April, 1773.

[1] Common Hall Book, No. 8, fo. 176b.
[2] This was something in the nature of a "whip," the custom being for the Speaker to send notice to the sheriffs to summon all their members to attend on a certain day.
[3] Watkin Lewes and Oliver.
[4] Journal House of Commons, xxxiv, 283; Walpole, Journal, i, 194-197.

The powers of the livery defined, 1773.

When Midsummer-day (1773) came round Plumbe and Kirkman were for the fourth time rejected for the shrievalty in favour of Plomer and Sayre. Plomer paid fine and Lee was elected in his place. The livery being determined more than ever to win their independence and to break away from the authority of the mayor, took the opportunity of their meeting together to consult the new Recorder upon the question "whether the livery of London legally "assembled in Common Hall, either on this or any "other day, have not a right to enter upon any "matter of public grievance they may think proper?" Glynn at once replied that they had an undoubted right, and that it was "beyond dispute that the right is inherent in them."[1] This important *dictum* negativing, as it did, a decision of Glynn's predecessor,[2] was afterwards used by Wilkes with effect in his famous letter to Lord Hertford (2 May, 1775).

Plumbe's case.

The aspirations of the livery were (at least for a time) damped by the decision given a few weeks later in a case known as "Plumbe's case." It will be remembered that in 1770 certain livery companies had objected to the tone of a recent remonstrance, and had in consequence passed resolutions forbidding their members to attend Common Halls except for the purpose of elections. A joint committee of the livery and the Common Council had thereupon been appointed to take counsel's opinion upon the rights of the livery.[3] Among the counsel consulted on the question was Glynn, and he and his brethren had given it as their opinion (June, 1771) that the mayor for the

---

[1] Common Hall Book, No. 8, fo. 176b.
[2] Gentleman's Magazine, xliii, 300.   [3] *Supra*, p. 94.

time being might legally summon a Common Hall; that it was the duty of those livery companies to whom precepts were sent by the mayor to execute those precepts, and that a wilful refusal was punishable by disfranchisement, the procedure being by way of information filed by the common sergeant in the mayor's court. Informations had accordingly been filed against the masters or wardens of the several companies of Goldsmiths, Weavers and Grocers by order of Common Hall,[1] but only one, viz., that against Alderman Plumbe, of the Goldsmiths, was proceeded with. The question was tried before a jury on the 14th July of this year (1773) with the result that Plumbe was convicted and adjudged to be disfranchised.[2]

The powers of the livery were further defined in a legal opinion delivered about this time by the Recorder and Common Sergeant on the questions (1) Whether the lord mayor, aldermen and livery of London in Common Hall assembled could do any corporate act except under the powers given them by Acts of Parliament; (2) Whether an order of the livery in Common Hall to the Town Clerk to affix his signature to such a document as the last remonstrance would be a sufficient justification for him in a court of law in case of a criminal prosecution; and lastly (3) Whether individuals signing such a remonstrance be liable to a prosecution of libel? To the first two

<small>Counsel's opinion on the powers of Common Hall.</small>

[1] Common Hall Book, No. 8, fos. 162-163.

[2] This judgment was reversed in 1775, and from that day to this the lord mayor has been unable to compel the attendance of the livery at Common Hall.—Journal 66, fos. 36b, 349b-350b. See also "Case of Mr. Alderman Plumbe" (Guildhall Library) where the judgments of the several judges in error are set out with comments by James Roberts, the city solicitor.

questions counsel made the following answer;—"From "the best information wee can get of the usage and "constitution of the City the Common Hall is not "empowered to do any act strictly corporate not "having the direction of the City Seal. They can do "no act that binds the estate of the City or that "effects the admission or removal of any of its "members." Then, referring to the former opinion of the Recorder just mentioned, they proceeded to say;—"wee did in concurrence with Mr. Solicitor-"General and Mr. Dunning upon consideration give "an opinion that a Common Hall was a lawful "assembly vested with legal powers. Wee find that "opinion warranted by Lord Coke's authority, and "therefore without more research and enquiry than "can now be made, wee cannot alter our opinion." They were further of opinion "that no Act of Common "Hall can endanger the Charters or Franchises of the "city, and wee think that the right of petitioning a "necessary consequence of a lawful assembly." As a result of their answer to the first question they believed that the Town Clerk, being by office the clerk of a legally convened meeting of the Common Hall, would not render himself criminally liable by giving his signature to the acts and resolutions of that assembly. As to the question of libel, that depended upon a variety of circumstances, but in their private opinion counsel believed that no one presenting the late remonstrance could be treated legally as a criminal.[1]

Bull, mayor, elected M.P. for the City, Dec., 1773.

At Michaelmas, Wilkes again put up for the mayoralty, but although he was again returned at the

[1] This opinion was ordered to be entered in the Repertory of the Court of Aldermen (19 Oct., 1773).—Repertory 177, fos. 439-445.

head of the poll he was again rejected by the Court of Aldermen in favour of his friend Bull.[1] Before the end of the year Bull was also chosen member for the City in the place of Ladbroke, who had died. A petition was laid before Parliament against his election, and in favour of his opponent, John Roberts, a court candidate, but was afterwards withdrawn.[2] The king had at one time expressed himself to North as thinking it best not to offer any opposition to Bull's election as member for the city, unless there was a good hope of success. "If Alderman Bull can be with success "opposed, I should think it eligible; but if that is "not pretty certain it is best not to interfere."[3] On learning, however, that Roberts, a former director of the East India Company, was about to stand he wished him success.[4] Previous to his election Bull signed an engagement (formulated by the livery at their meeting in March), to use his best endeavours to shorten the duration of parliaments; to exclude pensioners and placemen from the House; to establish a fair and equal representation of the people in Parliament; and to redress the grievances and secure the constitutional rights of his fellow subjects in Great Britain, Ireland and America. He also solemnly promised not to accept from the crown or its ministers any place, pension, contract, title, gratuity or emolument whatsoever.[5]

---

[1] Common Hall Book, No. 8, fo. 178. The contest was so equal that Wilkes only lost the election by the casting vote of Townshend.—Walpole, Journal, i, 262.

[2] Walpole, Journal, i, 275, 297, 301, 325; Gentleman's Magazine, xliv, 291.

[3] The king to North, 31 Oct., 1773.—Correspondence, i, 153.

[4] The same to the same, 12 Nov., 1773.—*Id.*, i, 155-156.

[5] Common Hall Book, No. 8, fo. 183.

England and the American colonies, 1765-1774.

It was during Bull's mayoralty that the relations between England and her American colonies became so strained that in 1775 the two countries were at open war. For the past ten years the colonies had displayed more or less resistance to the British government. In 1765 the Stamp Act was passed, and in the following year it had to be repealed. The irritation caused by its imposition remained, however, and the colonists began to ignore the authority of British Acts of Parliament. In 1767 another Act was passed by Parliament imposing import duties in America upon certain articles, and among them upon tea; but the Act was rendered from the outset almost a dead letter through the resistance offered to the execution of its provisions. Matters were not improved by the repeal of all the duties, except that on tea, three years later (1770), more especially when the Americans learnt that Lord North openly acknowledged that he retained the tea duty, not on account of its value, but simply in order to assert the right of England to tax her colonies. The crisis came in 1773, when the tea-ships lying in Boston harbour were attacked, and their cargo flung into the sea. In September of the following year (1774) all the American colonies agreed to combine in stopping commercial intercourse with Great Britain until their grievances were redressed.

The city and the Quebec Bill, 1774.

In the meantime a Bill had passed the Lords, and been sent down to the Commons, giving a constitution to Canada. The City presented a strong petition against the Bill (3 June) as unduly favouring the Roman Catholics, and begged the king to withhold his assent after the Bill had passed both Houses.[1] It was to no purpose. The country generally, and the clergy of the Established Church more particularly, showed great indifference,[2] and the Bill became law. The mayor received a letter of thanks from the Protestant settlers in Quebec, through Francis Maseres, (Cursitor Baron) for what the City had done in the matter; and the City thus encouraged resolved to continue its efforts and endeavour to get the Act repealed as soon as possible.[3] The king was strongly of opinion that the agitation in the City was merely got up "just to make a noise" at the coming elections in Common Hall,[4] and Walpole appears to have been much of the same opinion. He believed it was a move on the part of Wilkes in order to carry the election of sheriffs. By getting two friends appointed sheriffs he would be in a position to get Reynolds, his own attorney and election agent, appointed under-sheriff, and so "be more sure of the returning officer against the general election," which was fast approaching.[5] If this were so his scheme was frustrated for his nominees failed to get elected.

His star nevertheless was soon to be again in the ascendant. At the next election to the mayoralty, he was not only again returned at the head of the poll, but second to him was Bull, his friend, and actual mayor. The other candidates who went to the poll were James Esdaile and Brackley Kennet,

Wilkes elected mayor, 8 Oct., 1774.

[1] Journal 66, fos. 105b-106; Journal House of Commons, xxxiv, 765, 803; Gentleman's Magazine, xliv, 247, 283.
[2] Walpole, Journal, i, 376, 377.
[3] Journal 66, fos. 170-172, 178, 179.
[4] The king to Lord North, 18 June, 1774.—Correspondence, i, 192.
[5] Walpole, Journal, i, 380-382.

both of them senior to Wilkes. Hallifax and Shakespeare, the senior of all did not even go to the poll. Sawbridge who was next below Wilkes did not press his candidature, as the latter—according to Walpole—" had regained him by promising to bring him into parliament for the city." According to the same authority Wilkes "made" Bull decline the chair a second time, and hence it came to pass that when these two were returned to the Court of Aldermen, eleven voted for Wilkes, whilst only two, viz., Townshend and Oliver, voted for Bull. "Thus, " after so much persecution of the court, after so many " attempts on his life, after a long imprisonment in a " goal, after all his crimes and indiscretions, did this " extraordinary man, of more extraordinary fortune, " attain the highest office in so grave and important " a city as the capital of England."[1] That night Alderman Harley, an old opponent of Wilkes, had his windows broken, and the culprit was carried before Wilkes himself.[2]

<small>Takes his seat as M.P. for Middlesex, Nov., 1774.</small>

Nor did his success end here. The mayoralty election was still pending when parliament was dissolved (30 Sept.), and writs issued for a new one to meet on the 29th November. Wilkes was again returned for Middlesex and with him his friend, Glynn, the Recorder. The popularity of Wilkes was indeed now so great that he was believed to be capable of carrying no less than twelve seats. Prior to their election both candidates signed an undertaking to use their best endeavours to shorten the duration of parliaments, remove placemen and

---

[1] Walpole, Journal, i, 420.
[2] Gentleman's Magazine, xliv, 491.

pensioners from the House, advocate the repeal of the Quebec Act, and generally to follow the line of policy adopted by the livery of London, and recently accepted by Bull.[1] When the City elections came on, Bull and Oliver kept their seats, although Oliver declined to enter into any engagement. Wilkes kept his promise with Sawbridge (if any were really given), and Sawbridge was returned together with Wilkes's own brother-in-law, George Hayley. The irrepressible demagogue was at last allowed to take his seat without any opposition. Had he been permitted to have done so five years before, he would probably have sunk into insignificance, but now he "forced his way triumphantly, and came "vested with the insignia of the first magistracy in "England, and supported by half a dozen members "of his own nomination."[2] His triumph was complete in 1782, when he succeeded in getting the House to stultify itself by rescinding its proceedings touching the Middlesex elections.[3] In the dogged persistence with which he fought the House of Commons and finally came off victorious, he reminds us of no one so much as of the late Charles Bradlaugh, member for Northampton; in other respects the two characters will not bear comparison.

[1] Gentleman's Magazine, xliv, 444.
[2] Walpole, Journal, i, 427.
[3] Journal House of Commons, xxxviii, 977

CHAPTER XXXIX.

Wilkes and the Court of Aldermen.

Wilkes had not long occupied the mayoralty chair before he came into serious collision with the Court of Aldermen. In November (1774) an election of an alderman for the Ward of Bridge Within took place, and John Hart, one of the sheriffs, was returned at the head of the poll, defeating his opponent, William Neate, by four votes. A scrutiny was demanded, and, in spite of an objection raised by Hart on technical grounds, was allowed to proceed. Whilst the scrutiny was proceeding Hart appeared before the Court of Aldermen and claimed to be admitted to his seat. Neate was also in attendance, but the Court declined to hear him. Wilkes thereupon adjourned the Court until after the result of the scrutiny was known. On the 24th November the votes were cast up in the presence of Wilkes and his predecessor in office (under whom the original wardmote for the election had been held), when there appeared 95 votes for Neate, as against 84 for Hart. The result of the poll was thus reversed. Nevertheless, when the Court of Aldermen met the next day they insisted upon Wilkes putting the question for Hart to be called in and sworn, whilst they persistently refused to hear Neate or his attorney, Reynolds—Wilkes's own friend and election agent. This he positively refused to do, and the matter was allowed to stand over, both parties having in the meantime applied to the King's Bench for writs of *mandamus*.[1]

The proceedings of the aldermen were published in the *Public Advertiser* of the 28th November, and were severely commented upon, whilst the action of Wilkes was highly approved of. "The spirit of "injustice and violence which influenced the pro-"ceedings of the Court of Aldermen on Tuesday"— it was reported—"predominated stronger on Friday by "the arrival of Mr. Harley. One of the candidates for "the vacant aldermanship of Bridge Within, William "Neate, Esq., was refused to be heard, and likewise "his agent, Mr. John Reynolds. Mr. Houston, the "attorney who officiated at the wardmote, was not "suffered to make his report of the election. Mr. "Alderman Kirkman acquainted the Court that he "had been served with a *mandamus* from the Court "of King's Bench to swear in Mr. Neate, but no "attention was paid to him. Mr. Townshend and "Mr. Oliver insisted on the swearing in of Mr. Hart "immediately, and Mr. Harley's natural violence and "rage were brought in aid to the intemperate and "unjust spirit of the other two aldermen. The lord "mayor, however, had too much firmness to yield to "an act of palpable partiality and injustice, and "prevented the disgrace, which otherwise that Court "would have received, by repeatedly refusing to put "the question."[2] The whole passage reads very much as if inspired by Wilkes himself; but whether this were so or not, Wilkes entered his protest against a resolution of the Court that the paragraph was

Comments of the Public Advertiser, 28 Nov., 1774.

---

[1] Repertory 179, fos. 10-14, 17-20, 54-65.
[2] *Id.*, fos. 24-25.

injurious to the honour of the Court and "not founded in truth," because he apprehended that it *was* "founded in truth."

<small>Refusal by Wilkes to put a question reflecting upon himself, 29 Nov., 1774.</small>

Before the aldermen again met (29 Nov.) the city solicitor, acting (apparently) upon instructions from Wilkes, had defended Hart's *mandamus*, and at the next Court that officer was severely questioned on the matter, and was told that the Court would not allow him his costs. A motion was at the same time made to the effect that the lord mayor having refused to put a question which the Court of Aldermen was competent to decide, had violated the right of election in the freemen of the city, as represented in that Court. It was, of course, the business of Wilkes to put this question, but unlike Trevor, the Speaker, who stultified himself before the House of Commons in 1695, Wilkes positively declined, telling his brother aldermen that he thanked God he was "not quite idiot enough" for that.[1] A week later (6 Dec.) the Court passed a resolution to the effect that Neate had not been duly elected, and Wilkes again protested. The Court thereupon proposed to swear in Hart, but Wilkes again refused to put the question for the reason that the parties had not been heard.[2] Matters were thus brought to a deadlock. At length—on the 17th January, 1775—the Court put itself in order by hearing Neate, and immediately afterwards passed a resolution for calling in and swearing Hart. Wilkes no longer raised any objection, and Hart was sworn.[3] Hart did not long enjoy his victory, for by a judgment

---

[1] Repertory 179, fo. 24. [2] *Id.*, fos. 65–68. [3] *Id.*, fos. 96, 97.

of the King's Bench, pronounced in Easter term, 1776, he was excluded from inter-meddling with the aldermanry, and on the 18th June Thomas Wooldridge (*not* Neate) was admitted in his place.[1] As between Wilkes and the Court of Aldermen the honours certainly lay with the former, and he did not hesitate to tell the Court that he intended to pursue the same line of conduct throughout his year of office in spite of all the Court might think or do;—"I declared that "I never would put a question to decide the merits of "a cause before this Court until both the parties had "been heard. The Court at last consented that Mr. "Neate should be heard, and only after he had been "heard did I put the question. . . . The same "line of truth and impartiality I will steadily pursue "thro' the whole course of my mayoralty, regardless "of any resolutions of this Court which are repugnant "to the great principles of justice or the fair rights of "the chief magistrate."[2]

The new Parliament and the American colonies, 1775.

The result of the recent general election proved to be in favour of the ministry, and distinctly anti-American. The nation had declared for war, and nothing that the City could do was of any avail to prevent it. As soon as Parliament met (19 Jan., 1775) Chatham went down to the Lords and urged the advisability of addressing the king for the removal of the troops from Boston as a conciliatory measure. He was determined, he said, not to let the matter rest, but would labour to bring the country to a sense of the impending danger:—"I wish, my lords, not to "lose a day in this urgent, pressing crisis; an hour

---

[1] Repertory 180, fos. 288-294. [2] Repertory 179, fo. 194.

"now lost in allaying ferments in America may
"produce years of calamity; for my own part, I will
"not desert, for a moment, the conduct of this
"weighty business from the first to the last, unless
"nailed to my bed by the extremity of sickness. I
"will give it unremitted attention; I will knock at
"the door of this sleeping and confounded ministry,
"and will rouse them to a sense of their impending
"danger."[1] The citizens of London were among the
few who supported Chatham at this momentous crisis
in the country's history, and they despatched the
Town Clerk to the earl's country seat with an address
of thanks, which was acknowledged in very flattering
terms.[2] So far from showing any disposition to conciliate the colonies by withdrawing troops and repealing
obnoxious Acts, the new House proceeded to consider
a Bill for cutting off the inhabitants of Massachusetts
and other parts from the Newfoundland fishery. To
this the Common Council at once entered their protest,
both before the Lords and Commons. It was not to
be supposed, they plainly told Parliament, that a great
number of men, naturally hardy and brave, would
quietly submit to a law which would reduce them to
the verge of famine.[3] The warning was to no purpose.
The Bill passed.[4]

Remonstrance of livery, 5 April, 1775.

At length matters looked so serious that the livery of London met in Common Hall on the 5th April and drew up a respectful but solemn warning to the king himself against the fatal policy pursued by

---

[1] Chatham Correspondence iv, 378, note.
[2] Journal 66, fos. 179, 181b.
[3] Journal 66, fos. 185-185b, 188b-190, 191-192.
[4] Journal House of Commons, xxxv, 182, 241; Journal House of Lords, xxxiv, 365.

his ministers towards America. The measures which the government had recently adopted were declared to be "big with all consequences which can alarm a free and commercial people." They inflicted (said the livery) a deep and perhaps fatal wound to commerce; they ruined manufactures; they reduced the revenue and increased the taxes; and they alienated the colonists. Here, as ever, commercial interests were placed by the citizens in the foreground. But commercial interests did not form the sole motive for this remonstrance. The City's own liberties were at stake if the liberties of the subject in any part of the kingdom were infringed;—"Your petitioners con-"ceive the liberties of the whole to be inevitably "connected with those of every part of an empire, "founded on the common rights of mankind. They can-"not, therefore, observe without the greatest concern "and alarm the constitution fundamentally violated "in any part of your majesty's dominions. They "esteem it an essential, unalterable principle of liberty, "the source and security of all constitutional rights "that no part of the dominion can be taxed without "being represented."[1] The livery resolved that this address or remonstrance should be presented by the lord mayor, the city members, the Court of Aldermen (*not* the Common Council) and the sheriffs, and that they themselves should also attend the presentation in a body (and not by deputation, as in 1771 and 1773). Having settled this business, they next proceeded to pass votes of thanks to the Lords and Commons

[1] On the 7th March a pamphlet had been published entitled "Taxation no Tyranny; an Answer to the Resolutions and Address of the American Congress,"—from the pen of Dr. Johnson. —Boswell's Life of Johnson (Napier), ii, 289.

who had opposed "the impolitic and inhuman Bill for "prohibiting the people of New England from the "Newfoundland fishery, and for their opposition to " other arbitrary, cruel and anti-commercial measures" against their fellow subjects in America. They also thanked Chatham and Burke for the plan they had proposed for conciliating the American colonies; and lastly, they passed a vote of thanks to such of the Commons as had recently voted on Wilkes's oft repeated motion for expunging the resolutions of the late Parliament respecting Wilkes and the Middlesex election.[1]

The king's reply, 10 April, 1775. Notwithstanding the absence of the Common Council and the inordinate number of the livery that had expressed their intention of being present, the king submitted, rather than risk a contest with the City with Wilkes in the mayoralty chair. With Wilkes's personal behaviour at court the king was agreeably surprised, and owned that he had never seen "so well-bred a lord mayor."[2] The conduct of the mayor, however, took nothing off the asperity of the king's reply. He expressed the "utmost astonishment" that any of his subjects should be capable of encouraging the rebellious spirit which had displayed itself in some of the colonies in North America. As to the Parliament, which the livery had recently

[1] Common Hall Book, No. 8, fos. 186b–188.
[2] Walpole, Journal i, 484. Wilkes's winning manner was never more conspicuous than when, a year later (15 May, 1776), he first met Dr. Johnson at dinner. The story how he succeeded in completely winning over the learned lexicographer who had hitherto looked upon Wilkes as little more than a low demagogue, is admirably told in Boswell's Life (iii, 108–117). They afterwards became very good friends, and Johnson was fain to confess that "Jack was a scholar" and "Jack had the manners of a gentleman," and that "although Jack had always been at him, he would do Jack a kindness rather than not."— (*Id.*, iii, 208.)

characterised as a "formidable instrument of arbitrary power," instead of being the guardian of liberty, he declared that he had every confidence in it and intended to carry out its measures.

The next day (11 April) the Earl of Hertford, the lord chamberlain, wrote to Wilkes by the king's command, giving him notice that in future his majesty would not receive on the throne any address, remonstrance or petition except from the body corporate of the City. *(Letter from the lord chamberlain to Wilkes, 11 April, 1775.)*

The lord chamberlain's letter drew forth a long and spirited reply from Wilkes[1] as to the legal position of Common Halls and the powers and rights of the livery, in which he refers Lord Hertford to the opinions of counsel delivered in 1771 and 1773.[2] He reminds his lordship that the claim which he was making on behalf of the livery of London to the right of presenting addresses to the king on his throne was of no little importance, and not to be lightly abandoned or set aside;—"When his majesty receives on the throne any "address it is read by the proper officer to the king "in the presence of the petitioners. They have the "satisfaction of knowing that their sovereign has heard "their complaints. They receive an answer. If the "same address is presented at a levée, or in any other "mode, no answer is given. A suspicion may arise "that the address is never heard or read, because it is "only received, and immediately delivered to the "lord in waiting." It was on the throne (the letter continued) that the king and his predecessors had *(The lord mayor's reply, 2 May, 1775.)*

---

[1] Common Hall Book, No. 8, fos. 189b-191.
[2] See Plumbe's case. *Supra* pp. 138, 139.

constantly received addresses of the livery, and "on the most exact research" not a single instance had been found to the contrary. Wilkes concluded by expressing his fears lest the unfavourable answer the king had returned to the remonstrance should be considered by the American colonies as a fresh mark of the king's anger towards them, as well as of his displeasure against the faithful citizens of London. The livery would comfort themselves with the assurance of the king's sense of justice, which would sooner or later restore them to royal favour; but the Americans might be driven to despair unless by the merciful interposition of Providence the hearts of ministers were turned. Wilkes took care that his letter received the necessary publicity.[1]

Appeal from New York to the City, 5 May, 1775.

The warning came too late; open hostilities had already commenced. The attitude of the colonies towards the mother-country was clearly defined in a letter addressed to the City of London by the committee of Association of New York on the 5th May.[2] All the horrors of a civil war, the letter protested, would never compel America to submit to taxation by authority of Parliament, although it was perfectly ready to make voluntary contributions "as Englishmen" to assist the king if properly requisitioned. The writers appealed to the City of London, well knowing its attachment to the cause of justice and liberty, and they concluded their letter with an expression of confidence that it would use its utmost exertions "to restore union, mutual confidence and

[1] Walpole's Journal i, 487. It is printed in the Gentleman's Magazine, xlv, 220-222, and in the Volume of Addresses, etc. (ed. 1778) in the Guildhall Library.
[2] Journal 66, fos. 236-237b.

peace to the whole empire." The letter was laid before the Common Council on Friday, the 23rd June, when it was ordered to be printed, and a copy to be sent to every member of the Court.[1]

The next day being Midsummer-day the livery met as usual in Common Hall for the purpose of electing sheriffs and other officers. Alderman Hayley, the brother-in-law of Wilkes, was one of the sheriffs elected and Alderman Newnham the other. The ordinary business of the day having been got through Wilkes formally reported to the Common Hall the king's reply to the last address of the livery, and next proceeded to lay before them Lord Hertford's letter and his own reply. These having been read the Town Clerk was ordered to enter both letters in the City's Records, and a vote of thanks was passed to Wilkes "for his very able, judicious and spirited defence of the rights and privileges of the livery." The livery next proceeded to pass a resolution condemning the conduct of those ministers who had advised the king not to receive in future on the throne any address, remonstrance or petition from the livery of London, as being subversive of the right of the subject to petition the throne, and as calculated to alienate the minds of Englishmen from the Hanoverian succession. Then turning from their own grievances to those of America they passed a vote of thanks to the Earl of Effingham for his courageous conduct in throwing up his commission in the army rather than draw his sword against the lives and liberties of his fellow subjects, and next proceeded to prepare

Proceedings of Common Hall, 24 June, 1775.

[1] Journal 66, fo. 238.

another remonstrance to the king on the American war.[1]

This new remonstrance was, if possible, stronger and more plain spoken than any yet presented. The king was told that the power which he and his ministers claimed to exercise over the colonies, under the specious name of "dignity," was nothing less than "despotism," and that as the livery of London would not suffer any man, or any body of men, to establish arbitrary power over themselves, so they would not acquiesce in an attempt to force it upon any of their fellow subjects. They did not hesitate to declare that the majority of the members of that Parliament, in which the king had recently avowed he placed entire confidence, were "notoriously bribed to betray their constituents and their country."[2] Notwithstanding Lord Hertford's recent letter, they insisted upon the king receiving their address upon the throne, and intimated their intention of attending the presentation in a body. This was more than the king could stand, and he determined to put his foot down. The address not being an address of the Corporation of London, he expressed his intention of receiving it at his next levée, and when objection was raised by the sheriffs to this course, he told them that he was judge where to receive it.[3] This decision being reported to the livery they resolved (4 July) to publish their remonstrance, and not to present it. They at the same time passed a number of resolutions condemning the king's

[1] Common Hall Book, No. 8, os. 188b–191. [2] *Id.*, fos. 191–192.
[3] Walpole, Journal i, 495.

advisers, and ordered the sheriffs to place in the king's own hands a copy of these resolutions as well as of those passed on Midsummer-day, signed by the Town Clerk.[1]

On Friday, the 7th July, the Common Council took into consideration the letter from New York, which had been read to the Court on the 23rd June, and which had by this time been printed and circulated among the members of the Council, as ordered. A motion was thereupon made that a humble address and petition should be presented from the Court to his majesty praying him to suspend hostilities in America, and adopt such conciliatory measures as might restore union, confidence and peace to the whole Empire. The motion was carried, but only by a majority of fifteen; and the address having been drawn up by a committee appointed for the purpose, was in due course read and approved.[2] It is clear that the Common Council was half-hearted in the matter. According to Walpole, it only voted the address in order to satisfy the Americans who had appealed to London.[3] No doubt Court influence had been at work;—"If the Common Council can on "Friday be prevented from taking any step with "regard to the rebellion in America"—wrote the king to Lord North—"it would be desirable," at the same time he comforted himself with the thought that anything that the Common Council might do would have but little real effect.[4]

City address to the king for cessation of hostilities, 7 July, 1775.

---

[1] Common Hall Book, No. 8, fos. 192b, 193.

[2] Journal 66, fos. 239b-240b.

[3] "They could not help doing it, to satisfy the Americans on their address to them."—Walpole, Journal i, 496.

[4] The king to Lord North, 5 July, 1775.—Correspondence i, 253.

The king's reply, 14 July, 1775.

The king received the address on the throne with becoming dignity, and returned for answer that it was a duty he owed his faithful subjects to enforce respect for the constitutional authority of the kingdom on those of his American subjects who had openly resisted it. This answer appears to have had considerable effect upon the Common Council, for when, a week later, a motion was made to send a reply to the letter from New York, together with a copy of the City's late address, and the king's answer, the motion was lost.[1]

Address of the livery to electors of Great Britain, 29 Sept., 1775.

On Michaelmas-day, when his successor in the mayoralty chair was chosen by the livery, Wilkes, who had recently refused to countenance by his presence the proclamation of the Americans as rebels (23 Aug.),[2] produced a letter he had received from the Congress at Philadelphia appealing to the city of London, as the "patron of liberty," to mediate for the restoration of peace. Thereupon an address to the electors of Great Britain (prepared at a previous meeting of the livery held at the Half Moon tavern in Cheapside) calling upon them to assist the livery to bring to justice the authors of the evils that had arisen in this country and America was also produced and read. The document pointed to the increase of national debt and the decrease of national resources that must supervene if a ruinous and expensive war was to be undertaken against the American colonies. What was the object of the war? It could not be the security of England's commerce, for that was not in danger; neither could it be to bring the colonies

[1] Journal 66, fo. 241.
[2] Walpole, Journal i, 500; Gentleman's Magazine xlv, 405.

into due subordination to the mother-country, for the colonies themselves had repeatedly and solemnly acknowledged their subordination and submission to England. It appeared, then, that the object of the war was nothing else than to establish the arbitrary power of the crown over their fellow subjects in America—a measure which would greatly endanger the constitution at home and increase the number of placemen and pensioners. All that the colonies asked for was peace, liberty and safety. They had pledged themselves to be ready and willing in time of war to show their loyalty to the king and to assist him with money and men to the utmost of their ability. What more could in justice be required? They had recently made a final appeal in the hope that the effusion of blood might be stayed, but to this appeal no answer had been vouchsafed. "This, gentlemen," the address continued, "is the alarming state of America, which "fills us with anxiety and apprehensions. We lament "the blood that has been already shed; we deplore "the fate of those brave men who are devoted to "hazard their lives—not against the enemies of the "British name, but against the friends of the prosperity "and glory of Great Britain; we feel for the honour "of the British arms, sullied—not by the misbehaviour "of those who bore them, but by the misconduct of "the ministers who employed them to the oppression "of their fellow subjects; we are alarmed at the "immediate, insupportable expense and the probable "consequences of a war which, we are convinced, "originates in violence and injustice, and must end "in ruin. These are the sentiments, gentlemen," concluded this impassionate address, "which we take

"the liberty of communicating to you as the reasons
"upon which we have acted; trusting that if they
"meet with your approbation you will co-operate with
"us in endeavouring to bring the authors of those evils
"to the justice of their country." This "decent but
very strong address," as Walpole called it,[1] was at
once adopted as "the address of the lord mayor,
"aldermen and livery of London in Common Hall
"assembled," and was ordered to be published in the
papers.[2]

Petitions of Common Council in favour of peace, 25 Oct., 1775.

The day before Parliament re-assembled in October the Common Council backed up the livery and prepared addresses to both Houses in favour of a cessation of hostilities; but the nation was so distinctly in favour of war that the City could avail nothing, and its petitions were ordered to lie on the table.[3]

Arrest of Sayre, an ex-sheriff of London, Oct., 1775.

The tension of men's minds at this crisis was so great that all kinds of rumours gained credit, and a certain comical element was introduced in the midst of the prevailing gloom. A young American officer named Richardson, who was confined in the Tower, solemnly declared on oath that Stephen Sayre, an ex-sheriff of London, had paid him a visit and privately offered him a large sum of money to assist in seizing the Tower. This was only a part of the conspiracy. The king himself was to be seized on his way to the House of Lords and forced to call a new Parliament. Everybody, except the ministers, laughed at the folly

---

[1] Walpole, Journal i, 503.

[2] Common Hall Book, No. 8, fos. 193b–195b.

[3] Journal 66, fos. 259b–260b; Walpole, Journal i, 501, 502; Journal House of Commons, xxxv, 405; Journal House of Lords, xxxiv, 489.

of such a charge. A council was summoned, and by order of the Earl of Rochfort, secretary of state, Sayre was arrested and—in compliment to the City, so it was said—committed to the Tower. He was, however, shortly released.[1]

Parliament met on the 26th without any disturbance, and the king in his address showed a determination to prosecute the war with vigour. Sawbridge, who had been elected successor to Wilkes in the mayoralty chair, took occasion to compare the conduct of Lord Effingham with that of Lord George Germaine, formerly Lord Sackville, who had behaved so discreditably at the battle of Minden in 1759, and who had recently accepted office under the ministry. The one had thrown up his commission rather than engage in civil war, whilst the other "had turned pale at the head of squadrons."[2] In the last week of November, Alderman Oliver, in accordance with a resolution of the livery of London of the 4th July, moved the House to address his majesty, that he might be pleased to inform the Commons who were the advisers of the several measures so obnoxious to the American Colonies. The motion, however, found but little support except from Wilkes and Sawbridge, and upon being pressed to a division, was lost by an overwhelming majority.[3]

Proceedings of Parliament, Oct.–Nov., 1775.

At the close of Wilkes's mayoralty he received the thanks of the City for the splendour and hospitality that had marked his year of office, as well as for "his

Expenses of Wilkes's mayoralty.

---

[1] Walpole, Journal i, 508, 509; Walpole to Mann, 28 Oct., 1775; Letters vi, 277; Annual Register xviii, 167, 239–243.

[2] Walpole, Journal i, 523.

[3] Journal House of Commons, xxxv, 462. Walpole, Journal i, 524.

"vigilant and steady attachment to, and his very able "vindication of the constitutional rights of his fellow "subjects."[1] It would never have done for one who had so severely taken Trecothick to task for failing to maintain the City's reputation for hospitality, to have himself been deficient in that respect, whilst occupying the mayoralty chair; but setting this aside, Wilkes was naturally prone to lavish expenditure whether in or out of office. The result was that the close of his mayoralty found him in serious pecuniary difficulties. The lord mayors of that day derived their income from various sources, among them, being the sale of those places under the Corporation which happened to fall vacant during their year of office.[2] No two mayors therefore enjoyed precisely the same income, whilst their expenditure was then, as now, only limited by their individual tastes, or the length of their private purses. Wilkes's receipts during his year of office had amounted to £4,889 0s. 6½d., whereas his expenditure had been no less than £8,226 13s.[3] He was therefore out of pocket to the amount of nearly £3,500, or perhaps we ought rather to say that he would have been out of pocket to that extent, had he actually disbursed the money.

[1] Journal 66, fo. 261b.

[2] In November, 1776, an alteration was made in this respect, and it was ordained that for the future the sum of £1,000 should be paid to each mayor in lieu of the sale of offices. Journal 67, fo. 8b.

[3] Journal 67, fo. 9. The respective amounts of receipts and expenditure by some of his more immediate predecessors in office, are recorded as having been as follows:—

		Receipts.			Payments.		
1768.	Turner	£5,731	5	10	£7,749	12	4.
1770.	Crosby	4,251	11	6	6,685	10	11.
1772.	Townshend	3,896	0	0	7,592	16	9.
1773.	Bull	5,647	13	8	9,293	10	0.

This he had not done, for the simple reason that he had none to disburse.

His impecuniosity led him to consider seriously the advisability of becoming a candidate for one or other of the more lucrative posts in the gift of the citizens. Hitherto he had been averse to taking such a course, but matters had now come to such a pass that when the Chamberlainship of the City happened to fall vacant in February, 1776, through the resignation of Sir Stephen Janssen, he followed the advice of his friends, and became a candidate for the post. He was unsuccessful, however, being defeated by Benjamin Hopkins, a brother alderman. This being an *interim* election, Hopkins had again to seek the suffrages of the livery at Midsummer. Wilkes again opposed him, and was again defeated; this time by a crushing majority. Here it would have been well if he had rested satisfied, and not offered any further opposition when his more successful rival offered himself annually for re-election, the appointment being virtually during good behaviour. He was not, however, a man to let any scruples of delicacy stand in his way, and, moreover, he was being sorely pressed by creditors. Accordingly, he offered himself as a candidate, in opposition to Hopkins, at Midsummer, 1777, and again in 1778, but on both occasions he was defeated.[1]

Wilkes a candidate for the Chamberlainship, 1776–1778.

In the meantime his creditors had again and again applied to him for the discharge of his mayoralty debts, but could obtain no satisfaction, beyond a cool assurance that he had expended the

His creditors appeal to Common Council, Oct., 1777.

Common Hall Book, No. 8, fos. 199, 200, 205–205b, 211.

whole of the allowance made him by the City in executing the duties of the mayoralty; that their claims exceeded this allowance and he could not therefore discharge them! Was ever impertinence more sublime? Any other man they would have had laid by the heels, without further ado, but Wilkes they feared to touch. After much patience and long suffering, they made so bold as to appeal to the Common Council. This was in October, 1777. Someone suggested the bestowal of an annuity of £500 upon Wilkes for his public services, but the City wisely decided that the granting of any annuity to him, or the payment of his debts whether contracted in or out of office, would establish a bad precedent.[1]

<small>Wilkes elected Chamberlain. Nov., 1779.</small>

At Midsummer, 1779, Hopkins offered himself, as usual, to the livery for re-election to the Chamberlainship, and this time he was returned unopposed. Wilkes had at last seen the futility of continuing the struggle. Possibly the state of Hopkins's health may have had something to do with Wilkes's withdrawal. This, however, is only conjecture. All that we know is that in the following November Hopkins died, and his rival at last succeeded in obtaining the much coveted post.[2] This post—described by Wilkes himself as one of "profit, patronage and extensive usefulness, with rank and dignity," and sufficient, after the payment of his debts, to gratify every wish he could form at the age of fifty-three[3]—he continued to fill with credit to the City (as his friend Dr. Johnson

---

[1] Journal 67, fos. 85b, 100.
[2] Common Hall Book, No. 8, fo. 217b.
[3] Almon, Wilkes's Correspondence v, 37.

predicted he would) until the day of his death (26 Dec., 1797), no one being found bold enough ever to oppose his annual re-election.

Early in 1776 England and America were startled by the appearance of a small treatise entitled "Observations on the nature of civil liberty, the principles of government and the justice and policy of the war in America." The writer was Dr. Richard Price, a Dissenting minister, who had devoted much of his leisure to the consideration of questions of public interest, and more especially finance. The demand for his latest work was so great that it outran the supply. The Freedom of the City in a gold box was voted the author,[1] and two years later he received an invitation to become a citizen of the United States, ample provision being promised him for the rest of his life if he would go to America and undertake the regulation of the finances of that country. The offer was, however, declined on the score of old age.

The Freedom of the City to Dr. Richard Price, 14 March, 1776.

The day that the Common Council voted Dr. Price the Freedom of the City (14 March, 1776) it resolved once more to address the king with the view, if possible, of obtaining the postponement of any further military operations until America had had an opportunity of definitely refusing such just and honourable terms as this country was willing to offer. If this were done, England would free herself of any taint or suspicion of injustice and oppression, whilst the refusal of the colonies would then become rebellion. The king's reply was brief. He avoided giving a direct answer to the City's proposal, but contented himself

City address and king's reply, 22 March, 1776.

---

[1] Journal 66, fos. 296, 354.

with expressing his deep concern at the misery which the colonies had brought upon themselves, and his readiness to extend mercy and clemency as soon as the "existing rebellion was at an end."[1]

<small>Declaration of Independence, 4 July, 1776.</small>

The king's answer shows how little he was acquainted with the real feeling of the colonists at this time. With them it was no longer a question of clemency or redress. The idea of a total separation from the mother country had already taken shape. France had shown a disposition to assist them, and thus avenge herself on England for the Seven Years' war; but with or without France the colonies were bent on separation, and on the 4th July the Declaration of Independence was signed.

<small>Refusal of Sawbridge and Hallifax to back press warrants, 1776–1777.</small>

In anticipation of France openly declaring war against England, the government caused warrants to be issued for pressing seamen. These were executed with great cruelty, and met with much opposition. When Parliament met on the last day of October, Wilkes took the opportunity of an amendment being moved to the address to inveigh against press warrants, as well as against the "savage and piratical, as well as unjust, war" into which the country had been plunged by the king's ministers. He told the House that the press-gangs did not dare enter the City, knowing full well the character of Sawbridge, the lord mayor.[2] "It is "certain," he said, "that no pressing has at this time "been carried on in the city of London or its liberties. "No press-gangs have dared to make their appearance "in that jurisdiction. . . . The city has hitherto "remained in perfect tranquility by the vigilance,

---

[1] Journal 66, fos. 296–297, 299b.
[2] Walpole, Journal ii, 77.

"intrepidity and noble love of liberty which are "conspicuous in its present worthy chief magistrate."[1] Sir Thomas Hallifax, who succeeded Sawbridge in the mayoralty chair,[2] was equally stern in refusing to back press warrants in the City, and on two occasions received a formal vote of thanks for so doing from the Common Council, the first time being in February (1777) and the second when he quitted office.[3]

In 1777 the Habeas Corpus Act was suspended against all Americans, and in 1778 public subscriptions were set on foot in support of the war. The City did all it could to prevent the suspension of Habeas Corpus, and absolutely refused to subscribe to any bounties or to in any way countenance, or be instrumental in, the continuation of the war.[4] The king expressed to Lord North the mortification he felt at the City's attitude;—"I feared the city was not yet enough "returned to sobriety to be persuaded heartily "to support the cause, and therefore think the "friends of government would have acted wiser in "adopting a public subscription unattended with the "mortifying circumstance of a defeat in the Cor-"poration."[5]

The City refuses to countenance the war.

At last the ministers themselves began to show a change of front, and conciliatory measures were

City address, 13 March, 1778.

---

[1] Parliamentary History, vol. xviii, cols. 1,402, 1,403. Notwithstanding Wilkes's statement, instances are recorded of men having been pressed in the City; but their instant discharge was demanded.—Journal 67, fos. 12b-13, 43-43b.

[2] On coming into office Hallifax invited the ministers to his banquet. They had not been asked to the lord mayor's banquet for the last seven years.—Walpole, Journal ii, 84.

[3] Journal 67, fos. 42b, 95.

[4] Journal 67, fos. 42, 107.

[5] The king to Lord North, 17 Jan., 1778.—Correspondence ii, 122.

introduced and passed.¹ Whilst the consideration of these measures was pending, the Common Council drew up another address to the king exhorting him to give effect to those concessions which they feared might have been granted too late.²

Announcement of alliance between France and America, 13 March, 1778.

The fears entertained by the citizens were well founded. On the very day that their address was presented, the French ambassador delivered to Lord Weymouth a declaration that the king of France had entered into a treaty of commerce and amity with the Independent States of America, and that any attempt to interfere with that commerce between those two countries would be resented by his master. A few days later Benjamin Franklin was formally received at Versailles as ambassador for the United States of America.³ In the face of this new danger, both Houses rallied round the throne, with vows of support in maintaining the honour and dignity of the crown and nation, although in both Houses there were not wanting those who were in favour of petitioning the king for the removal of those ministers who had brought about all the mischief. The insulting message sent by France touching interruption of commerce with America, had in fact rather strengthened the ministry than otherwise, and a proposal in the Court of Aldermen to summon a Common Hall for the purpose of agitating for their removal fell flat.⁴

The death of Chatham, 11 May, 1778.

Chatham now became one of the foremost advocates for the maintenance of the supremacy of Great Britain over its dependencies, however opposed

¹ Walpole, Journal ii, 222, 223.   ² Journal 67, fos. 126-8.
³ Walpole, Journal ii, 223.   ⁴ Repertory 182, fo. 184.

he had been to the fatal policy that brought the country to such a crisis; and it was to him that Lord North, who had long wished to withdraw from the ministry, advised the king to apply for aid. Even if the king had been willing to trust Chatham, which he was not, the state of the Earl's health would scarcely have allowed him to accept a position of such responsibility. His days were in fact numbered. On Tuesday, the 7th April, he unexpectedly appeared in the House of Lords, having risen from a sick bed with the sole object of opposing a motion of the Duke of Richmond, virtually conceding the independence of the American Colonies. When the Duke had finished his speech, Chatham, slowly and with difficulty, rose from his seat. In words that at first were scarcely audible he explained that ill-health had prevented him from attending, at so important a crisis, to his parliamentary duties. He had that day made an effort, almost beyond his strength, to attend the House where, perhaps he might never speak again, and to express his indignation at the suggestion that had been made of yielding up the sovereignty of America. "My lords," he said, "I rejoice that the grave "has not closed upon me : that I am still alive to lift up "my voice against the dismemberment of the ancient "and most noble monarchy," and he concluded a spirited and affecting speech by exhorting his countrymen to make an effort to maintain their supremacy [that supremacy to which he himself had contributed so much] and, if they fell, to fall like men.[1] Even as he spoke, his words began to falter, and on rising to make a second speech, he

[1] Parliamentary History xix, 1,022, 1,023.

staggered and fell back in a fit of apoplexy. To all appearance he was in a dying state. He rallied however, but only for a few weeks, and on the 11th May he died.

His funeral. 9 June, 1778.

The City lost no time in petitioning Parliament that the remains of the statesman " whose vigour and " counsels had so much contributed to the protection " and extension of its commerce," might rest in St. Paul's, and the Lord Chamberlain was asked to give timely notice of the funeral in order that the Common Council might pay their last token of respect. The Chamberlain promised to accede to this request, but the City's petition to Parliament met with no further notice than an order that it should lie on the table.[1] Having failed in this direction the City determined to approach the king himself on the subject, and a "remarkably decent and respectful" address was prepared for the purpose in the Common Council.[2] Unfortunately the City had incurred the king's displeasure not only on account of its recent addresses, but also for the respect and affection it had always entertained towards Chatham, who for years had been the object of his special aversion. When asked to name a day for the reception of the address, the first question was as to its nature. He was afraid of having to listen to more "stuff." His curiosity, however, on the point was not gratified. The sheriff (Clarke) respectfully declined to inform him of the nature of the address, and for his "prudent conduct" was rewarded with the thanks of the Common Council.[3]

[1] Journal 67, fos. 137b–138b, 149b. Journal House of Commons, xxxvi, 990.
[2] Journal 67, fo. 148.
[3] Journal 67, fo. 150; Annual Register xxi, 243.

At length Friday, the 5th June, was appointed for receiving the address. By that time arrangements had been made for the interment to take place in Westminster Abbey, and the king notified the citizens of the fact in a somewhat dry and ungracious manner.[1] Although the ceremony was fixed for the 9th no notice had been sent to the City, notwithstanding the Lord Chamberlain's promise. The Common Council therefore, finding themselves thus trifled with, rescinded their resolution to attend.[2] Indeed the attitude taken up by the king and his ministers throughout the whole business was singularly childish and undignified.

The citizens, on the other hand, though prevented from showing their respect at the grave-side of the deceased statesman, were resolved to erect a memorial to one who, when in power, had never (as they declared) allowed them to return from the throne dissatisfied. A sculptured monument by Bacon, with an inscription from the pen of the great Edmund Burke, was in due course erected in the Guildhall, for the express purpose that citizens might "never meet for the trans-"action of their affairs without being reminded that "the means by which Providence raises a nation to "greatness are the virtues infused into great men; "and that to withhold from those virtues, either of "the living or the dead, the tribute of esteem and "veneration, is to deny themselves the means of "happiness and honour."

The City's monument to Chatham.

[1] Journal 67, fo. 149b.   [2] *Id.*, fo. 150.

CHAPTER XL.

Court martial of Admiral Keppel, Jan., 1779.

The extension of the sphere of war owing to the French alliance with America brought great difficulties to the ministry. A powerful fleet under Keppel was sent into the Channel, and in July engaged the French fleet off Ushant, but the action was indecisive, and both fleets retired, the one to Brest, and the other to Plymouth. Keppel had signalled Sir Hugh Palliser, his second in command, to bear up with his squadron, and renew the action, but Palliser's ship was much crippled, and he was either unable or unwilling to comply. Mutual recriminations followed, and as both admirals were in Parliament and political adversaries, Keppel being in Opposition, whilst Palliser was a Lord of the Admiralty, the charges led to a fierce Parliamentary war, and eventually Keppel had to submit to a court martial. The trial took place at Portsmouth, and lasted over a month. The result was anxiously awaited by the City and the country. At length, late in the evening of the 11th February (1779), a courier brought the news that Keppel had been honourably acquitted. The whole of London was at once one blaze of illuminations. Palliser had to make his escape out of Portsmouth for fear of violence, and a house in Pall Mall once occupied by him was completely gutted by the mob and its contents burnt in St. James's Square. The gates of the Admiralty were taken off their hinges. Lord

Sandwich had his windows smashed, so had Lord North, and greater damage would have been done but for the interference of the military.

The next day (12 Feb.) the Common Council passed a vote of thanks to Keppel "for his spirited "behaviour on the 27th of July last in his attack on "the French fleet, for his glorious and gallant efforts "to renew the engagement in the afternoon of that "day, efforts rendered unsuccessful thro' the want of "obedience to his orders by the Vice-Admiral of the "Blue."[1] They further voted him the Freedom of the City in a box of heart of oak, in testimony of the respect and gratitude which they entertained of his long and faithful services to his country.[2] That night the illuminations were repeated, but stringent measures were taken to prevent tumult.[3] The vote of thanks was conveyed to the admiral without delay, but circumstances prevented the Freedom being conferred on him until the following December. On the first occasion, Keppel was entertained with a few of his most intimate friends at the London Tavern;[4] on the second the admiral entertained a deputation from the Common Council at his own house in Audley Square. He and Lord Howe had by that time become so disgusted with the government that they had signified their intention of withdrawing their services from the navy so long as the ministers remained in power;[5]

Vote of thanks and Freedom of City to Keppel, 12 Feb., 1779.

---

[1] Walpole makes the following comment upon this paragraph:—
"The French will not like the *éclaircissement* of the court martial "by which it is clear that they were beaten and fled. The city which "does not haggle, has expressed this a little grossly in their address to "Keppel."—Walpole to Mann, 18 Feb., 1779. Letters vii, 179.

[2] Journal 67, fo. 200b.   [3] Walpole, Journal ii, 345.

[4] Journal 67, fos. 209b-212.

[5] Walpole to Mann, 9 March, 1779. Letters vii, 182.

but he assured his guests that his zeal for the public good had in no wise abated, notwithstanding his withdrawal from the command of the fleet.¹ The friendly attitude of the City towards Keppel could not have been otherwise than distasteful to the king who looked upon "poor" Palliser as an ill-used man, and had even suggested his appointment to the command of the North American fleet until the recent affair had blown over.²

Spain declares war, 17 June, 1779.

The situation in which ministers found themselves was daily becoming more difficult, when Spain rendered it worse by allying herself (June, 1779) with France and America against Great Britain. North had again and again intimated his readiness to resign, but the king would not hear of it, and the minister yielded to his master's stronger will and consented to remain in office against his own convictions. With this increase of danger Parliament again rallied round the throne, and voted loyal addresses. At the same time the leading Whig lords protested against the affairs of the country being left in the hands of a ministry that had proved itself so incapable;—"In " such a situation a change of system appears to us to " be our indispensable duty to advise."³ This too was the opinion of a large body of citizens, but the Common Council declined to hamper the king with another address on the subject.⁴

Economical reform.

The country for the most part was in favour of prosecuting the war with vigour, notwithstanding the

---

¹ Journal 67, fos. 329b–331b.
² The king to Lord North, 29 Jan. and 19 Feb., 1779.—Correspondence ii, 224, 232.
³ Journal House of Lords, xxxv, 802.
⁴ Journal 67, fo. 268–271.

addition of a fresh enemy. At the same time there was increasing dissatisfaction at the national expenditure and the excessive use of court influence over Parliament. The Opposition took advantage of this feeling, and in December motions were brought before the House of Lords in favour of economical reform. These were rejected, and the further consideration of the matter was postponed until the 8th February (1780). The Common Council sympathised with the Dukes of Devonshire, Grafton, Manchester, Portland and other Whig lords in their endeavours to promote reform, and passed them a vote of thanks. The Corporation was convinced that the cause of all the existing trouble lay in the "enormous and undue influence of the crown," and promised them support. Each of the lords wrote to acknowledge the vote of thanks, and their answers were given a wide circulation.[1]

Before the question came on again the country had become thoroughly roused. Committees of Association—as they were called—sprang up in all directions, their object being to impress upon Parliament the necessity of economy and the abolition of sinecures. Petitions flowed in from all parts. Yorkshire took the lead, but was closely followed by London.[2] The day that the City's petition was laid before the House (11 Feb.) Burke introduced a Bill for carrying out economical reform, but the measure had to be abandoned owing to the opposition it met with in committee.[3]

Committees of Association, 1779.

[1] Journal 67, fos. 331b–333b. Journal 68, fos. 5b 12b.
[2] Journal 68, fo. 13.
[3] Walpole, Journal ii, 366, 367, 374.

Dunning's motion, 6 April, 1780.

Although Burke's Bill had failed to pass, the movement continued to gain force both in and out of Parliament, and on the 6th April Dunning moved his famous resolution that "it is the opinion of this "committee that the influence of the crown has in- "creased, is increasing, and ought to be diminished." This resolution, with but a slight variation, was, after a hot debate, carried by a majority of eighteen.[1] It was followed by two other resolutions in the same direction, one (moved also by Dunning) to the effect that it was competent for the House to reform the Civil List, the other (moved by Thomas Pitt) that it was the duty of the House to remedy the abuses mentioned in the petitions. Both were carried, and the movers were accorded the thanks of the City (which they in due course acknowledged[2]), but when it came to taking further action on these resolutions the House raised so many objections that all thought of carrying them into effect had to be abandoned.

The City's letter to Lord Shelburne, 7 April, 1780.

As time went on the Committees of Association, not content with their legitimate work—the work for which they were originally established—viz., economical reform, took upon themselves to push parliamentary reform, a matter on which the country was not as yet agreed. The City approved of their action, having long been anxious to see a recurrence to short parliaments and a change made in the mode of representation, but in other places the new departure

---

[1] When that staunchest of Tories, Dr. Johnson, was asked by his friend Boswell if he had not felt vexed at the passing of such a resolution he characteristically replied, "I would have knocked the factious dogs on the head, to be sure, but I was not *vexed.*"—Boswell's Life of Johnson (Napier) iv, 154.

[2] Journal 68, fos. 47–47b, 49–50.

caused alarm. In Wiltshire, Lord Shelburne's county, the Association had been disavowed[1] owing to its recent action, and his lordship had in consequence written a letter to the county upholding the Association. Soon after this Shelburne was wounded in a duel, and upon his recovery the City took the opportunity of sending him a letter of congratulation, and at the same time of testifying their appreciation of his letter to the county of Wilts;—"The noble and "manly proof which your lordship has given in your "letter to the county of Wilts of your decided "concurrence in the undoubted right of the people to "short parliaments and the necessity of a more equal "representation cannot but increase our regard, "esteem and confidence; and your lordship in your "further prosecution of those great constitutional "objects may depend on the most firm and deter- "mined support of the city of London."[2]

The earl in reply assured the Common Council that the support of the City of London was the most honourable incentive he was capable of feeling, as well as the strongest preservative against despondency. As regards the proposals for shortening the duration of parliaments and a more equitable representation, which the counties, cities and boroughs of England were combining to obtain, they would certainly meet his zealous concurrence whenever they should appear "to be the public sense." Without wishing to influence others, he was bound at so critical a juncture to confess that his own opinion was in favour of both proposals.[3]

Lord Shelburne's reply, 12 April, 1780.

---

[1] Walpole to Mason, 13 and 17 April, 1780.—Letters vii, 352, 353; Walpole, Journal ii, 378, 379.

[2] Journal 68, fo. 46b.   [3] *Id.*, fo. 49.

The City accepts a Form of Association, 13 April, 1780.

The day that the earl's answer was read before the Common Council (13 April) a Form of Association was submitted for their approval. It followed the lines of the Yorkshire Association, and subject to certain alterations it was recommended for acceptance by the City of London.[1] The main point was that subscribers to the form pledged themselves to support only those parliamentary candidates who were in favour (1) of cutting down public expenditure, (2) of shortening the duration of parliaments, and (3) of establishing greater equality in parliamentary representation by allowing the several counties of Great Britain to elect in a due proportion 100 members at least in addition to their present number. The Common Council at once approved of the form, and ordered the Town Clerk to subscribe to it in the name of the Corporation. The citizens were to be recommended also to subscribe to it as being the best plan for effecting the objects in view. The Court at the same time deemed it opportune to place on record the passage in Chatham's letter to Lord Temple of the 17th April, 1771, in which the writer signified his approval of shorter parliaments and more equal representation, and this was accordingly entered on their Journal.[2]

Outcry against Sir George Savile's Act.

Scarcely had the ministry managed to escape from Dunning's attack before they were threatened by a new danger. This time they did not stand alone; the strife of parties ceased in the presence of a

---

[1] "The Form of Association prepared by the committee appointed by the Court of Common Council to correspond with the committees appointed or to be appointed by the several Counties, Cities and Boroughs in the kingdom."—Journal 68, fo. 51.

[2] Journal 68, fo. 52.

common danger. For some time past an agitation had been set on foot against a Bill which Sir George Savile had carried in 1778, for the relief of Catholics from some of the hardships inflicted upon them by law. The cry of "No Popery" had been raised, and in March last a motion had been made in the Common Council against any proceedings in Parliament calculated to favour Papists. The consideration of the motion was adjourned, and did not come on again until the 31st May, when the court came to a resolution that the passing of any Acts of Parliament in favour of Papists, or the repealing of any Acts against Popery, was repugnant to the true interests of the country. It, at the same time, directed the City's representatives in Parliament to support any movement for the repeal of Savile's Act, so far as it related "to the establishment of seminaries for the "education of youth, and the purchasing of lands "within the realm."[1] Protestant associations were formed in different parts of the country, and on all sides a cry was raised against catholic emancipation.

The chief leader of the movement was the crack-brained fanatic, Lord George Gordon, who led a mob some thousands strong, wearing blue cockades, through the city to Westminster with a petition which he desired to lay before the House of Commons. A motion that the petition should be brought up was seconded by Alderman Bull. This took place on Friday, the 2nd June. Whilst Lord George was thus engaged, the mob clamoured to be admitted into the House and would have forced an entrance, but for the arrival of a party of horse and

Lord George Gordon at Westminster, 2 June, 1780.

[1] Journal 68, fos. 29-29b, 61.

foot guards. Foiled in their attempt to intimidate the House, the mob dispersed in various directions, and proceeded to sack and burn the Roman Catholic chapels attached to the Sardinian and Bavarian embassies, standing in Duke Street, Lincoln's Inn Fields, and Warwick Street, Golden Square, and having so far wreaked their vengeance they retired to rest for the night.[1]

Riot in Moorfields, 4 and 5 June, 1780.

Matters were not allowed to rest here. On Saturday afternoon (3 June), Kennet, the lord mayor, received a letter from Lord Stormont, secretary of state, forewarning him of the likelihood of tumults arising within his jurisdiction and strongly recommending him to take the necessary steps for preserving the peace. The day passed off quietly, however. A few people gathered in Ropemakers Alley, Little Moorfields, where stood a Roman Catholic chapel, but no disturbance took place. On Sunday afternoon (4 June) matters took a turn for the worse, and the mayor, being informed that a very great concourse of people had assembled in Moorfields in a riotous manner, and was threatening the chapel, at once sent for the marshals and their men and instructed them to procure as many constables as possible, and disperse the mob. In the evening the mayor himself went to the scene of riot, and stayed there until three o'clock in the morning. In the course of the night he received another and more urgent letter from Lord Stormont;—
" I cannot but hope, and trust from your lordship's
" known zeal and activity that every effectual legal

---

[1] Walpole to the Countess of Ossory, 3 June, 1780.—Letters vii, 377.

"method will be used by you to preserve the public peace by guarding it against those dangers to which it stands exposed." The mayor was quick to grasp the situation. There were not nearly sufficient constables procurable to put down the riot, and those that were present declined to exert themselves to save the property of Roman Catholics. Kennet therefore took the only course open to him, and sent to the Tower for military assistance. The commander, however, was slow to give the aid required, and could be prevailed upon to send no more than 73 men, all told, and even these were sent in detachments. The force was utterly inadequate to cope with the crowd, but fortunately the mob were by this time ready to listen to the appeals of the mayor and aldermen, and quiet was at length restored. The mayor went home to seek a much needed rest, leaving one of the sheriffs on the spot in case of emergency. On Monday morning (5 June) a fresh riot broke out, and the mayor sent again to the Tower. A detachment of horse and foot was despatched to his assistance, but by the time it arrived the chapel and several houses adjoining had been burnt and destroyed.[1] The principal object of attack outside the city was Savile House in Leicester Fields, the house of Sir George Savile himself, the indirect author of all the mischief, and this was sacked by the mob.

Upon hearing of this fresh outbreak the secretaries of state, Lords Stormont and Hillsborough, wrote a joint letter to the mayor expressing concern and surprise that houses in the city should be

The conduct of the civic authorities impugned.

---

[1] Repertory 184, fos. 204-207.

demolished in broad daylight, and—as they were informed—" without the least interposition of the civic magistrates to preserve the public peace."[1] This was scarcely true. The mayor, aldermen and sheriffs appear to have done their duty, but they experienced no little difficulty in getting the marshalmen and constables—who were no friends to the Catholics, and had no real wish to save them from the mob—to do theirs. One marshalman, in fact, openly refused to obey the summons that was sent him, declaring that he would not go to protect any such Popish rascals, and for this he was suspended from office.[2] The mayor, in reply, justified himself (and with reason) by laying the blame upon the commanding officer at the Tower, who had failed to supply him with the requisite assistance. Lord Stormont accepted the mayor's explanation, and immediately sent copies of his letter to the field officer of the guards with directions to send to the city forthwith a detachment of foot guards and light dragoons, as well as to the commanding officer at the Tower, directing him to supply the lord mayor with such assistance as he might require.[3]

More rioting, 6 June, 1780.

On Tuesday morning (6 June) a Court of Aldermen sat, and the mayor reported all that had taken place since the previous Saturday. He was recommended to take the most effectual methods he could devise for preventing further tumult, and the Court promised to defray all expenses.[4] During the day the city was quiet, but at night the rioters split themselves up into various parties, and whilst one party was engaged in

---

[1] Repertory 184, fo. 207. [2] *Id.*, fo. 209.
[3] Journal 68, fos. 65, 65b. [4] Repertory 184, fo. 210.

sacking and burning Lord Mansfield's house in Bloomsbury Square, another attacked the house of Sir John Fielding, and others broke into old Newgate and Clerkenwell prisons, and set free the prisoners.

Writing to Lord North late that night the king expressed surprise that Lord Gordon was still allowed to be at large, and complained of the "great supineness of the civil magistrates," whereby the rioters received encouragement;—"I fear without more "vigour that this will not subside; indeed, unless "exemplary punishment is procured, it will remain a "lasting disgrace, and will be a precedent for future "commotions."[1] The fact was that many justices of the peace had run away, and it was with the greatest difficulty that a magistrate was found to read the Riot Act in Bloomsbury, and when found it was too late to save Lord Mansfield's house.

The king's letter to Lord North, 6 June, 1780.

Early next morning (7 June) the mayor despatched a letter to the secretaries of state asking for more troops, and at half-past two o'clock a reply was sent that he should have such additional force as could be spared. In the meanwhile he was urged to take every possible measure for protecting the Bank of England, which there was reason to believe was about to be attacked.[2] On receipt of this letter the mayor summoned a Common Council to meet that evening at six o'clock. It was at once resolved to direct the sheriffs to raise the *posse comitatus*. The services of the Military Association were offered and readily accepted. Many officers of the City's militia volunteered for duty, and they were

The City in the hands of the mob, 7 June.

---

[1] The king to Lord North, 6 June, 1780.—Correspondence ii, 324.
[2] Journal 68, fo. 65b.

desired to place themselves at the disposal of the sheriffs, who were instructed more particularly to protect the Mansion House, the Guildhall and the Bank of England.[1] The measures were not taken a whit too soon. Two attempts were made on the Bank, but in each case the rioters were repulsed. The King's Bench and Fleet prisons were fired; and as many as thirty-six fires, all blazing at one time and in different quarters of the city, might be seen from one spot. Houses were pillaged in all directions. In Broad Street the Artillery Company and the London Association were ordered to fire on the mob, and several were killed.[2] The streets were flooded in many places with raw spirits from wrecked distilleries, and as many (if not more) perished from excessive drink as from the firing of the military, although by an order of Lord Amherst, the adjutant-general, the latter were authorised to act without waiting for directions from the civil magistrates.[3] The return of the number of killed and wounded during the disturbances was 458.[4]

City petition for repeal of Savile's Act, 8 June, 1780

In the meanwhile troops had arrived in London from their various quarters in the country, and were encamped in the public parks. Their presence served to intimidate the rioters and order began to be

---

[1] Journal 68, fo. 66. Notwithstanding these precautions—and it is difficult to see what more could be done—Walpole declares that "the Lord Mayor Kennet and Sheriff Pughe behaved shamefully."—Journal ii, 408.

[2] This incident is depicted in a well known engraving, where the Mayor is represented, with his hat off, giving the command to fire. A prominent figure in the group is the surgeon, Sir William Blizard, tending a wounded man, whilst an attempt is being made on his own life by one of the rioters.—See Raikes's History of the Hon. Artillery Company ii, 68.

[3] Repertory 184, fo. 246; Walpole, Journal ii, 407-409; Walpole to the Countess of Ossory, 7 June, 1780.—Letters vii, 386-389.

[4] Annual Register xxiii, 262.

restored. Before the Common Council of Wednesday evening broke up, it resolved to petition Parliament for a repeal of Savile's Act, and the next day (8 June) the petition was drawn up. It set out, in effect, that since the Act made in the 11th and 12th years of King William III, entitled "an Act for the further preventing the growth of Popery," the Papists had experienced no persecution, and the state had enjoyed perfect tranquility, and that the repealing of part of the Act had occasioned much discontent and produced dangerous tumults. The petitioners therefore prayed that the repealing Act should be itself repealed as being in their opinion "the most probable means of immediately quieting the minds of the people." The sheriffs and the remembrancer were instructed to present the petition to the House of Commons without delay, but rather than listen to a debate for a repeal of the Act, of which General Conway had given notice, the House suddenly adjourned until the 19th.[1]

On Friday morning (9 June) the Lords of the Council issued a warrant for the arrest of the arch-mover in the recent troubles, and before night-fall Lord George Gordon was lodged in the Tower. Their lordships at the same time directed the lord mayor to make diligent search for all idle and disorderly persons, and to commit them for trial. All guns, pistols, and other offensive weapons were to be seized. A difficulty arose as to where to keep prisoners or those awaiting trial, now that Newgate and the other prisons were no longer serviceable. The mayor suggested the Tower, but the Lords of

Instructions of Lords of the Council, 9 June, 1780.

---

[1] Journal 68, fo. 67. Walpole, Journal ii, 409, 410.

the Council would not hear of such a thing. They recommended him to commit his prisoners to some of the city halls or other public buildings, as he might deem most fit, and they (the lords) would furnish a sufficient force to guard these temporary prisons. The Court of Aldermen lost no time in carrying out the instructions thus given.[1] That evening the mayor was desired to meet the Lords of the Council at the Cockpit, Whitehall. What took place at the interview does not appear to be recorded.[2]

<small>The civic and military authorities at variance, June, 1780.</small>

A proposal to form an armed association of householders for future protection, brought the City into variance with the military authorities. No sooner was the proposal set on foot than Colonel Twistleton who was in command of the troops in the city, informed the adjutant-general of it. The latter at once signified his disapproval on the ground that "no person can bear arms in this country but under officers having the king's commission," and he instructed Colonel Twistleton (13 June) to see that all arms in the hands of persons who were not of the City militia, or authorised by the king to be armed, were given up. The existing London Association which had been on duty since the beginning of the

[1] Repertory 184, fos. 228-236.

[2] *Id.*, fo. 232. According to the Gentleman's Magazine (Vol. 50, p. 295) it would appear that the mayor was put on his defence for we read: "The lord mayor of London was summoned before the privy council; but discharged the same evening." A modern writer goes so far as to say "the lord mayor was tried and convicted of criminal negligence." (Bright, Hist. of England iii, 1,094). Another goes still further, and states that he was "prosecuted by the attorney general for a gross neglect of duty and was convicted, but his death "prevented the passing sentence." (See note by editor of Letters of George III to Lord North, ii, 324). As a matter of fact Kennet did not die until two years later, and he continued to perform his civic duties to the last.—Repertory 186, fo. 196.

riots, on learning this order, flatly refused to surrender their arms, on the ground that by the articles of the Bill of Rights, all his majesty's Protestant subjects were permitted to have arms for their defence suitable to their condition and as allowed by law.[1] The Court of Aldermen could not understand this interference of the military in the City's affairs, and directed the lord mayor to apply to Colonel Twistleton for a copy of the orders under which he acted in the city. Thereupon that officer produced the original orders of the 7th June, signed by the adjutant-general.

This did not satisfy the Aldermen, and by their directions the lord mayor addressed a letter to Earl Bathurst, the president of the Council (14 June), informing him that in pursuance to his orders they had made diligent search for disorderly persons implicated in the late riots, and had " taken to their " assistance the house-keepers in each district, who " have armed themselves" under the directions of the Court for the purpose of supporting the civil magistrate, but the Court's attention having been drawn to Lord Amherst's letters to Colonel Twistleton, they desired some explanation, as those letters militated against former orders from the Lords of the Council. The Court further desired to know whether Lord Amherst's order of the 7th June was to continue in force.[2]

Letter to Lord Bathurst, 14 June, 1780.

---

[1] Highmore, Hist. of Hon. Artillery Company, p. 332. On the 16th June, the Court of Aldermen passed a vote of thanks to the association, as well as to the corps of light horse volunteers, serving under Alderman Kirkman, who had been the first to call the attention of the Court of Aldermen to Lord Amherst's orders. (Repertory 184, fos. 251-253.) The Common Council also acknowledged the services of both bodies, by resolving to present the first mentioned corps with a handsome pair of colours, and the second with a pair of standards. —Journal 68, fos. 72b-73.

[2] Repertory 184, fos. 243-248

Lord Bathurst's reply, 15 June.

In reply to this letter, the President of the Council explained that Lord Amherst's letters had been misunderstood, "for when he speaks of the "arms in the hands of the city militia or other "persons authorised by the king to be armed, he "certainly includes the arms in the hands of the "citizens and house-keepers, who by virtue of an "order of the Court of Lieutenancy are required to "keep them in their houses." As regards the order of the adjutant-general of the 7th June, he was of opinion that it had better remain in force so long as the presence of the military in the city was necessary for the preservation of peace. His letter concluded with a warning lest the armed house-keepers should expose themselves to the military, who in a tumult would have difficulty in distinguishing them from the rioters.[1]

The City's second letter to Lord Bathurst. 17 June, 1780.

This reply being deemed unsatisfactory, the lord mayor wrote a second letter (17 June) pointing out that Lord Amherst's orders to Colonel Twistleton, of the 13th, would, if literally executed, disarm those very persons without whose assistance it would have been impossible for the civic authorities to have executed the Order of Council of the 9th instant. This (he explains) is what was meant in his former letter, when he said that Lord Amherst's letters militated against the orders first received from the Lords of the Council, and the Court of Aldermen now desired him to submit to his lordship's consideration "whether some further explanation might "not be necessary to prevent a construction which "would leave the civil magistrate without power to "act at all, for want of necessary support."[2]

[1] Repertory 184, fos. 249-250.   [2] *Id.*, fos. 254-256.

The lord mayor's letter having been submitted to the Lords of the Council, the President replied, three days later (20 June), that in the opinion of their lordships the matter had been fully explained in his letter of the 15th. With regard, however, to the alleged impracticability of executing the Orders of Council of the 9th instant without the assistance of the inhabitants of the several wards who had armed themselves, the Council was of opinion that in times of danger "a reasonable number of inhabitants, armed "according to the nature and circumstances of the "case, may attend the peace-officers, as assistants to "them, for the preservation of the public peace, until "the danger be over." He concluded by reminding the aldermen that the privilege enjoyed by subjects of carrying arms under the Bill of Rights (to which they had referred in the mayor's last letter) did not extend to mustering and arraying armed bodies without the king's permission.[1] The next day (21 June) the Duke of Richmond moved in the Lords that the adjutant-general's orders contravened the Bill of Rights, but the motion was negatived without a division.[2]

Lord Bathurst's reply, 20 June, 1780.

Still the Court of Aldermen were far from being satisfied. They foresaw that difficulties were likely to arise in the execution of their duty if the military were to be allowed to act independently. They desired, therefore, the lord mayor once more to address the President of the Council with the view of getting the order of the adjutant-general respecting the military acting without previous directions from

Another letter to Lord Bathurst, 24 June, 1780.

---

[1] Repertory 184, fo. 267.   [2] Journal House of Lords, xxxvi, 151.

the civil magistrates, withdrawn. Accordingly on the 24th June Kennet wrote again to this effect,[1] but the only answer vouchsafed to this was the passing of a Bill of Indemnity for the acts of the military.[2] It was useless, therefore, for the Court of Aldermen to proceed further in the matter, and they had the wisdom to ignore a series of propositions which one of their number introduced later on (18 July) touching the rights of the citizens to bear arms and the non-interference of the military powers.[3]

<small>Speech of Wilkes in the House, 19 June, 1780.</small>

When Parliament resumed its sitting on the 19th Wilkes, who had displayed great zeal during the riots, not only made an attack on the lord mayor for not having taken proper precautions to prevent their occurrence in the city, but he declared that the petition drawn up and approved by the Common Council on the 8th had been improperly procured, having been moved in the Court after many of the members had gone home under the impression that business was over. He next proceeded to attack his former friend and colleague, Alderman Bull, who (he said) had not only omitted to take steps to quell the rioters, but had allowed the constables of his wards to "wear the ensigns of riot in their hats," and had been seen leaving the House of Commons arm-in-arm with Lord George Gordon himself. Bull could only reply that it was true that constables of his ward had worn the cockades, but he had made four of them remove them.[4] Permission was eventually given for bringing in a Bill for securing the Protestant religion.

[1] Repertory 184, fo. 270. [2] Journal House of Commons, xxxvii, 929.
[3] Repertory 184, fos. 309-312.
[4] Hansard, Parliamentary History xxi, 701, 702 ; Walpole, Journal ii, 418.

On the 8th July a motion was made in the Common Council for presenting an address to the king "expressing the grateful thanks of this Court for "his majesty's care and attention to the citizens of "London in granting them such aid as became "necessary to subdue the late dangerous riots, they "being too formidable for the control of the civil "authority." To this the previous question was moved and lost, and the original motion was at length carried, but when it came to nominating four aldermen and eight commoners to draw up the address, there were not found sufficient aldermen present, and the matter had to be postponed.[1] It was eventually passed on the 24th, and presented on the 28th, when the king made a suitable reply.[2]

City address to the king on late riots, 28 July, 1780.

The riots over, and the ring-leaders (all except Lord George Gordon himself) brought to justice, it remained to pay the costs. To make good all the damages involved much time and expenditure. The new gaol at Newgate on which so much money had been spent, and which was approaching completion at the outbreak of the riots, was completely "gutted," only the external walls being left standing. The keeper's house was demolished, and much damage done to the neighbouring Sessions House. For all this the City sent in claims for compensation,[3] and in course of time succeeded in getting from Parliament three several sums of £10,000 to assist in defraying the expense of rebuilding Newgate.[4] The cost of maintaining the military force quartered in the city

City claims for damages during the riots.

---

[1] Journal 68, fo. 338. The entry is misplaced.
[2] *Id.*, fos. 70, 74b.   [3] *Id.*, fos. 71, 77b-78.
[4] *Id.*, fos. 159b, 196b, 296. Journal 69, fo. 257b.

during the riots was no slight one, and had to be provided for by the Common Council. One ward alone, that of Farringdon Within, sent in a bill exceeding £350 for victuals supplied to a party of light horse quartered at the Oxford Arms in Warwick Lane, and the Sessions House, to a detachment of foot guards quartered in St. Paul's, and several companies of militia at Christchurch, Newgate.[1] There were, moreover, legal expenses incurred by the City in defending actions brought against the sheriffs by various inhabitants of the city for damage done to houses.[2]

A new Parliament, 31 Oct., 1780.

Whilst the riots brought a respite to Parliament from the importunity of associations, their suppression brought temporary support to the king, who embraced the opportunity of dissolving Parliament before the court party lost ground.[3] Parliament was accordingly prorogued on the 8th July, and on the 1st September, was dissolved, another being summoned to meet on the last day of October. Only two of the old city members were re-elected. These were Bull and Hayley. The places of Sawbridge and Oliver were taken by two other aldermen, namely, Kirkman— who commanded the light horse volunteers during the riots—and Nathaniel Newnham. Sawbridge, however, recovered his seat upon Kirkman's death, which occurred within a few days after his election. A year later (Sept., 1781) Hayley died, and Lord George Gordon, whom a jury had recently acquitted of high treason, made some show of contesting the seat. He soon, however, discovered that the

---

[1] Journal 68, fos. 164b, 165.   [2] *Id.*, fo. 152b.
[3] Walpole, Journal ii, 425.

City would have none of him, and withdrew before the election came on. The seat was won, after a severe contest, by Sir Watkin Lewes the outgoing lord mayor.[1]

The late riots had somewhat cooled the ardour of the associations. Many of them, according to Walpole,[2] had been formed chiefly with a view to the coming Parliamentary elections, and now that these were over, the various committees became less active. The City's Committee of Correspondence was dissolved, and the civic authorities after some wavering refused to allow country associations the use of the Guildhall for fear of renewed disturbances.[3]

The City's Committee of Correspondence dissolved, 15 March, 1781.

The news of the capitulation of Cornwallis and his army at Yorktown which reached London on Sunday, the 25th November (1781), induced the livery to urge the king once more to put an end to the war. A Common Hall was summoned by special request to meet on Thursday, the 6th December. Alderman Bull being too ill to attend and to consult his constituents as he wished, contented himself with addressing a letter to the "Gentlemen of the Livery" calling upon them to continue to be an example to the nation, as they always had been. With their assistance he hoped to see a change effected which should put an end to the evils from which the country was suffering. This letter having been read to the livery they proceeded to consider the terms of a new remonstrance, which was produced ready cut and dried. After expressing concern at the king's

Proceedings of Common Hall, 6 Dec., 1781.

---

[1] Walpole, Journal ii, 468-471.　　[2] *Id.*, 453.
[3] Journal 68, fos. 127-128.

recent speech in Parliament, declaring his intention to persevere in a system of measures which had already proved so disastrous, the document plainly told the king that he had been deluded by his ministers, and the consequences of that delusion had been the almost total extinction of trade and commerce, and the annihilation of public and private credit. "Your " majesty's fleets"—it went on to say—" have lost " their wonted superiority. Your armies have been " captured. Your dominions have been lost." The petitioners expressed a desire publicly to declare not only to the king, but to Europe and to America itself, their abhorence of the continuation of the unnatural and unfortunate war, which could only tend to the alienation of the American colonies with whom they still hoped to live on terms of intercourse and friendship so necessary to the commercial prosperity of the kingdom; and they concluded by imploring his majesty to dismiss his present advisers as a pledge to the world of his determination to abandon a system incompatible with the interests of his crown and the happiness of his people.[1]

The remonstrance was ordered to be presented by the lord mayor, the city members, the Court of Aldermen [*not* the Common Council], the sheriffs and ten of the livery—the number permitted by Stat. 13, Chas. II, c. 5—attended by the Recorder and city officers; and notwithstanding all previous objections on the part of the king it was resolved that the sheriffs should enquire when his Majesty would be pleased to receive it on the throne. The result was such as might have been, and no doubt was, expected. When those

[1] Common Hall Book, No. 8, fos. 227b–228b.

"fellows in fur,"[1] as George called the sheriffs, attended at court to deliver their message, the king told them he would consider the matter, and would let them know; and in due course Lord Hertford addressed (10 Dec.) the following letter to the mayor:—"It is well known to be the settled custom "for the King to receive upon the Throne an address "from the City of London only in their corporate "capacity, and the same was signified by a letter "written by me, in obedience to His Majesty's "command, on the eleventh of April, 1775, to the "then Lord Mayor. In consequence thereof I am "commanded by His Majesty to acquaint you that " His Majesty will receive at the levée on Friday the "14th inst. the Address, Petition and Remonstrance "of the Lord Mayor, Aldermen and Livery in Com- "mon Hall assembled. I have, etc." To this the mayor replied by referring the lord chamberlain to Wilkes's letter of the 2nd May, 1775, as to the question of custom. With regard to the present address, petition and remonstrance he contented himself with representing to his lordship that as the resolution of the livery was that it should be presented to the king on the throne, the persons directed by the said resolution to present it could not dispense therewith by presenting it in any other mode.[2] The remonstrance was in consequence never presented, although Walpole believed it to have been presented at the levée.[3]

Thus baulked in their design the livery proceeded at another special Common Hall (31 Jan., 1782) to pass a number of resolutions condemning the king's

Resolutions of Common Hall, 31 Jan., 1782.

---

[1] Walpole, Journal ii, 484.   [2] Common Hall Book, No. 8, fo. 229.
[3] Walpole, Journal ii, 484.

advisers and maintaining the necessity of shorter parliaments and fairer representation. They declared that the Committee of Correspondence appointed by the Common Council in February, 1780 (and since abolished) had "proved themselves firm friends to the people," and they resolved to appoint a similar committee from among themselves, and to petition the Common Council to grant the use of their new council chamber[1] to the committee for the purpose of occasionally meeting therein.[2] When the petition was laid before the Court on the 5th February it was refused, but in the following April it was granted, and the Committee of Correspondence was permitted to meet in the council chamber, or in any other part of the Guildhall that might be most convenient.[3]

The fall of North's ministry, 20 March, 1782. The ministry was now fast tottering to its fall. On the 22nd February General Conway moved the House of Commons to address the king for the purpose of restoring peace and giving up all thoughts of subduing America by force. After prolonged debate the motion was lost by one vote only.[4] Five days later (27 Feb.) the City agreed to a petition to the House imploring the Commons to interpose and prevent the continuation of the war,[5] and that same day the attack was renewed by Conway, who moved that the use of force to put down the colonies was impracticable. This time he was more successful.

[1] Now known as the old council chamber.
[2] Common Hall Book, No. 8, fos. 229-230.
[3] Journal 68, fos. 198, 221b.
[4] Journal House of Commons xxxviii, 814.
[5] Journal 68, fo. 217b.

His motion was carried by a majority of nineteen,[1] and a few weeks later (20 March) North resigned.

Much to his annoyance, the king found himself compelled to place the Opposition in office, with Rockingham as prime minister and Fox and Shelburne as secretaries of state, and to consent to negotiations for peace being opened on the basis of an acknowledgment of American independence. As soon as the change of government had taken place the Common Council presented a loyal address to the king expressing their warmest thanks for having complied with the wishes of the people and taken into his confidence men who were respected by the country for their constitutional principles. They trusted that with the assistance of these new advisers, and with the blessing of Providence, the dignity of the crown would be restored, and prosperity and unity promoted throughout the king's dominions. The king thanked the City for their address, and assured them that the dignity of the crown, the union of his people and the interests and prosperity of his dominions must ever be the principal objects of his care.[2]

City's address on change of ministry, 12 April, 1782.

The new ministers were pledged to do something towards purifying Parliament, and accordingly they carried a measure disqualifying contractors from sitting in the House of Commons, unless their contract should have been made at a public bidding. It was thought that government contractors might be too easily moved to support the party that happened to be in power. Alderman Harley, who sat with Sir

Parliamentary reform, 1782.

---

[1] Journal House of Commons, xxxviii, 860, 861; Walpole, Journal ii, 505-509.

[2] Journal 68, fos. 221-221b, 226.

George Cornewall for the county of Hereford, was one of those whom the Bill affected, inasmuch as he held a contract for supplying the army in Canada, Nova Scotia, Carolina, New York and the West Indies with money. He rose from his seat in the House and boldly defended himself. He had never (he said) asked for the contract; he was not in the habit of asking favours of ministers; "he got his contract in "consequence of an address which the late Lord "Suffolk intended to have moved to the king, that "his majesty would be pleased to confer upon him "some mark of his favour . . . . he was after-"wards offered a pension which he would not accept, "saying at the same time that he had rather have "something in the way of his profession; on this he "got the gold contract, which he fulfilled for twelve "years with the fairest character, and he now felt "himself hurt indeed that he should be treated as if "he were a criminal, in being forced to give up a "valuable branch of his business, or renounce the "honour, which he held so high, of sitting in Parlia-"ment."[1] The measure was carried on the 1st May. As Harley retained his seat, and continued to hold it until 1802, it is presumed he gave up his contract. On the 7th, William Pitt, the second son of the late Earl Chatham—who had already displayed such oratorical powers in defence of Burke's economical reform Bill that Burke himself, no less delighted than surprised, had declared him to be not a chip of the old block, but "the old block itself"[2]—moved for a committee to examine into the state of the

[1] Hansard, Parliamentary History xxii, 1,335.
[2] Walpole, Journal ii, 446.

representation of the country. The motion was rejected by only a majority of twenty, the closest division that the reformers ever achieved until 1831, the eve of their ultimate success.

The ministers now turned their attention to a reform of another kind. On the same day that Pitt made his motion in the House, Lord Shelburne, one of the secretaries of state, sent a letter to the lord mayor enclosing copies of a plan for augmenting the home force, and of a circular thereon he had sent to the chief magistrates of principal towns. His majesty (the letter said) expected that "his faithful citizens of London" would set an example to the rest of the kingdom, as they had so often done before, in gathering forces for the protection of their sovereign and their country; the more so, as the city of London had greater interests at stake. The Common Council not only voted (17 May) a sum of £5,000 to put the City militia on a proper footing, but resolved to invite subscriptions in the several wards of the city, and to send copies of Shelburne's letter to all the chartered and trading companies of the city.[1] The matter had already (9 May) been laid before the Court of Aldermen, and the lord mayor had been requested to wait upon Lord Shelburne, to thank him for the letter, and to assure him that the Court would at once proceed to accomplish his majesty's wish "and to do "justice to his majesty's most gratifying sentiments of "the exemplary loyalty and zeal of his faithful citizens "of London."[2]

Military reform, May, 1782.

On the 18th May, news arrived that the French fleet under De Grasse had been defeated by Rodney in

Rodney's naval victory, 12 April, 1782.

[1] Journal 68, fos. 226b-228.   [2] Repertory 186, fos. 187-194.

the West Indies (12 April). The City presented a congratulatory address to the king, who in reply (5 June) assured his "good city of London" of his constant attention to their commerce and happiness.[1] Rodney who had previously been in disgrace was now raised to the Peerage; but a proposal to entertain him at a public banquet at the City's expense fell through.[2] In October, however, the Common Council unanimously passed a vote of thanks to him for the service he had rendered to the commercial interests of the City, and the committee appointed to convey the same entertained him and his friends at a banquet given at the London Tavern—[3] an event which Horace Walpole had cause to remember, for the windows of his house in Berkeley Square were smashed by the mob which accompanied Rodney home from the City.[4]

The wreck of the Royal George, Aug., 1782.

In the meantime the British navy suffered a severe loss by the capsizing of the Royal George off Spithead. The vessel was reckoned the finest ship in the navy. The unfortunate circumstances, which carried her to the bottom with 800 souls, including Kempenfelt, the admiral, who was at the time writing in his cabin, have been immortalised in Cowper's well known lines:—

> "Toll for the brave!"
> The brave that are no more!
> All sunk beneath the wave
> Fast by their native shore!

It was, possibly, this loss which prompted the Common Council to consider the question of raising

---

[1] Journal 68, fos. 230, 238b.   [2] *Id.*, fo. 251.
[3] *Id.*, fos. 265, 290.
[4] Walpole to Mann, 26 Nov., 1782.—Letters viii, 309.

a sum of money (the Corporation itself contributing £10,000) for the purpose of presenting the king with a man-of-war, to be called the "City of London." It will be remembered that in 1665, when the ship "London" suddenly blew up on her way up to the Hope from Chatham, the City made good the loss then sustained by the navy. It was proposed now to follow the precedent then set, but after several adjournments the proposal was allowed to drop.[1]

In September Lord Howe set sail to relieve Gibraltar, which had endured a siege of three years and more. It was defended by General Elliot, afterwards raised to the peerage as Lord Heathfield, and the sufferings of the garrison had at times been terrible. When Shelburne succeeded to the premiership, on the death of Rockingham in July, negotiations for a peace with America and her allies were far advanced, but before a peace was signed France and Spain were anxious above all things to regain Gibraltar. Accordingly on the 13th September a tremendous attack was made on the fortress by the combined fleets. The forts replied with red hot shot, and eventually succeeded in destroying the floating batteries. Just when these were silenced Lord Howe appeared in the bay, and the combined fleet, not venturing to attack him, withdrew. The siege had attracted the eyes of all Europe, and in February (1783) the Common Council appointed a committee to consider the most suitable mode to be adopted by the City to express their respect to Elliot and Howe and the officers of the army and navy employed in "the glorious defence and relief of Gibraltar."

The relief of Gibraltar, Sept., 1782.

[1] Journal 68, fos. 273b, 284, 293, 296.

Copley's picture at the Guildhall.

Two artists were consulted on the matter, namely, West and Copley. The former was of opinion that it would be better to have two pictures instead of one, inasmuch as the defence of the Rock by Elliot and the relief by Howe were two distinct subjects. Copley, on the other hand, thought that both subjects could be treated in one picture of sufficient size to fill one of the side windows of the Common Council Chamber. The cost of such a picture he estimated at £1,500, but rather than lose the commission he was prepared to paint it for 1,000 guineas. His offer was in course of time accepted,[1] and his picture now adorns one entire wall of the Guildhall Art Gallery.[2]

The Peace of Paris, 3 Sept., 1783.

This great success, following so close upon Rodney's victory in the West Indies, convinced the allies that England was not by any means so prostrate as her failures in America had led them to believe, and they now showed a disposition to negotiate. Accordingly in January (1783) preliminaries of peace were signed at Paris. A provisional treaty had already been concluded with America, by which the

---

[1] Journal 68, fos. 298, 317. Considerable additions having been made to the picture as originally designed, a further sum of 300 guineas was voted to the artist, on condition, however, that he repaid Alderman Boydell the sum of 200 guineas which the worthy alderman had advanced to enable him to proceed to Germany for the purpose of painting certain portraits of Hanoverian officers for his picture. Copley objected to the Common Council taking cognisance of what was a private pecuniary transaction, and declined to pay Boydell out of the sum voted by the City. Thereupon the Common Council rescinded its vote, and paid 200 guineas to Boydell direct. This was in March, 1794. Five years later Copley changed his mood, and petitioned the Court for the other 100 guineas and for the return of the sketch of his picture. Both requests were granted.—Journal 70, fo. 259; Journal 74, fos. 63, 164b, 221; Journal 75, fo. 108; Journal 79, fo. 33. In 1817 this picture was lent to the British Institution for exhibition.—Journal 91, fo. 89b.

[2] The picture is so large, measuring over 24 feet in length, that it necessitated certain structural alterations in the old Council Chamber, where it was originally placed in 1793, at a cost of £300.—Journal 73, fo. 309b.

independence of the United States was formally acknowledged. The news was received in the city with the greatest joy, and the Common Council congratulated the king on his having paid "final attention" to the petitions of his faithful citizens and people. They took the opportunity of expressing their firm conviction that the commercial interests of this country and of North America were inseparably united—a sentiment with which the king declared in his reply that he entirely concurred—and hoped that the stipulations of the treaty would restore commercial intercourse between the two countries.[1] The preliminaries of both treaties were converted into definitive treaties on the 3rd September, and on the 6th October the peace was proclaimed in the city of London in the same manner as at the proclamation of peace with France on the 22nd March, 1763.[2]

[1] Journal 68, fos. 307-307b, 310-310b.
[2] Repertory 187, fos. 310, 311.

CHAPTER XLI.

The City and Fox's East India Bill, 1783.

Before the preliminaries of peace became converted into definite treaties, the Shelburne ministry had been forced to give way to a coalition with Fox and North as secretaries of state, and the Duke of Portland as nominal head. The new ministry found little favour with the City, firstly on account of its Stamp Act—imposing a duty upon all receipts for sums of forty shillings and upwards—which the citizens (wrongly, as it turned out) believed would be a hindrance to trade;[1] and secondly on account of Fox's attack on the chartered rights of the East India Company. If Fox's East India Bill were passed, what, they asked, was to become of their own chartered rights and privileges? Every corporation in the kingdom was solemnly warned of the consequences to themselves if the Bill were allowed to pass. "Our property and charter are invaded, look to your own" was the message the Company sent, together with a copy of Fox's Bill, to every borough in the country. The Bill passed the Commons, but when it came before the Lords the king declared himself so strongly against it that it was thrown out, and before the close of the year (1783) the ministers were suddenly and somewhat unceremoniously

---

[1] Journal 69, fos. 15, 16b-18b, 20-21. Commmon Hall Book, No. 8, fos. 239b-240. In May, 1784, the Common Council petitioned Parliament for its repeal. Journal 69, fo. 113b.

dismissed. For the first time in history we find the City unanimously supporting the king in the exercise of his prerogative. The Common Council hastened to assure his majesty that his faithful citizens had "lately beheld with infinite concern the progress of "a measure which equally tended to encroach on the "rights of your majesty's crown, to annihilate the "chartered rights of the East India Company, and to "raise a new power unknown to this free government "and highly inimical to its safety. [As the dangerous "measure was warmly supported by your majesty's "late ministers, we heartily rejoice in their dismission, *Vide* Printed "and humbly thank your majesty for exerting your addresses. "prerogative in a manner so salutary and consti- "tutional."] Finally they assured the king that as the prerogatives of his majesty's high office were intended for the good of the people, the citizens of London would always support the constitutional exercise of them to the utmost of their power. In other words, the king might always look to the City for support so long as he was content to exercise his prerogative for the preservation of "parliamentary engagements" and chartered rights.[1] The livery and the Common Council, so long opposed to each other, became allies again, and the former body passed a formal vote of thanks at a special Common Hall (13 Feb., 1784) to the representative body of the City for the address they had carried up to the throne "thereby setting an example to the whole kingdom."[2] Truly, as Macaulay remarks, "the successors of the old Roundheads had turned courtiers." Not content with thanking the Common Council for its attitude in

---

[1] Journal 69, fo. 65.   [2] Common Hall Book, No. 8, fo. 246.

the matter, the livery passed resolutions of their own in support of the just prerogative of the crown, the privileges of Parliament and the rights of the people, whilst they ordered that the city members should be instructed to advance in every way the business of the House, and particularly by the granting of supplies.[1]

Pitt's struggle with the Coalition, 1783-1784.

Fox's East India Bill had been strongly opposed by Pitt, who at the early age of twenty-three had been Chancellor of the Exchequer and leader of the House of Commons under the Shelburne ministry. It was to this youth that the king now appealed for assistance, and although the task of forming a ministry of any stability was almost beyond hope, Pitt undertook the struggle. As it was useless to look for any support in the Commons he chose his cabinet entirely from the Upper House, reserving for himself the post of First Commissioner of the Treasury and Chancellor of the Exchequer. Even before Pitt was able to take his seat as prime minister (a new election being necessary on his accepting office), it was evident that the Opposition intended to show him no pity or favour. It was not until the 12th January (1784)—the day that the House re-assembled after the Christmas recess—that he made his first appearance as prime minister. He came prepared with an India Bill, similar in most respects to that which he afterwards succeeded in carrying, but the Bill was now rejected although by a small majority. For weeks he struggled against the violent attacks of the Opposition, refusing either to resign or to dissolve

[1] Common Hall Book, No. 8, fo. 246b.

Parliament until he could take his opponents at a disadvantage.

At length, the nation at large became attracted by the indomitable courage and unflinching honesty of the young minister and began to rally round him. The city of London had been from the outset one of his staunchest supporters. On the 10th February (1784), the Common Council voted him the Freedom of the City and a gold box for his zeal in "supporting "the legal prerogative of the crown and the con- "stitutional rights of the people."[1] On the 28th, he was made free of the Grocers' Company and hospitably entertained by them in their hall. There are members of the Grocers' Company still alive who can recall the time when "the immortal memory of William Pitt" was honoured in solemn silence at all public gatherings in Grocers' Hall, and the esteem in which the company continues to hold one of the greatest statesmen that England has ever produced recently manifested itself afresh, when on the 28th February, 1884, the Grocers celebrated the "Pitt Centenary" by a banquet in their hall.

Civic honours for Pitt, Feb., 1784.

As soon as the minister perceived the attack of the Opposition wearing itself out, and the balance of parties becoming more equal, he seized the opportunity of dissolving Parliament and appealing to the country. One of the first elections to take place was, as usual, that for the City. Without his knowledge or consent Pitt himself was nominated among others; he declined, however, to stand, and was eventually returned for Cambridge University, a seat he continued

Dissolution of Parliament and defeat of Whigs, 1784.

---

[1] Journal 69, fos. 67, 128. The gold box was not presented until the 5th Feb., 1785. *Id.*, fos. 265b-266b.

to hold for the remainder of his life. The result of the City election was that all the old members were returned,[1] although Sawbridge nearly lost his seat in consequence of his attachment to Fox.[2] It soon became evident that the country was with Pitt. No less than 160 of Fox's friends and supporters—"Fox's martyrs," as they were popularly called—lost their seats, and Fox himself had, for a time, to content himself with a seat for a close borough, although he was eventually returned for Westminster, after one of the severest contests ever known.

<small>Pitt's East India Bill. 1784.</small>

When the new Parliament met (18 May) three subjects more especially demanded attention. These were the finances of the country, the affairs of the East India Company, and the state of Ireland. The first two were immediately taken in hand. Having in an incredibly short time placed the finance of the country on a firm basis, Pitt again introduced his East India Bill. This Bill, it must be borne in mind, differed essentially from Fox's Bill, which had recently excited such fears in the City, inasmuch as it merely proposed to establish a board of control for political purposes, and did not lay a finger upon the company's material possessions. The chartered rights of the company being left untouched, the directors offered no opposition, the fears of the City for their own chartered rights and possessions were lulled, and the Bill was allowed to pass. The dual system then established proved to work so well that it continued to be the

---

[1] Alderman Bull had died during the Christmas recess, and his place had been taken by Brook Watson.—Annual Register xxvii, 179.

Wraxall, Memoirs iii, 433, 434.

system under which India was governed from that day down to 1858.

In the course of the session Sawbridge brought forward his perennial motion in favour of short parliaments, but although it received the support of Pitt, notwithstanding his deeming it inopportune, the motion was lost.[1] In the following spring (1785) Pitt himself for the third, and, as it proved, for the last, time attempted to carry a measure for parliamentary reform, but this, too, was defeated, and, strange to say, by the same majority as Sawbridge's motion.[2] The Common Council had previously passed a resolution urging every alderman who had a seat in the House to do his utmost to secure shorter parliaments,[3] but it was all in vain, and Pitt, disappointed at his failure, again turned his attention from parliamentary to financial reform.

Pitt's Reform Bill, 1785.

One of the many schemes which he proposed for filling the exchequer was a tax on retail shops. As soon as the proposal got wind the City was at once up in arms, and a committee was appointed (14 May, 1785) to confer with Pitt on the matter. Upon the citizens objecting that they would have to bear nearly the whole burden of the tax, they were told they could recoup themselves by raising the price of their goods to the consumer.[4] Disappointed in this quarter, they resolved to lay their case before Parliament; and accordingly a petition was drawn up, which set forth that the citizens of London had always been

The City and the Shop Tax, May, 1785.

---

[1] Parliamentary History xxiv, 975-1006.

[2] The votes against Sawbridge's motion had been 199 to 125, whilst those against Pitt were 248 to 174, or a majority of 74 in each case.—Journal House of Commons, xl, 216, 863.

[3] Journal 69, fo. 223b.   [4] *Id.*, fos. 248-249.

ready and willing to bear their fair share of the necessary burdens of the state, but that the tax now proposed was partial, unjust and oppressive to trade; that the inhabitants and traders of the city were already overburdened with taxation; that London and Middlesex paid 80 parts out of 513, or more than one-sixth of the whole Land Tax annually raised in the kingdom; and that, finally, it was a grave mistake to suppose that a tax on trade eventually fell on the consumers, for the price of every commodity was regulated by supply and demand.[1] This petition was laid before the House on the 19th May, but with little effect, and on the 30th the Bill passed the Commons[2] in spite of the strong protest against it made by the city members, who received the thanks of the Common Council for their spirited and manly opposition to a tax "universally condemned for its partiality and injustice."[3]

<small>Efforts to get it repealed, 1785-1789.</small> No sooner was the Bill passed than a committee of shopkeepers was formed to get it repealed, and in this they were assisted by the committee appointed by the Common Council on the 14th May. The costs incurred by the latter committee were to be discharged to the extent of £300 out of the City's Chamber.[4] In November (1785), the Common Council instructed their committee to prepare a petition to Parliament for a repeal of the obnoxious Act. This was accordingly done and the petition duly laid before the House, but with no better

---

[1] Journal 69, fos. 249b-250.
[2] Journal House of Commons, xl, 1000, 1032.
[3] Journal 69, fo. 250b. [4] *Id.*, fos. 288b-290.

success than before (27 Jan., 1786).¹ In the meantime a split had occurred among the commissioners whose duty it was to carry out the provisions of the Act. Some of them had duly qualified themselves for the purpose, whilst others had not, and so long as disagreement continued among the executive officers, the City shop-keeper ran the risk of incurring a double assessment.² Early in 1787, the agitation was renewed, and the mayor was asked to allow of a meeting of the discontents in the Guildhall on the evening of Friday, the 19th January. The mayor was willing enough, but the Court of Aldermen were afraid of a disturbance and the meeting was put off.³ A fortnight later (31 Jan.) the Common Council resolved to present another petition to Parliament for the repeal of the Act. Further experience, they assured the House, had confirmed their opinion of the partiality and oppression of the Act, and of the impossibility of shifting the burden upon the consumer.⁴ The petition was presented the following day, but the House remained obdurate.⁵ The shop-keepers passed a vote of thanks to the Common Council for the pains they had taken in the matter.⁶ For another two years the City agitated for the repeal of the tax, receiving the support of Fox, among others,⁷ but all their efforts proved futile,

[1] Journal 69, fos. 330, 338b–339, 355. Journal House of Commons, xli, 151.
[2] Journal 69, fos., 297b–298, 302–305.
[3] Repertory 191, fos. 74–79.   [4] Journal 70, fos. 132–133.
[5] Journal House of Commons, xlii, 289.
[6] Journal 70, fos. 134, 134b.
[7] Journal 71, fos. 48–49, 74b, 75, 93, 99–99b.

until in April, 1789, they were at last crowned with success and the Act was repealed.¹

Convention with France, 1787.

The Shop Tax was not the only point in Pitt's financial schemes which tended to bring him into direct opposition to the City, as we shall shortly see; but as a whole his schemes were eminently successful, and not the least successful of them all was his commercial treaty with France. Duties were lowered in each country on the productions of the other and both England and France were the better for the change, but the treaty as originally drafted threatened unfortunately to diminish the revenues of the city of London. Pitt's attention having been drawn to the matter, a proviso was inserted in a subsequent convention signed at Versailles (15 Jan., 1787) whereby the City's rights were safeguarded.² The convention was followed in October by a joint declaration whereby England and France mutually agreed to discontinue warlike operations.³

The City and the slave trade, 1788-1792.

The year 1788 witnessed the first steps taken in Parliament for the abolition of the slave trade. Wilberforce a prominent leader in the movement succeeded in winning over Pitt to the cause, and the City threw its influence into the scale. On the 4th February, the Common Council petitioned the House to take the matter into its consideration.⁴ Little however was done beyond the introduction of

¹ Journal House of Commons, xliv, 276.

² Journal House of Commons, xlii, 266, 289. The city solicitor and comptroller were specially commended for their services in preserving the city's rights in the treaty.—Journal 71, fos. 17b-18b.

³ Journal 70, fo. 303b.

⁴ Journal 71, fo. 47b. Journal House of Commons, xliii, 166, 167.

THE CITY AND THE SLAVE TRADE. 213

a temporary measure for improving the sanitary condition of vessels employed in the slave traffic. The Bill passed the Commons, but underwent such a change in the House of Lords that it became practically useless. In 1789, and again in 1790, Wilberforce urged the Commons to abolish the slave trade in its entirety, and in 1792, Pitt supported the proposal in a speech which surpassed all his previous oratorical efforts. It was to no purpose. The Liverpool merchants, whose interests in the nefarious traffic were enormous, succeeded in frustrating every attempt to put it down. At last, even the city of London refused to petition Parliament any further on the matter.[1]

Pitt's Regency Bill, 1788-1789.

In the meanwhile an event had occurred which for the moment threatened to overthrow the ministry. In November, 1788, the king who had previously shown signs of mental derangement became so seriously ill that a regency seemed inevitable. That the Prince of Wales ought to be Regent all parties were agreed, but whether he should be allowed to take upon himself the regency as a matter of right, or whether he should accept it at the hands of Parliament and with such limitations as Parliament might think fit to create, opinions differed. Pitt was strongly in favour of upholding the authority of Parliament in the matter and introduced a Regency Bill. The Bill passed the Commons, but before it passed the Lords the king unexpectedly recovered, and further proceedings were stayed. For having thus maintained "the important right of the Lords " and Commons of this realm to provide the means

[1] Journal 73, fo. 87.

"for supplying the defect of the personal exercise of "the royal authority arising from his majesty's indis- "position," the Common Council passed a vote of thanks to Pitt and his supporters, which the minister duly acknowledged;[1] but when it was proposed to present an address to the prince condoling with him on the king's illness, and congratulating him upon his being invested with the government "by the united wisdom of the two Houses," a debate of three hours ensued and the motion was eventually lost.[2]

Gift of £1,000 by Prince of Wales for poor of city, Jan., 1789.

It speaks well for the prince that he not only bore the City no ill-will, but was careful to forward to the city Chamberlain the sum of £1,000 for the poor of the city, who were suffering from the inclemency of the season, as he feared that his father's illness might prevent the king sending his usual annual gift. The Common Council were touched with the prince's thoughtful act of charity, and sent to Carlton House to thank him. His highness took the opportunity of assuring them that no one was more sensible than himself of the attention of the City, and no one would be more ready to show regard "towards the most respectable city in Europe."[3]

City addresses on king's recovery, 19 March, 1789.

Towards the end of February (1789) the king was himself again. The news of his recovery was a cause of sincere joy to the city of London, as well as to the nation at large, however disappointing to those who had built their hopes upon a regency. On the night of the 10th March the whole of London was

---

[1] Journal 71, fos. 179b, 180, 188. [2] *Id.*, fos. 190, 190b.
[3] *Id.*, fos. 186b-187, 190.

illuminated. From one extremity of the town to the other and far out into the surrounding suburbs there was one blaze of light. Two days later the Common Council prepared congratulatory addresses to the king and queen. These were presented to their majesties at Kew on the Thursday, the 19th March, and were graciously received, the City on this occasion, in compliance with the king's wishes, who was still far from strong, waiving their right to present the address to him on the throne.[1]

A solemn thanksgiving service was held at St. Paul's on Thursday, the 23rd April—St. George's day—and was attended by the king and queen, the royal family, the members of both Houses and great officers of state, as well as by the lord mayor, the aldermen, the sheriffs and members of the Common Council. In carrying out the preparations for the king's reception in the city everything was done with the view of sparing the king all unnecessary exertions.[2] The Earl of Salisbury, in his capacity as lord chamberlain, suggested that if the lord mayor and sheriffs and those aldermen who represented the city in Parliament were to meet the king at Temple Bar and conduct him to St. Paul's it would be more agreeable to his majesty than the attendance of a greater number of persons. For the same reason it was decided that no more than four members of the Common Council should attend. The formal presentation to the king of the City's sword at Temple Bar and of its re-delivery into the hands of William Gill, the lord mayor, was

Thanksgiving service at St. Paul's, 23 April, 1789.

---

[1] Journal 71, fos. 212–213b, 216–216b, 221.
[2] Journal 71, fos. 221b, 222b–223b, 231b; Repertory 193, fos. 193–201, 206–215.

made the subject of a large oil painting, mounted on a screen of six panels, by Ralph Dodd.[1]

<small>Pitt's Bill for excise duty on tobacco, 1789.</small>

As soon as the king's health allowed of Parliament resuming its ordinary course of business Pitt consented to remit the Shop Tax, which had caused so much bad feeling in the city. Scarcely was this done, however, before he again gave umbrage to the citizens by a proposal to transfer the duty on tobacco from the customs to the excise. Walpole had endeavoured to carry out a similar change in 1733, but the opposition he met with was so overpowering that he was obliged to give way. Pitt was more successful. The City withstood his Bill, as it had withstood Walpole's, but in spite of all opposition Pitt's Bill passed, and all subsequent efforts to get it repealed proved futile.[2]

<small>Negotiations for the removal of the Bank guard, 1788–1790.</small>

The king's illness had interrupted negotiations that had been opened for the withdrawal of the guard of soldiers that had been accustomed ever since the Gordon riots, to pass through the city daily for the purpose of protecting the Bank of England. In 1787 a citizen had complained to the Court of Aldermen of his having been pushed off the footway by soldiers of the guard passing to the Bank on the

---

[1] The picture was painted as a private speculation by the artist, and was offered for sale to the Corporation in 1791. The committee to whom the matter was referred suggested that the City might give 200 guineas for the picture, not so much on account of its intrinsic merit as because the artist was an industrious and promising man with a numerous family. This suggestion did not meet with the approval of the Common Council. It preferred to give the artist half that sum in acknowledgment of his pains and to allow him to keep the picture. Whether the artist thought himself thus sufficiently paid for his work is not clear, but the picture for many years stood in the Long Parlour at the Mansion House, where it served as a screen. It has recently been restored, and is now hung in the lobby of the Guildhall.—Journal 72, fos. 357b, 431–431b.

[2] Journal 71, fos. 253, 272, 274b; Journal 72, fo. 55.

evening of the 5th July; and the Court had thereupon instructed the lord mayor to request the secretary at war to give such directions as he might think proper that the guard might in future march in single file and not two abreast as they hitherto had done.[1]

The secretary at war (Sir George Yonge) had replied that the lord mayor's suggestion would be likely to lead to great inconvenience; that he undertook to promise that the officers of the guards would for their part endeavour to conduct their detachments on the march in a quiet, decent and soldier-like manner, but that from representations that had been made to him by officers commanding the guards as to the treatment the detachments sometimes met with in their passage through the city, he felt bound to ask the lord mayor to take such steps as he might deem fit to prevent any cause of complaint arising in future on either side.[2] This letter had been referred to a committee, with instructions to report their opinion as to the best way of affording sufficient protection to the Bank and at the same time of avoiding the inconveniences complained of. The committee showed no haste in the matter, and it was not until the following May (1788) that they reported in favour of furnishing the Bank with a guard of the city's militia, in place of the detachment of foot guards. The Court of Aldermen on receiving this report wished to know what the directors of the Bank of England thought of the suggestion,[3] but all the answer they got was that if the existing mode of protecting the Bank were discontinued, the directors

---

[1] Repertory 191, fos. 363-364.   [2] *Id.*, fos. 381-383.
[3] Repertory 192, fos. 201-203.

would not "put the city to the trouble of providing any other." The Court scarcely knew how to treat this answer. At length, after several adjournments, it resolved (21 Oct.) that the lord mayor should write to the secretary at war and request that the guard at the Bank should be withdrawn.[1] Four days later Sir George Yonge informed the lord mayor by letter that the matter had been referred to his majesty's ministers, that the directors of the Bank had been desired to attend Lord Sydney on the subject, and that further information would be given as soon as the king's pleasure should be known.[2]

The king's severe illness served as an excuse for letting the matter drop, and nothing more was done until January, 1790, when Pickett, the lord mayor, on his own responsibility and without any authority from the Court of Aldermen, wrote to Grenville, then secretary of state (having previously solicited an interview with Sir George Yonge), desiring to know the king's pleasure as to the removal of the Bank guard. Grenville replied by asking the lord mayor to specify on what grounds his application was made, and whether the resolution of the Court of Aldermen of the 21st October, 1788 (referred to in his letter), was based on " any legal right or exemption claimed by the City."[3] The secretary was told in reply that no reasons were assigned for the resolution of the Court of Aldermen, nor had any been desired by the late secretary of state when approached on the subject; but the lord mayor volunteered some reasons of his own (27 Jan). He apprehended that "the

[1] Repertory 192, fos. 296, 308, 344, 394.
[2] Repertory, 193, fo. 34.   [3] Repertory 194, fos. 128-132.

"unnecessary introduction of the military into the civil "government of this nation" was unconstitutional. The Bank guard was originally adopted at the time of an extraordinary crisis. It was no longer needed, or if needed, could be more constitutionally furnished by the city's militia. The introduction of the regulars was considered an infringement of the ancient privileges of the City,[1] and their presence was an annoyance to his majesty's peaceable and commercial subjects. This answer of the lord mayor seemed far from satisfactory to the secretary of state as it ignored the question whether the City claimed any privilege. As soon as the mayor satisfied him on this point, he promised to take an early opportunity of consulting the king. The correspondence having been laid before the Court of Aldermen, the Court showed a disposition to let the matter rest. The mayor, however, wrote another letter to Grenville (notwithstanding the Court's request that he should do nothing more without instructions from them), intimating that he would still have to press the withdrawal of the guard as "unconstitutional, unnecessary, and offensive," but its only effect was to draw forth a formal acknowledgment of its receipt by the secretary of state, and there the matter was allowed to drop.[2]

[1] To this day the secretary of state for the home department requests the sanction of the lord mayor before despatching troops through the city, and when permission is given, it is on the understanding that all troops (with the exception of the "buffs," who claim to be directly descended from the ancient trained bands), march without colours flying, drums beating, or bayonets fixed. As a further token of the lord mayor's supremacy in the city, we may add that the pass-word of the Tower is sent to him quarterly.

[2] Repertory 194, fos. 132–137, 150-152.

Outbreak of the French Revolution.

Just at a time when there seemed a fair prospect of the country enjoying a long spell of prosperity the whole of the civilised world was moved by the outbreak of the French Revolution. Englishmen were at first disposed to look upon the movement with interest, if not with approval, as of a nation struggling to be free. But in course of time the sparks of sedition crossed the channel, and it became necessary to suppress by royal proclamation (21 May, 1792) the numerous pamphlets with which the country was flooded. Fox was one of the few statesmen who still believed in the honesty of purpose underlying the revolution, and he signified publicly his disapproval of the proclamation. The City supported the king, however, and its example was widely followed by other corporate bodies throughout the kingdom.[1]

The September massacres, 1792.

Pitt had hoped to save England by preserving a strict neutrality, and for a time he was successful, although frequently urged to declare war. The massacres of September (1792) rendered his peace policy almost hopeless by the shock they gave to English public opinion. The streets of London swarmed with French refugees, and subscriptions had to be opened for their relief.[2] How imminent was the danger which threatened England was brought home to the citizens by the appearance of a placard—headed *A House to let*—affixed to Newgate Prison, and bearing these words:—" Peaceable pos- " session will be given by the present tenants on or " before the first day of January, 1793, being the " commencement of the first year of liberty in Great

---

[1] Journal 73, fos. 144b-145; Annual Register xxxiv, 36.
[2] Annual Register xxxiv, 36, 39.

"Britain. The Republic of France having rooted out despotism, their glorious example and eventful success against tyranny render such infamous bastiles no longer necessary."[1]

With the spirit of revolution thus rife in the city the new lord mayor (Sir James Sanderson) had his hands full. He proved himself, however, equal to the occasion, and the Common Council thanked him (29 Nov.) for his pains in suppressing seditious meetings,[2] and promised him every assistance in the work of carrying into execution his majesty's late proclamation. The council at the same time passed a series of resolutions touching the duty of every corporation and every freeman to suppress seditious assemblies, and to bring to justice every disturber of the peace, and gave orders to the aldermen and common councilmen of each ward to take steps for the preservation of tranquility and for securing obedience to the law. These resolutions were to be printed in all the public papers of the United Kingdom.[3] The officers and men of the London militia had already received orders to be ready at short notice to be under arms for the purpose of suppressing riot and tumult.[4]

Resolutions of Common Council, 29 Nov., 1792.

In anticipation of war being sooner or later declared by one side or the other the Common Council resolved on the 10th January (1793) to offer bounties for seamen for a term not exceeding one

War declared by France, 1 Feb., 1793.

---

[1] Annual Register xxxiv, 44.

[2] At the close of his mayoralty he again received the thanks of the Common Council for having hazarded his life in putting down seditious meetings.—Journal 74, fo. 2.

[3] Journal 73, fo. 218.   [4] Annual Register xxxiv, 46.

month from that date.¹ Before that month expired the blow had fallen. Instead of England declaring war France took the initiative, and after sending her king to the scaffold declared war against England (1 Feb.). The citizens immediately extended their bounties for another month,² and pledged themselves to stand by the king and constitution.³ They furthermore contributed the sum of £500 to the fund that was being raised by merchants of the city for privateering purposes.⁴

The campaign of 1793.

In the course of the spring a British force, under the command of the Duke of York, landed at Ostend, and having joined the imperial army under the Prince of Saxe-Coburg, contributed in no small measure to the success achieved against the French during the earlier part of the campaign. Later on the Duke of York attempted the siege of Dunkirk, but was compelled to retire. A ward committee was appointed in the City for the purpose of raising subscriptions for providing the troops with warm clothing and other necessaries during the winter, and the Common Council voted the sum of £500 for the same purpose.⁵ Subscriptions came in from various parts of the country. Some towns, like Wigan and Hereford, sent clothing, but most of them sent cash. The result was that the City was able to despatch to the army a large number of greatcoats, trousers, shoes, stockings, shirts, mittens and other articles of apparel to the value of nearly £4,000. An offer made by the Grocers' Company to furnish the troops with a supply

---

¹ Journal 73, fo. 237.   ² *Id.*, fo. 249b.
³ *Id.*, fos. 255b–257.   ⁴ *Id.*, fo. 273.
⁵ Journal 74, fo. 2b.

of "porter" was declined by the committee with thanks, as it appeared to them that "the advantage thereof could only be partial and temporary at best."[1] The Duke of York, writing from Ghent (10 Jan., 1794) to acknowledge the gift, paid a high tribute to the patience and courage of the troops under his command.[2]

The campaign of 1794 proved disastrous to the allies, and before the end of the year the Duke of York resigned his command. The want of success on the continent was in part compensated by Howe's victory over the French at sea. The French had resolved to dispute the sovereignty of the seas, and had prepared a fleet at Brest. In course of time Howe fell in with it, and on the 1st June a general engagement took place, in which the enemy, although far superior to the English fleet in weight of metal, was completely worsted. For this victory Howe received the thanks of Parliament and of the City, and also the Freedom of the latter in a gold box.[3] The City, moreover, voted a sum of £500 for the relief of those wounded in the engagement, and of the widows and children of those who had been killed. Howe acknowledged the honour conferred upon him and the liberality and benevolence of the City towards those who had served under him in most gracious terms.[4] Success also attended our arms in the West Indies, where Admiral Sir John Jervis and Lieutenant-General Sir Charles Grey

The "Battle of the 1st of June," 1794.

---
[1] Committee Book, 21 Dec., 1793. [2] Journal 74, fos. 126b–129b.
[3] Journal 74, fo. 172; Journal 75, fo. 33.
[4] Journal 74, fos. 172b, 174b.

captured Martinique and other French islands. For these exploits the Common Council voted both gallant officers the Freedom of the City and gold boxes,[1] and presented a congratulatory address to the king.[2]

<small>Riots in the city, Aug., 1794.</small>

In the meantime (17 April) proceedings had been taken to raise a regiment of infantry and a troop of cavalry to be called "The Loyal London Volunteers." Their chief duty was to be the defence of the city, but they were to be ready to enter the service of the government whenever occasion might require. A committee was nominated to raise subscriptions, and an Act of Parliament was passed for placing the Militia of the City on a better footing.[3] Scarcely was this done before riots again broke out, and on the 20th August the mayor (Paul le Mesurier) had to send for the Honourable Artillery Company for the protection of houses where recruits were being enlisted for the army. The military remained on duty all night in the neighbourhood of Whitecross Street, and effectually checked the rioters in the wanton destruction of property. The next night they were again on duty, this time in Shoe Lane, where they succeeded in dispelling a mob. For these services they were not only thanked by the mayor, but, more formally, by the Common Council, the latter body extending its acknowledgments to the light horse volunteers, as well as to the Military Association at Grocers' Hall, for their respective services during the crisis.[4]

[1] Journal 74, fos. 156b-157, 195b; Journal 75, fo. 5.
[2] Journal 74, fos. 170b-172.
[3] Stat. 34 Geo. III, c. 81; Journal 74, fos. 133b, 145b, 153, 178.
[4] Journal 74, fos. 187-187b; Raikes, History of Hon. Artillery Company ii, 130, 131; Annual Register xxxvi, 25.

To add to the City's troubles a famine was threatening, and on the last day of the year (1794) the lord mayor received instructions to confer with the Duke of Portland (he had recently joined the ministry) as to the best means of averting the calamity.[1] In the course of the next twelvemonth the City voted two sums of £1,000 for the relief of the poor.[2] There was even some talk of discontinuing all Corporation dinners for one whole year, in order that the money thus saved might be devoted to the poor; but the civic fathers had not the courage to adopt such a self-denying ordinance, although they consented to a compromise. They agreed that no committee should dine at the City's expense between the 16th July and the 1st October.[3] More than this they could not do.

Scarcity of wheat, 1795.

In the hope of affording some relief the Lords of the Council proposed to put a stop to the use of fine flour for baking purposes, and to substitute a coarse but wholesome bread known as "standard wheaten bread" for the better class of bread. Their lordships themselves set an excellent example by signing a document pledging themselves and their families to use no other bread than standard wheaten bread until the following 1st October (by which time the harvest would have been gathered in), and to avoid as far as possible the use of flour in other articles of food. They further expressed a hope that their example might be generally followed. There was a difficulty, however, in adopting the standard wheaten bread in the city, where the assise of bread was

"Standard bread."

---

[1] Repertory 199, fo. 39. [2] Journal 75, fos. 38, 239b.
[3] *Id.*, fos. 181, 243.

regularly set by the mayor and aldermen. One reason against it was that its price as fixed by Statute was so low that bakers could not afford to make it, and penalties were attached to its sale at a higher price. The Lords of the Council were asked if they would indemnify bakers against such penalties if they infringed the Statute? They replied that this was beyond their power, but they suggested that the City might well make good any loss the trade might sustain, out of public subscriptions.[1]

The City's desire for peace, Jan., 1795.

The scarcity of wheat and the prospect of a bad harvest in 1795, had already predisposed the citizens for a cessation of hostilities abroad. As early as the 23rd January, 1795, a special Common Hall had been summoned by request, and a petition to the House of Commons had been drawn up praying the House to disclaim all right of interference in the internal concerns of France, and to take such measures as it should seem fit to bring about a speedy peace. The war, they said, ought never to have been entered upon and was based on a wrong principle.[2] The Common Council were more reserved, and, whilst assuring the king of their support, expressed a desire for such a peace only as could be procured with dignity and honour.[3]

Assault on the king, 29 Oct., 1795.

As the year wore on and distress increased, the cry for peace became more general, and the government resolved upon an Autumn Session. Matters indeed had become so serious that when the king

---

[1] Repertory 199, fos. 363-366, 369-371, 387-395. Journal 75, fos. 238b-247.

[2] Common Hall Book, No. 9, fo. 50b.

[3] Journal 75, fos. 43b-44b.

drove down to Westminster to open Parliament he was assailed on all sides with cries of "bread, bread! peace, peace!" and his carriage window was broken by a pebble or bullet. On his return he was again met with similar shouts, and he escaped with difficulty to Buckingham Palace. The Common Council at once offered their congratulations on his providential escape, and expressed their horror at the attack that had been made upon him. They at the same time embraced the opportunity, thus afforded, of thanking him for the declaration he had made of giving "the fullest and speediest effect to a negotiation for a general peace," whenever the condition of affairs in France would allow of it.[1] In consequence of this ebullition of public feeling, Pitt introduced and passed two Bills, commonly known as the Sedition and Treason Bills. The severity of these Bills was thought by many to be unreasonable, and brought much obloquy upon the minister; but the necessity of some such steps being taken to put down sedition was acknowledged by the Common Council.[2]

In December (1795), Pitt brought a royal message to Parliament declaring that the establishment of a new constitution (viz., the Directory) in France offered facilities for negotiations,[3] and in the following March (1796), overtures were made through the British envoy in Switzerland. They were, however, ungraciously received, and matters remained as

Negotiations for peace, 1796.

---

[1] Journal 75, fos. 312–313b.   [2] Journal 76, fos. 25–26.

[3] A proposal had previously (5 Nov.) been made in the Common Council to beseech the king "not to consider the Directory as incapable of maintaining the relations of peace and amity." The motion was, however, negatived.—Journal 75, fo. 312.

they were until the following October, when the king notified his intention to the new Parliament of despatching a minister to Paris for the purpose of re-opening negotiations. By a certain section of the Common Council the news was received with anything but favour, and they would gladly have seen Pitt dismissed. The majority, however, preferred to present a loyal address to the king, assuring him that in the event of the negotiations failing he might depend upon the City for future support in any crisis that might arise. The king thanked the City.[1] As was feared, the negotiations again proved fruitless. France was all the while preparing to make a descent on Ireland, and as soon as these preparations were complete, the British ambassador was abruptly ordered to quit Paris (19 Dec.).

The "Loyalty Loan" of £18,000,000, Dec., 1796.

Thanks to the minister at the head of affairs the crisis did not find England unprepared. Fresh levies had already been made, both for the army and the navy; supplementary corps of militia had been raised, and plans laid for forming bodies of irregular infantry and cavalry. One thing only was wanting, and that was money. In order to raise this, Pitt at first thought of introducing a Bill to compel all persons enjoying a certain amount of income to subscribe one-fourth for the service of the country. On second thoughts, however, he preferred to trust to the patriotic spirit of the nation. He believed that many would be found ready to contribute even a larger proportion of their income if only an example were set by the Bank of England and the Corporation of

[1] Journal 76, fos. 309-311, 314.

London. The sum required was large, being no less than £18,000,000, and the terms he had to offer were scarcely remunerative. On the last day of November he addressed a letter to the governor of the Bank of England, desiring him to lay the proposal before the directors, and at the same time expressing a hope that they might "not be disinclined to take "the lead in a measure which must have the most "beneficial effect on public credit and the most "evident tendency to accelerate the restoration of "peace on secure and honourable terms."[1]

The next day (1 Dec.) he wrote to the lord mayor, urging him to lay the matter before the Common Council;—"The repeated proofs which the "citizens of London have given of their zeal and "public spirit leave me no doubt that if it appears "likely to promote the interests of the country at "this important crisis, it will receive their cheerful "support in their individual capacity, as well as that "of the corporate body and of the different public "companies. It is unnecessary for me to state the "effect which such an example would produce "throughout the kingdom." To this the mayor (Brook Watson) replied that previous to the receipt of the letter he had been desired by a number of members to call a Common Council as soon as possible to consider the grant of an aid to government at the present crisis, and that he had in consequence summoned a court for the following Monday (5 Dec.).[2]

Pitt's letter to the lord mayor, 1 Dec., 1796.

For once the Corporation found themselves left in the lurch. Long before the time named for the

The loan subscribed.

[1] Journal 77, fos. 14b-15.   [2] *Id.*, fos. 14-16.

Common Council to consider Pitt's proposal the directors of the Bank of England had met, public subscriptions had been invited, and the whole loan of eighteen millions had been subscribed. Here is an account by a contemporary writer of the scene witnessed in the Bank on Thursday, the 1st December, and two following days[1] :—"At ten "o'clock this morning [1 Dec.] the parlour doors "were opened, before which time the lobby was "crowded. Numbers could not get near the books "at all; while others, to testify their zeal, called to "the persons at the books then signing to put down "their names for them, as they were fearful of being "shut out. At about twenty minutes past eleven "the subscription was declared to be completely full, "and hundreds in the room were reluctantly obliged "to go away. By the post innumerable orders came "from the country for subscriptions to be put down, "scarcely one of which could be executed. And long "after the subscription was closed persons continued "coming, and were obliged to depart disappointed. "It is a curious fact, and well worth stating, that the "subscription completely filled in fifteen hours and "twenty minutes: two hours on Thursday, six ditto "on Friday, six ditto on Saturday and one ditto and "twenty minutes on Monday—fifteen hours and "twenty minutes." The directors of the Bank subscribed one million in their corporate capacity and £400,000 individually. The Common Council finding themselves left out in the cold, scarcely knew what to do. At first a somewhat pompous proposal was made for a committee to "prepare a plan for assisting the

[1] Annual Register xxxviii, 44.

exigencies of the state in the present conjuncture." This, however, fell through, and the court finally contented itself with voting a sum of £100,000 towards the loan.¹

Pitt's method of disposing of public money, when he got it, was not always approved by the citizens, more especially when it went to subsidise foreign mercenaries, without any authority from Parliament. Here, again, the livery and the Common Council entertained opposite views, and whilst the former called upon the city members to move or support a motion for censuring the ministry for sending money to the Emperor of Germany during the sitting of Parliament without the consent of Parliament,² the latter gave public testimony of their opinion that such payments as had been made to the Emperor had been beneficial to the country.³

The City and foreign subsidies, Dec., 1796.

The constant drain of gold to the continent under Pitt's administration again began to affect the Bank of England as it had formerly done in 1793. On the previous occasion the difficulty had been got over by the issue of Exchequer Bills. Since that time the financial state of the country had been going from bad to worse. A run on country banks set in, resulting in demands being made on the Bank of England, which threatened to exhaust its reserve. At this crisis the Bank applied to the government. Pitt, with his usual promptitude, summoned a council, although it was Sunday (26 Feb., 1797), and a proclamation was issued suspending cash payments until Parliament should decide what should be done. The

Suspension of cash payments, 1797.

¹ Journal 77, fo. 16. ² Common Hall Book, No. 9, fo. 72b.
³ Journal 77, fo. 34b.

next day a meeting of the leading merchants of the city was held at the Mansion House under the presidency of the lord mayor. They at once grasped the situation, and unanimously consented to accept bank-notes as legal tender.[1] The Order in Council was subsequently approved by Parliament, and though intended only as a temporary expedient, the Act then passed continued in operation for twenty-two years, the resumption of cash payments not taking place until May, 1819.

Naval victory off Cape St. Vincent, 14 Feb., 1797.

At a time when England seemed on the verge of bankruptcy, she seemed also likely to lose her supremacy at sea. A plan was set on foot for a junction of the French and Spanish fleets, whereby an overwhelming force might be brought into the English Channel and an invasion rendered comparatively easy. Both the king and the citizens expressed the greatest confidence in the navy,[2] although there were not wanting signs of discontent among the seamen. Fortunately the Spanish fleet was intercepted by Sir John Jervis off Cape St. Vincent; the British sailors forgot their grievances in the presence of the enemy, and a signal victory was won (14 Feb.), for which Jervis received the thanks of the City and a sword of honour, whilst Nelson and others serving under him were voted the Freedom and gold boxes.[3]

Address of the livery, 23 March, 1797.

Although the Common Council—*i.e.*, the City in its corporate capacity—were satisfied that the king had done all that was possible to procure an honourable peace, the livery were far from content. Again, they drew up an address to the king demanding

---

[1] Annual Register xxxix, 9.   [2] Journal 77, fos. 23, 36.
[3] Journal 77, fos. 83b-84.

the instant dismissal of his ministers, and once more they made an attempt to get their address received by the king on the throne. The king, however, stood out, and all that the livery could do was to pass resolutions in their Common Hall to the effect that they had always possessed the privilege they claimed, and that it had never been questioned "except under the corrupt and infamous administration" of those who were responsible for the American war.[1]

All immediate danger from the foreign enemy being over, the crews of the Channel Fleet at Portsmouth broke out into open mutiny. Their grievances were real, and as soon as they were assured of a remedy they returned to their duty. No sooner was one mutiny quelled, however, than another broke out at the Nore and threatened danger to London. The two movements were entirely distinct, and the sailors at Spithead expressed their strong disapproval of the conduct of their fellow seamen at the Nore. The danger was none the less. The Common Council resolved (6 June) to form ward associations for the defence of the city, but only one association, viz., the "Cornhill Military Association," appears to have been actually formed, and that comprised no more than fifty-three members.[2] *Mutiny at the Nore, May, 1797.*

The mutiny soon spread to the fleet off the Texel where Admiral Duncan was stationed for the purpose of preventing a junction between the French and the Dutch. Many of the ships sailed away to join *Duncan's victory off Camperdown, 11 Oct., 1797.*

---

[1] Common Hall Book, No. 9, fos. 75-76, 80b.
[2] Journal 77, fos. 195-196b, 353-354.

the fleet at the Nore and Duncan was left in great straits. Nevertheless he still continued to make a show of force, and after the suppression of the mutiny, had the satisfaction of defeating the Dutch fleet off Camperdown (11 Oct.), and so putting an end to another projected invasion of Ireland. The Common Council presented a congratulatory address to the king; passed votes of thanks and presented swords of honour to Duncan and Sir Richard Onslow, and contributed £500 for the relief of the wounded and the widows and orphans of those who had fallen.[1]

Thanksgiving service at St. Paul's, 19 Dec., 1797.

Three such naval victories as those achieved by Howe, Jervis, and Duncan, deserved a solemn service of thanksgiving at St. Paul's, and on Saturday, the 25th November, the lord mayor received orders from the Duke of Portland to prepare for the king's reception in the city.[2] Tuesday, the 19th December, was the day fixed for the ceremony, and on that day the king and queen, the royal family, the cabinet and foreign ministers, the two Houses of Parliament, and a large body of naval officers and seamen came in solemn procession to the city, being met at Temple Bar by the mayor, sheriffs, and a deputation of the Common Council.[3] The gallant Duncan received an ovation, but Pitt was so grossly insulted on his way

---

[1] Journal 77, fos. 264–266, 277, 305b, 388.

[2] Repertory 202, fo. 36. Journal 77, fo. 300b.

[3] Repertory 202, fos. 167b–169b. A picture by John Graham representing the reception of his majesty at Temple Bar was offered to the City by the artist for the sum of £300, but the offer was not accepted. In 1798, after the battle of the Nile, Alderman Boydell presented to the City portraits of Howe, St. Vincent, and Duncan, together with one of Nelson, and these were gratefully accepted.— Journal 78, fos. 61b, 94, 107.

to the city that after the ceremony, instead of returning in his own carriage as he came, he betook himself to some friends in Doctors Commons and there dined, being afterwards conveyed home under military escort.[1]

Dispute as to command of London militia, 1797-1798.

The occasion caused a re-opening of the question as to the command of the London militia. Was the command vested in the lord mayor or in the Court of Lieutenancy?[2] The latter body had claimed to have the disposition of troops brought into the city to keep order on thanksgiving day. The lord mayor conceived such a claim to be opposed to his own prerogative, and he at once communicated with the Duke of York desiring his royal highness to order up the regiment of militia then quartered at Greenwich, and to place it for the day under his (the mayor's) command, and that had accordingly been done.[3] The question whether the lord mayor, for the time being, could on his own individual responsibility, and without consulting the Court of Lieutenancy, call out the London militia except in cases of emergency, was afterwards submitted to the law officers of the City, and they unanimously pronounced an opinion in favour of the lord mayor's contention.[4]

Military associations in the city, 1798.

Except for the naval victories of Jervis and Duncan the year 1797 had been one of the darkest in the nation's history. The war had lasted over four years, and although it had already added a hundred

---

[1] Annual Register xxxix, 83.
[2] The question had arisen in the month of July, when the Court of Lieutenancy took upon itself to change the quarters of the East and West regiments without consulting the lord mayor, but no decision had been arrived at.—Journal 77, fos. 222b, 238b. Journal 78, fos. 60, 152b.
[3] Repertory 202, fos. 162-166.   [4] *Id.*, fos. 308-316, 423-428.

and thirty-five millions to the National Debt, Pitt found it necessary early in 1798 to make another appeal to the country for a voluntary loan. Determined not to be behindhand again, the Common Council at once resolved (13 Feb.) to subscribe £10,000; but the money had to be borrowed.[1] A third invasion was threatening under the command of Napoleon Bonaparte himself. The Duke of York sent for the lord mayor to learn what military associations had been formed in the city, and was disappointed to find that only one existed (viz., the Cornhill Military Association just mentioned), and even that had threatened to dissolve itself when it found the rest of the city wards doing nothing. It now resolved, however, to put itself into active training. In April Secretary Dundas wrote more than once to the lord mayor urging the necessity of forming as many military associations as possible. The municipal authorities and the Court of Lieutenancy buried their differences, and vied with each other in inspiring the inhabitants of the city with military ardour. The Phœnix Fire Office offered its firemen for military training, and every effort was made to bring the militia regiments up to their full strength.[2]

The Battle of the Nile, 1 Aug., 1798. Instead of making a descent on England Bonaparte sailed to Egypt, seizing Malta on his way, and there he was forced to remain, owing to the destruction of his transports by Nelson at the battle of the Nile (1 Aug.). Nelson, a freeman of the City, presented to the Corporation the French admiral's (Blanquet)

---

[1] Journal 77, fo. 369.
[2] Journal 78, fos. 7-8, 82b; Repertory 202, fos. 231, 268-281.

sword, which lies in the Guildhall Museum.[1] The Corporation, on their part, presented Nelson with a sword of honour, and Captain Berry with the Freedom of the City in a gold box. They also passed a vote of thanks to the officers and men engaged in the action, and contributed the sum of £500 for the relief of the widows and orphans of those who had fallen.[2] The City further proposed to erect a suitable memorial of Nelson's victory. Several suggestions were offered. Copley recommended pictures to hang in the Council Chamber opposite his siege of Gibraltar, others were in favour of sculpture.[3] All suggestions were set aside, however, when it became known that a national memorial, in the shape of a Grand Naval Pillar, or *Rostra*, to be set up on Portsdown Hill, was proposed, and subscriptions invited. The Common Council at once resolved to subscribe 100 guineas to the fund.[4] Contributions, however, came in so slowly that the idea of a national monument had to be abandoned, and subscriptions were returned, the City's 100 guineas being paid over to the Marine Society by order of the Common Council.[5] On the 17th January (1799) the Honourable Mrs. Damer, a daughter of General Conway, and a clever artist, offered to execute a bust of Nelson for the Corporation, either in bronze or marble, in commemoration of his recent victory. The offer was gracefully made and no less gracefully

---

[1] Journal 78, fos. 100, 100b. It was originally placed in the Council Chamber with the medal struck by order of Alexander Davison, Nelson's friend and agent, and presented by him to the city.—*Id.*, fos. 105b, 287b-288.

[2] *Id.*, fos. 103, 106-107, 258b.

[3] *Id.*, fos. 147, 150, 165b, 171-172, 196, 244, 267.

[4] *Id.*, fos. 299b-301; Journal 79, fos. 160b-161.

[5] Journal 85, fos. 165b-166b.

accepted;[1] and the City's Art Gallery is enriched by an admirable specimen of that lady's handiwork.[2]

Pitt's Income Tax Bill, 3 Dec., 1798.   Soon after Parliament met in November (1798) Pitt introduced his financial scheme for the coming year. The principal feature of this scheme was a Bill for imposing a tax upon all the leading branches of income. The tax was professedly of a temporary character and was to be employed solely to meet the exigencies of the war. Some little opposition was made to the Bill both before and after it passed, as well in the city as in Parliament. The Common Council objected to it on the ground that it drew no distinction between the precarious and fluctuating income arising from labour, trade and professions and the more settled income arising from landed and funded property. They were afraid also that unless the assessors were bound to secrecy a man's credit might be unduly prejudiced.[3] In spite of all opposition the Bill passed the Commons by a large majority on the last day of the year, and early in 1799 was accepted by the Lords.

The Siege of Acre raised, 21 May, 1799   In the meantime the situation of Bonaparte and the French army—shut up as they were in Egypt—had become very critical. To complete his scheme of Eastern conquest Bonaparte had marched into Syria. After capturing Joppa, where he massacred his prisoners, he advanced to Acre, the key of Syria. There he was met by Sir Sidney Smith, who

---

[1] Journal 78, fos. 159b, 168.

[2] In May, 1817, Mrs. Damer obtained permission to have the bust removed from the city in order to allow her to make an alteration, and it was not returned until March, 1820.—Journal 91, fo. 159b; Journal 94, fo. 73b.

[3] Journal 78, fos. 157b–158, 204b–205.

succeeded in throwing himself into the town, and at length compelled him to raise the siege (21 May).[1] For his extraordinary gallantry in defending the fortress Sir Sidney was accorded the thanks of the City and a sword of honour.[2]

On the 21st June (1799) the king himself came to the City, accompanied by the Dukes of York, Gloucester, Kent and Cumberland, and officers of the Life Guards, for the purpose of reviewing the several volunteer corps of the City, drawn up in Bridge Street, Blackfriars, at St. Paul's, the Bank, the Royal Exchange and on Tower Hill. The royal party were met on the south side of Blackfriars Bridge, where the City's jurisdiction commenced, by the mayor, sheriffs and city marshals on horseback, followed by the grenadiers of the East Regiment of London militia. The ceremony of delivering the City's sword into the king's hands having been gone through, the inspection of the regiments took place. The royal party afterwards repaired to Finsbury to hold an inspection of the Artillery Company in their own ground;[3] and in Sun Street, the limit of the City's jurisdiction, the mayor took leave by lowering the sword. The Duke of Portland was subsequently commissioned by the king to express to the mayor the gratification the visit had given his majesty.[4]

Royal review of City volunteers, 21 June, 1799.

Pitt, in the meanwhile, though failing in health, had succeeded in forming a new coalition, and in August (1799), the whole of the Dutch fleet fell into the hands of Sir Ralph Abercromby and Admiral

Capture of the Dutch fleet, Aug., 1799.

---

[1] Annual Register xli, 35.   [2] Journal 78, fo. 320.
[3] Raikes, History of Hon. Artillery Company ii, 216.
[4] Repertory 203, fos. 308, 340–343; Journal 78, fos. 298–299.

Mitchell. A series of reverses, however, quickly followed, and before the end of November the allied forces, English and Russians, were glad to accept terms and quit Holland. Some members of the Common Council were for presenting a strongly worded address to the king demanding an enquiry into the cause of the failure of the expedition, and the punishment of the authors, but the motion was eventually allowed to drop.[1] The Council had previously congratulated the king upon the capture of the Dutch fleet.[2]

<small>French overtures rejected, Jan., 1800.</small>

As soon as Bonaparte heard of the new coalition that had been formed against him he hurried to Paris, leaving his army behind him in Egypt to shift for itself. Soon after his arrival he succeeded in putting an end to the Directory, and in getting himself appointed First Consul. He was now practically supreme, and on his own responsibility made overtures to England for peace. These overtures were declined, to the great disappointment of the livery of London, who again petitioned Parliament against the prolongation of the war, which had been undertaken, they said, for no other purpose than for restoring the Bourbon family to the throne.[3]

<small>The Act of Union, 1800.</small>

The disaffection that had so long manifested itself in Ireland led at last to the passing of an Act of Union. The subject was brought before Parliament by the king on the 2nd April (1800). A Bill was subsequently introduced and read a first time on the 17th June. On the 24th it passed the Commons.[4]

---

[1] Journal 79, fo. 28b.   [2] Journal 78, fo. 314.
[3] Common Hall Book, No. 9, fos. 118-119.
[4] Journal House of Commons, lv, 362, 667, 694.

The assent of the Irish Parliament was necessary for the scheme to take effect. This occasioned some difficulty, but by a wholesale system of bribery and corruption, such as was only too common in those days, it was at last obtained, and it was agreed that the union of Great Britain and Ireland should commence from the 1st January, 1801. Thenceforth there was to be but one Parliament for the two countries.

In the meantime distress in England had been increasing to an alarming extent owing to the bad harvests and the consequent scarcity of wheat. At the commencement of the year (1800), the price of flour had risen to such an extent that the Court of Aldermen resolved to enforce the consumption of the standard wheaten bread according to the Statute (13 Geo. III, c. 62).[1] As time went on matters became worse. In September the city was threatened with riot. On the night of Saturday the 13th, the following placard was stuck up on the Monument[2]:—

Bread riots in the city, 15–20 Sept., 1800.

"Bread will be sixpence the quartern loaf if "the people will assemble at the Corn Market on "Monday.

"Fellow countrymen.

"How long will ye quietly and cowardly suffer "yourselves to be thus imposed upon and half starved "by a set of mercenary slaves and government "hirelings; can you still suffer them to proceed in "their extensive monopolies and your families are "crying for food? No, let them exist not a day "longer. Ye are the sovereignty. Rouse then from

---

[1] Repertory 204, fos. 58–60. [2] *Id.*, fo. 412.

"your lethargy and meet at the Corn Market, "Monday."

As soon as the attention of the lord mayor (Harvey Combe) was drawn to the placard, he forthwith took steps to put down any disturbance that might arise. The city constables were posted in the neighbourhood of the Corn Market. The West Regiment of the city militia was held ready for action under the command of Alderman Newnham, at their head quarters in the Old Bailey, whilst the South-East Division of Loyal London Volunteers under the command of Alderman Curtis took up its station at Fishmongers' Hall. The fact of inflammatory papers having appeared posted on the Monument, and the steps he had thus taken to prevent disturbance, were duly reported by the mayor to the Duke of Portland, who signified his approval of the chief magistrate's conduct.[1] At eleven o'clock on Monday morning word was brought to the lord mayor that a crowd had collected at the Corn Market in Mark Lane, and that business was impeded. He immediately set out, accompanied by Alderman Hibbert, for Mark Lane. At the Corn Market they were joined by Sir William Leighton and Sheriff Flower. Finding a large number of people assembled who had no business in the Corn Market, his lordship ascended the staircase and proceeded to address the assembly, entreating them to go home, as that was the best way of getting rid of their grievance. Thereupon he was met with loud cries of "bread, bread, give us bread, and don't starve us!" On the whole, the mob

[1] Repertory 204, fos. 413, 418–420.

appeared fairly good tempered and cheered the mayor as he left for the Mansion House. In the afternoon, however, his presence was again required, and the Riot Act had to be read. Still nothing very serious occurred; one man suspected of being connected with the corn trade received rough treatment at the hands of the mob, and a few rioters were committed by the mayor to the Compter for attacking the city marshal with bludgeons, but matters soon quieted down and the mayor again returned to the Mansion House to write a report of the day's doings to the Duke of Portland as before. Whilst thus occupied, he was again sent for. This was at half-past six in the evening. As the mob were at that time beginning to display signs of mischief, he sent to Colonel Newnham to have his men ready at a moment's warning, whilst he drew the volunteers from Fishmongers' Hall, and with their assistance succeeded in clearing the whole of Mark Lane and guarding its approaches. The East India Volunteers, the Bishopsgate Volunteers, and the Portsoken also rendered assistance. In the course of the evening the Loyal London Volunteers were relieved by the militia; but nothing serious happened, and at one o'clock in the morning the troops were withdrawn.

On Tuesday (16 Sept.) the lord mayor gave a full account of all that had taken place to the Court of Aldermen, and informed that body that he had caused advertisements to be published offering a reward of £100 for the apprehension and conviction of the person or persons who had written or caused to be stuck up the inflammatory placards on the

Proceedings of Court of Aldermen, 16 Sept., 1800.

Monument.[1] At the suggestion of the Duke of Portland the amount of the reward was afterwards raised to £500.[2] The Court of Aldermen passed a vote of thanks to the mayor for what he had done. They also placed on record their opinion that, but for business in the Corn Market being hindered by the mob, the price of wheat and flour would have experienced a greater fall than it actually had done on the 15th, and further, that as nothing would more tend to the reduction of the existing high price of the principal articles of food than the affording protection to dealers bringing corn and other commodities to the market, the Court was resolved at once and by force (if necessary) to put down any attempt to impede the regular business of the markets of the metropolis.[3]

<small>Letter of the Duke of Portland to the mayor, 16 Sept., 1800.</small>

Whilst the mayor was presiding over the Court of Aldermen a letter was placed in his hands from the Duke of Portland, informing him that the duke had instructed Colonel Herries, commanding the London and Westminster light horse volunteers, to lose no time in placing his services at the lord mayor's disposal. The duke at the same time seemed to suggest that the lord mayor had been somewhat remiss in apprehending the ringleaders in yesterday's disturbances.[4] The mayor sent a reply that evening. He thanked the duke for his offer of assistance; but he had no occasion for it, as the city was perfectly quiet. As to his grace's suggestion that the arrest of some of the ringleaders might have been useful, the mayor begged to inform him that four of them had been arrested, and had been committed for trial. If

---

[1] Repertory 204, fos. 414-418.   [2] *Id.*, fos. 423-425.
[3] *Id.*, fos. 427, 428.   [4] *Id.*, fo. 423.

his grace thought that their prosecution by the crown would be more efficacious than by the city, he would forward the minutes of evidence that had been taken. The letter concluded by an assurance that at the time of writing (5 p.m.) the mayor had not the smallest intimation of any disorder in any part of the city.[1]

Notwithstanding the apparent tranquillity of the city, the mayor received notice three hours later that a mob had gathered in Bishopsgate Street and was threatening the premises of Messrs. Wood, Fossick and Wood. In anticipation of some further outbreak he had already massed troops in Drapers' Hall Gardens and at the Royal Exchange, whilst he had given orders to Colonel le Mesurier to hold the Artillery Company in readiness in the Artillery House. The colonel thought fit to disobey orders—to the mayor's great indignation—and on his own responsibility marched 150 men to Bishopsgate Street, and sent orders for a party of the light horse to follow him. The troops continued to parade the streets until nearly one o'clock in the morning, when all fear of a disturbance having passed away, they were withdrawn for the night, and the mayor went home to write another report to the Duke of Portland.[2] Disturbances continued to occur in different parts of the city between Wednesday, the 17th September, and the following Saturday, but they were not of a serious kind, the damage being chiefly confined to the breaking of street lamps.[3] After Saturday the streets resumed their wonted appearance, and business was carried on at Smithfield and the Corn Market as usual.

Precautions taken by the lord mayor.

[1] Repertory 204, fos. 432–434.   [2] *Id.*, fos. 434–437.
 Id., fos. 439–446, 469–472.

The lord mayor's speech to Common Council, 14 Oct., 1800.

The lord mayor of London for the time being has, as we have seen, always jealously guarded his right to the supreme control over all military forces within his jurisdiction. Harvey Combe was no exception. When the colonel commanding the Artillery Company ventured to disobey his orders during the recent riots Combe was justly indignant. He was more indignant when, a few weeks later, the military associations were called out without his orders on information of a likelihood of a riot sent by the Duke of Portland to the police officers of the city, and not to himself; and he laid the matter before the Common Council in the following speech,[1] delivered on the 14th October:—

"Gentlemen of the Common Council,

"After the disturbances which existed within this "city a month ago it is very natural for everyone to "be alarmed by the appearance of the least symptom "of their return. I have the satisfaction to state to "this Court that from the time I had the honor to "sit here last [27 Sept.] to the present moment I "have not received the slightest information of that "tendency, nor has any one person expressed to me "an apprehension on that head. I should not have "thought it necessary to have made this declaration "had it not been that a considerable agitation prevailed "in the city yesterday because the police officers round "the city had ordered out various military associations "to assist the civil power in consequence of information "received from the Secretary of State that riots were "expected—no such information was given to me."

[1] Journal 79, fo. 209b.

The same day that the lord mayor thus addressed the Common Council the Court resolved to present an humble address to the king praying him to hasten the meeting of Parliament in order to consider the enormously high price of provisions. To this the king replied that he was always desirous of recurring to the advice and assistance of Parliament on any public emergency, and that previous to receiving the City's petition he had already given directions for convening Parliament for the despatch of business. This was scarcely the reply the City looked for, and it gave rise to much debate in the Common Council. When the usual motion was made and question put that his majesty's gracious answer should be entered in the Journal of the Court, an amendment was moved reflecting upon the character of the answer received as one disrespectful to the Court and regardless of the extreme sufferings and distress of his majesty's subjects. This amendment was, however, negatived.[1] When Parliament at last met, the question of remedial measures was at once referred to select committees of both Houses. Nevertheless, the high price of bread continued to exercise the minds of the civic authorities for some time to come.[2] *City petition to king to summon Parliament, 16 Oct., 1800.*

Early in the following year (1801), Pitt resigned. It had been his intention to introduce a Bill into Parliament—the first united Parliament of Great Britain and Ireland—for the full emancipation of Roman Catholics, and thereby to fulfil a pledge he had given before the Union was effected. The king, *Pitt's resignation and the king's illness, Feb., 1801.*

---

[1] Journal 79, fos. 215-217, 218-218b.
[2] Repertory 205, fos. 85, 319-328. Journal 80, fos. 113b, 125.

however, displayed so much opposition to the proposal, that Pitt could not do otherwise than send in his resignation, which the king reluctantly accepted. The excitement caused by recent events brought on a recurrence of the king's insanity, and measures were taken for appointing a regent on the terms formerly insisted on by Pitt. The king's illness, however, again proved to be only of a temporary character, and when he recovered, the Common Council who had recently presented him with a congratulatory address on the Union,[1] deemed it best to take no notice either of his illness or recovery.[2]

Battle of Alexandria, 21 March, 1801.

The new ministry, with Addington, the late Speaker, at its head, was fortunate so far as the war was concerned. In March (1801) an expedition under Sir Ralph Abercromby landed in Egypt and succeeded in defeating the French army left there by Bonaparte. Abercromby was killed, but General Hutchinson, who succeeded him, continued to act with vigour, and was backed up by Admiral Lord Keith. The Common Council voted (23 July) a sum of £500 towards the relief of the widows and orphans of those who had perished in the expedition.[3] A month later the town of Alexandria capitulated, and the French army was allowed to evacuate Egypt. For these services the Freedom of the City was conferred on Keith and Hutchinson, and the thanks of the Common Council voted to the officers and men of the army and navy under their command, as well as to Sir Sidney Smith, who had recently been mixed up in the El Arish Treaty.[4]

[1] Journal 79, fos. 255, 256, 283.   [2] *Id.*, fo. 325.
[3] Journal 80, fo. 46b.   [4] *Id.*, fos. 97-97b.

At sea the British government was no less successful. A few days after the battle of Alexandria it became necessary to despatch a fleet to the Baltic in order to break up a Northern confederacy formed between Russia, Sweden, and Denmark, which threatened the interests of this country. The fleet was placed under the command of Sir Hyde Parker. Thanks to Nelson's insubordination in declining to obey the Admiral's signal to discontinue action, the battle of Copenhagen was won. The Common Council voted another sum of £500 for the relief of the wounded and the widows and orphans of those who had died in the action, but Nelson's name is not even mentioned.[1]

Battle of Copenhagen, 2 April, 1801.

Defeated in Egypt, and thwarted in her Northern policy, France was now willing to accede to terms, and on the night of the 1st October, Lord Hawkesbury, foreign secretary, was able to inform the lord mayor by letter that preliminaries of peace had been signed that evening. On the 10th, he wrote again informing the mayor that the preliminaries had been ratified.[2] The news caused immense satisfaction. Some time, however, was still to elapse before the final ratification took place. Negotiations to this end were carried on at Amiens, and although a number of outstanding questions were still left unsettled, peace was finally concluded on the 27th March, 1802, and proclaimed in the city on the 29th April, amid general rejoicing.[3] The termination (as it was thought to be) of a war which left the British navy "more proudly pre-eminent" than

Peace of Amiens, 27 March, 1802.

---

[1] Journal 80, fos. 46–46b. [2] Repertory 205, fos. 644–646.
[3] Repertory 206, fos. 292–293, 458–465.

the termination of any former war, called forth another of that long series of loyal addresses which the citizens found it their duty to present to the king in the course of his long and eventful reign.[1]

[1] Journal 80, fos. 219b, 237b-238b.

CHAPTER XLII.

The peace proved to be no more than a temporary suspension of hostilities, and England's refusal to surrender Malta, which she had recovered in 1800, and which she had covenanted by the terms of the treaty to surrender to France under certain guarantees, served Napoleon for an excuse to renew the war. On the 12th May, 1803, Lord Whitworth, the British ambassador, quitted Paris, where he had been subjected to much rudeness by the First Consul, and at the same time the French ambassador was directed to leave London. Much as the City disliked war, and eager as it had been for peace, the Common Council were among the first to express their determination to support the king and country "against the insatiable ambition of the French Republic."[1] *Resumption of hostilities, May, 1803.*

As soon as war was declared Pitt, after a prolonged absence in the country, re-appeared in the House, and in an impassioned speech, lasting two hours and a half, expatiated upon the justice and necessity of the war. This took place on the 3rd May. Two months later (22 July) he urged the House to take measures for the fortification of London itself:—" If the "fortification of the capital can add to the security "of the country I think it ought to be done. If by "the erection of works such as I am recommending "you can delay the progress of the enemy for three *Defensive operations.*

[1] Journal 81, fo. 142.

"days, it may make the difference between the safety "and the destruction of the capital."[1] An army of reserve was already in course of formation, and on the 28th June the secretary at war (Charles Yorke) wrote to the lord mayor expressing a hope that a contingent of 800 men might easily be furnished by "the first city in the world." The letter having been laid before the Common Council it was at once resolved to furnish the quota desired.[2] In addition to this army of reserve, which was to be 50,000 strong, the militia, to the number of 70,000, were embodied, whilst 300,000 volunteers were enrolled. In the city the *employés* in the Bank of England formed themselves into a regiment of volunteers, and the Guildhall became a drill-hall for the various military associations.[3] Besides ten regiments of volunteers and a cavalry corps, there were associations of River Fencibles and Harbour Marines. The Common Council voted two field pieces to the "Loyal London Cavalry" and colours to the other corps.[4]

Renewal of the Income Tax.

By way of raising supplies Addington brought forward a plan for the renewal of the Income Tax, which had been abolished at the conclusion of the Peace. The plan involved a distinction between incomes derived from land and funded property and incomes derived from the more precarious sources of trade and commerce—a distinction previously advocated by the City—but Pitt offered so strong an opposition to the proposal, although beaten on a division, that Addington gave way.

[1] Parliamentary History xxxvi, 1,661, 1,662.
Journal 81, fos. 166-167.   [3] *Id.*, fos. 171-172, 204.
[4] *Id.*, fos. 219b, 231b.

A sharp look-out was kept in the Channel to prevent the embarkation of the forces gathered on Boulogne heights, and all French and Dutch ports were closly blockaded by Cornwallis, Nelson and other naval commanders, whose services in this direction were handsomely acknowledged by the City in March (1804).[1] Nelson alone, of all the officers, showed dissatisfaction, and found fault with the City, because, forsooth, he had been described as "blockading" Toulon. Blockading Toulon! he had been doing "quite the reverse," so he informed the lord mayor by letter, written on board the "Victory" the 1st August;—"Every opportunity had "been offered the enemy to put to sea, for it is there "that we hope to realize the hopes and expectations "of our country, and I trust they will not be dis- "appointed." Not only did he ungraciously decline the City's vote of thanks, but he found fault with the civic authorities for having omitted to pass similar votes of thanks to Rear-Admiral Sir Richard Bickerton and Rear-Admiral Campbell, an omission which the writer imputed to wilful negligence in making proper enquiries.[2] The letter was referred to a committee to consider and report thereon. As regards the first objection raised by Nelson, viz., his having been represented as "blockading" the port of Toulon, the committee failed to see in this representation, although perhaps not technically correct, any solid reason for his not accepting the vote of thanks, more especially as others who had been similarly employed in different parts of the world had gladly accepted this mark of the City's gratitude. The Common Council, however, preferred

Nelson's ungraciousness towards the City, 1804.

[1] Journal 81, fos. 345-345b.   [2] Journal 82, fos. 54-55.

to ignore the objection altogether and to let the matter drop, whilst they tendered a handsome apology to Rear-Admirals Bickerton and Campbell for having unwittingly omitted their names in the vote of the Court of the 26th March.[1] This apology, coupled with an assurance that there did not exist a body of men in his majesty's dominions more sensible of the distinguished services of these two officers than the Corporation of London, was duly transmitted by the lord mayor to Nelson. That gallant admiral remained, however, still dissatisfied, and before the close of the year (27 Dec.) he again wrote from Toulon, complaining of other omissions on the part of the City, and recommending that for the future the municipal authorities should apply to the secretary of the Admiralty for the names of all officers in fleets intended to be thanked, and so avoid "such very unpleasant omissions." This savoured too much ot dictation. The consequence was that instead ot remedying the defect pointed out in the admiral's letter, the Common Council merely thanked the lord mayor for having communicated the letter to them.[2]

Resignation of Addington and recall of Pitt, May, 1804.

Meanwhile the state of affairs required a stronger man at the helm than Addington. There was only one man equal to the task. That man was Pitt. Between these two statesmen there was no comparison, except such as Canning wittily drew:—

> "Pitt is to Addington
> As London is to Paddington."

For some time past the country had displayed impatience of Addington's weak ministry and a

---

[1] Journal 82, fos. 97-98.   [2] *Id.*, fos. 181-182.

desire for Pitt's recall; but Addington was loth to acknowledge his own incompetence and stuck to office. The prime minister of to-day has happily hit off Addington's ministerial method in a single sentence. Addington's father had been a respectable and respected family physician to Pitt's family, and the son—writes Lord Rosebery in his excellent monograph on Pitt (p. 230)—"carried into politics "the indescribable air of a village apothecary in-"specting the tongue of the state." More than once indeed he went so far as to open negotiations with Pitt through a third party, but the terms offered were such as Pitt could not possibly entertain without loss of self respect. Now that England was embarked on a fresh war, the country became fairly aroused and the minister was forced to bow to public opinion and resign (10 May). Pitt undertook to form a ministry, but was at once confronted with difficulties from the king. It was Pitt's wish that the new ministry should be a large and comprehensive one, embracing both Fox and Grenville, but the king positively refused to admit Fox, although he offered no great opposition to Grenville. As Grenville refused to accept office without his friend, both were excluded, and Pitt had to form a government as best he could on a narrow Tory basis.[1]

Soon after the formation of the new ministry, an attempt was made in the Common Council (19 June) to pass a vote of thanks to Addington for his recent services, but an amendment was proposed to thank the late minister for having resigned office as soon as he discovered that he no longer enjoyed the con-

Proceedings of Common Council, 19 June, 1804.

---

[1] See Appendix to Stanhope's Life of Pitt, Vol. iv, pp. iv–xiii.

fidence of the country. The amendment further expressed regret that the late "partial changes" in the government appeared so little calculated to promote the interests of the nation and to secure the confidence of Parliament and the nation at so momentous a crisis. Before the amendment, however, could be put to the vote, it was found that a *quorum* was not present, and so "no decision was made thereon."[1]

<small>Review of city volunteers at Blackheath, 18 May, 1804.</small>

On the 18th May, Pitt resumed the reins of government, having submitted himself for re-election to his constituents at Cambridge. That same day the First Consul, Pitt's arch enemy, was solemnly proclaimed sovereign of the French under the title of the Emperor Napoleon. That same day, too, witnessed the presentation of colours which the Common Council had in October last (1803) voted to the London regiments. The presentation took place at Blackheath, the lord mayor being conveyed down the river in the City's state barge, accompanied by the commander-in-chief and a brilliant staff of officers, and the troops being conducted to Greenwich by the River Fencibles. One officer, viz., Colonel Kensington, commanding the third regiment of Loyal London Volunteers, declined to accept the colours, for what reason we are not told. The ceremony passed off without any accident or confusion, but a banquet which it was proposed to give the commander-in-chief and his staff after the review could not take place in consequence of the London Tavern being previously engaged, and time

[1] Journal 82, fos. 27-28.

did not allow of another suitable place being sought for.¹

It was quite clear that if the country was to be saved from invasion, the military forces of the kingdom would still have to be greatly strengthened. Before consenting to form a ministry, Pitt did not disguise from the king the serious character of the situation. "It is in the first place, evident"—he wrote to Lord Eldon for communication to the king—"that zealous and united as the country "appears to be at this moment [2 May] in its "efforts against the enemy, the present contest may "probably be of very long duration, attended with "great and heavy burdens, and likely to press "severely on the resources and conveniences of all "classes of persons." Filled with these sentiments, Pitt, as soon as he returned to office, prepared a measure for the better defence of the country and for substituting a more permanent military force for the existing militia. The Additional Force Bill, as this measure was called, was no sooner laid before the House than it met with the most strenuous opposition. The City, according to the provisions of the Bill, would have had to furnish 1,600 men for military service, but the Remembrancer, whose business it is to watch Bills in Parliament affecting the City's interests, applied to have the clause affecting the City struck out by an amendment in the House of Lords, "it having been uniformly the practice for "the city of London to have separate Bills for "such purposes." Two of the city members also

Pitt's Additional Force Bill, June, 1804.

¹ Journal 82, fos. 34b–36.

made similar applications. They were told that the objection came too late to allow of any omission or addition being made to the Bill, but that if the Corporation were desirous of having a separate Bill on this occasion "they might prepare the same with such "powers for raising the men or money required as "were more consonant to their accustomed forms and "practice."[1] In spite of the opposition of Addington, Sheridan, and Fox, the Bill eventually passed the Commons by a majority of forty-two, and was carried up to the Lords. There it was again strongly opposed and was only carried by a majority of thirty-four. The City took the advice offered and introduced a separate Bill on its own account, and this also passed.[2]

<small>Artillery practice in Finsbury.</small>

Nothing could exceed the energy of the prime minister in superintending personally the defences of the country, and although some of his measures (as for instance the erection of martello towers along the south coast and the cutting a canal from Hythe to Rye) could have done little to check the advance of the French army had a landing been once effected, the real value of such measures lay in the confidence and energy which they excited in the people. Nor were the citizens less energetic. The Artillery Company and the London militia, instead of marching out to the suburbs for practice took to discharging their field pieces in their own grounds in Finsbury, causing the houses in the vicinity to shake and windows to be broken by the concussion. The noise of their discharge frightened the horses of the frequenters of the City

---

[1] Journal 82, fos. 33-34.
[2] Journal House of Commons, lix, 406-422.

Road—the Rotten Row of the East end—and disturbed those who had sought ease and quiet, in what was in those days a respectable if not an aristocratic suburb of the city. In July (1804) the annoyance became so great that a formal complaint was made to the Common Council, who agreed that the practice complained of should not be continued.[1]

Whilst the City and the country were for the most part inspired with Pitt's enthusiasm, there were not wanting some who ridiculed the prime minister for intermeddling in military matters, and for the anxiety he displayed at the prospect of an invasion which they thought to be in the highest degree improbable. "Can he possibly be serious in expecting Bonaparte now!" —wrote Grenville to Lord Buckingham on the 25th August—although it was well known that Napoleon had himself gone recently to Boulogne to view the army that had long been encamped on its heights. He had even gone so far as to order a medal to be prepared, bearing the words *Frappée a Londres*, in commemoration of his expected conquest. Circumstances eventually led him to postpone his descent on the English coast, but the project was far from abandoned.

The French camp at Boulogne.

Strong as Pitt was in the country he was weak in parliament. Before the end of the year (1804) he sought at once to gratify the king and strengthen his own position in the House by becoming reconciled with Addington, who entered the ministry as President of the Council and was created Viscount Sidmouth. The coalition lasted, however, but a short time. On the

Disgrace of Lord Melville, April, 1805.

[1] Journal 82, fos. 44, 69b.

8th April (1805) Henry Dundas, now Lord Melville and first lord of the admiralty, was charged with peculation, and had to stand his trial in Westminster hall. The lord mayor claimed to have a certain number of tickets allowed him to witness the trial, on the ground that a former lord mayor had been allowed them to witness the trial of Warren Hastings. He experienced, however, some difficulty in getting them as he could produce no record of the mayor having established his claim at the former trial.[1] Although the trial resulted in Melville's acquittal, Pitt could not do otherwise than advise the removal of his old friend from the Privy Council. It was a bitter blow and one that he must have felt the more keenly when he found his old supporters, the citizens of London, animadverting in no measured terms upon his friend's conduct and congratulating the king on his having rid himself and his councils of so obnoxious a minister.[2] The unfortunate affair again caused an estrangement between Pitt and Sidmouth, which ended in the latter withdrawing from the ministry (7 July).

The battle of Trafalgar, 21 Oct., 1805. Although misfortune continued thus to follow Pitt in the House, his foreign policy promised well. Spain it is true had thrown in her lot with France. On the other hand, Pitt had succeeded in forming a strong coalition against the Emperor on the continent, and on the 21st October, Nelson succeeded in vanquishing the French and Spanish fleets off Cape Trafalgar, although at the cost of his own life. On the 13th November, the Common Council drew up an address to the king, congratulating him upon the

---

[1] Repertory 210, fos. 375-376. [2] Journal 82, fo. 253.

recent victory, whilst expressing sincere sorrow at the loss of so brave a commander.[1] A fortnight later they resolved to bestow the Freedom of the City with swords of honour upon Collingwood and others who had distinguished themselves in this action.[2]

Nelson's funeral afforded an opportunity for a solemn water pageant such as has seldom been seen. On Wednesday, the 8th January (1806) his remains were borne up the Thames, by barge from Greenwich to Whitehall, and thence to the Admiralty. The mayor, aldermen and city officers drove down to Greenwich after breakfast, and were there received by Lord Hood. The City's barge had been sent on, and the barges of the Drapers' Company, the Fishmongers, the Goldsmiths, the Skinners, the Merchant Taylors, the Ironmongers, the Stationers and the Apothecaries were already there. The lord mayor's barge immediately followed the royal barges and the barge containing the lords commissioners of the Admiralty. As the procession made its way up the river, with a slow hanging stroke befitting the solemnity of the occasion, minute guns were fired. The body lay at the Admiralty that night, and the next day (9 Jan.) was brought to its last resting place in St. Paul's. The whole of the military arrangements for keeping the streets of the city were left in the hands of the lord mayor, and no question as to his authority was raised, such as had been raised in 1797. On the other hand, a controversy had arisen as to the position allotted to the lord mayor in the procession, after its entrance in the city; the mayor claiming to take precedence of all subjects of the crown within his

The funeral of Nelson, 8 and 9 Jan., 1806.

[1] Journal 82, fos. 368–368b.   [2] *Id.*, fos. 381–382.

own jurisdiction in the city and liberties, whether the king was present or not. The king was not to attend on this occasion; nevertheless the mayor claimed the same precedence as if his majesty were present, on the ground that in all commissions of gaol delivery he was named before the chancellor, the judges and all other subjects whatever. Time did not allow of the question being fully enquired into at the Heralds' College, and the difficulty had to be solved by a special royal warrant to Garter King-at-arms, authorising him to allot the same place to the lord mayor that he would have enjoyed had the king himself been there to receive the City's sword. When the procession entered the city, the mayor accordingly took up his position between the carriage of the Prince of Wales and the funeral car. At the moment the remains were lowered into the crypt volleys were fired by the troops, in Moorfields, by signal given from the gallery on the top of the dome of the cathedral.[1]

Nelson's monument in the Guildhall. The City having resolved to erect a monument to the deceased admiral, the Hon. Mrs. Damer again offered her services. Her offer, however, was not accepted, the Common Council preferring to submit the matter to public competition. A number of designs were sent in, one of which was especially recommended by a committee of so-called experts (not being themselves artists). This was, however, eventually rejected on a ballot being taken, and a design accepted, which proved to be by James Smith, an artist who had studied under Flaxman, and who had

[1] Repertory 210, fos. 54–62, 65, 102–168; Journal 82, fo. 393b; Journal 83, fos. 120b–128b.

assisted Mrs. Damer. His estimate of cost was the lowest of five selected by the committee of experts.[1]

Although the victory of Trafalgar had established England's supremacy at sea and had effectually put an end to Napoleon's project of invasion, the victory he subsequently gained (2 Dec.) over the allied forces on the field of Austerlitz, completely shattered the coalition, and made him all-powerful on the continent. The shock was too much for Pitt, whose health had long been failing. Last lord mayor's day, when news of Nelson's victory and death had recently arrived, he had attended the banquet at the Guildhall, but at the cost of much personal suffering. Once more he was received with acclamation, and his coach was drawn in triumph. It was for the last time. When the lord mayor proposed his health as "the Saviour of Europe," he replied in one of the shortest, and under the circumstances perhaps one of the most effective speeches ever delivered on the occasion by a prime minister :—" I return you many thanks," he said, addressing the mayor, " for the " honour you have done me ; but Europe is not to be " saved by any single man. England has saved her-" self by her exertions and will, I trust, save Europe " by her example."[2] With only these two sentences— the last words spoken by him in public—Pitt sat down. A month later (7 Dec.) he set out for Bath, and there he received the fatal news. From that day his health rapidly declined. He recovered sufficiently to be removed to a house he had hired at Putney, but on the 23rd January he died.

Death of Pitt, 23 Jan., 1806.

[1] Journal 82, fo. 380 ; Journal 83 fos. 117–118b, 144–144b.
[2] Stanhope " Life of Pitt," iv, 345, 346.

His funeral, 22 Feb., 1806.

A month later (22 Feb.) the deceased statesman, whose praises Canning had sung as "The pilot that weathered the storm," was laid to rest in Westminster Abbey. The City expressed no wish, as at his father's death, to be present in their corporate capacity, but the lord mayor attended in state, and that there might not be wanting in after years (as in the case of Hastings's trial), a record of his attendance and of the precedence allotted him on this occasion, he caused the facts to be entered in the minutes of the Court of Aldermen.[1]

Pitt's monument in the Guildhall.

In the meantime (6 Feb.) a motion had been made in the Common Council to erect a monument in the Guildhall to the late minister. After long debate, the motion was carried, but only by a majority of six votes. A ward committee was thereupon appointed to carry the same into execution. On the 28th, an attempt was made to stop all further proceedings, but the court after further debate, decided otherwise, and unanimously resolved that the committee should submit such models and designs as they might think worthy, together with estimates of expense. On the 18th September, five models were submitted to the Common Council,[2] the estimates varying from £3,675 to £5,500. Eventually, the lowest estimate was selected. The artist who had sent in the model at this estimate, proved to be J. G. Bubb, of whom little is known, except that he carved the sculptures in front of the Custom House, and modelled the figures adorning the façade of the Opera House, in the Haymarket, recently pulled

[1] Repertory 210, fos. 373-375.
[2] Journal 83, fos. 11b-12, 45b-46, 225-226.

down. The monument occupied the artist for more than six years, and it was not set up in the Guildhall until 1813. The inscription, written by Canning, bears testimony to the affectionate regret with which the City of London cherished Pitt's memory.

Upon the formation of a new ministry with Grenville as prime minister, and Fox as foreign secretary, the Common Council presented an address to the king, offering their sincere thanks and congratulations "on the formation of an administration, com-"bining men of the highest consideration and talents"—the administration was known as "the ministry of "all the talents"; they hoped that by such an union of wisdom and energy in his majesty's councils, a policy of "vigour, vigilance, and economy" would be pursued, and they promised the king the City's support in every demand necessary for resisting the unreasonable pretensions of Napoleon and for effecting a permanent and honourable peace.[1]

City address to the king, 19 Feb., 1806.

Whilst Napoleon was bent on forming on the continent a western empire, England succeeded in securing the sea route to India by the re-capture of the Cape of Good Hope from the Dutch. The importance of this exploit by the British navy, under the command of Sir Home Popham, was misconceived by the City, and a vote of thanks to Popham moved in the Common Council was lost. The capture of Buenos Ayres, on the other hand, by the same officer, was welcomed by them with extravagant joy as opening a new source of commerce to British manufacturers, and the Common Council not only accorded

The City and Sir Home Popham, 1806.

---

[1] Journal 83, fo. 16.

Popham and the fleet a vote of thanks, but voted that officer a sword of honour of the value of 200 guineas.¹ Yet Buenos Ayres was shortly afterwards lost and never recovered, whereas the Cape still remains one of the most valuable possessions of the country.

Battle of Maida, 3 July, 1806.   The only military success of the Grenville ministry besides the conquest of the Cape of Good Hope, was gained in the south of Italy, where Sir John Stuart beat the French general Regnier at Maida. The victory was the more welcome, because it proved to the world that "the boasted prowess" of the French could not stand against well disciplined British soldiers when fairly put to the test. The Common Council, ever ready to recognise merit, voted Stuart the Freedom of the City and a sword.²

Fall of the Grenville ministry, March, 1807.   The Grenville ministry did not last long. It showed a singular inaptitude for war, but it fell on the question of Catholic emancipation, the same question that had caused Pitt to resign in 1801. In consideration of the king's increasing age and bad health, Fox had given his word immediately on assuming office, not to bring the question forward. Fox died in September, 1806, and early the following year Grenville, who had given no such pledge, notified his intention of bringing forward a Bill for throwing open all ranks of the army and navy to Catholics and Protestants alike. The king looked upon any assent that he might give to Catholic emancipation as nothing less than an infringement of his coronation oath, and he conscientiously and consistently opposed every

---

¹ Journal 83, fos. 154, 233-4.   ² *Id.*, fo. 234.

measure tending in that direction. A certain section of the Common Council was also opposed to the Bill as subversive of the constitution, but a motion to move parliament against the Bill was rejected.[1] Not satisfied with the withdrawal of Grenville's Bill the king in his morbid sensibility, insisted upon a promise that he would never bring forward a similar measure again — a promise that no constitutional minister could give. Thereupon he was summarily dismissed (March, 1807), and the Duke of Portland became nominally prime minister, although the leadership was virtually assumed by Spencer Perceval.

Once more the "successors of the Roundheads" congratulated the king upon his having vindicated "the glorious independence of the crown." Owing to the state of the king's health, and more particularly his defective eyesight, the City waived its right to present the address on the throne; and only a deputation of the Common Council was present.[2] A dissolution took place soon afterwards, when it was found that not only the City but the country supported the king.

City address, 22 April, 1807

Having devastated the continent to such an extent that both London and the kingdom were called upon to contribute towards the alleviation of the prevalent distress,[3] the Emperor had recently aimed a direct blow at England by issuing the famous Berlin Decree (21 Nov., 1806), forbidding all intercourse with this country, and confiscating all English merchandise found on the continent. This was the commencement of the "continental system" which

The Berlin Decree, 21 Nov., 1806.

---

[1] Journal 83, fo. 352b.   [2] *Id.*, fos. 382, 384b, 388.
[3] *Id.*, fos. 67, 151, 170–170b, 171b.   Journal 84, fo. 96b.

ultimately proved more injurious to Napoleon himself than to England.

<small>Napoleon and Spain, 1807-1808.</small>

The system was accepted everywhere except in Portugal, and Napoleon, who had long fixed his eyes on the Peninsula, seized the opportunity afforded by Portugal refusing to close its ports to England to wage war not only upon that country but upon Spain. The city of London became more than ever alive to the danger which threatened this country from the "vast gigantic confederacy" established mainly for the destruction of England, and the citizens set an example, as the king himself graciously acknowledged (30 March, 1808), "of union and public spirit" at this important crisis.[1] When Napoleon succeeded by a gross piece of chicanery in setting his own brother Joseph on the throne of Spain (15 June), the high-spirited Spaniards, rebelled, and sent envoys to England asking for assistance. They were everywhere received with enthusiasm, and the City offered them its customary hospitality.[2]

<small>City's address to the king, 20 July, 1808.</small>

Their appeal was not in vain. Money and arms were promised, to the great delight of the citizens, who formally offered their thanks to the king for granting his protection and support to a "high-"minded and gallant nation in defence of their "dearest rights and privileges." They declared that the king's solemn recognition of the Spanish nation as a friend and ally against "the common enemy of all established governments"—as they styled

---

[1] Journal 84, fos. 197b-198b, 201.

[2] Upon the lord mayor (Ansley) quitting office a vote of thanks was moved for the hospitality he had shown the Spanish envoys, but the motion was negatived. Affairs had not gone so well in Spain as the City had hoped.—Journal 84, fo. 357b.

Napoleon—had excited in their breasts the most lively and grateful sensations, and they assured him that they would spare no sacrifice to assist in preventing "twelve millions of fellow freemen from "being accursed with the most galling and profligate "despotism recorded in the history of the world."[1]

A force was despatched to Portugal under the command of Sir Arthur Wellesley; but no sooner had he achieved some success than he found himself superseded by Sir Harry Burrard, who in turn had to give place to Sir Hugh Dalrymple. The consequence was, that the good accomplished by one commander was quickly undone by another, and in August a Convention—known as the Convention of Cintra—was signed, and the French army was allowed to return home scot free. This raised a storm of indignation among the citizens, and the king to pacify them promised an enquiry. He little liked, however, the City's interference in the matter, and said so :—" I should have hoped "—he told the Common Council who waited upon him—" that recent occurrences "would have convinced you, that I am at all times "ready to institute enquiries on occasions in which "the character of the country or the honor of my "arms is concerned; and that the interposition of the "city of London could not be necessary for inducing "me to direct due enquiry to be made into a trans-"action which has disappointed the hopes and "expectations of the nation."[2] Wellesley and his two official superiors were thereupon ordered home to give an account of their conduct, the command of the army in Portugal being left in the hands of

The City and the Convention of Cintra, 1808

---

[1] Journal 84, fo. 294b.   [2] *Id.*, fos. 333, 336b.

Sir John Moore, who soon afterwards lost his life at Corunna.

Scandal of the Duke of York, 1809.

The Convention of Cintra and the retreat of Sir John Moore, successful as that retreat had been, although costing him his own life, discouraged the government which now was called upon to meet an attack from another quarter. Early in the spring of 1809, the Duke of York, commander-in-chief, was charged by a militia colonel named Wardle, member for Okehampton, with having allowed his mistress, Mrs. Clarke, to dispose of commissions, and having himself participated in the proceeds of this nefarious traffic. The scandal was aggravated by a public investigation before the entire House of Commons, and although the duke was eventually acquitted of personal corruption, he felt compelled to resign his post. His acquittal disgusted the Common Council, who desired to place on record their belief that it was greatly due to that "preponderating influence" of which they had formerly complained. On the other hand they voted Wardle the Freedom of the City in a gold box (6 April).[1] In the course of a few months Wardle was himself sued by a tradesman for the price of goods with which he had furnished a house for Mrs. Clarke. This put a new aspect on the charges Wardle had brought and greatly diminished the feeling against the duke, who was soon afterwards restored to office. The City, however, still upheld Wardle, and not only refused to rescind their vote of the 6th April, but placed on record an elaborate statement showing how by his means, and in the face of unexampled threats and difficulties, a system of

[1] Journal 85, fos. 79b-80b.

"scandalous abuse and corruption, not only in the army, but in the various departments of the State" had been brought to light. This statement they ordered to be published in the morning and evening papers.[1]

The ministry had scarcely recovered from the effects of the scandal before it received a fatal shock from the disastrous failure of the Walcheren expedition, owing chiefly to senseless disputes between the naval and military commanders. Canning and Castlereagh—the foreign minister and the war minister—endeavoured to throw the blame on each other's shoulders. They both resigned office and then fought a duel. Their resignation was followed by that of the Duke of Portland, whose failing health had from the first rendered him unfit for his position, and who shortly afterwards died. His place was taken by Spencer Perceval. *The Walcheren expedition, July–August, 1809.*

The City was greatly depressed at the result of the expedition, and there was some talk of the Corporation taking no part in the celebration of the king's jubilee, his majesty being about to enter upon the 50th year of his reign on the 25th October of this year. To some members of the Common Council it seemed out of place to set apart a day for public rejoicing at a time when the country was involved in so much disgrace.[2] The majority, however, thought otherwise, and the City joined with the rest of his majesty's subjects in offering congratulations. The citizens could forgive much, if only trade were good, and as to this they were in a position to assure the *The king's Jubilee, 25 Oct., 1809.*

[1] Journal 85, fos. 201b-205. See Annual Register li, 457.
[2] Journal 85, fo. 258.

king that notwithstanding the unexampled struggles through which the country had passed since the day of his accession, its commerce was "flourishing to an extent unknown in any former war."[1] A thanksgiving service was held in St. Paul's, which the municipal authorities attended in state. The City contributed £1,000 for the relief of poor debtors, whilst twice that amount was forwarded by the king for the same purpose. Resolutions were passed to illuminate the Guildhall and to go to the expense of a City banquet, but they were afterwards rescinded.[2]

City address re Walcheren expedition, 13 Dec., 1809.

The jubilee over, the City drew up and agreed to an address to the king complaining that no proper enquiry had been made into the circumstances under which the Convention of Cintra had been signed, as his majesty had promised, and urging another enquiry into the causes of the recent Walcheren disaster. The address was agreed to at a special Court of Common Council held on the 5th December. On the 13th, however, this address was set aside, and another and more temperate address substituted for it.[3]

The king's reply, 20 Dec.

Upon the latter address being presented to the king, a short, dry answer was returned, such as he was accustomed to give when displeased. He had not judged it necessary, he told the citizens, to direct any military enquiry into the conduct of the commanders of the expedition at sea and on shore; but it rested with parliament to ask for such information

---

[1] Journal 85, fo. 279b.   [2] *Id.*, fos. 277b-278, 291.

[3] *Id.*, fos. 322-325b, 350. The substitution of a new address in the place of one already agreed to was afterwards (8 Feb., 1810) declared irregular.—*Id.*, fo. 397.

or to take such measures as they thought best for the public good.[1]

Before the presentation of the City's address a special meeting of the livery took place (14 Dec.), when the original address agreed to by the Common Council and afterwards discarded was adopted by the livery as their own, and ordered to be presented to the king at the next public levée. Then followed another of those unseemly wrangles we have had so often to record. When the sheriffs proceeded to carry out the wishes of the livery they found that for some years past no public levée had been held owing to the king's failing eyesight, and when asked to do as all others did—with the exception of the corporation of London and the two Universities—and to leave the address with the principal secretary of state, who would in due course lay it before the king, they refused.

Address of the livery, 14 Dec., 1809.

The matter being reported to the livery (9 Jan., 1810), they proceeded forthwith to draw up resolutions condemning the king's advisers, and these the sheriffs were ordered to deliver "into his majesty's hands." The secretary of state very naturally objected to trouble the king any further in the matter, as there was, in reality, no difference between presenting an address and presenting resolutions. At the same time, he signified his willingness to lay a copy of the resolutions before the king in the manner adopted since the cessation of public levées. This offer was refused. An attempt was then made to have the document presented at a private levée, and

Resolution of the livery, 9 Jan., 1810.

[1] Journal 85, fo. 355b.

the sheriffs wrote a joint letter to the secretary of state informing him of their intention of attending for the purpose at the next private levée, unless it should be his majesty's pleasure to receive them at some other time and place. To this the secretary replied that no one was admitted to private levées without the king's permission; that he had laid their letter before the king and that his majesty saw no reason for drawing a distinction between the resolutions and the address; that had the sheriffs been deputed by the body corporate of London, his majesty would have received them differently, but he could not receive them at the levée or elsewhere for the purpose of presenting proceedings not adopted at any meeting of the corporation as such, without allowing others the same privilege, and thereby exposing himself to that personal inconvenience which the discontinuance of public levées was intended to prevent. Thus baffled, the livery had to content themselves with entering a formal protest against what they still believed to be a "flagrant violation of city rights."[1]

The City opposes proposed Wellington's annuity, Feb., 1810.

A few weeks later (23 Feb.) when a Bill was before the House for granting an annuity to Wellesley (recently created Viscount Wellington for his victory at Talavera) the Common Council took the matter up and complained to Parliament of the recent failure of the livery to get their address received by the king owing to the misconduct of his majesty's ministers, who had "placed a barrier between the king and the people," and whose conduct was now aggravated by the proposal respecting Wellington, made "in defiance of public opinion." Whilst petitioning against the

[1] Common Hall Book, No. 9, fos. 237b–243.

Bill the City assured the House that they did so from no motives of economy, but from a sense that, notwithstanding Wellington's indisputable valour, his military conduct was not deserving national remuneration. What were the facts? That in the short period of his service in Europe, not amounting to two years, they had seen his gallant efforts in Portugal lead only to the "disgraceful and scandalous" Convention of Cintra; while in Spain, notwithstanding his defeat of the French at Talavera, he had been compelled to retreat and leave his sick and wounded to the care of the enemy. No enquiry had been made into either of these campaigns, although it was but due to the nation that a most rigid investigation as to why so much valour should have been uselessly and unprofitably displayed should first take place before the nation's pecuniary resources should be thus applied. In India Wellington had received ample remuneration for his services, and at home he had held valuable appointments. As for making provision for his family, none had been made for the family of Sir John Moore, who had so nobly died.[1] This attitude of the City towards the Bill becomes the more intelligible when we consider that Wellington at that time had many enemies, both in and out of Parliament, and that his military genius had not yet awakened recognition. When, a year later, it was found that, owing to his skill, his patient self-reliance (for he received but little encouragement from the government at home) and his foresight, not a single French soldier remained in Portugal, the City, like the rest of the nation, were ready to acknowledge his

[1] Journal 85, fos. 420-422b.

"consummate ability, fortitude and perseverance," and presented him with the Freedom and a sword of honour, despatching at the same time the sum of £1,000 for the relief of poor Portuguese.[1]

Sir Francis Burdett committed to the Tower, 9 April, 1810.

In the spring of this year (1810) the question of parliamentary reform was (after an interval of twenty-five years) again brought into prominence by the committal of Sir Francis Burdett to the Tower by order of the House of Commons. The House had recently committed to Newgate a man named John Gale Jones for having published an attack on its proceedings, and Sir Francis Burdett had questioned its right to commit any man to prison. The consequence was that on the 6th April a warrant was issued for the committal of Burdett himself to the Tower. Burdett resisted the warrant as illegal, and had to be conveyed to the Tower by an armed force (9 April). The ministry anticipated a riot, and made application to the lord mayor for permission to quarter troops in the government storehouses situate on the banks of the river. The mayor, in reply, assured the secretary of state, through whom the application had been made, that the city was perfectly quiet, but he would consult his brother aldermen on the matter. The next day—the day that Burdett was to be conveyed to the Tower—he wrote again to the secretary, assuring him that the city continued quiet, but that if necessity arose for military assistance to protect the government stores he (the mayor) would allow the premises to be occupied by troops, but only on the express condition

[1] Journal 86, fos. 380, 380b.

that they acted under his own directions or the directions of one of the city marshals.¹

Unfortunately the day did not pass off without bloodshed. Notwithstanding the care taken to conduct their prisoner by a circuitous route instead of by the direct way through Eastcheap to the Tower, the troops were severely handled by the mob both going and returning. For a long time the soldiers exhibited the greatest patience, but at length they were forced in sheer self-defence to fire, and a man named Thomas Ebrall was killed and others wounded. The Court of Aldermen were asked to offer a reward of £200 for the discovery of the man who had shot Ebrall, on whose death a jury had brought in a verdict of wilful murder against a guardsman, name unknown, but the Court declined. They instituted an enquiry, however, into the whole of the proceedings of the day, and after taking numerous depositions and giving the matter their best attention they came to the conclusion that the firing by the soldiers was justified.² *Riots in the city.*

The livery in the meanwhile had insisted upon a special Common Hall being summoned for the purpose of taking into consideration "the alarming assumption "of privilege by the honourable the House of Com- "mons, of arresting and imprisoning during pleasure "the people of England, for offences cognisable in the "usual courts of law," and on the 4th May, they passed a cordial vote of thanks to Burdett for having resisted the Speaker's warrant, and for having upheld the right of freedom of speech. They also thanked *Petition of the livery to Parliament, 4 May, 1810.*

¹ Repertory 214, fos. 307–311.   ² *Id.*, fos. 336–339, 373–477.

the lord mayor for his "constitutional endeavours "to preserve the peace of the city without the aid of "the military." Furthermore, they resolved that the only means left to save the constitution and the country was parliamentary reform, which must be both speedy and radical, and they called upon the people of the United Kingdom to join them in endeavouring to bring this reform about. A petition to the House was then read and adopted, the language of which was so strong that even the petitioners themselves felt constrained to offer some kind of apology, and to declare that by it they intended no disrespect to the House. After commenting upon what they deemed an illegal and totally unjustifiable act of the House, in committing Jones and Burdett to prison without legal process, they proceeded to remind the Commons that so far from representing the people, they were known to have been sent to Parliament "by the absolute nomination or powerful influence of about 150 peers and others;" that they had refused to examine the charge brought against Lord Castlereagh and Spencer Perceval, two ministers of the Crown, of trafficking in seats; that when, on a former occasion, it was averred before the House "that seats for legislation in the House of Commons "were as notoriously rented and bought as the "standings for cattle at a fair," the House had treated the assertion with affected indignation, and ministers had threatened to punish the petitioners for presenting a scandalous and libellous petition. The petitioners, nevertheless, had lived "to see a House of Commons "avow the traffick and screen those accused of this "breach of law and right, because it had been equally "committed by all parties, and was a practice as "notorious as the sun at noon-day." Where, they asked, was the justice of the House? Where its dignity? Jones was confined to prison for an alleged offence which if committed against any subject of the realm, or even the king himself, would have been made the subject of legal investigation; Lord Castlereagh continued to be a principal minister of the Crown, and was at that very time a free member of Parliament; Sir Francis Burdett had been dragged from the bosom of his family and committed to the Tower, for exercising the right of constitutional discussion, common and undeniable to all, whilst Spencer Perceval continued a member of the House, taking a lead in its deliberations, the first minister of the Crown, and the chief adviser of the royal council. There was no need, the petitioners said, to recapitulate to the House the numerous instances of neglect to punish public delinquents, to economise the public money, to obtain redress for the lavish profusion of blood and money in the late Walcheren expedition. These and similar proceedings required no comment. Under these circumstances the petitioners called upon the House to expunge from its Journal all its orders respecting Jones and Sir Francis Burdett, and in conjunction with the latter to adopt such measures as would effect an immediate and radical parliamentary reform.[1]

Such strong language addressed to the Parliament of the United Kingdom was more than some of the livery then present in Common Hall could approve of, and they adjourned to the London Tavern where

The petition dismissed.

[1] Common Hall Book, No. 9, fos. 245-248b.

they drew up a formal protest against what they conceived to be nothing less than an attempt "to degrade "the legislature, to alienate the affections of the people "from the Government, to produce contempt and "distrust of the House of Commons, to introduce "anarchy, and to subvert the constitution." The petition nevertheless was presented to the House, but after considerable debate, and after a motion that it should be allowed to lie on the table had been lost by a large majority, it was dismissed.[1]

Proceedings of Common Hall, 21 May, 1810.

The rejection of their petition occasioned the holding of another Common Hall for the purpose of maintaining the rights of the livery constitutionally assembled. As soon as the Hall met (21 May), the livery proceeded to pass a number of resolutions. They declared that the recent protest had been signed by "contractors, commissioners, and collectors of taxes, place-men, and place-hunters," and that its object was "the excitement of civil dissension, the "increase of public abuses, and the further and fuller "participation in the wages of corruption," by many of those who had signed it; that the right of petitioning, which had been denied to the subject in 1680, and allowed and confirmed in 1688 by the Bill of Rights, had again been invaded, and a new race of *Abhorrers* had sprung up, and that it behoved every real friend of the country "to resist their mischievous "designs by recurring to the genuine principles of the "constitution, and by using every legal means for "obtaining a full, fair and free representation of the "people in Parliament." They resolved, notwithstanding the rejection of their last petition, to give

[1] Journal House of Commons, lxv, 346.

the House of Commons every opportunity of hearing and redressing the grievances of the people, and sanctioned the presentation of another humble address, petition and remonstrance. This new petition, which differed but slightly from the last, was presented to the House on the 25th, and instead of being rejected, was ordered to lie on the table.[1]

Just as lord mayor's day was approaching the king suffered a sudden relapse, owing in a great measure to the loss of his favourite daughter, and became hopelessly insane. The question thereupon arose whether the new lord mayor could, under the circumstances, be sworn before the barons of the exchequer. Counsel were of opinion that this was the proper course to pursue and the incoming mayor was so sworn.[2] There was no pageant owing to the death of the princess.[3]

The king's illness, Nov., 1810.

A few days prior to the king's seizure the City resolved to place his statue in their council chamber, in token of their sense of his " endearing and amiable qualities."[4] The work was entrusted to Chantrey who had already executed a bust of the younger Pitt for the Trinity House Brethren.[5] The artist undertook to complete the statue in three years, but it was not until 1815 that it was ready to be set up. It originally bore an inscription written by Samuel Birch, who was mayor at the time, but upon the removal of the statue

His statue in the Council Chamber.

---

[1] Common Hall Book, No. 9, fos. 249b-253b. Journal House of Commons, lxv, 410, 411.

[2] Repertory 214, fos. 772-812.   [3] *Id*, fos. 761-762.

[4] Journal 86, fo. 216b.

[5] Journal 86, fo. 332.—See minutes of committee relative to the king's statue, 19 April, 1811.

to the new council chamber, in 1884, the pedestal bearing the inscription was left behind.

The Regency Bill, Feb., 1811. The necessity of a regency soon became manifest, and in January, 1811, a Bill was introduced for the purpose of appointing the Prince of Wales. When Pitt introduced a similar Bill in 1788 he had displayed no little courage in upholding the authority of parliament and imposing certain restrictions and limitations upon the regency of the prince whose character was none of the best, and the City had acknowledged the wisdom of his policy and passed him a vote of thanks. At that time it was a matter of uncertainty whether the king might not recover, as recover he did, and there was danger of prematurely paying court to the rising sun. More than twenty years had since passed away. The king was now an old man and the Prince of Wales must, in the ordinary course of things, succeed to the throne before long. Parliament still wished to impose restrictions upon the regency, but in a more modified form than in the former Bill. The prince, however, was adverse to any restrictions and the City sided with the prince against parliament.[1] In spite of their protest the Bill, with its limitations, was passed (5 Feb., 1811) and the prince submitted to take the oaths. A few days later the City offered him an address of condolence and congratulation, and at the same time appealed to him for redress of grievances and more especially for parliamentary reform.[2]

The Freedom declined by Prince Regent. In May the Common Council offered him the Freedom of the City, but this he declined on the strange

[1] Journal 86, fos. 262b–268. Common Hall Book, No. 9, fos. 259–261b.
[2] Journal 86, fos. 290–291b.

plea that its acceptation would be incompatible with his station as Regent. He made, however, a gracious reply to the deputation which waited upon him to learn his pleasure (he declined to receive more than the lord mayor, the sheriff, the recorder, and the remembrancer, as being contrary to precedent), and assured them that it was his earnest desire at all times to promote the interest and welfare of the ancient corporation.[1]

The regency being thus settled the "friends of parliamentary reform" appointed a committee (May, 1811) to organise a meeting in London. The meeting was to take place on Whit Monday (3 June) and was to be attended by delegates from all parts of the kingdom. The Common Council were disposed to accede to a request for the use of the Guildhall for the purpose of the meeting, but upon representation being made to them by the Court of Aldermen, and by some of the livery, that such a course would be without precedent as well as dangerous to the peace of the city, the permission was withdrawn.[2]

Proposed reform meeting at the Guildhall, 3 June, 1811.

As time wore on and the livery who had confessedly looked upon the regency as the "dawn of a new era" found their hopes disappointed, no change being made in the ministry and no reforms carried out, they resolved to address themselves to the Regent. They accordingly drew up a petition after their kind, and appointed a deputation of twenty-one liverymen to attend its presentation (26 March, 1812). Not a word was said about the petition being presented to

Address of the livery to the Regent, 26 Mar., 1812.

---

[1] Journal 86, fos. 373b–374, 384–385b.

[2] *Id.*, fos. 386b–387b, 400–405; Repertory 215, fos. 345–350; Common Hall Book, No. 9, fos. 263–265.

the prince on the throne. When the sheriffs attended at Carlton House on Wednesday, the 1st April, to learn when the Regent would be pleased to receive it, they were told that he would receive it at the levée on the following Thursday week (9th) in "the usual way." When asked if he would receive the deputation appointed by the livery, the prince demurred. There were "certain forms attending that," but he would communicate with the secretary of state who would give them an answer. The next day (2 April), secretary Ryder informed the sheriffs by letter, that no persons beyond "the number allowed by law," to present petitions to his majesty, would be admitted to the levée on the 9th, except the lord mayor, aldermen, sheriffs, and city officers. The sheriffs, on the receipt of this letter again came to the charge and represented to the secretary of state—apparently for the first time, and on their own responsibility—that the livery had expected that the Regent would have received their address on the throne. What, moreover, did the Regent mean when he said that he would receive it in "the usual way"? To this query, the secretary replied that by the words "in the usual way," the prince meant "the way in which the petitions of "persons in general were received, and not in which "the addresses or petitions of the livery of London "had been received in some instances previous to the "year 1775." He also added that the address and petition would not be read at the levée nor would any answer be given, and, further, that only a deputation of the livery, not exceeding ten persons, might attend. On being informed of all this the livery were furious, but had to content themselves as before, with passing a number of resolutions against the advisers of the crown, etc., etc., and these the sheriffs were ordered to deliver into the prince's own hands.[1]

Ten days later (17 April), the Common Council drew up an address to the prince, which proved to be such a formidable indictment of the government that it was characterised by his highness (who presumably received it on the throne) as one that involved "the "total change in the domestic government and foreign "policy of the country." This address did not appear in the *London Gazette*, as it ought to have done according to custom, and upon enquiry as to the reason for this omission, answer was made that "the *London Gazette* was the king's paper," and nothing appeared therein without the order of government; that no such order had been received in this case; that nevertheless, as it had been found to be usual to insert addresses of the Corporation presented to the king with the answer thereto, the secretary of state would give directions for inserting the last address and answer "on account of the usage," and not as a matter of right.[2] *Address of Common Council to regent, 28 April, 1812.*

Dissatisfied as the citizens were with the ministry, they nevertheless viewed with horror the dastardly assassination of Spencer Perceval in the lobby of the House of Commons (11 May), and both the Court of Aldermen and the Common Council presented addresses on the subject to the Prince Regent.[3] As soon as news of the outrage reached the lord mayor, he despatched messengers to the House for confirmation of *Assassination of Spencer Perceval, 11 May, 1812.*

---

[1] Common Hall Book, No. 9, fos. 272–277b.
[2] Journal 87, fos. 195, 196b, 204b.
[3] Journal 87, fos. 228b–231b; Repertory 216, fo. 340.

the report, and at the same time sent his chaplain to the secretaries of state for further particulars. The city marshals were immediately ordered to take steps for calling out the watch and ward, and to report every half-hour to the Mansion House. All that night a double patrol was kept, and half-hourly reports sent in until daylight. At eight o'clock the following morning, the East Regiment of London militia mustered at head-quarters in case of an outbreak,[1] but it soon became known that the outrage was the work of a single individual—one Bellingham, a Liverpool broker, with some real or fancied grievance —and not of a political conspiracy as was at first believed. The assassin was convicted and hanged within a week. All the ministers resigned, and an attempt was made to construct a Whig cabinet, but it failed and Lord Liverpool became premier.

The Battle of Salamanca, 22 July, 1812. In June, Napoleon entered Russia, and Wellington prepared to carry out offensive operations in Spain. In the following month (22 July) the latter defeated the French general, Marmont, at Salamanca, and afterwards entered Madrid in triumph. For his victory at Salamanca, the Common Council added a gold box to the Freedom of the City already accorded to him but not yet conferred;[2] whilst later on they voted a sum of £2,000 in aid of the sufferers from Napoleon's Russian invasion.[3]

The "Shannon" and "Chesapeake," 1 June, 1813. The year 1813 found England at war, not only with France but with America. For some time past the United States had felt aggrieved at certain Orders

---

[1] Repertory 216, fo. 338–339.   [2] Journal 87, fo. 397b.
[3] *Id.*, fo. 438b.

in Council which had been issued by way of retaliation for the famous Berlin decree; and in contravention of these orders they had insisted on the doctrine that a neutral flag made free goods. The orders had been revoked in favour of America in June, 1812, but the concession came too late, and war had been declared. An attempt to draw off Canada from her allegiance failed, but at sea the Americans succeeded in capturing some of our frigates. At length, a duel was, by arrangement, fought outside Boston harbour, between the English vessel "Shannon," Captain Broke in command, and the American frigate "Chesapeake." The vessels were well matched, but the action which took place on the 1st June (1813), lasted little more than a quarter of an hour. It was reported at the time that an explosion took place on the "Chesapeake," and that it was owing to this rather than to any superiority in courage or tactics on the part of the crew of the English vessel that the American was made a prize.[1] But, however, this may have been, the honour of the day rested with Captain Broke, who was presented with the Freedom of the City and a sword of the value of 100 guineas.[2] The unhappy war was not brought to a close until December (1814).

In the meantime, Napoleon had met with a series of unprecedented reverses, and been forced to abdicate; Louis XVIII had succeeded to his murdered brother's throne, and peace between England and France had been signed at Paris (May, 1814). The City presented

Treaty of Paris, May, 1814.

---

[1] See letter from Commodore William Bainbridge to the secretary of the navy. Dated Charleston (Mass.), 2 June.—*Examiner*, No. 294.

[2] Journal 88, fos. 114, 171.

a long congratulatory address to the Prince Regent, on the fall of Napoleon and the accession of Louis to the throne.[1] Swords of honour were showered on foreign officers,[2] whilst our royal allies, the czar of Russia and the king of Prussia, as well as the new French king were presented with congratulatory addresses, and with the Prince Regent magnificently entertained by the citizens at the Guildhall (18 June).[3] Two days later the peace was proclaimed in the city with the same formalities as those used in the proclamation of peace with France and Spain, in 1783,[4] and on Thursday, the 7th July, a solemn thanksgiving service was held in St. Paul's, and was attended by the Regent.[5]

The Duke of Wellington at the Guildhall, 9 July, 1814.

The entertainment at the Guildhall was followed at a short interval (9 July) by another given to the Duke of Wellington, when opportunity was taken of presenting him with the Freedom of the City, which he had hitherto been unable to "take up," as also with the sword of honour and gold box already voted to him. The second entertainment was scarcely less brilliant than the former, the general arrangements and decorations being the same on both occasions.[6]

Petition Common Council for abolition of slave trade, 4 July, 1814.

Before the terms of peace were actually settled, the House of Commons embraced the opportunity of addressing the Regent upon the advisability of pro-

---

[1] Journal 88, fo. 285b.   [2] Journal 89, fos. 45b–46.
[3] Journal 88, fos. 295b, 297b; Journal 89, fos. 42–45, 47–47b, 50, 52b, 307b–320; Repertory 218, fos. 448–453, 472–481. A plaster of Paris bust of the Czar was presented to the lord mayor, and set up in the centre niche of the Egyptian Hall, in the Mansion House. Journal 89, fo. 93b; Journal 90, fo. 47.
[4] Repertory 218, fos. 485–487.
[5] Journal 89, fos. 39b, 56.   [6] Journal 90, fos. 71–80b.

vision being made against the revival of the slave trade in those parts which were about to be ceded to France.[1] Ever since 1792 Bills had from time to time been introduced, with the view of putting down or at least suspending the nefarious traffic, but with little or no success, until in 1807 an Act was passed prohibiting the slave trade, under a penalty of heavy fines. As this Act was not sufficiently deterrent, another Act had been passed in 1811, making slave trading a felony, and so the trade had, after a long struggle, been finally abolished throughout the British dominion. Since 1792 the civic fathers do not appear to have taken any active part in the matter; but when it became known that the peace had been concluded, not only without any guarantee against the revival of the slave trade in parts where it had been abolished by England, and which were now to be ceded to France, but with express stipulations that the traffic should and might be exercised in those parts for a certain number of years, the City again took the matter up. A strong petition was drawn up by the Common Council (4 July), and submitted to both Houses of Parliament. They expressed the deepest regret that by such stipulations " all the labours and exertions " of the wise and virtuous in this country, and all the " enactments of the legislature," for the abolition of the slave trade had been rendered useless and unavailing. After such a formal recognition in the treaty of the right of France to carry on the abominable traffic, it would be preposterous for the British government to ask the assistance of other powers to put it down. The petitioners, therefore, humbly prayed

[1] Journal House of Commons, lxix, 231.

both Houses to take speedy steps to impress upon his majesty's government the necessity of having the obnoxious clauses rescinded.[1] A week later (11 July) the prince, who, when originally applied to on the matter by the House of Commons, had returned what was then considered a favourable answer, now assured Parliament that he would endeavour to carry out its wishes.[2]

<small>Battle of Waterloo, 18 June, 1815.</small> Early in the following year, whilst a congress was sitting at Vienna to regulate the affairs of Europe, news was brought that Napoleon had made his escape from Elba. Louis XVIII, the restored Bourbon king, who had already become unpopular, fled to Lille, and Napoleon became once more emperor of the French. His reign was, however, cut short on the field of Waterloo (18 June). The allies entered Paris in triumph (7 July), Napoleon took refuge on board the "Bellerophon," a British man-of-war, and claimed the hospitality of the Prince Regent. It was, however, only too clear that the peace of Europe would be constantly menaced were he to be allowed his liberty. He was, therefore, removed to St. Helena, and kept under guard. Louis XVIII was again restored, and negotiations were resumed, which resulted in a second treaty of Paris (20 Nov.). Once more the City offered congratulations to the Regent,[3] and as the swords of honour, voted last year to Blucher and other distinguished foreign officers, had not yet been presented, the lord mayor (Samuel Birch) proposed going to Paris himself, with a small deputation of the

---

[1] Journal 89, fos. 61b-64b.
[2] Journal House of Commons, lxix, 450.
[3] Journal 89, fos. 352-353b.

Common Council, and making the presentation—as he said—"in the face of the world." Although he had received assurances that every possible respect would be shown him, he eventually abandoned the idea, and contented himself with despatching the swords to the Duke of Wellington for delivery to their respective owners.[1]

[1] Journal 89, fos. 368-368b ; Journal 90, fo. 57b.

CHAPTER XLIII.

The City opposes renewal of Income Tax, Feb., 1816.

Now that the war was over, a period of tranquillity, prosperity and retrenchment was eagerly looked for. The country therefore experienced bitter disappointment when, on the resumption of the parliamentary session in February (1816), the government declared its intention of continuing to levy the income or property tax (which, from the first, had been avowedly a war tax) although the assessment was to be reduced by one-half. The citizens were among the first to express their indignation at such a proceeding. The Common Council and the livery passed a number of resolutions against the continuance of a tax that was at once inquisitorial, unjust and vexatious, and both bodies presented petitions to parliament against its renewal.[1] The Common Council submitted to the House that having patiently endured great burdens and privations during a war of unexampled difficulty they had naturally expected that on the return of peace "they " should have been relieved from the burthens of war " establishments and war taxes, that at least the most " obnoxious and oppressive of them would have been " removed, and they confidently hoped that by such " reductions in the public expenditure with the neces- " sary reformations and the abolishing of all unnecessary " places, pensions and sinecures, there would have been " no pretence for the continuance of a tax subversive

[1] Journal 90, fos. 123–125; Common Hall Book, No. 9, fos. 339–340.

"of freedom and destructive to the peace and happiness of the people." The livery for their part reminded the House that the first imposition of the tax was accompanied by "the most unequivocal and solemn declaration that the same should be withdrawn immediately after the termination of the then existing hostilities," and they expressed the utmost surprise and indignation at the government proposing to continue the oppressive and odious tax now that peace had been restored. As for the proposed reduction from ten to five per cent. the change so far from being likely to render the tax less vexatious would produce the opposite effect, and would, in their opinion, "be the occasion of the most degrading and inquisitorial proceedings, worse, if possible, than have been experienced under the former pressure of this heavy burden." The outcry of the city was quickly taken up by the country, and such a flood of petitions against the renewal of the tax poured in that the government had to give way and the tax was abandoned.

At the opening of the session the Prince Regent had congratulated the country upon the prosperity of the revenue and of all branches of trade and manufacture.[1] As a matter of fact both the commercial and agricultural interests of the country were in a very bad way. The high prices produced during the latter part of the war by the continental system, which virtually excluded foreign competition, had been most disastrous to agriculture by encouraging a bad system of farming, whilst they inflicted the greatest hardship upon all but the wealthiest class. In 1811 the price of a quartern loaf—as set from time to time by the Court of Aldermen,

Agricultural depression, 1811–1815.

[1] Journal House of Commons, lxxi, 4.

according to the custom of the city,¹ "within the city "and the liberties thereof, and the weekly Bills of "mortality, and within ten miles of the Royal "Exchange"—had risen to such a height that the Common Council presented an address to the Regent (18 Dec.) praying him to take measures for re-opening commercial intercourse with foreign, and especially neutral, nations. To this the Regent replied that nothing should be wanting on his part towards restoring commercial intercourse between this country and other nations "to the footing on which it has been usually conducted, even in the midst of war."² The average price of the quartern loaf, from this period until the autumn of 1813, when the country was blessed with a rich harvest, may be set down at 1s. 6d. It then began to fall rapidly. Flour, however, kept up in price for some time owing to the dryness of the summer, which prevented many mills near London from working, whilst several of the mills which could work "were engaged in answering the demands of govern-"ment for the army abroad, and the prisoners of war "confined in this country."³

The City and the first Corn Law, March, 1815.

No sooner had the price of wheat fallen than a Corn Law Bill was introduced into Parliament, in the interests of the landed gentry, to raise it again. The Bill was brought in on the 1st March (1815), and rapidly passed the Commons, in spite of protests from the Common Council, as well as the livery of London, who objected to the landowner, who had benefited

---

¹ The custom of setting the assize in the city continued until 1822, when it was abolished by Stat. 3 Geo. III, c. cvi.

² Journal 87, fos. 68, 104b.

³ See Report of Special Committee on the continued high price of bread, 24 March, 1814.—Journal 88, fos. 262b–268b.

by the war, being made richer at the expense of the tradesman and merchant, whose burdens the war had so much increased.[1] On the 21st the Bill passed the Lords, and only awaited the Regent's assent to become law. Determined to make one more effort the Common Council presented an address to his royal highness begging him to withhold his assent.[2] They complained of the "precipitancy" with which the Bill had been passed, and of the utter disregard of public feeling and opinion which both Houses—composed as they were of landed proprietors, to whom the war had been a source of emolument—had throughout displayed. The Bill had been passed (they repeated) in the interest of landowners, who already enjoyed sufficient immunities, whereas the manufacturer and the merchant, who had done so much to make England what she was, had to suffer from foreign competition and the recent introduction of machinery. The Bill, if passed, would keep up the price of food, and so drive the manufacturer and artisan to foreign parts, and transfer the skill, industry and capital of the kingdom to other nations. They prayed his highness, therefore, to exercise his prerogative of refusing his assent to the Bill. This he refused, however, to do, and the Bill became law. As to the merits or demerits of free-trade, opinions are still divided; but for thirty years after the passing of the first Corn Law the City never lost an opportunity of declaring its opposition to the principle involved,[3] and never rested until in 1846 the first

---

[1] Journal 89, fos. 216b, 217b-219, 237b; Common Hall Book, No. 9, fos. 316-318b.

[2] Journal 89, fos. 242b-244.

[3] Journal 99, fos. 101-105; Journal 100, fos. 113b-115; Journal 117, fos. 225-226; Journal 118, fos. 438b-441.

steps were taken for the abolition of all corn duties. However much others have benefited by their repeal, one cannot shut one's eyes to the fact that to the agricultural class the result has been little short of disastrous.

<small>A year of general depression, 1816.</small>

Unfortunately the depression was not confined to agriculture, as the Common Council took an early opportunity of pointing out to Parliament in their petition against the renewal of the income tax (8 Feb.) : " Your petitioners are deeply sensible "— they told the House of Commons—" of the depressed " state of the agricultural interests and of the ruinous " effect of such a burthen thereon, they nevertheless " beg to state that the manufacturing and trading " interests are equally depressed and equally borne " down with the weight of taxation."¹

<small>Address of the livery to Regent, 21 Aug., 1816.</small>

As time went on matters became worse, and in August the livery resolved to present another address to the Regent, calling his attention to the prevalent distress, which they characterised as " unparalleled in the history of our country," and which they declared to be "the natural result of a corrupt system of administration," as well as of the profligate waste of public money during the late war. An address was accordingly drawn up (21 Aug.) praying his highness to lose no time in recommending to the serious consideration of Parliament (1) the distressed state of the country; (2) the prompt abolition of all useless places and pensions; (3) the immediate and effectual reduction of the standing army; (4) a system of the most rigid economy in every public department, and

¹ Journal 90, fo. 124b.

last, but not least, (5) such a reform of Parliament as should restore and secure to the people their ancient constitutional rights. This address they ordered to be presented to the Prince Regent "seated on his throne." The address was never presented, for the reason that the Regent refused to receive it in any other way than at a levée or through the medium of his secretary of state. The livery therefore had once more to console themselves with passing a number of resolutions after the usual manner.[1]

The streets of the city, meanwhile, swarmed not only with artisans out of work, but, what was worse, with discharged soldiers and sailors. A large proportion of the last mentioned class were foreign seamen. At the close of the war the government had taken steps to send to their respective countries all foreign seamen who had served on British vessels. Many of them, however, had either declined the government offer, or, having accepted it and obtained a passage home, had come to England with the view of entering the English merchant service or obtaining some other employment in this country. It was in vain that the lord mayor (Matthew Wood)[2] applied to the foreign consuls to send them home. The

The city flooded with vagrants.

---

[1] Common Hall Book, No. 9, fos. 343-345, 346b-347.

[2] He had just entered upon his second year of office, and had given no little offence to Lord Sidmouth—at that time high steward of the city and liberties of Westminster, as well as secretary of state for the home department—by returning from Westminster after being sworn in, through the streets of Westminster instead of by water, without having given notice to the high steward. Wood justified his conduct to Sidmouth in a letter in which he protested against the claim of the high steward to dictate to the lord mayor, the city of London, and the sheriffs of London and Middlesex, the particular course they were to take in going or returning on the occasion of the lord mayor being sworn before the Barons of the Exchequer.—Journal 90, fos. 348b-349b.

answer was that they had "forfeited all claim on "their native country and violated the allegiance "they owed to it by entering the service of Great "Britain." The consequence was that great numbers of these unfortunate men wandered about the city in an utterly destitute condition. Oftentimes when opportunity offered for sending some of them to their own country their consuls could not find them. The lord mayor, who was in communication both with Lord Sidmouth and Lord Melville, suggested the advisability of mooring an old vessel in the Thames for the reception of foreign seamen until they could be sent home. Lord Melville, as first lord of the admiralty, signified his approval of the plan and promised to supply a suitable vessel. In the meanwhile, matters daily grew worse. The lord mayor complained to Lord Sidmouth (16 Nov.) that he had frequently been engaged from nine in the morning until six in the evening attending to destitute cases :—" I have had " before me two hundred in a day, of whom the greater " number have come from Wapping and the out " parishes, and not one in twenty has slept in " London." If only the magistrates (he declared) would examine into the cases of their own districts, " it would divide the labour and prevent the daily " assemblage of from one to two hundred of these poor " creatures around the Mansion House, some of whom " linger about it all night." In conclusion he begged to draw his lordship's attention once more to the situation of the foreign seamen who were found on the bridges and in the streets "literally starving," and to ask that the government should do something to relieve the City of the heavy expense which their presence entailed. The only reply which the secretary of state vouchsafed to this appeal was a *non possumus*. The government had done all they could do, and relief could only be looked for at the hands of the foreign consuls, whose duty it was to provide for their own poor.[1]

Moved at the sad spectacle which met them on every side, the livery of London again met in Common Hall on the 29th November. They felt that it was useless to attempt to get an address received by the Regent in the manner they deemed proper; so they again passed resolutions urging all counties, corporate bodies, towns, wards and parishes throughout the kingdom to lay their grievances at the foot of the throne and before Parliament in a firm, temperate, and peaceable manner, with the view of eventually obtaining that economical and parliamentary reform they had so long and so anxiously desired.[2] *Resolutions of the livery, 29 Nov., 1816.*

In the meanwhile a series of riots had taken place in various parts of the country. In agricultural districts ricks had been fired, and in manufacturing towns machinery had been wantonly destroyed. In December, a riot known as the "Spa Fields Riot" broke out, but was repressed without much difficulty, thanks to the courage of the lord mayor. The first intimation that Matthew Wood received that anything was wrong, was about mid-day on Monday, the 2nd December. He was then told that a mob some thousands strong was approaching the city by way of Aldersgate Street; that a man had already been shot *Lord Mayor's report of Spa Fields Riot, 3 Dec., 1816.*

[1] Journal 90, fos. 345b- 348.
[2] Common Hall Book, No. 9, fo. 348b-350b.

in a gun-maker's shop in Skinner Street, and that the shop had been cleared of a large quantity of arms. What subsequently took place is best told in Matthew Wood's own report[1] to his brother aldermen :—" I "immediately signified my intention of going out "to meet them and instantly Sir James Shaw and " Mr. White offered their services. On enquiring for " Police Officers, only two were to be found. We " hurried to Guildhall, where we met with only three "more, and attended by these five we advanced " by the back streets in the hope of reaching the top "of Cheapside before the Mob ; in Lad Lane we " were told that they had already entered Cheapside "in great force with Colors, and the firing was " distinctly heard by us, we returned therefore imme- " diately with all imaginable speed by the way of " Princes Street into Cornhill, with the view of " heading them in that direction ; in this however we " were again foiled, for in reaching the West end of " Cornhill, we saw them pressing [*sic*] the front of " the Exchange. We followed them close, and seeing "the head of their Column crossing into Sweeting's " Alley we rushed thro' the Royal Exchange in order " to take them in front and we succeeded. We met "them on the North of the Royal Exchange near the " Old Stock Exchange, on seeing me they cheered, " we immediately attacked them, upon which they "began to seperate in all directions and some laid " down their arms. Sir James Shaw intrepidly seized " the Flag and its Bearer, Mr. White seized one man " and I another. The Mob were now seen flying in " all directions : about this time Mr. Favell and Mr.

[1] Repertory 221, fos. 6-18.

"Hick joined us, a man with a tricolored Cockade in "his hat (Hooper) came up to me with a desire to "explain. I made him go before me into the Ex-"change which he did without resistance. I had him "in the centre when two fellows levelled their Musketts "at me. I said, 'fire away, you Rascals.' One of "them fired. I then gave Hooper into the Custody "of the Officers, who found in his pockets two "Horse Pistols, one loaded with Ball, the other with "Slugs. A cry that the mob had rallied was heard "just as we were making arrangements for securing "the Prisoners. I ordered the gates of the Exchange "to be shut, which we accomplished with some "difficulty and not before several guns loaded with "shot were fired under the gates at our feet, but "without any effect. Information being now received "that a portion of the Rioters had gone towards the "East end of the City, it was determined to follow "them, directions having been first given to put the "prisoners into the custody of the Master of Lloyd's, "with whom Sir James Shaw also lodged the Stand-"ard. I proceeded accompanied by Sir James and "a few Constables up Cornhill and Leadenhall Street, "but here we were told, the Mob had wholly dis-"persed; which induced us to return to the Mansion "House, where I found Sir William Curtis, who in his "zeal for the Public Service, had lost sight of all "personal ailments, and had come, ill as he was, to "offer me his best services, by this time also the "Dragoons had reached the City. Mr. Alderman "Atkins who had been sitting in the Justice Room "for me also joined us, and it being suggested, that it "would be proper that the different Wards should

"collect as many of their respectable Inhabitants
"as possible, to be sworn in Special Constables, I
"immediately gave directions to that effect. Sir
"James Shaw and Mr. Alderman Atkins tendered
"their Services to convey my wishes to Lloyd's and
"the Stock Exchange and these Gentlemen informed
"me that the proposition was received and accepted
"at each of these places by the Gentlemen with
"cheers. These Gentlemen next proceeded to the
"Bank where they saw the Governor, and had the
"satisfaction to learn he had anticipated their wishes;
"a division of the Bank Corps being then actually
"under arms. From the Bank they proceeded to the
"India House and met with several of the Directors
"in attendance who immediately gave orders for 500
"of their men to be selected as a Guard on their
"warehouses, who were soon after sworn in Con-
"stables by Mr. Alderman Atkins. When these
"Gentlemen returned to the Mansion House there
"were assembled Sir John Eamer, Sir John Perring,
"Sir William Leighton, Sir Charles Flower, Alderman
"J. J. Smith, Alderman Scholey, Alderman Birch,
"Alderman Magnay, Alderman Heygate, Alderman
"Cox and Sheriffs Bridges and Kirby with their
"Under-Sheriffs. About 3 o'clock information was
"brought me, that the Mob had broken into the
"Warehouses of Messrs. Branden and C$^{o.}$ and Mr.
"Rea's and had taken from each a quantity of arms,
"and almost at the same moment I received intelli-
"gence that the plunderers had been met and
"dispersed by the Dragoons, who had made some
"Prisoners, and recovered most of the arms. During
"the absence of Sir James Shaw and Mr. Alderman

"Atkins Mr. White of Bishopsgate Street had arrived
"with a Troop of Light Dragoons which he had
"fetched from the Light Horse Stables, Grays Inn
"Lane, and Mr. Goldham having been dispatched
"with a few of them to reconnoitre, now returned
"with a Coach loaded with Musketts, Swords,
"Blunderbusses, Pikes, Halbuts, and a brass Cannon
"which had been taken from the Mob in the Minories
"by the Life Guardsmen and three Prisoners were
"sent into Aldgate Watchouse and committed to the
"care of a Constable, who by a shameful dereliction
"of his duty suffered them to escape. Mr. M^C Lean
"of Brunswick Square, who had not long left the
"Mansion House, returned about four o'Clock and
"informed me, that, the Meeting in the Fields had
"broken up, and that, there were 15,000 people
"coming down Holborn and passing to Fleet Market.
"I determined to go and meet them; Sir James Shaw
"and Mr. M^C Lean tendered their Services, when
"taking some Police Officers some Special Constables
"and a Detachment of Dragoons with us we moved
"on in a quick pace by the North side of St. Paul's
"Church Yard where we met about 2,000 persons,
"but seeing they were without arms of any kind and
"perfectly peaceable, we allowed them to pass on.
"We proceeded Westward and nearly to the middle
"of Fleet Street when meeting another party of
"Dragoons, who informed us every thing was quiet
"in that Quarter we returned to the Mansion House,
"I having first directed a party of the Horse accom-
"panied with Police Officers to make the Circuit of
"the Prisons and to report to me when they had so
"done. The City was quiet from this time. About

"12 o'Clock at Night some papers taken by the
"Constable out of the Pocket of the Man who shot
"Mr. Platt were shown to me, by which I learned
"that Hooper was connected with Preston the Secre-
"tary of the Spa Fields Meeting. These papers state
"that subscriptions towards defraying the expences
"of erecting Hustings, Printing &c., will be received
"by J. Hooper No. 9 Graystock Place Fetter Lane
"signed Preston Secretary. About one in morning
"accompanied by Mr. Sheriff Kirby, Mr. Under-
"Sheriff Kearsey and others with some Constables, I
"went to No. 9 Graystock Place and made the
"Householder come down, who proved to be Preston
"the Secretary. We searched the House and found in
"it very few papers—one an Hymn, and another a
"letter of exhortation on the subject of 'England
"expects every Man to do his duty.' There was
"likewise a small quantity of Tricolored Ribbon.
"Preston had two daughters and there were only
"two Beds on the floor in the same room, the whole
"house in a most wretched condition—with scarsely
"a chair; in the room used by Hooper for the
"reception of subscriptions there was no other furni-
"ture but a table. Preston said Hooper did not
"lodge there nor did he know where he lived. It is
"supposed Watson Jun[r.] was the Person who fired
"the Pistol at Mr. Platt, as Hooper says he did not
"see Watson for some time after they left the Fields,
"and it appears that he went into the Shop alone.
"The Officer was induced to let him escape through
"the entreaties of Mr. Beckwith's family who were
"apprehensive should he be detained that the house
"would be pulled down. I have no doubt had the

"Mob not been prevented it was their intention to
"have collected a great number of fire arms and then
"to have returned to Spa Fields and from thence to
"Carlton House. Hooper admits that they intended
"to go to Carlton House, but not with fire arms.
"Hooper said that Watson Junr· gave him the Pistols
"on Sunday night at Preston's House and in his
"presence said that if they were opposed by the Civil
"power, they were to use them."

The lord mayor closed his narrative with a handsome acknowledgment of the services rendered by his brother aldermen, the special constables and others, whilst he expressed a desire more particularly to call the attention of the Court to the conduct of Sir James Shaw, "whose zeal, activity, coolness and undaunted courage," had rendered him such valuable assistance throughout the day.

On the 9th December—just one week after the riot—the Common Council presented an address to the Regent praying for a reformation of abuses, a speedy meeting of Parliament, and a more equitable system of representation. The address was received with "surprise and regret." His highness expressed his opinion, shared as he said, by a large portion of his subjects, that the prevailing distress was the result of "unavoidable causes." He was confident that the good sense, public spirit, and loyalty of the nation would prove superior to the attempts that had been made to "irritate and mislead" his subjects. And he declared his readiness to meet Parliament at the time appointed and not before.[1]

The City's address to Regent on state of affairs, 9 Dec., 1816.

[1] Journal 90, fos. 377-380b, 384-384b.

Reflections on the Regent's reply

When it came to recording the Regent's "most gracious" answer on the Journal of the Common Council, an amendment was made and carried, to leave out the words "most gracious." The Council went further than this. It passed a resolution expressing its own "surprise and regret," that his highness should have been advised to return such an answer at such a time; that he should have imputed to those who sought only a reformation of abuses, a desire to "irritate and mislead" the people, and that he should have attributed to "unavoidable causes" what was in reality due to reckless public expenditure, sanctioned by a corrupt Parliament.[1]

Outrage upon the Regent, 28 Jan., 1817.

The general discontent vented itself by a personal attack on the Regent as he drove from Westminster after opening Parliament in January (1817), and one of the windows of his carriage was broken by a missile. The City at once expressed its indignation at the outrage and offered addresses congratulating the prince on his escape.[2]

City petitions to Parliament for Reform, Feb., 1817.

Parliament had not sat many days before the Common Council and the livery presented strongly-worded petitions to both Houses for Reform. The Common Council pointed out—as an example of one

---

[1] Journal 90, fos. 383-384.

[2] Repertory 221, fo. 175. Journal 91, fo. 18. A curious incident is recorded in connection with these addresses. Owing to the requisition for a Common Council having referred to the attack on the Regent as an act of some "rash and intemperate" individuals only, and not as a treasonable outrage, the Recorder declared the Common Council to be illegal, and the Court at once broke up, there being no aldermen present. The Common Council resented what they considered to be an unjust attempt on the part of the aldermen to dictate to them in the exercise of their duty, and an unwarrantable attack upon their privileges, and a few days later (13 Feb.) passed resolutions to that effect, and ordered them to be published in the morning and evening papers.—Journal 91, fos. 33b, 34.

of the most glaring anomalies—that Cornwall alone returned more borough members than fifteen other counties together including Middlesex, and more than eleven counties even including county members,[1] whilst the livery referred all the evils which the country was suffering—"the prodigious amount of the National "Debt, the enormous and unconstitutional military "establishments, the profusion of sinecure places and "pensions, and a long course of lavish expenditure of "the public money"—to one source, viz., "the corrupt, "dependent, and inadequate representation of the "people in Parliament." They disclaimed all wild and visionary plans of Reform. All they desired was "to see the House of Commons in conformity with "pure constitutional principles, a fair and honest organ "of the public voice exercising a controuling power "over the servants of the Crown, and not an instru-"ment in their hands to oppress the people."[2]

It was to no purpose. The outrage on the Regent frightened the ministers, and instead of following the advice offered by the City and appeasing the public by showing a willingness to correct abuses, they proceeded to suspend the Habeas Corpus Act and to pursue a cruel system of repression, which only served to increase the evil.[3] *Repressive measures of the Government, March, 1817.*

Not only were seditious actions proceeded against but seditious writings. A quiet and inoffensive bookseller of Old Bailey, named Hone, was prosecuted on three several charges for which he was put on trial three several days. The charges were professedly for having published pamphlets of a blasphemous character, but *The trial of Hone, the bookseller, Dec., 1817.*

---

[1] Journal 91, fo. 12. [2] Common Hall Book, No. 10, fo. 9.
[3] Journal 91, fos. 34b-40. Common Hall Book, No. 10, fos. 14–22.

the persistency with which they were pressed after a first and second acquittal, sufficiently showed that the prosecution had been undertaken from political and not from any religious motives, and the City did not hesitate to tell Parliament as much.[1] They declared that they had viewed with indignation and horror the vindictive cruelty with which ministers had exercised their power since the suspension of the Act. Numerous individuals (they said) had been torn from their wives and families, dragged to distant prisons and kept in irons, and afterwards released without being brought to trial, or even knowing the nature of the charges against them. The country had been flooded with spies and informers in the pay of the government, and these inhuman wretches had endeavoured to excite simple and deluded men into acts of outrage and treason. The petitioners did not disguise their belief that "the groundless alarms "excited by ministers were solely for the purpose "of stifling complaints and protecting abuses."

The Indemnity Bill, 13 March, 1818.

When the Habeas Corpus Act was again allowed to come into force (29 Jan., 1818), after nearly a year's suspension,[2] the ministers were anxious to cover their recent proceedings under a Bill of Indemnity. A sealed bag of papers was laid upon the table of the House which the government demanded to be referred to a secret committee, but as this committee was virtually nominated by the government itself, the citizens of London lost no time in declaring that they for-

---

[1] Journal 92, fos. 57b-58.

[2] Journal House of Commons, lxxiii, 11. The suspension had been renewed in June (1817), notwithstanding the City's continued opposition.—Journal 91, fos. 187-189b.—Common Hall Book, No. 10, fos. 23-31.

their part, would have no confidence in any report such a committee might think fit to make.¹

The City had its revenge in the following June, when parliament was hurriedly dissolved and a new election took place. Three of the old city members, —Sir William Curtis, Sir James Shaw, and John Atkins, —all of them aldermen with ministerial proclivities, were rejected, and four liberals were returned, the best known being Matthew Wood, who had sat in the last parliament on the withdrawal of Harvey Combe, and Robert Waithman, afterwards an alderman. In the country the elections were attended with the bitterest party strife, but as the representation then stood, no great change was possible, and the ministers found themselves still in possession of a large majority.

The City and the parliamentary election, June, 1818.

Although the harvest of 1817 had been a good one, and commercial activity had succeeded a period of extraordinary depression, the year 1818 was marked with great distress among artisans, owing to overproduction. As is usually the case at such times, demagogues were at hand urging the sufferers to revolutionary measures. Among them was the Rev. Joseph Harrison, a schoolmaster at Stockport, who, after making a violent speech in that town on the 28th June (1819), was arrested on a warrant at a mass meeting held in Smithfield, on the 21st July.²

Mass meetings in Smithfield, 21 July, 25 Aug., 1819.

Another of these demagogues was Henry Hunt, commonly known as "Orator" Hunt, who had offered

The "Manchester massacre" or "Peterloo," 16 Aug., 1819.

---

¹ Addresses of Common Council and Common Hall to parliament, 23 and 27 Feb., 1818.—Journal 92, fos. 54b–58b.—Common Hall Book, No. 10, fos. 48–55.—Journal House of Commons, lxxiii, 90, 106.

² See report of lord mayor to Court of Aldermen on the public meetings held in Smithfield, 21 July, and 25 Aug., 1819.—Repertory 223, 627–632.

himself as a candidate for Westminster at the last general election, and figured in the Spa Fields commotion. He was a man, however, more ready to stir up others to deeds of violence than risk his own skin. An attempt to arrest him at a meeting which he was about to address in St. Peter's Fields, near Manchester, led to five or six being killed by the military, and to a number of others being wounded. The affair, which was caused by magisterial blundering, came to be known as the "Manchester massacre" or "Peterloo," and proved a formidable weapon against the government. Hunt was taken, but liberated on bail, and on the 13th September was conducted in great triumph from Islington to the Crown and Anchor Tavern, in the Strand.[1]

City address to Regent, 9 Sept., 1819. The Common Council expressed much sympathy with the sufferers, whose only fault had been to assemble for the purpose of lawfully and peacefully discussing public grievances, and they petitioned the Regent for a full and immediate enquiry into the outrage and for the punishment of the authors. They assured his highness that he had been deceived by false representations, otherwise he would never have been induced to express approval of the conduct of the abettors and perpetrators of the late atrocities.[2] The Prince in reply flatly told the citizens they knew nothing about the real state of the case, and this "most gracious" answer was ordered to be entered in the Journal of the Court.[3]

The six Acts, 1819. The passing of a series of suppressory enactments, known as "The Six Acts," at an autumn session, gave

[1] Repertory 223, fos. 629–630.
[2] Journal 93, fos. 156b–157b. [3] *Id.*, fos. 159b–160.

the Common Council another opportunity for recommending parliamentary reform. It at the same time suggested—as reformers of the present day will do well to remember—*the extension of the municipal form of government* as a better panacea for existing evils than more drastic measures.[1] The Court of Aldermen, on the other hand, kept silence. They had, however, already passed a number of resolutions upholding the magistracy in putting down seditious meetings, and calling upon the labouring classes to have confidence in themselves, and not to be led by agitators, but to wait patiently until the present difficulties—"springing alone from the termination of a protracted war"—should pass away.[2]

The city itself presented signs of uneasiness. On Michaelmas-day, when the election of a lord mayor took place, a great commotion had been raised in Common Hall by sheriff Parkins, alderman Waithman, "Orator" Hunt and others, who wished to introduce violent resolutions against the government. The sheriff made himself especially obnoxious to the out-going lord mayor (Atkins), chiefly, it appears, on account of the Court of Aldermen having refused to recognise him (Parkins) as the senior sheriff. His conduct in Common Hall, as well as the conduct of Waithman and certain others, was deemed so bad by the Court of Aldermen that legal proceedings were ordered to be taken against them.[3] The Common Council expressed disapproval at any proceedings being taken, and recommended their withdrawal. The Court at the same time directed the City Chamberlain

Proceedings in Common Hall, 29 Sept., 1819.

---
[1] Journal 93, fos. 332-335b. [2] Repertory 223, fos. 656-659.
[3] *Id.*, fos. 635-636, 758-764.

not to pay any costs of the proceedings.[1] The Court of Aldermen were not unnaturally indignant at this,[2] but declined to withdraw from their position, and eventually a judgment was obtained in the King's Bench, which completely justified the position they had taken up. It was laid down by the judges that when a Common Hall has been summoned for a particular purpose, the livery have no right to introduce matter for consideration distinct from that for which they were assembled. The defendants in this case, however, were exonerated on the ground that they had been misled by an opinion given by Glynn, the City's Recorder in 1773, as to their rights.[3]

Conduct of Sheriff Parkins.

In the meantime, sheriff Parkins had continued to make himself as obnoxious as he could. He refused to attend at church on Michaelmas-day, and on the following day, when he should have accompanied his fellow sheriff, to be presented at Westminster to the Barons of the Exchequer, he wrote a rude letter to the mayor, excusing himself joining the procession on the score that he was busily engaged in his duties at the Old Bailey, and could not be "at two places one and the same time." Later in the day, he presented himself at Westminster, but without any state, and declined to invite the Barons of the Exchequer to the entertainment usually provided by the sheriffs on such occasions. He, in fact, gave no entertainment at all. He ought to have accompanied the mayor to the Court of Aldermen on the 8th October, but he again excused himself, on the plea of

---

[1] Journal 93, fos. 323b–325.   [2] Repertory 224, fos. 26–34.
[3] Repertory 225, fos. 61–69, 907, *seq.* For Glynn's opinion *vide sup.*, p. 138.

a headache, which he had the coolness to attribute to "the incessant noise and dreadful screams" at the last Common Hall. The mayor complained to the Court of Aldermen, and the sheriff was called upon to explain his conduct at the next Court.[1] When the Court met, Parkins read a long statement, which for sheer impudence will bear comparison with some productions of Wilkes or Junius, whilst lacking their cleverness. The reason he gave for not having accompanied the lord mayor to Westminster was that he did "not choose to divide with the lord "mayor those marks of popular feeling which every- "where follow the track of the city state carriage "during the present mayoralty." The lord mayor and the other sheriff had made the best part of the journey to Westminster by water, as was then the custom, but Parkins had reverted to the more ancient custom of riding thither on horseback.[2] It was true (he said) that he was not accompanied by any member of his company, but that was because "it would have been "neither decorous nor prudent to have set on foot or "even on horseback any rival procession, since it might "have been deemed by the lord mayor a demonstra- "tion of hostility against his own supremacy," and so on and so on. His whole defence was after the same manner, but all that the Court of Aldermen did was to refer his conduct to a Committee of Privileges (12 Oct.), and there the matter appears to have ended.[3]

[1] Repertory 223, fos. 636–645.
[2] Sir Gilbert Heathcote is said to have been the last mayor (1710–11) to have ridden to Westminster on horseback for the purpose of being sworn in.
[3] Repertory 223, fos. 660–672.

Accession of George IV, 29 Jan., 1820

On the evening of Saturday, the 29th January, (1820) George III passed away, and on Sunday morning his death was notified to the lord mayor. A special Court of Aldermen was immediately summoned to sit at the Mansion House, when the mayor laid before them two letters from Lord Sidmouth, one informing him of the king's decease, and the other desiring his attendance at Carlton House, at one o'clock that afternoon. He also laid before the Court another letter which he had subsequently received. This was a letter from the Clerk of the Privy Council, stating that the lords of the Council would meet at one o'clock, at Carlton House, and that the lord mayor and Court of Aldermen might attend, if they thought proper. Thereupon the lord mayor, the aldermen, and the high officers of the city proceeded in state (the black sword being borne before the mayor) to Carlton House, where they heard and subscribed the proclamation of King George IV. On their return to the Mansion House, the York herald delivered a copy of the ceremonial to be observed the next day, when the king should be proclaimed. Upon the arrival of the procession the following day at Temple Bar, the lord mayor took up his position in his state coach immediately before the archbishop of Canterbury; the aldermen, sheriffs, chamberlain, common serjeant, town clerk and city officers immediately after the lords of the Privy Council. The proclamation was publicly read at Carlton House and Charing Cross and at three different places within the City's jurisdiction, viz.: at the corner of Chancery Lane, the corner of Wood Street, Cheapside, and at the Royal Exchange.[1]

---

[1] Repertory 224, fos. 181-193.

When sheriff Parkins and his brother sheriff, Rothwell, attended at Carlton Palace to learn when it would be convenient for the king to receive addresses from the City, they found his majesty much indisposed. Monday, the 28th February, was fixed for receiving the addresses of the Courts of Aldermen and Common Council, but an intimation was given to the sheriffs (privately, it appears) that the state of the king's health would require the addresses to be presented in a room adjoining his majesty's bedroom by a small deputation from each Court. When Rothwell, the senior sheriff, communicated the result of their mission to the aldermen and the Common Council, Parkins again made himself obnoxious, declaring that *he* had heard nothing about the addresses being presented by small deputations, and that as a matter of fact "his majesty "did not appear to him to be so unwell as he had been "led to expect from the various reports he had heard." No notice was taken of this exhibition of bad taste, and both Courts agreed to present their addresses by deputation. To each of them the king made gracious replies, promising that the welfare and prosperity of the City and the maintenance of its rights and liberties should be objects of his constant care.[1]

City addresses to George IV, 28 Feb., 1820.

The coronation was originally fixed for Tuesday, the 1st August, but was subsequently postponed to Thursday, the 19th July, 1821.[2] The City lost no time in sending in its customary claim of services; and the masters and prime wardens of the twelve principal livery companies were invited, as usual, to assist the lord mayor in his duties at the coronation

The coronation of George IV, 19 July, 1821.

[1] Journal 94, fos. 32-34, 71b-73b; Repertory 224, fos. 193-200.
[2] Repertory 224, fos. 333-341; Repertory 225, fo. 499.

banquet.[1] These services were now performed for the last time, the coronation banquet and all ceremonial in connexion therewith in Westminster Hall being dispensed with, by royal proclamation, at the accession of William IV.[2]

City addresses to Queen Caroline, June, 1820.

The ceremony was somewhat marred by an injudicious attempt of the unhappy queen to force her way into the abbey. Whatever may have been the extent of her folly or her guilt no one can question the misfortune of Queen Caroline. From the first moment of their meeting she was treated by her husband with scant courtesy and was soon forced to quit his side and lead a life of retirement at Blackheath. A watch was set on her movements and her conduct made the subject of a private enquiry by the lords. The City was no less indignant than the princess herself at such a proceeding. The livery presented her with an address of sympathy,[3] and at the close of the enquiry the Common Council congratulated her upon having escaped from a "foul and atrocious conspiracy against her life and honour."[4] The Court of Aldermen, however, once more held aloof. This was in 1813. In the following year she withdrew disgusted to the continent and there remained until her husband succeeded to the throne. Again the livery and the Common Council presented addresses and testified their attachment to one whom most people looked upon as an injured woman, who had in vain

---

[1] Repertory 224, fos. 342-343, 350, *seq.* 427; Repertory 225, fos. 502-514, 582-584.

[2] Repertory 235, fos. 551-557.

[3] Common Hall Book, No. 9, fo. 285; the address was not allowed to be printed in the Gazette; *Id.*, fos. 287b-288b.

[4] Journal 87, fo. 508.

challenged her accusers to appear before a public and impartial tribunal.¹ Her wish was now to be gratified.

Another secret enquiry into her conduct was held by the lords, at the king's command, and upon evidence thus scraped together and unsupported by oath a Bill of Pains and Penalties was introduced into the House of Lords for depriving the queen of her title and dissolving her marriage. The Common Council entered a strong protest and appealed to both Houses to reject the Bill,² but in vain. The queen was put on her defence, and after a protracted trial succeeded with the help of her learned counsel—Brougham, Denman and Lushington—in placing her conduct in such a light that the Bill had to be abandoned.

The queen's trial, Aug.-Nov., 1820.

The news of the queen's triumph was received with the wildest delight, and for three nights in succession London was illuminated. Addresses began to flow in upon her in such quantities that a special day of the week had to be set apart for their reception.³ The Common Council assured her that they had never entertained the slightest doubt as to what would be the result of a trial unconstitutionally instituted and unfairly carried on; and expressed a hope that she would continue to reside among them.⁴ The Freedom of the City was voted to counsel engaged in her defence.⁵

City address to the queen, 21 Nov., 1820.

In acknowledging the City's address the queen referred to her late victory as a triumph for the people. "If my enemies had prevailed"—she said—"the "people who are now feared would have been despised,

The queen's reply, 24 Nov., 1820.

---

¹ Journal 94, fo. 182b; Common Hall Book, No. 10, fos. 92-93.
² Journal 94, fos. 199b-203b.
³ Annual register lxii, 482, 483, 498.
⁴ Journal 94, fo. 277b.   ⁵ *Id.*, fos. 291b-292.

"their oppression would have been indefinitely in-
"creased." She declared that it was to the sympathy
and support of the people and of the Press that she
was chiefly indebted for her escape from a conspiracy
such as had never before threatened an individual, and
although she doubted whether her presence in the
country was conducive to the national welfare, as
seemed to be generally supposed, she expressed herself
as being always ready to conform to the will of the
community at large :—" The people have made many
sacrifices for me, and I will live for the people."[1]

The queen at Brandenburgh House. The Court of Aldermen, as a body, had rigidly withheld their support from the unfortunate queen. Nevertheless, there were two members of the Court who thoroughly believed in her innocence, and who rendered her every assistance in their power. These were Matthew Wood, in whose house in South Audley Street she first found shelter on her return from abroad, and Robert Waithman. Matthew Wood continued to attend her at Brandenburgh House, where she kept her court, and where he dined with her the day that the Bill against her was thrown out. The motley character of her attendants elicited a satirical poem from Theodore Hook, in which the alderman comes in for his share of ridicule in the following lines :—

> " And who were attending her—heigh ma'am ; ho ma'am?
> Who were attending her, ho?
> — Lord Hood for a man,
> For a maid Lady Anne,[2]
> And Alderman Wood for a *beau—beau*
> And Alderman Wood for a *beau*."

[1] Journal 94, fos. 278b-279b.   [2] Lady Anne Hamilton.

It was Matthew Wood whom the queen employed to write to the Corporation, whilst her trial was still pending, asking that body to accept her portrait in testimony of her attachment and gratitude to "the first city in the world" for the zeal they had manifested in her cause, and it was Waithman who laid the letter before the Common Council. The offer was graciously accepted, and Queen Caroline's picture, as well as that of her deceased daughter, the Princess Charlotte—a subsequent gift—are preserved in the Guildhall Art Gallery.[1]

Presents her portrait to the City.

An intimation which the Common Council received from the gentleman acting as the queen's vice-chamberlain that she proposed to attend the usual service held at St. Paul's on Wednesday, the 29th November, was received with mixed feelings. It was feared that her appearance in the city might cause inconvenience, and perhaps lead to riot. Nevertheless a special committee was appointed to give her a suitable reception.[2] A similar foreboding was felt by the Court of Aldermen as soon as they heard of the queen's intention, and a motion was made expressing regret; but before any vote could be taken on the matter, the Court was abruptly broken up by Wood and Waithman leaving.[3] On the 27th, the Court again met, when communications were read from the Dean of St. Paul's, and from Lord Sidmouth, touching the preparations to be made for her majesty's reception in the Cathedral, and the precautions to be

The queen at St. Paul's, 29 Nov., 1820.

---

[1] Journal 94, fos. 231b, 242, 275.

[2] *Id.*, fos. 273-275. She had originally proposed to attend on Sunday, the 26th Nov., but changed the day, lest her presence should lead to a desecration of the Sabbath.

[3] Repertory 225, fos. 25-28. Annual Register lxii, 499-500.

taken against injury being done by accident or otherwise within the sacred precinct or in the public streets. The lord mayor was promised the assistance of the military if necessary. Again, a motion was made expressive of regret at the queen's proposal, but with no better success than at the previous Court. Alderman Wood again got up and left the Court so as to reduce the number present to less than a *quorum*, and Alderman Waithman immediately moved a count out.[1] Fortunately the day passed off without any mishap. One of the chief grievances which the queen had been made to suffer had been the omission of her name from the Liturgy. On this occasion she desired that "the particular thanksgiving, which at "the request of any parishioner, it is customary to "offer up" might be offered on her behalf, but the officiating minister refused on the ground that the rubric directed that "those may be named, who have "been previously prayed for, but that the queen not "having been prayed for, could not be named in the "thanksgiving." After all was over, the queen communicated her thanks to the lord mayor and the committee for the trouble they had taken, and expressed herself as particularly obliged to his lordship for not yielding to alarm, and for declining all military assistance.[2]

<small>Address of Common Council to the king, 7 Dec., 1820.</small>

The queen's trial served only to increase the City's dissatisfaction with the ministers, and the Common Council once more urged their dismissal (9 Dec.). In their address to the king they referred

---

[1] Repertory 225, fos. 29–37. Annual Register lxii, 500.
[2] Journal 94, fo. 285b. Annual Register lxii, 503–506.

"with pain and reluctance" to the late proceedings against the queen—proceedings which (they said) had drawn forth "the reprobation of the great body of the people"—and they expressed indignation at the flagrant outrage that had been committed on the moral and religious feelings of the nation.[1]

The king's reply, 9 Dec. It is not to be supposed that the king would receive such an address very graciously. Indeed, he acknowledged that he received it "with the most painful feelings," and he vouchsafed no further answer than to tell the citizens that whatever might be their motives in presenting the address, it served no other purpose than to inflame the passions and mislead the judgment of the less enlightened of his subjects, and to aggravate the difficulties with which he had to contend.[2]

Address, Court of Aldermen. Very different had been the reception accorded the previous day (8 Dec.) to an address from the Court of Aldermen, in which they informed the king of their resolution to defend the monarchy and other branches of the constitution, at that time so bitterly attacked. The subject of the queen's trial was not mentioned, although an attempt had been made to introduce it into the address by some members of the Court. This "loyal and dutiful" address was graciously received with the king's "warmest thanks."[3]

The queen's death, 7 Aug., 1821. Early in the following year (Jan., 1821) the Common Council petitioned both Houses for the restoration of the queen's name in the Liturgy, and for making her a proper provision to enable her to

---

[1] Journal 94, fos. 287-289.　[2] *Id.*, fo. 304.
[3] Repertory 225, fos. 42-50, 59-60.

support her rights and dignities. It at the same time demanded an enquiry into the manner in which the queen's prosecution had been brought about.[1] As regards a provision to be made for the queen, she had previously declined to accept any at the hands of the ministry.[2] The Commons now voted her an annuity of £50,000,[3] which she accepted but did not long enjoy, for in the following August she died.

<small>Disgraceful scene at her funeral, 14 Aug., 1821.</small>

The circumstances attending her funeral were of a most disgraceful character. She had expressed a wish to be buried in her own country, and this wish was carried out. The citizens were extremely anxious to pay a last token of respect in the event of her corpse being brought through the city to Harwich, the port of embarkation, and the Remembrancer waited upon Lord Liverpool for the purpose of notifying to him the resolutions passed by the Common Council to that effect. As in Chatham's case, so in the case of this unfortunate queen, the wishes of the citizens were ignored. After some delay they were informed that the funeral arrangements were already completed, and had been laid before the king, and that it was not intended that the procession should pass through the city.[4] The people, nevertheless, decided otherwise, and succeeded in gaining the day. This was not accomplished, however, without bloodshed. In order to insure the funeral procession passing through the city, the roads not leading in that direction were blocked and the pavement taken up. At Knights-

---

[1] Journal 94, fos. 337-340b.   [2] Annual Register lxii, 491-492.
[3] Journal House of Commons lxxvi, 24, 73.
[4] Journal 95, fos. 327, 327b, 331-331b.

bridge the mob came into collision with the military quartered in the barracks there. Stones and mud were freely thrown, and the guards were tempted at last to fire on the mob, killing two of their number. After the procession had passed through the city, with the lord mayor at its head, it was allowed to continue its course without further opposition. This took place on Tuesday, the 14th August.[1]

On the 26th, when the funeral procession of the two men shot by the military had to pass in front of Knightsbridge barracks, another disgraceful scene occurred. Waithman, who was sheriff at the time, fearing lest the sight of soldiers outside the barracks might infuriate the people, had taken the precaution of asking the officers in command to keep their men within the gates until the procession had gone by, but the only answer he got was that "the sheriff "might be d—d, they would not make their men "prisoners for him." In the course of the day Waithman himself was struck. This led to a long correspondence with Lord Bathurst, one of the principal secretaries of state, but the sheriff failed to get any redress. The Common Council instituted an enquiry, and upheld his action.[2] The Court of Aldermen ignored the whole affair, but one of their number, viz., Sir William Curtis, a member for the City, made a violent speech in the House against the Common Council for having dared to institute an enquiry. The alderman himself was a member

The sheriff assaulted by the military, 26 Aug., 1821.

---

[1] Annual Register lxiii, 127.

[2] Journal 95, fos. 332, 370-375; Journal 96, fos. 21-22. After Waithman's death, in 1833, an obelisk was erected to his memory in Ludgate Circus, opposite to that erected to commemorate the mayoralty of Wilkes in 1775.

of the General Purposes Committee to which the matter had been referred, but did not attend its meetings. The Common Council voted his speech a gross and injurious reflection upon the members of the Corporation and an unfounded calumny upon the committee.[1]

The City and the Holy Alliance, 1823-1824.

The citizens appreciated too well the blessings of freedom not to sympathise with the struggles of others to obtain it, and they looked askance at the Holy Alliance which had been formed with the view of dictating to the rest of the world. In their eyes "national independence is to states what liberty is to individuals," and that being so the Common Council readily voted two sums of £1,000 to assist Spain and Greece in throwing off their respective yokes.[2] In 1823 the relations between the City and Spain, then threatened by France, were of such a friendly nature that a proposal was actually made to set up, in the centre of Moorfields, a statue of Don Rafael Del Riego, a patriotic Spanish general, who had lost his life in the cause.[3] In the following year (1824) the City again raised its voice against the pretensions of the Holy Alliance, and opposed the renewal of the Alien Act, mainly on the ground that its renewal would appear to countenance the action of the allies "against the "independence of nations and the rights and liberties "of mankind."[4]

Revival of trade followed by wild speculation, 1825-1826.

A revival of commerce, which commenced in 1821, was succeeded in 1825 by an era of wild speculation such as had not been seen since the days of the South

---

[1] Journal 96, fos. 101-102.
[2] Journal 97, fos. 168b, 170-171b, 172b-173b.
[3] *Id.*, fos. 313-314.   [4] Journal 98, fos. 40-43.

Sea Bubble. The civic authorities protested against the reckless formation of Joint Stock Companies, but in vain.[1] Before the end of the year a crash came, firms and companies began to break, credit was shaken, trade depressed, and a run on banks took place, resulting in many of them stopping payment altogether. In six weeks between sixty and seventy banks are said to have stopped payment, of which six or seven were London houses. The distress which ensued was widespread, so widespread indeed that it extended to Scotland, and brought to grief that "wizard of the North," whose writings have delighted, and continue to delight, so many thousands, both young and old —Sir Walter Scott. In the city of London the Spitalfield weavers were reduced to such straits that the Corporation had to come to their assistance with a grant of £500.[2] Although the worst was over by the end of 1825, bankruptcies were frequent during the following year, whilst the country was much disturbed by riots and attacks on all kinds of machinery, which the artisan foolishly regarded as the chief cause of all the misery. When Venables, the lord mayor, went out of office (Nov., 1826) and the Common Council passed the usual vote of thanks, they expressly referred to the decision, energy and judgment he had evinced "during a recent period of commercial embarrassment," and the prompt measures he had taken for relieving distress and restoring confidence.[3]

---

[1] Journal 99, fos. 83b-87b; Journal 100, fos. 116-118b.
[2] Journal 100, fo. 76.   [3] *Id.*, fo. 298.

CHAPTER XLIV.

Repeal of Corporation and Test Acts, May, 1828.

In November (1826) a new Parliament met. Of the old city members only one—viz., Matthew Wood, the popular alderman—retained his seat. He was joined by two other aldermen, one of them being the no less popular Waithman, and a commoner. The questions most pressing were Catholic Emancipation and Parliamentary Reform. The latter had been long urged by the City. As regards the emancipation of Catholics, the City had at one time shown considerable opposition. In 1790, the Common Council expressed itself as anxious to strengthen the hands of those friends of the established church who had twice successfully opposed in Parliament the repeal of the Corporation and Test Acts—a necessary preliminary to Catholic emancipation—and had called upon the city members and those of the Common Council who had seats in Parliament, to resist any future attempt that might be made in the same direction.[1] Since that time the citizens had changed their minds, and we find them now (May, 1827), passing resolutions against the iniquity of making the solemn ordinance of the Lord's Supper "a qualification and passport for power," and congratulating the king upon his having placed Canning, a notorious friend of Catholic emancipation, in power.[2]

Canning unfortunately died before he was able to accomplish anything in this direction, and his successor,

[1] Journal 72, fo. 70. [2] Journal 101, fos. 174-177, 180.

Goderich was deficient in moral backbone; but early in 1828 the Duke of Wellington became Prime Minister, and upon a motion made by Lord John Russell, a Bill was introduced for the repeal of the Corporation and Test Acts. A simple declaration that an applicant for office would not compromise the Established Church, was to be substituted for the old sacramental test. During the passage of the Bill through the Lords, the City endeavoured to get certain amendments introduced, for the purpose chiefly of protecting members of the Common Council from incurring penalties and forfeitures imposed by the Bill, but in this they failed.[1] The Bill passed, and a great step towards Catholic emancipation was thus gained. The same principle which prompted the City to urge the repeal of these Acts, also prompted them in later years to petition Parliament, and themselves to pass resolutions in favour of the abolition of unnecessary oaths.[2]

Renewed activity on the part of the Catholic Association in Ireland, and the return of O'Connell for County Clare, hastened Catholic emancipation. The question was taken up by Peel, hitherto an anti-Catholic. He succeeded in winning over the Duke of Wellington, and the latter at last persuaded the king to promise some concession at the opening of Parliament on the 5th February, 1829. The City voted Peel the Freedom in a gold box and thanked the Duke of Wellington.[3] The Common Council at

The Catholic Emancipation Bill, April, 1829.

---

[1] Journal 102, fos. 152–153.
[2] Journal 104, fos. 196b–198b. Journal 106, fos. 236-237, 239b–241b.
[3] Journal 102, fos. 377–377b.

the same time presented addresses to both Houses praying them to support the measures about to be introduced.[1] A Bill, giving effect to the intentions of the Government, was brought in on the 5th March. The king who had reluctantly consented to its introduction resisted to the last, but was compelled to give way, and on the 14th April the Bill became law.

Addresses on accession of William IV, June–July, 1830.

The other pressing question of the day, viz., Parliamentary Reform, awaited settlement under a new king and a new Parliament. On the 26th June, 1830, George IV died, and his eldest surviving brother, the Duke of Clarence, was welcomed by the City as his successor under the title of William IV. The City—both Aldermen and Common Council lost no time in presenting the usual congratulatory addresses,[2] but not a word was said on the subject that was about to move the country from one end to the other. A month later (28th July) the livery prepared a long address, in which, disclaiming "the fulsome strains of unmeaning flattery," such as they declared had been poured into the royal ear "from more than one body of men in the city of London already," they respectfully but firmly laid before the new king a representation of what they believed to be the true state of affairs. The chief grievance of the country, they said, lay in the fact that the great body of the people who paid taxes, had no control whatever over those who falsely called themselves the representatives of the people; and they expressed their long-confirmed and deep-rooted conviction that this and all other evils had arisen from the people not being properly

---

[1] Journal 102, fos. 376–376b.
[2] Journal 104, fo. 201. Repertory 234, fo. 743.

represented in the House of Commons. Notwithstanding former rebuffs they desired that their address should be received by the king on his throne. As this could not be—although the king expressed his willingness to receive it at the next levée, or through the secretary of state—the address was not presented at all.[1]

The accession of a new king necessitated the dissolution of Parliament and fresh elections. These took place amid great excitement, for already the country was agitating by means of political unions for Parliamentary reform. At their close it was found that the Government, although losing many seats, still retained a majority. No change was made in the city members. *A General Election, July, 1830.*

When parliament met on the 2nd November, the country was on the tip-toe of expectation as to what the ministry would do. Would the Duke of Wellington continue to ignore the manifest will of the nation or would he give way? He did the first. He not only declared that the country was satisfied with the existing state of things, but he pledged himself to oppose any measure of Parliamentary reform that might be proposed by others. Here was a distinct challenge to the reformers, a challenge which they were not slow to take up. That same night Brougham, who had been returned to Parliament for Yorkshire, free of expense, gave notice that on the 16th, he would bring forward a motion for reform. Before that day arrived the ministry had resigned. *Opening of the new parliament, 2 Nov., 1830.*

In the meanwhile, the new king had received a cordial invitation to dine at the Guildhall on any *The king's visit to the city postponed.*

---

[1] Common Hall Book,·No. 10, fos. 274–280, 283–284.

day most convenient, and his majesty had graciously accepted the invitation, and had named the 9th November, lord mayor's day.[1] He chose that day for the reason probably that it was customary for a new sovereign to honour the citizens with his presence on the first lord mayor's day after his accession. Extensive preparations had already been made to give the king a befitting reception, when on the 7th November, Sir Robert Peel informed the outgoing mayor by letter, that his majesty had been advised to forego his visit to the city, for fear lest his presence might give occasion to riot and tumult, and endanger the property and lives of his subjects. The fact was, that the lord mayor elect (Sir John Key) had, on his own responsibility, written to the Duke of Wellington warning him of danger. A copy of his letter was read before the Common Council on the 8th, when exception was taken to it as being "indiscreet and unauthorised." After considerable debate, a resolution was at length drawn up to the effect that in the opinion of the court "neither riot nor commo-"tion was to be apprehended had his majesty and his "royal consort . . . condescended to honour the "city of London with their presence ; and that had "evil disposed and disaffected persons made attempts "to excite commotion or disturbance on that occasion, "the most perfect reliance might have been placed "on the good feeling and spontaneous exertions of the "great mass of the population of London to co-"operate with the civil power in effectually suppressing "such attempts and preserving the public tranquility."[2] This was all very well. Nevertheless, in spite of all

[1] Journal 104, fos. 321-322, 323.   [2] *Id.*, fos. 364b-366.

precautions taken by the civic authorities, and although the king and his ministers, who had given so much offence by opposing the popular will, refrained from entering the city, an affray actually took place at Temple Bar, in which one of the city marshals was severely wounded in the head.[1]

On the 15th November, the day that the Wellington ministry received its *coup de grace*, a Common Council was summoned to sit at the Mansion House, in order to consider Brougham's motion, which was to be made in parliament the following day. It then passed the following resolutions :—[2]

Resolutions of Co. Co. re Reform, 15 Nov., 1830.

" RESOLVED that this court, as the representative
" body of the citizens of London, having at various
" times expressed its opinion of the propriety and
" necessity of a revision of the present state of the
" representation of the commons in parliament, is
" called upon in an especial manner at the present
" moment (after the declaration of the first minister
" of the crown, that the representation is satisfactory
" to the country), to make a renewed avowal of its
" conviction that the House of Commons as at present
" constituted is as far from being satisfactory to the
" country as it is from being a real representation
" of the people.

" RESOLVED that the power now exercised by
" various peers and other interested persons of return-
" ing a large portion of the members, is wholly incom-
" patible with the true end and design of a House of
" Commons, which in principle and in practice, ought
" to be a representation not of a private, but of general

[1] Repertory 235, fo. 13.   [2] Journal 104, fo. 374.

"interests, an effectual control upon taxation and "the public expenditure, and the organ by which the "commons of the realm may fully exercise that share "in the legislature to which, by the constitution they "are entitled.

"RESOLVED that petitions founded upon these "resolutions, be forthwith presented to both Houses "of Parliament, praying them to institute a full and "faithful inquiry into the state of the representation "with the view to the remedying of such defects therein "as time and various encroachments have produced, "so as to give real effect to the essential principles of "the constitution, namely, that members of parlia- "ment shall be freely chosen, that peers shall not "interfere in elections, and that in the House of "Commons, the king may with truth, be said to meet "his people in parliament." Before the petitions could be laid before parliament,[1] the ministry had resigned.

The Reform Bill introduced, 1 March, 1831.

The new prime minister was Lord Grey, who, as a young man, had urged the necessity of parliamentary reform as early as 1792. Among those who were content to accept office under the new ministry, although in an inferior capacity, was Lord John Russell, who had also done good service for the cause, and who was now to be entrusted with the task of introducing the long looked for Bill. On the 1st March (1831) the first Reform Bill, which for the last sixty years the City had been anxiously

---

[1] The petition to the commons was presented on the 16th Nov.—the day that the Duke of Wellington resigned; that to the lords on the 25th.—Journal House of Commons, lxxxvi, pt. I, 87; Journal House of Lords, lxiii, 128.

awaiting, and for which it had agitated with all the forces at its command, was at length brought in.

As soon as the provisions of the Bill became known the Common Council, who had hitherto refrained from expressing any opinion upon the nature of the change that had taken place in the ministry, hastened to express their satisfaction to the king at the policy adopted by his new ministers;— "We beg to assure your Majesty that having long "entertained a deep and increasing conviction of the "necessity of a reform in the representation of the "people in the Commons House of Parliament, we "have looked forward with the greatest anxiety to "the course which your Majesty's ministers would "adopt in reference to that important subject; and "we now feel ourselves imperatively called upon, "humbly and dutifully, to express to your Majesty "our entire satisfaction at the principles of the "measure that has been introduced, under their "sanction, to the Honorable House of Commons."[1] The livery, too, presented an address in much the same terms, although by the provisions of the Bill non-resident liverymen were threatened with exclusion from the franchise. The Bill, they said, afforded a clear proof of the sincerity and honesty of his majesty's ministers, and entitled them to the best thanks and lasting gratitude of the country. They further presented addresses in the same strain to both Houses of Parliament.[2] The Court of Aldermen, on the other hand, were as little enamoured of reform as the Lords, and thought it best to say nothing beyond

The Bill approved by Common Council and Livery.

---

[1] Journal 105, fo. 133.
[2] Common Hall Book, No. 10, fos. 295-299.

what they were committed to in the address of the Common Council.

<small>Dissolution of Parliament, 22 April, 1831.</small> The debate on the first reading lasted seven nights. When the second reading came on the Bill passed, but only by a bare majority. A hostile amendment was subsequently carried in committee by a majority of eight, and thereupon the government withdrew the Bill, and Parliament was dissolved in order that the question might be submitted to the country (22 April). A special Court of Common Council was summoned to meet on the 27th, when the committee which had been recently appointed to watch the proceedings in Parliament relative to the Bill, reported the fact of the dissolution, and recommended the City to place on record its "cordial gratitude" to the king for having thus given the country an opportunity of expressing its wishes. A resolution was thereupon passed to that effect. This was followed by another resolution expressing a fervent hope that at the general election about to take place all minor considerations might give way to the one great duty of promoting the country's welfare, and that only such members would be returned as would unequivocally pledge themselves to support his majesty's ministers in carrying the great question of reform to a successful issue. By so doing they would overthrow "a faction arrayed in "hostility against the liberties of their country, and "seeking to maintain themselves in the usurpation of "a power unknown to the constitution, and no less "injurious to the prerogatives of the Crown than dis- "tinctive to the legitimate rights of the People."[1] The

---

[1] Journal 105, fos. 258–259b.

lord mayor had already received notice that in view of the elections which were to take place in the city on the 29th orders had been given that no troops should enter or be quartered in the city for one day at least previous to the day of election nor until one day at least after the closing of the poll. These steps were taken pursuant to Stat. 8 George II, c. 30, but the Court of Aldermen affected some surprise and the Town Clerk was instructed to ascertain whether similar orders had usually been given on the occasion of previous elections.[1]

The elections, which were carried on amid the greatest excitement, and no little riot and disorder, proved strongly in favour of the reformers. In the city the three aldermen, viz., Wood, Waithman and Thompson, who sat in the last Parliament, were again returned, but Willliam Ward, who had been one of the city's representatives since 1826, was strongly advised not to put up again for fear of some personal violence being offered him,[2] and his seat was taken by Venables, another alderman. The Bill, in a slightly amended form, was again brought in, and eventually passed the Commons (21 Sept.). *The Reform Bill passes the Commons, 21 Sept., 1831.*

The livery of London, as well as the Common Council, had been anxious to petition the Lords to give their assent to the Bill, even before it had left the Commons. The livery, indeed, had drafted their petition two days before the Bill passed the Commons.[3] The Common Council were less precipitate, and waited until the 27th before they drew up their petition.[4] The *The Bill rejected by the Lords, 8 Oct.*

---

[1] Repertory 235, fos. 376, 377.   [2] Annual Register lxxiii, 154.
[3] Common Hall Book, No. 10, fos. 304-306.
[4] Journal 105, fos. 376-377, 379b-380, 387b-389.

Court of Aldermen again kept silence. The country waited with anxiety to see what the Lords would do. It had not long to wait. On the first reading the Bill was thrown out by a majority of forty-one (8 Oct.).

City address to the king on rejection of Bill by Lords, 8 Oct., 1831.

The opponents of the measure believed and hoped that the fate of the ministry was now sealed. The day that the Bill was rejected by the Lords another Common Council was summoned for the purpose of taking into consideration what under the circumstances was best to be done. It forthwith resolved to draw up an address to the king expressive of the City's bitter disappointment at the Lords "having turned a deaf " ear to the nation's voice, and thrown out the great " Bill for consolidating the peace, prosperity and " liberties of the people," and of its continued confidence in his majesty's ministers. The address concluded with a solemn warning that unless the country received some assurance that a Bill, similar to that which had been just rejected, would soon be passed, nothing could prevent "the most fearful national commotions."[1]

The king's reply, 12 Oct.

The king received the address very graciously and thanked the City for its expressions of confidence and loyalty. He assured the citizens of his desire to uphold the just rights of the people, and of his determination to further the promotion of such measures as might seem best calculated for that purpose; and he concluded by recommending those present to use all their influence with their fellow citizens for the purpose of preventing acts of violence and commotion.[2]

---

[1] Journal 105, fos. 389b–391b.   [2] *Id.*, fo. 392.

The livery were scarcely less prompt in assuring the king of their loyalty, and their confidence in the existing government:—"We venture humbly to "represent to your majesty our belief that under "the present trying and difficult circumstances, the "security of public credit and the preservation of "the public peace depend upon their continuance "in office." No other ministers, they went on to say, would possess the same esteem and confidence of the country, and they only were in a position to carry the Bill.[1] At the same time they passed a vote of thanks to the ministers "for their honest, firm, and patriotic course of conduct."

Address of the livery, 10 Oct., 1831.

The City's prognostications of evil arising out of the Lords' refusal to bow to the will of the nation were fully justified. The streets of London and other large towns became the scenes of disorderly riots. At Derby the houses of those opposed to reform were attacked by the mob and their windows smashed. The ancient castle of Nottingham, once a royal residence, was fired and reduced to a pile of smoking ruins. At Birmingham a meeting was held at which those who were present pledged themselves to pay no taxes if the Reform Bill were again rejected,[2] whilst at Bristol, nearly a whole square was burnt by the mob.[3] The political unions that had sprung up all over the country resolved to increase their strength by the formation of a National Political Union, which should have its headquarters in London. To this end, a meeting was

Agitation in the country, Oct.-Nov., 1831.

---

[1] Common Hall Book, No. 10, fo. 312.
[2] Annual Register lxxiii, 281, 282.   [3] *Id.*, lxxiii, 291-294.

held in Lincoln's Inn Fields, on the 31st of October, with Sir Francis Burdett in the chair. The proceedings, however, took such a radical turn that before long Burdett withdrew his name from the association. The government, too, became alarmed at the prospect of a meeting announced to be held on the 7th November. Orders were given to swear in special constables, the whole of the recently established (1829) police force was to be held in readiness, and a large body of troops was quartered in the neighbourhood of the capital ready to put down any disturbance that might arise. On the 4th November —three days before the proposed meeting—a royal proclamation was read before the Court of Aldermen calling upon all his majesty's liege subjects to assist the civil magistrates in putting down disturbances as soon as any should appear, and to aid in the preservation of the peace. Thereupon a resolution was passed to the effect that each member of the Court in his respective ward should immediately enroll and swear in a number of special constables to assist the magistracy upon any tumult, riot, outrage or breach of the peace occurring within the city.[1] Thanks to the precautions thus taken, and to the advice given to the leaders of the movement by Lord Melbourne, the meeting was not held.[2]

Votes of thanks to Sir John Key, mayor, Nov., 1831.

On the 9th November, Sir John Key, the lord mayor, entered upon his second year of office, having been re-elected by the livery, and forced upon the

---

[1] Repertory 235, fos. 711-714.
[2] Annual Register lxxiii, 296, 297.

THE BILL AGAIN BROUGHT IN.

Court of Aldermen for a second term.[1] The Common Council, as was usual, acknowledged his services of the past year, and more particularly his "vigilant superintendence of the police," which had conduced so much to the peace of the city, with a formal vote of thanks.[2] Two days previously (15 Nov.), when a similar vote had been proposed in the Court of Aldermen, it failed to pass for lack of a *quorum*,[3] and the matter was allowed to drop. The livery had already tendered him their thanks, not only for the zeal he had displayed in the cause of parliamentary reform, but also for his consenting to undertake another year of office and for upholding the election rights of the livery against the "secret tribunal" of the Court of Aldermen.[4]

On the 12th December (1831) the Bill was again brought in by Lord John Russell and on the 23rd March (1832), it passed the Commons. The second reading of the Bill took place in the Lords on the 14th April, and was carried by a majority of nine; after which both Houses rose for the Easter recess. Before they met again the Common Council had voted Earl Grey and Viscount Althorp, the chancellor of the exchequer, the Freedom of the City, (both of whom graciously acknowledged the

Lords Grey and Althorp voted the Freedom of the City, 26 April, 1832.

---

[1] On Michaelmas-day the livery returned Key and Alderman Thorp. The Court of Aldermen selected Thorp, but he declined to take office. At a subsequent election the livery again returned Key and with him Alderman Thompson. The Court of Aldermen thereupon called upon Thompson, but he also declined to serve, and a third election had to take place. Again Key was returned, together with Alderman Kelly, and the Court of Aldermen finding the livery bent on having their own way, selected Key.—Common Hall Book, No. 10, fos. 308-310, 313-320.

[2] Journal 106, fo. 1.   [3] Repertory 236, fos. 4, 5.

[4] Common Hall Book, No. 10, fo. 320.

compliment), and had drawn up a petition to the Lords, to be presented by the Duke of Sussex, praying them to pass the Bill with the least possible delay.[1]

Resignation of the ministry, 9 May, 1832.

When, after the recess, the Bill came again before the Lords (7 May), the government found themselves beaten on an amendment introduced by Lord Lyndhurst, who had been chancellor in Wellington's ministry.[2] Grey who had been constantly urged to advise the king to create a sufficient number of new peers to insure the passing of the Bill, now asked him to cut the Gordian knot by the creation of fifty new peers. The king, however, was becoming frightened at the determined attitude of the country, and declined. Thereupon the minister tendered his resignation (9 May).

City petition to Parliament, 10 May, 1832.

The news that the ministers had resigned was received with howls of indignation throughout the country. The papers appeared with a black edge of deep mourning. The National Union decreed that whoever should advise a dissolution was an enemy to the country. The day following the resignation of the government a special Court of Common Council met and drew up a petition to the House of Commons, expressing their mortification and disappointment at finding that his majesty had refused his ministers the means of carrying the Bill through the House of Lords. They, too, like the National Union, were of opinion that whoever advised his majesty to withhold from his ministers the means of ensuring the success of the Reform Bill, had proved themselves the enemies of their sovereign, and had "put to im-

---

[1] Journal 106, fos. 245b–248.   [2] Annual Register lxxiv, 155.

"minent hazard the stability of the throne, and the "tranquillity and security of the country," and they prayed the House to withhold all supplies until the Bill had passed.[1] The city members and those of the Common Council who had seats in Parliament were urged to support the prayer of the petition, and to decline voting any supplies until the Reform Bill should have been satisfactorily secured, and a joint committee of all the aldermen and commoners of the city was appointed to sit from day to day, to promote the object they had so much at heart.[2]

The next day (11 May), the livery met in Common Hall and drew up an address to the king. The defeat of the Bill, to pass which the electors of the country had specially sent their representatives to Parliament—the defeat of the Bill by a small majority in the House of Lords, had (they said), "spread terror and dismay" among his majesty's subjects, and threatened the credit, the tranquillity, the institutions of the country. At such a crisis the livery of London could not do less than pray his majesty to "adopt such measures as are provided by the constitution" (in other words, create a sufficient number of peers) for the purpose of removing all obstacles to the Bill.[3] Not content with appealing to the king, they called upon the House of Commons to exercise their right, given them for the good and welfare of the nation, and to refuse any further supplies until the Bill should have become law.[4] They, further, passed a number of resolutions upholding the conduct of Lord Grey and his colleagues

Proceedings of Common Hall, 11 May, 1832.

---

[1] Journal 106, fos. 275–276.   [2] *Id.*, fo. 276b.
[3] Common Hall Book, No. 10, fos. 327–332.   [4] *Id.*, fos. 332–333.

in the ministry, and condemning those, who like the Duke of Wellington and others, were at that moment attempting "to mislead and delude the people by pretended plans of reform," after defeating "the people's Bill."[1]

<small>Another City address to the king, 14 May, 1832.</small>

For a whole week the country was kept in a state of suspense, anxiously waiting to see whether the Duke of Wellington, who had declared his willingness to accept office and to give his support to a less complete measure of reform, would succeed in forming an administration or not. Whilst negotiations were being carried on the Common Council met (14 May), and drew up a long and strongly-worded address ending with a declaration that they—the lord mayor, aldermen and Common Council of the city of London —would be wanting in their duty to themselves and to posterity, if they did not express their overwhelming sorrow at the resignation of his majesty's late honest ministers, and their serious apprehension that unless Lord Grey and his colleagues were promptly recalled and allowed to pass the Reform Bill unmutilated and unimpaired, the country would witness those "calamities which have affected other nations when struggling to be free."[2] There would, in fact, be a revolution, such as had been witnessed in France at the close of the last century.

<small>Re-call of Earl Grey's ministry, 18 May, 1832.</small>

When the sheriffs applied for an appointment to be made for the reception of the address, they were put off from time to time. Thereupon, the matter was taken up by the recently appointed joint committee, and on the 18th, they had an interview

---

[1] Common Hall Book, No. 10, fos. 328–329.
[2] Journal 106, fos. 280b–283.

with Earl Grey, but by that time matters had been accommodated, and there was no longer any occasion for presenting the address. The Duke of Wellington had three days before (15 May), communicated to the king his inability to form a ministry, and on the evening of the 18th, formal announcement was made to both houses that Earl Grey and his colleagues had been re-called and were in a position to carry through the Bill unimpaired in efficiency and without mutilation.[1] The Common Council took an early opportunity of expressing their utmost satisfaction at the turn of affairs, and passed resolutions to that effect, which were ordered to be delivered to the secretary of state, and also to be published in all the morning and evening newspapers.[2]

The question naturally arose whence this confidence of the re-called ministry? Was the House of Lords to be swamped by the creation of a batch of new peers, or had an arrangement been made for securing the withdrawal of the requisite number of opposition peers? The answer was soon forthcoming. When the Bill again came before the lords, the Duke of Wellington left the house, and was followed by about a hundred other peers. The bishops withdrew in a body, and the Bill, with some trifling alterations, which the Commons readily accepted, was passed by a large majority (4 June), and three days later received the royal assent. *The Reform Bill becomes law, 7 June, 1832.*

The Bill as introduced in December last, had to undergo some alterations in order that the proposed plan of reform might embrace the livery franchise *The rights of the livery saved.*

---

[1] Journal 106, fos. 326b–328. Annual Register lxxiv, 175, 185.
[2] Journal 106, fos. 328–328b.

peculiar to the city of London. The necessity of amendments in this direction did not escape the attention of the committee appointed on the 21st April (1831), to watch the course of the Reform Bill and to give support to Earl Grey's ministry; and the day after the Bill had received the royal assent, this committee had the satisfaction of reporting to the Common Council that the most important of the amendments proposed by them had been adopted and introduced in the Act.[1]

Celebration of Reform at Guildhall, 11 July, 1832.

The citizens were immensely pleased at the success which, after so long a struggle, had at last attended their efforts to secure a better representation of the people in the House of Commons. The measure was not and could not be final, but it was a step, and a long step in the right direction, and as such, the Common Council resolved that it should be publicly celebrated, and honour given to those to whom honour was due in effecting its accomplishment. An Irish and a Scottish Reform Bill were still before parliament, but as the passing of these measures was looked upon as a foregone conclusion, they were not allowed to stand in the way of the City's proposed celebration of the passing of the English Bill. Earl Grey and Lord Althorp had not yet received the Freedom of the City voted in April last. It was therefore arranged that the Freedom should be conferred upon these ministers with all the pomp and ceremony that befitted the occasion on Wednesday, the 11th July,[2] and that

[1] Journal 106, fos. 377–377b.
[2] Just a twelvemonth had elapsed since the freedom had been conferred on Lord John Russell (9 July, 1831), for undertaking the introduction of the Reform Bill. Ten years later (1841), he was returned as one of the members for the city, and continued to represent it until his elevation to the peerage.

the presentation should be followed by an entertainment at the Guildhall, given to all those members of the House of Commons who had voted for the third reading of the Bill, as well as to those peers who had voted against Lord Lyndhurst's amendment, and such other noblemen and gentlemen as had lent their aid to the cause. In acknowledging the honour conferred upon him Earl Grey paid befitting tribute to the City's influence in the commercial world, its loyalty to the constitution, and its love of freedom "never more conspicuously manifested" than during recent events.[1] A book containing the autographs of the principal guests, among whom was the Duke of Sussex, is preserved in the Guildhall library, as well as a medal struck in commemoration of the passing of the Bill.[2]

With this signal triumph of the people, to which the city of London had contributed so much, the present work is brought to a close. No good end would be served by entering the domain of contemporary politics. Enough has been set out in these pages to convince the impartial reader that the city of London is no mean city; that it possesses a record equal, if not indeed superior, to that of any other city in the Universe, ancient or modern, and that its wealth and influence have ever been devoted to the cause of religious, social and political freedom. Notwithstanding anything its detractors may say, the City has not only marched with the age, it has for the most part been a leader of public opinion, and has shown itself in advance of the

A retrospect.

---

[1] Journal 106, fos. 378–379b. Journal 107, fos. 119b–129b.

[2] For description of this medal and of other medals struck from time to time by order of the Corporation, see *Numismata Londinensia*, edited with descriptive notes by Mr. Charles Welch, F.S.A., the Guildhall Librarian, (London, 1894).

age. It is to three notable aldermen of the city, viz., Oliver, Crosby, and Wilkes, be it remembered, that the country is indebted for the liberty of the press, and the freedom of reporting Parliamentary debates, so long jealously withheld. Had it not been for the determined attitude of these aldermen the country might have waited still longer for Parliament to be brought to realise that its proceedings are (so to speak) public property. It was Wilkes, again, and his brother aldermen who made a successful stand against the pernicious, if lawful, custom of pressing men for the king's service, the result being that whilst the rest of the kingdom was over-run with press-gangs, the city of London was quit of them, or if any ventured to seize the person of a citizen, they were soon made to surrender their prey.

Enfranchisement of Jews.

If other evidence, beyond what appears in these pages, were wanting in proof of the enlightened policy pursued by the Corporation of London, it will be found in the fact that Jews were enfranchised and admitted into the city's council and to all municipal offices long before they gained admission into the council of the nation. In December, 1830, the Common Council passed a Bill for extending the Freedom of the City to all natural born subjects, not professing the Christian religion but in other respects qualified, upon their taking the Freeman's oath according to the forms of their own religion.[1] Five years later David Salomons, a Jew, was admitted to the shrievalty. In 1847 he was elected alderman, and in 1855 became lord mayor. In the meanwhile, repeated attempts had been made to get Parliament to pass a Bill for altering the oaths of allegiance and supremacy, in such a manner that

[1] Journal 105, fos. 5–6.

Jews might be relieved of the necessity of making a declaration "upon the true faith of a Christian." The House of Commons had again and again passed Bills to this effect, but they had always been rejected by the Lords, who steadily refused to give their assent to the admission of Jews, notwithstanding the entreaties of the city of London.[1] The election of Alderman Salomons to the mayoralty was regarded by the livery of London as "a triumph to liberal principles," and as affording a prospect "of the ultimate triumph of the "cause of toleration by the admission of the members "of the Jewish persuasion to the legislature, and the "highest offices of the State."[2] Their hopes were now destined to be soon realised. A compromise was at last effected, and three years later (23 July, 1858), a Bill was passed allowing either House by a resolution to modify the form of oath required from its members.

For years the City had been content to suffer for its principles. Ever since 1847 it had continued to return a Jew to Parliament, in the person of Baron Lionel Rothschild, in spite of the fact that he was not allowed to take his seat. As soon however as the Bill became law, the House of Commons passed the necessary resolution, and on the 26th April the Baron took his seat, and the City recovered its full representation in Parliament. Both Alderman Salomons and Baron Rothschild commemorated their respective victories by endowing scholarships in the City of London School, open to candidates of every religious persuasion; and a like scholarship was founded by a

Baron Rothschild, M.P., for the City.

---

[1] Journal 126, fo. 31. Journal 127, fo. 345. Journal 129, fo. 379.
[2] Common Hall Book, No. 10, fo. 637.

committee known as the "Committee of the Jewish Commemoration Fund."[1]

The City's finances.   The city of London was, as we have seen, known in earliest times as the king's "Chamber," and the Chamberlain was the king's officer. The City in fact served as the purse of the nation, until such time as the establishment of the Bank of England did away with the necessity of direct applications to the Corporation for loans, to enable the government of the kingdom to be carried on. Like the nation itself, the City has had its times of pecuniary distress, and nothing but the most careful nursing of its estate has enabled it to tide over its difficulties. More especially was this the case at the close of the civil war, and again, for some years after the Great Fire, as well as at the commencement of the reign of Queen Anne.

The City's public spirit.   The City has not wasted its substance. Large sums have been expended upon local improvements, upon the erection of markets, upon bridges, not forgetting that latest marvel of engineering skill, the Tower Bridge, upon the City's schools, upon the erection of the Guildhall library with its adjacent Museum and Art Gallery, as well as upon the establishment and maintenance of one of the most successful Schools of Music ever known in this country. At the close of the year 1882, the Corporation had, within a comparatively recent period, expended nearly six and a half millions, out of its own funds, upon improvements within the city and liberties—improvements which benefited the inhabitants of the metropolis generally no less than the citizens

---

[1] Hust. Roll, 372 (2), 373 (3), (4).

themselves.[1] Nor has the Corporation stayed its hand at the city's boundaries. During the short period of ten years preceding 1882, a sum of more than £300,000 was expended out of the city's cash for providing open spaces for the people, including Epping Forest, Wanstead Park, West Ham Park, and Burnham Beeches, but irrespective of the later acquisitions of Coulsdon and other adjacent commons in the county of Surrey, since dedicated to the public.[2] An area exceeding 6,000 acres in all, has thus been preserved for posterity and placed beyond risk of purprestures and encroachments.

From the time when the Metropolitan Board of Works was first established in 1855, down to its disestablishment in 1889, the Corporation contributed large sums of money to assist that body in carrying out the stupendous work of the Thames Embankment, a work of which Londoners may well be proud, and were engaged jointly with the Board in freeing from toll the bridges of Staines, Walton, Hampton Court, Kingston and Kew, on the Thames, as well as Tottenham Mills and Chingford bridges on the Lea. *The City and the Metropolitan Board of Works.*

Since the abolition of the coal and wine dues in 1889, the whole of which had been devoted to carrying out improvements, erecting public buildings, and freeing bridges, in and near the metropolis,[3] the work of the Corporation, as well as of the London County Council *Abolition of coal and wine dues, 1889.*

---

[1] See prefatory note to returns made by the Chamberlain pursuant to an order of the Court of Common Council, 26 Oct., 1882. (*Printed.*)

[2] Chamberlain's returns (*Sup.*).—"Expenditure for benefit of metropolis, etc." pp. 12, 13.

[3] For a list of metropolitan improvements and public works carried out by means of these dues, see "Ten years' growth of the City of London"—being a report of local government and taxation committee of the Corporation (1891), James Salmon, Esq., Chairman, pp. 130-139.

(the successor to the Metropolitan Board of Works), in this direction has been sorely crippled. It was popularly supposed that the coal dues affected the price of coal and gas, and that as soon as the dues were abolished the price of these commodities would at once go down. The result has proved to be far otherwise. An income of more than half a million sterling, produced in such a way as to afford the minimum of burden to the taxpayer, and expended in such a way as to produce the maximum of benefit to the whole of the metropolis, has been lost to the City and the London County Council, whilst the consumer not only pays the same price as before for his coal and gas (the middle-man pocketing the tax), but finds himself saddled with an increased rate.

The City as Port sanitary authority. One more remark and we have done. As conservators of the river Thames, the Corporation did much to improve its navigation, but in 1857 the conservancy was taken away from the City and became vested in a board. In 1872, however, the Corporation became the sanitary authority of the Port of London under somewhat remarkable circumstances. When the Public Health Bill of that year was framed, the Local Government Board long hesitated as to whom the duty of acting as the sanitary authority of the Port of London should be committed. At the last moment the Corporation stept in and volunteered to undertake the duty free of expense. The government readily accepted the offer, and to this patriotic act on the part of the municipality as well as to the energy of its executive officers, it is largely due that this vast metropolis enjoys comparative immunity from cholera and zymotic diseases and that the city itself, besides being the best paved and the best lighted, is also the most healthy city in the civilised world.

END OF VOL III.

APPENDIX A.

TABLE OF CONTENTS.

No. 1. Reply from the City to a letter from King Henry V (Printed in *Memorials*), asking for wine and provisions for the army at Rouen. Dated 8 Sept. [1418].

No. 2. Proclamation for speeding men to the English army in Normandy. [1418.]

No. 3. Letter from King Henry V to the City, notifying the capture of Pontoise. Dated Mantes, 5 Aug. [1419].

No. 4. Reply to the above. Dated 6 Sept. [1419].

No. 5. Letter from the Duke of Clarence to the City on the same subject. Dated Mantes, 5 Aug. [1419].

No. 6. Reply to the above. Dated 6 Sept. [1419].

No. 7. Letter from Henry V to the City, informing the citizens of his movements in France. Dated Mantes, 12 July [1421].

No. 8. Reply to the above. Dated 2 Aug. [1421].

No. 9. Letter from the Duke of Bedford to the City, claiming the government of the realm at the death of Henry V. Dated Rouen, 26 Oct. [1422].

No. 10. Letter from the Mayor and Aldermen of the City to the Duke of Bedford. No date [1424].

No. 11. Another letter from the same to the same. No date [1424].

No. 12. Letter from the Earl of Salisbury and of Perche to the City, announcing the success of the war in France. Dated 5 Sept. [1428].

No. 13. Reply to the above. Dated 12 Oct. [1428].

No. 14. Letter from Henry VI to the City, asking for a loan. Dated Rouen, 10 Nov. [1430].

No. 15. Letter from Cardinal Beaufort, notifying the Mayor, Sheriffs and Aldermen of the City, of his intention to return forthwith to England. Dated Ghent, 13 April [1432].

No. 16. Letter from the Mayor and Aldermen of Calais to the City of London, asking for assistance. Dated 27 June [1436].

No. 17. Letter from Henry VI to the Mayor, Aldermen and Sheriffs of London, touching the peace of the City. Dated Lichfield, 3 Sept., 35 Hen. VI [1456].

No. 18. Letter from the same to the City, ordering the seizure of certain ships of war in the Thames. Dated Coventry, 10 March [1456-7].

No. 19. Letter from the same to the same, touching the peace of the City. Dated Kenilworth, 22 March [1456-7].

No. 20. Letter from the City to Henry VI, touching the capture of Sandwich by the French. Dated 3 Sept. [1457].

No. 21. Reply to the above. Dated Northampton, 5 Sept. [1457].

No. 22. Reply of Bishop Waynfleete, the Chancellor, to letter from the City, similar to No. 20 *supra*. Dated Waltham, 5 Sept. [1457].

No. 23. Letter from the Earl of Kendal, Lord Scales and others besieged in the Tower, to the Lord Mayor, asking why war was being made upon them. No date [*circ.* July, 1460].

No. 24. Reply to the above. No date.

No. 25. Agreement touching the surrender of the Tower by the Earl of Kendal, Lord Scales and others. Dated 16 July, 38 Hen. VI [1460].

No. 26. Minutes of the proceedings of the Common Council upon the return of the Earl of Warwick to England and the flight of King Edward IV. October, 1470.

No. 27. Letter from Thomas Fauconberge (commonly known as the "bastard Falconbridge,") to the City, declaring his peaceable intentions towards the City. Dated Sittingbourne, 8 May [1471].

No. 28. Reply to the above. Dated 9 May [1471].

No. 29. Account of the invasion of the City by the Kentish rebels. 12 May, 1471.

No. 30. Letter from King Henry VII to the City, announcing the betrothal of his daughter, the Princess Mary, to Charles of Castile. Dated Richmond, 28 Dec. [1507].

No. 31. Petition of Dean Colet to the Common Council that he might be allowed to purchase certain lands and tenements for the purpose of enlarging his school; 15th Jan., 3 Henry VIII [1511-12].

No. 32. Letter from Henry VIII to the City, desiring 300 men for the navy against a threatened invasion by the King of France. Dated Greenwich, 30 Jan. [1512-13].

APPENDIX A.—CONTENTS. 355

No. 33. Letter from Cardinal Wolsey to the City, touching a loan of 4,000 marks. Dated 3 Sept. [1522].

No. 34. Letter from Henry VIII to the City requesting a benevolence. Dated Greenwich, 25 April [1525].

No. 35. Order of obsequies to be celebrated in the City on the death of the Lady Jane Seymour, 10 Nov., 1537.

No. 36. Extract from letter from Sir Richard Gresham to Thomas Cromwell, lord Privy Seal, touching the purchase of certain houses in Lombard Street belonging to Alderman Monoux, for the purpose of a site for an Exchange. Dated 25 July [1538].

No. 37. Letter from Henry VIII to Alderman Monoux, desiring him to part with the property above-mentioned. Dated Chichester, 13 Aug. [1538].

No. 38. Another letter from the same to the same, on the same subject. No date.

No. 39. Letter of thanks from Henry VIII to Alderman Monoux for acceeding to the King's former request. Dated Westminster, 25 Nov. [1538].

No. 40. Proclamation of Henry VIII, forbidding public hunting and hawking in the suburbs of London. Dated Westminster, 7 July, 37 Hen. VIII [1545].

No. 41. Letter from King Edward VI and the Protector Somerset to the City, asking for a force of 1,000 men as a protection against conspirators. Dated Hampton Court, 6 Oct. [1549].

No. 42. Letter from Lords of the Council to the City, touching the conduct of the Duke of Somerset. Dated 6 Oct. [1549].

No. 43. Letter from Queen Mary to the City, desiring a contingent of 1,000 men to be ready for active service at a day's notice. Dated Richmond, 31 July, 1557.

No. 44. Another letter from the same to the same, asking for 500 men to be immediately despatched for the relief of Calais. Dated Greenwich, 2 Jan. [1557-8].

No. 45. Letter from Queen Elizabeth to the City, desiring 250 soldiers for service at sea under the High Admiral, Lord Clinton, against the French. Dated Greenwich, 17 May, 2 Eliz. [1560].

No. 46. Letter from the same to the same, desiring that Sir Thomas Gresham might be discharged from serving the offices of Mayor, Alderman and Sheriff. Dated Westminster, 7 March, 5 Eliz. [1562-3].

No. 47. Proclamation against the Earls of Northumberland and Westmoreland or their rebellion against the Queen's majesty. Dated Windsor Castle, 24 Nov., 1569.

AA 2

No. 48. Letter from Queen Elizabeth to the City on the occasion of the discovery of the Babington conspiracy. Dated Windsor Castle, 18 Aug., 1586.

No. 49. Speech delivered by a member of the Common Council upon the same occasion.

No. 50. List of ships furnished and victualled by the City to meet the Armada, 1588.

No. 51. Government order to victual ships furnished by the City against the Armada. 24 July, 1588.

No. 52. List of all the ships furnished by the City against Spain in 1558.

No. 53. Letter from King James I to the City, upon his accession. Dated Holyrood House, 28 March, 1603.

No. 54. Reply to the above. Dated 29 March, 1603.

No. 55. Another letter from King James I in answer to the foregoing. Dated Newcastle, 11 April, 1603.

No. 56. Letter from the Lords of the Council to Sir Arthur Chichester, Deputy in Ireland, as to the course to be pursued with the City's Commissioners appointed to view the Irish Estate. Dated Whitehall, 3 Aug., 1609.

No. 57. Letter from Speaker Lenthall to the Lord Mayor, asking, on behalf of Parliament, for a City loan of £60,000. Dated Covent Garden, 15 Jan., 1640-1.

No. 58. Another letter from Speaker Lenthall, on the same matter. Dated Covent Garden, 6 Feb., 1640-1.

No. 59. A third letter from the same, on the same matter. Dated Charing Cross, 19 Feb., 1640-1.

No. 60. Letter from the Earl of Essex to the City, desiring a loan of £100,000 for the maintenance of the Parliamentary army. Dated Northampton, 13 Sept., 1642.

No. 61. Letter from the same, announcing the appointment of Skippon as Sergeant-Major-General in the Parliamentary army. Dated Hammersmith, 16 Nov., 1642.

No. 62. Resolution of the Common Council for putting the City and suburbs into a posture of defence; 23 Feb., 1642-3.

No. 63. Letter from the Mayor, &c., of Gloucester to the City of London, touching the removal of Colonel Massey. Dated 29 May, 1645.

No. 64. Letter from the Mayor, &c., of Plymouth, to the same, enclosing copy of petition to Parliament for relief against the depredations of the Royalists. Dated 5 Sept., 1645.

No. 65. The City's petition to King Charles I, in reply to His Majesty's letter of the 19 May, 1646.

No. 66. Letter from Fairfax and the Council of War to the Commissioners of the City of London, forbidding further enlistments. Dated 14 June, 1647.

No. 67. Letter from the same to the Mayor, Aldermen and Common Council of the City, touching the removal of the army and the safety of the King's person. Dated St. Albans, 15 June, 1647.

No. 68. The City's reply to the two preceding letters. Dated 18 June, 1647.

No. 69. Letter from Fairfax to the City in answer to the above. Dated St. Albans, 21 and 22 June, 1647.

No. 70. Letter from the City to Fairfax, informing him that Commissioners had been despatched to remain at the head-quarters of the army. Dated 25 June, 1647.

No. 71. Letter from Fairfax to the City, notifying the removal of the army to the bridge. Dated Berkhamstead, 25 June, 1647.

No. 72. Letter from Fairfax to the City, enclosing copy of proposals forwarded to Parliament from the army. Dated Reading, 8 July, 1647.

No. 73. Letter from the City to Fairfax, deprecating any attempt to intermeddle with the liberties and privileges of the City. Dated 28 July, 1647.

No. 74. Minutes of Common Council touching a recent disturbance in the City; 11 April, 1648.

No. 75. Letter from Fairfax to Skippon upon his re-appointment to the command of the City's forces. Dated Windsor, 10 May, 1648.

No. 76. A narrative of the proceedings of the Court of Common Council held the 13 Jan., 1648-9, presented by order of the Court to the House of Commons.

No. 77. Letter from the Council of State to the Mayor and Aldermen of the City, for defacing statues of James I and Charles I. Dated Whitehall, 31 July, 1650.

No. 78. Another letter from the same, ordering the entire removal of the statue of Charles I at the Royal Exchange. Dated Whitehall, 14 Aug., 1650.

No. 79. Letter from the Council of State to the City, for removal of ordnance to the Tower. Dated Whitehall, 19 Nov., 1653.

No. 80. The City's humble Petition and Representation to the Lord Protector, promising to stand by him against the enemies of the nation; 16 March, 1657-8.

No. 81. Letter from Sir John Langham to the Court of Aldermen, declining to resume the Aldermanry from which he had been deposed by Parliament, on the score of ill-health. Dated Crosby House, 18 Sept., 1660.

No. 82. Letter from the Earl of Manchester to the Court of Aldermen, desiring that the Butchers of the City might continue to supply offal to the King's "Game of Bears" as formerly. Dated Whitehall, 29 Sept., 1664.

No. 83. The City's address to King Charles II, congratulating him upon his escape after the Rye House Plot. 2 July, 1683.

No. 84. Letter from the Duke of Newcastle to the Lord Mayor, informing him of the Pretender having set up his Standard in Scotland. Dated Whitehall, 4 Sept., 1745.

No. 85. Another letter informing the Lord Mayor of the Pretender having entered Derby, and desiring him to put the City into a posture of defence. Dated Whitehall, 6 Dec., 1745.

No. 86. Proceedings relative to the expunging of the recognisance entered into by William Witham, Messenger of the House of Commons, as narrated by James Morgan, Clerk to the Lord Mayor, to the Committee appointed to assist in defending Crosby, Wilkes and Oliver. 22 March, 1771.

No. 87. Letter from Charles Fox, Chairman of the Westminster Committee, to the Town Clerk of London, suggesting a general meeting of the Committees of Association. Dated St. James's Street, 20 Feb., 1780.

No. 88. Letter of thanks from Edmund Burke to the same, for the City's approval of his Bill for Economical Reform. Dated St. James's Square, 6 March, 1780.

No. 89. Letter from Charles Fox to the same, forwarding copy of proceedings of the Westminster Committee of Association, and giving particulars of the proceedings of the House of Commons upon Dunning's motion. Dated St. James's Street, 10 April, 1780.

APPENDIX A.

No. 1.

Reply from the City to a letter from King Henry V [Printed in *Memorials*] asking for wine and provisions for the army at Rouen. Dated the Feast of Nativ. of B.V.M. (8 Sept., 1418).

Letter Book I, fo. 216.

Our most dred most soveraign lord and noblest kyng to the soveragn highnesse of your kyngly mageste with all maner of lowenesse and reverence mekly we recomende us Nat oonly as we oughte and shulde but as we best can and may with alle our hertes thankynge your soveraign excellence of your gracious lettres in makyng gladsom in understondyng and passyng confortable in favoring of our poure degrees which ye liked late to send us from your hoost afore the cite of Roan. In which lettres after declaracōn of your most noble entent for the refresshing of your hooste ye recorde so highly the redinesse of our wille and power at alle tymes to your plesaunce and thankyn us therof so hertely that treuly save oonly our preier to hym that al good quiteth never was it ne mighte it halfe be deserved. And after suing in your forsaid gracious lettres ye praye us effcuelly [*sic*] to do enarme as mani smale vessels as we may with vitaille and specially with drinke for to come up as fer as they may in to the river of Seyne. And nat only this but in the conclusion of your soveraign lettres forsayd ye fede us so bounteuesly with behest shewyng of your good lordship to us in tyme comyng as ye have ever don that now and ever we shulle be the joyfuller in this life whan we remembre us on so noble a grace. [O how may the simplesse of pouere lieges better or mor clerly conceyve the graciouse love and favorable tendresse of the kyng her soveraign lord than to here how your most excellent and noble persone more worthi to us than alle wordly richesse or plente in so thynne habondance of vitaill homly disposed so graciously and goodly declare and uttir un to us that ar your liege men and subgitz yor plein luste and plesaunce as it is in yor sayd noble lettres worthily conteyned. Certein trewe liege man is þer non ne feithful subgit coude þer non ne durste tarie or be lachesse in any wyse to the effectuell praier or comaundement of so soveraign and high a lord which his noble body peineth and knightly aventureth for the right and welfare of us alle].[1] Oure most dred most soveraign lord and noblest kyng plese it your soveraign hignesse to understonde how that your forsaid kyngly praier as most strait charge and comaundement we willyng in alle pointes obeye and execute anon fro þe resceit of your of your [*sic*] sayd gracious lettres which was þe XIX day of August nigh none unto þe makyng of þese symple lettres what in getyng and enarmyng of as many smale vessels as we myght doyng brewe boþe ale and bere purveing wyne and oþer vitaillee for to charge with þe same vessels we have don our besie deligence and cure as god wot. In which vessels wiþoute gret plente of oþer vitails þat men of your cite London aventuren for refresshing of your host to þe costes where your soveraign presence is Inne we lowely send wiþ gladdest wille unto your soveraign excellence and kyngly mageste by John Credy[2] and John Combe poure officers of your sayd cite bringers of these lettres tritty botes of swete wyne that is to seye ten of Tyre, ten of Romeney ten of Malvesy and a

---

[1] The passage here placed in parenthesis was, we learn from a marginal note, for divers causes omitted from the original letter.

[2] He was esquire to the mayor *(Armiger Maioris)*. After he had served the City faithfully for 20 years, and become incapable of further work, he was, in February, 1420, allowed an annuity of 40 shillings and his clothing or livery of the City in the same manner as the sergeants of the Chamber.—Letter Book I, fo. 238b.

thousand pipes of ale and bere with thuo thousand and five hundred coppes for your hoost to drinke of which we besech your high excellence and noble grace for our alder comfort and gladnesse benignely to resceyve and accepte nat havyng reward to þe litelhed or smale value of the gifte it self which is simple but to þe good will and high desir þat þe poure yevers þerof hav to þe good spede worship and welfare of yor most soveraign and excellent persone of which spede and welfare and al your oþer kyngly lustes and plesaunces we desire highly be the sayd berers of thes lettres or oþer whom your soveraign highnesse shal like fully to be lerned and enfourmed. Our moost dred most soveraign lord and noblest kyng we lowely besech the kyng of heven whos body refused nat for our savacōn wordly peyne gilteles to endure þat he your graciouse persone which for our alder good and proffit so knythly laboureþ litel or noght chargyng bodily ease in al worship and honure evermore to kepe and preserve. Writen at Gravesende under þe seal of mayralte of your sayd cite London on þe day of þe Nativite of our Lady the Blisful Mayde [8 Sept.].

No. 2.

Proclamation for speeding men to the English army in Normandy.
6 Henry V, A.D. 1418.

Letter Book I, fo. 217.

Be ther a proclamacōn made that al maner men þe which wil toward the Cite of Roan or any other place in the coste of Normandie þere to bein service sould or wages wiþ þe kyng our soveraign lord whom god save and kepe or wiþ ony other persone of his host or retenu make and apparale hem redy in alle haste betuen this and souneday þat next comith atte ferthest for to be wiþ inne shipbord in their best and most defensable harneys and covenablest ariaye to Seyle toward þe costes above sayd an in þe mene while come they to þe Mair of þys Citie and heshal ordeyne and dispose hem redy Shippyng in this port and vitaill free toward þe costes abovesayd.

No. 3.
Letter from King Henry V to the City notifying the capture of Pontoise. Dated Mantes, 5 Aug. [1419].

Letter Book I, fo. 236

By þe kyng.

Trusti and welbeloved we grete yow wel and late you wete to your comfort that we been in good heele and prosperite of our persone blessed be god which graunte you always soo to bee Ferthermore as touching tithing we signifie unto yow þat god of his grace worshiped be he hath sent in to our handes our toun of Pontoyse and hough proffitable þe havyng of it is unto us John Palyng þe bringer of þis can enfourme you. And we pray you thankeþ god þerof and of alle his gracious soondes þat he sendeth us and for asmoch as our adverse partie wool noo pees nor accord have wiþ us but finally have refused al meenes of pees We be compelled ayein to werre thorough þair default as he wot þat al knoweþ, To whoos mercy we trust for our good wil and redinesse to þe pees to have þe better spede heraftur þe which we recomende to your good prayers wiþ al our herte and god have you in his kepyng Yeven under our Signet at our town of Mant þe v day of Augst.

No. 4.
Reply to the above. Dated 6 Sept. [1419.]

Id. Ibid.

Our most dred and most souveraign ertly lord we recomande us unto þe souveraign excellence of your kyngly mageste in þe most humble and lowely wyse þ^t any pouere or simple lieges can best imagine or devise lowely thankyng your souveraign excellence and noble grace of þe right gracious and right confortable lettres which ye liked late to sende us fro your town of Maunt be Johan Palyng. The which lettres with al maner of honour and lowely reverence we have mekly resceyved and understonde. And trewely most dred and souveraign lord gladder ne moor confortable tithinges might never have come nor in better tyme for to satisfie and refresche þe fervent desir of your poure lieges þat have loong thrusted aftur knowlech of your prosperite than were your sayd gracious lettres the which amongs al oþer special graces most principalich for our hertly confort conteyned þe souveraign helþ and parfit prosperite of your most souveraign and gracious persone. The which Crist of his souveraign mercy and noble pite plese alwey to kepe in al maner of worship and joye. Our most dred and souveraign erthly lord whan we remembre us hough þat your kyngly might and power grounded in the trewe pees of god is so vertuosly soonded wiþ þe spirit of meknesse in devout and continuel thankyng of god in al his soondes and trust of good prayers of your peple as your said lettres make gracious mencõn: Trewely we ar meved be as gret consideracõn and as resonable cause as ever were liege men to pray as we have and shulle yet god will for þe good and gracious spede of your most excellent and gracious persone and to thanke god lowely þat ever he sent us so gracious and so vertuose a souveraign lord to regne and have lordship up on us. Our most dred and most souveraign lord yef it like your souveraign highnesse to here of þastat of your citee London plese it your kyngly mageste to conceyve þat in more quiet ne pesibler rest as ferforth as absence of you þat ar our most gracious and most souveraign lord may suffre was never erthly citee nor place blessed be god. Our most dred and most souveraign lord we lowely beseche god the kyng of pees whos grace excedeth þe merit of hem þat pray þat he vouche sauf your kyngly mageste stabilissh in al vertu and evermore kepe your most excellent and souveraign persone in al joy and prosperite to his plesaunce. Writen at your said citee of London under þe seal of mairalte þerof þe vi^e day of September.

No. 5.

Letter from the Duke of Clarence to the Mayor and Aldermen of London notifying the capture of Pontoise. Dated Mantes, 5 Aug. [1419]

Letter Book I, fo. 236b.

Right trusty and Welbeloved We grete you well often tymes with al our herte And forasmoche as it is confortable and likyng to you to here of þe tithinges in this parties We do you to understonde þat the morwe after þat the werre began at this tyme by twene my lord þe kyng and his adversaire of Fraunce by cause þat he wolde naught applie nor accorde to right and resoun he assigned certein peple to passe to Pountoise Where the Frensh kyng lay during the time of this convencõn. And so thei have wonne the forsaid toun by assaulte ithonked be god thorough the whiche wynninge my forsaid lord hath passage to Parys Ferthermore We do you to understonde that Roger Tillyngton, Skynnere, our welbeloved servaunt desurth gretly to be freman and enfranchised amongs you at þis tyme Wherefor We pray you entierly With al our herte þat ye wol for contemplacõn and favour of us to admitte and resceyve the forsayd Roger to be enfraunchised amongs you so þat he may knowe þat þis our praier may availle hym and stonde in stede as our gret trust is in you Right trusty and Welbeloved þe Holy Trinite have you evermore in his kepyng Iwriten at Maunt Under our Signet the v day of Augst.

No. 6.

Reply to the above. Dated 6 Sept. [1419]

Id. ibid.

Right High right mighty Prince and excellent lord We recomaunde us unto þe high lordship of your gracious excellence in as humble Wyse as any poure men best can or may ymagine and devise Thakyng your lordly excellence in as lowely maner as office of writing may conteyne for þe high and favorable remembraunce

which your gracious Lordship hath to þe Citee of London in signi-
fieng to us be your gracious lettres writen at Maunt the v day of
Augst of our most dred and most souveraign erthly lordes prosperous helth and victorious spede and eke of youres The Which
god of His souveraign grace and noble pite With encrees of al
honur and Joye ever kepe & mainteigne. Right high right
mighty Prince and excellent Lord yef it like your lordly excellence
to here of thastat of the Citee of London. Plese it your gracious
Lordship to conceyve þat in moor quiet ne pesibler rest blessed
be god was never erthly Cite nor toun in absence of her most
souveraign & gracious Lord. Right high right mighty Prynce
and excellent lord þe Prynce of all hevenly knyght hood have you
in his holy kepyng Writen at þe sayd Citee London under þe
seal of Mairalte þerof þe vj^e day of September.

No. 7.

Letter from Henry V to the City informing the citizens of his
movements in France. Dated Mantes, 12 July [1421].

Letter Book I, fo. 263.

Trusty and welbeloved we grete yow wel And for asmuch as
we be certein that ye wol be joyful to here good tiding of oure
estat and welfare we signiffie unto yow that we be in good heele
and prosperite of oure personne and so been oure brother of
Gloucestre oure beluncle of Excestre and al the Remenant of
lordes and other personnes of oure oost blessed be oure lorde
whiche graunte yow soo for to bee witting moreover that in oure
comyng by Picardy we hadde disposed us for to have taried
sumwhat in the cuntre for to have sette hit with goddes help in
better gouvernance and whils we were besy to entende therto
come tidinges unto us that he that clepeth hym Daulphin was
commen doun with a greet puissance unto Chartres and thoos
parties purposinge hym for to leye siege as we were enfourmed
unto the saide toun of Chartres Wherefor we drow us in al
haste unto Paris as wel for to sette oure fader of France as the

saide good toune of Paris in seure gouvernance and from them
unto this oure toun of Mante at whiche jolace we arrived on
Wodnesday last to thentente for to have yeven secours with goddes
grace unto the saide toun of Chartres and hider comme unto us
oure brother of Burgoigne with a faire felaship for to have goon
with us to the saide secours the whiche oure brother of Burgoigne
we fynde right a trusty lovyng and faithful brother unto us in al
thinges. But in oure comyng from Paris unto this oure toun of
Mante we were certified uppon the weye by certain lettres that
were sent unto us that the saide pretense Daulphin for certein
causes that meved hym hath reised the saide siege and is goon
in to the cuntre of Touraine in greet haste as hit is saide and we
truste fully unto oure lord that þorow his grace and mercy al
thinges here that we shall have to doo with shall goo wel from
hensforth to his plesance and worship whom we beseche devoutely
that hit soo may bee and to have yow in his keping. Yeven under
oure signet in oure oost at oure toun of Mante the xij day of Juyl.

No. 8.

Reply to the above. Dated 2 August [1421].

Letter Book I, fo. 263.

Our most dred and most soveraign erthly lord we recomaunde
us un to your kyngly power and soveraign highnesse in as meke
wyse and lowly maner as eny simple officers or pouere lieges most
hertly can ymagine or divise Thankyng with al our hool myght
and konnyng your soveraign excellence and noble grace of þe
right confortable and joyfull lettres which ye liked late to sende
us from your town of Mante þe which lettres with al maner of
humble reverence we have lowly resceyved and understonde.
By whos tenure amonges al other blessed spede and gracious
tithynges. For which we thanke highly and ever shall þe lord
almyghty ware we most inwardly comforted and rejoysed whan we
herd þe certeinte of your prosperouse helth after which we have
longe desired and which god of his eendles pite ever kepe and

mainteign And of þestate of your cite London yef it like your soveraign highnesse to heere and understonde Plese it your kyngly Mageste to conceyve þat in pesibler degree tretabler governance ne joyfuller rest as ferforth as absence of yow þat are our lord most soveraign under god may suffre was never erthly cite nor place blessed be god in whos vertu stondeth al kyngly gladnesse which of his infinit power and most habundaunt grace alwey dresse and continue your spede to his high worship and plesaunce and sende yow grace with report of wordly victorye upon us and all your other lieges longe for to regne. Writen at your saide cite of London under þe seal of þe Mairalte þerof þe ij day of Augst.

No. 9.

Letter from the Duke of Bedford to the City claiming the government of the realm at the death of Henry V. Dated Rouen 26 Oct, [1422].

Letter Book K, fo. 2.

Right trusty and welbeloved we grete yow wel with al oure herte And for asmuche as hit liked our lord but late a goo to calle the kyng our souverain lord that was from this present world un to his pardurable blisse as we truste fermely by whos deces during the tendre age of the king oure souverain lord that is nowe the gouvernance of the Reaume of England after the lawes and ancien usage and custume of þe same Reaume as we be enfourmed belongeth un to us as to þe elder brother of our saide souverain lord that was And as next unto þe coroune of England and havyng chief interesse after the king þat is oure souverain lord whom god for his mercy preserve and kepe We praye yow as hertely and entirerly as we can and may and also requere yow by þe faithe and ligeance that ye owe to god and to þe saide coroune that ye ne yeve in noo wyse assent conseil ne confort to any thing that myght be ordenned pourposed or advised in derogacõn of þe saide lawes usage and custume yif any suche be or in prejudice of us Lattyng you faithfully wite that our saide prayer and requeste procedeth not of ambicion ner of desir that we might have of worldly worship other of any singuler comodite or prouffit that we might resceyve thereby but of entier desir and entente that we have that the forsaide lawes usage and custume ne shulde be blemysshed or hurt by oure lachesse negligence or deffaulte ner any prejudice be engendred to any personne souffisant and able to þe whiche the saide gouvernance myght in cas semblable be longyng in tyme comyng Making pleine protestacõn that it is in no wise oure entente any thing to desire that were ayenst the lawes and custumes of the saide lande ner also ayenst the ordonnance or wil of oure saide souverain lorde that was savyng our right to þe whiche as we trowe and truste fully that hit was not oure saide souverain lordes entente to deroge or doo prejudice And god have you in his keping Writen under oure signet at Rouen þe xxvj day of Octobre.

No. 10.

Letter from the Mayor and Aldermen of the City of London to the Duke of Bedford. No date [A.D. 1424.]

Letter Book K, fo. 18b.

Right high right myghty and right honourable Prince we recomaunde us un to your Lordly excellens in þe most humble and servisable maner that we can best ymagine and devise Thankyng lowly your noble grace of þo gracious lettres in makyng gladsom in undyrstandyng and passyng comfortable in favoring of our pouer degrees Whyche you liked late to sende us from Craille upon case[1] [sic] in Normandie be þat worshypfull and wel avised man John Salveyn your esquier whyche hath made us notable report and right comfortable exposiciõn of þestate and tidinges of þat londe blessed be god Bot amonges alle other more gladder ne more comfortable tidinges myght now have come nor in better tyme to satisfie and refressh þe fervent desire of us that long have thursted after knowlech of your prosperite þan were seid gracious lettres þat yaven us ful enformacõn and singler comfort of þe

---

[1] Creil (Oise).

gode hele and disposicõn of your persone whyche Crist of his soveraign mercy and pite infenite ever preserve and mainteigne in Joye and honoure to his plesaunche. Right high right myghty and right houourable Prince of þat þat your lordly clemence so benigly voucheþ sauf as is purported in þe parclose of your seid lettres to have assercion be comers be twene of your gode desires enclinyng your excellence to þaccomplissement of hem at alle tymes, it excedeth in estimablich our power and konnyng to yeve you thankynges þerof recompensable in every wyse. Bot god þat is guerdoner of every gode dede quite rewarde yow in stede of us where we may not And for we truste and knowe verilich þat hit pleseth yow to here of þestate of þe Cite of London to whiche ye have evyr be right gode Lorde and favorable we certefie un to your gracious Lordship þat in more quiete ne pesibler reste was never Cite nor place blessed be god whiche of his incomperable bounte send you gode and graciouse lif to þe plesaunche of hym and comfort of us and alle your oþer welvillers long for to lede Writen at London.

No. 11.

Another letter from the same to the same. No date [A.D. 1424.]

Letter Book K, fo. 21.

Right high right mighty And right honurable Prince we recomaunde us to þestate of your lordly excellence in as humble maner as eny ordyr of writing can expresse for bountees & bienfaites innumerable which þe liberal grace of your high and gracious lordship without our meryt or desert hath ever shewed us heretofore but at þis tyme in especial for þo passing gladsom and confortable letters of credens þat plesyd you late to sende un fro Vermeil[1] on perche be þat worshipful & wel avised esquier Stephen Hatefelde on of your kervers which made us noble assercõn ioyfull report and comendable credence of þe cronicable and victoriouse esploit þat our lord almyghty be special influence

[1] Verneuil.

of his grace as it semeth and singler mediacon of your knyghtly corage sent un to þat blessed innocent and gracious Prince our soveraign Lord whiche esploit and victorie as devoutly as we can or may we yelde and ever shall humble þankinges and grace to þe lord of hevenis which in þe balance of his infenit merci and pite as it semyth so favourably weyeth þe right and Innocence of our seid soveraign lord during his tendre age þat he will not suffre hym in nowise to be Injuried be malice or circumvencon of his enemyes Bot hath purveid sent and stablisshed you right high right myghty and right honourable Prince to be a special mene and supporter in þis parte for tuicon and conservacon of his right and Innocence to singler comfort and consolacon of all his people blessid be god whiche of his incomperable bounte send you good and graciouse lif to þe plesaunche of hym and comfort of us and all your oþer Welvillers Long for to lede. Writen at London &c.

No. 12.

Letter from the Earl of Salisbury and of Perche to the Mayor and Aldermen of the City of London announcing the success of the war in France. Dated 5 Sept. [1428]

Letter Book K, fo. 55b.

Right trusty & entierly welbeloved frendes we grete you hertely wel And for asmuche as we trust fully that ye desire to here of þe good tydinges of þat which vureth wel to oure sovereing lord in the conquest of his enemys here in þis lande We do yow to witte þat þe vure & spede seth our last comyng in to þis lande hath be so good that I am ever behold to þanke god besechyng hym to continue hit for his mercye and after þe Wynnying of many diverse tounes castelles & Forteresses we laied siege afor þis toune of Yenville and after diversez aprochemenes made þerto as was on sonneday sevenyght which was the xxix day of August we gate þe said toune of Yenville be þe most notable assault þat evere we sawe. And sethen þe castell was yolden un to oure grace and many oþer tounes castelles & stronge chirches god hath sent hem in to þobbeissaunce of oure sovereing lord blessed most god be somme yolden to oure grace somme to our wil somme wonne be assault & somme oþer wyse þe nombre of whiche is more þan xl And so þanked be god þer comyth in dayly places to þobbeissaunce to þe Recovering of which we þenke to do all diligence as we behold with out sparyng of labour or pein. And for our gret & singler comfort We pray you oft tymes to signifie us be wryting of youre Welfare And þat we may fynd your faveur and Frendship in alle þinges þat we have or shal have to don in oure absence and so to continue your good frendship like as hit liked yow to do what tyme we were þer present For which we thanke yow and hold us muche behold to do for yow what we can or may to which we wol ever be redy with al our power And þe holie trinite have yow always in his blessed keping Writen at Yenvile the v day of Septembre.

Item we do you to wite that seth the wryting of þis we have had tydinges frome our brother Sire Richard Haukeford whome we had sent to Ride afore þe toune and castel of Meun sur leyre* þat blessed be god he hath do so good diligence that he hath goten þe sayd toune castel & peuple yolden to þobbeissaunce of oure soverein lord Which toune & castell ben ryght notable & hugely fourneshed of peuple and vitaile yuoughe blessed be god for alle þe kyngis puissaunce here a good while And to þe sayd toune is a faire brigge overe þe gret River of leyre which ys bot v leges oute of þe cite of Orliens.

[A schedule of 38 towns follows]

No. 13.

Reply to the above.   Dated 12 Oct. [1428]

Letter Book K, fo. 55b.

Right worshipful & ryght mighti lord we recomaunde us to your gret lordsship & noble grace in as humble maner as we can or ought Thankyng it fro þe deppest of our hertis of þe gentill

* Meun on the Loire.

lettres writene at Yenvile þe v day of Septembre last þᵗ ye liked to sende us be your herauld   Which lettres after the resceit of hem whith dhue reverence And after þat thei were publisshed and redde to fore þe Commens of þis Cite putte us all in singler comfort & Joye because of þe fervent & special desir we hadde afore to here comfortable tidynges of your good spede and welfare   And mekely we þanke our lord of heven for þe gret & greüx oevre þat it liked hym to sende you of his mercy so sone after youre First comyng at þis tyme in to þo parties as your seid lettres make noble mencioun Beseching hym of his infinit pite continue & encrese it to his plesaunce   Right worshipful & ryght mighty lord of þat þᵗ it liketh youre high lordship so favorably to wryte & desire in yoʳ seyd lettres to here & know of oure welfare & offre us your good lordship in tyme comyng plese it yow to wite þat þe sayd Cite is in gret pees tranquillite & good accorde and we þat are þe simple governors þerof in good hele & disposicõn of our personnes blessed be god   And be cause we perceyve wel þat þis desire & ofre procedeth of your gret gentilesse & good grace & not of our merit ne desert so þᵗ it excedeth incomparablich our puissaunce to recompense it be thankinges or ought elles   Therefore we pray to god þat is almyghti to acquite & guerdone it in stede of us   But we & suche service as we can do þough it be simple or mene of value shal ever be Dressed & apparailled to your plaisirs   Whiles we lyve God knoweth which of his endles grace kepe & preserve your noble lordship in alle þe actes of knyghthode to Hys plesaunche.   Wrytten at London þe xii day of Octobre.

No. 14.

Letter from King Henry VI to the City asking for a loan of 10,000 marks.   Dated Rouen, 10 Nov. [1430].

Letter Book K, fo. 84.

Trusty and welbeloved we grete yow wel and signiffie un to yow þat amonge alle þevident tokens of trewe affeccioun and of kyndenesse þat our sugettes of oure Roy^me of England hav shewed and shewen un to us for þavantyng forward of oure present voiage þe tender love and kynde acquitail of oure goode and trew cite of London bothe un to our progenitours of noble memoire in like cas, and al so un to us is noȝt owt of our remebrance but writen and wel emprinted þeryn for þe which we have and purpos to have our said citee as þe principalle and most notable of our said Roy^me and yow as our kynde and trewe suggettes þe moore specialy recommended and can yow singuler thank and as owre entencioun is to shew yow perseverance of goode lordship semblably we trust þat on yowre part ye wol put yow in yowre trewe dewire and kynde acquitaille un to us att alle tymes and namely at our nede as ye have wel done al weyes hedir toward and soþe hit is þat be cause of many costlew charges long to declare our necessitee is at þis tyme suche þat on lesse þan it be in short tyme releved suche inconveniences þat god defende been noȝt unlike to falle boþe til us and oures, as shuld be right displesant til alle oure trewe suggettes and to yow in special whom we wold entierly desirous of our welfare. Wherfore siþ we have founden yow redy and welwilling to chevese us of good at alle tymes ar þis, þat nede hape required, and oure necessitee is suche at þis tyme as was never gretter. We pray yow hertely and also right entierly, as ye desiere þe seurte of oure personne and þe wel and worship of boþe oure Roy^mes þat continuing un to us þe kynde tendirnesse in oure absence þat ye shewed un to us in oure presence ye wol at þis tyme make un to us a prest of x^ml marc repaiable at suche tyme and of seure repaiment as may bee accorded be twix our counsaille þer and yew of which chevance we trust ye wol not faille us consideryng þat þe said some may do us more ese and service in our present necessite þan perventure shuld þe double and muche more an oþer tyme whan þat whan þat [*sic*] our nede war lasse To þe whiche loone we trust þat our personel beyng here among our enemyes in þis our tendir age shal muche þe more meve yow for to take yow nigh to serve oure desire Wyting for certain and withouten dowte þat in perfourming at þis tyme of our prayer ye may do un to us soo notable and þanklewe service þat we wol wel considre hit in tyme comyng and be þe more enclined to shewe you favorable and good lordship Wyting also þat we wold noȝt desire of yow þis charge as nowe be cause of þe charges þat ye have borne un to us ar þis, ner urgent and verray necessite required us þer to and our lord have yow in his kepyng. Yeven under our signet at our toun of Rouen þe x day day of Novembre.

No. 15.

Letter from Cardinal Beaufort to Mayor, Sheriffs and Aldermen of the City informing them of his intention of returning to England. Dated Ghent, 13 April [1432].

Letter Book K, fo. 105.

My ryght trusty and with al myn herte entierly welbeloved frendis I grete yow wel as hertily as I can. Desiring evermore to knowe of the welfare and prosperite of yowe alle and of ech of yow and of al þe good commune of þe noble citee of þe which ye bee for my singuler joye and gladnesse. Biseching oure blessed lord evermor to give yow as good welfare as ye can desire and as I wold for my self. And wol ye wite þat nought wiþstanding divers adversitees þat I soeffre ayeinst Reson and gentilesse I hadde pourposed me to have goon to þe court of Rome to doo þe duetee þat loongeþ to myn astat trustyng always þat þe moost xr̃n prince my souverain lord of whos disposicioun I ne have noo doubte and also his wise counsail of his Royaume in engeland wel advised wolde have doon me Right and favour also al þing considered aswel in myn absence as yn my presence. Nevertheless as in to þis tyme I feele right littel or noon as me þenkeþ And þerfore nought wiþstanding þat oure holyfader haþ sent un to me for to come to hym in haste I wol leeve al þing for a tyme and retourne agein into engeland and bee þer yif god wol a boute þe bigynnyng of þis parlement to knowe þe causes why I am þus straungely demeened and declare my self as a man þat have nought deserved soo to be treted. Mi right trusty and wiþ al myn herte entierly welbeloved frendis I þanke yow wiþ al þentierness of my herte of youre good love favour and will wich I have ever founden in yow paying you of youre good continuance and douteth not ye schull þerinne doo to god plesance for he is al trouþe to þe Kyng my soverain lord noo trespas nor offence but to hym comen to more age which with goddis mercy shal in haste growe singuler plesir, and to your self worshipp. My right trusti and wiþ al myn herte entierly welbeloved frendis yef I can or may goodly eny thing doo to your ese ye certiffie me þerof as to hym þat to my trewe pouer wol faithfully parfourme hit right gladdly and wiþ al myn herte þat knoweþ our blessed lord whom I hertily beseche to have yow evermor in his gracioux proteccioun and keping. Written att þe good town of Gaunt þe xiii^e day of Averil.

No. 16.

Letter from the Mayor and Aldermen of Calais to the Mayor and Aldermen of the City of London asking for assistance. Dated 27 June [1436].

Letter Book K, fo. 148.

Ful worshipfull wise & discrete sires we recommaunde us un to you in as goodli wise as caan be þought and in as mochell as we fynde of olde governaunce of þis toun that oure predecessours hadde in cours to wryte to your worshipfull estate to be mene and movers toward þe kyng our souveraigne lord and þe gracious lordes of is counseill for þe relevying & sustentacioun of þis said toun the yeveth us occasioun to wryte to yow attys tyme. Of which it were to longe to wryte the particuler circumstaunces of þe mischiefs and disese þat is suffred here to our unportable distresse and hevynesse. With more þ^t we sende to yow at this time how þarmynakz[1] þ^t been in Rewe prese fast and have prayhed a boute Samme de boys[2] and takyn mony prisouners and brent þe toun of

---

[1] The Orléans or Armagnac party (so called from the Duc d'Armagnac, Constable of France) the deadly enemy of the Dukes of Burgundy.

[2] Samer au bois, near Boulogne.

Staples. And as it is said of presumpcioun þey purpose & avaunte to override þe lordshipes heere of Guysnes & oþer and to renne heere a fore þis toun. So ferforth þat þe pore tenauntz forsake þe land & drawe þeim in to þe said toun & castelx and leve þe villages desolate the which yef þei were destruyed that god defende were pryved of our sustenaunce of levying and conforte & þe people anyentysed for evyr prayeng & besechyng you as ye þ^t be þe principall of all þe citees of þe Roiaulme of Engelond that it like to yor trew affeccioun that ye have & owe to have to þe said toun to contynue & exercise þe commendable promocioun as your said worthy predecessours hadden in use for þe salvacioun of þe said toun. As ye þat were trust singulerly in and as a principall membre oweth to do & ministre to is parties atte reverence of god whom we be sech preserve you ever & graunt yow parfite conclusyoun of yor desires with good lyf and long. Wrytene at Cales þe xxvij day of Juyn.

No. 17.

Letter from Henry VI to the Mayor, Aldermen and Sheriffs of London touching the prevention of disturbance within the City. Dated Lichfield, 3 Sept., 35 Hen. VI [1456].

Letter Book K, fo. 287.

By the king.

Right trusty and trusty and welbeloved we doubt not but that it is in yor remembraunce what inconvenience have late fallen and more were likly to have falle if it had not myghtly have be resisted not oonly by suche as with multitude of people otherwise then that their power & degree wold have entred oure chambre and citee of London by what meanes it is not unknowen unto you, but also by thinsolence of evil disposed and mysgoverned people of our saide citee whereof as nowe ye have þe governaunce the which thing hath be to the breche of our peas and grete trouble of our people and whereof we have had cause to be gretely displeased. And we willyng to eschew all suche inconveniences from hensforward will and charge you straitely that considered that our saide citee is called and named oure chambre and so we holde it wherein shuld be rest and peas and the whiche ought to be of goode governaunce to ensample of all this oure Reaume that from hensforthward ye ne suffre any persone or persones of what estate degree or condicioun that he or they be of at any tyme to entre into oure saide cite and chambre but peasiblie and with moderate nombre of people according to his and their estate and degree. And also þat not onely aftre their entree into our saide citee and chambre ye have suche awaite & and [*sic.*] attendaunce that they ne make any assemblees nor gadringes of any suche evil disposed people as is abovesaide but also þat ye have suche awaite & attendaunce to oure saide citee and chambre þat by the people beyng in or resorting to oᵣ saide citee no gadringes nor assemblees be made the which in any wise may sowne or shuld be to þe breche of oᵣ peas or trouble of our people. And if any suche hap to be as god defend þat ye lette it as ye wol answere unto us at your perill. And furþermore we wolle and charge you on þe feith and ligeance that ye owe unto us þat ye kepe oᵣ saide citee in due obeisaunce unto us as ye ought to doo. And not to suffre any such multitude of people entre into our saide citee neiþer to be in þe same but as ye may be at alle tymes of power to suppresse them and to be governours for us of þe same as reason wille ye shuld. Yeven under our privee seal at Lychefeld the iij daye of Septembre the yeer of oᵣ regne xxxvth [1456].

No. 18.

Letter from King Henry VI to the City ordering the seizure of foreign ships of war in the Thames. Dated Coventry, 10 March [1456–7].

Letter Book K, fo. 288b.

By the king.

Trusty and welbeloved We be enfourmed by a full grevous and a lamentable complainte made unto us and our counseill by marchantz estraungiers of Italie beyng heere within þis that where as they nowe late by vertue of our lettres patentz have shipped certeyn wolles wollencloth and other marchandises in diverse shippes of Zeland and paied truely alle duetees belongyng unto us And upon that have their Cokettes[1], there have certeyn shippes of werre aswell of Caleis as of Sandewiche encountred the said shippes of Seland within the Themyse at Tilbery or there nigh. And in maner of werre assaulted them and doo their werst to take and despoile them the whiche demeanyng is full gretely ayenst our honeur and worship in especial sith the saide marchantes been heere undre our sauf conduit and ligue. It is so also an example to discorage every marchaunt, and thereof must ensue not onely grete disclaundre to this our land but also the subversion of then-trecourse of marchandise. Wherin resteth gretly the welefare of our subgettes, With the whiche horrible dede, we be right gretely displeased as we have cause so to be And will in no wise suffre that it passe over unpunysshed, And forasmuche at this straunge demeanyng is commytted and doon undre the boundes of yor franchises and in suche place where ye have jurisdiccõn and power by suche franchises as ourre noble progenitours and we have graunted unto you as it is doon us to understande. It is yor parte to resiste correct and reforme the said wronges wherefore we by thavise of o^r grete Counseil woll that callying to yor remembraunce our lawes made in þ^t behalve and in especial the statue made by our noble progenito^r King Edward the third in the ixth yeer of his regne and oþer statutes made in þat behalve ye immediatly aftre pereceivyng of thees our lettres sette remedye in þe matier abovesaid. And þat ye take þe said shippes of Werre and male-factours and commytte theym to prisoun there straitely to be kept and to have as they have deserved, And provide that þe said shippes of Seland and marchandise be at their full fredome, and restored to their goodes if any be take fro them. Letyng you wite for certeyn if ye be remysse or necligent in þe punisshing of

---

[1] Cockets or seals delivered to merchants in token of their merchandise having passed the Custom-house.

þis mysgovernaunce and executyng this our comaundement, as we thinke ye have be in oþere afore this, ye shall renne into þe peyne provided by our lawes aswele in yor franchise as oþerwise. Wherto we shall entende withoute any grace to be shewed to you. And if so bee ye doo effectuelly yor devoir in this matier þat sitteth us right nigh to hert we shal thanke you And lete you have knowliche þat ye have doon us singler pleasir. Yeven undre o{r} privee seal at our citee of Coventre the x daie of Marche.

No. 19.

The same to the same touching the peace of the City. Dated Kenilworth, 22 March [1456-7].

Id., ibid.

By þe king.

Trusty and welbeloved we grete you wele and late you wite that certeyn of yor breþeren aldermen of our cite of London hath shewed unto us by þe declaracõn of your Recorder of þe good diligence that ye entended to have put you in to þe performyng of our commandement yeoven unto you by our lettres of prive seal in case our said lettres had come unto you in convenable tyme as for tharrest and attachement to have be made of certeyn shippes and persones þat late in our Ryver of Thamyse made gret attemptatz ageynst our ligue and sauf conduct of þe which yor goode disposicioun and benivolence we hold us wele content and can you þerfore right goode thankes charging you that if it hapne any of þe said shippes or mysdoers to repaire herafter unto o{r} saide citee or unto þe franchise þerof that thenne ye doo put them undre arrest and to be kept in sure warde abiding the determinacon of our lawes the which we wol in all wise be executed. And over this we charge you in yor effectuel devoir to see that our peas be kept at alle tymes within our saide citee And if any misgoverned persone of what estate or condicioun so ever he be make any stiring riot or attempt any thing to þe breche of o{r} paix within oure saide citee and franchise of þe same þat thenne ye doo yor peyne to suppresse them and to put hem in warde and so þat they be duely punisshed according to their demerites. In which thing doyng ye shal mynistre unto us cause of grete plaisir and deserve of us perfore right good and especial thanke in tyme to come. Yeven under our signet at o^r Castell of Kenelleworth the xxij daye of Marche.

No. 20.

Letter from the City to Henry VI, touching the capture of Sandwich by the French. Dated 3 Sept. [1457].

Letter Book K, fo. 292.

Of al erthely princes our moste high moste redoubted sovereyn lord and moste Christian kyng. We youre symple officers and feithfull humble lieges Mair and Aldermen of yor true citee and chambre of London recomande us unto yor most souvereyn excellence & noble grace in als humble and lowly wise as we moste hertly canne ymagine and devise humblely besechyng yor moste noble grace to be enformed of þe full piteuous and lamentable tidings þat late have comen unto o^r knowliche bothe by writing in certeyn and credible reaporte made to us touching thynfortunate entrepruise late hadde upon yor towne of Sandewiche by yor enemyes and adversaires of France and Bretaigne whiche in a grete armee and with grete noumbre of shippes on Sondaie last passed aboute vj of the clok in þe mornyng arrived to lande at y^r saide towne of Sandewiche And there after diverse scarmysshes gate and entred þe towne and it have dispoiled and pilled unto thuttermoste they have also full cruelly slayne diverse and many of your people and taken prisoners þe moste parte of the þrifty men of þe same towne and also have taken & ladde awaie þe shippes in the haven þere aboute þe nombre of xxxij grete and smale diverse of theym charged with wolles and oþere marchandises of no litle estymacõn and value to þe grete hurt of all this your reaume, and suche othir shippes as they myght not with them wele convey from thens have broken fired and brent and many oþere grete and outrageous violences have there commytted

APPENDIX A.

and doon þat pitee is to hire like as in þe copies of ij lettres entreclosed within thise is made expresse mencõn And thise doon yor saide enemeys with their vessels pillaige and prisoners withdrowe them unto the Downes where they dailie encrecen in gretter nombre both of people and vessels entending not as it is seide therby to ceasse of their cruell and malicious purpose but utterly to destroye þe navire of this yor land as it sheweth in open experience by that they have late also attempted and doon at yor towne and porte of Fowey and oþere places And then to take an entrepruise upon this yor royalme þe whiche if it ne were þe sonner myghtly lette and manly withstonde by yor saide highnesse and myghti power myght of liklihode growe unto þe grete jeoparde of your saide reaume as god defende In eschewing of whiche daungerous myschiefz and grete perils we yor said humble lieges wiþ grete & undelayed diligence have had rype comynycacõn with þe grete partie of yor comons of yor saide citee whom to þe pleasir of god and of you sovereyn lord and to þe defence and saufgarde of this yor reaume we fynde to their power full welewilled and towardly disposed to take upon them the charge in hasty wise to vitaille manne and setteforthe diverse shippes heer beyng in yor ryver of Thamyse with þe nombre of m^t m^t persones or neer thereby they to be redy to attende & assist such armee and power as shall like yor highnesse by thavise of yor Counsell to provide and ordeyne to þe resistence recountre and rebuke of yor saide enemyes by goddis mercy. So þat it may like yor moste high and noble grace to comaunde them so to doo And þeruppon to yeove them sufficient auchorite undre yor grete seal. And to open and declare þe premisses unto your saide higenesse more at large We send towardes þe same at this tyme o^r broþer Thomas Cook, alderman pleynly instruct of o^r entent in this behalve. To whom in moste humble wise we besiche yor said highnesse to give full feith & credence in the premisses Moste high moste redoubted sovereyn lorde and most Christian kyng we devoutly besiche þe kyng of all kynges whos reaume shall endelesly last and endure your blessed soule and noble body from either of þeir enemyes evermore to protect kepe and defende þat ye mowe in þis world upon us and alle yor oþer lieges wiþ reporte of worldly joye and victorie long tyme regne & endure to þe singuler conforte of us all   Written at yor saide citee of London þe third daie of Septembre.

No. 21.

Reply to the above.   Dated Northampton, 5 Sept [1457].

Id. Ibid.

Trusty and welbeloved we grete you oftentymes wele   And lete you wite þat this same daie o^r welbeloved Thomas Cook oon of your brethren hath in yor behalve presented yor lettres and also declared full notablie yor credence unto us by the which we have understande the fervent desire and true ligeaunce þat ye tendirly and humbly bere unto o^r royal estate, the whiche hath gretely renoveled and recomforted us Whereof aswele as of the notable aide that ye have graunted at this tyme unto us in right notable nombre of men of werre shippes and all other necessaires expedient for theym to þe repressing and rebuke of thoultrageous malice of oure enemyes of Fraunce now travarssing the narwe Se as it is saide we thanke you with as goode wille and hert as we can trusting for undoubted and also praying you þat considering þis Somer season passeth fast ye wille in all possible haste prepare and advaunce yor saide exploit for the whiche we have comaunded Chauncellor of Englond to yeove you auctorite so to doo undre oure grete seal   And have written to o^r port of Hull and oþere to drawe them and their ships towardes þe Se in their moste defensible and warrely araye and to ioigne and accompaignie theyme with you under the leding and guiding of god and of suche lordes and capitaignes proved in þe werre as we have full hope shall be to the grete renõmee of us and seurtee of you and alle our true subgettes and to thutter confusioun and reproche of o^r auncien enemy adverse of Fraunce   Yeoven undre oure Signet at our towne of Northampton the v daye of Septembre.

APPENDIX A.

No. 22.

A letter similar to No. 20 (*supra*) was sent to Bishop Waynfleete the Chancellor, to which was made the following reply. Dated Waltham, 5 Sept. [1457].

Letter Book K, fo. 292b.

Right Worshipfull and right entierly welbeloved sirres I recommende me unto you in þe moste herty wise Puttyng you in knowliche þat I have receved yoʳ lettres direct unto me by Roger Tonge yoʳ comon clerc in þe whiche I have understande not onely yoʳ grete trouth to þe king our aller sovereigne lord and to this his Reaume but also I see and cleerly understand yoʳ worshipfull coraige special love tendernesse and affeccõn þat ye bere to his highnesse and to þe defence prosperite and wele of this his Land to my special reioysing and conforte for þe whiche I thank you all as entierly as it is possible to me so to doo I am certeyn that þe kinges highnesse will yeove you a grete Laude & speciall thankinges & alle the land hath cause to do þe same Your worshipfull Demeanyng in this case and in this tyme of so straite necessite shall be an example to all þe land aftre I besiche you right hertly to contynue yoʳ saide goode & worshipfull entent to yoʳ perpetuell laude & worship hereaftre In suche tyme as I shall come next to þe kinges high presence & to thassemblyng of þe lordes of his land I shall not forgete but I shall remembre open and declare yoʳ worshipfull demenyng at this tyme And where as I have ever be wele willyng to þe wele of þe cite afore this tyme by occasioun of this yoʳ so thankfull demeanyng ye shall have me Doutelese ever heraftre more redy & right glade to doo suche thinges as may be to þe welefare honer and prosperite of þe same And how be it þat this may be thought a burthyn and a charge for þe season I doute not but þe goodenesse of almyghty god sha encrece you þe more for this so meritory a werk in tuicioun & defence of þe land and in eschewing of inconveniences happely muche gretter than as yet ben knowen Furthermore I pray you to yeve feith & credence to suche thinges as þe said Roger shall open unto you in my behalf   And þe Holiegoste have you alwey in his guydyng   Written at Waltham þe vth day of Septembre.

No. 23.

Letter from the Earl of Kendal, Lord Scales & others in the Tower to the Mayor asking why war was being made upon them. No date [*circ.* July 1460].

Journal 6, fo. 250b.

Sirs it is yor saying that ye be the kinges trew liegemen and soo be we wherfore we wul desire of you to wite the cause why ye make us werre   And that we may understande how ye may joyne your sayinges and youre dedes togiders,   And also what shuld bee the cause that ye take prisouners and we shuld nat defende us ayenst you and of this abovesaid we pray of you an answer for we cast us no more to accomber you w^t oure writing, &c.

No. 24.

Reply to the above. No date.

Id. ibid.

Like it your lordshipps to understande and with for certain that according to oure sayn . . we have ever bee, nowe we bee, and ever will bee the kinges treu subgettes and hum . . . liegemen   And where ye by youre bill desire of us to wite þe cause why we mak . . you werre, &c.   Therto we answer and seye that ye and your ffelesship have began and made no werre by diverse assault shetyng of gonnez and otherwise by the which the kinges treu liege people aswell the inhabitauntz of this eitee men women and children as oþer have be murdred slayn maemed and myscheved in sundry wise   And soo that þat hath be doon by us is onely of youre occasioun in oure defence.   And suche as we take for prisouners been for the attemptatz occasiouns and assaultz by theym doon as aforesaid in breche of the kinges peas, and for dispoillyng of the kinges treu people of their vitaillz and goodes without due contentacõn or paiement hadde in that behalve contrary to good equite and all lawe, &c.

No. 25.

Agreement touching the surrender of the Tower by the besieged Lords. Dated 16 July 38 Hen. VI [1460].

Id. fo. 256.

Be it remembred that we William Hulyn maire of the citee of London and the aldermen and þe comunes of the same agree us by thise presentz to holde ferme and stable and to performe in every pointe in that that in us shall bee alle suche appoyntementz touchyng the gyvyng over of the Toure of London by therle of Kendale the lord Scales the lord Lovell the lord Hungerford and Sir Edmond Hampden and oþer nowe beyng w'in the same tour, and the receyving of the tour aforesaid by the erle of Salisbury to the kinges use as be made by the same erle or his deputees on that one partie, and the said erl of Kendale lord Scales, lord Lovell, lord Hungerford and Sir Edmond Hampden and oþer or that othre partie. In witnesse wherof to thise same presentz we have put our comon seal writen at London aforesaid the xvj day of July the xxxviij[th] yeer of the reign of King Henry the vj[te] [1460].

No. 26.

Minutes of proceedings of the Common Council upon the return of the Earl of Warwick to England and the flight of King Edward IV. Oct., 1470.

Journal 7, fos. 223b–224.

Translation.

Be it remembered that on the 1st day of October it was noised abroad throughout the city that Edward the Fourth King of England had fled, for which cause the Queen Elizabeth who had fortified the Tower of London quitted the same Tower and fled to the sanctuary at Westminster and sent the Abbot of Westminster to Richard Lee the Mayor and the Aldermen to inform them on the Queen's behalf that the men of Kent and many others from divers parts of England in great numbers were purposing to enter the city and lay siege to the said Tower and the men at arms whom the said Queen had left behind in the same Tower; that the same Queen desired that the said Tower should be delivered into the hands of the Mayor and Aldermen because the said Queen was afraid, it was said, that unless the said Tower was so surrendered the said Kentishmen and others would invade the said sanctuary of Westminster to despoil and kill the said Queen. And be it remembered that the said Tower was on the Wednesday next following delivered into the hands of the Mayor and Aldermen and of Geoffrey Gate, knight & others of the council of the lords Clarence and Warwick on condition that all who were then within the said Tower should remain safe & secure with their goods and be conducted in the city of London either to the Sanctuary at Westminster or Saint Martin according as they might wish. And be it remembered that the lord Henry the Sixth who on the said Wednesday and for many years past had been confined in a certain cell (*in quodam Argastulo*) within the said Tower, was conducted by the said mayor and Aldermen to a certain chamber adorned with handsome furniture which the said Queen Elizabeth had fitted up and in which, being *enceinte*, she purposed being brought to bed. And be it remembered that the aforesaid Mayor and Aldermen for the safe custody of the said Tower and the said lord the King Henry the Sixth then living in the same placed in the said Tower the persons underwritten, namely

[Here follows a list of names.]

And each of the said Commoners had with him in the same Tower 2 men at arms to wait upon him.

And be it remembered that all the foregoing was executed by authority of the common council assembled in the church of Saint Stephen in Walbrok.

Also be it remembered that on the 5th day of October the Archbishop of York entered the Tower of London with a large band of men at arms and took command of the said Tower and relieved the said Aldermen and Commoners of the custody of the same And be it remembered that on Saturday the 6th day of October George Duke of Clarence and Richard Earl of Warwick entered the City by Newgate about the third hour after noon with a large army and rode through *le Chepe* to the said Tower of London and took away the lord the King Henry the Sixth and brought him the same day before nightfall to the Bishop of London's palace.

Be it remembered that as soon as it was notified that Edward the Fourth had fled the Mayor and Sheriffs every day to wit for 10 days rode about the City with armed men both before nine and after nine; the following men being sent by the masters and wardens of the misteries to the Guildhall every morning to attend upon the said Mayor and Sheriffs.

[Here follows a schedule of the number of men sent by each mistery.]

No. 27.

Letter from Thomas Faucomberge, captain of Kent, to the City of London. Dated "Sydyngbourne," 8 May [1471].

Letter Book L, fo. 78.

To the worshipfull my feithfull trusty and welbeloved frendes the Comminaltie of the Citee of London youre feithfull trewe lover Thomas Faucomberge Capteyn and leder of oure liege lorde king Henrys people in Kent at this tyme sendith hertly recommendacioun lettyng witte that I am enfourmed howe the partie of the usurper of our saide liege lordes Crownne hath made you to understande that I with the kynges people shulde purpose to robbe ryfell and despoile the Citee of London if I came therein. Wherefore they exorted you to make us werre and kepe us oute of the Citee. Certaynly frendes god knoueth whome I calle to recorde It was never myn entent ne purpose and therfore I beseeche you to give no credence to theire false suggestioun and surmyse. But trusty frendis sethen it is soo that I have taken upon me with the helpe of Almyghty god and the true comons to revenge his quarell ayenst the saide usurper and his adherentis and to sike hym in whate parties he be within the Reaume of Enland to abrigge the peynfull labour and to shorte the wey of the kinges people hertly sette and disposed ayenst the saide usurper desire and praye you courteisly to passe through the Citee in oure wey And we shall neiþer take vitaille ne ware withouten payment be ye therof certayne And that I promytte you on myn honour for he is not within the kyngis hoste in my company that breketh the kyngis crye but he shal have execucioun accordyng to his offences. No more unto you at this tyme saffe we have desired of the Maire and Aldermen to have an answere hereof by Fryday ix of the clokke at the blak ethe. And Almyghty Jesus have you and the goode Citee in his blessed garde. Writene at Sydyngbourne hastely the viij[th] day of Maij.

No. 28.

Reply to the above. Dated 9 May [1471].

Id. ibid.

Worshipfull sir we receyved your lettres writen at Sydyngborn the viij[th] day of the present month of Maij by the whiche we understande that it is comyn unto youre knoulege that if ye and youre ffeleaship w[t] the which ye be accompanyed shulde come unto the Citee of London like as ye write ye entende to doo that thanne ye wolde rifell and dispoile the saide citee ye desire us by the saide lettre that we shulde yeve no eredence to noon suche surmyse seiyng and takyng recorde of god that ye never entended so to doo. Prayng us to suffre you and youre saide ffeleaship to passe through the saide Citee of London uppon youre journey to perfourme and execute suche thinges as in your saide lettres ben more largely expressed. Sir we lette you witte that whanne the kgng kyng Edward þ[e] fourth oure soveraigne lord after his grete victorye hadde uppon Ester day last passed beside Barnet daparted oute of the saide Citee of London   He charged and commaunded us upon oure aligeaunce that we shulde kepe the same saffely and suerly to his beof and use not suffryng any persone what degree or condicioun or estate whereof gaderyng or makyng assembles of any people contrary to his lawes w^t oute auctorite of his high commaundement to entre therin   ffor the whiche cause and many oþer we ne darre may ne wille suffree you to passe through the same Citee, lettyng you witte for certayne that we understand that if ye and youre saide feleaship shulde come and entre in to the same that youre saide feleaship wolde beof like condicioun as other of like disposicioun have bene in tyme passed as by sondry precedentis it appereth unto us right largely   And it shulde not lye in youre power to lette your saide feleaship frome dispoilage and robery.   Wherefore we advertise you for that love and service that we afore tyme have ought unto that noble knyght youre ffader[1] and oure goode lorde whose steppes we wolde that ye shulde folowe and for verrey favour that we have born and bere unto you for the goode disposicioun and vertue that in tyme passed we have knouen to be in you that ye spare and absteyne you self from suche unlawfull gaderyng & asumbleng of people the whiche if ye soo doo we doubte not but it shal not onely be unto you grete honour and worship but also to youre prevaile and cause the kyng the rather to be youre goode and graciouse lorde.   Moreover Sir we have receyved a proclamacioun sent from you in the whiche amonge oþer articles we understand that ye by the commaundement of Henry late kyng of this Reaume Margarete late quene and Edward late called Prynce by thavise of the Erle of Warwyk whom ye suppose to be alyve[2] as we ben enfourmed and oþer ye be ordeigned Captayne of the Navye of Englond and men of warre both by þ^e See and by lande.   Right worshipfull Sir we mervaile gretely that ye beyng a man of soo grete wisdame and discrecioun

---

[1] Sir William Neville, Lord Falconbridge & Earl of Kent.
[2] He had been killed at Barnet.

shulde be disceyved by simple seynges and fayned tales we certifie you upon oure worshippes and trouthes that bothe the saide Edward late called Prynce and therle of Warrewyk ben slayne and dede for we knoue for certayne not onely by the reaporte of men of grete credence bothe of this citee and by other which were w^t the saide Erle of Warrewyk in the felde whanne he and his brother Marqueys Montagu were slayne but also by open lying of theire bodyes in the chirche of Poules by the space of ij dayes whiche many of us didde see and understand for certayne to be the bodies of the saide Erle of Warrewyk and Marqueys Also Sir the saide Edward late called Prince Therle of Devynshire lord John of Somerset lord Wenlok Sir Edmund Hampden Sir Robert Whityngham, Sir John Lewkenore, John Delves w^t other moo were sleyne upon Saturday last passed at Tewkesbury. And the Duke of Somerset lord of Seint Johannys Sir Gerveys of Clifton Sir Thomas Tresham w^t oþer moo to the noumbre of xij persones ben taken and ben beheded on Monday last passed as we ben veryly enfourmed at Tewkesbury aforsaide where god yaffe the kyng oure saide soverayn lord the victory as we certeynly understande not onely by lettres signed with oure saide soveraigne lordys owne hande whereof we sende yow a copye herein enclosed and by writynges senden from lordes and gentilles there beyng present unto divers and many persones beyng w^{t}in in the saide Citee of London but also by the reaporte of many credible persones and men of worship and by oþer servauntes of the same Citee. Whereof some were sent unto the hooste of oure saide soveraigne lord the king and some unto the hooste of the saide Edward late called Prynce to see and understand the disposicioun of bothe þe saide hoostes and to make reaporte unto us accordyng to the trouth whiche faiethfully have made reaporte unto us of the disposicioun and gugdyng of bothe the saide hoostis and howe and in what manere and fourme the saide Edward late called Prynce and oþer were taken and slayne. Wherefore we fryndely exorte you and stire you not onely to absteyne youre silf from suche unlawfull gaderynges and assembles of people and gevyng feith and credence

APPENDIX A. 391

to any symple feyned and forged tales contrary to trouth as it is rehersed, but also to take accepte and obey the kyng, kyng Edward the iiij[th] for your soveraigne lord the grete victories aforerehersed which god hath gevyn hym by his myghty power considered like all the lordes spirituell and temporell of this lande and we also have agreed for to doo. And ye soo doyng shal cause the kyng rather to be youre goode lorde and therby ye shal eschewe grete ieobardies parelles and inconveniences that myght enshewe of the contrary. And also ye shal not onely have oure good willes and benevolences in all thinges that hereafter ye shall have to doo w[t] us but also we shall be meane to the kynges highnesse trustyng that by oure praier he shal be unto you the rather goode and graciouse lord lettyng you witte for certayne that ye nor youre hooste shal not come within the said Citee. Writen at London in the yeldehall the ix day of Maij.

No. 29.

Account of the invasion of the City by the Kentish rebels on Sunday the 12th May 1471.

Journal 8, fo. 7.

Translation.

Be it remembered that the Mayor and Aldermen with the assent of the Common Council fortified the banks of the river Thames from Castle Baynard as far as the Tower of London with men at arms, bombards, and other implements of war to prevent an attack by the seamen who had brought a large fleet of ships near the Tower, and the said bank was held by the Aldermen and the rest of the citizens in great numbers. Be it remembered also that on Sunday viz: the 12th day of May in the eleventh year of Edward IV, [1471] Kentish seamen and others, rebels of the lord the king made an attack upon London bridge and on the new gate there and set fire to divers houses called *berehouses* near the hospital of Saint Katherine; and afterwards on the 14th day of May being

Tuesday the eleventh year aforesaid about eleven o'clock in the morning of the said Tuesday the said Kentish seamen and other rebels made an attack with great force and set fire to 13 tenements upon London bridge. The said Kentish seamen and others to the number of 5000 persons also made an attack from the Thames upon the gates of Aldgate and Bishopsgate and set fire to divers tenements. The citizens, however, sallied out of the gates and made a stout resistance and put them to flight, and nearly 300 men fell in battle and in flight besides those who were drowned in endeavouring to get on board their ships at Blakewall &c. And afterwards viz: on the eve of the Ascension the aforesaid eleventh year our said lord King came with a great multitude of armed men to the city of London and there to the honour of the same city created knights John Stokton the Mayor, Richard Lee, Matthew Philip, Ralph Verney, John Yong, William Tailor, aldermen, Thomas Urswyk the Recorder, George Irlond, William Hampton, Bartholomew James, Thomas Stalbrok and William Stokker, aldermen. And the same lord the King conferred upon them knights' badges.

No. 30.

Letter from King Henry VII to the City announcing the betrothal of his daughter the Princess Mary to Prince Charles of Castile. Dated Richmond, 28 Dec. [1507].

Letter Book M, fo. 138.

By the king

Trusty and welbeloved we grete you well. And forasmoche as wee doubt not but yt is and shalbe to you and to all other our true subiectes right joyfull and confortable to here and understande from tyme to tyme specially of suche causes and matiers as redounde to the grete honour exaltacioun universall weal suertie and restfulnes of us this our realme and our subiectes of the same we signifie unto you that by o^r grete labour studie and police thys grete and honourable aliaunce and mariage betwixt the prince of Castile and o^r right dere doughter the lady Marie ys nowe o^r

lorde bethanked betwixt o^r ambassadours and the oratours aswell of o^r brother and cousyn the king of Romans as of the seid yonge prince at o^r towne of Calays accorded aggreed concluded and finally determyned w^t a grete ample and large amitie and consideracioun to the suertie strenght defence and comfort aswell of us and of the seid prince as of either of our realmes contrayes dominions and subiectes and considering the noble lynage and blode whereof the seid yong prince ys descended whiche ys of the grettest kinges and princes in Cristendome remembring also the regions landes and contrays by rightfull enheritaunce he shall succede with the manyfolde commodities and goodenes that may folowe and ensue to us and this o^r realme aswell by the seid aliaunce and amitie as also by the free and sure entercourse of merchaundise that our and hys subiectees may and shall have in the regions and contrayes of us bothe specially being soo nye joyned togeder as they be we thinke verraly that thought the same shalbe right chargeable yet for the hono^r suertie weale and profite of this o^r seid reame noon so noble mariage can any where be founde So that by meane therof and thother aliaunce whiche we have w^t o^r good son the King of Scottes[1] this o^r reame ys nowe environd and in maner closed on every side w^t suche myghti princes o^r good sonnes frendes confiderates and alies that by the helpe of o^r lorde the same ys and shalbe perpetually establisshed in rest and peace and welthy condicioun to o^r grete hono^r and pleaso^r the reioysing and comfort of all o^r loving frendes confiderates and alies, the feare and discomfort of o^r enmyes that wold entende or presume to attempt any thing to the contrary The premisses therefore considered we do advertise you of the same to thentent that like as we doubt nat but ye and every of you wol take pleaso^r and comfort in hering thereof So with convenient diligence uppon the sight of these o^r lettres ye wol cause demonstraciouns and tokens of reioysing and comfort to be made in sundry places w^t in o^r citie there aswell by making of

---

[1] Margaret, daughter of Henry VII, married to James IV of Scotland.

ffyres in suche places as shall thinke convenient as otherwise in the best and confortable maner that ye can so that therby it may be evidently knowen what gladnesse and reioysing ys generally takyn and made by you and other o^r subiectes for perfecting of the seid hono^{r}able matiers like as we knowe right well that the subiectes of the seid yong prince for their parte have doon and wol semblably do accordingly lating you wite that we have directed o^r like lettres to diverse other cities and townes w^{t}in o^r seid reame semblably to do for theyr part Yeuen under o^r Signet at our maner of Richemond the xxviij day of Decembre.

No. 31.

Petition of Dean Colet to the Common Council that he might be allowed to purchase certain lands and tenements for the purpose of enlarging his School; 15 Jan. 3 Henry VIII. [1511–12].

Journal 11, fo. 147b.

To the hono^{r}able Comon Counsell of the Citie of London.

Shewith unto you the Hono^{r}able Comyn Counsell of the Citie of London yor lover and Bedman John Colet Deane of poules That where he hath made sute unto you afore this tyme for certeyn mesuage or tenement in the olde Chaunge and ye have not sufficiently yitt knowen his mynde in that behalf that it woll nowe lyke you to understande his mynde more plainly whiche ys this, That ys to sey That where he hathe edified and ordeyned a scole for your Childern bothe for lernyng and for good made maners in poules Churche and nowe to the more examplefying and makyng profite of the same in every pointe And also the more commoditie and weale of yor sonnes that nowe and hereafter shall resorte to the seid Scole because he sethe that it moche behoveth hym to his purpose to have suche house and tenement in the old Channge lying at the bakside of the said scole in the Est parte of the same that is to sey betwixt the tenement nowe in the tenour of Reynold Pwe Citezen and Marchaunt haberdassher of London on the South parte and the tenement nowe in the tenure of John

Evers Citezein and Marchaunt haberdassher of London on the North parte conteynyng in lenght from the South to the North xxviij fote of assise and in brede from the Est to the West x fote ix Inches and a half of assise nowe being in the tenure of the seid John Evers paying a yerely Rent of xxxv s̃. Therfore he instantly praieth you and requireth you that ye wyll voutesave to lett hym have the seid tenementes for convenient and reasonable price suche as shalbe sene to indifferent men according to the true valour of the seid tenementes and and [*sic*] this grauntyng ye shall doo the seid John Colet a gret pleaso^r and also a thing of gret commoditie to your childern, and the seid John Colet Deane of poules shall pray for your good prosperious contynuance to almyghty God all way who ever kepe you amen.

No. 32.

Letter from King Henry VIII to the City desiring 300 men for the service of the Navy against a threatened invasion of England by the King of France. Dated Greenwich, 30 Jan. [1512-13].

Journal II, fo. 1.

Trusty and welbeloved we grete youe well And forasmoche as we have perfite knowleage that o^r enemye the Frenche kyng hathe prepared a strong navye furnysshed w^t men of warre to entre and lande in diverse parties of this o^r realme in this nexist moneth of Februarij for to brenne slee robbe and distroye all that they may overcome We entendyng to prevent his conspired malice and to defende o^r reame and subgiettes from all suche invasions by strength of a navye to be shortly sett to the see Wol therefore & commaunde youe that almaner excuses utterly sett a parte ye furthw^t upon the sight hereof doo prepare and arredye the number of ccc able persones sufficiently harneysed to serve us on the see so that they be here at Grenewiche by the xvth day off Februarij nexist commyng at the farthest any o^r former lettres wrytinges to contrary notw{t}stondyng and that in the mean season ye do send unto us some persone to receyve money for jakettes and conducte money and that ye faile not hereof as ye tender our hono{r} the suertie & defence of this o{r} realme and woll annswer therefore unto us at their utturmost perill. Yeven under o{r} Signet at o{r} mano{r} of Grenewiche the xxx day of Januarij.

No. 33.

Letter from Cardinal Wolsey to the City, touching a loan of 4000 marks. Dated Westminster, 3 Sept. [1522].

Journal 12, fo. 196b.

Right honorable and my welbelovid frendes I parceyve by the relacõn of Sir John Dauncy howe towardly and benevolently ye at this present tyme of necessite, do use applye and endevo{r} yor selfes to shewe gratuite hono{r} and pleasure unto the kynges grace, and that the rather at my contemplacõn and desire, ye be mynded and contentid nowe to avaunce unto his highnes by way of lone the summe of iiij{ml} merkes which is not only a manyfest and evydent demonstracõn of the perfite zele that ye have to the furtheraunce of the kynges affaires, but also therbye I do see what good inclynacõn and lovyng myndes ye be of to do unto me acceptable and thankfull pleasure assuryng you that the kynges highnes woll not faile so to remembre this yor gentill demeano{r} as ye shall have cause to thynk the same well employed and bestowed. And for my parte I thank you asmoch as though an other season ye gave unto me thries that valure, offeryng that eny goodes of myn or that I can make of my frendes shalbe as alliable unto yor commodities weales and profites hereafter as ye do shew you to be unto the satisfacõn of my desire and request, promysyng you also that w{t}in xv dayes next ensuyng I shall see you entierly repayed of the same   And in all such thynges as may concerne thadvauncemet and comon weale of you and that Citie ye shall assuredly have my favo{r} and good furtheraunce as thise yor merites condyngeiely do requyre   At my place besides Westmynster the iij^(de) daye of Septembre.

Yo^r assured lovyng ffrende
T. Cardinalis Ebor.

No. 34.

Letter from Henry VIII to the City requesting a benevolence. Dated Greenwich, 25 April [1525].

Letter Book N, fo. 278.

Trusty and right welbiloved we grete you well.   Lattyng you wytte that by the reaporte and relacioun of the moost reverende fadre in God our most trusty and mooste enterly welbiloved counsaillor the lorde legate Cardynall Archebisshope of Yorke Primate of Englande and Chauncellor of the same   Whom we appoynted to practyse w^t you for an amyable graunte to be made unto us towards the supportacõn of o^r charges for our intended vyage in to Fraunce for recoverey and atteignynge of our crown and rightes there   We to our singuler contentation understonde that ye lyke most lovynge and kynde subgettes have shewed yor selffes as confo^rmable and well mynded to accomplyshe our desire purposed and shewed unto you by the sayde moost reverende fadre in that behalffe as cowde be imagined or devised   And that there lakketh yn none of you any maner towardnes or herty good wille with all effecte to perfo^rme the same   For the whiche your good demontracõn evidently provynge the feithfull and mooste lovynge myndes that you alwaies have borne and contynually doo bere unto us, ye do geve us right good cause to devise and studie howe we may be as gracious soverayne lorde unto yow, as ye bee good subgettes unto us: and surely yor towarde conformytes & demeano^rs heryn be so imprynted in our harte and mynde that we shall never forgett the same but yn all your resonable causes and pursuytes woll have suche consideracõn and respecte therunto as shalbe to yor comfortes gevyng you for this yor benevolent demeano^r our right hartye thankys.   Nevertheless in asmoche as by reaporte and informacõn of the said moost reverende fader we perceyve that albeyt ye be of this towarde molinacõn and disposicioun as is aforesaid, yet your powers and abilities be not equyvalent and correspondent unto yor good myndes ne ye may commodiously performe the same without your grete detryment and extreme hynderance & decay: We moche more esteme the prosperite of this our realme and the weale of you o^r lovynge and kynde subgettes then we doo ten suche realmes as Fraunce is. And not willynge you in any wise to be so overcharged in this benyvolent graunte as shulde be to yor extreme impoverishing have of our herty affeccõn and love towardes you at this tyme directed our other lettres and instruccõns unto the said most reverend fader willyng and desirynge hym to shewe and declare unto you what waies of moderacõn we have devysed to be taken with you in this behalff. By whome ye shall perceyve that we noo lesse doo tendre your weales then we doo the attaynynge of o^r said rights and crown whiche of necessite in avoydynge the greate dishono^r that by the contrary may ensue to us and this our realme and subgettes we must attempte to recover. Trustyng therefor verelye that lyke as we have tendre respecte unto you and your commoditie soo ye will as liberall and good subgettes regarde the importance of our said intendyd viage with the hono^r and Reputacõn of us and this own realme accordyngly Yoven undre our Signet at o^r Maner of Grenewiche the xxv day of Aprill.

No. 35.

Order for Obsequies to be celebrated in the City on the death of the lady Jane Seymour, 10 November 1537.

Letter Book P, fo. 135b.

At thys courte yt ys agreed that a Solempn herse shalbe made in poules wyth iiij great Candlestickes wth iiij great Tapers and the herse to be garnysshed wth xxx other great Tapers wth ij Braunches of vyrgyn waxe and the same to be garnysshed wth blacke clothe and wth the Quenes armys and upon Monday next at after noone the great belles in Every churche at one of the Clocke to be Ronge and so contynue tyll three and then all the belles in Everye churche to Rynge tyle vj of the clocke And my lorde Mayre and the Sheryffes to contynue by the space of xiiij dayes And also agreed that all the Aldermen shall goo in blak and agreed that at twoo of the clocke at after noone to assemble here upon Monday next and that at after noone a Solempn Obytt to be kept at powles and on the morrowe the Masse And that of every Churche twoo preestes shall gyve attendance Every one in theyre Surplesses and the said Preestes to be devyded in fyve places in our Lady Chappell Saint Georges Chappell and Saint The Great Chappels on the North and South partes and that warnynge be gevyn by the clerkes of Every churche to the churchewardens of Everye Churche and one offycer of my lorde mayres to goo west and an other easte Also to gyve warnynge to the churchewardens and that the belles of Every churche upon Tuesday next shall begynne at ix of the clocke and contynue untyll xj of the clocke afore noone And than the great belles of every churche to rynge alone tyll xij of the clocke be strycken And that my lorde for hys Offycers viij blacke Gownes shall have and Every one of the Sheryffes to have iiij a pece At the costes of thys Cytie And that Mr Recorder shall have xxxiij^s iiij^d. The Chamberleyn the under-chamberleyn and the Towne clerk Every one of them xx^s a pece by the commaundement of my lorde Mayre.

No. 36.

Extract from letter from Sir Richard Gresham to Thomas Cromwell, lord Privy Seal, touching the purchase of certain houses in Lombard Street belonging to Sir George Monoux, Alderman of the City of London, for the purpose of a site for an Exchange. Dated 25 July [1538].

Brit. Mus. MS. Cotton, Otho E x, fo. 45.

* * * "The Last yere I shewyd yor goode lordeshipe a Platte that was drawen howte for to make a goodely Bursse In Lombert strete for merchaunts to Repayer unto I doo suppose yt wyll coste ij m^l/ and more wyche shalbe very beautyful * * and allsoo for the honor ow^r soveragne * * ther ys serteyn howssys in the sayd * * longyn to Sir George Monnocks and excepte * * maye purchesse them the sayd Bursse can [not] be made Wherefor yt maye please yor good lordshipe [to] move the kynges highnes to have his most gracious letty^{r}s [di]rectyd to the sayd Sir George Wyllynge and allsoo [co]maundynge hym to cawsse the sayd howssys to be [so]led to the Mayer and Comminaltye of the City of London for suche prices as he dyd purches them for and that he fawte not but to accomplyshe hys gracious commaundement the Letty^r must be sharply made for he ys of noo jentyll nature and that he shale gyffee Further credens to the mayer I wyll delyver the Letty^r and handyll hym the best I can, and yf I maye obtayngne to have the sayde howyssys I dought not but to gather oon m^l/ towarde the buildynge or I departe howte of myn office ther shale lacke noo goode wylle In me. And thus o^r lorde preserve yor goode lordshippe in prosperous helthe long to contynew   At London the xxv daye Juylly.

No. 37.

Letter from King Henry VIII to Alderman Monoux desiring him to part with certain property whereon to erect an Exchange. Dated Chichester, 13 August [1538].

Journal 14, fo. 124.

By the Kynge

Trusty and welbelovyd we grete you well And where as we under stande that ye have certeyn howsyng and tenementes abowt lombard strete in our Citye of london whiche ar veray mete and expedyent for certeyn intended purposes to the weale and commen furtherance of merchauntes and entreocours of the same w^{t}yn that o^r Cytye lyke as o^r trusty and Ryght welbelovyd servaunt Sr Rychard Gresham maio^r of the same and other hys brethern there can declare unto you   Forasmoche as we tender moche that theyre good mynde and purpose in that byhalf may take effect   And not dowbtyng but beyng brought up there ye have a good zeale and affeccõn to the same we have therfore thought hartely to requyre you that nowe shewyng the same ye woll nowe vouchesave at o^r intercessyon to bestowe upon suche a common weale and furtheraunce so moche of yor sayd howsyng as shall nede for thaccomplysshement of the same freely and frankely   Or at the least w^t so reasonable an agreament indelayedly to be made betwene you and the sayd Gresham as they maye have cawse to thynke that ye want no good affeccõn towardes the sayd cytye   And also that ye have suche good respect to our requisicõn herein as apperteigneth   Assuryng you that yor gentle confirmite so to doo shalbe by us thankfully accepted and remembred accordyngly   Yeven under o^r signet at o^r citye of Chichestre the xiij daye of August.

No. 38.

Another letter from King Henry VIII to the same urging him to part with property required for an Exchange, on reasonable terms.   No Date [1538].

Id. ibid.

By the Kyng

Trusty and welbelovyd we grete you well   And where as we have lately dyrected to you o^r letters hartely desyeryng you at o^r request frankely and frely to gyve certeyn yor howses that ye have in lombardstrete yn that o^r Cytye of London for a burse or place apte for merchauntes to resorte to orelles upon suche a reasonable agreament and convencõn as ye cowlde fynde yn your harte for o^r sake to conclude w^t theym yn that byhalf wheryn ye shulde doo unto us acceptable pleasure not to be forgotten whensoever oportunytye shall requyre   Wherupon as we be enfo^{r}med o^r trusty and Ryght welbelovyd servaunt Sir Rychard Gresham Knight late Maio^r of o^r sayd Cytye have w^t other of hys brethern Aldermen of the same bene lately w^t you for thaccomplysshement therof at whiche tyme ye hooly remytted the matter to thorderyng of o^r trusty and welbelovyd counsailo^r Sir Richard Ryche chauncelo^r of o^r co^{r}te thaugmentacõns of o^r crowne w^t whome also the sayd Sir Rychard Gresham w^t other of hys brethern thaldermen of that o^r Cytye concluded and agreed to pay yerely for ever an annuall rent of twenty markes by yere for the sayd howses yet thys notw^{t}standyng thorough the evell counsayll and dethortacõn of certayn persones of frowarde disposicõn whiche lytle regarde o^r pleasure and yor estymacõn contrary to o^r expectacõn and lesse to the furtherance of the common wealth of that o^r Cytye have dysturbed the sayd good purpose to o^r no lytill marvell we therfore muche desyeryng the same to take effect do eftsones desyre and hartely requyre you that ponderyng and weyng w^t yo^{r}self the benefite and commodytye that shall ensue therof to o^r common wealth and to the beautifitye of that o^r cytie and chamber of London to condescende to o^r desyre and conclude the sayd graunte accordyngly w^{t}out further delaye Requyryng you that of yor gentle conformytie herein to be used on yor behalf (the contrary wherof we nothyng loke for) ye woll advertyse us w^t convenyent dylygence by thys brynger Sir Rychard Gresham to thintent that accordyng to yor procedynges hereyn we maye gyve unto you o^r condigne thankes and also remember the same whan occasyon shall serve to yor no lytle benefit accordyngly Yeven under o^r Signet &c.

No. 39.

Letter of thanks from Henry VIII to Alderman Monoux for acceding to the King's former request. Dated Westminster, 25 Nov. [1538].

Journal 14, fo. 124b.

By the Kynge

Trusty and welbeloved we grete you well And perceyvyng by the relacõn of o^r Ryght trusty and Right welbelovyd counsailo^r

the lorde privie seale howe at the contemplacõn of o^r lettres lately
dyrected unto you for yor lovyng graunte to be made unto the
merchauntes of o^r citye of London for theyre reasonable money
to have of you suche yor howses and tenementes situate and lyeng
yn Lombardstrete as shulde be mete for a burse wherunto the
merchauntes of o^r said Cytye shulde for the trafique of mar-
chaundyses have dayly conco^{r}se and accesse to the beautifyeng of
o^r sayd Cytie and the advauncement of o^r common wealth of the
same ye have lyke a lovyng subiect confo^{r}med yo^{r}self unto the
same And have of yor owne gentlenes shewed and declared more
conformitye unto theyre sute and Request than we desyred of you
by o^r sayd lettres lyke as for yor gentle Accomplysshement thereof
we geve unto you o^r cordyall and condynge thankes So we
assure you we shall have the same yor towardnes yn the perfo^{r}myng
hereof yn suche remembrance as whan occasyon shall serve yn
yor lawfull pursuytes the same shall redownde unto yor benefyte
accordyngly Yeven under o^r signet at o^r Royall palace of Westminster the xxv day of Novembre.

No. 40.

Proclamation by Henry VIII forbidding public hunting and
hawking in the suburbs of London. Dated 7 July, 1545.

Journal 14, fo. 240b.

Forasmoche as the Kynges moste Royall Maistey is moche
desyrous to have the Games of hare partriche ffesaunte and
heron preserved in and abowte his hono^r at his paleys of Westmynster for his owne disporte and pastyme That is to saye from
his said paleys at Westmynster to saint Gyles in the feelde and
from thens to Islyngton to o^r ladye of the Oke to Hyghegate to
Harnesey parke to Hampstede Hethe and from thens to Shote-
hophyll to Wyllesdon to Acton to Cheseweke to Chelsehethe and
so from thens to his said paleys of Westmynster to be preserved
and kepte for his owne disporte pleasure and Recreacõn. His
Highnes therefore straytlye chargethe and Commaundeth all &

singuler his subiectes of what Estate Degree or condicõn soever they be that they ne any of them do presume or attempte to hunte or hawke or in any manener of meanes to take or kyll any of the said Games wthin the precincte aforesaid as they tender his favour and wull exchewe further punysshement at his Maiestyes wyll and pleasure. * * * Dated Westminster, 7 July, 37 Henry VIII [1545].

No. 41.

Letter from King Edward VI and the Protector Somerset to the City asking for a force of 1000 men as a protection against conspirators. Dated Hampton Court, 6 Oct. [1549].

Letter Book R, fo. 39b.

Trustye and welbeloved we greate yowe well we charge and commaunde yowe moste ernestlye to gyve order wth all spede for the defence & preservacõn of that o^r Cytie of London for us. And to levye owte of hande & to putt in order as menye as convenyentlye yowe maye well weaperred & arayed keapyng good watche at the gates And to sende us hether for the defence of o^r person one thousand of that o^r cytie of trustye & faythfull men to attende upon us & o^r most intyerly belovyd uncle Edwarde Duke of Somersett governo^r of o^r personne and protecto^r of o^r realmes domynyons and subiectes well harnessed & wth good & convenyent weapon. So that they do make their repayer hether unto us this night if yt be possyble or at the leaste tomorrowe before none. And in the meane tyme to do what as apperteyneth unto yor duetye for ours & o^r seid uncles defence agayns all suche as attempte anye conspyracie or enterpryse of vyolence against us or o^r seid uncle, and as yow knowe best for o^r preservacõn & defence at this presente Yoven under o^r Signett at o^r hono^r of Hampton co^{r}te the vjth of October the third yere of o^r reign.

Poscript—Ye shall further gyve credyte to o^r trustye & welbeloved Owen Claydon the bearer herof in all suche thynges as. he shall further declare unto yowe on the behalf of us & o^r seid uncle the lord protecto^r.

No. 42.

Letter from Lords of the Council to the City touching the conduct of the Duke of Somerset. Dated 6 Oct. [1549].

Letter Book R, fo. 40.

After o^r right hartye comendac͠ons unto yor good lordship knowyng yor hartye loves & earnest zeales to the preservac͠on of the person of the kynges maiestie & of this realme : and other his maiesties realmes & domynyons we have thought good to advertyse yowe that notwthstanding all the good advyse & counseyll that we cowde geve to the Duke of Somerset to steye hymself wthin his reasonable lymyttes and to use his governement nowe in the tender age of his maiestye in suche sorte as might tende to his highnes suertye to the conservac͠on of his estate & to his owne hono^r The seid duke neverthelesse styll contynuing in his pryde covetousnes & ambycyon ceaseth not daylie by all the wayes & meanes he can devyse to enryche hymself wthowte measure and to empoveryshe his ma^{tie} he buyldeth in iiij or v places moste sumptuouslye & leaveth the poore souldiers unpayed of their wages onvyttaylled and in all thynges so unfurnysshed as the losses lately susteyned to the greatest dyshono^r that ever came to the kynge & this realme do declare ; he soweth daylie dyvysyon bytwene the nobles & gentlemen of the commens he rewardeth & enterteyneth a number of those that were capteyns of the commens in this late insurecc͠ons & fynally in such wyse subverteth all lawes justyce & good order as yt is evydent that puttyng his truste in the commens & perceyving that the nobles and gentlemen shuld be an impedyment to hym in hys dyvyllyshe purposes he laboureth fyrste to have theym destroyed & thyncketh after easelye inough to achive his desyer wth yt appeireth playnly is to occupye the kinges maiesties place for his doinges who so ever lyste to beholde theym do manyfestlye declare that he myndeth never to render accompte to his maiestie of his procedynges. These thynges wth manye moo to large to recyte consydered we pondred wth o^{r}selfes that eyther we muste travayle for some reformac͠on or we muste in effecte as yt were consent wth hym to the destruccyon of o^r soveraign lorde & cuntreye, wherepon laying aparte all respectes and restyng only upon o^r duetyes we joyned in counseyll & thought quyetlye to have treated the matter wth hym, who perceyvyng that we joyned for the kynge & wold have suche order as might be for the suertye of his ma^{ties} person & the commen welthe streight put hym self in force & resteth at pleyn point as yt appereth eyther to go thurrough wth his detestable purpose in sorte as he hathe done or to trye yt by the sworde. Nowe for asmoche as we see presentlie that onles there be a reformacõn the person of the kinges ma^{tie} is in moste certeyn daunger & this realme o^r naturall countrey lyke to be destroyed wth o^r posteryties, lyke as we have agayne fully resolved wth godes helpe eyther to delyver the kynges ma^{tie} & the realme from this extreme ruyne & destruccyon or to spend o^r lyves for the declaracõn of o^r faythfull hartes and duetyes so knowinge yor hartye good wylles & troth to his maiestye & therefore nothinge doubtyng of yor redynes to joyne wth us in o^r godly purpose we thought good to lett yowe knowe the verye trouthe of o^r enterprice & in the kynges ma^{ties} behalf so requyre yowe not onlye to put good & substancyall order for watche and warde but also to have an earnest contynuall regarde to the preservacõn wthin yor cytie of all harneys weapons & munycõns so as none be suffred to be conveyed to the seid duke nor any others attendyng aboute hym and besydes that yow from hensforth obey no letters proclamacõns nor other commaundements to be sent from the seid duke and thus we byd yor L. moste hartely farewell from London the vjth of October.

No. 43.

Letter from Queen Mary to the City, desiring a contingent of 1,000 men to be held ready for active service at a day's notice. Dated Richmond, 31 July, 1557.

Journal 17, fo. 54b.

By the Quene

Trustie & welbeloved we grete yow well and lett yow wete y^t the warres beinge open betwixte us and Fraunce and the Kynge our deerest Lorde & husband passed the seas in persone to pursue the enemye we have gyven order as mete is (o^r hono^r and suertie so requiering) to have a convenyent force putt in a perfytt readynes to attend upon o^r persone aswell for the defence & suertie thereof as to resiste suche attempes as may be by any forrein enemye or otherwise made agaynst us & o^r Realme and therefore will & comaunde yow that of the hole manred of that o^r Cytie of London aswell in lyberties as wthowt yow do appoynte the nomber of one thousand hable souldyers wherof as many to be horsemen as may be and the resydewe to be hable footemen the horsemen to be well horssed & armed & of the footemen the fourthe parte to be harquebutiars or archers One other fourthe parte or more to beare pykes and the residewe of the said footemen to be bylles all well harnessed and weaponed to serve us in o^r saide defense having & kepinge the same nomeber in suche order as under the leadynge of mete Captaynes gentlemen of enherytaunce or their heires apparaunte by yow lykewyse to be named they may be readye by the xvjth of August nexte at the furthest and from thensfourthe to contynue in suche a redynes as at all tymes after they maye be hable upon one dayes warninge to repaire unto us or suche other place as we shall appoyncte for our servyce Takinge also suche order as the said Captaynes to bee by yow named may in the meane tyme knowe and be acquaynted wth theire soldiers and the soldyers lykewyse withe their Captaines And because we have wrytten o^r specyall lettres to the persones named in the scedule inclosed to furnyshe for o^r servyce suche nombers of men as they ar hable to make Our pleasure is yow shall forbeare in the settinge fourthe of theis numbers to take any the tenaunts or others under the rules or offyces of the said persones or of any others appoynted lykewyse to serve us And our pleasure is yow shall have also lyke respecte to the tenaunts & others under the rules and offyces of those noble men and gentlemen now gon with o^r armye into Fraunce And of yor doinges herein o^r pleasure is yow shall advertise us by yor Lettres wth as muche spede as you possibly maye And theis o^r Lettres Shalbe unto yow suffycient warraunte and dyscharge for yor doinges in that behalfe   Yoven under o^r Sygnet at o^r mano^r of Richemond the last of July the fourth and fyveth yeres of o^r raignes [1557].

No. 44.

Letter from Queen Mary to the City asking for 500 men to be immediately dispatched for the relief of Calais. Dated Greenwich, 2 Jan. [1557-8].

Journal 17, fo. 55.

Trustie and welbeloved we greate you well and where ye did this last Sommer put in a readynes the nomeber of one thowsande men to attend upon o^r person at all tymes whan we shuld calle for the same   Havinge receyved certein advertisementes from o^r Towne of Callice that the Frenche hathe approched theither and myndeth to attempte sum exployte on o^r said Towne and other o^r pieces there we have thought good for the better metinge wth suche attemptates as shalbe by them offered to sende a furder supplye of men thither and therfore requyre & comaunde yow furthwth upon the recipte of theise o^r letters wth as muche dylygente spede as ye may possyblye to putt in a reddynes the number of fyve hundreth hable footemen and to se them furnyshed wth armure and weapon, whereof as many of them to be harquebutters as yo^w can gett and the rest to be furnyshed wth bowes and pykes so as the said number be ready to sett fourthe towardes o^r said Towne under the conducte of suche captaynes as we shall appoynte by Frydaye nexte at the furthest   For whose conducte money we have alredy given order they shall receyve the same at o^r said Towne of Callyce at their arryvall there   And because this o^r servyce requyrethe moche expedycōn and haste, ye shall not neade to staye for the makinge of any cotes for the said number but to send them fourthe withe all spede   Wereof we requyer you not to fayle as we specyallye truste yo^w   And theise o^r lettres shalbe yor suffycient warraunte & dyscharge in this behalfe.

Yeoven under o^r Sygnet at o^r Manno^r of Grenewiche the seconde of January in the fourth and fyfthe yeres of o^r raignes [1557–8].

No. 45.

Letter from Queen Elizabeth to the City desiring 250 soldiers for service at sea under the High Admiral, Lord Clinton, against the French. Dated Greenwich, 17 May, 2 Eliz. [1560].

Journal 17, fol. 238b.

ELIZABETH R.

Right Trustie and welbeloved we grete you well Because we certaynly understand that notwthstandinge our desire and good contentacõn at diverse tymes declared to have a treatie wth the frenche for the redresse and staye of the notable Iniuries and attemptes commytted agaynst us and the right of our Crowne and for the wthdrawinge of their forces out of Scotland the whiche can not be permytted there as they be wthout greate daunger not onlie to o^r towne of Barwick but also to the state of o^r realme consideringe the false pretence made and certeyne other depe practises by them agaynst this Realme To the furderaunce of whiche treatie they offer in speche and good wordes accesse of personages to mete wth somme of ours; yet their preparations to the seas be daylie so great as greater can not well be whiche surely with convenient providence on our parte and by goodes goodnes we nede not feare. Thearfore meanynge to be ready for the defense and honour of o^r Realme aswell to treate wth the frenche for accorde and quietnes as for wthstandinge of there furder attemptes specially by sea we have by advyse of our Counsell thought convenient to send our navie furthwth to the seas, and therwth o^r right trustie and right welbeloved Counsellor the lord Clynton our highe Admirall to governe the same, and wth o^r said Navie to wthstande suche force as he shall fynde on the frenche parte upon the seas to damage either our owne subiectes and marchauntes tradynge the seas or the subiectes of any other our frendes or to invade or attempte to lande upon any parte of o^r sea costes And for the better furnyture of o^r said navie wth souldiores we will that there shalbe levyed wthin that our Cytie of London and the liberties of the same the nomber of two hundred and fyftie hable men whereof o^r meanynge ys, that the one halfe shoulde be archers and thother harquebuttiers, and as sone as ye have levied the same, our pleasure is that ye shall commytt them to several captaynes for every hundred, and cause them to be arrayed wth armoure and weapon mete for that service to be redy in o^r Cytie of London the xxiiijth of this monethe and to departe to o^r navie wth o^r Admirall at suche tyme as he shall prescribe and for their conducte money the same shalbe delivered to you by order of o^r Treasorer of Englande And theise o^r lettres shalbe yor sufficient warrant for the levyenge of the said nomber of two hundred and fyftie men accordinglie. Yeoven under o^r signet at our mannor of Greneiwiche the xvijth of Maye the seconde yere of o^r reigne [1560].

No. 46.

Letter from Queen Elizabeth to the City, desiring that Sir Thomas Gresham might be discharged from serving the offices of Mayor, Alderman and Sheriff. Dated Westminster, 7 March, 5 Eliz. [1562–3].

Journal 18, fo. 137.

Trustie and welbeloved we gret you well; And wheras our faythfull servante Sr Thomas Gresham knighte is one of the citizens and fredome of o^r citie of London, and by reason therof maye perchance hereafter be called upon or elected to serve in the office of maio^r alderman or shref wthin our saide citie of London or countye of Middlesex Forasmuche as the same Sr Thomas Gresham not onlye in tymes past hathe ben employed in o^r service about our weightye affayres in the partyes of beyond the sea concerninge the state of o^r Realme But also hereafter duringe his lif muste and shalbe employed aboute o^r like weightye affayres in o^r service concerninge the state of oure realme from tyme to tyme as our pleasure shalbe to appoynte. These ar to signifye unto you that those & other speciall consideracõns us movinge our request and expresse pleasure is that at yor nexte comen assembly or comen counsayle daye to be holden wthin our saide cittye ye do cause it to be fyrmely and perfectley ordered and of recorde emongest yon regestred by an absolute acte of comen counsell that o^r saide servante Sr Thomas Gresham from hensfourth duringe his life shalbe free and clerely discharged of and from the saide offices of maio^r, alderman and shriff afore mencõned and of and from every of them and not at any tyme to be elected or charged wth the same offices or any of them And that ye fayle not herof as ye tender o^r favo^r And of yor procedinges in observacõn of this our request, that ye do furthwith after yor nexte comen counsell daye assertayne us by writing from you to the intent we maye have consideracõn of the same as shall appertayne. And sowe bidd you fare well from o^r palace at Westminster the vijth daye of Marche in the fyveth yere of our reigne [1562-3].

No. 47.

Proclamation against the Earls of Northumberland and Westmoreland for their rebellion against the Queen's Majesty. Dated Windsor Castle, 24 Nov., 1569.

Journal 19, fo. 202b.

By the Queene.

The Queenes maiestie was sundry wise aboute the latter ende of this sommer infourmed of some secrete whisperinges in certaine places of Yorkshire, and the Bishopricke of Durham that there was lyke to be shortly some assemblies of Lewde people in those partes tendinge to a rebellyon : Whereof, because at the first the informacõns conteyned no evident or direct cause or proofe therfore her Maiestie had the lesse regarde therto, untill upon certayne convencõns and secrete meetinges of the Earles of Northumberlande and Westmerlande, wth certen personnes of suspected behavor, the formor reportes were renewed and thereof also the

saide two Earles were in vulgare speaches from place to place
expresslye noted to be the auctors, whereupon the Earle of Sussex,
lorde President of her Maties councell in those north partes, gave
advertisment of the like brutes, addinge nevertheles (to his
knowelege) there was no other matter in dede but lewde rumors,
sodaynly raised and sodaynly ended   And yet shortely after he
sent for the two Earles wth whom he conferred of those rumors :
who as thei could not deny but that thei had harde of suche, yet
(as it nowe afterward apperethe) falsely then dissemblinge, thei
protested themselves to be free from all suche occasions, offeringe
to spende theire lyves against any that shulde breake the peace
and so muche trusted by the said lorde president upon theire
othes, they were licensed not only to departe, but had powre geven
to examyn the causes of the said brutes. Neverthelesse the fire
of theire treasons wch thei had covered was so greate, as it did
newly burst out mo flames. Whearupon her Maiestie beinge
alwais lothe to enter in any open misport of any of her nobilitie,
and therfore in this case desirous rather to have bothe the saide
Earles cleared from suche sclaunders and her good people that
lived in feare of spoile to be quitted comaunded the lord President
(as it semed) havinge than discovered somewhat further of theire
evill purposes, dyd onely at the first write to them to come to hym
to consult upon matters apperteynynge to that councell, whereunto
they made delatory and frivolous answeres : and so beinge once
agayne more earnestly required, thei more flatly denyed   And
last of all her Maiestie sent her owne private letters of comaundement to them to repaire to her presence all wch notw^{th}standinge,
thei refused to come : And havinge before the delivery of her
Maties letters to them assembled as great numbers as they could
(wch were not many, for that the honester sorte dyd refuse them)
thei did enter into an open and actuall rebellion armynge and
fortifyinge them selfes rebelliously in all warlike maner and have
invaded houses and churches and published proclamacõns in there
owne names to move her Maties subiectes to take theire partes, as
personnes that meane of theire private auctorite to breake and

subvert Lawes threateninge the people that if thei cannot atchive theire purposes, then strangers will enter the Realme to fynyshe the same   And wth this they adde, that they meane no hurte to her Maties personne a pretence always first published by all traitors   And as for reformacõn of any greate matter, it is evident thei be as evill chosen two personnes (if there qualities be well considered) to have creditt, as can be in the whole Realme   And nowe her Maiestie manifestly percyvinge in what sorte these two Earles beinge both in povertie, the one havinge but a very small porcõn of that wiche his auncesters had and lost, and the other havinge almost his whole patrimony wasted, do go aboute throughe the perswasion of a nomber of desperat persons associated as parasites wth them to satisfie there privat lacke and ambicioun wch cannot be by them compassed w^thout coveringe at the first certeine highe treason against the quenes Maties person and the Realme, longe hidden by suche as have heretofore provoked them, wth the cover of some other pretended generall enterprises hathe thought good that all her good lovinge subiectes shulde spedely understand howe in this sorte the said two Earles contrary to the naturall propertie of nobilitie (wch is instituted to defende the prince beinge the head and to preserve peace) have thus openly and traitorrously entred into the first rebellyon and breach of the publique blessed peace of this Realme that hath heppened (beyonde all former examples) duringe her Maties raigne wch nowe haithe contynued above eleven yeares, an acte horrible against god the only gever of so longe a peace; and ungratefull to there soveraigne Lady to whom thei two particularly have heretofore made sundry professions of there faith and lastely most unnaturall and pernicious to theire natyve cuntrey that hath so longe enyoied peace, and nowe by there only mallyce and ambicioun is to be trobled in that felicitie   And herew^th also her Maiestie chargeth all her goode subiectes to employ there hole powers to the preservacõn of comon peace (wch is the blessinge of almightie god) and spedely to apprehend and suppresse all maner of personnes that shall by any dede or word shewe them selfes favorable to this rebelliouse entreprise of the said two Earles, or any there associates who as her Maiestie hath already willed and commaunded to be by the forsaid Earle of Sussex, her liefetenaunt generall in the northe, published rebells and traitors against her Crowne and dignytye so dothe her Matie by these presentes for avoidinge of all pretences of ignoraunce reiterat and eftsonnes notifie the same to her whole Realme, wth all their adherentes and favorers to be traitors, and so to be taken and used to all purposes not doubtinge but this admonicõn and knowlege geven, shall suffice for all good subiectes to retaine them selves in there dwetes, and to be void from all seducinge by these foresaid rebells and traitors or there adherentes and favorers, whatsoever there pretences shalbe made or published by them selves, or suche as have not the grace of god to delighte and lyve in peace, but to move uprores to make spoile of the goodes and substances of all good people, the true proper fruytes of all rebellions and treasons geven at the Castell of Windsor the xxiiij daie of November 1569 in the twelfth yere of her Maties raigne.

god save the quene.

No. 48.

Letter from Queen Elizabeth to the Mayor and Aldermen of the City of London on the occasion of the discovery of the Babington conspiracy. Dated Windsor Castle, 18 August 1586.

Journal 22, fo. 52.

Right trustie and welbeloved we grete you well being given tunderstand howe greatlie our good and most Loving subiectes of that Cittie did reioyce at the apprehension of certayne develish and wicked mynded subiectes of ours that through the greate and singuler goodnes of god have of late ben detected to have most wickedlie and unnaturallie conspired not onelie the takinge awaie of our oune lief, but also to have stirred upp (as mutche as in them laye) a generall rebellion throughout our whole realme : we could coulde [*sic*] but by our owne lettres witnes unto you the grate and singuler contentment we receyved uppon the knowledge thereof assuringe you that we did not so mutche reioyce at the escape of the intended attemp against our owne person, as to see the greate Joye our most Lovinge subiectes tooke at the apprehension of the contrivers thereof, w^{ch} (to make their Love more apparent) the have (as we are to our greate comfort enformed) omitted no outwarde shewe, that by anie externall acte might witnes to the worlde, the inward love and dutifull affeccion they beare towardes us, and as we have as greate cause wth all thankfulness, to acknowledge godes greate goodnes towardes us throughe the infinit blessinge he layeth uppon us as manie as ever Prince hadd, yea rather, as ever creature hadd; Yet doe we not for anie worldlie blessinge receyved from his devine Matie so greatlie acknowledged them, as in that it hath pleased him to inclyne the hartes of our subiectes Even from the first begynninge of our reigne, to carrie as greate Love towardes us, as ever Subiectes carried towarde Prince, whiche ought to move us (as it dothe in verey deede) to seeke wth all care and by all good meanes that apparteyne to a christian Prince, the conservacion ot so loving and dutifull affected subiectes. Assuringe you that we desire no longer to Live, then while we maie in the whole course of our governement carrie our self in sutche sorte, as maie not onelie nourish and contynewe their Love and goodwill towardes us, but also increasse the same we thinke meete that theise our lettres should be also commynicated in sum generall assemblie to our most Lovinge subiectes the commons of that cittie. Geven under our signet at our castell of Wyndesor the xviijth daie of August 1586 in the xxviij yere of our Reigne.

No. 49.

Speech made by a member of the Common Council 22 Aug., 1586, upon the occasion of the discovery of the Babington conspiracy.

Journal 22, fo. 52.

Right worshipfull my good countreymen & citezens of this most noble cittie of London. Since the late brute and report of a most wicked and tray terouse conspiracie, not onelie to take awaie the leif of our most gracious soveraigne whom god graunt longe to lyve & raigne over us but also to stuer upp a generall rebellion throughout the whole realme ; the greate and universall ioye of you all of this cittie, uppon the apprehension of divers of that most wicked conspiracy a late declared and testified by manie outward actes & shewes hathe wrought in the quenes most excellent maiestie sutche a gracious contentement, that it hathe moved hir highnes, by hir letters signed wth hir owne hand to signifie unto my L. Maior of this cittie, and his bretherein, her most noble and pricelie acceptacioun thereof And that in sutche sorte as there by maie appeare that hir highnes hath not more no not so mutche reioyced at the most happie escape of the wicked mischeif intended against hir owne person as att the ioye wch her lovinge subiectes and namelie you of this cittie of London looke at the apprehension of the practizers of that intended treason By occasion whereof hir highnes brought to a thankfull rememberance, and acknowledginge of godes infinite blessing bestowed on hir, comparable wth anie prince or creature in the worlde no worldly thinge more or like accompteth of them of the heartie love of hir lovinge faithfull subiectes many wayes and many tymes before nowe but especially by this our greate ioye in this sorte at this tyme and uppon this occasion shewed.

And that hir exceadinge greate love and exceptacion of our reioycinge maye the more appeare unto you, it hath pleased hir highnes in the same letter to declare that she desireth no longer to live amonge us, then she shall maynteyne contynue norish & increase the love and goodwill of her subiectes towardes hir And this her highenes hath willed to be made knowen unto you all wth this, that she will not faile wth all care and by all good meanes that apperteyne to a Christian prince to seke the conservacion of you all so lovinge and dowty full affected subiectes This hir maiesties pleasure in parte nowe declared & more to be made knowen to you by hir owne letters, wch you shall heare redd, my lorde maior and his bretheren have required me to declare unto you all that they doe hartelie reioyce and thank god for the happie daie of the good acceptacion of this your greate ioye   And my L. himself hathe willed me to give you all hartie thankes in his name for that in the tyme of his service your dutifull behaviours have gotten to the cittie so noble & worthie a testimonie of dewtie & loyaltie of so worthie & noble a quene.

Now for asmutche as godes blessinges wonder fullie abounde & one ioye cometh uppon an other let us not be unthankfull to god but acknowledge his goodnes, attribute the same (as in deede we ought) to the sincere religion of allmightie god most godlie established by the quenes most excellent ma^{tie} wch hath taught us to knowe god a right our dowtie to our soveraigne and to love our countrey, and hath made us dutifull & obedient subiectes reioycinge att all good thinges happeninge to hir ma^{tie} hir realme or to anie in hir noble service the true effectes of a true & good religion. Whereas the contempners thereof & the immoderate affectors of the Romish religion & suspersticions, beinge voide of the true knowledge of god, have declyned from god, their allegiance to their prince their love to their countrey, And have become inventors of mischifes, brutors and spreaders abrode of false and sediciouse rumors, sutche as ioye at no good thinge but contrarie wise reioyse at everie evell successe, the badges and markes of their profession, who have before this, & in this realme and other hir highnes dominions stirred upp rebellion forrein invasion, and manie tymes practized the verey deathe & destruccion of the quene hir self the ruyne & subversion of the whole realme the proper effectes of their romishe religion.

We have behelde thes thinges & seene in our daies the ruyne and mischeifes invented against others fall uppon the inventors themselves & have knowen the wicked and violent handes of divers of them devilishlie to kill & murdre them selves whom most trayterouslie then woulde, and most happilie the could not slea the Lordes annoynted.

As we have knowen all thes thinges, so god be thanked, that by a better religion, havinge ben better taught, we have ben no partakers of their wicked devises, But have put to our helpinge handes as occasion hath served, and over redie to ever throwe the auctors & devisers there of.

And I have no doubt, but we of this noble cittie, who hetherto have ben alwaies redie redie dutifullie & faithfully to serve hir maiestie uppon all occasions (her highnes now so graciouslie acceptinge onely of our reioycinge at the apprehension of her enemies ever the least parte of the dutie of a good subiecte to so good a quene) wilbe redie everie one wth all y^t we can make, & wth the uttermost adventure of all our lives spedilie to be revenged uppon all sutche as shall vilanouslie & trayterouslie attempe or put in ure anie mischeif to her noble person, and in the meane tyme will have a better eye and eare to all suspicious miscontented persons to their sayenges and doinges to their false brutes and reportes, to the places and corners of their haunt & resort, to their harbours companions, ayders & maynteyners.

God upholde and contynue his religion amonge us & increase our zeale therein wch hathe made us so lovinge & loyall and so beloved & acceptable subiectes to so worthie a prince, & roote out the wicked & romishe religion that hath made so manie disloyall & trayterous subiectes, to whom is bothe odious & irkesome the longe lief and prosperouse reygne of our most noble quene Elizabeth. God confounde all sutche traytors and preserve hir hignes longe to live and raigne over us.

No. 50.

List of ships furnished and victualled by the City to meet the Armada, 1588.

State Papers Dom. Vol. ccxii. No. 68.

At Plymmowthe xix^{no} Julij 1588.

A note of all the shipps nowe at sea under the chardge of the Lorde Admerall wth their nombers of men and tyme of victuallinge wch is reduced nowe to ende in them all together the xth of Auguste.

*   *   *

APPENDIX A.

		Men.	
	The Hercules	120	
	The Tobie	110	
	The Senturyon ...	90	Theis shipps
	The Marget and John	84	beinge set furthe
	The Mynyon	84	by the Cyttie are
	The Assention ...	84	victuallid by them
	The Red Lyon ...	84	alreadie until the
	The May Flower ...	84	xth of Auguste and
The London	The Primrose	80	shalbe here fur-
Shippes	The Teger	72	nyshid with a
	The guyfte of god ...	64	moneths victuall
	The B. Burre ...	64	more at the
	The Brave	64	Cytties chardge
	The golden Lyon ...	64	accordinge to yor
	The Royall defence ...	60	Lo: order.
	The Thomas bona ventur	60	
	The releif	16	
	The Moneshine ...	30	instead of theis to
	The Pasporte	30	have 2 pynnasses
	The Dyana ...	16	

No. 51.

Government order to victual ships furnished by the City; 24 July, 1588.

State Papers Dom. Vol. ccxiii. No. 15.

Mr. Quarleis theis are to praie you presentlie to victuall theis shippes hereunder written nowe at the seas wth my Lo: Admirall wth one moneths victuall of xxviij daies to begyn the xth of August 1588 and to end the vijth of September followinge both daies included Of wch monnethes victualls you are to victuall the said Flete for the fyrst xiiij daies at Portesmouth The other xiiij daies he victuall to be sent to Dover. This to be doune with all spede possible and so fare you well from my house at Stroude the xxiiij[th] of Julie 1588

* * *

1	The Hercules ...	
2	The Tobie ...	
3	The Senturion ...	
4	The Marget and John...	
5	The Mynion ...	
6	The Assention ...	
7	The Red Lion ...	
8	The Tygar ...	
9	The Mayflower ...	Of London.
10	The Prymrose ...	
11	The gift of god ...	
12	The bark Burle ...	
13	The Brawle ...	
14	The golden Lion ...	
15	The Riall defence ...	
16	Thelen Nathan ...	
20	The foure pynnasses ...	

No. 52.

List of all the ships furnished by the City against Spain in 1588.

State Papers Dom. Vol. ccxxxvii, fos. 15b-16b.

The whole flete sett out in 88 against the Spaniards and w[ch] were payed by Q. Eliz: and how many were payed by London and the Porte Townes

Queene Eliz: whole armye at Sea against y[e] Spanish forces in anno 1588.

* * *

Shippes set forth and payde upon y[e] charge of y[e] City of London anno 1588

APPENDIX A.

	Men.	
The Hercules	120	George Barnes
The Tobie	110	Robert Barratt
The May flower	90	Edw: Bankes
The Mynion	90	John Dale
The royall defence	80	John Chester
The Assention	100	John Bacon
The Guift of God	80	Thom: Luntlowe
The Prime Rose	90	Rob: Bringborne
The Margarett and John	90	John Fisher
The goulden Lyon	70	Rob: Willton
The Dyana	40	
The B. Burre	70	John Sarracole
The Tigar	90	Willm Cæsar
The Brane	70	Willm Furth
The Red Lyon	90	Jarvis Willes
The Centurion	100	Samuel Foxcraft
The Pastporte	40	Chr. Colethurst
The Mooneshine	30	John Brough
The Tho. Bonaventure	70	William Alldrige
The Releife	30	John King
The George Noble	80	Henery Billingham
The Anthony	60	George Harper
The Tobie	70	Chr. Pigott
The Sallamander	60	Damford
The Rose Lyon	50	Barn. Acton
The Antellope	60	Dennison
The Jewell	60	Rowell
The Paunce	70	Willm Butler
The Providence	60	Rich. Chester
The Dolphin	70	Willm Hare

30 Shipps and Barques   2130 men.

No. 53.

Letter from King James I to the City upon his accession to the throne. Dated Holyrood House, 28 March 1603.

Journal 26 fo. 75b.

Trustie and welbeloved we greit you hartelly well beinge informed of youre great forduartnes in that iuste and honorable action of proclaminge ws youre Souverane lord and King immediatlye after the deceas oure late darrest Sister the quene, wherin yo^u have gevin a singulare good proufe of your ancient fidelitie, a reputation hereditarie to that oure Citie of Lundon, beinge the Chamber of oure Imperiall crowne and ever free from all shedowes of tumultous and onlawful courses wee could not omitt wth all the speid possible wee might to give you hereby a teast of oure thankfull mynde for the same and withall assurance that yo^u cannot crave anie thing of ws fitt for the mentenance of yow all in generall and everie one of yow in particulare but it shalbe moast willingly performed by ws whose speciall care shall ever be to provide for the continewance and incresse of your present happines desiringe yow in the meane tyme to goe constantly forduart in doinge all and whatsumer things yow shall find necessary or expedient for the good goverment of oure said Citye in execution of Justice as yow have bene in wse to doe in oure said darrest Sisters tyme, till oure pleasure be knowen unto yow in the contrare This not douting but ye will doe as ye may be fully assured of oure gratious favour towards yow in the hieghest degrie, we bid you hartely farewell Halyrudhous the 28 of Marche 1603.

No. 54.

Reply to the above. Dated 29 March, 1603.

Id., fo. 76.

To the most high & mighty Prince our most dread & gracious Soveraigne Lord King James ye First King of England, Scotland, France & Ireland.

APPENDIX A.

Most mighty prince & our most dread & gracious Soveraigne Wee cannot expresse the great comfort and exceeding ioy conceived here for this great blessing of Almighty God in preserving yor sacred Matie for this yor right and yor right for y^u and y^u for us yor Liege people of this yor Realme wch is increased & redoubled by the perfect union and concurrence of all yor Maties faithful subjects throughout yor Realme especially of this yor Highnes City in harty love & loyall affeccōn towards yor Highnes a Prince so famous and renowned through the world for yor great wisdome piety iustice Magnanimity & other great & princely vertues whereby our selves and all other yor Loyall Subjects of this your Land are made assured of ye continuance and increase of that happy peace holy religion & other great & infinite blessings of Almighty God, which wee have enjoyed soe many yeares by the happy governm^t of o^r late gracious and glorious Queene of famous memory.

What thancks sufficient can wee render to Almighty God for this his mercy and unspeakable goodnes towards this Land whoe hath thus tempered o^r great sorrow wth a great^r comfort & repaired this o^r great losse of a Mother with the advantage of a greater gain in the succession of yor Highnes as a Father which is accompanied wth the union of both Kingdoms to the great Strengthening of yor Highnes and noe lesse terror of ye Enemies (if any be) of yor Highnes person & estate.

Touching o^r selves to whom the Charge & preservacōn of this yor Chamber and principall City is comitted as wee have endeavored with all o^r powers to advance yor Highnes most iust clayme and rightfull title to the Succession of this yor Kingdome soe o^r future care & indeavour shall extend it selfe to ye very uttermost of our witts & power to preserve ye same wth all humble duty & circumspeccōn for yor Highnes use ag^t all power & opposicōn both of this Land (if any happen as God forfend) and the whole world. For assurance of wch o^r Loyalty & devoted loves towards yor Highnes Wee have sent unto y^u o^r speciall Messenger to witt o^r Secretary & Remembrancer Mr. Doctor Fletcher a man (wee heare) non unknowne unto yor Highnes As alsoe to returne unto us the Significacōn of yor Highnes pleasure and direccōn in such matters as shall conduce to the well ordering of this yor Chamber W^{ch} wee humbly pray Almighty God & intreate yor Highnes for yor owne and yor peoples sake may be accelerate wth all safety and due caucōn of yor person to the publique ioy both of o^r selves and yor whole Realme From London this xxixth of March 1603.

Your Maties most humble & loyall Subjects

The Maior & Aldermen of your Highnes Citty & Chamber of London.

Robert Lee Maior

John Hart	Tho : Bennett	John More
John Spencer	Tho : Lowe	Robt. Hampton
Stephen Slaney	Wm Glover	Roger Larke
Henry Billingsly	Wm Romeney	Humf. Weld
Stephen Soame	Leonard Halliday	Tho : Cambell
John Garrard	John Watts	Wm Craven
Jo: Croke Recorder	Rich. Goddard	Henry Anderson
	Henry Rowe	James Pemberton
	Edw. Holmden	Jo: Swinarton, Sherriffe

No. 55.

Letter from King James I to the Mayor and Aldermen of the City of London, in reply to the foregoing. Dated Newcastle, 11 April 1603.

Journal 26, fo. 80.

JAMES R.

Right trustie and welbeloved wee greet you well Althoughe before the Comeynge of yor Lettres and this gentleman sente unto us wee had wth greate Contentment by Comon reporte understood of your forwardnes in Joyninge wth ye nobillitie of this our Realme

APPENDIX A. 425

in the publishinge of oure righte to the succession of this Crowne Yet weare wee not a little gladd to finde ye same confirmed by soe honeste and diutifull a testimonie thereof under yor owne handes and by ye speeche of a persone of soe greate truste wth you and chieflie that you are not lead into this devosion onlie by the undoubted belief of oure righte, but alsoe for ye assurance you have of oure zeale to ye preservacõn of Religion for that wee have alwaies accompted those accõns that aryse oute of religious groundes to be the beste founded. And as wee doubt not but that in that poynte we shall give you and ye reste of o^r people satisfaction Soe maie you be assured that in all other thinges, wherein wee shall understande that anie breache or wronge hath bene done to ye liberties and priviledges of that o^r Cittie wee wilbe readie to restore whatsoever shalbe justelie expected of us as we have more at lardge spoken to this gentleman and will by oure actes when wee shalbe amongest you make knowne to yor selves esteeminge yo^u worthie to be helde in noe lesse accompte of us then you have byne to anie of o^r progenitors whoe esteemed you moste. Given under o^r Signet at o^r Towne of Newcastle ye xj^th daie of Aprill 1603 in ye firste yeare of o^r raigne of England.

No. 56.

Letter from the Lords of the Council to Sir Arthur Chichester, Deputy in Ireland, as to the course to be pursued with the City's Commissioners, appointed to view the Irish Estate. Dated Whitehall, 3 Aug., 1609.

Transcripts, &c., Irish Government (Public Record Office), Vol. I, fo. 500.

After o^r very harty comendacõns to yor Lp. we have written unto yo^ur Lp. and the Counsell there a letter wherein we have in generall recommended certaine cittizens appointed by the Citty of London to view the Derrye and Colrane and the cuntrie between them; And in this have thought it expedient to declare o^r minde somewhat more particulerly, because we shoulde be sorry that any endeavo^r or informacõn should be lacking that might either satisfie or encourage them For when we consider how slowly this busines hath yet gon forward since it was first intended, how fit & able the Citty is for a work of y^t importaunce, of what good use their example wilbe to draw on others and lastly what reputacōn it will give both abroad and at home to ye action y^t is like really to be effected we are moved to recommend them the more earnestly unto yor Lp. to take order that all occasions of discouragement may be prevented which som indiscreete persons may unprovidently suggest, if choice be not made of such to conduct and accompany them, who for their experience and understanding shalbe able both by discourse and reason to controule whatsoever any man shall reporte, either out of ignorance or mallice, and to give the undertako^{rs} satisfaccōn when they shalbe mistaken or not well informed of any particuler For which purpose the conductors must have care to lead them by the best waies and to lodge them in their travaile, where if it be possible, they may have English entertainement in Englishmens howses. And howsoever we have had the opportunitye heere to lay the first hand upon this offer, and to make the project unto the Cittie thereby to drawe them on to entertaine the same for an entraunce into the business yet that it may be both begun and well followed we send the same here inclosed and must leave it to your lordship to perfect Wherein we thinck it fit That those y^t be sent in their company be so well prepared before hand to confirme and strengthen every part thereof by demonstracōn as they may plainely apprehend & conceive the comodities to be of good use and profit ; on the other side, that matters of distast as feare of the Irish, of the souldiers, cess and such like be not so much as named, seeing you knowe that discipline and order will easilie secure them. And if there be any thing conteyned in the Project, whether it be the Fishing, the Admiralty or any other particuler wch may serve for a motyve to enduce them ; Although yor lordship or any other have interest therein yet you shall make no doubt but his Ma^{ty} will have such consideracōn thereof that no man shalbe a looser in y^t wch he shall parte wth for the furtheraunce of this service. And thus not doubting of yor L^{ps} discreete carriadge of this busines y^t cannot besides your generall dutie but be glad in your owne particuler to have so good neighbo^{rs} to yor plantacõn we byd yor Lp. very hartely Farewell. From Whitehall the third of August 1609.

No. 57.

Letter from Speaker Lenthall to the Lord Mayor asking, on behalf of Parliament, for a City loan of £60,000. Dated Covent Garden, 15 Jan., 1640-1.

Journal 39, fo. 167.

My Lord,

The greate necessetie of supplyinge the Kinges Army and providinge for the Northen Counties without which the peace of the Kingdome wilbe much endangered is such that the Howse of Commons is inforced to thinke upon a more present way of raysinge moneyes then can bee effected in the Course of Subsidies. Whereupon they have directed mee to pray your Lorpp. to call a Coñion Hall with as much speede as conveniently you may and to comend to the Cittizens of London the Loane of £60000 by such as shall freely and willingly contribute thereunto. Which they intende not as any burthen unto them, but as an occasion of further expressinge of theire good affeccõns to the publiq. Whereof they have soe often had experience and they will soe provide that the Suñie now desired to bee lent shalbe truly repaide out of the Subsedies wth interest for the time it shallbe forborne wherein not doubtinge of yor Lopp^s Care in the best way you may to further this request for ye Coñion safetie of the Kingdome and to receyve an answer as speedily as the bussines will permitte. ffrom my house in Covent Garden this instant 15th of Januarij 1640.

I rest Your Lopp^s. verie loveinge ffreind

Wm Lenthall, Speaker.

No. 58.

Another letter from Speaker Lenthall on the same matter. Dated Covent Garden, 6 Feb., 1640-1.

Id. ibid.

My Lord,

The present necessity requiringe the sume of £60000 for the good of the Kingdome to be advanced sooner then by way of subsidies it can be levied as hath bin formerly signified vnto yor Lo^rpp. by Ald^ran Pennington The house hath commaunded me this day againe to intimate vnto you their desire that wth the help of such Citizens as are willing to lend particuler sumes you will take such Course that £60000 may presently be paid into the Chamber of London that soe it may be disposed of as the house shall direct Wherein not doubting of yor Lo^rpps care I rest from my house in the Coven garden the sixth of ffebruary 1640.

Yo^r Lo^rpps very loving freind
Wm Lenthall, Speaker.

No. 59.

A third letter from Speaker Lenthall on the same matter. Dated Charing Cross, 19 Feb., 1640-1.

Journal 39, fo. 180.

My very good Lord and Gentlemen,

I have formerly by my lr̃es directed by order of the house of Com̃ons vnto yor Lo^rpp signified their desire to borrow of the City sixty thousand pounds for the presente supply of the Kings Army and releif of the Northern partes conceived to tend principally to the gen'all safety of the whole kingdome.

We could not but take notice of the forwardnes of the Citty to comply and albeit there hath bin some protraccõn, yet we now expect the expression of it in a speedie payment. I am therefore required by the house of Commons to desire yor Lo^{pp} forthwth to call a Comon Hall, and in that to signifie vnto them our desires,

Their former ingagement by promise and the expectacōn of the present performance the urgent and instant necessity of the Kingdome admitting of no delay w^{th}out great hazard of insueing danger to us all wch we desire may be prevented.

We have taken care for the secure payment of this £60000 by the bill of subsidies already passed whereof I thought it fitt to Certifie yor Lorpp resting

Yo^r Loving faithfull freind to serve you
Wm Lenthall, Speaker.

from my house at Charing
Crosse 19 ffebruarij 1640.

No. 60.

Letter from the Earl of Essex to the City desiring a loan of £100,000 for the maintenance of the Parliamentary army. Dated Northampton, 13 Sept. 1642.

Journal 40, fo. 38.

My lord and gentlemen   I receaved so great expressions of affeccōn both to ye cause, and to myselfe from ye cittye of London at my departure from you, that I cannot dispaire but to obtayne any suite from you that shalbee an advantage to ye Comon wealth Upon a true judgment of ye condicōn of our affaires and of that of ye enemye, I am confident that wee may bringe this business to a quick and happy conclusion God doth blesse us wth so good successe dailey & the other parte by their plundring and burninge of townes and houses grow so odious, that they grow weaker wee stronger everywhere, Yet are wee in one great straight, and such a one as if it bee not speedily remedyed, may quash all our hopes, and endanger that peace, and libertie which wee so much strive for. Our treasure wch must maintayne ye army grows neere an ende, and yo^u well know our army consists of such as cannot bee kept one day togeather w^{th}out pay, what a ruine it would bringe uppon us all if a disbandinge should happen I leave to your judgments.

My desire unto yo^u is that yo^u would supply us wth the speedy loane of one hundred thousand pounds which I am confident would wth Gods blessinge bringe these unhappy distraccõns to an ende quickly. Your citty hath hitherto had ye honor (next to God) to bee the chiefest safetye of the Kingdome and Parlyament This will render yo^u to all posterity the ffinishers of this great worke. If any thinge of particuler love or respect to mee may bee any argument herein I shall take it for ye greatest honor that hath befalne mee and will oblige myselfe to acknowledge it by the utmost and most faithfull indeavors of your ffaithfull ffriend Essex From the rendez-vous att Northampton 13° Sept. 1642.

No. 61.

Letter from the Earl of Essex to the City on the appointment of Skippon to the rank of Sergeant-Major-General in the Parliamentary army. Dated Hammersmith, 16 Nov. [1642].

Journal 40, fo. 41b.

My lord and gentlemen   Havinge a due regarde both to the publique trust and to the good and wellfare of the cittye of London I have made choice of Serjeant Major Skippon to bee Serjeant Major Generall of the army under my comaund beinge well assured of his fidellitye and abillity to discharge that trust   And yet knowinge of what concernement his present imployment in ye citty may be I have thought fitt to give your Lor^pp and yo^u gentlemen notice hereof wth this assurance that in this choice I have had a speciall regard as to the publique so particulerly to the securetye of the cittye of London   And that in it I do not intende wholy to deprive yo^u of him but so as his service may be rendered usefull both to this armye and to your cittye whose good and wellfare I shall carefully provide for ye uttmost of my power and do rest your ffaithfull ffriend Essex. From my quarter at Hammersmith this 16th day of November 1642.

No. 62.

Resolution of the Common Council for putting the City and Suburbs into a posture of defence, 23 Feb. 1643.

Journal 40, fo. 52.

That a small fort conteyning one bulwark and halfe and a battery in the reare of the flanck be made at Gravell lane end. A horne worke wth two flanckers be placed at Whitechapell windmills. One redoubt wth two flanckers betwixt Whitechapell church and Shoreditch. Two redoubts with flanckers neere Shoreditch church wth a battery. At the windmill in Islington way, a battery and brestwork round about. A small redoubt neere Islington pound. A battery and brestwork on the hill neere Clarkenwell towards Hampstead way. Two batteries and a brestworke at Southampton house. One redoubt wth two flanckers by St Giles in the Feilds, another small work neere the turning. A quadrant forte wth fower halfe bulwarks crosse Tyborne high way at the second turning that goeth towards Westminster. At Hide parke corner a large forte wth flanckers on all sides. At the corner of the lord Gorings brick wall next the fields a redoubt and a battery where the court of Guard now is at the lower end of the lord Gorings wall, the brestwork to be made forwarder. In Tuttle feilds a battery brestworke, and the ditches to be scowred. That at the end of every street wch is left open to enter into the suburbs of this citty defenceable brestworkes be made or there already erected repayred wth turnepikes muskett proof, and that all the passages into the suburbs on the northside the river except five vizt The way from St. James towards Charing Crosse, the upper end of Saint Giles in Holborne, the further end of St. John Street towards Islington Shoreditch church and Whitechappell be stopped up. That the courtes of guard and the rayles or barrs at the utmost partes of the freedome be made defensible and turnepikes placed there in lieu of the chaynes all muskett proof. And that all the shedds and buildings that joyne to the outside of the wall be taken downe. And that all the bulwarkes be fitted at the gates and walls soe that the flanckes of the wall and streets before the gates may be cleared and that the gates and bulwarks be furnished with ordnance.

No. 63.

Letter from the Mayor, &c., of Gloucester to the City of London, touching the removal of Colonel Massey. Dated 29 May 1645.

Journal 40, fo. 132.

When we were in suche distresse by a close seige, that our freindes held our condicõn desperate, and our enimies did assure themselves of prevailing over us; by Gods providence we had reasonable releif from your famous and ever renowned citie wch doth now embolden us to present unto you our present estate, which is in breife. That our heartes wth the heartes of the country in generall are surrounded wth feare and greife for the removall of Collonell Massey from us, whose endeavors amongst us God hath soe wonderfullie prospered. Wee represented our sadd sense thereof and our reasons in particuler by peticõn to the hono^{ble} houses of parliament, but such meanes was used by some for the accomplishment of their owne ends therein that our peticõn was not read in the howses. So that wee are like to be deprived of him, and thereby much distraccõn, if not confusion sorely threatned to us and this countrey, thereby to the encouragement of the enimy and discouragement of o^r friends, Therefore we doe humbly apply ourselves unto you desiring you to interpose for us to the Parliament for his contynuance wth us. Wherein you will not only doe us a singuler favour, but we are confident much further the publique service thereby, and which shalbe most gratefully acknowledged by

Your humble Servants

Gloucester 29 of May 1645.   Luke Nurse Maior

[and seven others.]

APPENDIX A.

No. 64.

Letter from the Mayor, &c., of Plymouth to the City of London, enclosing copy of petition to Parliament for relief against the depredations of the Royalists. Dated 5 Sept. 1645.

Journal 40, fo. 144b.

The greate zeale you have ever manifested for the good of the kingdome, and the forwardnes you shewed to contribute your assistance to us upon all occacõns doth imbolden us at this tyme of our extremity to beseech you to stretch out yor helping hand to us you know we have bin long beseiged, and we have often moved the Parliam^t, the Committee of the West, and the Generall for releif, and all this summer it hath bin promised, but o^r hopes are hitherto frustrate. We have therefore sent the peticõn (whereof the enclosed is a copie) to Sir John Young and Mr. Waddon Burgesses for this towne, and indeed this is the last and only visible meanes that unde God is left us. We beseech you that you wilbe pleased to second our peticõn by your owne desires in our behalf And wee shall not cease to pray for the contynuance of yor peace and encrease of all other blessings and rest

Plymouth at the Committee for Goverm^t, 5 Sept. 1645.	Yo^r most humble servants Justinian Pearde Maior [and four others.]

No. 65.

The City's petition to King Charles I in reply to His Majesty's letter of the 19th May 1646.

Id., fo. 187.

Most humbly acknowledging the speciall grace and favour of yor ma^{tie} in condescending soe particulerly to communicate unto this city yor royall and pious resolucons to comply wth your Houses of Parliament for setling of truth and peace in this distracted kingdome signified by yor late gratious lettre of the 19th of May last to the representative body thereof In wch as the pet^{rs} cannot but see the speciall hand of Almighty God soe they must and doe from the bottome of their hearts blesse his holy name that at length he hath opened such a dore of hope by enclyning your ma^ties heart to looke downe upon the afflicc͠ons of yor people and from thence take comfort to themselves that he will confirme and increase those good resolucons in yor ma^tie.

As for this city the pet^rs esteeme it their duty now againe as they have formerly done to declare unto yor royall mat^ie and the whole world, that, according to their Protestac͠on and Covenant they have alwayes, and doe still reteyne the same loyall thoughts towards yor mat^ie as ever and as becometh subiects to doe from which they shall never recede.

And as next unto the good guidance of Almighty God they doe humbly comitt and submitt the meanes and maner of their future peace and happines unto yor ma^ts great and faithfull Councell the two Houses of Parliament.

So they shall contynue their instant prayers to the Throne of all Grace to dispose yor ma^ties royall heart to comply with such proposic͠ons as from them shalbe represented unto yor ma^ty for the settlement of true religion and peace in all yor kingdomes and the mainteynance of the union betweene the two nations. And then the pet^rs shall not doubt but yor ma^tie (wch is their earnest prayer) will with honor and joy returne unto this yor antient city, and that yor throne shall in yor royall selfe and your posterity be established in all yor kingdomes to the great honour of yor mat^ie and to the comfort of all yor good subiects amongst whome the petic͠on^rs shall alwayes strive to approve themselves inferiour to none in loyalty and obedience.

And as in dutie bound shall pray &c.

No. 66.

Letter from Fairfax and the Council of War to the Commissioners of the City of London forbidding further enlistments. Dated 14 June, 1647.

Journal 40, fo. 222.

Being informed that divers souldiers are daily listed under offic^rs, in and about the cities of London and Westm^r, and parts thereto adiacent, besids the trayned bands and usuall auxiliaries. We strongly apprehend that (notwithstanding all your desires and labour of peace) the kingdome is like to be precipitate by some persons into a new warr. Therefore (before we can answere that part of yor cities lettre to remove to 30 miles distance from London) we desire the citie would use their indeavo^{rs}, to prevent all such listings, and therein deale soe effectually as that nothing be for future done towards such listinge or raising any forces, and those already raised may be forthwith discharged. But if this cannot be done, we shalbe forced by an unwilling necessitie to apply our indeavo^{rs} to breake all designes of that kinde. And therein we hope to receive the concurrance of yor citie, professing, we have nothing else in our eye, but yo^{rs} our owne, and this poore kingdomes good and quiett.

Hereof we desire to here speedily from you, but so from time to tyme, as oft as may be, which we shall owne as a seale of that reciprocall love, wch the cities lettre purports to this army, and shall on our part be most earnestly endeavoured to be maynteyned.

June 14th 1647.

No. 67.

Letter from the same to the Mayor, Aldermen and Common Council of the City, touching the removal of the army and the safety of the King's person. Dated St. Albans, 15 June, 1647.

Journal 40, fo. 222b.

We are very glad our lettre from Royston of the tenth of this instant June had soe good a recepcõn wth you: whereof you have given us assurance by yor lettre of the twelfth of this instant,[1] and by those worthy aldermen and others the members of yor citie whome you sent unto us, to whose hands we yesterday returned such answere (to that part of yor lettre for our removal to thirty miles distant from London) as the present exigence of affaires

---

[1] Printed in Rushworth's Collections.

could possibly admitt. To wch we add this sincere assurance that soe soone as we shall receive the next resolucōn from the Parliament in relacōn to the proceedings upon the papers nowe given in unto them (whereof likewise yor comissioners have received a coppie from us) We shall then imediately give you such further answere and satisfaccōn to that particuler, as the nature of those results will permitt, wth respect only had to the necessary prosecution of those pressing concernements of the kingdome, comprized in those papers (whereunto) (for) the iustnes and reasonablenes of our desires, and their consistance wth the true honour, iust power and priviledges of parliament, the liberty of the subiect and safety of yor citie and kingdome we do referr you.

As to yor desire (expressed in the instruccōns to yor comissioners) of o^r care for the safetie of his ma^ties person, while amongst us. We had upon his first comeing into our quarters assigned, and have since contynued in attendance about his ma^ty, a guard of two regim^ts of horse, of as faithfull men, and under as trustie a commaund as this army doth affoard, neyther shall our future care be wantinge in any further provision necessary for the safetie of his royall person. And nowe we cannott but take notice, as of the past, most free and forward ingagem^ts of yor famous citie in the same cause, wch we are now desiring to see a period to, and accomplishment of, soe of yor contynued readines to close wth us in our iust and necessary desires to the same ends: as alsoe of yor present professed averssenesse to ingage in any thing that may tend to any further warr or distraccōn in this kingdome. For all wch we cannott but returne (after our praises to God) thankes to you and yor citty. And we assure you that the sence thereof hath a deep impression in our spiritts to find (as we doe hitherto) the hand of God working all mens hearts to go cleere, and unanimous concurrence wth our owne, in our desires for the present setling and securing the rights liberties and peace of the kingdome, beyond wch we have noe aymes or ends of our owne.

St. Albans June 15th 1647.

APPENDIX A. 437

No. 68.

The City's reply to the two preceding letters. Dated 18 June 1647.

Journal 40, fo. 224b.

Yo^r answere of the 14th and lettre dated the 15th of this instant June, wth copies of the papers given into the Parliam^t we the maior aldermen and commons in common councell assembled have received and perused, and by our committee we have ben further informed of them, and of yor many seasonable expressions of the reallity of yor intencõns to promote the peace and welfare of the Parliam^t and kingdome, and in particuler of this city, wch how acceptable it is to us will best appeare by our proceedings thereupon.

We take it very kindely that though you were informed divers souldiers were daily listed under offic^{rs} in and about the Cities of London and Westm^r and parts thereto adiacent, besides the trayned bands and usuall auxiliaries, yet you conceived (and that most truly) it was wthout the privity or consent of this Court, and did not suspect the sincerity of our heartes in what by o^r last was represented unto you, wherein for yor further satisfaccõn be pleased to take notice that since the returne of our comittee from St. Albans, yor said answere and lettre and a narrative of the severall passages twixt you and our committee, and yor desire that the citie should use their indeavo^r to prevent all such listings and therein deale soe effectually, as that nothing be for the future done towards such listings or raising any forces, and that those already raised might be forthwth discharged: and the resolucõn of this court, and the Committee of the Militia of this city and parts adiacent upon the whole being all by our direccõn made knowne to both Houses of Parliam^t they were pleased to make severall votes thereupon; whereunto (as to those thinges) we desire to be referred.

By all which we hope the great desire of this court and citie to cherish a right understanding and keep a good correspondence twixt yo* Excellencie yo* Councell of Warr, Armie and this Citie will evidently appeare, and shortly draw from you a more full answere satisfaccōn and assurance, that your army shall noe way preiudice the Parliament (whose power and priviledges are the principall meanes to preserve the liberties of the subiects of this kingdom) nor this Citie (who have lost soe much blood and spent soe much treasure in defence thereof) and in order thereunto that it shalbe forthwith removed to, and contynued at a further distance from London.

London 18 of June 1647.

No. 69.

Letter from Fairfax to the City acknowledging receipt of letter of the 18th June. Dated St. Albans, 21 and 22 June, 1647.

Journal 40, fo. 225b.

Wee received yo^{rs} of the eighteenth of this instant, whereof though all passages were not soe answearable to our expectacōn as wee hoped yet we apprehend the same good affeccōn in you towards this armie as was expressed in yor former letter And that not onelie from the assureance of the worthy gentlemen, (yor comissioners) againe sent to us, But alsoe from that informacōn we have received of yor extraordinarie indeavo^{rs}, to procure monie for the armie; To prevent further raysinge or listinge of souldiers and to procure those alreadie listed to be disbanded, (some persons of yor militia onelie, haveinge bin active for the raysinge of them without yor privitie) As likewise from that letter (fild with respecte) which you prepared and intended to us, And beinge sent to the Parliament was obstructed by some persons, who (labouringe to imbroyle the kingdome in a new warre) would not have the fforces alreadie raised to be disbanded who excepted against yor discoverie to the House, That some persons onelie of the militia had ioyned in the raysinge of the new forces, who alsoe would prevent a right understandinge betweene yor cittie, and this armie, knowinge a firme corrospondence betweene them would

APPENDIX A.

make the designes of all such men hopeles, And though our takinge notice of these thinges seemes not regular, yet beinge soe publiquelie done, we thought fitt to mind you of them.

Now although wee have confidence of the reall and cleare intentions of yor lor^{pp} and ald$\tilde{r}$en, and the commons of yor cittie to promote the peace of this kingdome, and the iust desires of this armie, alsoe to prevent all tendencies to a new warre, or anie further blood, and therefore hold our selves obliged to yeeld all possible compliance to what you desire of us, yet addinge to the former grounds the manie informac$\tilde{o}$ns which daylie come to us of the continued underhand workings of some persons still to list men, that divers agents are sent into severall parts of the kingdome to leavie forces and Worcester the place appointed for a generall randezvouz, whither the fforces designed for Ireland (that were parte of this armie) are by some of the committee at Darbie House[1] ordered to march: And severall of those companies who went out from us for the service of Ireland, havinge it intimated to them, and by divers carriages perceiveinge they were intended a foundac$\tilde{o}$n for a new armie and a new warre, they so much abhorred the thoughts of it as both the officers and souldiers of divers companies are of late entirelie returned to us : likewise that noe meanes is lefte unattempted to bringe in fforces from Ireland, France and Scotland against the peace of this poore kingdome.

Wee (upon the whole matter) offer to yours, and all mens considerac$\tilde{o}$ns, whether with yo^{rs} ours or the publique safetie we can remove further backward, untill upon yor and our ioynt indeavo^{rs} with the Parliament, those things of imediate and pressing necessitie be provided for, which wee desired in our paper last given in to the Parliam^{ts} Comissioners in order to the better proceedinge upon the heads of the Representac$\tilde{o}$n and Charge, with more hopes of safetie, and of a timelie and happie issue to our selves, and the kingdome (vizt.) That the persons

---

[1] Derby House, Cannon Row, Westminster, erected in 1598 by William, Earl of Derby. It was surrendered to Parliament *temp.* Charles I, and was used for Parliamentary Committee meetings and other state purposes.

impeached by us may not continue in power and capacitie to obstructe due proceedings against themselves; And for their owne escape from justice to threaten ruine to the whole nation.

That all fforces latelie raised or listed in or aboute the cittie may be forthwith discharged except the usuall nomber of trained bands and auxiliaries and that all endeavo^{rs} publiquely or privatlie to rayse anie further forces may cease and be supprest.

And that the same measure maybe allowed to this armie in payinge them upp to the same ffoote of accompte as is alreadie given to those who have diserted the same.

And for the things exprest in our Representation though of weightie importance yet because they will require time they shalbe noe occasion to impead our remove, and in the meantime both by Proclamacõn from his Excellencie and all other wayes wee shall indeavo^r, that the accustomed supplies to yor cittie may be freelie sent up.

To conclude, wee say from o^r hearts that as oure espetiall ends are the glorie of God, and the good of this whole land, soe our indeavo^{rs} shalbe to prosecute the same without preiudice to the beinge or welbeinge of Parliaments in generall, (the mayntenance whereof wee value above our owne lives) or (as wee have formerlie said) of this Parliament in particular, but altogeather in order to the good and peace of this nation, and with a most tender regard to yor cittie to which wee professe we shall by all actions make good all ingagements tending to the securitie thereof in what way yo^{r}selves shall desire consistinge with the good of the whole kingdome you makeinge good your mutuall correspondencie with us not doeing anie thinge to our preiudice in the prosecucõn of our iust desires, and endeavo^{rs}.

St. Albans June 21, 1647.

Wee heare (even now) since the writinge of this letter, that (yesterday) divers of the Reformadoes came againe (in a threatninge manner) to Westm^r the house of Commons then sittinge to the greate affrightment and terror of divers faithfull members then present, and to discouragement of others from their attendance there, soe that we cannot but perceive, that the freedome of this Parliament is noe better then that those members who shall accordinge to their consciences endeavo^r to prevent a second warre, and acte contrarie to their wayes, who, (for their own preservacõn) intend it they must do it with the hazard of their lives : which indeed is a thinge soe destructive to Parliamen^{ts} and freedome that we conceive our selves in dutie bound, to endeavo^r to the utmost to procure redresse therein.

June 22th 1647.

No. 70.

Letter from the City to Fairfax in reply to recent letters and informing him that Commissioners had been despatched to remain with the army at head-quarters. Dated 25 June, 1647.

Journal 40, fo. 229b.

We the maior aldermen and commons in common councell assembled having received yo^{rs} to us of the 21th and 22th and yor excellencies to our committee of the 23th instant wth a coppie of a Remonstrance directed to the Parliam^t, did send three of that nomber yesterday to acquaint you wth our resolucõns thereupon, since wch we have caused coppies of those lettres to be presented to both Houses, desiring their direccõn concerning the resideing of some of that committee continually wth you in the head quarter, and that according to yor former requests the Reformadoes and other offic^{rs} and souldiers raised for the service of the Parliam^t might be required forthwith to repair into their severall counties there to receive such satisfaccõn as is or shalbe appointed by Parliament, and that if any souldiers be listed uppon the votes of the committee of Lords and Commons, and committee of the militia that they may be forthwth discharged whereupon severall votes were made, unto which we desire to be referred.

We have also taken those lettres wth another received from those we sent yesterday and copie of a lettre dated the 24th instant delivered to the Comm^{rs} of Parliam^t, and yo^{rs} of the 25th instant into further consideracõn thereby observing the constancie of yor

expressions to doe nothing in preiudice either of the Parliam{t} or the citie, and of your purpose by proclamacon and otherwise to indeavour that the accustomed supplies of this citie may be freely sent upp. All which we do with due thankfulnes acknowledge, And to performe a right understanding with you we have appointed the said committee, or six of them at the least continually to reside in yor Head quarter, and do intend to make it our further request to the Parliam{t} that whoever have or shall endeavour to raise any forces to ingage this kingdome in a new warr, may be discovered and prevented therein, and that you may receive satisfaccon equall to those that have left the armie, soe soon as it is possible for the Parliam{t} to performe the same, believing upon the assurance you have given us that yor speciall ends are the glory of God the good of this whole land, and the safety of Parliam{t} and citie. To conclude the neare approach of yor armie to this citie causeth us once more to desire you to take it into yor most serious consideracon, for albeit you do not come to offer any violence to us, yet wee have and shall suffer very much in our trade and price of victualls by reason thereof, wch we hope you wilbe so sencible of as to prevent it in the future by removing further of, and by takeing such a course that we may receive no further preiudice either in thone or thother, wch is our earnest desires, and that in yor indeavo{rs} to save the kingdome from ruine, you doe not overthrow the fundamentall constitucon of Parliam{t} wch is essentiall to the well being thereof.

London 25 June 1647.

No. 71.

Letter from Fairfax to the City notifying the removal of the army to Uxbridge. Dated Berkhamstead, 25 June, 1647.

Journal 40, fo. 230.

Wee have in all things dealt cleerly and plainely wth you, and hope wee shall still continue to doe so. As soone as the worthy alderman and the other two gent{s} yor com{rs} came the last night to us, we acquainted them wth our purpose to draw the head quarter to Uxbridg That soe we might contract our quarters wch have hitherto lyen scattered. At which place we hope to receive that wch wilbe satisfaccõn to the kingdome and will remove obstruccõns out of the way of justice, wherein if right were done, wee should let you and all the world see that we would be soe farr from pressing neere yor citie of London, it should be indifferent to us to march not only to the distance already prescribed, but to any part of the kingdome we should be commanded to by the Parliament. Wee have asked nothinge hitherto but right in the things that are knowne, as if they were proved an hundred times before them from whome wee have sought them, wch if graunted would not only be a justice to the armie, but would lett the kingdome see the ffountayne in a way to be cleered without wch nothing of force or power would be a securitie to any man. We wish the name of priviledges may not be in the ballance wth the safetie of a kingdome, and the reality of doing justice, wch as we have said too often, we cannot expect whilest the persons we had accused are the kingdomes and our judges. A little delay will indanger the putting the kingdome into blood, notwithstanding what hath bin said, if it be considered that in Wales (besides underhand workings in yor citie) and other places men are raised and that in noe small nombres. And are not those men in the Parliam^t who have contynued faithfull to the principles of common interest from the beginning of the Parliam^t to this very day still awed by the concourse of Reformadoe offic^{rs} and others to their doores. Expence of time will be their advantage only who intend to bring evill purposes to passe. We have written this to you for yor satisfaccõn that soe nothinge may be done without giving you a perfect account of our intencõns and ends. And still to contynue our assurance to you, that should necessity bring us neerer to the citty our former faith given you shall be observed inviolably, there being nothing more (next the good of the kingdome) in our thoughts and desires than the prosperitie of yor citty.

Barkhamsteed June 25 1647.

No. 72.

Letter from Fairfax to the City enclosing copy of proposals forwarded to Parliament from the army. Dated Reading, 8 July, 1647.

Journal 40, fo. 234.

My Lord and Gentlemen

To the end we may contynue a right understanding betweene you and us all along in the manadgm^t of this great busines, wth the Parliam^t (the happie proceeding whereof so much concernes the safety and peace of this Kingdome) We have given yor Commission^{rs} this day, the copie of a paper wch we presented to the Commissioners of Parliam^t residing wth us. Wherein we take notice of the true reasons of the slowe progresse in the Treaty, and declare where the stoppe remains. And to the end that nothing be wanting in us wch might work towards the speedy settlem^t of the quiett of this Kingdome, wee have humbly offered what we conceive will most effectually tend to remove those incombrances and lettes, wch stand betwixt us, and this universall good to the Kingdome; and till that be done, it cannot be expected that we should procure the peace of this nation by a Treatie, but rather give occacōn and opportunity thereby to others to ingage us in a second warr, wch must necessarily hazard the ruine of this Kingdome, as also ascertayne the destruccōn of Ireland, the relief whereof we should most effectually apply unto, were the affaires of England, but once put into a hopefull way. It is a sound and substantiall settlement of the whole we desire, in a generall safe and well grounded peace, and the establish^{mt} of such lawes, as might duly and readily render to every man their iust rights and liberties: And for obteyning of theis, not only our intencōns have lead us, but we thinke that all the blood, treasure, and labour spent in this warr was for the accomplishm^t of theis very things, wch are of that concernem^t both to our selfs and posterity, that neither we nor they cane live comfortably without them. And thereof we hope yor selfes will have the same sence, and therefore improve your interest for the obtayning of our iust desires in the proposalls now sent to the Parliam^t, wch being graunted, and we secured from the danger of a warr, we shall proceed wth cheerfulness to the Treaty; and doubt not in a short time to see a happy conclusion to the satifaccõn of all honest mens expectacõns: And that in all our undertakeings we shalbe found men of truith, fully and singly answering the things we have held forth to the Kingdome in our severall declaracõns and papers, without bye or base respects to any private ends or interests whatsoever.

July 8th 1647 Readinge.

No. 73.

Letter from the City to Fairfax, deprecating any attempt to intermeddle with the liberties or privileges of the City. Dated 28 July, 1647.

Journal 40, fo. 242b.

Our Committee being all returned from the Army contrary to o^r expectacõn we are yet well satisfied therewth, because, that it was at your request. They have communicated unto us severall papers from you dated on and betweene the 17th and 23th present, by one whereof, being a lettre to this Court, we take notice of the sence the army hath of a printed paper wch had come to their hands out of the Citie, and have perused the same, but in regard the originall hath not bin yet presented to this Court, it is not thought fitt to declare our sence thereupon, but we esteeme it our duty to rest in that wch both Houses of Parliam^t have resolved, upon consideracõn of this paper, wch we conceave also wilbe sufficient to stopp the further proceeding thereof. But truly we cannot conceale from yor Ex^{cie} that (forasmuch as we can collect) this paper was occasioned from intelligence wch came from the army, that there was some intencõn there, to move the Parliament for the change of the Militia of this Citie, and we doubt not but you have heard what great distemper the alteracõn wch the Parliam^t

made of our Militia upon yor desire did lately produce in this Citie, wch being now againe upon our humble peticōn put into the same hands it was, at the tyme the mocōn came from you, we hope all things are well appeased and setled. And we are confident it cannot be offensive unto the armie, if we desire them not to intermeddle wth any the Liberties or Priviledges of this Citie or interpose in the point of our Militia, but that wee may enioy that trust quietly wch wee shall assure you we shall take care shalbe managed to no other end but for the Parliam^{ts} and our owne defence, and shall give no iust provocacōn to any person whatsoever. We shall conclude wth this profession that we shall alwayes detest all occasions of a new warr, and we are not conscious to ourselves, that any thing that hath passed in this business can deserve the expressions of yor lettre, as if it were probable to involve the whole Kingdome in bloud, or that it must necessarily begin within our bowells or draw the seat and misery of warr upon us and our Citie. For all other thinges we referr you to our Committees.

London 28 July 1647.

No. 74.

Minutes of Common Council touching a recent disturbance of soldiers in the City; 11 April, 1648.

Journal 40, fo. 267.

Att this common Councell Mr. Aldr̄an Fowkes and Mr. Aldr̄an Gibbs (by direccons of the comitte of the milicia for London) did make a large relacōn of the greate tumult insurreccōn and mutinie which happened in this Citty on the last Lords day and on Monday last by many evill disposed persons wch first began on the Lords day in the afternoone in the Countie of Middlesex. Where they seazed the colours of one of the trayned bands of the said countie who were there imployed for the suppressing of such persons as did prophane the Lords day And being dispersed by some some of the genālls forces did gather togeather within the citty of

APPENDIX A.

London and Libties thereof   And in a riotous manner did breake open divers houses and magazens of armes and amunicõn and tooke away armes plate money and other things   And did seaze vpon the drums of the trayned bands of this Citty which were beating to raise their companies and armed themselves and beate vp drums and putt themselves in a warlike posture   And seazed vpon the gates chaynes and watches of the Citty and then marched to the Lord Maiors house and there assaulted the Lord maio^r sheriffs comitte of the milicia of London and other magestrates of the same   And did shoote into the Lord maiors house beat backe his guard killed one of them wounded divers others and seazed and tooke away a peece of ordinance from thence with which they did afterwards slay and wound divers persons and comitted many other outrages   All which matters being largely debated and many particulars insisted vpon both for the discovery and punishment of the said outrages and misdemeanours and alsoe for the preventing of the Like for tyme to come   It was at the last concluded and agreed by this common Councell as followeth, ffirst this common Councell do generally conceive that this Citty was in great danger by Reason of the said outrages and misdemeanours   And that if the same had not bine soe tymely prevented and stayed the whole citty would have benn exposed to the fury and rage of the said malefactors   And this comon Councell doth declare that the same misdemeanor and outrage was an horrid and detestable Acte tending to the destruccõn of the City and that they do disavow the same and with an vtter detestacõn doe declare their dislike therof   And this common Councell doe appoint the comitte of the milicia of London to make the same knowne to the honãble houses of Parliament   And alsoe to make an humble request vnto them that an order may be issued forth from them to the sevãll ministers of this city and the places adiacent that they may be directed to give publique thankes to Almighty God the author of this greate and wonderfull delivãnce from that eminent danger wherein this Citty and parts adiacent were involved   And further the said comittee was appointed by this court to apply themselves to the honāble houses of Parliament for the obteyning of a speciall Comission of Oyer and Terminer for the trying and punishing of all the malefactors that had a hand in this detestable accōn according to the knowne Lawes of this land   And this court with thankfull harts doe acknowledge the instruments (vnder God) by wch they obteyned this delivãnce to be by the forces raised and continewed by the Parliament vnder the command of his excellency the Lord Genāll Fairefax And to manifest the same this common Councell doe alsoe order that the said comitte of the millitia in the name of the City as a thing agreed vpon by an vnamious Consent shall returne their harty thankes to his excellency for his speedy and seasonable aide afforded the Citty in this their greate straight and danger   And this court with a genāll consent doe well approve of the endeavours of the said comitte of the milicia for London for the raising of the forces of the City And in their procuring of the said Ayde and helpe from his excellency in this extreamity and what els they have doun for the appeasing and suppressing of the said tumults And this courte doe give thankes to the said comitte of the millicia for their care and paines taken by them taken vpon this sadd occasion And they doe appointe Mr. Adrīan Fowkes to declare the same their thankes to such of the said comitte as are not of this Court And this Court doth alsoe with all thankfulnes acknowledge the paines and care of the right honāble the Lord Maior and the right Worshiplull the Sheriffs of the Citty therin And this court doe genāally declare that it is the duty of every Citizen of this Citty by himselfe & all that doe belong vnto him or is vnder his comand to be ready vpon all occasions to be ayding and assisting vnto the Lord Maior and the rest of the magistrates of this City for the suppressing of all tumults and disorders within the same And the sevāll persons now present att this comon councell by the holding vp of their hands have promised that for the tyme to come they will vse their vtmost endeavours and be ready vpon all occasions to doe the same.

Vpon the late sadd occasion which happened by reason of the tumult and insurreccōn that was within this Citty and places adjacent this courte entred into consideracōn of some meanes to be vsed and prepared to prevent and suppres the Like for the future   And to that purpose it was propounded that the number of 100 horses might be in readinesse within this Citty furnished with all things fitting for service to be drawe forth vpon any occasion by the Comand of   for the tyme being for the suppressing of any tumult or other disorder as occasion should require   And after some debate had thervpon it was genãlly conceived that the proposicōn was fitt to be entertained   And to that purpose itt was thought fitt and soe ordered by the courte that the Comitte of the milicia for London shall consider how the said horses shalbe raised and the charge therof   And how they shalbe kepte maintained and disposed of for the service of the Citty   And of all other matters and circumstances concerning the same   And to report to the next common councell in writing their opinions therin   That soe this courte vpon their report may doe thervpon what they they shall think fitt and may be best for the good and saftie of this Citty.

No. 75.

Letter from Fairfax to Skippon upon his re-appointment to the command of the City's forces.   Dated Windsor, 10 May, 1648.

Journal 40, fo. 275.

I received yours and understand by severall gentlemen of the millitia of London how much you are desired and importuned to accepte of the comand of the forces in and aboute the cittie of London.   I must needs say I cannot but be sorry to parte with one who hath upon all occasions doun such good service for the Parliament and Kingdome.   But my private respects ought to give place unto the publique   And since it is so generally desired by the cittie and severall millitia, I cannot but be glad they have made soe good a choice and hope it will tend to the furtherance of union and good agream^t for the advantage of the Parliament, Cittie and Kingdome.   The consequences whereof I apprehend to be such that I cannot but denie my selfe and frely leave you to

your selfe and doe disingage you from any tye to my selfe or the
army under my comand in case you accepte of the aforesaid
comand in the cittie Wishing you much hapiness in your under-
takings I remayne &c.
Windsor 10th May,
1648.

No. 76.

A narrative of the proceedings of the Court of Common Council
held in Guildhall, London, the 13th of January, 1648–9,
presented by order of the Court to the House of Commons.

Journal 40, fo. 314.

A common councell beinge lawfully summoned to meete at
eight of the clocke in the morneinge upon the day above written,
Wee commoners of the citty of London members of the said courte
in obedience to the said summons and for discharge of the trust
reposed in us made our appearance att the vsuall place of meetinge
for the saide courte about the time appointed. Aboute eleven of
the clocke the Lord Maior accompanied onely with two of the
Aldermen tooke the chayre Wee then desireinge the lord mayor
that the acts of the last courte might be reade accordinge to the
vsuall course of the saide courte and for the further confirmacōn
of the said acts could not obtcyne the same (though earnestly
desired) for above an howres space after which some members of
the said courte (being parte of a committee formerly chosen by the
said courte) tendered a peticōn therevnto to bee reade, and considered of which peticōn (beinge the same now presented to this
honoble House) was drawne vpp by them in referrence to an order
of the said courte and received the approbacōn of the major parte
of the quorum of that comittee and though itt was often and
earnestly prest for a long time by the major parte of the courte
that it might be reade to receive the sence of the courte, yett the
Lord Maior wholly refused to suffer the same or that the question
should be putt whether it should be reade yea or noe After the
fruitelesse expence of many howres another question beinge drawne

vpp the major parte of the courte required itt to be putt, to be putt [*sic*] to be decided according to the right and custome of the courte and beinge denyed therein declared how vnjust and of what a destructive nature to the beinge of the courte such a denyall would bee yet notwithstandinge the Lord Maior with the two Aldermen departed and lefte the courte sittinge to the greate greife and generall dissatisfaccõn of the same Beinge thus deprived of our ordinary assistance for our proceedings, wee did then require and command the Common Serjeant and Towne Clarke officers of the said courte to stay in the courte and putt the question both which they contemptuously refused and lefte the courte sittinge likewise Wherevpon in discharge of our trust and in our tender care of the common good of Citty and Kingdome Wee did stay and remaine a courte wherein was thrice reade debated and voted (*nemine contradicente*) the peticõn hereunto annexed to be as this day presented to this honoble Howse

Havinge given this honoble Howse this breife, but true, narrative of parte of our sufferings for eight howres at least In the breadth (as wee conceive) of our vndoubted rights & priviledges and conceiveinge the like obstruccõns would render our meetings in councell altogether fruitlesse for publiq benefitte and service for the future Wee are forced to appeale vnto this honoble Howse for such consideracõns hereof and direccõns herein, as may make the commons of London in common councell assembled vsefull to the ends for which they were chosen.

No. 77.

Letter from the Council of State to the Mayor and Aldermen of the City for defacing statues of James I and Charles I. Dated Whitehall, 31 July, 1650.

Repertory 60, fo. 213.

My Lord and Gentlemen.

In pursuance of an Order of Parliament wee desire you forthwith to give order that ye two Statues that Stand at ye west end of Paules above yᵉ worke borne up by yᵉ Columnes sett upp to represent King James and the late King may forthwith bee throwne downe. Alsoe yᵗ yᵉ head of that Statue at yᵉ Exchainge sett there to represent yᵉ late King be broaken off, and yᵉ Septer broaken out of his hand And this inscripcon put upp by it *Exit Tyrannus Regum ultimus Anno Libertatis Angliæ restitutæ primo Annoque Domini 1648 Januarij 30°* And yow are alsoe to take care that yᵉ inscripcon under those Statues at Paules be cutt out of yᵉ stones and that this be doune before Saturday the tenth of August next and yᵗ yᵉ Councell bee then certified of your proceedings therein.

Whitehall
31 July 1650.

Signed in yᵉ name and by order of yᵉ Councell of State appointed by Authority of Parliament

Jo: Bradshawe P'sidᵗ.

No. 78.

Another letter from the same ordering the entire removal of the statue of Charles I at the Royal Exchange. Dated Whitehall, 14 Aug., 1650.

Id., fo. 220b.

My Lord and Gentlemen

By a łre from yᵉ Councell beareing Date yᵉ 31ᵗʰ of July last order was given for yᵉ throwing downe of the two Statues at ye west end of Paules & likewise for yᵉ takeing of yᵉ head & Septer out of yᵉ hand of yᵗ wᶜʰ stood at yᵉ Exchainge in Lond wᶜʰ according to yᵉ desire of the Councell Wee understand is put into Execucõn, Since which the Councell haveing taken yᵗ matter into further consideracõn they have thought fit to order that that yᵉ whole of what is remayneing of yᵉ Statue of yᵉ late Kinge at yᵉ Exchainge be taken downe and that yᵉ Inscripcõn which was ordered to be placed neere unto it be now written in ye place wher ye said Statue did stand.

Signed in ye name & by ord^r of
y^r Councell of State appoynted
by Authoritye of Parliam^t
Jo: Bradshawe
Prsid^t.

Whitehall 14th
of August 1650.

No. 79.

Letter from the Council of State to the City for removal of ordnance to the Tower. Dated Whitehall, 19 Nov., 1653.

Journal 41, fo. 90b.

The Councell of State have considered that there are severall great guns belonging to the Citie of London which are now remayning at Leadenhall, and severall other partes of the Cittie, and for the better secureinge thereof have thought fitt that the L^t of the Tower should draw them in thither on Tuesday next, wherein yor Lordship is desired to give yor assistance, and to cause the same to be delivered accordingly takeinge a receipt from the officers of the Ordnance by an inventory indented conteyning the numbers and quallities. And the Councell doth hereby declare, and give yor Lordship assurance that this is not at all intended as a disrespect to the Citty, or in prejudice to their interest in the said guns, but in order to their safeguard, and to be returned back to the Citty when they shall have occasion for them and desire them.

Whitehall 19th November 1653.

No. 80.

The City's humble Petition and Representation to the Lord Protector promising to stand by him against the enemies of the Nation; 16 March, 1657–8.

Id., fo. 170b.

Sheweth

That the peticoners are deepely sensible of the manie mercies & signall providences that these three nations have received from

Almightie God in subduing his and their Enemyes in the times of our late warres, in which it pleased our wise and Gratious God to vse your highnes as the most speciall & eminent Instrument in his hand as chosen out and fitted by him for those great & subsequent workes by which his name mightbe Glorifyed, the three Nations & in speciall his owne people therein protected and preserved from their enemies att home & abroad. And not only soe, but the Continued goodnes of god hath followed vs in soe much that after a sharpe & bloody warre seuãll yeares together, for some yeares last past those cloudes have bine brooken, and the Sun of peace hath shined vppon vs with a great measure of hope putt into our harts of a happie lasting & well grounded forme of goverment, according to the peticõn and advice of the late Parliam^t consented to by your highnes for which wee doe as in duty bound blesse the Lord and desire a long and happie continuance of the same. But yet your peticõners taking notice from your Hignes late gracious speech to them that the old restles enemy is reviving his almost dead hopes of prevailing to execute his wrath and malice against god your highnes & the good & peacefull people of the three Nations, partly from the discontents of a Brain sicke party at home and especially from the aides of the popish inveterate enemy abroad and have laid designes to themselves hopefull, by insurreccons from within and invasions from without vs to raise newe troubles & kindle the flames of warre againe amongst vs, by which to change our Government & therein ruine the three Nations The premisses considered the peticoners do professe vnto all both frinds and Enemyes That we shall vppon our antient principales of love & fidelitie to God your Highnes & the good people in the three nations with all readines oppose this enemy to the vtmost with our lives & fortunes

And therefore we doe most humbly pray that your highnes will please with all cheerefulnes as supreme Maiestrate to God & in the Goverment of these three Nations for preservacõn of religion the lawes libties peace & safety thereof And as your peticoners doe blesse God for you soe they shall

APPENDIX A. 455

(as in duty bound) faithfully and constantly in their seuãll places not only yeild obedience to you therein but bee Enemyes to yours & the Nations Enemyes, and freinds to yours & the Nations friends.

And ever pray &c.

No. 81.

Letter from Sir John Langham to the Court of Aldermen, declining to resume the Aldermanry from which he had been deposed by Parliament, on the score of ill-health. Dated Crosby House, 18 Sept., 1660.

Remembrancia ix, 8.

My Lord & Gentlemen,

By a copy of a vote of Common Councill held ye 4th of September present (wch was left at my house) I find my selfe declared to bee an Aldr̃an of London, & invited to ye execucõn of that place. The knowledge of my vnfitness for y^t imploym^t by reason of my great age of 77 yeares, & those infirmities y^t accompany it, did soon put me upon ye resolucõn of getting my discharge from it. But ye death of my eldest sonn's wife & child, did overwhelme me as well as him wth that greife, wch permitted not my goeing abroad untill the last Thursday, when I hoped to have found at Guildhall a full court of Aldr̃en. But those expectacõns failing me, I forbore ye declaring my Intencõns & desires then. And being this day upon my retreat into the Country for the necessary refreshm^t of my selfe & sonn I thought it my duty to acquaint yor Lord^p : & this Court wth my Condicõn & most earnest Request. I have now beene laid aside about 12 yeares; The Rump Parliam^t haveing first imprisoned me in ye Tower (ye 24th of 7^{ber} 1647), cheifly (as was conceived) to prevent my being chosen Lord Mayor the Michãs following, where I remain'd vntill the 6th of the next June, when I was enlarged wth out so much as Peticõning But afterwards to satisfye y^e Ambicõn of some that had a mind to bee in our seats, Sr John Gayre, Aldr̃an Adams, my selfe & Bro^r Bunce, by a resolve of that Remain of a House of Commons that presumed to sitt as a Parliam^t, were disenabled & discharged from being Ald$\tilde{r}$en, & others chosen in our steds. Notwthstanding wch displeasure of those who usurped the Government & my being out of their sight, in y^e Country, y^e City retained those kind remembrances of me & my sufferings as to choose me 2^{ce} one of their Burgesses, in those Convenc$\tilde{o}$ns, wch wee called then Parliam^{ts} wch as they are argum^{ts} that I enjoyed their favour, so they are Reasons that I take not ill w^t this Court, or y^e Common Councill complyed in ag^t my Right, out of a feare of those who had made themselves Masters of the Three Kingdomes as well as this Citty: And that sense of my duty wch made me accept of serving this City (where God hath blest me) when called to it, & continue in that service whilst permitted, would now alsoe command my returne to the executing of my place, as an Ald$\tilde{r}$an, upon that Invitac$\tilde{o}$n I have re$\bar{c}$d, did not my finding and dayly discovering my disabilityes perswade me that you in Justice ought not to require, what I out of Conscience ought not to accept, ffor, both my age hath a legall excuse from the troubles of Magistracy, & yor affaires need that presentness of parts, wch a life so much worne out as mine is, cannot afford. I doubt not but I might have obteyned my discharge elswhere, but because yor Lord^p & this Court, are those to whome ye memb^{rs} of it especially are to betake themselves I thought it unbecoming me so farr to despair of yor Justice & ffavour, as to look for it in any other place. Wherefore, I make it my importunate request to your Lord^p & this Honble Court, that I may be discharged, for ever, from being an Ald$\tilde{r}$an, & part of that tyme that yet remaines of my life shall be spent in pray^{rs} for the happiness & flourishing of this Renowned Citty And when I shall have yor dismission into y^t privacy, wherein I may vndisturbedly prepare for the other & better world I am hasting into, I shall not cease to be a fervent Lover of that place, wherein I have received so manyfold mercyes from y^e Divine goodness, nor to bee my Lord and Gentlemen, yor affecc$\tilde{o}$nate ffreind and humble servant.

Crosby House the 18th Septem^{br} 1660.

No. 82.

Letter from the Earl of Manchester to the Court of Aldermen, desiring that the Butchers of the City might continue to supply offal to the King's "Game of Beares" as formerly. Dated Whitehall, 29 Sept., 1664.

Original Letter.

My very good Lord and the rest
of my very good ffreinds the Court
of Aldermen.

Being informed by the Master of his Maties Game of Beares and Bulls and of others that very well remember that the Company of Butchers did formerly cause all their Offall in Eastcheape and Newgate Markett to bee conveyed by the Beadle of their Company vnto two Barrow Houses conveniently placed on the Riverside to receave the same for the provision and feeding of his Maties Game of Beares And that that Custome hath beene interrupted in the late Troubles when the Beares were killed. And that his Maties Game being now againe by the order of the King and Councill removed to the usuall place on the Bank side at the very great charges of the Master of the Game I shall therefore earnestly recommend it to your Lo^{pp} and the rest of my very good freiends the Court of Aldermen and desire you to give such order to the Master and Wardens of the Company of Butchers that their offall may bee duely conveyed to the aforesaid houses as formerly it was for the feeding of his Maties said Game which the under officers at present are forced to provide by extraordinary and very chargeable meanes soe not doubting of your Care herein I rest

Court at Whitehall   Your humble Servant
  Septemb: 1664
   Michaelmas day   (Signed) Manchester.

No. 83.

The City's address to King Charles II congratulating him upon his escape after the Rye House Plot; 2 July, 1683.

Journal 50, fo. 83b.

To the Kings most Excellent Matie

The humble Addresse of the Lord Mayor, Aldermen and Commons of the City of London in Common Councell assembled Sheweth

That wee your most Loyall and dutifull subjects haveing with astonishment received ye discovery of a most traterous and horrid Conspiracy of diverse ill affected and desperate persons to compasse ye death and destrucçõn of your Royall person and of your Dearest Brother James Duke of Yorke, and that to effect ye same theis have held Severall Treasonable Consultaçõns to Levy men and to make an Insurrecçõn and made great provision of Armes; A designe notoriously tending to ye present destrucçõn not only of your best Subjects but of ye Sacred Person of your Ma^{ty} ye best of Princes and to involve this and ye future Generaçõn in Confusion blood and misery carryd on notwthstanding their Specious pretences by knowne dissenting Conventicles and Atheistical persons.

And haveing in ye first place Offered up our Solemn thanks to Almighty God for his Watchfull Providence in bringing to Light this impious and Execrable Machination.

We doe in ye next place humbly offer to your Matie ye deepe resentments of our Loyall hearts concerning ye same and begg your Matie to rest fully assured that as no interest in this world is valuable to us in comparison of your Ma^{tyes} service and safety so wee are determined readily to Expose our lives and fortunes in defence of your Ma^{tyes} person your heires and successors and your government establisht in Church and State and particularly for discovering Defeating and destroying all such Conspiracys assotiations and attempts whatsoever.

All which Resolutions are accompanyd wth our daily and fervent prayres that your Ma^{ty} may Vanquish and overcome all your enimyes and that the yeares of your happy reigne over us may be many and prosperous.

No. 84.

Letter from the Duke of Newcastle to the Lord Mayor informing him of the Pretender having set up his Standard in Scotland. Dated Whitehall, 4 Sept., 1745.

Journal 58, fo. 377.

His Majesty having received an Account, That the Eldest Son of the Pretender after having been some time in Scotland, has traiterously assembled a considerable Number of Persons in Arms, who have Set up a Standard in the Name of the Pretender, resisted and attacked some of His Majesty's Forces, and are now Advancing towards Perth or Edenburgh ; And there being the greatest Reason to Apprehend, That these Attempts have been Encouraged, and may be supported by Foreign Powers ; The King has commanded Me to Acquaint Your Lordship therewith, And His Majesty being fully persuaded of the Abhorrence and Detestation that must be raised in the Minds of all his faithful Subjects, at this Audacious Attempt, to Subvert Our most excellent Constitution both in Church and State under which Alone the Liberties and Properties of these Protestant Kingdoms can be preserved, And being Particularly convinced of the Zeal and Loyalty of his good City of London His Majesty Orders Me to assure You, That he has the firmest Confidence, that Your Lordship, pursuant to the great Trust reposed in you, will in Conjunction with the other Magistrates of his said good City, exert your Authority with the utmost Care and Vigilance on this important Occasion, for the Preservation of the Publick Peace ; The Security of the City of London ; and the Disappointment as far as depends upon You, of these wicked and Traiterous Designs. I am &c. Whitehall, September 4th 1745.

No. 85.

Letter from the Duke of Newcastle to the Lord Mayor informing him of the Pretender having entered Derby, and desiring him to put the City into a posture of defence. Dated Whitehall, 6 Dec., 1745.

Repertory 150, fo. 40.

I am commanded by the King to Acquaint Your Lordship; That His Majesty has, this day, received certain Advice, that the Rebels, with the Pretender's Son, Arrived, on Wednesday last, at Derby, in their way, as they give out towards London; That His Royal Highness the Duke of Cumberland upon this New motion of the Rebels towards Derbyshire, had made the necessary Disposition for getting before them, with the utmost Expedition; And had determin'd for that purpose, to March, the direct way for London. Part of the Cavalry of His Royal Highness's Army will be this Night at Northampton, and the Remainder to Morrow, And the Foot will Encamp to Morrow also near Northampton so that His Royal Highness did not Doubt, but he should be able to reach Northampton so as to be between the Rebels and London; But in order that the Peace and Security of the City of London, may be provided for, in all Events, His Majesty has commanded me to recommend it to Your Lordship, That imediate Directions may be given for augmenting the Guard of the City, in such manner as shall be thought proper; And that a sufficient Number of the Train'd Bands may be constantly out in the day time, as well as at Night, to preserve the peace of the City. Your Lordship will also be pleas'd to take Care, that Orders may be given to the Commanding Officers of the Parties employ'd in that Service, to be very vigilant in preventing, or suppressing any Disorders, or Tumults; And to Seize any Persons that may be assembled together in a riotous manner: And also that a Guard may be constantly posted in the Squares and open Places of the City; And that there may be daily Meetings of the Magistrates appointed in proper places to See, that these Services are perform'd.

Your Lordship will likewise be pleas'd to Cause an Exact Account to be taken of all Horses (as well Coach and Saddle Horses) in the several Stables within the City; where Horses are kept for hire; and transmit an Account of the same, to be laid before His Majesty.

The King thinking, that it may be of great Service, that proper Signals should be made, in case of any Commotion or Alarm, and also that Alarm Posts should be appointed, within the City, and Suburbs; His Majesty has commanded, that the same should be forthwith done, And that Your Lordship should have imediate Notice of it.

His Majesty has also given directions to the Master General of the Ordnance, to appoint forthwith proper Persons, to Inspect the several Entrances into the City, and to Consider, in what manner, in case of an Emergency the same may be obstructed.

I am to desire your Lord[p] would be pleased to transmit to me, to be laid before the King an Account of the Number of Men, that are at present, appointed for the several Guards to the City, and of the Places, at which they are posted; As also of what Number of Men you would propose to add, for that Service, And in what parts of this City, they may most usefully be posted.

His Majesty having been inform'd, that a considerable number of his good Subjects, Inhabitants of the City, out of Zeal for His Majesty's Service, and for the preservation of Our Excellent Constitution, are desirous of appearing in Arms, on the present occasion; His Majesty has ordered me to recommend it to your Lord[p] to give all possible Encouragement to such laudable designs, And if Your Lord[p] will transmit to me the Names of any Persons that shall be willing to Engage in the manner above-mentioned, I will imediately procure a proper authority from His Maj[ty] for that purpose.

The Zeal, which your Lo[p] & the City of London have shew'd for the Defence of His Maj[tys] Person and Government, and the Abhorrence and Detestation You have express'd, for the present unnatural Rebellion, give His Majesty the strongest Assurance, that you will Exert your utmost Endeavours in Opposition to the bold and dangerous Attempts, now making by the Pretender and his Adherents ; which threaten the Peace and Tranquility of this great and flourishing City

I am &c.

Whitehall Decm^r 6th 1745.

No. 86.

Proceedings relative to the expunging of the recognizance entered into by William Witham, Messenger of the House of Commons—as narrated by James Morgan, Clerk to the Lord Mayor, to the Committee appointed to assist in defending Crosby, Wilkes and Oliver; 22 March, 1771.

Committee Book.

Mr. James Morgan Clerk to the Lord Mayor acquainted the Committee that he was served on Wednesday Morning last the twentieth instant with an order of the House of Commons dated the nineteenth March 1771 to attend that House with the Minutes taken before the Lord Mayor relative to the Messenger of the House of Commons giving security for his appearance at the next General Quarter Session of the Peace for the City of London to answer such Indictments as may be preferred against him for the supposed assault and Imprisonment of J. Miller. In consequence of this Order he attended the House of Commons on Wednesday the twentieth instant with the book from between two and three o'clock in the Afternoon—that he was called in between two and three o'clock the next Morning and was asked by the Speaker who he was—he said he was Clerk to the Lord Mayor of London— The Speaker ask'd for the Minutes that were taken, then he produced the book at the Bar. The Speaker sent for the book to him and ordered that part relating to Miller to be read. He was likewise ordered up to the Table and the Minutes were read. That a Motion was then made that those Minutes should be expunged which was carried in the Affirmative. That he was ask'd by a Member whether Mr Aldⁿ Wilkes and Mr Aldⁿ Oliver were there. He answered they were. He was then ordered to the Bar and was served with an Order of the House of Commons as follows—Ordered that Mr James Morgan Clerk to the Lord Mayor of London do expunge from the Minute Book kept by him at the Mansion House the entry relative to William Whitham a Messenger of this House giving security for his appearance at the next General Quarter Sessions of the Peace for the City of London. That he answered he had no Indemnity for so doing. The Speaker said he was ordered so to do. He then did expunge that Minute accordingly. He was then ordered to withdraw.

This Committee doth desire the Right Honourable the Lord Mayor to call a Court of Common Council for Tuesday next and lay the whole transaction of the above affair before the said Court, when Mr Morgan is to attend with the Minute Book.

No. 87.

Letter from Charles Fox, Chairman of the Westminster Committee, to the Town Clerk of London suggesting a general meeting of the Committees of Association. Dated St. James's Street, 20 Feb., 1780.

Minutes of City Committee of Correspondence.

Sir,

The Westminster Committee observing that the London Committee are instructed ' to meet such Members of the Com-"mittees of the several petitioning Counties, Cities and Boroughs "as are now in London, or who may be deputed for the purpose "of presenting, or supporting their Petitions, and who may think "it necessary to confer, on the means of promoting the common "object of the said Petition" have directed me to acquaint you that it is their opinion, that nothing is so desireable in the present Stage of the business as a general meeting of the several Committees by their Agents or Deputies. From the correspondence they have had with the other Committees they have reason to think this opinion is pretty general; and therefore if the London Committee should concur in that opinion they would wish to know in what manner the London Committee think such a measure may be best effected.

It has been suggested that the London, Middlesex and Westminster Committees, might meet by their Deputies and that a joint invitation from them to the other Committees would come with more propriety and weight than such a proposal from any single Committee: But altho' this mode has been thought of, any other that is equally adapted to bring about the measure proposed, will be equally acceptable to the Westminster Committee. I have the honor to be &c.

St. James's Street
    February 21st 1780.

No. 88.

Letter of thanks from Edmund Burke to the same for the City's approval of his Bill for Economical Reform. Dated St. James's Square, 6 March 1780.

Ibid.

Sir,

I receive with great satisfaction and very humble acknowledgement, the honour which the Committee of the Common Council of London have been pleased to confer on me, by their Resolution of the 3^d Inst., which you have been so obliging as to transmit to me. Their approbation of the plan which I submitted to Parliament;—the effects which they expect from its being carried into execution,—these secure to me the co-operation and support of the greatest Corporation in the World, thro their very respectable Committee. Be so good, Sir, as to assure that Committee, that I shall be unwearied in my endeavours, to carry into execution the measures which they have approved, and which, under such a sanction, I am entitled to consider as leading to the attainment of some part of the desires, which they, in common with multitudes of our fellow subjects have lately express'd. I say some part, because I am sensible that much more is wanting; and I protest to the Committee, with great sincerity, that I shall be, as active, as industrious, and as zealous in supporting the constitutional and salutary measures, already proposed, and such as may be hereafter proposed, by other Gentlemen, as I have been in endeavouring to give effect to my own humble, but, certainly, well intended conceptions. The people alone can procure the final attainment of the just and temperate requests which they have made. Their interference as constitutional always, as it was now necessary, has already produced a visible effect. A continued watchfulness, on their part, will beget an active attention in the Representative body, to the Interests of their constituents. Let us continue true to ourselves, and we shall not find many that will dare to be false to us. Let each, in his station of public trust, give the best Counsel his capacity suggests, and let our whole collective and united efforts be applyd to execute whatever is wisely plann'd, be the Proposer who he may. Let us do this and the People cannot remain long unsatisfy'd in their just and reasonable desires. I have the honour to be &c.

    Charles Street,
      St. James's Square,
        6th March, 1780.

No. 89.

Letter from Charles Fox to the Town Clerk of London forwarding copy of proceedings of the Westminster Committee of Association, and giving particulars of the proceedings of the House of Commons upon Dunning's motion. Dated St. James's Street, 13 April, 1780.

Ibid.

Sir,

    I have the honour of transmitting to you a copy of the proceedings in Westminster Hall on the 6th inst. in which you will observe that the form of Association adopted by the City of Westminster, is nearly similar to that of the County of York.

    There never was a time when Union was more necessary than the present, as the only hopes of those who wish to defeat the wishes of the people, are confessedly founded upon supposed disagreements among the true friends of their country.

I should long ago have transmitted to your Committee, lists of the Members who have voted in the late important questions, but have been unable to procure any on which I could depend. That which was printed in the Newspapers, was to my knowledge very incorrect.

I cannot close my letter without informing you that the three following Resolutions were agreed to by the House of Commons on the 6th instant.

"That it is necessary to declare, that the Influence of the "Crown has increased, is increasing, and ought to be diminished."

"That it is competent to this House, to examine into and "correct Abuses in the Expenditure of the Civil List Revenues, "as well as in every other branch of the Public Revenue, when- "ever it shall appear expedient to the Wisdom of this House so "to do."

"That it is the Duty of this House, to provide, as far as may "be an immediate and effectual redress of the Abuses complained "of in the Petitions, presented to this House from the different "Counties, Cities and Towns of this Kingdom."

The number who voted for them were 233

Against them 215

so that in one of the fullest houses that we have ever known a complete approbation has been given to the sentiments of the Petitions, with a promise to attend to their Prayers. How that promise will be performed, it is our duty to watch; If we persevere in our exertions, I think there is little or no doubt of obtaining our objects, but if we are lulled into Security by Success, it is but too probable that the Representatives of the People may relapse into their former inattention to their constituents.

I am &c.

St. James's Street,
    April 10th 1780.

APPENDIX B.

Knights and Burgesses of the City of London.

The list of members representing the City of London in Parliament from 1284 down to the present day, here given, has been compiled mainly from the Blue Books of Parliamentary returns (printed in 1878 and 1879), but with large additions gathered from the City's own Records. It may fairly claim to be a more perfect list of City members than has hitherto been published.

The number of representatives of the City in Parliament has varied from time to time. In a treatise known as *Modus tenendi Parliamentum*, ascribed to the early part of the xiv[th] century, the number of members for London, York and other Cities is given as two, the same as the number of Barons of the Cinq Ports and knights of shires.[1] The more usual number as gathered from the City's Archives was either two or four, although there have been occasions (as in the Parliament of 1284 and more especially during the Commonwealth) when it amounted to six and (as in Barebone's Parliament) even to seven. Frequently it happened that when the writ prescribed the election of two members, four or more were elected, although not more than two or, perhaps, three, were to attend.[2] It is in 1346 that we meet for the first time with a writ commanding the election of four members. In the following year a writ was issued for the election of the old number (two), but this was apparently a mistake, for another writ was soon afterwards issued stating that the number should be four. The City, however, displayed great

---

[1] *Modus tenendi Parliamentum* (ed. T. Duffus Hardy), p. 10.
[2] Letter Book E, fos. 20, 22, 88b, 89.

apathy in the matter—the attendance in Parliament interfered no doubt with the commercial pursuits of the members—and, although four were elected, it was distinctly provided that any three or even two might attend.[1] On the other hand, when the City was called upon to elect two members for the Parliament of 1348, it returned four.[2] From 1351 to 1354 the writs prescribed only two members, and the City returned only two, but from 1355 down to the passing of the Redistribution of Seats Act in 1885[3]—that is to say, for a period of more than 500 years—the City of London has, if we except the Parliament of 1371, never been represented in the council of the nation by less than four members.

So long as the City was represented by two members, both were usually aldermen.[4] When four were returned, two were, as a rule, aldermen, and two commoners. The Recorder, who in earliest times was also an alderman of the City, was frequently returned with another alderman, and continued to be so returned long after he had ceased to be elected from the body of aldermen. Indeed, for two centuries—viz., from 1454 to 1654—the Recorder for the time being seldom failed to be elected one of the City's members; but from the time of the Restoration no Recorder has sat for the City, nor has the ancient custom of the City to be represented by an equal number of aldermen and commoners been followed. Prior to the Restoration the custom was so strictly observed that when a member who was a commoner happened to be elected alderman, he resigned his seat in Parliament in order that another commoner might be elected.[5]

[1] Letter Book F, fo. 145b.   [2] *Id.*, fo. 150.
[3] Stat. 48 & 49 Vict., c. 23, which prescribed that after the end of the Parliament then existing the City should return two members and no more.
[4] An exception appears to have been made in 1352, when a commoner was returned with an alderman.—Letter Book F, fo. 215.
[5] Two instances of the kind are recorded, one in 1509 and another in 1534.—See Repertory 2, fo. 77. Letter Book M, fo. 166b. Repertory 9, fo. 79b. On the other hand, there are cases recorded where members of Parliament for constituencies other than the City, having been elected aldermen of the City, have claimed exemption from service owing to their privilege as members.—Repertory 60, fos. 199b, 211b, 245b. Repertory 95, fo. 81.

APPENDIX B.

The parliamentary elections were originally carried out by the mayor and aldermen and a deputation specially summoned from each ward, but the choice of members practically lay with the mayor and aldermen. In course of time the commoners came to be elected by the Common Council, but the aldermen still kept a hold on the elections by nominating certain individuals of whom the citizens were to make their choice.[1]

In 1523 we find an election taking place at the [court of] Husting[2] in the Great Hall. One alderman and the Recorder were nominated by the Court of Aldermen and their nomination was subsequently confirmed by the Common Council in the Guildhall; whilst two commoners were nominated by the commonalty attending at the Husting. But even the latter nominations appear to have been in this instance confirmed by the Common Council.[3] Six years later (viz., in 1529) the election proceedings are recorded somewhat differently. The election took place as before at the [court of] Husting in the Great Hall, the aldermen were nominated by the mayor and aldermen in the Inner Chamber of the Guildhall [*i.e.*, in the Court of Aldermen] and were afterwards ratified and confirmed by a large gathering of the commonalty (*immensa communitas*) in the Great Hall, but the commoners were elected by the commonalty without any subsequent ratification by the Common Council.[4]

At what date the Livery—as distinct from the citizens at large—began to usurp the functions of the commonalty and claim the exclusive right of electing City members, is not clear; but that they did so monopolise the Parliamentary franchise long before it was restricted to them by the Election Act of 1725, there is ample evidence,[5] and they continued to enjoy this monopoly until the passing of the Reform Act of 1832.

---

[1] Repertory 2, fos. 75b, 77, 125b. Letter Book M, fos. 166b, 186.

[2] Hence the name "Hustings" as applied to Parliamentary elections at the present day.

[3] Repertory 6, fo. 20b. Letter Book N, fo. 222.

[4] Letter Book O, fo. 157.

[5] As early as 1539 we find the citizens "in their grand livery" summoned for a Parliamentary election (Repertory 10, fo. 85b); usually it was the "commons" who were summoned.

The City members enjoyed, as we have seen,[1] certain allowances by way of "duties," "fees" or "wages," for their attendance in Parliament, besides gowns, robes or liveries for themselves and their servants, and a reasonable sum of money for expenses. According to Coke (4 Inst., p. 46) the fee or wage paid "time out of mind" to a knight of the shire was four shillings a day, whilst that to a citizen or burgess was half that sum;[2] and these same fees the City Chamberlain paid in 1584 to the alderman and the Recorder representing the City in Parliament, presumably, in their capacity as knights of the shire (the City of London itself constituting a county), and to the two commoners, sitting as burgesses, respectively.[3] In 1628 a question was raised in the House as to whether the aldermen representing the City in Parliment ranked as knights, but no decision appears to have been arrived at.[4]

When the City members attended Parliament, they went as befitted the representatives of the capital of the kingdom. Alderman and commoner alike wore scarlet gowns richly trimmed with fur, for which they received allowances, according to their dignity, of cloth and money. An alderman was allowed ten yards of cloth for his gown, a commoner five. Again, an alderman who had served as mayor received an allowance of 100 shillings for fur; an alderman who had not passed the chair was entitled to no more than 5 marks, whilst commoners received only half that sum.

[1] Vol. i, pp. 273, 274.
[2] Coke's statement is not strictly accurate. Before 1327 knights of the shire were in the habit of receiving sums varying from 1s. to 6s. 8d. a day. From the year 1327 their allowance was 4s. a day exclusive of travelling expenses, and this sum appears to have been paid as long as members received payment for attendance in Parliament.—See Preface to *Modus tenendi Parliamentum*, p. viii and Notes to the same, pp. xxvii, xxviii.
[3] Chamber Accounts (Town Clerk's Office), Vol. II, fos. 21b, 22. The same fees had been authorised by the Court of Aldermen three years before.—Repertory 20, fo. 183. After the Restoration, when more than two aldermen were frequently returned, the junior members (whether aldermen or commoners) received the burgess fee of two shillings a day, as witness the case of Sir John Robinson—the only City member sitting in the first Parliament after the Restoration whose name has come down to us.—See Chamber Accounts, Vol. $\frac{1}{11}$, fo. 145. The expense was defrayed, in early days, by the exaction of one penny in the pound from every individual who had been assessed for the last fifteenth.—Letter Book E, fos. 20, 22.
[4] Journal House of Commons, i, 894.

APPENDIX B.

One "livery" a session was the usual allowance, provided that there was not more than one session within the year; but when, as in 1532, Parliament continued to sit for a number of years, an allowance in cash was made to the members in lieu of another livery for themselves and their servants. This cash payment amounted to £6 13s. 4d.[1]

In addition to wages and allowances already mentioned, the City members were allowed a certain amount of travelling (and other) expenses. From the ancient treatise already referred to we gather that in this respect (if in no other) they were customarily placed on an equality with the knights of shires.[2] When Parliament sat at Westminster, these travelling expenses amounted to little more than a shilling a day—the sum allowed them for boat-hire;[3] when, on the other hand, Parliament sat in some remote town, as it frequently did, they were greater. Thus in 1296, when Parliament was to meet at Bury St. Edmunds, the citizens voted their representatives 20 shillings a day for travelling expenses.[4] The two aldermen who represented the City in the Parliament held at York in 1298 were each allowed 100 shillings and no more.[5] On the other hand when nearly a century later (1388), Parliament sat at Cambridge, the City members were not only allowed their travelling expenses, but the cost of their board and lodging, and even their washing bills were discharged by the Corporation, the whole amounting to upwards of £100, a large sum in those days.[6]

In the middle of the 15th century, viz., in Thomas Chalton's mayoralty (1449-1450), the Common Council resolved that

---

[1] Repertory 8, fo. 210b. Repertory 20, fo. 183.

[2] "Solebant cives esse pares et equales cum militibus comitatuum in expensis veniendo morando et redeundo."—*Modus tenendi Parliamentum*, p. 13.

[3] Repertory 20, fo. 183. Chamber Accounts, Vol. II, fos. 21b, 22.

[4] Letter Book C, fo. 22b. See Frontispiece. The writ and proceedings thereon are printed from the City's Records in Palgrave's Parl. Writs, Vol. I, p. 49.

[5] Letter Book B, fo. 93b. (xxxviiib.)

[6] Letter Book H, fo. 245. (See "Memorials," pp. 511, 512).

thenceforth the allowance for expenses should not exceed 40 shillings a day, but ten years later, when Parliament was to meet at Coventry, it showed a more liberal spirit and undertook to repay any further disbursements that the members might make for the honour and benefit of the City.[1] It did the same in 1464, when Parliament was to have sat at York.[2]

How long the City continued to make payments and allowances to its members is not clear. No doubt, as wealth increased and a seat in the House was looked upon less as a burden, men were found ready to undertake the duties on their own responsibility and without any extraneous assistance, and the custom of payment of members by the City became gradually obsolete. Take, for instance, the case of two of the City's representatives in the Parliament of 1661. Whilst, on the one hand, we find the Court of Aldermen authorising the Chamberlain to pay to John Jones, a burgess, a daily allowance of four shillings—a sum usually allowed knights of the shire—and this amount is recorded in the City's Chamber Accounts as having been duly paid;[3] on the other hand, we find alderman Sir John Frederick (elected member for the City *loco* alderman Fowke deceased) returning the fees and allowances paid to him by the Chamberlain "for his full allowance for diett and boate hire . . . and for his Robes alsoe."[4]

Lastly, it is to be noted that on the occasion of the opening of a new Parliament, the members for the City claim, and generally exercise, the privilege of sitting on the Treasury or Privy Councillor's bench; but on what grounds such privilege is claimed and allowed is not clear.[5]

---

[1] Journal 6, fo. 166b.   [2] Journal 7, fo. 52.
[3] Repertory 69, fo. 319b.   Chamber Accounts, Vol. $\frac{1}{11}$, fo. 224.   Vol. $\frac{1}{11}$, fo. 52b.
[4] Chamber Accounts, Vol. $\frac{1}{12}$, fos. 51, 65.
[5] Sir Erskine May's Parliamentary Practice, (8th ed.) p. 212.

MEMBERS OF PARLIAMENT FOR THE CITY OF LONDON,

1284—1895.

1284.[1] Henry le Waleys.
Gregory de Rokesle.
Philip Cissor.
Ralf Crepyn.
Joce le Acatour.
John de Gisors.

1296.[2] Stephen Eswy.
William de Hereford.

1298. Walter de Fynchyngfeld.
Adam de Foleham.

1300.[3] Geoffrey de Norton.
(March) William de Betoyne.
John le Bancker.
William de Red.
[the first two returned.]

1305. William de Combemartin.
Walter de Fynchyngfeld.

1307. William de Combemartin.
Henry de Durham.

1309. Henry de Durham.
William Servat.

1312.[4] Nicholas de Farndon.
John de Wengrave.
Robert de Kelseye.
John de Sellyng *or* David de Cotesbrok.

1312.[5] Nicholas de Farndon.
John de Wengrave.
Robert de Kelseye.

1313. Nicholas de Farndon.
William de Leyre.
William Servat.
Stephen de Abyndone.

1314.[6] John de Gisors.
William de Leyre.
Robert de Kelseye.
Richer de Refham.
[or two of them.]

---

[1] Chron. Edward I and II (Rolls Series No, 76). Introd. p. xxxiii.
[2] Letter Book C, fo. 22b. [3] *Id.* fo. 41b.
[4] Letter Book D, fo. 149b. [5] *Id.*, fo. 151.
[6] Letter Book E, fos. 20, 22. It appears that at this election three aldermen were nominated for the mayor and aldermen to elect two, and four commoners were nominated for the mayor and aldermen to elect two.

1315. William de Leyre.
Henry de Durham.
1316.[1] William de Combe-
martin.
John de Burford.
Ralph de Walcote.
William de Flete.
Simon de Abyndon.
1318. John de Cherleton.
William de Flete.
Roger le Palmere.
1319.[2] Hugh de Waltham.
William de Flete.
William de Hacford.
Michael Mynot.
John Waldeshef.
[or three of them.]
1320. Nicholas de Farndon.
Anketin de Gisors.
Henry Monquoi.
Roger Hosebonde.
1321.[3] Nicholas de Farndon.
Hamo Godchep.
John Sterre.
Thomas Prentiz.
[three or two of them.]
1322. Robert de Swalclyve.
(May) Reginald de Conduit.
William de Hacford.
Gregory de Norton.
[three or two of them.]

1322. Walter Crepyn.
(Nov.) Thomas de Chetyng-
don.
1324. Anketin de Gisors.
Henry de Seccheford.
1325. Anketin de Gisors.
Henry de Seccheford.
1327. Anketin de Gisors.
(Jan.) Henry de Seccheford.
Reginald de Conduit.
Thomas de Leyre.
Edmund Cosyn.
John Steere [Sterre?].
[two to attend.]
1327. Benedict de Fulsham.
(Sept.) Robert de Kelseye.
1328. Richard de Betoyne.
(Feb.) Robert de Kelseye.
John de Grantham.
John Priour, jun.
1328. Richard de Betoyne.
(April) Robert de Kelseye.
1328. Stephen de Abyndone.
(Oct.) Robert de Kelseye.
1330. Stephen de Abyndone.
(Mar.) John de Caustone.
1330. John de Grantham.
(Nov.) Reginald de Conduit.
Stephen de Abyndone.
[or two of them.]

---

[1] Letter Book E, fo. 46b. Elected to attend a Parliament at Lincoln in Jan. 1316, for the special purpose of considering the establishment of a Staple near Calais.

[2] Letter Book E, fo. 89. The writ was endorsed with two names only, viz., William de Leyre and William de Flete. *Id.*, fo. 88b.

[3] *Id.*, fo. 123b.

APPENDIX B. 475

1332. (Mar.) Anketin de Gisors.
John de Caustone.
John Priour, jun.
Thomas de Chetyngdon.
[three or two of them.]

1332. (Sept.) Reginald de Conduit.
John de Caustone.
Anketin de Gisors.
Thomas de Chetyngdon.
[three or two of them.]

1332.[1] (Dec.) Richard de la Pole.
Thomas de Chetyngdon.
Henry Monquoi.
[or two of them.]

1334. Reginald de Conduit.
John de Caustone.
Roger de Depham.

1335. Richard de Rothingge.
Richard le Lacer.
Roger de Forsham.
[or two of them.]

1336.[2] (Mar.) Henry de Seccheford.
Thomas de Chetyngdon.

1336. (Sept.) John de Caustone.
Richard de Hakenaye.

1337. (Jan.) Reginald de Conduit.
John de Caustone.

1337. (Sept.) Reginald de Conduit.
Benedict de Fulsham.

1338. (Feb.) John de Grantham.
Andrew Aubrey.
Ralph de Upton.
Richard de Rothingge.

1338. (July) Ralph de Upton.
Bartholomew Deumars.

1339. (Jan.) Simon Fraunceys.
John de Northalle.

1339. (Oct.) Simon (Fraunceys).
John (de Nort) halle.

1340.[3] (Jan.) William de Brikelesworth.
John de Mockyng.
Adam Lucas.

1340. (Mar.) William de Brikelesworth.
Richard de Rothingge.
Richard de Berkyngge.
[or two of them.]

1341. Simon Fraunceys.
William de Brikelesworth.

1344. John de Northalle.
John Lovekyn.

1346. Geoffrey de Wychyngham.
Thomas Leggy.
John Lovekyn.
Thomas de Waldene.
[four, three or two of them.]

---

[1] Letter Book E, fo. 236. The Blue Book omits Richard de la Pole.
[2] *Id.*, fo. 245b. The Blue Book gives in addition the name of 'John Priour, and adds "or two of them."
[3] Letter Book F, fo. 29b.

1348. John Lovekyn.
(Jan.) Richard de Berkyngge.
William de Iford.
Richard de Wycombe.
[three or two of them.]

1348. John Lovekyn.
(Mar.) Richard de Berkyngge.
William de Iford.
Richard de Wycombe.
[three or two of them.]

1351. Thomas Leggy.
William de Iford.

1352.[1] Simon Fraunceys.
(Jan.) Simon de Bedyngton.

1352.[2] Adam Fraunceys.
(Aug.) John Lytle.

1353. Thomas Leggy.
Thomas Dolsely.

1354.[3] John de Stodeye.
Thomas Dolsely.

1355.[4] Adam Fraunceys.
John de Stodeye.
Simon de Bedyngton.
Adam de Acres.

1357.[5] Adam Fraunceys.
John de Stodeye.
Simon de Bedyngton.
William de Essex.

1358. Thomas Dolsely.
William de Welde.
William de Essex.
Richard Toky.

1360. Bartholomew Frestlyng
Stephen Cavendyssh.
Walter de Berneye.
Richard Toky.

1361. Adam Fraunceys.
John Pecche.
Simon de Benyngton.
John Pyel.

1362.[6] Adam de Bury.
(Oct.) John Lytle.
John Hiltoft.
John Tornegold.

1363.[7] William Holbech.
John de St. Alban.
Simon de Benyngton.
John Tornegold.

1365. Adam Fraunceys.
(Jan.) John Lovekyn.
Simon de Benyngton.
Richard de Preston.

1365.[8] Adam Fraunceys.
(May) John Wroth.
Simon de Benyngton.
John de Worstede.

[1] Letter Book F, fo. 207.
[2] *Id.*, fo. 215. Summoned to attend a Council.
[3] Letter Book G, fo. 18.   [4] *Id.*, fo. 39.
[5] *Id.*, fo. 58.
[6] *Id.*, fo. 101. In the Parliamentary Blue Book, Bartholomew Frestlyng appears in place of Adam de Bury.
[7] *Id.*, fo. 112b.   [8] *Id.*, fo. 175.

APPENDIX B.

1368. John Wroth.
Bartholomew Frestlyng
John Aubrey.
John Organ.

1369. John Pecche.
(June) John Tornegold.
Nicholas de Exton.
John Hadele.

1369.[1] Adam Fraunceys.
(Nov.) John Stodeye.
John Aubrey.
John Philipot.

1370.[2] John Pecche.
(Jan.) William Walworth.
Fulk Horewode.
John Fyfhide.

1370.[3] John Tornegold.
(Feb.) Bartholomew Frestlyng
John Philipot.
William Essex.

1371. Bartholomew Frestlyng
John Philipot.

1372. John Wroth.
John Pecche.
William Venour.
William Kelshull.

1373. Adam Stable.
John Warde.
John Birlyngham.
Adam Carlile.

1376.[4] John Pyel.
William Walworth.
William Essex.
Adam Carlile.

1377. John Hadle.
(Jan.) John Organ.
William Tonge.
William Venour.

1377. Adam Carlile.
(Oct.) Walter Sibill.
William Walworth.
John Philipot.

1378. John Hadle.
Geoffrey Neuton.
John de Northampton.
William Venour.

1379.[5] Adam Carlile.
Walter Sibill.
John Hadle.
William More.

1380.[6] John Philipot.
(Jan.) Robert Launde.
John Boseham.
Thomas Cornwaleys.

1380.[7] John Organ.
(Nov.) John Rote.
Thomas Welford.
William Tonge.

1381. Sir John Philipot.
John Hadle.

[1] Letter Book G., fo. 238b. Summoned to attend a Council.
[2] *Id.*, fo. 240. A Council. [3] *Id.*, fo. 262b.
[4] Letter Book H, fo. 28. [5] *Id.*, fo. 105b.
[6] *Id.*, fo. 117. [7] *Id.*, fo. 125.

William Baret.
Hugh Fastolf.

1382. John More.
(Oct.) Thomas Carleton.
William Essex.
Richard Norbury.

1383. Sir Nicholas Brembre.
(Feb.) John More.
Richard Norbury.
William Essex.

1383. William Walworth.
(Oct.) Sir John Philipot.
William Baret.
Henry Vanner.

1384. John Hadle.
(Apr.) John Organ.
John Rote.
Henry Herbury.

1384. John Hadle.
(Nov.) John Organ.
Thomas Rolf.
Henry Herbury.

1385. John Hadle.
Nicholas Exton.
Henry Herbury.
William Ancroft.

1386. John Hadle.
John Organ.
Adam Carlile.
Thomas Girdelere.

1388. William More.
(Feb.) John Shadworth.

William Baret.
John Walcote.

1388. Adam Bamme.
(Sept.) Henry Vanner.
William Tonge.
John Clenhand.

1390. William More.
(Jan.) John Shadworth.
Adam Carlile.
William Brampton.

1390.[1] John Hadle.
(Nov.) John Loveye.
Thomas Newenton.
John Botesham.

1391. William Shiringham.
William Brampton.
William Staundon.
John Walcote.

1394.[2] William Staundon.
John Fresh.
Thomas Exton.
John Wade.

1395. Adam Carlile.
Drew Barantyn.
Geoffrey Walderne.
William Askham.

1397. William Staundon.
(Jan.) William Brampton.
William Hyde.
Hugh Short.

---

[1] *Id.*, fo. 253. On fo. 255 William More is given in place of John Loveye.
[2] *Id.*, fo. 288b.

1397. Andrew Neuport.
(Sept.) Drew Barantyne.
Robert Asshecombe.
William Chychely.

1399. John Shadworth.
(Oct.) William Brampton.
Richard Merlawe.
William Sonnyngwell.

1402.[1] John Hadle.
(Sept.) William Parker.
John Prophete.
William Norton.

1403.[2] William Staundon.
Drew Barantyn.
William Marcheford.
John Prophete.

1406. William Staundon.
Nicholas Wotton.
John Sudbury.
Hugh Ryebrede.

1407. William Askham.
William Crowemer.
William Marcheford.
John Bryan.

1410.[3] Drew Barantyn.
(Jan.) Henry Halton.
John Reynewell.
Walter Gawtron.

1410.[4] Richard Merlawe.
(Nov.) Thomas Fauconer.

John Sutton.
John Michell.

1413.[5] Drew Barantyn.
(Feb.) William Askham.
William Marcheford.
Walter Gawtron.

1413. Drew Barantyn.
(May) William Askham.
William Marcheford.
Walter Gawtron.

1414.[6] Richard Merlawe.
(Jan.) Robert Chichele.
William Burton.
Alan Everard.

1414. William Waldern.
(Nov.) Nicholas Wotton.
William Olyver.
John Gedney.

1415. Robert Chichele.
William Waldern.
John Reynewell.
William Michell.

1416.[7] Richard Merlawe.
(Mar.) Thomas Fauconer.
William Weston.
Nicholas Jamys [James]

1416.[8] Richard Whitington.
(Oct.) Thomas Knolles.
John Perneys.
Robert Whityngham.

[1] Letter Book I, fo. 18b. [2] Letter Book I., fo. 35b.
[3] Id., fo. 88b. [4] Id., fo. 105b.
[5] Id., fo. 119. [6] Id., fo. 130.
[7] Id., fo. 160b. [8] Id., fo. 172b.

1417. William Crowemer.
William Sevenoke.
John Welles.
John Boteler, jun.

1419. Nicholas Wotton.
Henry Barton.
Richard Meryvale.
Simon Sewale.

1420. Thomas Fauconer.
John Michell.
Salamon Oxneye.
John Hi[g]ham.

1421. William Waldern.
(May) William Crowemer.
William Burton.
Richard Gosselyn.

1421. Thomas Fauconer.
(Dec.) Nicholas Wotton.
John Whateley.
John Brokley.

1422. Thomas Fauconer.
John Michell.
Henry Frowyk.
Thomas Mayneld.

1423.[1] Thomas Fauconer.
John Welles.
Henry Frowyk.
Thomas Boteler.

1425. Nicholas Wotton.
John Welles.
"Eborardus" Flete.
Thomas Bernewell.

1426. John Michell.
John Welles.
"Eborardus" Flete.
John Higham.

1427. John Michell.
John Welles.
William Melreth.
Walter Gawtron.

1429. Nicholas Wotton.
Nicholas James.
William Melreth.
Walter Gawtron.

1431. William Estfeld.
Nicholas James.
John Higham.
John Abbot.

1432. John Gedney.
William Melreth.
John Levyng.
Philip Malpas.

1433. John Reynewell.
John Welles.
John Hatherle.
Thomas Catteworth.

1435. John Michell.
Robert Large.
John Bederenden.
Stephen Forster.

1437. Henry Frowyk.
Thomas Catteworth.
John Carpenter, jun.
Nicholas Yeo.

[1] Letter Book K, fo. 8.

APPENDIX B. 481

1442. Sir William Estfeld.
John Bowys.
Philip Malpas.
William Cottesbroke.

1447. Henry Frowyk.
William Combys.
Hugh Wyche.
William Marowe.

1449. Thomas Catteworth.
(Feb.) John Norman.
Geoffrey Boleyn.
Thomas Billyng.

1449. Stephen Broun.
(Nov.) John Norman.
John Nedham.
John Har[e]we.

1450. Henry Frowyk.
William Marowe.
John Harewe.
Richard Lee.

1453. Stephen Broun.
William Cantelowe.
John . . . .
. . . . . .

1455. Geoffrey Feldyng.
William Cantelowe.
John Harewe.
John Yonge.

1463.[1] William Marowe.
Thomas Urswyk, Recorder.
Thomas Wynselowe
John Bromer.

1467. Sir Ralph Josselyn.
Thomas Urswyk.
John Warde.
John Crosseby.

1469.[2] Ralph Verney.
George Irlond.
Stephen Fabyan.
Thomas Stoughton.

1472. Sir Ralph Verney.
George Irlond.
John Brampton.
Stephen Fabyan.

1478. Sir William Hampton.
Richard Gardyner.
William Bracebrigge.
John Warde.

1483.[3] Sir William Heriot.
Robert Tate.
John Marchall.
William Bracebrigge.

1485.[4] John Warde, Mayor.
Thomas Fitz-William Recorder.
John Pekeryng.
William Spark.

[1] Letter Book L, fo. 11b. Journal 7, fo. 21, 23b.
[2] Journal 7, fo. 199.   [3] Journal 9, fo. 24.
[4] *Id.*, fo. 91b.

1487.[1] Sir Henry Colet, Mayor.
Thomas Fitz-William, Recorder.
Hugh Pemberton.
John Pekeryng.
William White *loco* Thomas Fitz-William.[2]

1491.[3] Robert Tate.
William Capel.
Nicholas Alwyn.
Thomas Bullesdon.

1497.[4] [Richard] Chawry.
Sir Robert Sheffeld. Recorder.
. . . .
. . . .

1504.[5] Sir John Shaa.
Sir Robert Sheffeld, Recorder.
Thomas Cremour.
John Paynter.
Sir John Tate[6] *loco* Sir John Shaa deceased.

1510.[7] John Tate.
John Chaloner, Recorder.

James Yarford.
John Brugys.
Thomas More *loco* James Yarford, elected alderman.

1512.[8] Sir William Capel.
Richard Broke, Recorder.
William Calley.
John Kyme.

1515.[9] Sir William Capel.
Richard Broke, Recorder.
William Calley.
John Kyme.

1523.[10] George Monoux.
William Shelley, Recorder.
John Hewster.
William Roche.

1529.[11] Sir Thomas Seymer.
John Baker, Recorder.
John Petyte.
Paul Wythypol.

[1] Journal 9, fo. 157b.
[2] Elected member for Lincolnshire. [3] Journal 9, fo. 279.
[4] Repertory 1, fo. 10. Elected by the Aldermen. The names of those elected by the Commonalty have not come down to us.
[5] Journal 10, fo. 301. [6] Elected 29 Dec., 1503.—Repertory 1, fo. 150.
[7] Letter Book M, fos. 164b, 166b.
[8] Journal 11, fo. 147b, Repertory 2, fo. 125b.
[9] Letter Book M, fo. 231b, Journal 11, fo. 204b. [10] Letter Book N, fo. 222.
[11] In Jan., 1534, the Court of Aldermen voted the usual allowances to the Recorder, Mr. Wythypol and Mr. Bowyer, the City members.—Repertory 9, fo. 41b. In October of the same year Robert Pakyngton was elected in place of William Bowyer chosen an Alderman.—(Blue Book, Appendix p. xxix), and in December Sir Thomas Seymer asked leave to resign his seat on account of ill-health.—Repertory 9, fo. 141b.

APPENDIX B.

1542. Sir William Roche.
Sir Roger Cholmeley, Recorder.
John Sturgeon.
Nicholas Wylford.

1545. Sir William Roche.
Sir Roger Cholmeley, Recorder.
John Sturgeon.
Paul Wythypol.
Sir William Forman *loco* William Roche.[1]
Sir Richard Gresham[2] *loco* Sir William Forman.
Robert Broke, Recorder.[3]

1547. Sir Martin Bowes,
Robert Broke, Recorder.
Thomas Curteis.
Thomas Bacon.

1553. (Mar.) Sir Martin Bowes.
Robert Broke, Recorder.
John Marsh.
John Blundell.

1553. (Sept.) Sir Rowland Hill.[4]
Robert Broke, Recorder.
John Marsh.
John Blundell.

1553. (Oct.) Sir Rowland Hill.[5]
Robert Broke, Recorder.
John Marsh.
John Blundell.

1554. (April) Sir Martin Bowes.
Robert Broke, Recorder.
John Marsh.
John Blundell.

1554. (Nov.) Sir Martin Bowes.
Ralph Cholmeley, Recorder.
Richard Grafton.
Richard Burnell.

1555. Sir Martin Bowes.
Ralph Cholmeley, Recorder.
Philip Bold.
Nicholas Choyne [Chune].

1558. William Garrard.
Ralph Cholmeley, Recorder.
John Marsh.
Richard Grafton.

---

[1] Roche had been committed to prison.
[2] Elected 10 Nov., Forman being unable to attend through illness.—Repertory 11, fo. 244 (221).
[3] Elected 17 Nov., *loco* Cholmeley, appointed King's Sergeant—Wriothesley, p. 162.
[4] Letter Book R, fo. 259b.   [5] *Id.*, fo. 270b.

1559.[1] Sir Martin Bowes.
Ralph Cholmeley, Recorder.
John Marsh.
Richard Hills.[2]

1563. Sir William Chester.
Ralph Cholmeley, Recorder.
Laurence Withers.
John Marsh.

1571.[3] Sir John White.
Thomas Wilbraham, Recorder.
John Marsh.
Thomas Norton.

1572. Sir Roland Heywood.
William Fletewood, Recorder.
John Marsh.[4]
Thomas Norton.

1584.[5] Sir Nicholas Woodrooff.
William Fletewood, Recorder.
Walter Fisshe.
Thomas Aldersey.
Henry Billingsley,[6] *loco* Walter Fisshe, dec^{d.}

1586. Sir Edward Osborne.
William Fletewood, Recorder.
Thomas Aldersey.
Robert Saltinstall.

1589 Sir George Barnes.
William Fletewood, Recorder.
Thomas Aldersey.
Andrew Palmer.

1593. Sir John Harte.
Edward Drewe, Recorder.
Andrew Palmer.
George Sotherton.

1597. Sir John Harte.
John Croke, Recorder.
George Sotherton.
Thomas Fettiplace.

1601. Sir Stephen Soame.
John Croke, Recorder.
Thomas Fettiplace.
John Pynder.

1604.[7] Sir Henry Billingsley.
Sir Henry Montague, Recorder.
Nicholas Fuller.
Richard Gore.
Sir Thomas Lowe, *loco* Sir Henry Billingsley.[8]

---

[1] Journal 17, fo. 161.
[2] Hyde in the Parliamentary Return.   [3] Journal 19, fo. 356b.
[4] A Writ was issued (28 Sept., 1579), for the election of a member *loco* John Marsh, deceased.—Journal 20, part 2, fo. 516b.
[5] Journal 21, fos. 388b, 390.
[6] Date of Return, 29 Sept., 1585.—Letter Book, &c., fo. 60b.
[7] Journal 26, fo. 171; Letter Book BB, fo. 226b.
[8] *Ob.*, 22, Nov. 1606.

APPENDIX B.

- 1614. Sir Thomas Lowe.
  Sir Henry Montague Recorder.
  Nicholas Fuller.
  Robert Middleton.
- 1621. Sir Thomas Lowe.
  Robert Heath, Recorder.
  Robert Bateman.
  William Towerson.
- 1624. Sir Thomas Middleton.
  Sir Heneage Finch, Recorder.
  Robert Bateman.
  Martin Bond.
- 1625. Sir Thomas Middleton.
  Sir Heneage Finch, Recorder.
  Robert Bateman.
  Martin Bond.
- 1626. Sir Thomas Middleton.
  Sir Heneage Finch, Recorder.
  Sir Maurice Abbott.
  Robert Bateman.
- 1628. Thomas Moulson.
  Christopher Clitherowe
  Henry Waller.
  James Bunce.
- 1640. (April) Thomas Soame.
  Isaac Pennington.
  Matthew Cradock.
  Samuel Vassall.
- 1640. (Nov.) Thomas Soame.
  Isaac Pennington.
  Matthew Cradock.
  Samuel Vassall.
  John Venn, *loco* Matthew Cradock.[1]

CROMWELLIAN PARLIAMENTS.[2]

- 1653. Robert Tichborne.
  John Ireton.
  Samuel Moyer.
  John Langley.
  John Stone.
  Henry Barton.
  Praise-God Barebone.
- 1654. Thomas Foot.
  William Steele, Recorder.
  Thomas Adams.
  John Langham.
  Samuel Avery.
  Andrew Ricaut or Riccard.
- 1656. Thomas Foot.
  Sir Christopher Pack.
  Thomas Adams.
  Richard Brown.

[1] *Ob.*, 27 May, 1641.
[2] Taken from Browne Willis's "Notitia Parliamentaria."

Theophilus Biddulph.
John Jones.
1659. William Thomson.

Theophilus Biddulph.
John Jones.
Richard Brown.

1660. Sir John Robinson.[1]
1661. John Fowke.
Sir William Thompson.
William Love.
John Jones.
Sir John Frederick, *loco* John Fowke.[2]

1679. Sir Robert Clayton.
(Mar.) Sir Thomas Player.
William Love.
Thomas Pilkington.

1679. Sir Robert Clayton.
(Oct.) Sir Thomas Player.
William Love.
Thomas Pilkington.

1681. Sir Robert Clayton.
Thomas Pilkington.
Sir Thomas Player.
William Love.

1685. Sir John Moore.
Sir William Pritchard.
Sir Samuel Dashwood.

Sir Peter Rich.
1689. Sir Patience Ward.
Sir Robert Clayton.
William Love.
Thomas Pilkington.
Sir William Ashurst, *loco* William Love, deceased.

1690. Sir William Pritchard.
Sir Samuel Dashwood.
Sir William Turner.
Sir Thomas Vernon.
Sir John Fleet, Mayor, *loco* Sir William Turner.[3]

1695. Sir Robert Clayton.
Sir John Fleet.
Sir William Ashurst.
Thomas Papillon.

1698. Sir John Fleet.
Sir William Ashurst.
Sir James Houblon.[4]
Thomas Papillon.

---

[1] The only member for the City sitting in this Parliament yet discovered. The sum of £37 4*s.* is recorded as being paid to him for his attendance as a "burgess" for the City.—Chamber Accounts, $\frac{1}{11}$, fo. 145.

[2] *Ob.*, 22 April, 1662.

[3] *Ob.*, 9 Feb., 1693.—Luttrell, Diary, iii, 32.

[4] *Ob.*, Oct., 1700.—Luttrell, Diary, iv, 701.

APPENDIX B.

1701. (Feb.)
- Sir Robert Clayton.
- Sir William Ashurst.
- Sir William Withers.
- Gilbert Heathcote.
- Sir John Fleet, *loco* Gilbert Heathcote, disqualified.

1701. (Dec.)
- Sir Robert Clayton.
- Sir William Ashurst.
- Sir Thomas Abney.
- Gilbert Heathcote.

1702.
- Sir William Pritchard.
- Sir John Fleet.
- Sir Francis Child.
- Gilbert Heathcote.

1705.
- Sir Robert Clayton.
- Sir William Ashurst.
- Sir Gilbert Heathcote.
- Samuel Shepheard.
- Sir William Withers Mayor,[1] *loco* Sir Robert Clayton.[2]

1708.
- Sir William Withers, Mayor.
- Sir William Ashurst.
- Sir Gilbert Heathcote.
- John Ward.

1710.
- Sir William Withers.
- Sir Richard Hoare.
- Sir George Newland.
- John Cass.

1713.
- Sir William Withers.
- Sir Richard Hoare.
- Sir John Cass.
- Sir George Newland.[3]

1715.
- Sir John Ward.
- Sir Thomas Scawen.
- Robert Heysham.
- Peter Godfrey.

1722.
- Francis Child.
- Richard Lockwood.
- Peter Godfrey.
- John Barnard.
- Sir Richard Hopkins, *loco* Peter Godfrey, deceased.

1727.
- Sir John Eyles.
- Humphrey Parsons.
- John Barnard.
- Micaiah Perry.

1734.
- Humphrey Parsons.
- Sir John Barnard.
- Micajah Perry.
- Robert Willimot.

1741.
- Daniel Lambert, Mayor
- Sir John Barnard.
- Sir Robert Godschall.
- George Heathcote.
- William Calvert, *loco* Sir Robert Godschall.[4]

1747.
- Sir John Barnard.
- Sir William Calvert.

---

[1] Elected 22 Nov., 1707.—Luttrell, vi, 237.
[2] *Ob.* 16 July, 1707.
[3] *Ob.*, March, 1714.
[4] *Ob.*, 26 June, 1742.—Gentleman's Magazine, vol. 12, p. 831.

1747. Slingsby Bethell.
Stephen Theo. Janssen.

1754. Sir John Barnard.
Sir Robert Ladbroke.
Slingsby Bethell.
William Beckford.
Sir Richard Glyn, Mayor, *loco* Slingsby Bethell.[1]

1761. Sir Robert Ladbroke.
Sir Richard Glyn.
William Beckford.
Thomas Harley.

1768. Thomas Harley, Mayor
Sir Robert Ladbroke.
William Beckford.
Barlow Trecothick.
Richard Oliver, *loco* William Beckford.[2]
Frederick Bull,[3] *loco* Sir Robert Ladbroke.[4]

1774. John Sawbridge.
Richard Oliver.
Frederick Bull.
George Hayley.

1780. George Hayley.
John Kirkman.
Frederick Bull.
Nathaniel Newnham.
John Sawbridge, *loco* John Kirkman.[5]
Sir Watkin Lewes, *loco* George Hayley.[6]
Brook Watson, *loco* Frederick Bull.[7]

1784. Brook Watson.
Sir Watkin Lewes.
Nathaniel Newnham.
John Sawbridge.

1790. William Curtis.
Brook Watson.
Sir Watkin Lewes.
John Sawbridge.
John William Anderson *vice* Brook Watson.[8]
William Lushington, *vice* John Sawbridge.[9]

1796.
1801. *First Parliament of the United Kingdom of Great Britain and Ireland [1801].*
William Lushington.

---

[1] *Ob.*, 1 Nov., 1758.—Gentleman's Magazine, vol. 28, p. 556.
[2] *Ob.*, 21 June, 1770.
[3] Elected 5 Dec., 1773.—Walpole's Journal, i, 275.
[4] *Ob.*, 31 Oct., 1773.—Gentleman's Magazine, vol. 43, p. 581.
[5] *Ob. circ.*, Sept., 1780.
[6] *Ob.*, 30 Aug., 1781.—Gentleman's Magazine, Vol. 51, p. 443.
[7] *Ob.*, 10 Jan., 1784.—Gentleman's Magazine, Vol. 54, pt. i, p. 73.
[8] Accepted the Stewardship of the Manor of East Hendred, co. Berks. Appointed Commissary General of Forces in March, 1793.—Journal 73, fo. 273b.
[9] *Ob.*, 20 Feb., 1795.—Gentleman's Magazine, Vol. 65, pt. i, p. 175.

APPENDIX B.

William Curtis, Mayor.
Harvey Christian Combe.
John William Anderson

1802. Harvey Christian Combe.
Charles Price.
William Curtis.
Sir John William Anderson.

1806. Harvey Christian Combe.
James Shaw, Mayor.
Sir Charles Price.
Sir William Curtis.

1807. Sir Charles Price.
Sir William Curtis.
James Shaw.
Harvey Christian Combe.

1812. Harvey Christian Combe.
Sir William Curtis.
Sir James Shaw.
John Atkins.
Matthew Wood, Mayor, *loco* Harvey Christian Combe.[1]

1818. Matthew Wood.
Thomas Wilson.
Robert Waithman.

John Thomas Thorp.

1820. Matthew Wood.
Thomas Wilson.
Sir William Curtis.
George Bridges, Mayor.

1826. William Thomson.
Robert Waithman.
William Ward.
Matthew Wood.

1830. William Thompson.
Robert Waithman.
William Ward.
Matthew Wood.

1831. Robert Waithman.
William Thompson.
Matthew Wood.
William Venables.

1833. George Grote.
Matthew Wood.
Robert Waithman.
Sir John Key.
George Lyall, *loco* Robert Waithman.[2]
William Crawford, *loco* Sir John Key.[3]

1835. Matthew Wood.
James Pattison.
William Crawford.
George Grote.

[1] Accepted the Chiltern Hundreds.
[2] *Ob.*, 6 Feb., 1833.—Gentleman's Magazine, Vol. 103, pt. i, p. 179.
[3] Accepted the Chiltern Hundreds.

1837. Matthew Wood.
William Crawford.
James Pattison.
George Grote.

1841. John Masterman.
Sir Matthew Wood.
George Lyall.
Lord John Russell.
James Pattison, *loco* Sir Matthew Wood.[1]

1847. Lord John Russell.
James Pattison.
Baron Lionel N. de Rothschild.
John Masterman.
Sir James Duke, Mayor, *loco* James Pattison, deceased.

1852. John Masterman.
Lord John Russell.
Sir James Duke.
Baron Lionel N. de Rothschild.

1857. Sir James Duke.
Baron Lionel N. de Rothschild.
Lord John Russell.
Robert Wigram Crawford.

1859. Lord John Russell.
Baron Lionel N. de Rothschild.
Sir James Duke.
Robert Wigram Crawford.
Western Wood, *loco* Lord John Russell.[2]
George Joachim Goschen, *loco* Western Wood.[3]

1865. George Joachim Goschen.
Robert Wigram Crawford.
William Lawrence.
Baron Lionel N. de Rothschild.

1868. George Joachim Goschen.
Robert Wigram Crawford.
William Lawrence.
Charles Bell.
Baron Lionel N. de Rothschild, *loco* Charles Bell, deceased.

1874. William James Richmond Cotton.
Philip Twells.
John Gellibrand Hubbard.
George Joachim Goschen.

---

[1] *Ob.*, 25 Sept., 1843.—Gentleman's Magazine, Vol. 20, N. S., p. 541.
[2] Accepted the Stewardship of the Manor of Northstead, co. York.
[3] *Ob.*, 17 May, 1863.—Gentleman's Magazine, Vol. 59, N. S., p. 810.

APPENDIX B.

1880. William J. R. Cotton.
Robert Nicholas Fowler.
Rt. Hon. John G. Hubbard.
William Lawrence.

1885. Sir Robert N. Fowler.
Rt. Hon. J. G. Hubbard.

1886. Sir Robert N. Fowler.

1886. Rt. Hon. J. G. Hubbard.
Thomas Charles Baring,[1] *loco* Hubbard, raised to the peerage.
Henry Hucks Gibbs,[2] *loco* Baring, dec^{d.}
Sir Reginald Hanson,[3] *loco* Fowler, dec^{d.}

1892. Sir Reginald Hanson.
Alban G. H. Gibbs.

---

[1] Elected 27 July, 1887. [2] Elected 18 April, 1891.
[3] Elected 3 June, 1891.

INDEX.

Abbey of Graces, or New Abbey, suppressed, i, 398.

Abercromby, Sir Ralph, captures the Dutch Fleet, iii, 239; his death, 248.

"Abhorrers," party name of, ii, 460.

Abingdon, occupied by Essex, ii, 205.

Abney, Thomas, sheriff, knighted, ii, 574; M.P. for the City, 609; unsuccessfully contests the City, 613.

Abyndone, Stephen de, M.P. for the City, i, 178.

Acatour, Joce le, M.P. for the City, i, 118.

Acre, the seige of, raised by Sir Sidney Smith, iii, 238.

Acton, Sir William, elected mayor and discharged by Parliament, ii, 130; imprisoned in Crosby House, 173.

Adams, Thomas, his conduct as mayor approved, ii, 235; sent to the Tower, 266; impeached, 273; deprived of his aldermanry, 308; restored, 383.

Addington, succeeds the younger Pitt, iii, 248; proposes a renewal of the income tax, 252; resigns and is succeeded by Pitt, 254; proposed vote of thanks of Common Council to, 255-256; joins Pitt's ministry and is created Viscount Sidmouth, 259; withdraws from the ministry, 260.

"Addled" Parliament, the, ii, 61.

Adrian, John, elected mayor, i, 104.

Agincourt, battle of, i, 259.

Aislabie, Chancellor of the Exchequer, convicted of bribery, iii, 21; expelled from Parliament, 22.

Aix la Chapelle, treaty of, iii, 56.

Aldermen, assessed as barons, i, 217; elected for life, 243; created justices by James I, ii, 58; removal of several, 308; restored, 383; several removed and others appointed by Charles II, 396; appointed by James II, 504; to be in future nominated by the court of, 519; fined for non-attendance at swearing-in of lord mayor, 573; disputed elections of, 640-645; iii, 146-149.

—— Court of, first mention of, i, 72; its claim to veto proceedings of Common Council, ii, 304-305, 448-451, 454; matters of difference with the Common Council, 334, 448, 556; standing counsel appointed for, 454; reformed by James II, 519, 520; thanks the king for Declaration of Indulgence, 520; Jeffreys attends, with restitution of City's liberties, 530; charged with obstructing the City's business, 643; its claim to veto proceeding of Common Council confirmed by statute, iii, 27, 29; resolution of, in favour of short parliaments, 135.

Alexandria, battle of, iii, 248.

Aleyne, Thomas, elected mayor, ii, 356; knighted by Charles II, 380; the citizens take the oath of allegiance at the house of, 381.

Alfred the Great, "restores" London, i, 12.

Aliens, taxation of, i, 280, 319.

Allen, Francis, M.P., reports to the House proceedings of the Common Council, ii, 229; elected alderman, 230.
—— Sir John, mayor, particulars of, i, 394 n.
—— Sir William, mayor, i, 517.
Alphage, Archbishop of Canterbury, murder of, i, 18; interred in St. Paul's, 19; removed to Canterbury, *id.*
Althorp, Lord, the freedom of the City conferred on, iii, 339, 344.
Alva, Duke of, seizes English merchants in Antwerp, i, 508; his envoy in the City, 511.
Amadas, Robert, goldsmith, discharged alderman, i, 371.
Amcotes, Sir Henry, mayor, i, 431.
America, commencement of war with, iii, 142; war opposed by Chatham and the City, 149; the Massachusetts Bill, 150; New York appeals to London, 154; City address to the king for cessation of hostilities with, 157; the king's reply, 158; motion to send a reply to the appeal from New York negatived, *id.*; Philadelphia appeals to the City, *id.*; address of livery to electors against war with, 158–160; declaration of independence of, 166; subscriptions in aid of war with, refused in the City, 167; alliance with France, 168; the independence of, recognised, 202–203.
Amherst, Lord, adjutant-general, his order for the military to fire without waiting for directions from civil magistrate, iii, 184; objections raised by the City, 187, 188.
Amicable Loan, the, i, 374–376.
Amiens, the "Mise" of, i, 95; peace of, iii, 249.
Andrews, Thomas, mayor, placed on commission for trial of Charles the First, ii, 301; Commonwealth proclaimed by, 311; proposal to confer knighthood on, 312.
Anne, Queen of Richard II, her assistance invoked by citizens for a charter, i, 224, 225; her death, 243, 244.
—— Queen of Richard III, coronation of, i, 323.
—— Queen, accession of, ii, 610; City addresses to, 610, 616, 623, 626, 629, 630, 635, 647, 649; her picture at the Guildhall and her statue at the Royal Exchange, 611; coronation of, *id.*; her Tory proclivities, 612; attends the lord mayor's banquet, 613; at St. Paul's, 614, 616, 621, 624, 647; attends the trial of Dr. Sacheverell, 634; dismisses the Whigs, 636; her indisposition, 648; her death, 650.
—— Boleyn, her marriage with Henry VIII, i, 388; the City's welcome to, 388, 389; her coronation, 389; her execution, 395.
—— of Brittany, assisted by Henry VII against the king of France, i, 329, 330.
—— of Cleves, her passage through the City, i, 397.
Ansgar, sheriff of Middlesex, i, 32.
Antoninus Pius, his itinerary, i, 5.
Antwerp, decline of, i, 505; English merchants seized in, 508; fall of, 530, 531.
Archers, Archery, the effectiveness of the long-bow, i, 190, 192, 197; archery practised in Finsbury Fields, 190; archers furnished by the City against France, 190, 204; the City's gates to be guarded by, 220; a detachment sent by the City to put down the Pilgrimage of Grace, 304; mounted archers for defence of Calais, 480.
Armada, the, preparations in the

City to meet, i, 534; ships set forth by the City, 536n.; sighted off the Lizard, 537; the fate of, 537–541.
Argyle, Earl of, defeats the Earl of Mar at Sheriffmuir, iii, 8.
Armagnac, Count of, constable of France, i, 262.
Arms, assize of, i, 120.
Army, the, a tax imposed by Parliament for maintenance of, ii, 176; objection to tax, 181; petition for reforms in, 199; rendezvous at Aylesbury, 200, 201; establishment of a standing, 208; the New Model, 214; City petition for disbandment of, 239, 240, 242; its relation to Independents and Presbyterians, 222, 240; correspondence between the City and, 243, 245, 247, 248, 249, 251, 252, 255; the Declaration of, 246; City Commissioners appointed to remain with, 248; moves to Uxbridge, 249; new Commissioners sent to, 257; another Declaration of, 258; the City surrenders to, 259; enters London, 260; demands money from the City, 263; further correspondence with the City, 268, 269; ill-feeling between the City and, 275; another Declaration of, 293; returns to London, 294; pay demanded for, 296, 297; a mutiny in, 310; free quarters to be found in the City unless money be found for, 314, 315; the City consents to furnish a contingent of cavalry, 332; Parliamentary vote for disbandment of, 456; encamped at Hounslow, 518; disaffection in the camp, 528; Pitt's army of reserve, iii, 252; his Additional Force Bill, 257.
Army Plot, the, ii, 139.
Arthur, son of Henry VII, marries Catherine of Aragon, i, 335, 336

Arundel, Edmund, Earl of, i, 158.
—— Henry, Earl of, i, 456.
—— Richard, Earl of, i, 234, 235; arrested, 244.
—— Thomas, Archbishop of Canterbury, his opposition to the Lollards, i, 255.
—— Sir Thomas, i, 411.
Ascue, or Ascough, Anne, trial and execution of, i, 415.
Ashurst, Sir William, stands for the City, ii, 553; elected sheriff, 565; elected mayor, 573; his unpopularity, id.; at the head of the commission for the Bank of England, 585; M.P. for the City, 598, 607, 609, 622n., 629; unsuccessfully contests the City, 613.
Assandun, victory of the Danes at, i, 24.
Association, the, the City called upon to raise troops for protection of, ii, 220; in defence of William the Third, 600.
Aswy or Eswy, Stephen, taken prisoner, i, 122; M.P. for the City, 126.
Athelstan, his Mansion House in the City, i, 16; his encouragement of commerce, id.
Atkin or Atkins, Thomas, M.P., committed to prison ii, 123; released, 125; placed on commission for trial of the king, 301; proposal to confer knighthood on, 312; desired by City to make communication to Parliament, 369.
Atkins, John, M.P. for the City, loses his seat, iii, 309.
Atte Bowe, Alice, condemned to be burnt alive, i, 119.
Atterbury, Francis, Bishop of Rochester, arrested for complicity in Jacobite plot, iii, 25.
Audley, James, Lord, defeated at Blore Heath, i, 296.
—— John, Lord, i, 380.
—— Sir Thomas, the building and

site of the priory of Holy Trinity bestowed on, i, 387 ; his death, 408.
Austin Friars, i, 399, 400.
Austrian Succession, war of the, iii, 49, 56.
Aylesbury, rendezvous of Parliamentary forces at, ii, 200, 201.
Aylmer, John, Bishop of London, advocates the appointment of special preachers in the City, i, 526, 527, 528 n.
—— Lawrence, mayor, imprisoned, i, 338.
Aylyff, Sir John, barber-surgeon, first alderman of Bridge Ward Without (1550), i, 443, ; particulars of, 443 n.
Ayres, Deputy, ii, 590.

Babington, Anthony, his conspiracy against Elizabeth, i, 532.
Backwell, Edward, alderman, assists the City with money, ii, 439 ; reduced to bankruptcy, owing to closing of the Exchequer, 445.
Bacon, Sir Nicholas, i, 510.
Badlesmere, Sir Bartholomew de, executed at Canterbury, i, 151.
—— Lady, insults the queen, i, 151.
Bagnall, Sir Samuel, i, 559.
Bailey, Sir William, mayor, i, 376.
Baker, John, recorder, M.P. for the City, i, 381.
Baldock, Chancellor, his house sacked, i, 158.
Baliol, Edward, surrenders the crown of Scotland to Edward III, i, 197.
Bamme, Adam, goldsmith, a candidate for the mayoralty, i, 239 ; mayor, 240 ; dies during his mayoralty, 244.
Bankes, Sir Henry, stands for mayoralty, iii, 127, 132.
Bank of England, the, foundation of, ii, 584–586, a run on, 603 ; makes an advance to William III,

id.; refuses to render assistance during South Sea troubles, iii, 19 ; " Black Friday " at, 52, 53 ; threatened by Gordon rioters, 184 ; negotiations for removal of the military guard of, 216–219 ; suspension of cash payments, 231 ; a regiment of volunteers formed by employés of, 252.
Bannockburn, defeat of Scots at, i, 141.
Barclay Conspiracy, the, ii, 599.
Bardi, the, their banking house sacked, i, 158.
" Barebone's " or the " little " parliament, ii, 346.
Barentyn, Drew, first alderman of Farringdon Within, i, 243 ; mayor, takes horse to meet the Duke of Lancaster, 245.
Barnard, Sir John, M.P. for the City, opposes passing of Election Act (11 Geo., i, c. 18), iii, 28 ; opposes Walpole's Excise Bill, 36 ; re-elected M.P. for the City, 47 ; again elected, 56.
Barnes, Sir George, mayor, signs "counterfeit will " of Edward VI, i, 453.
Barnet, battle of, i, 314.
Barons, the, revolt of, i, 59 ; meeting of, at St. Paul's, 63, 72 ; at Bury St. Edmunds, 73 ; elect Robert Fitz-Walter as their leader, 74 ; admitted into London, 77 ; war between John and, 78 ; invite Louis the Dauphin over, 79 ; supported by London, 89 ; reject the Mise of Amiens, 95 ; in league with the citizens of London, *id.* ; refuse to go abroad with Edward I, 127 ; insist upon a confirmation of their charters, 128 ; elect ordainers, 133 ; admitted into the City, 136 ; the City's gates barred against, 138 ; Edward II comes to terms with, 141 ; in the City, 167.

Barrington, Lord, burnt in effigy on Tower Hill, iii, 118.

Barton, Elizabeth, executed, i, 390.

—— Henry, mayor, appointed commissioner for victualling the navy, i, 261.

Basing-House, siege of, ii, 196.

Basset, Philip, appointed chief justiciar, i, 91.

—— Robert, alderman, his gallant resistance to the Kentish rebels, i, 316.

Bateman, Sir Anthony, mayor, the French Ambassador insulted at the banquet of, ii, 404.

—— Sir James, subscribes to loan to Prince Eugene, ii, 624.

—— Robert, ii, 25.

Batencurt, Luke de, sheriff, goes to Paris to confer with King Edward I, i, 116.

Bathurst, Lord, President of the Council, the City's correspondence with, touching the right of the citizens to arm themselves, iii, 187-190.

Baxter, Richard, trial of, ii, 510; his opposition to James II, 521.

Baylis, Robert, his contest with Richard Brocas for aldermanry of Bread Street Ward, iii, 15-16.

Baynard's Castle, Robert Fitz-Walter, owner of, i, 74.

Beachcroft, Sir Robert, mayor, ii, 642.

Beam, the Great, reconveyed by Henry VIII to the City, i, 387, 388.

Beam, the Small, granted to Jacobina la Lumbard, i, 124; granted to a friend of Hugh le Despenser, 133, 141.

Beaufort, Edmund. *See* Somerset.

—— Henry, Bishop of Winchester, quarrels with Gloucester, i, 270; goes to France, 271, 273, 277; created a cardinal, 271; his goods seized, 277.

Becket, Gilbert, Portreeve of London, i, 55, his tomb in St. Paul's Churchyard, 57.

—— Thomas, his birth, i, 55; made chancellor and archbishop, 56; his memory long cherished by the citizens, *id.*; St. Thomas de Acon and S. Thomas's Hospital dedicated to, 57; his image over the gate of Mercers' Chapel, 125; windows relative to, altered at the Reformation, 425.

Beckford, William, alderman, Pitt's letter to, iii, 67; causes Bute to be insulted at the Guildhall, 69; supports Wilkes in Parliament, 71, 72; supports Chatham's East India Bill, 79; re-elected mayor, 90; his magnificent entertainment, 98; his failure to "fix" Rockingham, 99; his famous speech, 102; the City's thanks to, 103; his last days, 105.

Bedford, Edward, Earl of, arrested for treason, i, 562.

—— John, Duke of, question of his precedence at the Guildhall, i, 257, 258; presides over parliament, 263; rivalry with the Duke of Gloucester, 268; appointed Protector during minority of Henry VII, 269; goes to France, 271; returns to defend himself before parliament, 278; sets an example of economy, *id.*; death of, 279.

Bekering, Thomas, engaged in the Trumpington Conspiracy, i, 248.

Belknap, Robert, refuses the City's claims at coronation of Richard the Second, i, 213.

Benevolence, a, opposed by the City, i, 411.

Benfleet, South co., Essex, Danish fortification at, i, 13.

Benn, Antony, recorder, ii, 67; knighted, 72.

Berkeley, Lord Thomas, i, 380.

KK

Berlin Decree, the, iii, 267.
Berry, Captain, the freedom of the City voted to, iii, 237.
Berwick, captured by Bruce, i, 141, recovered by Edward III, 197.
Bethell, Slingsby, sheriff, ii, 472, 473, 475; fined for creating a disturbance in Common Hall, 493; returns to England, 548.
—— Slingsby, elected M.P. for the City, iii, 56.
Bethlehem Hospital, conveyed to the City, i, 451.
Betoyne, Richard de, connives at Mortimer's escape from the Tower, i, 154; elected mayor, 159; appointed warden of the Tower, *id.*; accompanies City members to Parliament at Lincoln, 162; M.P. for the City, 163, 174; mayor of the Staple, disagrees with his colleagues at York, 174–176; his conduct approved, 177.
Bide, John, alderman and sheriff, ii, 269.
Bigod, Hugh, justiciar of the City, i, 89, 90.
—— Roger, his altercation with the king, i, 127.
Billers, Sir William, mayor, his unpopularity, iii, 38.
Billingsgate, the City's right to tolls at, i, 308.
Billingsley, Sir Henry, the daughter of Sir John Spencer committed to the charge of, i, 553; elected M.P. for the City, ii, 8.
Bill of Rights, ii, 553.
Bill of Rights Society, iii, 124.
Birch, Samuel, his inscription on statue of George III, iii, 281; his proposed visit to Paris to present swords of honour to Blucher and others after Waterloo, 290.
Bishops, the seven, sent to the Tower, ii, 526; trial and acquittal of, 527.
Black Death. *See* Plague.

Black Friars, Parliament meet in house of the, i, 133, 370; the legatine court at the house of the, 379, 380; their house suppressed, 398.
Blackfriars Bridge, formerly known as "Pitt Bridge," iii, 65.
"Black Friday," iii, 52.
Blackwell, William, town clerk, i, 473.
Blake, admiral, his victory over the Dutch, ii, 344.
Blenheim, battle of, ii, 616.
Blois, Henry de, Bishop of Winchester, acts as intermediary between Stephen and the Empress Matilda, i, 47; his speech before the Synod at Winchester, 48.
Blore Heath, defeat of Lord Audley by the Earl of Salisbury at, i, 295, 296.
Blound, John le, mayor, knighted, i, 130.
Bludworth, Sir Thomas, nominated alderman by Charles II, ii, 396; his conduct at the Fire of London, 415, 418; elected sheriff, 470.
Boleyn, Thomas. *See* Rochford.
Bolingbroke, Henry St. John, afterwards Viscount, forms a Tory Ministry, ii, 638; takes refuge in France to avoid impeachment, iii, 5; assists the Pretender, 6.
Bolton, Peter, iii, 13.
—— Sir William, elected mayor, ii, 425; Courts of Aldermen held at his house, 429; proposal to appoint him surveyor-general for the rebuilding of the city, 432; convicted of embezzlement, 432 n.
Bond, Sir George, mayor, summons the citizens to church at the approach of the Armada, i, 538.
—— Martin, his monument, in St. Helen's, Bishopsgate, i, 545.
—— William, alderman, owner of Crosby House, i, 512.
Bonner, Edmund, Bishop of London,

deprived of his see, i, 438, 439; his sentence confirmed, 440; his bishopric conferred on Ridley, *id.*; re-instated, 458.
"Book of Sports," the, burnt in Cheapside, ii, 187.
Boroughbridge, battle of, i, 152.
Bosworth, battle of, i, 326.
Boulogne, captured by Henry VIII, i, 409-411; threatened by the French king, 414; surrendered by Warwick, 445; threatened by Spain, 556.
Bourne, Doctor, his sermon at Paul's Cross, i, 458.
Bowes, Sir Martin, mayor, improves the City's water supply, i, 416; member of Hospital Committee, 417; accompanies remains of Henry VIII to Windsor, 419.
Box, Henry, grocer, his school at Witney, co. Oxon, i, 353.
—— Ralph, a candidate for the shrievalty, ii, 473, 480; elected, 483; discharged, 486; knighted, 548.
Boy-Bishop, the, ceremony in connection with, discontinued in the City, i, 421.
Bradley, Matthew, ii, 138.
Bradshaw, John, heads the commission for trial of Charles the First, ii, 301; his letter to the City, touching its Irish estates, ii, 326.
Breda, the Declaration of, ii, 377; treaty of, 437.
Brembre, Nicholas, carries a letter from the City to the king, i, 206; appointed mayor by the king, 211; promulgates charter forbidding foreigners to traffic by retail, 214; opposes the Duke of Lancaster, 215; arraigned and fined, 216; subscribes to fund for winning back the nobility to the City, *id.*; knighted, 220; re-elected mayor, 224, 227, 228; confers with the king, 231; his complicity in the king's attempt upon the life of the Duke of Gloucester, 233; charged with treason, 234; his flight and capture, 235; his trial, 236; executed, 237.
Brentford, co. Middlesex, Charles I in possession of, ii, 175; withdraws from, 176; John Horne (Tooke), vicar of, iii, 87.
Bretigny, peace of, i, 199.
Breton, John le, warden of the City, i, 122, 128; assists in furnishing ships, 126.
Brice, Hugh, mayor, coronation cup of Richard III, in custody of, i, 323; re-elected mayor, 327.
Bridewell, Parliament sits at, i, 381; converted into a workhouse, 451.
Bridge House Estate, the, return of rental of, i, 252.
Bridge Ward Without. *See* Southwark.
Bridgen, Edward, iii, 13.
—— William, mayor, fails to assist the sheriffs in burning No. 45 of the *North Briton*, iii, 76; Wilkes proposes to use him as a stalking-horse, 126.
Broad, John, goldsmith, ii, 32.
Broad-bottomed administration, the, iii, 57.
Brocas, Richard, his contest with Robert Baylis for aldermanry of Bread Street Ward, iii, 15-16.
Broke, captain of the "Shannon," presented with the freedom of the City, iii, 287.
Bromfield, Sir Edward, ii, 125.
Brooke, Sir Basil, his plot for winning the City for the king, ii, 197.
Broom, coroner, arrests the mayor, ii, 501; is suspended, 502; reinstated, 549.
Brougham, his motion for Parliamentary reform, iii, 329.
Brown, John, elected alderman and discharged, i, 379.
Browne, Major-General Sir Richard,

ii, 206, 207, 216; arrested, 295; deprived of his aldermanry, 319; restored, 383; elected mayor, 384; appointed major-general of the City's forces, 385.
Bruce, Robert, captures Berwick, i, 141.
Bruges, recovery of, by the English army, ii, 629.
Brugge, Sir John, mayor, i, 367.
Bryan, William, engaged in the Trumpington Conspiracy, i, 248.
Buckingham, Edward, Duke of, his manor of The Rose in the parish of St. Laurence Pountney, the late site of Merchant Taylors' School, i, 366; his trial at the Guildhall and execution, 366–367.
—— George, Duke of, his unpopularity in the City, ii, 100, 105; his expedition to Rhé, 103; assassination of, 108.
—— Henry, Duke of, his harangue at the Guildhall in favour of Gloucester, i, 321; rebellion and execution of, 324.
—— Owen, sheriff, knighted, ii, 598; as mayor, entertains the Duke of Marlborough, 617; late alderman of Bishopsgate Ward, 644.
—— See Gloucester, Thomas, Duke of.
Bucklersbury, a mass-house in, sacked, ii, 533.
Bull, Frederick, alderman, elected sheriff, iii, 121; elected mayor and M.P. for the City, 141; seconds motion that Lord Gordon's petition do lie on the table of the House, 179; charged by Wilkes with having connived at Gordon riots, 190; again returned M.P. for the City, 192; his letter to the livery, 193.
Bulmer, his waterworks at Broken Wharf, ii, 19.
Bunce, James, alderman, committed to the Tower, ii, 266; impeached,

273; deprived of his aldermanry, 308; restored, 383.
Bunyan, John, his opposition to James II, ii, 521.
Burdett, Sir Francis, committed to the Tower, iii, 276; his committal followed by riots, 277; vote of thanks of the livery to, *id.*
Burgh, Hubert de, defeats French fleet off Dover, i, 81; causes Fitz-Athulf to be hanged, 82; in disgrace, 84.
Burgundy, Charles, Duke of, marries Margaret, sister of Edward IV, i, 309.
—— John, Duke of, murder of, i, 265.
—— Philip, Duke of, comes to terms with Henry V, i, 265; lays siege to Calais, 279, 280; commerce of London hindered by, 289.
Burke, Edmund, thanked by the livery for policy towards American colonies, iii, 152; writes the inscription for Chatham's monument in the Guildhall, 171; his Economical Reform Bill, 175, 176.
Burnell, Anne, i, 552.
Burnet, Bishop, his opinion on the parliamentary elections of 1710, ii, 637, 638.
Burrard, Sir Harry, iii, 269.
Burton, Henry, enters London with Prynne, ii, 134.
Bury, Adam de, alderman, deposed, i, 205.
Bute, Marquis of, appointed Secretary of State, iii, 67; insulted at Lord Mayor's banquet, 69; forced to declare war against Spain, 70, 72; resigns, 73.
"Bye" or "Surprise" Plot, the, ii, 7.
Byng, Admiral, his victory off Cape Passaro, iii, 40; outcry against, for loss of Minorca, 59, 60; tried and shot, 61.

INDEX.

501

Byron, Sir John, holds the Tower for Charles I, ii, 162.
Cade, Jack, rebellion of, i, 282-285.
Cadiz, capture of, i, 555; expedition to, ii, 94.
Caen, capture of, by Edward III, i, 191; by Henry V, 262; the citizens to send provisions to, free of duty, 263.
Cæsar, Sir Julius, Chancellor of Exchequer, ii, 22.
Calais, taken by King Edward III, i, 193; abortive attempt by the French to recapture, 195; besieged by the Duke of Burgundy, 279; appeals to London for assistance, *id.*; City forces sent to raise siege of, 280; the Duke of Gloucester appointed captain of, *id.*; the Duke of Somerset captain of, 287; the City again called upon to assist, 289; the loss of, 480; falls into the hands of Spain, 556.
Caleys, John of, enlists volunteers in the City, for France, i, 412.
Calthorp, Sir Martin, his charity to disbanded soldiers, i, 547.
Calvert, William, sheriff, knighted, iii, 50; M.P. for the City, *id.*; re-elected, 56.
Campden, Edward, Viscount, attends the Common Council, ii, 128.
Campeggio, Cardinal, his reception in the City, i, 362-364; presides over Legatine Court at the Blackfriars, in the matter of the divorce of Catherine of Aragon, 380.
Campion, the Jesuit, arrives in England, i, 525; execution of, 528.
Candler, Richard, his insurance business, i, 500.
Canning, the City's satisfaction at his accepting office, iii, 326.
Cantelowe, William, alderman, committed to prison, for complicity in an attack upon the Lombards. i, 292; particulars of, 292n.

Canterbury, Archbishop of, question of his precedency at the Guildhall, i, 257, 258. *See also* Alphage; Arundel; Chichele; Cranmer; Sudbury.
Cape Breton, capture of, iii, 56.
Capel, Sir William, alderman, fined, i, 338; M.P. for the City, 345 n.
Cardmaker, *alias* Taylor, John, burnt, i, 474.
Cardonel, Philip de, his scheme for raising money, ii, 447.
Caroline, Queen, wife of George IV, City addresses to, iii, 316, 317; her trial, 317; holds Court at Brandenburgh House, 318; presents her portrait to the City, 319; attends service at St. Paul's, *id.*; her death, 321; disgraceful scene at her funeral, 322.
Carpenter, John, town clerk, founder of the City of London School, i, 349, 350; picture of the Dance of Death in cloister of Pardon churchyard, painted at his expense, 427.
—— Dr. John, master of St. Antony's School, i, 349.
Carter, Robert, i, 385.
Carteret, George, afterwards Viscount Carteret and Earl Granville, iii, 48, 49; his want of patriotism, 52.
Casimir, Count, entertained by Sir Thomas Gresham, i, 520; the City's gift to, 521.
Cass, John, M.P. for the City, ii, 638.
Castro, Bartholomew de, builds the refectory of the Grey Friars, i, 402.
Caswall, Sir George, expelled from Parliament and committed to the Tower, iii, 20, 21.
Cater, William, ii, 71.
Catesby, Robert, plans the Gunpowder Plot, ii, 13.
Catherine of Aragon, preparations for her reception in the City, i,

335; her marriage with Prince Arthur, 336; her marriage with Henry viii, 344; City gift to, at coronation, *id.*; rejoicings at the news of her pregnancy, 354; proceedings at the Blackfriars relative to her divorce, 379, 380.

Catherine, of Braganza, City gift to, ii, 399.

—— Parr, queen of Henry viii, appointed regent, i, 409.

Catholic emancipation, at one time opposed, afterwards favoured by the City, iii, 326.

Caustone, John de, M.P. for the City, i, 178.

Cecil, Sir Robert, his house at Theobalds, ii, 2.

—— Sir William, Lord Burghley, i, 511, 514.

Chalgrove Field, battle of, ii, 188.

Chamberlain, Sir Leonard, appointed lieutenant of the Tower, i, 435.

Chambers, Richard, alderman, disputes the king's right to levy ship money, ii, 115; deprived of his aldermanry for not attending proclamation of Commonwealth, 311, 312.

Champion, Sir George, M.P, for Aylesbury, rejected for mayoralty for having upheld the Spanish Convention, iii, 42, 43, 45.

Chantrey, Sir Francis, his statue of George the third in the Council Chamber, iii, 281.

Chantries, suppression of, i, 414, 424.

Chapman, Sir John, appointed mayor by James II, ii, 530; re-elected by the citizens, 533; seized with apoplexy whilst trying Jeffreys, 537; death of 546.

Charles, Prince, afterwards King Charles I, joy of the citizens at his return from Spain without the Infanta ii, 84; his marriage with Henrietta Maria, 86, 93; his claim to tonnage and poundage, 108; goes to Scotland, 111; demands ship money, *id.*; his charter to the City, 118; City gift to, on return from Scotland, 121; attempts to force a loan from the City, 122; again goes to Scotland, 142; entertained in the City, 147; promises to restore the City's Irish Estate, 149; attempts to arrest the Five Members, 155; City's petition to, 158; his reply, 160; leaves London, 161; City's deputation to, at Oxford, 178–180; the Common Hall rejects his terms, 180; Parliamentary terms rejected by, 183; issues a commission of array to Gardiner, 187; besieges Gloucester, 193; retires to Oxford, 196; leaves Oxford, 206; re-enters Oxford, 212; betakes himself to Newark after defeat at Rowton Heath, 222; proposes to come to Westminster, 225; offers to compromise the religious question, 226; communicates with the City, 234; the City's reply, 235, 237; removed from Holmby House by Cornet Joyce, 242; his answer to propositions for peace, 257; negotiations for a personal treaty with, 282–285; Levellers' petition against negotiating with, 291; trial and execution of, 301; his statue removed from Royal Exchange, 330.

Charles Prince, afterwards King Charles II, birth of, ii, 109; letter and declaration of, sent to the City, 289; further correspondence with the City, 340, 377; issues the declaration of Breda, 377; the City's answer, 378; City gift to, 379; the City sends commissioners to, *id.*; proclaimed king, 380; enters London, *id.*; Richmond Park restored to, 381; the citizens take the oath of allegiance, *id.*; entertained by the City, 384; coronation of, 389-391; letter from, *re* election of Common Council, 398; his charter to the City, 403; his reception on return from a progress, 404; his efforts to suppress the Fire, 416; declares war with the Dutch, 445; his illness, 459; prohibits "tumultuous petitions," 460; livery petition to, *id.*; City petitions and addresses to, 461, 463, 465, 475, 498; reluctantly accepts an invitation to dinner on lord mayor's day, 474; issues writ of *Quo Warranto* against the City, 476; tries to obtain a royalist Common Council, 494; death of, 505.

Charles V of Spain, elected Emperor, i, 364; his visit to the City, 364, 365; enters into a league against France, 373.

Charles, Prince of Castile, married by proxy to Mary, daughter of King Henry VII, i, 339.

Charles Edward Stuart, Prince (the young Pretender), prepares to invade England, iii, 49; failure of expedition, 50; lands in Scotland, *id.*; his march to Derby, 51, 52; withdraws from Derby, 54; defeated at Culloden, 55.

Charleton, John de, opposes Betoyne at York, i, 175-177.

Charlotte, Queen, wife of George III, her picture at the Guildhall, iii, 70.

—— Princess, daughter of George IV, her portrait presented to the City by Queen Caroline, iii, 319.

Charter-house, the, suppressed, i, 390-393.

Chastillon, Cardinal, entertained by Gresham, i, 504.

Chatham Place, iii, 65.

Chauncy, Maurice, his account of the proceedings against the Charter-house, i, 390-392.

Cheapside, Queen Eleanor's cross in, i, 125; "Post of Reformation" set up in, 473; destruction of cross in, ii, 187.

Cheriton, Waller's victory at, ii, 199

"Chesapeake" the, defeated by the "Shannon," iii, 286, 287.

Cheshire, Royalist rising in, ii, 354.

Chester, siege of, ii, 224.

—— Ranulph, Earl of, i, 84.

Chetwyn, Philip, objects to Skippon being placed in command of City forces, ii, 276; charges Alderman Gibbs with lying, 292; committed to Warwick Castle, 319.

Cheyne, William, recorder, i, 230.

Chichele, Henry, Archbishop of Canterbury, i, 256.

—— Robert, mayor, ordered to make valuation of property in the City, i, 251; return of his own rental, 252.

Chichester, Sir Arthur, ii, 33.

Chigwell, Hamo de, elected mayor, i, 149, 150; deposed, 153; appointed tax collector, 162; re-elected mayor, 165; abused by a brother alderman, *id.*; trial of, at Guildhall, 169.

Child, Francis, alderman, knighted, ii, 552; elected sheriff, 555; M.P. for the City, 613; opposes passing of Election Act (II Geo. i, c. 18), iii, 28.

—— Sir Josiah, a director of the East India Company, ii, 575, 576; examined on the company's expenditure, 596; his security for a loan to the king, 603.

Chimney Tax. *See* Hearth Tax.

Chinon, death of Henry II, at, i, 61.

Chiverton, Richard, mayor, knighted by Cromwell, ii, 352.

Christchurch, Newgate, soldiers quartered in, during Gordon riots, iii, 192.

Christ's Hospital, founded by the City, i, 450.
Cintra, Convention of, the City's indignation at the, iii, 269; enquiry demanded, 272-274.
Cissor, Philip, or the tailor, M.P. for the City, i, 118.
Clarence, George, Duke of, intrigues with Warwick, i, 310.
—— Thomas, Duke of, informs the citizens of the king's success abroad, i, 262.
Clarendon, Henry, Earl of, recalled from Ireland, ii, 516.
Clark, Edward, alderman, knighted, ii, 552; elected sheriff, 555.
—— Sir George, sent to Charles I at Oxford, ii, 180.
Clarke, Sir Samuel, candidate for aldermanry of Langbourn Ward, ii, 642.
—— William, concerned in the Bye Plot, ii, 7.
Clayton, Sir Robert, alderman, M.P. for the City, ii, 458, 464, 538, 598, 607, 609, 622 n.; mayor, 460; attends presentation of address to Charles II, 475; declines aldermanry at the restoration of City's charter, 531; unsuccessfully contests the City, 553, 606, 613; witnesses presentation of a bribe to the Speaker, 590; M.P. for Bletchingly, 613; his death, 622 n.
Clements, Jaques, assassinates the French king, i, 548.
Clerkenwell Prison, inmates of, set free by Gordon rioters, iii, 183.
Cleve, Goscelin de, i, 195.
Cleveland, Thomas Wentworth, Earl of, brought prisoner to London, ii, 342.
Cleydon, John, executed for Lollardry, i, 256.
Clifford, Thomas, Lord, recommends Charles II to close the Exchequer, ii, 444.
Clinton, Edward, Lord, i, 491.

Closterman, his picture of Queen Anne, ii, 611.
Clothworkers of London, Dutch envoys to Elizabeth entertained by, i, 530; committee for fitting out ships against the Armada sit at the Hall of, 536; James I, a member of company of, ii, 12; the company's subscription to bounties for soldiers, iii, 64.
Clough, Richard, Gresham's agent in Antwerp, i, 496, 511.
Cnut, elected king by the Danish fleet, i, 20; takes refuge in Denmark, 21; returns, 22; attacks London, 23; his victory at Assandun, 24; agrees with Edmund for a division of the kingdom, *id.*; elected king of all England, 25.
Coal, an import laid on, for assisting to rebuild the City after the Great Fire, ii, 430-434; abolition of coal and wine dues, iii, 349, 350.
Cobham, Edward, Lord, marches to London with Richard, Duke of Gloucester, i, 287.
—— Eleanor, i, 271; tried as a witch, 281.
Cobold, Thomas, engaged in the Trumpington Conspiracy, i, 248.
Cockaine, Sir William, alderman, ii, 26, 68; governor of the Irish Society, 38, 42; entertains King James, 69.
Coleman, Edward, executed, ii, 458.
Colet, Henry, alderman, i, 348.
—— John, Dean of St. Paul's, i, 348; founder of St. Paul's, school, 350-352.
College, Stephen, the "Protestant joiner," trial of, ii, 467, 468.
Collett, James, sheriff, knighted, ii, 606.
Collier, Richard, mercer, his school at Horsham, i, 353.
Combe, Harvey, his conduct during bread riots, iii, 241-245.
Committee of Both Kingdoms,

formation of, ii, 199; draws up proposals for peace, 201; re-appointed, 203, 204.

Committee of Correspondence, formed by the City, iii, 175, 178; dissolved, 193; a committee formed by the livery, 196; the use of the Guildhall allowed the committee, *id*.

Committee of Grievances, report of, 541–543.

Committee of Safety at the Guildhall, ii, 244.

Committees of Association, formation of, iii, 175, 176; Lord Shelburne and the Wiltshire Committee, 177; the City accepts form of Association, 178; the use of the Guildhall refused to, 193.

Common Council, elected by the guilds, i, 206; the old system reverted to, 207; held in the Church of St. Stephen, Walbrook, 312; a loan extorted from, ii, 129; supports Pym, 152; Charles I demands the Five Members from, 157; petition for peace laid before, 177; sends a deputation to the king, 178; makes proposals for reduction of Newcastle, 189; parliament entertained by, 198, 234; their objection to present petitions to parliament unless drawn up by themselves, 217; petition to parliament by, *id.*; the Covenant taken by members of, 226; Scottish commissioners attend, 228; Fairfax invited to dinner by, 261; a personal treaty with Charles demanded by, 282; a purge administered to, 297; disorderly proceedings in, 298, 299; the claim of the Court of Aldermen to veto proceedings of, 304, 448–451; proceedings of, regulated by Act of Parliament, 304; a further purge administered to, 306, 307; more matters of difference with the Court of Aldermen, 334, 556–558, 643–645; dissolved by the Rump, 366; restored, 371; Charles II tampers with, 494; ceases to sit, 509, 519; resumes its sittings after restoration of City Charter, 532; opposes Election Bill (II Geo. i, c. 18), iii, 28; New York appeals to, 154; motion to send a reply to the appeal from New York negatived in, *id.*; Philadelphia appeals to, *id*.

Common Hall, votes £100,000 for Parliament, ii, 167; rejects terms offered by Charles I, 180; an Act touching elections in, 329, 330; petitions Charles II for parliament to be allowed to sit, 460; elections in, 469; presents an address to Charles II, 475; resolution of, to stand by King William, 601!; remonstrance on Luttrell being declared M.P. for Middlesex, iii, 88, 89; resolutions reflecting on Lord Holland, 91; another remonstrance, 91–93; remonstrance objected to by certain livery companies, 93; the king hesitates to receive it as being "entirely new," 94–96; the king's reply, 97; the remonstrance condemned by Parliament, 98; another remonstrance (1771), calling upon the king to dissolve Parliament, 119; the livery not allowed to attend in a body, 120; another remonstrance (1773), in favour of short parliaments, 135; the king's reply, 137; opinion of Glynn, Recorder, as to rights of livery in Common Hall, 138; Plumbe's case determining jurisdiction of Court of Aldermen over livery, 138–139; counsels' opinion as to power of the livery in, 139–140; another remonstrance (1775), against policy towards America,

150–152; thanks of the livery to Chatham and Burke, 152; the king's reply to remonstrance, *id.*; the king refuses to receive future addresses of the livery, on the throne, 153; resolution of the livery thereon, 155; vote of thanks to Lord Effingham for refusing to take part in the American war, *id.*; a new remonstrance to the king against war with America, 156; remonstrance not presented, the king refusing to receive it on the throne, *id.*; address of the livery to electors, against the war, 158–160; another remonstrance to be received on throne, 193-194; not presented, 195; a Committee of Correspondence formed by the livery, 196; the livery petition Parliament for a peace with France, 226; urges the king to dismiss his ministers, 232-233; address of the livery touching the Convention of Cintra, not received, 273–274; a vote of thanks to Sir Francis Burdett, 277; strong petition for Parliamentary reform, 278; petition dismissed, 280; another petition allowed to lie on the table, 281; address of livery to Prince Regent, not presented, 283–285; another address to the same for reformation of abuses, not presented, 296; judicial decision that the livery have no right to introduce matters for consideration in, other than those for which they are assembled, 311; address to William IV, not presented, 328–329; address to the king, praying him to create a sufficient number of peers to enable the Reform Bill to be passed, 341; the rights of the livery reserved in Reform Bill, 343–344.

Commonwealth, the, establishment of, ii, 303, 311.
Commune, a, granted to the Citizens of London i, 64.
Companies, Livery, contribute to a gift of £500 to the king, , 201; stand by Henry VI, against the Duke of York, 303; the Corporation deprived of the control of, 337; called upon by Wolsey to surrender their plate towards a loan, 368, 369; precept to, for contingent to oppose Pilgrimage of Grace, 394; subscribe to loans to Queen Mary, 467, 482; loan of £100,000 to Parliament by, ii, 167; £50,000 raised by, 193; arbitrary treatment of, by the king, 505; refuse to obey mayor's precept, 616. *See also* Ulster Plantation, Virginia Plantation, &c.
Compton, Bishop of London, signs invitation to the Prince of Orange, ii, 529.
—— William, Lord, marries "Rich" Spencer's daughter, i, 553, 554.
Concealed lands, commission to search for, i, 531; Statute (21, Jas. I, c. 2,) relative to, ii, 87.
Conduit, Reginald de, leader of city forces against Scotland, i, 180.
"Confirmatio Cartarum" the, i, 128.
Conyers, Gerard, elected alderman, ii, 640, 641.
Cook, Sir Thomas, alderman, governor of the East India Company, ii, 578; charged with misusing the Company's money, 593–595; sent to the Tower, 594, 596; elected mayor and discharged, 597; contests Colchester, 599.
Cooke, Osmond, City marshal, iii, 75.
Cooke or Coke, Sir Thomas, alderman, committed to prison, i, 310; seeks restoration of his lands, seized by Lord Rivers, 312, 313.
Cope, Sir John, defeated by the

Young Pretender at Preston Pans, iii, 51.
Copenhagen, battle of, iii, 249.
Copland, Rev. Patrick, his sermon at Bow Church, ii, 55.
Copley, Anthony, plots against James I., ii, 7.
—— John, his picture commemorating the relief of Gibraltar, iii, 202.
Cordell, Sir John, alderman, imprisoned in Crosby House, ii, 173.
Cordwainers of London, Wardmote held at Hall of, iii, 15.
Cornewall, Sir George, M.P. for co. Hereford, iii, 198.
Cornhill, Gervase de, sheriff of London, i, 45.
—— Henry de, sides with Longchamp, i, 62; joins the Barons, 77.
Cornish, Henry, Alderman, sheriff, ii, 464, 472, 473, 475; assaulted by the military at Guildhall, 489; a candidate for the mayoralty, 490; fined for creating a disturbance in the Common Hall, 493; trial and execution of, 512-514; his attainder reversed, 548.
Corn Law, introduction of the first, iii, 294-295.
Cornwall, Edmund, Earl of, regent during the absence of King Edward the First, i, 123.
Cornwallis, Lord, surrenders at Yorktown, iii, 193.
Coronations, City's claim to service at, i, 69, 213, 275, 307, 323, 389, 421, 485, ii, 389, 508, 540, 611; Coronation Cup of Richard III presented to the Commonalty, i, 323, 324; report of remembrancer as to manner of making City's claim at, iii, 32.
Coronation Stone, removed by Edward I, from Scone to Westminster Abbey, i, 126; proposal to reconvey to Scone, 163.
Corporation Act, the, passed, ii, 394; bill for repealing, 463, the mayor instructed to see its provisions enforced at coming election of Common Council, 494; Act for quieting corporations guilty of having neglected provisions of, iii, 11-12, attempt to obtain repeal of, 34, 35; repeal of, 326-327.
Corporations, taken in hand by James II, ii, 508, 509, 518, 519; bill for restoring, 552.
Cottington, Lord, attends the Common Council, ii, 126.
Cotun, John de, alderman, his abuse of Chigwell, i, 165.
Council of State, the, formation of, ii, 303.
Courtenay, William, Bishop of London, insulted by John of Gaunt, i, 209.
Covenant, the, taken by the Common Council, ii, 226.
Coventry, Sir William, ii, 409.
Cradock, Matthew, M.P. for the City, his speech in the house against Strafford, ii, 132; advocates the restoration of the City's Irish estate, 133.
Craggs, Secretary of State, expresses regret at insult offered to alderman Ward, iii, 16; convicted of receiving bribes from directors of South Sea Company, 21; his death, *id*.
Cranmer, Thomas, Archbishop of Canterbury, conducts service at St. Paul's, i, 431; letter from the Lords of the Council to, 435; sent to the Tower, 458; trial of, at Guildhall, 460; burnt at Oxford, 474.
Crayford, Britons defeated at, i, 7.
Creçy, battle of, i, 192.
Crepyn, Ralph, M.P. for the City, i, 118; his affair with Laurence Duket, 119.
Croke, or Crooke, John, recorder, chosen Speaker, i, 564.

Crombwelle, John de, Constable of the Tower, removed from office, i, 147.
Crome, Dr. Edward, rector of St. Mary, Aldermary, recantation of, at Paul's Cross, i, 415.
Cromwell, Oliver, re-appointed to command in the army after the Self-denying Ordinance, ii, 215; made Lieutenant-General, 318; opposed the army's approach to London, 252; goes to Wales, 277; success of, at Preston, 290; desires a loan of the Common Council, 310; City gift to, 313; success of, in Ireland, 326; welcomed on his return, 327; his victory at Dunbar, 328; his letter to the City, 331; his victory at Worcester, 341; returns to London, 342; summons a parliament, 346; nominated Protector, and entertained by the City, 347; declines the title of king, 349; nominates a House of Lords, 350; his death, 352.
—— Richard, proclaimed Protector, ii, 353.
—— Thomas, i, 381; his attitude toward the City, 386; appointed Vicar-General, 392; supervises the suppression of the monasteries, 397; institutes parish registers, 403; letters to, from Sir Richard Gresham, touching the erection of a Burse, 494.
Crosby, Brass, elected mayor, iii, 106; carries up an address to the king, 107; upholds the freedom of the Press, *id.*; orders the discharge of Miller, accepting his recognisance to prosecute the messenger of the House of Commons, 108, 109; defends his conduct before the House, 109-112, 115; committed to the Tower, 116; regains his liberty, 119; again stands for the mayoralty, 127; gift of plate to, 128.

Crosby House, the palace of Richard III, i, 320; the agent of the Duke of Alva lodged in, 512; delinquents committed to custody in, ii, 173.
Cross, Sir Robert, i, 562.
Crossed or Crutched Friars, the Corporation of London regarded as their "second founders," i, 401.
Crowmere, William, mayor, appointed commissioner to enquire into cases of treason, &c., in the City, i, 269.
Culloden Moor, victory of the Duke of Cumberland at, iii, 55.
Cullum, Thomas, sheriff, committed to the Tower, ii, 266.
Cumberland, George, Earl of, i, 560.
—— William, Duke of, endeavours to intercept the young Pretender, iii, 52, 53; presented with the freedom of the City, 54, 55.
Currency, the, debased, i, 445.
Curtis, Sir William, alderman, engaged in suppressing bread riots, iii, 242; loses his seat for the City, 309, inveighs against the Common Council before Parliament, 323; his speech voted an unfounded calumny, 324.
Customs of the City, charter of Edward III, granting right to vary, i, 188.
Cut, Richard, put in the pillory for circulating evil rumours, i, 466.

Dalrymple, Sir Hugh, iii, 269.
Dalton, James, his speech in Common Council upon discovery of the Babington Conspiracy, i, 532.
Dalyngrigge, Sir Edward, warden of the city, i, 242.
Damer, Hon. Mrs., executes a bust of Nelson for the City, iii, 237; her offer to execute a monument in honour of Nelson, declined, 262.
Danby, Thomas, Earl of, impeached,

ii, 458; signs invitation to Prince of Orange, 529. *See also* Leeds, Duke of.

Danegelt, first payment of, i, 17; revival of, 27; the City exempt from, 41; revived under a new name, 69.

Danelagh, the, i, 11.

Danes, the, in London, i, 11; expelled, 11, 12; attack of, repelled by the citizens, 13; their reappearance (896), *id.*; their return (*temp.* Ethelred II), 16, massacre of, 17; defeated at London Bridge, 20; victory of, at Assandun, 24.

Dangerfield, cruel punishment of, ii, 510.

Daniel, Peter, Sheriff, ii, 509.

Darc, Jeanne, the maid of Orleans, i, 272.

Dartmouth, Lord, receives the seals, ii, 637; a City deputation to, 645, 646.

Dashwood, Francis, elected mayor, ii, 613; knighted, 614.

—— Sir Samuel, M.P. for the City, ii, 509, 554; elected mayor, 613.

D'Assoleville, Monsieur, agent of the Duke of Alva, lodged at Crosby House, i, 511, 512.

Daubeny, Lady, her part in Waller's plot, ii, 188.

Dauntsey, William, mercer, his school at West Lavington, i, 353.

Deane, Admiral, killed in an engagement with the Dutch, ii, 345.

Declaration of the Army, ii, 246, 248.

Declaration of Indulgence, the, ii, 518; thanks to the king for, 520, 525; a second, published, 525; appointed to be read in churches, 526.

Declaration of Rights, the, ii, 539.

De donis, statute, i, 119.

De Grasse, Admiral, defeated by Rodney in the West Indies, iii, 199–200.

Dekker, Thomas, ii, 59.

Delinquents, imprisoned in Crosby House, ii, 173; City petition for payment of debts out of estates of, 208.

Delmé, Peter, elected alderman, ii, 642, 643.

Demesne, towns held in, i, 2–4.

Denmark, visit of king and queen of, i, 371; the king welcomed by the City, ii, 17.

—— George, Prince of, entertained at Guildhall, ii, 551; death of, 629.

Derby, the young Pretender enters, and seizes money that had been subscribed to oppose him, iii, 52.

Derby, *alias* Wright, John, bowyer, convicted of perjury, i, 343.

Derick, Antony, goldsmith, i, 507.

De Ruyter, Admiral, defeated off Portland, ii, 344.

Desmond, Earl of, rebellion of, i, 523.

Despensers, the, father and son, i, 92, 133, 141, 148, 150, 153, 154.

Devonshire, Thomas, Duke of, marches to London with Richard, Duke of York, i, 287.

Digges, Alice, i, 552.

Dixie, Sir Wolstan, skinner, his school at Market Bosworth, i, 353; appointed with Sir Thomas Pullison to prevent the price of provisions in the City being enhanced, 541.

Dobbs, Sir Richard, his zeal in foundation of Christ's Hospital, i, 450; particulars of, 450n.; signs "counterfeit will" of Edward VI, 453.

Dodd, Ralph, his picture of the entry of George IV into the City on his way to St. Paul's, iii, 216n.

Dodmer, Ralph, his mayoralty banquet, i, 380.

Dohna, Baron, sent by the elector Palatine to raise money in the City, ii, 74, 75, 84.
Dolben, Sir William, recorder, his opinion on the question of the aldermanic veto, ii, 455.
Donne, Dr., ii, 95.
"Doomsday" Book, i, 37.
Dorset, Thomas Grey, Marquis of, i, 380.
Dover, treaty of, ii, 443.
Drake, Sir Francis, his raiding expedition to Spain, i, 534; pursues the Armada, 541; again sets sail for Spain, 546.
Drapers of London, contribute to a gift of £500 to the king, i, 201; subscribe towards furnishing soldiers for war with France, 347; Knights of the Bath entertained by, ii, 69; conference at their Hall between Monk and the aldermen, 369.
Du Bois, John, proceedings relative to his election as sheriff, ii, 480–487.
Duckett, Lionel, mercer, sounds Gresham as to his intentions respecting the erection of a City Burse, i, 496.
Dudley, Edmund, his extortionate conduct in the City, i, 337, 338; executed, 343.
—— Lord Guildford, i, 453; executed, 465.
—— Sir John, i, 412.
Duket, Laurence, murder of, i, 119.
Dunbar, thanksgiving in the City for victory at, ii, 328.
Duncan, Admiral, defeats the Dutch fleet off Camperdown, iii, 233–234; a sword of honour voted to, 234.
Duncombe, Charles, goldsmith, ii, 603; a candidate for the mayoralty, 608; particulars of, 608 n.; seeks to represent the City in Parliament, 609; elected mayor, 630.

Dundas, Henry, secretary, afterwards Lord Melville, urges the Lord Mayor to form military associations in the City, iii, 236; charged with peculation, but acquitted, 260.
Dunkirk, sold to the French, ii, 403.
Dunkley, Robert, ii, 640.
Dunning, his motion for economical reform, iii, 176.
Durham, Borough of, surrenders its charter to the bishop, i, 4.
Dyos, "Mr." the Bishop of London's chaplain, his sermon at Paul's Cross, i, 527.

East India Company, to lend its ordnance for defence of the City, ii, 186; the rise of, 575–578; parliamentary examination of its accounts, 593; the old and the new companies united, 597; Fox's East India Bill, iii, 204–206; Pitt's East India Bill, 208.
Ebrale, Thomas, killed by the military in Burdett riots, iii, 277.
Economical Reform, the City urgent for, iii, 175; Committees of Association formed in favour of, id.; Dunning's motion, 176.
Edgar, King, his law, i, 10.
Edgar the Atheling, his claim to the throne supported by London, i, 31.
Edge-hill, battle of, ii, 174.
Edmonds, Simon, elected mayor and refuses to serve, ii, 336.
Edmund Ironside, chosen king in London, i, 23; divides the kingdom with Cnut, 24; his death, id.
Edward the Confessor, chosen king in London, i, 27; his death, 29.
Edward, Prince, afterwards King Edward I, supports the Barons, i, 90; seizes treasure in the Temple, 94; committed to Dover

INDEX.

Castle, 96; escapes, 98; crowned in London, 111; negotiates with the Countess of Flanders, 115-117; goes to Gascony, 123; his domestic troubles, 124; death of the Queen, 125; seizes treasure in monasteries, *id.*; his altercation with Roger Bigod, 127; sets sail for Flanders, 128; his victory at Falkirk, 129; receives a gift of £2,000 from the City, 130; his death, 131.

Edward II, his accession, i, 132; his foreign favourites, 132-133; marches against the Scots, 134; the City sends him 1,000 marks, *id.*; the birth of a prince, 138; takes the City into his own hands, 146; issues "a charter of service," 151; the City lost to, 155, 156; his death, 159.

Edward III, his birth, i, 138; the conduits run with wine in his honour, 139; his accession, 160; his charters to the City, 160, 180, 188, 196, 208; charges the citizens with having assisted in he revolt of Lancaster, 166; visits London, 167; sends copy of Lancaster's charges to be read at Guildhall, *id.*; his marriage, 171; pays homage to the King of France, 178; goes to France, 182, 185; his unexpected return, 187; makes a truce with France, 189; renews the war, 190; sets sail for France, 191; his success in Normandy, 191-192; returns, 193; again goes to France, 199; his death, 211.

Edward, Earl of March, afterwards Edward IV, enters the City with Richard, Duke of York, i, 290; attainted, 296; marches to London, 298, 299; admitted into the City, 305; his claim to the crown acknowledged by the citizens, 306; proclaimed king, *id.*; accession of, 307; his charters to the City, 307-308; his marriage, 309; takes flight, 311; returns and is admitted into the City, 313; recovers the throne, 314; prepares to invade France, 317; grants a general pardon to the City, 318; entertains the citizens with a day's hunting, *id.*; his death, 319.

Edward V, birth of, i, 317; preparations for his coronation, 319; welcomed by the City, 320; lodged in the Tower, *id.*; deposed, 322.

Edward VI, birth of, i, 396; his accession and coronation, 418, 420-421; conducted by the citizens to Westminster, 431; removed by Somerset to Windsor, 435; dines with Sheriff York, 439; his charter to the City *re* Southwark, 442; incorporates the four City hospitals, 452; his death, 453; his will disposing of the crown, *id.*

Edwards, Sir James, ordered to attend every evening at Whitehall during last illness of Charles II, ii, 505.

Edwin, Sir Humphrey, sheriff, ii, 530.

Effingham, Earl of, refuses to serve in the army against the American colonies, iii, 155; his conduct compared with that of Lord George Sackville, 161.

Eleanor, Queen, wife of Henry III, insult offered to, i, 94; presented with the custody of London Bridge, 101; her death, 125.

Eldred, John, ii, 71.

Eleven Members, the, the army's charge against, ii, 246; withdrawal of, 250; six members escape to the Continent, 262.

Elizabeth of York, married to Henry VII, i, 328; her coronation, 329; account of the manner of receiving her corpse, 336.

Elizabeth, Queen, birth of, i, 389; declared illegitimate, 396; reinstated in right of succession, 420; accession of, 484; coronation of, 485; her policy of moderation, 486; closes English ports to Flemish vessels, 492; opens the Royal Exchange, 499; refused a loan by the Merchant Adventurers, 506; seizes Spanish vessels, 508, 509; excommunicated, 516; her shifting policy towards Spain and France, 518; Dutch envoys to, 530; Babington's plot to murder, 532; visits the camp at Tilbury, 545; assists Henry IV of France, 548; her death, 566.
—— Princess, daughter of James I, married to the Elector Palatine, ii, 59.
Elliot, General, afterwards Lord Heathfield, his gallant defence of Gibraltar, iii, 201.
Elsing, William, mercer, founder of Elsing Spital, i, 386.
Eltham, Sir John de, i, 170.
Empson, Richard, his extortionate conduct in the city, i, 337, 338; executed, 343.
Engagement, the, taken by Lilburne with reservation, ii, 319. *See also* Treasonable Engagement.
Ermin Street, i, 5.
Essex, Robert Devereux, 2nd earl of, City present to, i, 548, 549; capture of Cadiz, 556; attempts to raise an insurrection in the City, 561–563.
—— Robert, 3rd Earl of, ii, 154, 191, 200, 202; takes command of parliamentary army, 172; applies to the City for a loan, *id.;* takes Reading, 188; his jealousy of Waller, 191; relieves Gloucester, 194; withdraws to Reading, 196; leaves Reading, *id.;* surrenders to the royalists, 210; resigns, 215.

Essex, Earl of. *See* Mandeville, Geoffrey de.
Estfeld, William, mayor, performs customary service at the coronation of Henry VI, i, 275.
Etaples or Estaples, treaty of, i, 330
Ethelred, alderman, made governor of London, i, 12–13.
Ethelred the "Unready," his weak government, i, 16, 17, institutes the payment of Danegelt, 17; betakes himself to Normandy, 19; returns to London, 20; expels Cnut, 21; his death, 22; his laws for regulating foreign trade, *id.*
Eton, Hugh, punished for making a disturbance in church, i, 422.
Eugene, Prince, obtains a loan from the citizens, ii, 624; visits London, 645.
Everard, John, gives information of proposed attack on the City, ii, 275; City's petition to parliament thereon, 276.
Evesham, battle of, i, 98.
Evil May-day, i, 355–357.
Ewen, John, mercer, his benefaction to the Grey Friars, i, 402.
Exchequer, the, closed by Charles the Second, ii, 444.
—— Court of, removed to York, i, 162.
Exclusion Bill, the, before the Commons, ii, 458; passed by the Commons, rejected by the Lords, 462.
Exton, Nicholas, deprived of his aldermanry, i, 223; elected mayor, 228, 229; continued in office, 232; stands aloof from the king's attempt on the life of the Duke of Gloucester, 233; an attempt to get him removed from mayoralty, 239.
Eyles, Sir John, mayor, ii, 530; summoned to attend proclamation of George II as king, iii, 31.

INDEX.

Eyre, James, recorder, refuses to attend presentation of address to the king, iii, 101.

Fabyan, Alderman, his chronicle, i, 313; placed in command of the city's gates, 332.
Fairfax, Sir Thomas, ii, 214, 216, 219; Parliamentary army under, defeated in the north, 189; Leicester surrenders to, 220; defeats Hopton, 233; correspondence between the City and, 243, 245, 247, 248, 249, 251, 255, 264, 265, 269; the City surrenders to, 259; entertained by the City, 261; appointed constable of the City, 262; endeavours to force a loan from the City, 264, 265, 268, 275; threatens to quarter troops on the City, 267; puts down rising in Kent, 280, 281; success of, at Colchester, 290; informs the City of his intention to enter London, 293; demands money from the City, 293, 296, 301, enters London, 294; seizes the treasury at Weaver's Hall, 295, 296; again entertained by the City, 312; gift of plate to, 313; superseded by Cromwell, 328.
Falaise, John de, announces birth of Edward the Third, i, 138.
Falconbridge, Thomas. See Fauconberg.
Falkirk, battle of, i, 129; General Hawley defeated at, iii, 55.
Falkland, secretary, ii, 179.
Farndon, Nicholas de, deposed from the mayoralty by the king, i, 146; placed in the mayoralty chair by the king *loco* Chigwell, 153.
Farringdon ward, divided, i, 243.
Farringdon, co. Hants, fortifications at, captured by King Stephen, i, 53.
Fauconberg, Thomas, rising in Kent under, i, 314; his letter to the City and answer, 314, 315; attempts to force London Bridge, 315, 316; beheaded, 316.
Fawkes, Guy, *alias* "John Johnson" joins Gunpowder Plot, ii, 13.
Felton, John, i, 516.
Fenton, John, Lieutenant-Colonel, ii, 339.
Fenwick, Sir John, bill of attainder against, ii, 600.
Ferdinand II, Emperor, loses the crown of Bohemia, ii, 74.
Ferrar, Nicolas, skinner, his bequest to the college in Virginia, ii, 48.
Fielding, Sir John, his house attacked by Gordon rioters, iii, 183.
Fifth-monarchy men, outbreak in the City of, ii, 386–388, 396.
Finch, Sir Heneage, recorder, chosen Speaker, ii, 97, 132.
—— Sir John, ii, 108.
Finchley, the camp at, iii, 52, 53.
Finsbury, Manor of, the City's lease of, i, 493.
Firebrace, Sir Basil, charged with mis-using the money of the East India Company and committed to the Tower, ii, 593, 595-596; reieves his liberty, 597; created a baronet, *id.*
Fire of London, the, ii, 414–425. *See also* London.
Fisher, John, Bishop of Rochester, committed to the Tower for denying the king's supremacy, i, 392; beheaded, 393.
—— Captain John, ii, 121.
Fishmongers of London contribute to a gift of £500 to the king, i, 201; attempt to break up the monopoly of free fishmongers, 222, 224; subscribe towards furnishing soldiers for war with France, 347; subscribe to bounties for soldiers, iii, 64.
Fitz-Athulf or Olaf, Constantine, hanged for treachery, i, 82.
Fitz-Eylwin, Henry, first mayor of London, i, 66.

LL

Fitz-James, Richard, Bishop of London, dies of the plague, i, 366.
Fitz-Otes, Hugh, Constable of the Tower, appointed warden of the City, i, 101, 103.
Fitz-Reiner, Richard, sides with John, i, 62.
Fitz-Thedmar, Arnald, compiler of *Liber de Antiquis*, i, 67 ; opposed to the Barons, *id.* ; deprived of his aldermanry, 90 ; opposed to popular policy of Fitz-Thomas in relation to City guilds, 93, 94 ; his prejudice against Walter Hervy, 107.
Fitz-Thomas, Thomas, mayor, organization of guilds under, i, 93 ; refused admittance to the mayoralty, 95 ; swears fealty to the king, 97 ; accused of meditating a wholesale massacre of citizens, 99 ; summoned to Windsor, 100 ; his fate, 101, 103 ; results of his policy, 110.
Fitz-Walter, Robert, Baron of Dunmow, elected leader of the Barons, i, 74 ; his duties as Castellain of London, 75 ; his feud with king John, 76, 77 ; fails to raise the siege of Rochester, 78 ; taken prisoner at Lincoln, 80 ; his death, 81.
Fitz-William, Thomas, recorder, his speech at the Guildhall in favour of Richard, Duke of Gloucester, i, 322.
—— William, made sheriff by Henry VII, i, 338.
Flanders, interruption of trade with, i, 113 ; Flemings expelled from England, 115 ; peace concluded with, 116 ; increase of trade with, 171 ; Flemish weavers invited to settle in England, 178 ; English ports closed to Flemish merchants by Elizabeth, 492 ; Flemish merchants seized in London, 510 ; forces under the Earl of Leicester sent to, 531.
Flanders, Countess of, seizes English merchandise, i, 112 ; negotiates for peace, 115, 117.
Fleet, Sir John, M.P. for the City, ii, 554, 598, 607, 613 ; mayor, 570 ; unsuccessfully contests the City, 609 ; his death, 642.
Fleet Prison, the, fired by Gordon rioters, iii, 184.
Fleetwood, Charles, Lieut.-Gen., confers with the City, ii, 357, 359 ; promises a free parliament, 360.
Fletcher, Dr., remembrancer, sent as special messenger to James I, ii, 2.
Flete, William de, i, 134.
Flower, Charles, sheriff, iii, 242.
Fogwell Pond, Smithfield, water supply taken from, ii, 20.
Folkmote, i, 13.
Foote, Sir Thomas, alderman, ii, 236 ; elected mayor, 316.
Forced Loan, the, ii, 100, 102.
Foreigners or strangers, in the country, i, 84 ; in the City, 475–476, 504, 532 ; iii, 297–299.
Fowke or Foulke, John, alderman, ii, 197, 218 ; placed on commission for trial of Charles the First, 301 ; charges brought against when mayor, 337 ; sent Commissioner to meet Monk, 365 ; reports to Court of Aldermen Monk's intention of leaving the City, 370 ; M.P. for the City, 392.
Fowlke, Christopher, sent to Guildford with food for the City's soldiers, i, 414.
Fox, Charles, joins the Newcastle Ministry, iii, 57, leader of the House of Commons, 60 ; assaulted by a mob, 115 ; appointed Secretary of State under Rockingham, 197 ; Secretary of State under the Duke of Portland, 204 ; his East India Bill, *id.* ; joins the ministry

INDEX.   515

of "all the talents," 265; his death, 266.

Fox, Stephen, supports Luttrell's candidature for Middlesex, iii, 87.

France, war with, *temp.* Edward III, i, 180, 190, 195, 197, 199, 201, 204; the crown of, claimed by Henry V, 257; war with, *temp.* Henry V, 257, 258, 262; a truce with *temp.* Henry VI, 281; French descent on south coast, 293; war with, *temp.* Henry VIII, 345, 347; league against, 373; the king of, taken at Pavia, 374; peace concluded with, 377; renewal of the war with, 408, 409; peace with, proclaimed, 415; Mary declares war against, 477; the king of, defeated at St. Quentin, 479; recovery of Calais by, 480; Elizabeth's war with, 489; peace with, signed, 492; assassination of king of, 548; Charles I at war with, ii, 102; a cry for war against (1678), 455; William III at war with, 559, 568; peace made at Ryswick with, 603; war conducted by Marlborough against, 614, 616, 621, 629, 630, peace with, 647; declaration of war with (1744), iii, 49; alliance with America, 168; convention with, 212; outbreak of revolution, 220; war declared with, 221; negotiations for peace, 227; the French army encamped at Boulogne, 259.

Franklin, Benjamin, Ambassador for the United States at Versailles, iii, 168.

Fraunceys, Adam, mayor, i, 197; contributes to a loan to the king, 202.

—— John, first alderman of Farringdon without, i, 243.

Fray, John, commissioner to enquire into cases of treason, &c. in the city, i, 269.

Frederick, Prince of Wales, his marriage, iii, 39; presented with the Freedom of the City in the Saddlers' Company, 40.

—— Elector Palatine, marries Elizabeth, daughter of James I, ii, 59; the City's present to, 60; elected King of Bohemia, 74; the City of London renders assistance to, 75, 77, 89; driven out of Bohemia, 77; a Londoner punished for insulting, 83.

Frederick, Sir John, mayor, ii, 397.

Freeman, Ralph, ii, 72.

Free Trade Bill, ii, 10.

Frestlyng, Bartholomew, M.P. for the City, i, 202.

"Frith-gild" of the City, i, 14–16.

Frobisher, Sir Martin, pursues the Armada, i, 541; monument to, in St. Giles's, Cripplegate, 544.

Frowyk, Henry, mayor, i, 279.

Fryer, Sir John, mayor, iii, 16, 17.

Fuller, Nicholas, M.P. for the City, ii, 8.

Fulsham Benedict de, M.P. for the City, i, 162; his contest for the mayoralty, 165.

Furnese, Sir Henry, subscribes to loan to Prince Eugene, ii, 624.

Galeys, Henry le. *See* Waleys.

Gardiner, Stephen, bishop of Winchester, liberated from the Tower by Queen Mary, i, 457; made chancellor, 458; severely reprimands the lord mayor, 466.

—— Sir Thomas, recorder, endeavours to obtain a City loan for Charles the First, ii, 124; his impeachment 124, 169; the king wishes to make him Speaker, 132; welcomes the king to the City, 148; is knighted 149; a commission of array addressed to, 188.

Garnet, Henry, trial of, at Guildhall, ii, 15.

LL 2

Garrard, Sir John, withdraws from the Militia Committee, ii, 171.
—— Sir Samuel, mayor, favours Dr. Sacheverell, ii, 632; evades burning his sermon, 635.
Garraway, William, i, 553.
Garrett, Sir George, sheriff, entertains Charles I, ii, 157; sent to the King at Oxford, 180.
Garway, or Garraway, Henry, mayor, ii, 122; speech of, at Common Hall, 181.
Gate, Sir John, the king's bailiff in Southwark, i, 442.
Gaunt, Elizabeth, burnt for being implicated in Rye House Plot, ii, 515.
Gaveston, Piers de, asks a favour of the City for his friend, i, 133; banished, id.; favoured by Edward II, 136; beheaded, 137.
Gayer or Gayre, Sir John, imprisoned by Charles I, ii, 123; released, 125; withdraws from the Militia Committee, 171; committed to the Tower, 266; impeached, 273; the "Lion Sermon" instituted by, 274; deprived of his aldermanry, 308.
Geffrey, Thomas, barber, i, 284.
George I, accession of, iii, 1; welcomed by the City, 2; attends lord mayor's banquet, 3; his picture and statue, 9; goes to Hanover, 10; his quarrel with the Prince of Wales, id.; his death, 30.
George, Prince of Wales, afterwards King George II, his quarrel with his father, iii, 10; his accession, 31; his coronation, 32; attends lord mayor's banquet, 33; impudent demand of his cup-bearer, id.; his portrait by Jervas, id.
George III, accession of, iii, 66; his statue at the Royal Exchange and his picture at the Guildhall, 70; his anxiety that Wilkes should be expelled the House, 82; indignant at the conduct of Crosby and Oliver, 109; his anxiety lest Wilkes should be elected mayor, 132; his letter to Lord North touching Lord Gordon, 183; his illness, and measures taken for a regency, 213; City address on his recovery, 214; thanksgiving service at St. Paul's for recovery of, 215; assault on, 226; celebration of his Jubilee, 271; becomes insane, 281; his statue in the Council Chamber, id.

George, Prince, afterwards King George IV, forwards to the City £1,000 for the poor, during his father's illness, iii, 214; appointed Regent, 282; declines the Freedom of the City, id.; refuses to receive addresses from the livery seated on the throne, 283–285, 296–297; entertained at the Guildhall after the Peace of Paris, 288; an outrage committed against, 306; his accession, 314; his coronation, 315.
Gerard, or Garrard, William, sheriff, attends proclamation of Lady Jane Grey as Queen, i, 454.
Gerrard, John, implicated in Gunpowder Plot, ii, 15.
—— Sir Thomas, i, 560.
Ghent, recovery of, ii, 629.
Gianibelli, Frederico, erects waterworks at Tyburn, ii, 19.
Gibbon, Edward, grandfather of the historian, his estate sequestrated, iii, 22.
Gibbs, Alderman, ii, 224, 292.
Gibraltar, relief of, by Lord Howe, iii, 201; Copley's picture of siege of, 202.
Gilbert, Sir Humphrey, i, 544.
—— Sir John, i, 562.
Gill, William, mayor, receives George the Fourth on his visit to St. Paul's after illness, iii, 215.
Ginkell, General, afterwards Earl of Athlone, ii, 563.

Gisors, Anketin de, i, 146.
—— John de, M.P. for the City, i, 118; desired by Edward II to hold the City, 136; taken into custody, 146; affords an asylum to Mortimer, 154; appointed Warden of the Tower jointly with Betoyne, 159.
Gloucester, siege of, ii, 193–195; letter from, touching the removal of Colonel Massey, 216, 217.
—— Gilbert, Earl of, defeats Montfort at Evesham, i, 98; takes possession of the City, 102; comes to terms with Henry III, 103.
—— Henry, Duke of, City gift to, at Restoration, ii, 379.
—— Humphrey, Duke of, question of his precedence at the Guildhall, i, 257, 258; vicegerent in England, 268; his position settled by Parliament, 269; quarrels with Beaufort, 270, 271, 277; loses the favour of the citizens, 271; appointed Captain of Calais, 280.
—— Robert, Earl of, exchanged prisoner for King Stephen, i, 52.
—— Thomas, Duke of, his house attacked, whilst Earl of Buckingham, i, 216; his persecution of Brembre, *id.*; plot of Richard II, against, 232, 233; charges five of the king's counsellors with treason, 233, 234; arrested, 244.
Glover, Richard *alias* "Leonidas," opposes the Spanish Convention, iii, 42; his poem "Admiral Hosier's Ghost," 44, 45; presides over Committee of Livery, 45, 46; drafts petition to Parliament touching insufficiency of convoys, 47.
Glyn, John, recorder, ii, 200, 260, 291; one of the Eleven Members, 246; expelled the House and committed to the Tower, 263; forced resignation of, 315; member of Cromwell's House of Peers, 350; accident to, 391.

Glynn, John, recorder, moves that Wilkes be heard at the Bar of the House of Commons, iii, 137; his *dictum* as to the rights of the Livery in Common Hall, 138, 140; returned M.P. for Middlesex, 144.
Godchep, Hamo, i, 153.
Godfrey, Sir Edmondesbury, supposed murder of, ii, 457.
—— Peter, elected M.P. for the City, iii, 4.
—— Thomas, opens the City's gates to Cade, i, 284.
Godolphin, Lord, dismissed from office, ii, 637.
Godrell, Paul, ii, 591.
Godsalve, John, the City's right of measuring cloth conferred on, i, 406.
Godschall, Sir Robert, a candidate for the mayoralty, iii, 45, 46; elected M.P. for the City, 47; mayor, *id.*; chairman of Parliamentary Committee to consider insufficiency of convoys, 47, 48.
Godwine, Earl, i, 26, 28.
Gold, Henry, rector of St. Mary, Aldermary, executed at Tyburn, i, 390.
—— Thomas, nominated for the mayoralty, ii, 476, 490.
Goldsmiths of London, their quarrel with the Weavers, i, 154; return of rental of, 252; their pageant at coronation of Henry VIII, 345; subscribe towards furnishing soldiers for war with France, 347; ordered to resume their old quarters in Goldsmith's Row, ii, 110; the Duke of Marlborough entertained by, 617, 618; mayoralty of Sir Owen Buckingham kept in Hall, 617; subscribe to bounties for soldiers, iii, 64; disapprove of remonstrance drawn up in Common Hall, 93.
Gondomar, Spanish ambassador, insulted in London, ii, 79.

Goodman, John, reprieve of, ii, 136.
Gordon, Lord George, presents petition to Parliament in favour of repeal of Savile's Act, iii, 179; riots in the City instigated by, 180–184; committed to the Tower, 185; offers himself as candidate for the City, 192.
Gore, Richard, merchant tailor, M.P. for the City, ii, 8.
—— Sir William, knighted, ii, 571; elected mayor, 608; stands for the City, 609.
Goring, George, Lord (Earl of Norwich), threatens Plymouth, ii, 221; takes the lead in the Kentish rebellion, 282.
Gracedieu, Bartholomew, sheriff, knighted, ii, 606.
Grafton, Duke of, his relations with Wilkes, 74, 80.
—— Richard, printer, i, 485.
Grantham, John de, elected Mayor, i, 165; M.P. for the City, 174.
Greenland House, siege of, ii, 205.
Greenway, Oswald, implicated in Gunpowder Plot, ii, 15.
Greenwich Park, muster of citizens in, i, 529.
Gregory, William, alderman, his chronicle, i, 287.
"Grenecobbe," Henry, i, 220.
Grenville, Sir John, carries a letter from Charles II to the City, ii, 377; City gift to, 379.
—— William, W., Secretary of State, his correspondence with the lord mayor touching removal of the Bank of England guard, iii, 218–219.
—— Lord, joins with Fox informing the ministry of "all the talents," iii, 265; the fall of his ministry, 266–267.
Gresham, Sir John, mercer, his school at Holt, co. Norf., i, 353; witnesses removal of Duke of Somerset to the Tower, 438; signs counterfeit will of Edward the Sixth, 453.
Gresham, Sir John, of Titsey, i, 511.
—— Sir Richard, mayor, his letter to Henry VIII, re Royal Hospitals, i, 404; particulars of, 404 n.; proposes to erect a Burse, 494.
—— Sir Thomas, erects the Royal Exchange, i, 495–499; particulars of, 495 n.; founder of Gresham College, 502; entertains Cardinal Chastillon, 504; suggests minting Spanish treasure, 512; entertains Count Casimir, 520; his death, 521.
—— College founded, i, 502.
—— House, municipal offices removed to, after the fire, ii, 421.
Grey, Sir Charles, the freedom of the City voted to, iii, 223.
—— Earl, succeeds the Duke of Wellington as prime minister, iii, 332; the freedom of the City voted to, 339, 344; resigns, 340; recalled, 342; succeeds in passing the first Reform Bill, 343.
—— Henry, Lord, repels invasion of Ireland, i, 523.
—— Lord, of Wark, fined for disturbance at the Guildhall, ii, 493.
—— Lady Jane, appointed successor by Edward VI, i, 453; proclaimed queen, 454; trial of, at Guildhall, 460; executed, 465.
—— William de, attorney-general, burnt in effigy on Tower Hill, iii, 118.
Grey Friars, of London, their house suppressed, i, 398; benefactions to, 402; their house vested in the City, 417; removal of altars and tombs from church of, 428; their buildings converted into Christ's Hospital, 450, 451.
Grocers of London, subscribe towards furnishing soldiers for war with France, i, 347; nominate weighers of the Great Beam, 387;

tumult at the Hall of, ii, 178; parliament entertained at the Hall of, 234, 356; Fairfax invited to dinner by, 261; the Commons and Council of State at the Hall of, 312; the Lord Protector entertained by, 347; Monk entertained at the Hall of, 372; a conventicle held by Sir John Shorter, mayor, at the Hall of, 525; lord mayor's banquet held at the Hall of, 533, 574; the Bank of England commences business in the Hall of, 586; subscribe to bounties for soldiers, iii, 64; disapprove of remonstrance drawn up in Common Hall, 93; the freedom of their company conferred on Pitt, 207; their offer to send a quantity of porter to the troops in Flanders, 222–223; the Military Association in Hall of, 224.

Guildhall, the, first mention of, i, 14–15; trial of Hamo de Chigwell at, 169; implements of war stored at, 184; trial of Anne Ascue at, 415; trials of Lady Jane Grey and Cranmer at, 460-461; trial of Nicholas Throckmorton at, 467, 468; trial of John Felton at, 516; the rebuilding of, after the Fire, ii, 429, 434; the Lords meet at, after James II's flight, 535; standards taken at Ramillies hung up in, 623: threatened by Gordon rioters, iii, 184.

Guildhall Library, books borrowed from, by Somerset, and never returned, i, 438.

Guilds, early organisation of, i, 93, 94; Hervy's regulations of, 107; their rising importance, 110; reorganisation *temp.* Edward III, 200; elections by, 206. *See also* Companies.

Gunpowder Plot, ii, 13–16.

Gurney, Richard, mayor, ii, 145, 146; knighted, 149; impeached, 168; refuses to give up the City's *insignia*, 169.

Habeas Corpus Act, passed, ii, 459; suspended, 599, 627; suspended for a whole year, iii, 25; again suspended, 307.

Hadley, John, appointed joint-treasurer of subsidy, i, 251.

Hainault, Jacqueline of, wife of the Duke of Gloucester, i, 270; her ill-treatment, 272.

Halifax, Lord, burnt in effigy on Tower Hill, iii, 118.

Hallifax, Thomas, stands for the mayoralty, iii, 127, 132, 133; refuses to back press warrants, 166.

Hamersley, Hugh, haberdasher, ii, 32.

Hampden, John, resists the levying of ship money, ii, 118; one of the Five Members, 155; killed at Chalgrove Field, 189.

Hanse Merchants, supply wheat to the City, i, 346.

Hardy, John, alderman, i, 379.

Harfleur, captured by Henry V, i, 258, 259.

Harley, Robert. *See* Oxford, Earl of.

—— Thomas, sheriff, superintends the burning of No. 45 of the *North Briton* at the Royal Exchange, iii, 75; receives the thanks of both houses of parliament, 76, 83; burnt in effigy on Tower Hill, 118; his windows broken, 144; defends himself in parliament, 197–198.

Harold, elected king, i, 29; his death, 30.

Harper, Sir William, merchant Taylor, his school at Bedford, i, 353.

Harrison, major-general, ii, 328.

—— Rev. Joseph, arrested for inciting to riot, iii, 309.

Hart, John, sheriff, his contest for the aldermanry of Bridge Ward, iii, 146–149.
Haslerigg, Sir Arthur, one of the Five Members, ii, 155; the City confers with, 360, 363.
Hastings, battle of, i, 30.
Haunsard, William, furnishes a ship to the king for war with France, i, 182; his gallantry in the battle of Sluys, 186.
Havre, or Newhaven, occupied and lost by Elizabeth, i, 489, 490, 491.
Hawkesbury, Lord, informs the lord mayor of preliminaries of peace with France having been signed, iii, 249.
Hawkins, Sir John, reports engagement with the Armada, i, 537, 538, 541; his monument in the church of St. Dunstan East, 544.
—— Katherine, wife of Sir John, i, 544.
Hawley, General, defeated at Falkirk, iii, 55.
Hayley, George, alderman, brother-in-law of Wilkes, elected M.P. for the City, iii, 145; elected sheriff, 155; again returned M.P. for the City, 192; his death, *id.*
Hearth or Chimney Tax, the, imposition of, ii, 399; abolished, 544–545.
Heath, Sir Robert, attorney-general, exhibits an information against the City, touching its Irish Estate; ii, 143.
Heathcote, George, elected mayor against his will, iii, 45; discharged, 46; elected M.P. for the City, 47; loses his seat, 56.
—— Sir Gilbert, elected M.P. for the City, but disqualified, ii, 607; re-elected, 609, 612, 622, 629; elected alderman, 612; knighted, 614; subscribes to loan to Prince Eugene, 624; urges the removal of Marlborough to Holland, 636;

governor of the Bank of England, 637; his conduct at the election of an alderman, 640.
Hende, John, mayor, summoned to attend the king at Nottingham, i, 241; dismissed from the mayoralty and committed to Windsor Castle, *id.*
Henrietta Maria, wife of Charles I. negotiations for her marriage, ii, 86; her arrival in London, 93.
Henry I, elected king at Winchester, i, 39; election confirmed by the City, 40; his charter to the City, *id.*
Henry of Anjou, afterwards Henry II, his arrival in England, i, 54; welcomed in London, *id.*; his accession, 56; charter of, to the City, 58; his son Henry crowned, 59; his domestic troubles, 59, 61; his death, 61.
Henry II, of France, death of, i, 488.
Henry III, takes the City into his own hands, 85, 99; extorts money from his subjects, 87; his coronation, 88; takes leave of the City 88, 90; returns from abroad, 90; makes peace with the barons, 92, 97; lodged a prisoner in the Bishop of London's palace, 96; his charter to the City, 103; his death, 105.
Henry of Lancaster, afterwards King Henry IV; return from exile, i, 244, 245; met by the citizens of London, 245; proclaimed king, 246; his debts, 270.
Henry IV of France, assisted by Elizabeth, i, 548.
Henry V, claims the crown of France, i, 257; goes to France, 258; discovery of a conspiracy against, *id.*; captures Harfleur, 259; welcomed by the citizens on his return, 260; prepares for another expedition to France, *id.*; letters from, to the City, 261, 262, 264, 265;

conquers Normandy, 263; coronation of his queen, 266; his death and funeral, 266, 267.

Henry VI, coronation of, i, 274; goes to France, 275; crowned at Paris, *id.*; his return and reception by the City, 275–277; his charter to the City, 281; his marriage, *id.*; his illness, 288; kept in custody at Bishop of London's palace after the battle of St. Albans, 291; loses the City's favour, 296; deputation from the City to, at Northampton, 298; brought prisoner to London, 302; regains his freedom after second battle at St. Albans, 304; restored, 312; removed from the Tower to the Bishop of London's palace by Warwick, *id.*; his death in the Tower, 316.

Henry of Richmond, afterwards King Henry VII, prepares to invade England, i, 324, 325; defeats Richard III at Bosworth, 326; welcomed by the City, *id.*; his coronation, 327; his marriage, 328; his visit to London, 329; assists Anne of Brittany against the French king, *id.*; decease of Edmund his infant son, 335; enters into alliance with the king of the Romans, 336; his charter to the Merchant Taylors, 337; his charter to the City, *id.*; his proposed alliance with Margaret, sister of Archduke Philip, 338, 339; his death and funeral, 340, 341; his chapel in Westminster Abbey, 340; his *obit* kept by the City, 342.

Henry VIII, visits the City as a boy, i, 334; the City's present to, at coronation, 344; at St. Paul's, 362; enters into a league against France, 373; his marriage with Anne Boleyn, 388; marries Jane Seymour, 395; the City, in difficulty with, 406; goes to France leaving Catherine Parr, regent, 409; returns, 411; his death, 417.

Henry, Prince, son of James I, becomes a Merchant Taylor, ii, 12.

Herbert, Sir John, secretary of state, ii, 22.

Hereford, Henry, Duke of. *See* Henry of Lancaster, afterwards King Henry IV.

—— Humphrey, Earl of, insurrection of, i, 147; seeks an interview with the City, 149.

—— Sir William de, member for the City, i, 126.

Heretics, Statute for burning, i, 249; re-enacted, 471.

Herne, Sir Joseph, security for a loan to William III, ii, 603.

Hertford, Francis, Earl of, lord chamberlain, his letter to Wilkes touching the king's refusal to receive in future addresses of the livery on the throne, iii, 153; Wilkes's reply, 154; his letter to the lord mayor touching presentation of livery address, 195.

Hervey, Lord, his account of trick played by Walpole on the Dissenters, iii, 34, 35; objects to City's address to George II, on occasion of marriage of the Princess Royal to the Prince of Orange, 39.

—— Sebastian, mayor, ii, 55, 72; opposes matrimonial alliance between his daughter and Christopher Villiers, 73.

Hervy, Walter, disputed election of, as mayor, i, 104–105; grants charters to the craft guilds, 107; quarrels with Gregory de Rokesley, 108; arrested, *id.*; charges against, 109; discharged from aldermanry, 110.

Heton, George, chamberlain, dismissed, i, 519.

Hewling, Benjamin, condemned to death at Bloody Assizes, ii, 521.

Hewling, William, ii, 521.
Hewlyn, William, mayor, i, 295.
Hewson, John, a member of Cromwell's House of Lords, ii, 350; quells a riot in the City, 358.
Hewster, John, M.P. for the City, i, 370.
Heysham, Robert, elected M.P. for the City, iii, 4.
Hill, Sir Rowland, mercer, his school at Drayton, co. Salop, i, 353; committed to the Tower for obstructing the Sergeant-at-Mace, 406, 407; particulars of, 406n.; enters on his Mayoralty, 427.
Hille, Sir Thomas, mayor, dies of the plague, i, 327.
Hillsborough, Lord, Secretary of State, urges the mayor to guard the City during Gordon riots, iii, 181.
Hoadley, Benjamin, Bishop of Salisbury, persuades the dissenters to postpone attempt to repeal Corporation and Test Acts, iii, 34, 35.
Hoare, Richard, knighted, ii, 614; M.P. for the City, 638; late alderman of Bread Street Ward, iii, 15.
Hockenhall, George, refuses to serve sheriff, ii, 472.
Hockenhull or Hocknell, Thomas, ensign in the guards, reprimanded for allowing his soldiers to insult an alderman, iii, 16, 17.
Holiday, Leonard, alderman, the Duke of Bedford committed to the custody of, i, 562.
Holland, the Dutch fleet defeated off Portland, ii, 344; war declared with (1665), 406; the victory of the Duke of York over Opdam, 409; naval engagement with the Dutch off the North Foreland, 414; the Dutch fleet in the Medway, 435; retires, 436; war declared with (1672), 445; the peace of Nimeguen, 456.
Holland, Henry, Earl of, his speech at the Guildhall, ii, 175; threatens a royalist rising in the City, 225.
—— Henry, lord, charged with peculation, iii, 89, 91; his hatred for the City, 90.
Holles, Denzel, one of the Five Members, ii, 155; attends the Common Hall, 200.
Holy Trinity, Aldgate, Priory of, confiscated by Henry VIII, i, 386; bestowed upon Sir Thomas Audley, 387.
Hone, William, bookseller, his trial, iii, 307–308.
Hooke, Robert, his scheme for rebuilding the City, ii, 427; appointed surveyor, 428, 431.
Hooper, John, informs against Bonner, i, 439; made Bishop of Gloucester, 441; burnt, 474.
Hopkins, Benjamin, elected City Chamberlain, iii, 163; his decease, 164.
Hopton, Ralph, defeats Parliamentary forces under Waller, ii, 189; surrenders to Fairfax, 233.
Horn, Andrew, counsel for the City at the Iter of 1321, i, 143, 147; chamberlain, 159, 161.
—— John, goes to Paris to confer with Edward I, i, 116.
Horne, John, Vicar of Brentford, iii, 87; claims to have written Beckford's famous speech, 102; his letter to Wilkes on being elected sheriff, 124.
—— Robert, alderman, committed to Newgate by rebels under Cade, i, 285.
Houblon, Sir James, knighted, ii, 571; accused of bribery, 590; M.P. for the City, 606.
—— Sir John, sheriff, ii, 548; knighted, 552; first governor of the Bank of England, 586, 602;

attends the Privy council on the Barclay conspiracy, 599; candidate for aldermanry of Broad Street Ward, 640.

Houghton, John, prior of Charterhouse, proceedings against, i, 390-392.

Howard, Admiral Lord, commands the fleet against the Armada, i, 537, 539, 541; captures Cadiz, 556.

Howe, Lord, threatens to leave the navy, iii, 173; his victory over the French, 223; the freedom of the City voted to *id.*

—— John, his opposition to James II, ii, 521.

Huberthorne or Hoberthorne, Henry, mayor, assists in proclaiming Edward VI king, i, 418; particulars of, 418n.; knighted, 420.

"Humble Representation of the Dissatisfaction of the Army," ii, 248.

Humphreys, Sir William, mayor, puts a stop to the spread of seditious literature, iii, 3.

Hundred Court, i, 13.

Hunt, Henry, known as "Orator Hunt," arrested for inciting to riot, iii, 309, 310; creates a disturbance in Common Hall, 311.

Hunter, William, burnt, i, 474.

Huntingdon, William, Earl of, i, 192.

Husting Court, i, 13.

Hutchinson, General, the freedom of the City voted to, iii, 248.

Income tax, introduced by Pitt, iii, 228, 238; renewal of, 252, 292-293.

Indemnity bill, the, opposed by the City, iii, 308.

Ingram, Sir Arthur, ii, 63.

Insurance against fire, City's scheme for, ii, 425.

Ipswich, Cardinal Wolsey's college at, i, 382.

Ireland, the Desmond rising in, i, 523; Tyrone's insurrection in, 559; Mountjoy's conquest of, 563; rebellion of 1641 in, ii, 146; proposed confiscation of Irish rebels' estates, 163; royalist successes in, 309; Ormond defeated before Dublin, 314; subdued by Cromwell, 326; Cromwell, welcomed on his return from, 327; letters of sympathy from, after the Fire, 420, 421; Tyrconnel appointed lord deputy of, 516; siege of Londonderry, 549-550; battle of the Boyne, 559.

—— Duke of, charged with treason, i, 234.

Irish estate, the City's ii, 28-45; commissioners sent to view the plantation, 32; their report, 35; the City consents to undertake plantation of Ulster, 37; the Irish Society formed, 37, 41; the City forced to surrender a portion of, 38; allotment among the companies, 39, 43; more commissioners sent to Ireland, 42; the right of the companies to sell, 44; declared forfeited by Court of Star Chamber, 115; judgment reversed, 143; the King promises to restore, 149; letter from the council of state touching, 326; the companies petition Charles II relative to, 386.

—— Society, formation of, ii, 37; incorporated, 41.

Ireton, Henry, ii, 252, 352.

—— John, knighted by Cromwell, ii, 352; nominated by parliament to be re-elected mayor, 354.

Isabel, wife of Edward II, sets out for France, i, 154; her return 155; confirms the City's rights, 158; becomes unpopular, 163; retires into privacy, 170.

Isleworth, manor of, devastated by the mob, i, 96.

Jakes, Robert, shearman, convicted of perjury, i, 343.

James I, his threat to remove Court and Parliament from London, i, 1; accession of, ii, 1; enters London, 3, 5; plots against, 6, 13; refuses to surrender rights of purveyance, &c., 9; at Merchant Taylors' Hall, 12, 61; rumour of the assassination of, 16; his financial difficulties, 56–59; the City declines a loan to, 63; entertained by Alderman Cockaine, 69; the City's reception of, on return from Scotland, 72; death of the queen, *id.*; state visit of, to St. Paul's, 76; his death, 91.

James, Duke of York, afterwards James II, christening of, ii, 111; the City's gift to, at the Restoration, 379; his victory over the Dutch, 409; his efforts to suppress the Fire, 416; vote of thanks to, 431; his action against Sheriff Pilkington, 478, 492; his picture at Guildhall mutilated, 479; accession of, 506; collects the Customs without leave of Parliament, 507; coronation of, 508; favours the Catholics, 516; issues a Declaration of Indulgence, 518; the Aldermen present an address to, 520; issues a second Declaration of Indulgence, 525; birth of prince James, 528; informs the lord mayor of the approach of William, 529; restores the City's charter, 530; sets out to meet the Prince of Orange, 533; attempted flight of, 535; goes to France, 537; lands in Ireland, 549; death of, 607.

James Edward, Prince (the old Pretender), birth of, ii, 528; his legitimacy questioned, 532; acknowledged king by Louis, 607; threatened invasion in favour of, 626; the Tories favour, 648; a reward offered for arrest of, 649; precautions taken against, iii, 3; prepares to invade England, 6; failure of conspiracy, 8; threatens another invasion, 24.

Jane Seymour, her marriage with Henry VIII, i, 395; preparations for her coronation, 396; her death, 397.

Janssen, Stephen Theodore, sometime City chamberlain, iii, 20; elected M.P. for the City, 56; resigns chamberlainship, 163.

—— Sir Theodore, director of South Sea Company, expelled from Parliament, iii, 20.

Jarman, or Jermyn, Edward, appointed surveyor for the rebuilding of the City, ii, 428, 431.

Jeffreys, George, suspended from office of common sergeant, ii, 451; his suspension referred to the king, 452; restored, 453; forced to resign the recordership, 461; made chief justice, 502; holds the "Bloody Assize," 512; president of Ecclesiastical Commission Court, 516; appears before Court of Aldermen, 519; carries the City's charter back, 530; taken in disguise, 537.

—— Sir Jeffrey, excused from being mayor, ii, 632.

Jenkin's ear, iii, 40, 41.

Jenner, Sir Thomas, appointed recorder by Charles II, ii, 504.

Jenyns, Stephen, merchant taylor, his school at Wolverhampton, i, 353.

Jervas, Charles, his portraits of George II and Queen Caroline, iii, 33.

Jervis, Sir John, admiral, the freedom of the City voted to, iii, 223; his victory over the French off Cape St. Vincent, 232; a sword of honour voted to, *id.*

Jessel, Sir George, his opinion

touching the City's right and title to Irish estate, ii, 45.

Jews, Henry III extorts money from, i, 87; expulsion of, 123; enfranchisement of, iii, 346-347.

Joanna, daughter of Edward II, called "Joanna of the Tower," birth of, i, 148.

John, Prince, afterwards king, rebels against his father, i, 61; opposes Longchamp, 62; admitted into the City, 63; grants the citizens their "Commune," *id.*; his accession, 72; resigns the crown and receives it as the Pope's feudatory, 73; meets the Barons in London, 74; signs Magna Carta, 77; open war between him and the Barons, 78; his death, 79.

Johnson, Robert, sheriff, removed by Henry VII, i, 338.

—— Dr. Samuel, his inscription on portrait of Chief Justice Pratt, iii, 78; his pamphlet "Taxation no Tyranny," 151 n.; his opinion of Wilkes, 152 n., 164-165.

Jolles, Sir John, mayor, ii, 66.

Jones, John, captain, M.P. for the City, ii, 392.

—— John Gale, committed to Newgate for publishing an attack on Parliament, iii, 276.

—— Sir William, attorney-general, his opinion taken on the question of the aldermanic veto, ii 454.

Josselyn, Ralph, mayor, created Knight of the Bath, i, 307.

Joyce, Cornet, carries off Charles I, ii, 242.

Joyner, William, mayor, builds the Grey Friars Chapel, i, 402.

"Jubilee," book called, burnt by order of Exton, mayor, i, 229.

Judd, Sir Andrew, skinner, his school at Tonbridge, i, 353; undertakes to forward provisions to the army, 414; summoned as mayor to attend the Lords of the Council, 445; signs "counterfeit will" of Edward VI, 453.

Junius, approves of remonstrance of the Livery, iii, 93; upholds the conduct of Crosby and Oliver, 115; offers to support Wilkes, 125; strenuously supports Sawbridge's candidature for the mayoralty, *id.*; expresses his opinion of Lord Mayor Nash, 130.

Justiciar, the citizens permitted to elect their own, i, 43.

Keith, Lord, admiral, the freedom of the City voted to, iii, 248.

Kelseye, Robert de, M.P. for the City, i, 162, 163, 174.

Kendale, Sir Robert de, king's commissioner, the City taken into the hands of, i, 146.

Kendricke, John, consents to accept the mayoralty notwithstanding diminished allowances, ii, 333.

Kennet, Brackley, mayor, his conduct during the Gordon Riots, iii, 180-184; summoned to attend Lords of Council, 186.

Kensington, Colonel, refuses to accept colours presented by the City, iii, 256.

Kent, revolt under Wat Tyler, i, 218-221; under Cade, 282; under Fauconberg, 314-316; royalist rising in, ii, 280, 282.

—— Edmund, Earl of, charged with treason and executed, i, 170.

Keppel, Admiral, court martial of, iii, 172; entertained at the London Tavern, 173; the freedom of the City voted to, *id.*

Ket, Robert, his rebellion, i, 432; taken and hanged at Norwich Castle, 433.

—— William, executed at Wymondham, i, 433.

Key, Sir John, Mayor, his letter to the Duke of Wellington, iii, 330;

re-elected mayor, 338, 339n.; vote of thanks to, 339.
Kiffin, William, appointed alderman by James II, ii, 521; reluctantly accepts office, 522; discharged, 523; subscribes (unwittingly) to an entertainment given to the Papal Nuncio, 524.
Kimbolton, Lord, impeachment of, ii, 155.
King's Bench, court of, removed to York, i, 162.
King's Bench prison, fired by Gordon rioters, iii, 184.
Kirkman, John, a candidate for the Shrievalty, iii, 138; elected M.P. for the City, 192; his death, *id*.
Kitson, Sir Thomas, sheriff, i, 391.
Kneseworth, Thomas, late mayor, committed to prison, i, 338.
Knighthood, proclamation enforcing, i, 240.
Knolles, Thomas, appointed joint treasurer of subsidy, i, 251; ordered to make valuation of property in the City, *id*.
Knyvett, Thomas, refuses to pay tax for maintenance of Parliamentary army, ii, 181.

Ladbroke, Robert, Sheriff, M.P. for the City, knighted, iii, 50; his death, 141.
Lagos Bay, disaster in, ii, 571.
La Hogue, battle of, ii, 569.
Lamb, Dr., assassination of, ii, 105.
Lambert, Daniel, elected mayor, iii, 47; M.P. for the City, *id.*; knighted, 50; loses his seat for the City, 56.
—— Col. John, ejects the Rump, ii, 356; marches northward to intercept Monk, 364.
Lambeth, treaty of, i, 81.
Lambyn, Edmund, i, 153.
Lancaster, Henry, Earl of, revolt of, i, 163, 164; the citizens charged by Edward III with having assisted, 166; his charges against the king read at the Guildhall, 167; his fall, 168; fined, 170.
Lancaster, John, Duke of, his quarrel with the citizens, i, 208–211; reconciled, 212; Philipot leads the opposition against, 215.
—— Thomas, Earl of, his house in Holborn, i, 149; taken prisoner at Boroughbridge and executed at Pomfret, 152; a tablet erected in St. Paul's by, 153; Queen Isabel proclaims herself avenger of, 155.
Landen, battle of, ii, 571.
Langham, Sir James, committed to the Tower, ii, 266; impeached, 273; deprived of his aldermanry, 308; restored and excused serving, 383, 384.
Langton, Stephen, Archbishop of Canterbury, produces before barons assembled at St. Paul's, a copy of Charter of Liberties granted by Henry I, i, 72.
—— Walter, Bishop of Chester, i, 129, 137.
Latimer, Hugh, Bishop of Worcester, sent to the Tower, i, 458; burnt at Oxford, 474.
Latymer, William, Parson of St. Laurence Pountney, informs against Bonner, i, 438.
Laud, Archbishop, attack made on his palace at Lambeth, ii, 124; impeached, 135.
Lauderdale, Lord, attends the Common Council, ii, 229; brought prisoner to London, 342.
Launde, Robert, knighted, i, 220.
Lawrence, Joseph, candidate for aldermanry, ii, 644.
Laxton, William, grocer, his school at Oundle, i, 353; knighted, 412; accompanies remains of Henry VIII to Windsor, 419.
Leathersellers of London, a portion of the suppressed Priory of St. Helen's, Bishopsgate, converted

INDEX.

into a hall for the Company of, i, 401.
Ledes, co. Kent, castle of, captured by Edward II, i, 151.
Lee, Sir Richard, i, 478.
—— Robert, mayor, first signatory to proclamation of James I, ii, 1.
—— Rowland, Bishop of Lichfield and Coventry, i, 391.
—— William, elected Sheriff, iii, 138.
Leeds, Thomas, Earl of Danby, afterwards Duke of, impeached, ii, 458; signs the invitation to the Prince of Orange, 529; bribed by East India Company, 594, 596; ordered to be again impeached, 596.
Legge, William, the Freedom of the City voted to, iii, 61–62; subscribes to bounties for soldiers, 64.
Leiburn, Sir Roger de, advises the City's submission to Henry III, i, 100.
Leicester, surrenders to Fairfax, ii, 220.
—— Robert, Earl of, sent to Flanders, i, 531; his opinion of London soldiers, 535.
Leigh, Sir Thomas, mayor, particulars of, i, 484n.
Leighton, Sir William, iii, 242.
Leman, Sir John, ii, 67, 71.
Le Mans, birth place of Henry II, i, 61.
Lenthall, William, appointed Speaker of the House of Commons, ii, 132; writes to the City for a loan, 135, 136; his bold speech to the king, 156; attends Court of Aldermen, 363.
Lepanto, battle of, 517.
Lethieullier, Christopher, elected sheriff, ii, 548; knighted, 552.
Leventhorp, John, executor of King Henry IV, i, 270.
Levett, Sir Richard, elected sheriff, ii, 565; knighted, 567; stands for the City, 609.
Lewen, William, alderman, candidate for aldermanry of Broad Street Ward, ii, 640.
Lewes, battle of, i, 96; the "Mise" of, id.
Leyre, William de, the captive Wallace lodged in the house of, i, 130.
Lieutenancy, Court of, commission granted to the City, ii, 67; address to Charles II, thanking him for dissolving parliament, 466; a new commission appointed by Queen Anne, 612; dispute with the Lord Mayor as to the control of the City's militia, iii, 235.
Lilburne, John, incites the army to mutiny, ii, 310; his trial at the Guildhall, 316–318; elected common councilman, 319; takes the Engagement with reservations, id.; election declared void by Parliament, id.
Lille, capture of, ii, 629.
Lilly, William, the Grammarian, master of Colet's School, i, 365.
Lincoln, John, executed for riot on Evil May Day, i, 357.
Littleton, Stephen, takes part in the Gunpowder Plot, ii, 14.
Livery of London, the. *See* Common Hall.
Livery Cloth, presented to the mayor, etc., on the decease of Henry VIII, i, 418; the City's claim to, allowed at Queen Mary's funeral, 483.
Loans, to Louis the Dauphin, i, 82; to Edward II, 140; to Edward III, 185, 189, 192, 198, 201; to Richard II, 214, 217, 225; to Henry IV, 250, 251; to Henry V, 258, 261; to Edward IV, 308, 310, 318, 319; to Richard, Earl of Warwick, 310, 312; to Richard III,

325, 326; to Henry VII, 328, 329, 330; to Henry VIII, 367, 369, 373; to Mary, 467, 477, 482; to Elizabeth, 519, 546, 549, 560; to James I, ii, 13, 57, 63, 69, 70; to Hugh Middleton, 25; to the Elector Palatine, 75, 77, 83; to Charles I, 92, 97, 104, 105, 119; the "forced loan," 100; Charles attempts to extort another loan from the City, 122; more applications for, 126, 127, 128; to Parliament, 135, 136, 138, 146, 162, 167, 172, 177, 182, 205, 214, 241, 263, 264, 290, 292, 310, 372; for payment of the Scottish army, 140, 219, 238; a loan for the siege of Chester, 224; to Cromwell, 314; to the Council of State, 373; to the Convention Parliament, 378; to Charles II, 385, 388-389, 399, 403, 406, 414, 436, 455, 456; to the Prince of Orange, 538; to William and Mary, 560, 563, 567, 568, 569, 570, 571; the last of the City loans, 587.

Locke, Sir William, i, 438.

Lockwood, Richard, M.P. for the City, opposes passing of Election Act (II Geo., i, c. 18), iii, 28.

Lollards, the, proceedings against, i, 221, 248-250, 253-257.

Lombards, the, a rising in the City against, i, 292.

London, Bishops of. *See* Aylmer; Bonner; Courtenay; Fitz-James; Maurice; Mellitus; Ridley; Tunstal.

—— Bridge, its erection during Roman occupation, i, 5; the Danes defeated at, 20, 21; repaired under William Rufus, 39; custody of, presented to Queen Eleanor, 101; attacked by Fauconberg, 315, 316; a false drawbridge ordered to be made in case of need in time of difficulty, 431.

London, City of, its geographical position, i, 1; the "emporium" of the world, 2; not in demesne, *id.*; its commercial greatness during the Roman occupation, 4; Roman relics in, 6; the metropolis of the East Saxons, 8, 9; its increasing importance under Egbert, 9-10; the same weights and measures used in, as at Winchester, 10; the headquarters of the Danes, 11; "restored" by Alfred the Great, 12; Ethelred, alderman of, 13; government of, similar to that of a shire, *id.*; gallant repulse of Danes by citizens, *id.*; the "frith-gild," 14-16; first mention of a Guildhall, 15; the mint in, 16; attacked by Sweyn, 17, 19; submits to Sweyn, 19; takes part in election of Edmund Ironside, king, 23; attacked by Cnut, 23; the "lithsmen" of, 25, 26; the capital of the kingdom, 27; gemóts held in, *id.*; declares for Earl Godwine, 28; favours Edgar the Atheling, 31; arrival of William the Conqueror in, i, 31; negotiates with, 32; submission of, 33; William's charter to, 34; the portreeve of, 35, 64; lost charter granting the shrievalty of, 36, 37 n.; not included in "Doomsday," 37; right to elect its own Justiciar, 43; its election of Stephen, 45; sends representatives to the Synod at Winchester, 48-50; the Empress Matilda in, 50, 51; Geoffrey de Mandeville, Earl of Essex, sheriff of, 53; holds the balance between Stephen and the Empress, *id.*; arrival of Henry of Anjou in, 54; destroyed by fire (1136), 55; charter of Henry II to, 58; disturbances in, 59, 60; Longchamp and the citizens of, 62; grant of a "Commune" to, 63; charters of Richard I to, 68, 71; the Barons admitted into, 77; charter of John granting annual election of mayor of, *id.*; its rights preserved by *Magna Carta*, *id.*; placed under an interdict, 78; arrival of Louis the Dauphin in, 79; invested by the Earl Marshal, 81; lends money to Louis, 82; protest of, against Papal claims, 85; taken into Henry III's hands, 85, 99, 111; persecution of Jews in, 87; Henry III, master of, 91; mediates between the king and barons, 92; the queen insulted by inhabitants of, 94; the mayor and chief citizens summoned to Windsor, 100; the Earl of Gloucester gains possession of, 102; charter of Henry III to, 103; arrival of Edward I in, 111; sends a deputation to confer with the king at Paris, 112, 116; taken into the king's hands, 122, 146; furnishes Edward I with ships and men, 125; its mayoralty restored, 128, 148; riots in, 135; the Barons admitted into, 136; the gates of, barred against the Barons, 138; the king's right to talliage, resisted, 139, 140; confirmation of ordinances of, by Edward II, 142; proceedings at the Iter at the Tower (1321), 143–148; taken into the king's hands, 146; assists Edward II in expedition against the castle of Ledes, co. Kent, 151; charter of exemption from foreign service to citizens of, *id.*; lost to Edward II, 155, 156; freedom of, conferred on Stratford, Bishop of Winchester, 158; Queen Isabel and the mayoralty of, *id.*; charters of Edward III to, 160, 180, 188, 196, 208; citizens of, urged to join the Earl of Lancaster in revolt, 164; charged by Edward III with having assisted Lancaster, 166; the mayor and citizens summoned to attend the king at Woodstock, 178; ships furnished by citizens of, 182, 183; charter of Edward III, granting privilege of using gold mace, 196; grievances of, laid before the king, 198; return made of number of parishes in, 203; an ecclesiastical centre, *id.*; opposed to John of Gaunt, 209–211; reconciled, 212; charters of Richard II to, 214, 224; foreigners forbidden to traffic in, by retail, 214; reforms in, under Northampton, 221–223; Richard II applies to, for assistance against Parliament, 233; the mayor and aldermen summoned to Windsor, 234; the Lords appellant admitted into, 235; absolved by the Archbishop of oath of allegiance, *id.*; refuses a loan to Richard II, 241; the mayor and sheriffs committed to prison, *id.*; fined, 242; the citizens go to meet Henry of Lancaster, 245; rental of the City's lands, 252; the citizens invited to send provisions to Caen free of Custom, 262, 263; sends provisions to Harfleur for the English army, 263, 264; the king's thanks for the same, 264, 265; famine in, 272; allowances to City Members of Parliament, 273, 274; parliamentary relief for poor of, 278; Calais appeals to, 279; forces sent for relief of Calais, 279, 280; charter of Henry VI to, 281; entrance to, denied to the Duke of York, 287; affected neutrality of, 288, 290, 291; again called upon to assist in defending Calais, 289; the Duke of York takes up his quarters in, 290; a rising against Lombards in, 292; letter from

Henry VI to the Mayor for safeguarding of, 293; thanks of Henry VI for offer of ships by, *id.*; commissions of array issued to mayor and sheriffs, 297; sends deputation to Henry VI, at Northampton, 298; opposes the entrance of the Yorkists, 299; deputation sent to meet the Yorkist Lords, 299, 300; shows signs of wavering, 301, 302; forsaken by Henry VI, 305; charters of Edward IV to, 307, 308; the Tower in the hands of municipal authorities, 312; the custody of the Tower removed from, *id.*; Edward IV re-enters, 313; letter of Fauconberg to and reply, 314, 315; grant of a general pardon to, 318; Edward entertains the citizens with a day's hunting, *id.*; Edward V welcomed by, 319, 320; the Duke of Buckingham's harangue at Guildhall in favour of Gloucester, 321; deputation to Gloucester offering him the crown, 322; gift to Richard III and his queen at coronation by, 323; bold speech of Londoners to Richard III, 325; reception of Henry VII by, 326, 329; precautions taken against Perkin Warbeck, 332; visit of Henry VIII to as a boy, 334; rejoicings in, on formation of league between Henry VII and the king of the Romans, 336; charter of Henry VII to, 337; gift to Henry VIII at coronation, 344; famine in, 346; foundation of City of London school, 349, 350; charges brought by Wolsey against, 354; Wolsey's advice to, touching payment of subsidy, 355; riots in, on Evil May Day, 355-357; obtains the king's pardon, 358; reception of Cardinal Campeggio in, 362-364; solemn procession in, on report of Scottish invasion, 372; rejoicings in, on news of defeat of the French, 374; the citizens and the Amicable Loan, 375-376; French ambassadors lodged in Bishop of London's palace in St. Paul's Churchyard, 377; deputation sent to Henry VIII, at Greenwich, touching Wythypol's discharge from aldermanry, 377-379; famine in (1529), 379; suppression of monasteries in, 386, 390-393, 397-401; the citizens show dissatisfaction at the king's marriage with Anne Boleyn, 388; sends a detachment to put down Pilgrimage of Grace, 394; increase of poor in, on suppression of Religious Houses, 404; offers to purchase the dissolved houses for relief of poor, 405; Edward VI welcomed to, 420, 421; the Reformation in, 421-430; redemption of charges for superstitious uses by, 424, 425; Edward VI passes through, 431; letter to, from Lords of the Council with charges against Protector Somerset, 433, 434; letter from Somerset to mayor of, 434; joins the Lords against Somerset, 435; the Lords explain their conduct to, 436; raises forces against Somerset, *id.*; charter of Edward VI to, granting rights in Southwark, 442; indignation in, on Warwick's arbitrary conduct, 446; Queen Mary proclaimed in, 454, 455; Queen Mary welcomed by, 456; put into a state of defence against Wyatt, 462; Philip and Mary welcomed by, 469-471; renewed opposition to foreigners in, 475, 476; accession of Elizabeth welcomed by, 484; havoc worked by reformers in, 487; protestant refugees in, 504; renders assistance to the Prince of

Orange, 505; Flemish merchants seized in, 510; measures taken for safeguarding of, during Northumberland Conspiracy, 515, 516; proceedings against Jesuits in, 524, 525; special preachers in, 526; foreigners in, 532; threatened famine in, 533; preparations in, to meet the Armada, 535; disbanded soldiers in, after defeat of Armada, 547; search in, for Spanish emissaries, 549, 550; refuses further supplies of ships, 557-559; threatened by another Armada, 560; the mayor of, the first signatory of document proclaiming James I king, ii, 1; James enters Tower of, 3; his passage through the City, 5; free trade opposed by citizens of, 10-12; water supply of 18-28; the Ulster Plantation, 28-45; the Virginia Company, 46-54; account of insult offered to the Spanish ambassador in, 79-82; joy of citizens at the return of Prince Charles from Spain, 84; plague of 1625 in, 95; called upon to supply ships for defence of the Thames, *id.*; ships supplied by, 98, 101; sickness and famine in, 109; ship money levied in, 111, 117, 125; loss of its Irish estate, 115; charter of Charles I to, 118; unpopularity of Strafford in, 132; refuses to advance money until execution of Strafford, 138; the "Protestation" accepted by, 139; day of thanksgiving in, 142; opposition to the bishops, 147, 150; Charles entertained in, 147; petition of, for removal of bishops, 151; Charles at the Guildhall, demands the five members, 156; petition to the king thereon, 158; a panic in, 159; Charles's reply to late petition, 160; supplies the army with arms, 170; defensive operations in, 170, 171; petitions for peace, 177; deputation to the king, 178; the king's terms rejected by, 180; weekly assessment in, 182, 184; propositions for peace, 183; scheme for fortification of, *id.*; Puritanism in, 187; scarcity of coal in, 189; the Tower committed to the custody of mayor and sheriffs, 191; sends relief to Gloucester, *id.*; "weekly meal" for payment of army, 199, 200; suspects banished from, 202; nvited by Parliament to frame proposals for peace, *id.*; thanked by Parliament, 204; difficulty in getting in arrears of monthly assessment and weekly meal account, 205; proposals submitted to Parliament, 209, 210; its trade ruined, 213; letter from the mayor of Gloucester to, 216; Plymouth appeals to, 220; royalist prisoners in, 221; Presbyterianism in, 223, 227, 232; letter from the Scottish Parliament to the Mayor of, 228; claims to govern the militia of the suburbs, 230-232; letter of Charles I to, 234; remonstrance by, presented to both Houses, 234-235; a counter remonstrance, 235; reply to King's letter, 235-237; petitions both Houses to redress grievances, 239; correspondence with the army, 243, 245, 247, 248, 249, 251, 252, 255, 264, 265, 269; sends commissioners to head-quarters, 248; beset by reformadoes, 250; petitions of apprentices to Parliament, 251; preparations for defence of, 254, 256; more commissioners to the army, *id.*; surrenders to Fairfax, 259; army enters, 260; at the mercy of the army, 262; more demands for money, 263-266; the mayor and others com mitted, 266; threat to quarter troops on, 267; petitions parliament for removal of the army to a greater distance, 269; petitions for release of aldermen, 270; Puritanism in the City, 271; its attitude towards the army, 275, 277; entrusted with the protection of Parliament, 277, 279; petitions for control of militia, 278; again petitions for release of aldermen, 280; aldermen released, 282; letter from Prince of Wales to, 289; urges parliament to come to an understanding with the army, 292; loan by, to assist negotiations with the king, *id.*; negotiations opposed by London "Levellers," 291; Fairfax announces his intention to enter, 293; demands money from, 293, 296, 301; the army enters, 294; the Commonwealth proclaimed in, 311; Richmond Park presented to, 313; threatened with free quarters for the army unless money be found, 314; economical measures taken by, 321; money raised for relief of the poor of, 322-324; removal of Royal emblems in, 330; assessed at one fifteenth of the whole kingdom, 331; another letter from Prince of Wales to, 340; Scottish prisoners brought to, after battle of Worcester, 341; reception of Cromwell in, 342; subscriptions for relief of wounded soldiers in, 344; precautions against a royalist rising in, 350-352; letter from Monk to the Common Council, 357; negotiations for the safety of, 357, 359, 360; rising of apprentices in favour of a free Parliament, 358; royalist hopes centered in, 361; reply sent to Monk, 363; desires a full Parliament, 364; another letter

from Monk, 364-365; deputation to meet Monk, 365; Monk enters, 366; confers with Court of Aldermen, 367, 368, 369; royal arms again set up in, 374; the City's declaration and vindication, 374-377; letter from Charles II to, 377; answer thereto, 378; commissioners sent to the king, 379; Charles II proclaimed in, 380; the king enters, *id.*; takes oath of allegiance, 381; rising of Fifth-monarchy men in, 386-388, 396; parliamentary election (1661), 392-393; desires confirmation of its charter, 394-396; reception of Russian ambassador in, 401-403; charter of Charles II to, 403; the French ambassador insulted at Lord Mayor's banquet, 404-406; the Great Plague, 409-414; estimate of population of, 413 n.; the Great Fire, 414-418; assistance sent from York and Ireland to, 420; the streets to be cleared, 423; the rebuilding of, 427-435; a special court of judicature created for settling disputes after the fire, 428; report on state of the Chamber of 438-439; Cardonel's proposals for raising money, 447; the Prince of Orange in, 443; effect of closing the Exchequer upon, 445; heavy assessment in, 446; petitions Parliament for pecuniary relief, 447; petitions and addresses to Charles II for summoning a Parliament, 460, 461, 463, 465, 475; elections (1681) in, 463; proceedings against, under writ of *Quo Warranto*, 476, 477, 478, 494-500; debate on question of City's surrender, 503; judgment entered, 503-504; bishop of, suspended, 516; agitation against Popery in, 516-517; dissenters supreme in, 525; rejoicings in, at birth of Prince James Edward, 528-529; the City charter restored, 530; the mayor and others attend Privy Council, 532; attacks on Catholics in, 533, 534; James sends for the mayor and aldermen on hearing of landing of Prince of Orange, 533; the Lords attend at Guildhall to draw up declaration in favour of William, 535; invited by Prince of Orange to send representatives to assembly, 537; reversal of judgment on *Quo Warranto*, 541, 543, 554-555; report of City Committee of Grievances, 541-543; William and Mary at the Lord Mayor's banquet, 551; elections (1690) in, 553; disputed municipal elections in, 556-558; assistance of, invoked against France, 559-561; William again at the Lord Mayor's banquet, 570; excitement in, on disaster in Lagos Bay, 572; address to the Queen, 573; address to William on death of Queen, 587; corrupt practices in, 589-596; Jacobite tumults in, 597, 598; elections (1695) in, 598; address on discovery of Assassination Plot, 599; Association in defence of the King, 600; opposes Election Bill, 601; resolution to defend the King, 601; rejoicings in, for the peace of Ryswick, 603; King's reception on return from Flanders, 604-606; address to William on death of James II, 607; addresses to Queen Anne, 610, 616, 623, 626, 629, 630, 635, 649; visits of the Queen to, 613, 614, 616, 621, 624; the Duke of Marlborough in, 617, 623; financial difficulties of, 618-621; standards taken at Ramillies presented to, 623; soldiers supplied to Anne, 624;

search for Papists in, 627; elections (1708 and 1710) in, 628, 637; Act for building new churches, 639; election disputes in, 640; Prince Eugene in, 645; records to be searched for customary procedure in communications with the Crown, 646; address to Queen Anne on peace of Utrecht, 647; loyal addresses to George I, touching Jacobite Conspiracy, iii, 6, 8. The City reprimanded by Parliament for defraying law costs in disputed elections out of the Chamber, 13-15; the action of Parliament towards South Sea Company approved by, 22; the Election Act, (11 Geo. i, c, 18) regulating elections in, 26-29; the freedom conferred on Frederick, Prince of Wales, 40; loyal addresses to George II, 49, 51, 54, 55; the freedom conferred on the Duke of Cumberland, 54, 55; opposes a proposed tax on plate, 58; urges the execution of Admiral Byng, 59, 60, 61; the freedom conferred on Pitt and Legge, 61, 62, offers bounties for soldiers, 63; addresses to the king on Capture of Quebec and conquest of Canada, 64; address on surrender of St. Lucia and capture of Martinico, 72; the freedom voted to Charles Townshend, 79; another remonstrance, 100, 101; the King's reply, 101; Beckford's famous speech, 102; address to King deprecating hostilities with America, 157; the King's reply, 158; the freedom voted to Dr. Richard Price, 165; another address deprecating war with America, *id.*; subscriptions in aid of war with America refused by, 167; advocates conciliatory measures, 168; freedom voted to

Admiral Keppel, 173; vote of thanks to Whig lords for supporting economical reform, 175; letter to Lord Shelburne touching Wiltshire Committee of Association, 176, 177; Lord Shelburne's reply, 177; accepts form of Association, 178; advocates repeal of Savile's Act, 179, 184; the Gordon riots in, 180–184; address to the king after Gorden riots, 191; claim for damages after riots, *id.*; address to the king on Rodney's victory in the West Indies, 200; proposal to present the king with a man-of-war in place of the Royal George by, 201; opposes Fox's East India Bill, 204–206; upholds the exercise of the king's prerogative, 205; opposes Shop Tax and obtains its repeal, 209–212; the city's rights saved in convention with France, 212; its efforts to abolish the slave trade, 212–213, 288–290; the Prince of Wales's gift of £1,000 to poor of, 214; sends clothing, etc. to troops in Flanders, 222; the freedom voted to Howe, Jervis and Sir George Grey, 223–224; riots in, 224; great scarcity in, 225; subscribes £100,000 to Loyalty Loan, 231; the freedom voted to Nelson and a sword to Jervis, 232; swords of honour voted to Duncan and Sir Richard Onslow, 234; the freeedom voted to Captain Berry, 237; a sword of honour voted to Nelson, *id.*; the same to Sir Sydney Smith, 239; bread riots in, 241–245; address to the king for meeting of Parliament to consider the high price of provisions, 247; Pitt's proposal to fortify, against Napoleon, 251; claims a separate Bill in matters military, 257; address to the king on the dismissal of Lord Melville, 260; the same on the formation of the ministry of "all the talents," 265; the freedom voted to Sir John Stuart for victory of Maida, 266; address on fall of the Grenville Ministry, 267; address of thanks to the king for assisting Spain against Napoleon, 268; its indignation at the Convention of Cintra, 269; the freedom voted to Colonel Wardle, 270; demands enquiry into cause of failure of the Walcheren Expedition, 271; opposes Wellington's annuity, 274; the freedom offered to the Prince Regent but declined, 282; address to Regent omitted from *London Gazette*, 285; address on assassination of Spencer Percival, *id.*; offers congratulations to Prince Regent after Waterloo, 290; the Corn Laws opposed by, 294–296; addresses to the Regent on the general depression, 294, 296; the lord mayor's report of the riot in Spa Fields, 299–305; address to Regent on the prevailing distress, 305; the Regent's "most gracious" reply, 306; opposes Indemnity Bill, 308; address to George IV on his accession, 315; address to king for dismissal of ministers, 320; lends pecuniary assistance to Spain and Greece against the Holy Alliance, 324; votes assistance to Spitalfields weavers, 325; resolutions of Common Council touching Parliamentary Reform, 331–332; the freedom voted to Lords Grey and Althorp, 339, 344; petition to Parliament not to vote supplies until the Reform Bill be passed, 340–341; examples of public spirit displayed by, 349–350; the Corporation appointed sanitary authority of London, 350.

London City Forces, supplied to Edward I, i, 126; to Edward II, 140, 152; to Edward III, 161, 179, 180, 182, 183, 185, 190, 195, 199; to Henry VI, 280-293; to Henry VIII, 346, 409-411, 412, 413, 414; to Queen Mary, 462, 464, 477, 478, 480, 481; to Queen Elizabeth, 489, 490, 491, 519, 531, 534, 546, 548, 549, 552, 555, 556, 557, 559, 560; reviewed in Greenwich Park by Queen Elizabeth, 518, 529; soldiers supplied for service in the Palatinate, ii, 89; to Charles I, 94, 98, 103, 126; musters in the City, 120; placed in command of Skippon, 161; additional forces raised for defence of the City, 170; the City offers to raise a force for the army, 175; the City again called upon to supply men, 185; ten volunteer regiments raised by the City, 186; Sir William Waller in command of, 191; horse raised for Waller, 193; mutiny amongst, 196-197; auxiliaries to join the Parliamentary army, 200; at siege of Greenland House, 205; City contingent to first standing army, 208; military activity in the City, 215; cavalry raised for the protection of the associated counties, 220; Massey commander-in-chief of, 257; Skippon again in command of, 276; reviewed in Hyde Park, 329; the City consents to raise cavalry, 332; Monk made sergeant-major-general of, 373; Sir Richard Browne appointed major-general, 385; auxiliaries raised in the City, 436; reviewed in Hyde Park, 569; City militia exempted from the National Militia Bill, iii, 57; the London Association and the Gordon rioters, 183, 184; refuses to lay down its arms, 186-187; proposal for an armed association of householders objected to, 186-190; the City militia to be placed on a proper footing, 199; the Loyal London Volunteers, 224, 252; thanks to the Military Association at Grocer's Hall, 224; the Cornhill Military Association, 233, 236; review of volunteers, 239; a contingent of 800 men furnished by the City against Napoleon, 252; the River Fencibles and Harbour Marines, *id.*; review of City volunteers at Blackheath, 256; the City included in the provisions of Pitt's Additional Force Bill, but claims a separate Bill, 257; objections to artillery practising in Finsbury Fields, 258. *See also* Militia and Trained bands.

London, City Records, order for expunging, ii, 398; defective condition of, 453; minutes of Common Council during Civil War expunged, 498; to be searched for customary procedure in communications with the Crown, 646.

—— City wall, i, 5.

—— Mayor of, first mention of, i, 66, 68; charter of John granting annual election of, 77; the title of "lord" mayor, 197; election of, by the guilds, 206; assessed as an earl, 217; election of, preceded by Divine Service, 252; takes precedence of the king's brothers at the Guildhall, 257; communion substituted for mass at election of, 429; mass substituted for communion, 459; election of, preceded by communion, 487; presented to the House of Lords in the absence of the king, ii, 267; expenses of his table cut down, 320; not to sell places, 321; his allowance reduced, 333-335; interference of Parliament in election of, 354, 355; proposal to omit pageant on lord mayor's day for fear of riot, 356 ; his claim to jurisdiction within the Temple, 440, 443 ; his prerogative in election of sheriffs, 470, 564 ; presented to the Constable of the Tower on election, 547 ; the question of his precedence in the City in the absence of the king, iii, 262 ; the new mayor sworn before the barons of the exchequer, the king being ill, 281.

London, Sheriffs, of, charter of William I, granting sheriffwick of London, i, 36; of Middlesex, 40-43; the appointment of, lost for a time to the City, 58; inquest of, *id.*; election of, by the guilds, 206; fines for discharge of, ii, 63, 338 ; their expenses cut down, 320 ; not to sell places, 321 ; allowances of, reduced, 335; mode of electing, 468-472 ; the mayor's prerogative to elect one of the, 470, 472, 563-566; tumultuous elections of, 479-488 ; James II sanctions the mayor's prerogative, 520; a bill to settle elections of, rejected, 565.

—— Ships, supplied to Edward I, i, 125 ; to Edward III, 182, 183, 189, 193, 195, 197, 199, 204 ; to Henry VI, 293 ; to Queen Elizabeth, 536, 549, 552, 555, 560 ; requisition of, resisted by the City of London, ii, 95; supplied to Charles I, 98, 101, 114; loss of the ship "London," 407 ; launch of the "Loyal London," 408 ; the same destroyed, 435.

—— Thomas of. *See* Becket.

Long, Sir Lisleborne, recorder, waits upon the Protector, ii, 352.

Longbeard, William Fitz-Osbert, called, rising in the City under i, 70 ; takes refuge in St. Mary-le-Bow, and is hanged, 71.

Longchamp, William, Bishop of Ely, appointed chancellor during absence of Richard I, i, 61 ; takes refuge in the Tower for fear of John, 62; deposed from chancellorship, 63.

Lorimer, Edmund le, grant of Small Beam to, i, 141.

Lotteries, the first public lottery, i, 506-508 ; a lottery in aid of the Virginia Company, ii, 49, 51.

Louis the Dauphin, lands at Sandwich, i, 79 ; deserted by the Barons and supported by London, 80 ; defeated at Lincoln, *id.* ; his departure, 81.

Louviers, fall of, i, 263.

Love, Christopher, executed on Tower Hill, ii, 383.

—— William, alderman, M.P. for the City, ii, 392, 458, 464, 538 ; removed from his aldermanry, 396.

Lovell, Salathiel, recorder, knighted ii, 570.

Lowe, Sir Thomas, ii, 13, 66.

"Loyalty loan," the, iii, 228-231 ; the City subscribes £100,000 to, 231.

Lucar, Emanuel, committed to Fleet prison, i, 468.

Lumbard, Jacobina la, the Small Beam granted to, i, 124.

Lumnore, Lumnar, or Lomner, Henry, grocer, his connection with the Great Beam, i, 387.

Lunsford, Colonel, Lieutenant of the Tower, removed at the Lord Mayor's request, ii, 153.

Luttrell, Colonel, declared M.P. for Middlesex, iii, 87, 88 ; burnt in effigy on Tower Hill, 118.

Lygons, Ferdinando, commissioned to raise 300 archers in the City, i, 480.

Lyndhurst, Lord, his amendment to the Reform Bill, iii, 340.

Lyons, Richard, alderman, deposed, i, 205 ; his death, 219.

Lyttelton, Sir George, Chancellor of the Exchequer, proposes a tax on plate, iii, 58.

INDEX.

Maghfeld, or Maunfeld, Gilbert, appointed sheriff by the king, i, 242.
Maida, battle of, iii, 266.
Malpas, Philip, his house sacked by Cade, i, 284; particulars of, 284 n.
Malplaquet or "Blaregnies," battle of, ii, 630.
Manchester, Edward, Earl of, ii, 215.
—— Henry. Earl of. *See* Montagu.
"Manchester Massacre," the, or "Peterloo," iii, 309–310.
Mandeville, Geoffrey de, Earl of Essex, justiciar of the City, i, 44; constable of the Tower, 51; won over by the Empress Matilda, *id.*; forsakes her, 52; justiciar and sheriff of London and Middlesex, 53; again joins the Empress, *id.*; his death, 54.
Mansfeld, Count. arrives in England, ii, 86, 87; failure of his expedition for recovery of the Palatinate, 90.
Mansfield, Lord, iii, 83; his house destroyed by Gordon rioters, 183.
Mansion House, the, threatened by Gordon rioters, iii, 184.
Mar, Earl of, defeated at Sheriffmuir, iii, 8.
Marchall John le, murdered in Cheapside, i, 156.
Mare, Peter de la, released from Nottingham Castle, i, 212.
Margaret, Princess, sister of Edward IV, married to the Duke of Burgundy, i, 309, 310.
—— of Anjou, her marriage with Henry VI, i, 282; collects a force in defence of her husband's crown, 303; defeats Warwick at St. Albans, 305; intrigues with Warwick, 311; defeated at Tewkesbury, 314.
Markets, monopoly of, granted to the City, i, 161; allotment of sites for, after the Great Fire, ii, 433.

Markham, Sir Griffin, plots against James I, ii, 6.
—— Sir John, Lieutenant of the Tower, removed, i, 435.
Marlborough, John, Duke of, deserts James II, ii, 534; his successes in the war with France, 614, 616, 621, 622; entertained at Goldsmiths' Hall, 617; sets out for Holland, 621; entertained at Vintner's Hall, 623; his victories at Oudenarde and Malplaquet, 629, 630; sets out to the war, 638; dismissed from his offices, 645.
Mary, Princess, daughter of Henry VII, married to Prince Charles of Castile, i, 339; marries Louis XII, 347.
Mary, Queen, birth of, i, 354; her marriage with the Dauphin, 361, 362; declared illegitimate, 396; her place in the succession acknowledged by statute, 420; proclaimed Queen, 454, 455; enters the City, 456; restores the mass, 457; City gift to, at coronation of, 460; harangues the citizens at Guildhall, 462; married to Philip II, 469; obtains the reconciliation of England to Rome, 424; her persecution of Protestants, 473–475; deserted by Philip, 477; declares war against France, *id.*; her death, 483; her statue at the Royal Exchange mutilated, ii, 534.
—— Queen of Scots, assumes the style of Queen of England, i, 488; proposed marriage with the Duke of Norfolk, 515; execution of, 533.
—— wife of William III, proclaimed Queen, ii, 539; coronation of, 540; attends the lord mayor's banquet, 551; again invited but unable to attend, 573, 574; City address to, 573; death of, 587; the City's rights at the funeral of, allowed, 588.

Maseres, Francis, cursitor baron, his letter to the City touching the Quebec Bill, iii, 143.

Mason, Robert, recorder, ii, 113.

Massey, Edward, colonel, ordered to leave Gloucester, ii, 216; made commander-in-chief of the City forces, 257; arrested, 295.

Matilda, the Empress, her claims to the throne acknowledged by the nobility, i, 44; disallowed by the City of London, 45; appeals to Rome, 46; acknowledged "Lady of England," 47; enters London, 50; driven out, 51; wins over Mandeville, *id.*; withdraws to the continent, 53.

—— Queen of Stephen, supported by Mandeville, i, 52; reduces Winchester and releases Stephen, *id.*

Matthias, the Emperor, loses the crown of Bohemia, ii, 74.

Maunay, Sir Walter de, commands expedition to Brittany, i, 189.

Maurice, Bishop of London, rebuilds St. Paul's, i, 38.

May, Hugh, king's commissioner for surveying the City after the fire, ii, 431.

Maynard, Sir John, his opinion taken on the question of the aldermanic veto, ii, 454.

Medicis, Mary de, welcomed by the citizens, ii, 141.

Melborne, John, mayor, i, 365.

Mellitus, first Bishop of London, i, 8.

Melville, Lord. *See* Dundas, Henry.

Mercers of London, image of Becket over gate of chapel of, i, 125; contribute to a gift of £500 to the king, 201; return of rental of, 252; subscribe towards furnishing soldiers for war with France, 347; the foundation of Mercers School, 349; foundation of St. Paul's School, 350-352; meeting of the Lords of the Council in Hall of, 435; trustees of Gresham College, 502; subscription for Prince Eugene opened at their chapel, ii, 624.

Merchant Adventurers, refuse to advance a loan to Elizabeth, i, 506; invited to subscribe to lottery, 507; bonds of the governor and company of, to be given up, 514; their company suppressed and afterwards restored, ii, 68.

Merchant-Taylors of London, contribute to a gift of £500 to the king, i, 201; return of rental of, 252; charter of Henry VII to the, 337; the French Ambassadors lodged in hall of, 362; their school founded on the site of the Duke of Buckingham's "Manor of the Rose," 366; refuse to part with property for erection of a City Burse, 497; take shares in first public lottery, 507; the House of Commons entertained by, ii, 12; Prince Henry enrolled a member of, *id.*; James I entertained by, 12; James I entertained by the City in Hall of, 61; Parliament entertained in Hall of, 198.

Merlawe, Richard, appointed joint treasurer of subsidy, i, 251; mayor, 263.

Merton, Walter de, chancellor, orders the arrest of Walter Hervy, i, 108; issues proclamation for expulsion of Flemings, 115.

Merttins, Sir George, mayor, iii, 27.

Mesurier, Paul le, mayor, iii, 224; engaged in suppressing bread riots, 245.

Michell, Robert, punished for insulting the Spanish ambassador, ii, 81.

Middlemore, Humphrey, Procurator of Charter-house, committed to the Tower, i, 391.

Middlesex, co., grant of, to the

City to ferm, i, 40; the shrievalty of, granted to the City, 41; the shrievalty of, exercised by sheriffs of London, 42; the shrievalty for a time lost to the City, 58; the ferm increased, 104; the ferm decreased, 160.

Middleton, Hugh, undertakes the formation of the New River, ii, 21; pecuniary assistance given to, by James I, 23; created a baronet, 25; City votes a gold chain to, *id.*; his death, 26; money grant to widow of, *id.*

—— Robert, surety for his brother Hugh, ii, 25.

—— Sir Thomas, mayor, ii, 23, 51; is security for a loan to his brother Hugh, 25; demurs at entertaining the king and court, 61; commands a regiment of trained bands, 66.

—— Thomas, poet, ii, 61.

Mildmay, Sir Walter, i, 514.

Militia, commission appointed for the City, ii, 165; committee of, 171, 215; its dispute with committee of Salters' Hall, 190; a new committee of, 241, 244; the City militia placed in the hands of a Parliamentary committee, 253, 254; restored to the City, 254; the City's claim to govern militia of the suburbs, 230-232; City's petition for control of, 278; militia committee appointed, 279; petition for amalgamation of City's militia with that of neighbouring counties, 286, 287; the committee of, increased, 339; the National Militia Bill (1756), iii, 57; the City's militia to be placed on a proper footing, 199, 236; Act of Parliament passed for the same purpose, 224; dispute as to the supreme control of the City's, 235.

Militia Ordinance, the, ii, 164.

Miller, John, printer of the *Evening Post*, arrested under the Speaker's warrant, but discharged, iii, 108.

—— Tempest, alderman, removed, ii, 396.

Mills, Peter, appointed surveyor for the rebuilding of the City, ii, 428, 431.

Milton, John, appointed Secretary for foreign languages to Council of State, ii, 303.

Minorca, loss of, iii, 59.

Mitchell, Admiral, captures the Dutch fleet, iii, 239-240.

"Mohocks," ii, 646.

Monk, General, his victory over the Dutch, ii, 344; prepares to march southward, 357; correspondence between the City and, 357, 360, 363, 364; City deputation to, 365; enters London, 366; another deputation to, *id*; confers with the Aldermen, 367, 368, 369; complains to Parliament of his treatment, 368; invited to take up his quarters at Whitehall, 369; remains in the City but changes his residence, 370; entertained at Grocers' Hall, 372; Sergeant-major-general of the City's forces, 373; resigns, 385.

Monmouth, duke of, rebellion of, ii, 511, 512, 513.

Monoux, Sir George, draper, his school at Walthamstow, i, 353; M.P. for the City, 370; re-elected mayor but discharged, 372; his gift to the City of a brewhouse in Southwark, 373; objects to part with property for the erection of a City Burse, 494, 495.

Mons, fall of, ii, 571; threatened by Marlborough and Eugene, 630.

Montagu, Chief Justice, i, 437.

—— Sir Henry, Recorder, afterwards earl of Manchester, welcomes James I to London, ii, 6; M.P. for the City, 8; urges the

City to grant loans to Charles I, 122, 128.
Montague, Charles, adopts Paterson's plan for a national bank, ii, 584.
—— John, lord, killed with his brother, the Earl of Warwick, at Barnet, i, 314, 315.
Montfort, Simon de, Earl of Leicester, refused admission into the City, i, 91; summons a Parliament, 97; killed at Evesham, 98.
Monument, the, inscription on, ii, 419, 420.
Moore, Sir John, elected mayor, ii, 476; his conduct in the election of sheriffs, 478, 479; M.P. for the City, 509; a candidate for the mayoralty, 547; accused of betraying the City's liberties, *id.*
Moorfields, riots in, ii, 271, 272; iii, 180.
Mordaunt, Lord, carries Charles II's letter to the City, ii, 377; the City's gift to, 379.
Mordon, Simon de, contributes to a loan to the king, i, 202.
More, John, sheriff, committed to the Tower, i, 227; attempts made to obtain his release, 228–229, 232.
—— Sir Thomas, his connection with the City, i, 348; welcomes the Emperor Charles I to the City, 365; elected Speaker, 370; the seals transferred from Wolsey to, 380; committed to the Tower for denying the king's supremacy, 392; beheaded, 393.
Morice, Peter, obtains permission to set up a water-mill at London Bridge, ii, 19.
Morley, Colonel, City commissioners to confer with, ii, 360, 363.
Mortimer, Sir John, sentenced to death, i, 269.
—— Roger, escapes from the

Tower, i, 153; joins Isabel in France, 154; returns with her, 155; visits the Guildhall, 159; governs the country, 160, 168; arranges terms of treaty between England and Scotland, 163; opposed by Lancaster, *id.*; his death, 170.
Mountjoy, Lord, defeats Tyrone, i, 563.
Mugg, John, rector of St. Clement Danes, i, 157.
Mundy, John, alderman, occasions riot on Evil May Day, i, 356.
Muntfichet, Richard de, taken prisoner at Lincoln, i, 80; his castle on the site of the Black Friars' house, *id.*
"Murder Committee," the, Dudley North examined before, ii, 548–549.
Murray, John, ii, 88.

Namur, fall of, ii, 571; taken by William III, 597.
Nantes, Edict of, revoked, ii, 515.
Napoleon, marches into Syria, iii, 238; appointed First Consul, 240; insults the British ambassador, 251; proclaimed Emperor of the French, 256; attacks Spain, 268; his fall, 288; escapes from Elba, 290; defeated at Waterloo, *id.*
Naseby, battle of, ii, 219.
Nash, William, alderman, iii, 121; elected mayor, 127; refuses to summon a Common Hall, 128; vote of thanks refused on his quitting office, 130.
Navigation Act, the, ii, 343.
Neate, William, his contest for the Aldermanry of Bridge Ward, iii, 146–149.
Nelson, Horatio, the freedom of the City voted to, iii, 232; his victory at the Nile, 236; presents the French admiral's sword to

the City, *id.*; a sword of honour voted to, 237; proposal to erect a national memorial of his victory at the Nile, *id.*; his bust at the Guildhall, 238; offended at the City, 253-254; his victory of Trafalgar, 260; his death and funeral, 261; his monument in the Guildhall, 262-263.

Netherlands, the, envoys sent to Elizabeth from, i, 530; recruits enlisted in the City for service in, *id.*; reinforcements for, 556.

Nevill, George, Archbishop of York, removes the custody of the Tower from the citizens, i, 312.

—— John de, of Raby, i, 228.

—— Richard. *See* Warwick.

Neville, Alexander, Archbishop of York, sent by Richard II to the City to ask for their support, i, 233; charged with treason, 233, 234.

Newark, the Scottish army invited to attack, ii, 222, 225.

Newburgh, Lord, acts as messenger between the King and the City, ii, 154.

Newbury, gallant conduct of City trained bands at, ii, 195; the second battle of, 212.

Newcastle, Thomas Pelham, Duke of, calls upon the lord mayor to assist in proclamation of war with Spain, iii, 43; informs lord mayor of the Pretender's landing in Scotland, and of his marching on London, 51, 53; administration of, 57, 58; makes a scape-goat of Admiral Byng, 59, 61; resigns, 60; his coalition with Pitt, 62.

—— William Cavendish, Earl of, governor of Newcastle, ii, 189.

Newcastle-on-Tyne, muster of forces at, i, 161; City proposals touching reduction of, ii, 189, 190; surrender of, 212.

Newgate prison, destroyed during Gordon riots, iii, 183-185; parliamentary grants for rebuilding, 191.

Newland, Sir George, M.P. for the City, ii, 638; candidate for aldermanry of Broad Street Ward, 640.

Newnham, Nathaniel, alderman, elected sheriff, iii, 155; elected M.P. for the City, 192; engaged in suppressing bread riots, 242, 243.

Newport, Isle of Wight, the treaty of, ii, 291.

New River the, Act for bringing water of, from Chadwell, ii, 20; Middleton undertakes the work, 21; the opening of, 23; inhabitants compelled to use water of, 24.

New River Company, the, desires transfer of Middleton's rights, ii, 27.

Newton, Thomas, appointed Sheriff by the king, i, 242.

Nicholas, Secretary, ii, 162, 382.

Nicholson, Humphrey, a candidate for the shrievalty, ii, 473.

Nile the, battle of, iii, 236.

Nimeguen, peace of, ii, 456.

Nore, the mutiny at, iii, 233.

Norfolk, Thomas, 9th Duke of, attends lord mayor's banquet, i, 380; liberated from the Tower by Queen Mary, 457.

—— Thomas, 10th Duke of, proposal of marriage with Mary Stuart, i, 515; committed to the Tower, *id.*

Normanby, Marquis of, his questionable transactions with the City, ii, 591-592.

Norris, Sir John, his expedition against Spain, i, 546.

North, Dudley, nominated sheriff by the mayor, ii, 479; declared elected, 482; sworn in, 488; the Mercers' Company refuse to recognise election, 488; elected alderman, 493; arrested at the suit of Papillon and Du Bois, 501; proceedings against, 548–549.

North, Lord, letter from George III to, touching expulsion of Wilkes from the House, iii, 82; consulted by the king as to manner of receiving City remonstrance, 97; assaulted by a mob, 115; the fall of his ministry, 196–197; secretary of state under the Duke of Portland, 204.

Northampton, battle of, i, 302.

—— John de, favours the Duke of Lancaster, i, 215; reforms of, during mayoralty, 221, 223; re-elected mayor, 223; proceedings against, 225–227; committed to Tintagel Castle, 227; efforts to release him, 228, 230; released, 230; re-appears in the City, 239; re-instated in his freedom, 240.

—— treaty of, i, 163.

North Briton, No. 45 burnt at the Royal Exchange, iii, 74–76.

Northbury, Richard, committed to the Tower, i, 227; attempt made to obtain his release, 228–229, 232.

Northumberland, Algernon, Earl of, attends a Common Council, ii, 267.

—— John, Duke of, formerly Earl of Warwick, overpowers Ket's rebellion, i, 433; summons the mayor and aldermen to confer with him at his house in Ely Place, 434, 435; leads the government after Somerset's fall, 440; his unpopularity with the City, 445–447; created Duke of Northumberland, 447; supports Lady Jane Grey, 453, 454; committed to the Tower, 455.

—— Thomas, Earl of, rebels against Elizabeth, i, 515.

Norton, William, i, 248.

Norwich, Earl of. *See* Goring.

Nottingham, Charles I sets up his standard at, ii, 169.

Oates, Titus, corroborates existence of a Popish plot, ii, 457; his punishment, 510.

Occasional Conformity Bill passed, ii, 640.

Offley, Thomas, alderman, signs "counterfeit will" of Edward VI, i, 453; performs the duties of sheriff at Dudley's execution, 465; mayor, 478; particulars of, 478 n.

Old Bailey, petition of grand jury at, for Charles II to summon a parliament, ii, 466.

Oldcastle, Sir John, Lord Cobham, proclamation for capture of, i, 249; committed to the Tower, but escapes, 254; is re-captured and executed, 257.

Oliver, John, appointed surveyor for rebuilding the City after the Great Fire, ii, 431.

—— Richard, alderman, a member of the society known as the "Supporters of the Bill of Rights," iii, 87; discharges Miller arrested by Speaker's warrant for printing parliamentary debates, 108; defends his conduct before the House, 109–112; committed to the Tower, 113; a "table" provided for him at the City's expense, 114; regains his liberty, 119; refuses to serve sheriff with Wilkes, 120; gift of plate to, 128; his motion in the House, *re* American Colonies, 161.

O'Neill. *See* Tyrone.

Onslow, Colonel, otherwise "Cocking George," burnt in effigy on Tower Hill, iii, 118.

Ordainers, the, i, 133.

Orleans, siege of, i, 272.

Ormond, James, Marquis of, defeat of his forces near Dublin, ii, 314.

—— James, 2nd Duke of, assists in capturing French fleet in Vigo

Bay, ii, 614; attends thanksgiving service at St. Paul's, 615; commands the English forces in the Netherlands, 645; takes refuge in France to avoid impeachment, iii, 5; assists the Pretender, 6.

Orphans, City, a Court of, established, ii, 543; petition of, for relief, 544; proposal to establish a fund for, 545; City petition to parliament for relief of, 579-581; Act for relief of, 582; the City's gift to the Speaker for procuring passing of the same, 589.

Osborne, Edward, mayor, particulars of, i, 528 n.

Oudenarde, battle of, ii, 629.

Owdeby, John, appointed joint treasurer of subsidy, i, 251.

Oxford, the "lithsmen" of London attend at, for election of king, i, 25; the Provisions of, 89, 91; Christchurch or "Cardinal College" at, 382; deputation sent to Charles I at, ii, 178-180; suspected royalists from, arrive in London, 202; Charles forced to quit, 206; endeavours to return to, 211; siege of, 216; siege abandoned, 219; thanks of the University of, sent to the City, 347.

—— John, Earl of, i, 380.

—— Robert Harley, afterwards Earl of, fails to form a Coalition, ii, 637; forms a Tory ministry, 638; impeached, iii, 5; his trial and discharge, 10, 11; founder of the South Sea Company, 17.

Oxford Arms, the, in Warwick Lane, soldiers quartered in, during Gordon riots, iii, 192.

Pack, Sir Christopher, alderman, his "remonstrance," ii, 348, 349; member of Cromwell's House of Lords, 350.

—— Deputy, sent Commissioner to Fairfax, ii, 248.

Package and Scavage, charter of Edward IV to the City granting the right of, i, 307.

Painters, strike of, in the City, i, 485.

Palatinate, the, the City assists Mansfeld to recover, ii, 89-91. See also Frederick, Elector Palatine.

Palliser, Sir Hugh, his quarrel with Admiral Keppel, iii, 172; his flight from Portsmouth, id.; the king's friendship for, 174.

Palmere, Roger le, i, 134, 153.

Papillon, Thomas, nominated for the shrievalty, ii, 480; declared duly elected, 481; petitions in favour of his election, 485, 486; Pritchard, the mayor, arrested at the suit of, 500; Pritchard obtains damages from, 502; returns to England, 548; deputy governor of the East India Company, 575, 576; M.P. for the City, 598.

Paris, Peace of (1763) iii, 72; (1783) 202; (1814) 287; (1815) 290.

Parish Registers, institution of, i, 403.

Parkhurst, Sir Robert, mayor, ii, 113.

Parkins, Joseph, sheriff, creates a disturbance in Common Hall, iii, 311, his unmannerly conduct, 312-313.

Parliament, the "mad," i, 89; summoned by Simon de Montfort, 97; at Shrewsbury, 118; at Bury St. Edmunds, 126; at the Black Friars, London, 133; at Lincoln, 162; at Northampton, 163; at Salisbury, removed to London, 164; at York, 173; the "good," 205; at Gloucester, 215; the "merciless," 238; allowances to City Members of, 273, 274; at Coventry, 296; the Duke of York's claim to the Crown allowed by, 303; benevolences declared illegal by, 325; at the Blackfriars, 370; at Bridewell, 381; objects to

Queen Mary marrying a foreigner, 460; the Commons entertained in the City, ii, 12; the "addled," 61; supplies granted by, on condition that negotiations be broken off with Spain, 85; the Short, 121; the Long, 132; a guard for, refused by Charles I, 154; attempt to arrest the Five Members, 155-156; orders the bringing in of plate, 168; City petitions for peace laid before, 178; entertained by the City, 198, 234, 312; besieged by reformadoes, 242; petitions of London apprentices to, 251; besieged by apprentices, 254; City's petition to, that the army might be removed further from London, 269, 270; the same for release of recorder and aldermen, 270; the City entrusted with the protection of, 277; City's petition that the king might be allowed to come to London, 282, 283; the Speaker insulted by a member of the City Militia, 285; compliments the citizens on their desire for peace, 286; complains of insufficiency of protection, 292; City's petition for relief from taxation, 331; the Rump dismissed by Cromwell, 337; the Barebones or little, 346; the first under the Protectorate, 348; number of City members, 348 n.; composition of Cromwell's House of Lords, 350; dissolution of second Protectorate, *id.*; the Rump restored, 353; entertained at Grocer's Hall, 356; the Rump ejected by Lambert, *id.*; London apprentices declare for a free parliament, 358; Fleetwood promises a free parliament, 359; the Rump again restored, 362; a deputation from, to the Aldermen, 363; the City demands a full and free parliament, 364; the Rump dissolves the Common Council, 366; Monk demands a full parliament, 368; the excluded members return to, 370; the Long dissolved, and Convention summoned, 373; entertained by the City, 384; the Cavalier parliament, 391, 458; City petition to for pecuniary relief, 447; a series of short parliaments, 458, 460, 462, 463, 465; petitions and addresses to Charles II for summoning, 460, 461, 463, 465, 475; Tory parliament of 1685, 508, 516; the Convention summoned, 538; meets, 539; dissolved, 553; elections (1690) *id.*; the Speaker convicted of bribery, 589-591; election of the first triennial parliament (1695), 598; Election Bill opposed by the City, 601; elections (1698), 606; elections (1701), 609; Statute permitting continuation of, notwithstanding demise of the crown, 611, 612; elections (1705), 621; Act for limiting exportation of corn, 631; elections (1710), 637; Act for building 50 new churches, 639; the Occasional Conformity Act, 639, 640; elections (1715), iii, 4; Septennial Act passed, 9; drastic measures against South Sea Company taken by, 20-21, 23-24; Election Act (11 Geo. i, c. 18), regulating elections in the City, 26-29; the City in favour of repeal of Septennial Act, 48; elections (1747) 56; the National Militia Bill, 57; instructions to City members, 70; declares Luttrell duly elected M.P. for Middlesex, 88; arrest of printers for publishing parliamentary debates, 107, 108; instructions to City members to support Sawbridge and shorter parliaments, 130-132; resolution of Court of Aldermen in favour of short parliaments, 135; City members made to sign undertaking to promote short parliaments, &c., 141, 144, 145; proceedings relative to Wilkes and Middlesex election expunged, 145; extract from Chatham's letter to Lord Temple touching shorter parliaments entered on the City's Journal, 178; elections (1780), 192; steps taken to purge Parliament of contractors, 197-199; the Act for Stamped Receipts, 204; elections (1784), 207-208; the Shop Tax, 209; Pitt's Sedition and Treason Bills, 227; his Additional Force Bill, 257-258; the livery urge Parliamentary Reform, 277-281; the use of the Guildhall refused to reformers, 283; City petitions for Parliamentary Reform, 306-307; parliamentary elections in the City, 309; the passing of the Six Acts, 310; elections (1826), 326; repeal of Corporation and Test Acts, 327; the Catholic Emancipation Bill, 327-328; elections (1830), 329; the first Reform Bill introduced, 332; rejected and Parliament dissolved, 334; Reform Bill again brought in and passed by the Commons, but rejected by the Lords, 335; City's petition to, urging Reform, 340; Reform Bill passed, 343; admission of Jews into, 346-347.

Parma, Duchess of, forbids importation of English wool into Flanders, i, 492-496.

Parsons, Humphrey, M.P. for the City, elected mayor for the second time, iii, 46; vote of thanks to, vetoed by aldermen, 46, 47; dies during his mayoralty, 47.

—— Sir John, mayor, ii, 619.

—— Robert the Jesuit, arrives in England, i, 525; escapes, 528.

Paterson, William, his scheme for a national bank, ii, 584.

"Paul of London" the, barge furnished by the City, i, 204, 205.

Paulet, William. *See* Winchester.

Pecche, John, alderman, deposed, i, 205.

Peel, Sir Robert, the Freedom of the City, voted to, iii, 327; his letter to the lord mayor touching the postponement of the king's visit to the City, 330.

Peers, Sir Charles, alderman, iii, 13.

Pelham, Henry, his ministry, iii, 57.

—— Sir John, executor of Henry IV, i, 270.

Pemberton, Sir Francis, his opinion taken on the question of the aldermanic veto, ii, 454.

Pembroke, Philip, Earl of, ii, 200.

Pennington, Isaac, alderman and M.P. for the City, ii, 102; a loan of £21,000 raised by his constituents, 134; offers the House a guard of citizens, *id.*; informs the House that the City refused to advance money on account of Goodman's reprieve, 136; sent to announce to the citizens the danger that threatened the Commons, 155; elected mayor, 168; orders the City's gates to be repaired, 171; re-elected mayor, 173; lieutenant of the Tower, 210; resigns the lieutenancy, 215; directed to summon a Common Hall for election of a mayor upon suspension of Gayer, 266; placed on the Commission for trial of King Charles, 301; member of the Council of State, 303; proposal to confer the honour of knighthood on, 312.

—— Sir John, his opinion of ships furnished by the City, ii, 102; letter to, from Thomas Wiseman touching the character of a London mob at Westminster, 151.

Perceval, Spencer, becomes Prime

NN

Minister, iii, 271; assassinated, 285.
Percival, Sir John, founds a school at Macclesfield, i, 352.
Percy, Thomas, takes part in the Gunpowder Plot, ii, 14.
Peters, Alice, mistress of Edward III, proceedings against, i, 207, 208; robs her paramour, 211.
Perry, Micaiah, M.P. for the City, opposes Walpole's Excise Bill. iii, 36.
Petitioners, party name of, ii, 460.
Petitions, the City's custom, touching presentation of, ii, 217.
Petyte, John, grocer, M.P. for the City, i, 381.
Pevensey, William I, lands at, i, 30.
Philip, Richard, grocer, i, 284.
Philip II of Spain, marries Mary, i, 469; leaves England, 476; induces Mary to declare war against France, 477; prepares to invade England, 534; the defeat of the Armada, 537–541; prepares another Armada, 559, 560.
Philipot, John, M.P. for the City, i, 202; apologises to the king for the City's attitude towards John of Gaunt, 210; waits upon Richard II at Kennington, 212; appointed joint treasurer of Parliamentary subsidy, 214; removed, 215; his expedition against pirates, id.; opposes the Duke of Lancaster, id.; subscribes to fund for winning back the nobility to the City, 216; knighted, 220; resigns or is deprived of his aldermanry, 223.
Philippa of Hainault, her marriage with Edward III, i, 171.
Philips, Sir Thomas, ii, 33.
Picard, Sir Henry, mayor, his banquet to four kings, i, 200.
Pickett, William, lord mayor, endeavours to obtain the removal of the Bank of England guard, iii, 218.

Pilgrimage of Grace, the, i, 394.
Pilkington, Thomas, M.P. for the City, ii, 458, 464, 538; empanels a jury favourable to Shaftesbury, 468; elected sheriff, 473; leader of the Whigs in the City, 478; the Duke of York's action against, 478, 492; committed to the Tower, 480; called to account for his conduct in the election of sheriffs, 487; fined, 493; elected mayor, 547; re-elected, 551; again stands for the City, 553; again elected mayor, 555.
Pindar, Paul, refuses to pay tax for maintenance of parliamentary army, ii, 181.
Pitt, William, afterwards Earl of Chatham, protests against the importation of mercenaries, iii, 58; opposes a proposed tax on plate, id; takes the lead on resignation of Newcastle, 60; dismissed, 61; the freedom of the City conferred on, 61, 62; his coalition with Newcastle, 62; subscribes to bounties for soldiers, 64; expresses delight at City's address on conquest of Canada, id; Blackfriars Bridge named after, 65; resignation of, 67; his letter to Alderman Beckford, id; City's vote of thanks to, 68; his acknowledgment, 69; attends lord mayor's banquet, id; his indignation at the conclusion of the Peace of Paris, 73; recalled to power and created Earl of Chatham, 79; introduces an East India Bill, id; recommends Beckford to make no attempt to "fix" Rockingham, 99; his eulogy of Beckford's speech, 102; the City's thanks to, 103; his opinion touching shorter parliaments, id; upholds the conduct of Crosby and Oliver in discharging printers arrested for printing parliamentary debates,

114; advises conciliatory measures towards America, 149, 150; receives the thanks of Common Council and the livery, 150, 152; his last speech in parliament, 168-170; his death and funeral, 170-171; his monument in the Guildhall, 171; extract from his letter to Lord Temple touching shorter parliaments entered in the City's Journal, 178.

Pitt, William, the younger, advocates economical and parliamentary reform, iii, 198-199; his struggle with the Coalition, 206; the freedom of the City and of the Grocers' Company conferred on, 207; returned M.P. for Cambridge, *id.*; his East India Bill, 208; his last attempt to carry parliamentary reform, 209; his Regency Bill, 213; imposes excise tax on tobacco, 216; his Loyalty Loan, 228-230; his letter to the lord mayor asking the City to subscribe, 229; his subsidies to the emperor, 231; mobbed in the City, 234-235; his income tax Bill, 238; resigns, 247; again takes office, 254; his difficulty in forming a ministry, 255; his Additional Force Bill, 257; his death, 263; his funeral and monument, 264.

Piwelesdon, or Puleston, Thomas de, accused of meditating a wholesale massacre in the City, i, 99.

Plague, the Black Death, i, 194, the sweating sickness, 326-327, 360; divers visitations of, 365, 407, 521; proposal to build a pest-house in the City, 551; (of 1603), ii, 3-5; (of 1625), 95; (of 1665), 409-414.

Player, Colonel, ii, 249.

—— Sir Thomas, chamberlain, M.P. for the City, ii, 458, 464; fined for creating a disturbance in the Common Hall, 493.

Plomer, William, elected sheriff but pays fine, iii, 138.

Plow-Monday, entertainment of lord mayor's household on, i, 418n.

Plumbe, Samuel, alderman, stands for the shrievalty, iii, 138; ordered to be disfranchised for refusing to obey lord mayor's precept, 139.

Plumbe's case, touching the jurisdiction of the Court of Aldermen over the livery companies, iii, 138-139.

Plymouth, appeals to London for relief, ii, 220.

Poitiers, battle of, i, 197.

Poll Tax (of 1379), i, 217; (of 1380), 218; established for disbanding the armies, ii, 139.

Pont de l'Arche, expected fall of, i, 263.

Pontoise, surrender of, i, 264.

Poor, the, weekly collections for, at St. Paul's Cross, i, 404; the house of, in West Smithfield, 417, 449; a brotherhood established in the City for relief of, 449; royal gift for relief of, iii, 214.

Poor debtors, Royal gifts for relief of, iii, 3, 33.

Popham, Sir Home, a vote of thanks to, for recapture of Cape of Good Hope, refused, iii, 265; for capture of Buenos Ayres, 266; a sword of honour voted to, *id.*

Popish Plots, ii, 6, 13, 134, 456-458.

Porter, Sir William Beauchamp, M.P. for Middlesex, iii, 81.

Portland, Duke of, prime minister, iii, 204; joins Pitt's administration, 225; his letter to the lord mayor offering military assistance during bread riots, 244; a slight passed on the lord mayor's authority by, 246; succeeds Lord Grenville as prime minister, 267; resigns, 271.

Porto Bello, capture of, iii, 44.

Portreeve, office of, i, 35; title of, changed to mayor, 64.
Postal System, attempt by City to establish a, ii, 322, 323.
Poter, Walter le, elected sheriff, i, 104; builds the chapter-house of the Grey Friars, 402.
Powis, Lord, i, 380.
Prat, "Mr.," king's commissioner for surveying the City after the Fire, ii, 431.
Pratt, chief justice, afterwards Lord Camden, discharges Wilkes, iii, 74; the Freedom of the City voted to, 78; his portrait in the Art Gallery, *id.*
Press Warrants, counsel's opinion as to legality of, iii, 107; refusal of Sawbridge and Hallifax to back, 166.
Preston, Lord, at the head of a Jacobite plot, ii, 562.
Preston Pans, Sir John Cope defeated at, iii, 51.
Price, Dr. Richard, the Freedom of the City voted to, iii, 165.
Pride, Colonel, purges the House of Commons, ii, 294; elected common councilman, 319; opposed to Cromwell assuming regal estate, 349; member of Cromwell's House of Lords, 350.
Priour, John, the younger, M.P. for the City, i, 174.
Pritchard, Sir William, elected mayor, ii, 490-492; arrested at the suit of Papillon and Du Bois, 500, 501; recovers damages against Papillon, 502; M.P. for the City, 509, 554, 613; stands for the City but is unsuccessful, 599.
Proby, Peter, sheriff, ii, 63; sent commissioner to Ireland, 64.
Prynne, enters London in triumph, ii, 134.
Puiset or Pudsey, Hugh de, Bishop of Durham, i, 61.
Pullison, Sir Thomas, mayor, his precept for raising volunteers for the low countries, i, 530; appointed jointly with Sir Wolstan Dixie to see that the price of provisions in the City was not enhanced, 541.
Pulteney, Sir John de, leader of the City's forces against Scotland, i, 180; gift to, for services in, obtaining City's charter, 181; taken into custody by order of the king, 187.
Purveyance, attempt to abolish, ii, 9.
Pym, John, supported by the Common Council, ii, 152; refuses to "discontent" the citizens, 153; one of the Five Members, 155; attends Common Hall and hears the king's reply to City deputation sent to Oxford, 180; accompanies a Parliamentary deputation to the Common Council, 184, 185.

Quebec, capture of, iii, 64.
Quebec Bill, the, iii, 142.
Quiney, Lieut.-Col., assaults Alderman Cornish in the Guildhall, ii, 489.
Quo Warranto, writ of, proceedings against the City under, ii, 476, 477, 478, 494-500; judgment entered, 503-504; reversal of judgment on, 541, 542, 543, 554-555.

Radyngton, Sir Baldwin de, warden of the City, i, 242.
Rainton or Raynton, Sir Nicholas, sent to prison by Charles I, ii, 123; released, 125; summons a Common Hall for election of mayor, 168.
Raleigh, Sir Walter, his expedition against Spain, i, 551.
Ramillies, battle of, ii, 622; Standards captured at, set up in the Guildhall, 623.
Rawlinson, Sir Thomas, mayor, ii, 623.

INDEX.

Ray, Daniel, whipt for insulting the Spanish ambassador, ii, 81.

Raymond, Sir Jonathan, a candidate for the mayoralty, ii, 547, 555.

Reading, taken by Essex, ii, 188; in the hands of the royalists, 196.

Recorder of London, the, customs of the City recorded by mouth of, i, 145.

Recusants, laws against, i, 525, 526.

"Redbridge," the ship, stoppage of, ii, 578-579.

Rede, Richard, alderman, sent to the war in Scotland for opposing benevolence, and taken prisoner, i, 411.

Refham, Richer de, mayor, obtains a confirmation of the City's liberties, i, 134-135; removed from mayoralty and aldermanry, 135, 136.

Reformadoes, City petition for removal of, ii, 250.

Reform Bill, the first, introduced, 332; approved by the City, 333; withdrawn, 334; again brought in and passed by the Commons but thrown out by the Lords, 335; City addresses on its rejection, 336-337; agitation in the country, 337-338; again brought in and passed, 343; the rights of the livery of London reserved, *id*; entertainment at the Guildhall to commemorate the passing of, 344.

Regency Bill, the, iii, 282.

Reynardson, Abraham, elected mayor, ii, 297; at variance with the Common Council, 299, 376; deposed from the mayoralty and sent to the Tower, 308; restored to his aldermanry, 383; re-elected mayor and declines office, 384.

Reynold, Robert, i, 422.

—— William, i, 284.

Reynolds, Father, executed, i, 392.

—— John, attorney, and election agent for Wilkes, iii, 100, 143, 146, 147.

Reynolds, Sir Joshua, his portrait of Chief Justice Pratt, iii, 78.

Rich, Sir Peter, a candidate for the shrievalty, ii, 486; elected, 487; sworn in, 488; M.P. for the City, 509; chamberlain, 538, 555.

—— Sir Thomas, alderman, ii, 396.

Richard I, his accession, i, 61; appoints Longchamp chancellor during his absence, *id.*; his charters to the City, 68, 71; returns to England, 68; crowned a second time, 69; his death, 71.

Richard II, the "Londoners' King," i, 212; charter of, forbidding foreigners to trade by retail, 214; another charter of, 224, 225; meditates an attempt upon the life of his uncle the Duke of Gloucester, 232; a commission of Regency appointed, 233; applies to the City for aid, *id.*; compelled to submit to Parliament, 234; deposed, 245; doubtful reports as to his death, 247.

Richard, Duke of Gloucester, afterwards Richard III, appointed Protector, i, 320; his schemes for obtaining the crown, 320-322; crowned, 323; bold speech of Londoners to, 325; escorted by citizens from Kensington to the City, 326; defeated at Bosworth, *id*.

Richard, King of the Romans, his manor of Isleworth devastated, i, 96; brought prisoner to the Tower, *id*.

Richmond Park, presented to the City, ii, 313; restored to Charles II, 381.

Ridley, Nicholas, bishop of Rochester, translated to London, i, 440; his letter of gratitude to Sir Richard Dobbs, mayor, 450; sent to the Tower, 458; burnt at Oxford, 474.

"Riffleres," street ruffians called, i, 135; ii, 646.
Riot Act, the, passed, iii, 7.
Ripon, treaty of, ii, 131; negotiations removed to London, 135.
Roberts, William, nominated sheriff by mayor's prerogative, ii, 471.
Robinson, "Jack," iii, 121.
—— Sir John, mayor, ii, 401.
—— Sir Leonard, elected chamberlain, ii, 565; knighted, 571.
Roche, Sir William, alderman, M.P. for the City, i, 370; committed to prison, 412.
Rochelle, expeditions for relief of, i, 204; ii, 103, 107.
Rochester, besieged by King John, i, 78; by the Barons, 96.
Rochford, Sir Thomas Boleyn, Lord, i, 380.
Rockingham, Lord, attends Beckford's famous entertainment, iii, 99; succeeds Lord North as prime minister, 197.
Rodney, Admiral, defeats the French fleet in the West Indies, iii, 199-200; entertained in the City, 200.
Rogers, John, burnt for heresy, i, 473, 474.
Rokesle or Rokesley, Gregory de, opposes Walter Hervy, i, 108; goes to Paris to confer with King Edward I, 116; again sets out for France, 117; master of the Exchange, 118; sent with a gift of money to the king, *id.*; member for the City, *id.*; declines to attend the king's justiciars, 120; builds the dormitory of the Grey Friars, 402.
Rooke, Sir George, encounters the French fleet in Lagos Bay, ii, 572; captures French fleet in Vigo Bay, 614.
"Roreres," street ruffians called, i, 135; ii, 646.
Rose, Miles, i, 361.
Rothschild, Baron Lionel, M.P. for the City, iii, 347; founds a scholarship in City of London School, *id.*
Rouen, siege of, by Henry V, i, 263.
Rowe, Owen, Colonel, made chairman of the Common Council, ii, 299; placed on commission for trial of Charles I, 302.
—— Thomas, mayor, particulars of, i, 511 n.
Rowley, John, the City's agent in Ulster, ii, 32.
Rowton Heath, Charles I defeated at, ii, 222.
Royal Contract, ii, 104.
Royal Exchange, the, building of, i, 494–499; insurance business carried on at, 499; music and football played in, 501; Royal arms removed from, ii, 330; again set up in, 374; statue of Queen Anne in, 611; the firing of guns under piazza, forbidden, iii, 2.
"Royal George," the, sunk off Spithead, iii, 200.
Rump, the, expelled by Cromwell, ii, 337; restored, 353; ejected by Lambert, 356; again restored, 362; dissolved, 373.
Rupert, Prince, expected in London, ii, 172; before Bristol, 184, 186.
Russell, Lord, i, 435.
—— Lord John, moves for repeal of Corporation and Test Acts, iii, 327.
—— Thomas, draper, his school at Barton-under-Needwood, co. Stafford, i, 353, 354.
—— Sir William, stands for the City, ii, 599.
Rutland, Edward, Earl of, attainted, i, 296.
—— Roger, Earl of, committed to the Tower for complicity in the Essex rebellion, i, 562.
Rye House Plot, the, discovery of, ii, 502; Burton outlawed for being concerned in, 515; Elizabeth

INDEX.

Gaunt burnt for being concerned in, *id.*
Ryswick, peace of, ii, 603.
Ryvers, Richard, Lord, i, 289.

Sacheverell, Dr., sermon preached by, ii, 631; impeached, 633; trial of, 634; obtains the living of St. Andrew's, Holborn, 648.
Sackville, Lord George, afterwards Lord George Germaine, his conduct at Minden as compared with that of Lord Effingham, iii, 161.
—— Sir Richard, i, 461.
Sadler, John, town clerk, removed, ii, 382.
St. Albans, the first battle of, i, 291; the second, 304.
St. Bartholomew, priory and Hospital of, the priory suppressed, i, 398; the master bound to keep the obit of the mayor and aldermen, 401; re-established, 409; the hospital vested in the City, 417; governors of, appointed, 449.
St. Clare, abbey of, called the Minories, injured by fire, i, 402.
St. Dunstan, East, insult offered to the mass in church of, i, 423.
St. Ewen, or Ewin, destroyed at the reformation, i, 428.
St. Helen's without Bishopsgate, priory of, suppressed, i, 400; the nun's chapel of, given to Sir Richard Williams, 401; the refectory of, converted into hall of the Leathersellers, *id.*
St. James, Garlickhithe, parish registers of, i, 403.
St. John, Henry. *See* Bolingbroke.
St. Martin Orgar, insult offered to the mass in church of, i, 423.
St. Mary without Bishopsgate, priory and hospital of, suppressed, i, 398. *See also* Bethlehem.
St. Mary Bothaw, parish registers of, i, 403.

St. Mary le Bow, its roof blown off, i, 39.
St. Mary Woolnoth, insult offered to the mass in church of, i, 423.
St. Nicholas Shambles, church destroyed at the Reformation, i, 428.
St. Paul's, Church of, founded by Ethelbert, i, 9; Alphage, Archbishop of Canterbury buried in, 19; Ethelred II buried in, 22; a gemót held in, 28; destroyed by fire (1087), 38; meeting of the barons and citizens in, 63, 72; Richard I returns thanks in, 68; Edward I seizes £2,000 found in, 125; a tablet set up by Earl of Lancaster in, 153; the treasure in, carried off by the mob, 158; Richard, Duke of York, swears allegiance to King Henry VI in, 288; a general reconciliation solemnized in, 294; the bodies of Warwick and Montagu killed at Barnet, exposed in, 315; Henry VI lies in state in, 316; the standards taken at Bosworth, deposited in, 326; the Earl of Warwick exhibited as a prisoner in, 328; marriage of Prince Arthur and Catherine of Aragon in, 336; the corpse of Henry VII brought to, 341; "children" of, 350; solemn thanksgiving in, for pregnancy of Catherine of Aragon, 354; Henry VIII and French Ambassadors at, on occasion of betrothal of the Princess Mary with the Dauphin, 362; the King and Queen of Denmark attend mass in, 371, 372; *Te Deum* celebrated in, for capture of French King at Pavia, 374; Convocation at, presided over by Thomas Cromwell, 396; solemn procession to, for health of Jane Seymour and infant prince, 396-397; obit of Jane Seymour celebrated in, 397; removal of images from, 427; the charnel house in

churchyard removed, *id.*; the cloister in Pardon churchyard destroyed, *id.*; Cranmer conducts service in, 431; order against cattle being led through, 471; the Lollards Tower at, a prison for heretics, 475; restoration of, *temp.* Elizabeth, 492; lease by the Dean and Chapter to the City, of the Manor of Finsbury, 493; the first public lottery drawn at west door of, 508; thanksgiving service at, for defeat of Turkish fleet at Lepanto, 517; the same for defeat of Armada, 543; state visit of James I to, ii, 76; riots in, 174; thanksgiving service for victory over the Dutch, 345; for peace of Ryswick, 606; for victories of Marlborough, 614, 615, 616, 621, 624; for peace of Utrecht, 647; for peaceful accession of George I, iii, 3-4; for suppression of Jacobite rebellion, 9; soldiers quartered in, during Gordon riots, 192; thanksgiving service for recovery of George III, 215; the same for naval victories of Howe, Jervis and Duncan, 234; Nelson's funeral in, 261; thanksgiving service for the Jubilee of George III in, 272; Queen Caroline attends service in, 319.

St. Paul's Cross, Dr. Shaw's sermon at, i, 320, 321; collections for the poor made every Sunday at, 404; recantation of Dr. Crome at, 414; sermon of Bonner against the King's supremacy preached at, 438; sermon preached by Hooper at, 439; Dr. Bourne's sermon at, 458; sermon by Bishop Gardiner's chaplain, at, 459; sermon by Dyos at, inveighing against the City, 527.

St. Paul's school, foundation of, by Dean Colet, i, 350-352.

St. Peter, Cornhill, the advowson of church of, conveyed to the City, i, 253.

St. Thomas of Acon, hospital of, suppressed, i, 398.

St. Thomas's hospital, suppressed, i, 398; purchased by the City, 449, 450.

Salamanca, battle of, iii, 286.

Salomons, David, the first Jew admitted to municipal offices, iii, 346, 347; founds a scholarship in City of London school, 347.

Salisbury, Richard, Earl of, enters the City with Richard, Duke of York, i, 290; defeats lord Audley at Blore Heath and crosses to Calais, 295, 296; attainted, 296; returns from Calais and marches to London, 298, 299.

—— William of, i, 84.

Sampson, David, whipt for insulting the Spanish ambassador, ii, 80.

Sandwich, John, Earl of, otherwise "Jemmy Twitcher," produces Wilkes's *Essay on Woman* before parliament, iii, 77; burnt in effigy on Tower Hill, 118.

—— Ralph de, warden of the City, i, 122.

Sauterie, Joan, wife of John, tried for speaking against the sacrament, i, 415.

Sautre, William, burnt for heresy, i, 250.

Savile, Sir George, his Act in favour of Roman Catholics, iii, 179; his house in Leicester fields sacked by Gordon rioters, 181.

Savoy, the, sacked by the mob, i, 218.

Sawbridge, Jacob, director of South Sea Company, expelled from parliament, iii, 20.

—— John, alderman, iii, 20; a member of the society known as the "Supporters of the Bill of Rights," 87; elected sheriff, 88; *Junius* urges his candidature for the mayoralty, 125; Wilkes's opinion of, 126; stands for the mayoralty, 127; elected M.P. for the City, 145; succeeds Wilkes in the mayoralty, 161; supports Oliver's motion in the House *re* war with America, *id.*; his refusal to back press warrants, 166; loses his seat in parliament but recovers it, 192.

Sawyer, Sir Robert, attorney-general, his speech in proceedings under writ of *Quo Warranto*, ii, 496, 497.

Say, James Fiennes, Lord, executed, i, 285.

Sayre, or Sayer, Stephen, elected sheriff, iii, 138; committed to the Tower for a supposed conspiracy, 160, 161.

Scales, Thomas, Lord, leads the citizens against Cade, i, 285; holds the Tower for King Henry VI, 300; endeavours to take sanctuary at Westminster, seized and murdered, 302.

Scawen, Sir Thomas, elected M.P. for the City, iii, 4.

—— Sir William, subscribes to loan to prince Eugene, ii, 624.

Schools, founded by citizens of London, i, 349-354.

"Scot," definition of payment of, iii, 15, 26, 29.

Scotland, rebellion of under Wallace, i, 129; renewal of war with, 140; Edward III takes the field against the Scots, 161; peace with, 163; preparations for war with, 179; England invaded by Scots, 372; proposed union with England, ii, 8; disorders in, 119; Scottish commissioners in London, 135; "friendly assistance" granted to the Scots, 140; Scottish commissioners attend the Common Council, 228; the union with, 625-626.

Scott, Sir John, ii, 640.

Scottish army, prepares to march southward, ii, 219, 222; offer to withdraw on terms, 238; news of a fresh army being raised, 274; defeated at Dunbar, 328; enters England, 338; defeated at Worcester, 341.

Scrop, Geoffrey le, the king's sergeant pleader at the Iter of 1321, i, 144.

Seberht, "sub-king" of London, i, 9; founder of Westminster Abbey, *id.*

Self-denying ordinance, the, ii, 214.

Semer, or Seymer, Thomas, opposition to his election as mayor, i, 359, 360; M.P. for the City, 381.

Senlac, battle of. *See* Hastings.

Serle, William, chamberlain to Richard II, execution of, i, 247.

Sevenoke, William, grocer, appointed commissioner to enquire into cases of treason, &c., in the City, i, 269; his grammar school, 353.

Seymour, Lord Henry, joins the fleet against the Spanish Armada, i, 538.

Shadworth, John, sheriff, i, 240; committed to prison, 241, 242.

Shaftesbury, Earl of, one of the suggesters of the closing of the Exchequer, ii, 444; proceedings against, 468.

Shakespeare, John, stands for the mayoralty, iii, 132, 133.

"Shannon," the, defeats the "Chesapeake," iii, 286, 287.

Sharplisse, or Sharplys, Thomas, wins chief prize in Virginia lottery, ii, 49.

Shaw, or Shaa, Sir Edmund, mayor, i, 320.

Shaw, Dr., his sermon at Paul's Cross, in avour of Gloucester, i, 320.

—— Henry, granted the right to

bring water from Fogwell Pond, ii, 20.
Sheerness, a City loan for fortifying, ii, 437.
Shelburne, Lord, letter from the City to, touching the Wiltshire Committee of Association, iii, 176, 177; his reply, 177; appointed secretary of state under Rockingham, 197; instructs the lord mayor to place the City Militia on a proper footing, 199; gives place to a coalition ministry, 204.
Shelley, William, Recorder of London, elected M.P. for the City, i, 370.
Shepheard, Samuel, M.P. for the City, ii, 622n.
Ship Money, demand for, ii, 111-115, 117, 125.
Shore, Jane, mistress of Edward IV, i, 321.
Shorter, Sir John, attends the presentation of an address to Charles II, ii, 475; nominated for the mayoralty, 476; appointed mayor by James II, 523.
Shrewsbury, Charles, Earl of, signs the invitation to the Prince of Orange, ii, 529.
—— Francis, Earl of, joins the lords against Somerset, i, 437.
—— George, Earl of, i, 380.
Shute, Samuel, as sheriff, empanels a jury favourable to Shaftesbury, ii, 468; elected sheriff, 473; committed to the Tower, 480; called to account for his conduct in the election of sheriffs, 487; fined, 493.
Sidney, Sir Philip, his death, i, 532;
—— Sir William, the Great Beam conveyed to him by Henry VIII, i, 387.
Simnel, Lambert, insurrection of, i, 328.
Six Acts, the, iii, 310.
Six Articles, the, i, 415, 422.

Skinners of London, contribute to a gift of £500 to the King, i, 201; return of rental of, 252, the Solemn Engagement signed at the hall of, ii, 252.
Skippon, Philip, in command of the City forces, ii, 161; attempts to win the garrison of the Tower, 162; refuses to obey the king's orders to go to York, 166; ordered to view the City for the purpose of defence, 171; appointed Sergeant-major-general under Essex, 176; makes terms with the royalist army, 211; wounded at Naseby, 219; City petition to parliament that he might be placed in command of City forces, 276; the protection of parliament confided to, 278; City opposes secret enlistments by, 287-288; appointed member of Council of State, 303; invited to dinner by the City, 328; member of Cromwell's House of Lords, 350.
Slaney, Sir Stephen, mayor, i, 555.
Slave Trade, the City's efforts to abolish, iii, 212-213, 288-290.
Slingsby, Captain, his account of King Charles's visit to the Guildhall to demand the arrest of the Five Members, ii, 157.
Sluys, battle of, i, 186.
Smith, Benjamin, a letter addressed to, miscarries, iii, 121.
—— Sir Clement, i, 424.
—— Sir Sidney, a sword of honour voted to, for raising the siege of Acre, iii, 238-239; the thanks of the City voted to, 248.
—— Thomas, sheriff, deprived of his office for complicity in the Essex rebellion, i, 562.
—— Sir Thomas, actively engages in promoting colony of Virginia, ii, 51, 54, 55.
Smithes, George, alderman, sent to view the Ulster plantation, ii, 42.

Smithfield, confirmation by Edward IV of City's right to tolls at, i, 308.
Smyth, Richard, carpenter, convicted of perjury, i, 343.
Soame, Sir Thomas, ii, 155, 237; committed to prison by Charles I, 123; released, 125; a candidate for the mayoralty, 130; deprived of his aldermanry, for not attending proclamation of Commonwealth, 311, 312; restored, 383.
Solemn Engagement of the City, signed, ii, 252.
Solemn League and Covenant, the, ii, 202.
Somerset, Edmund Beaufort, Count of Mortain, Duke of, raises the siege of Calais, i, 280; his rivalry with Richard, Duke of York, 286; arrested, *id.*; released and appointed captain of Calais, 287; killed at St. Albans, 291.
—— Edward, Duke of, appointed Protector, i, 420; his fall, 433–437; committed to the Tower, 438; liberated, 440; again arrested, 447; his trial and execution, 447–449; his widow released from the Tower by Queen Mary, 457.
—— Henry, Duke of, refused admission into the City, i, 294.
—— Robert Carr, Earl of, marriage of, ii, 61.
Somerset House, built, i, 427.
Southampton, Henry, Earl of, committed to the Tower for complicity in the Essex rebellion, i, 562.
South Sea Bubble, the, iii, 17–24.
Southwark, William I sets fire to, i, 32; charter of Edward IV confirming the City's jurisdiction over, 308; the City's difficulty in exercising its rights over, 441; the king's rights in, granted to the City by Edward VI, 442; the establishment of the ward of Bridge Without, 443–445; the borough desires incorporation with the City, ii, 324–326; prays the king to dissolve Parliament, 466.
Spa Fields, the lord mayor's account of the riot in, iii, 299–305.
Spain, Spanish vessels seized, i, 508; treasure melted down and goods sold, 512, 514; City courts closed to Spanish suitors, 513; claims between England and Spain referred to arbitration, 514; another breach with, 528; the defeat of the Armada, 534–543; search in the City for Spanish emissaries, 549, 550; ships furnished by the City, against, 552; the Spanish ambassador insulted, ii, 79; the City's opposition to the Spanish convention, iii, 41, 42; war declared with, 43; the mayor objects to taking part in the proclamation of the war, *id.*; the secret clause in the Family Compact, 67; war declared against, 72; joins France and America against England, 174; seeks the assistance of England against Napoleon, 268; supported by the City of London, *id.*
Spencer, Sir John, mayor, committed to the Fleet, i, 553; his daughter married to Lord Compton, *id.*; his "doggednes," 554; refuses to pay his quota towards Irish Estate, ii, 39.
Springham, Matthias, merchant-taylor, sent commissioner to Ireland, ii, 42, 64.
Spurs, battle of, i, 347.
Stable, Adam, mayor, removed, i, 211.
Stafford, Thomas, seizes the castle of Scarborough, i, 477.
—— William, Lord, execution of, ii, 462.
Stamp Act, enforcing stamped receipts for money, iii, 204.
—— —— Grenville's, iii, 142.
Stampe, Thomas, a candidate for the mayoralty, ii, 547.

"Standard wheaten bread" its use encouraged in time of scarcity, iii, 225.

Stanhope, Charles, implicated in the South Sea Company, iii, 21.

Stanier, Sir Samuel, mayor, unsuccessfully contests the City, ii, 628; candidate for aldermanry of Broad Street Ward, 640; letter from Queen Anne to, 648.

Staples, the, established in England, i, 171; the City opposed to removal of, to the continent, 174; temporarily abolished, 177.

Stapleton, Walter, Bishop of Exeter and king's treasurer. new weights and measures issued by, i, 146, 147; murdered, 156–157.

Staundon, William, appointed *locum tenens* during absence of mayor, i, 241.

Steele, William, recorder, appointment of, ii, 316; proposal to send him to Ireland, 348.

—— William, his opinion touching aldermanic veto, 454, 455.

Steelyard. the, merchants of, i, 22, 23, ; closed by order of Queen Elizabeth, 565.

Stephen, elected king by the City of London, i, 44, 45; his coronation, 46; made prisoner at Lincoln, 47; released, 52; crowned a second time, *id.;* makes peace with Henry, 54.

Stewart, Sir William, mayor, iii, 25.

Stillingfleet, Dr., preaches in the Guildhall chapel, ii, 525.

Stocker, William, mayor, dies of the sweating sickness, i, 327.

Stokker, John, Common Hunt, i, 332.

Stokton, Henry, fishmonger, convicted of perjury, i, 343.

—— John, mayor, his cautious policy, i, 313; knighted, 316.

Stormont, Lord, secretary of state, urges the mayor to preserve the peace in the City during Gordon riots, iii, 180, 181–182; orders the guards in the Tower to assist the mayor, 182, 183.

Stow-on-the-wold, defeat of the royalists at, ii, 233.

Strafford, Thomas, Earl of, his attitude towards the City, ii, 132; ordered into custody, 133; trial and execution of, 137.

Stratford, the bakers of, i, 379, 414.

—— John de, Bishop of Winchester, made free of the City, i, 158; instigates the citizens to join the Earl of Lancaster in revolt, 164.

"Straw," Jack, rebellion under leadership of, i, 219; his confession, 220; his death, 221.

Strode. William, one of the Five Members, ii, 155.

Stuart, Arabella, the Bye Plot in favour of, ii, 7.

Succession, Act of, passed i, 389; proceedings against those refusing to subscribe to, 390.

Suckley, Henry, committed to the Tower for obstructing the sergeant-at-mace, i, 406–407.

Sudbury, Simon de, Archbishop of Canterbury, beheaded on Tower Hill, i, 219.

Suetonius, the Roman general, leaves London to its fate, i, 4.

Suffolk, Charles, Duke of, attends lord mayor's banquet, i, 380; his mansion known as Southwark Place, 439, 442,

—— Michael, Earl of, sent by Richard II to the City to ask for support, i, 233; charged with treason, 234.

—— William, Earl of, effects a truce with France, i, 281; murdered, 282.

Sunderland, Charles Spencer, Earl of, dismissed from office, ii, 637; resigns, iii, 21.

Supremacy, Act of, i, 392; Elizabethan Act of, 486.

INDEX.

Swanlonde, Simon de, mayor, summoned to attend the king at Woodstock, i, 178.
Sweyn, attacks London, i, 19; his death, *id.*
Swinnerton, John, alderman, i, 399, 400; mayor, ii, 59, 60, 66.
Sword-blade Company, the, iii, 20, 21.
Symond, John, recorder, i, 274.
Sympson, William, fuller, convicted of perjury, i, 343;

Taillour, Philip le, elected sheriff, i, 104; candidate for the mayoralty, 105.
Talliage, the citizens of London resist exaction of, i, 139.
Taunton co. Somerset, the parliamentary army at, ii, 216, 217.
Taxation, of parishes, i, 203.
Tayllour, William, alderman, imprisoned, i, 295; mayor, entrusted with the custody of jewels pledged by the Earl of Warwick, 310, 311.
Taylor, Richard, punished for insulting the Spanish ambassador, ii, 81.
Temple, Earl, withdraws from the ministry, iii, 67; visits Wilkes in the Tower, 74.
Temple, the, treasure lying at, seized for the king, i, 94; affray between citizens and Templars, 295; the lord mayor's claim of jurisdiction within, ii, 440-443.
Test Act, passed, ii, 446; a new, 458; attempt to obtain repeal of, frustrated by Walpole, iii, 34, 35; repeal of, 326-327.
Tewkesbury, battle of, i, 314.
Thames, the, its sweet water, i, 1; wears to be removed from, 71; precautions taken for guarding, against foreign invasion, 182, 183; a bridge proposed at Gravesend, as a defence against Spanish fleet, 560.

Theobalds co. Herts, mansion house of Sir Robert Cecil, ii, 2, 3, 23.
Thirty Years War, the, beginning of, ii, 73.
Thompson, Sir Samuel, sheriff, ii, 530.
—— William, alderman, M.P. for the City, ii, 392.
Throckmorton, Nicholas, trial of, at Guildhall, i, 468.
Tichborne, Robert, alderman, explains to Parliament proceedings of Common Council (13 Jan. 1649) ii, 300; placed on commission for trial of Charles I, 302; despatched to the fleet with money for relief of seamen wounded in Dutch war, 345; member of Cromwell's house of lords, 350.
Tilbury, camp formed at, i, 535, 545.
Tillyngton, Roger, skinner, i, 264.
Tithes, disputes touching, i, 383-386.
Toleration, petition against, ii, 227.
Tomkins, Thomas, burnt, i, 474.
Tomson, Richard, his account of the Armada, i, 537, 539-540.
Tonge, Dr., rector of St. Michael, Wood Street, spreads report of a Popish plot, ii, 457.
Tonnage and Poundage, the king's claim to, ii, 108.
Tothill Fields, muster of City archers in, i, 191.
Tory, origin of the name of, ii, 460.
Tournay, siege of, by Edward III, i, 187; captured by Henry VIII, 347; reduced by Marlborough, ii, 630.
Tower, the, strengthened by William II, i, 39; the Iter of 1285 at, 120-122; the Iter of 1321 at, 143-148; the Iter of 1341 at, 187-188; held by Lord Scales and others for King Henry VI, 300, 301; surrendered to the Yorkists, 302; lost to Edward IV, 312; the young Princes lodged in, 320.

Townshend, Charles, secretary of state, thanks the lord mayor for stopping the spread of seditious literature, iii, 3; informs the lord mayor of Jacobite conspiracies, 6, 24; the Freedom of the City voted to, 79.
—— James, a member of the Society known as the "Supporters of the Bill of Rights," iii, 87; elected sheriff, 88; applies at court to know the king's pleasure touching receiving a remonstrance, 94–96; his speech to the king, 96, 97; stands for the mayoralty, 127; elected mayor, 132.
Tradesmen, Corporation of, ii, 117.
Trafalgar, battle of, iii, 260.
Trained Bands, their formation, ii, 64–67; called out, 120, 153; placed under command of Skippon, 161; review of, in Finsbury Fields, 166; twelve companies of, prepared to join Parliamentary Army, 173; their conduct at Edge-Hill, 175; at Newbury, 195; assist in recovery of Reading, 196; disaffection among the, 197, 206–207; sent to assist Waller in preventing the king's return to Oxford, 211; ineffectual attempt to call out the, 246, 247; the officers of, petition Parliament for a personal treaty with the king, 283; their want of discipline, 296; a muster of, in Finsbury Fields, 340, 341; new officers of, nominated, 361, 364; review of, in Hyde Park, 569. *See also* London, City Forces, and Militia.
Treasonable Engagement, the, ii, 345, 346.
Treby, Sir George, recorder, his speech in proceedings under writ of *Quo Warranto*, ii, 495; removed by Charles I, 504; restored, 531; welcomes the Prince of Orange, 537; lays before the Common Council letters seized on board a ship at Liverpool, 550, 551; made chief justice, ii, 570; intercedes for the officer who had allowed an insult to be offered to Alderman Ward, iii, 17.
Trecothick, Barlow, succeeds Beckford in the mayoralty, iii, 106; offends Wilkes by backing press warrants, *id*.
Tressilian, Chief Justice, charged with treason, i, 234; hanged, 238.
Tresswell, Robert, painter-stainer, ii, 32.
Trevillian, John, i, 283.
Trevor, Sir John, Speaker, accused of, corrupt practices, and expelled the House, ii, 589–591.
Tromp, Admiral, defeated off Portland, ii, 344.
Troyes, treaty of, i, 265.
"Trumpington" Conspiracy, the, i, 247.
Trussel, Sir William, in command of City ships of war, i, 183.
Tulse, Sir Henry, a candidate for the mayoralty, ii, 490; appointed mayor by Charles II, 504.
Tunstal, Cuthbert, Bishop of London, i, 372, 380.
Turin, the siege of, ii, 624.
Turk, Andrew, i, 195.
Turke, Richard, sheriff, i, 439.
Turner, Samuel, mayor, iii, 86; hesitates to accede to petition for summoning a Common Hall, 88.
—— Sir William, mayor, insulted in the Temple, ii, 440; his election as sheriff, 470; ordered to attend every evening at Whitehall during last illness of Charles II, 505; M.P. for the City, 554.
Turnham Green, City forces despatched to join Essex at, ii, 176.
Twistleton, Colonel, iii, 186, 187, 188.
Twyford, Nicholas, opposes Brembre for the mayoralty, i, 227; elected mayor, 239.

INDEX.

Tyburn, City's water supply from, ii, 24.

Tyler, Wat, the peasant revolt under, i, 218; killed by Walworth, 219.

Tyrconnel, Rory O'Donnel, Earl of, flight of, ii, 28.

—— Richard Talbot, Earl of, appointed lord deputy in Ireland, ii, 516.

Tyrone, Hugh O'Neill, Earl of, insurrection of, i, 559; defeated by Mountjoy, 563; flight of, ii, 28.

Ulster, plantation of. *See* Irish Estate.

Uniformity, enforced by Henry VIII, i, 415; Elizabethan Act of, 486, 503; Act of (1662), ii, 400.

Union, Act of, iii, 240-241.

Urling, Simon, recorder, knighted, iii, 50.

Urswyk, Thomas, recorder, i, 298; opens the City's gates to Edward IV, 313; gallantly fights against the Kentish rebels, 316; made a baron of the exchequer, 317.

Ushant, naval combat off, iii, 172.

Usk or Husk, Thomas, brings charges against Northampton, i, 226; appointed under-sheriff, 232; executed, 238.

Utrecht, peace of, ii, 647.

Uvedale, Sir William, commissioned to receive City subscriptions, ii, 137.

Uxbridge, treaty of, ii, 213; the Parliamentary army moves to, 249.

Vane, Sir Henry, ii, 126, 200, 270.

Vanner, Henry, sheriff, return made by, with a view of enforcing knighthood, i, 240; committed to prison, 241, 242.

Vassall, Samuel, M.P. for the City, ii, 237.

Venables, William, mayor, vote of thanks to, for his services during a commercial crisis, iii, 325.

Venn, John, M.P. for the City, ii, 150, 155, 184, 311.

Venner's plot, ii, 387, 396.

Venour, William, grocer, a candidate for the mayoralty, i, 239.

Vere, John de, earl of, i, 380.

Vernon, Admiral, captures Porto Bello, iii, 44; presented with the freedom of the City, *id*.

—— Sir Thomas, M.P. for the City, ii, 554; again stands for the City, 599.

Vesci, Eustace de, insulted by King John, i, 77.

Villars, Marshal, at Malplaquet, ii, 630.

Villiers, Christopher, ii, 73.

Vintners of London, the, royal banquet to five kings in hall of, i, 200 n.; contribute to a gift of £500 to Edward III, 201; the Duke of Marlborough entertained in hall of, ii, 623; meetings of the livery in hall of, iii, 45, 46.

Virginia Company, the, formation of, ii, 46-56; subscriptions of livery companies to, 47; a new charter granted to, 48; re-constructed, 49; lotteries in aid of, 49-52; vagrant children supplied to, 52; disagreement with the City, 54.

Vyner, Sir Robert, commissioned to provide new regalia for coronation of Charles II, ii, 390; borrows the City's plate for the coronation of James II, 508.

—— Thomas, mayor, commissioned to supply plate for the Protector, ii, 347; knighted by Cromwell, 348.

Wade, General, endeavours to intercept the young Pretender, iii, 52.

Waithman, Robert, elected M.P. for the City, iii, 309; creates a disturbance in Common Hall, 311; a supporter of Queen Caroline,

318, 319; assaulted at Knightsbridge during his shrievalty, 323.
Wake, Thomas, Lord, incites the citizens to join the Earl of Lancaster in revolt, i, 164.
Wakefield, battle of, i, 304.
Walcheren Expedition, the, iii, 271; enquiry demanded by the City, 272.
Waldene, William, appointed commissioner to enquire into cases of treason, etc., in the City, i, 269.
Wale, William, alderman, ii, 370.
Wales, rebellion in, ii, 277.
Waleys, or Galeys, Henry le, mayor, i, 108; goes to Paris to confer with King Edward I, 116; sent to the king with a gift of money, 118; M.P. for the City, *id.*; re-elected mayor, 129; builds the nave of the Grey Friar's church, 402.
Walker, Rev. George, his stout defence of Londonderry, ii, 550.
Wallace, William, rising of the Scots under, i, 129; carried prisoner to London, 130; tried and executed, *id.*
Waller, Edmund, his plot, ii, 187.
—— Sir William, appointed to command of City forces, ii, 191; his jealousy of Essex, *id.*; horse to be raised in the City for, 193; his success at Cheriton, 199; endeavours to prevent Charles returning to Oxford, 211; resigns, 215; arrested, 295.
Walpole, Horace, his indignation at the Common Council presuming to speak on behalf of the City, iii, 71 n; his account of Townshend's election as mayor, 132–133, 134; his opinion as to the cause of the City's agitation over the Quebec Bill, 143.
—— Sir Robert, married to Sir John Shorter's grand-daughter, ii, 524; measures taken against directors of South Sea Company at instigation of, iii, 24; his influence with Queen Caroline, 34; tricks the Dissenters, 34–35; the City's opposition to his Excise Bill, 35–38; mobbed, 37; reluctantly declares war with Spain, 43; resigns, 48.
Walsingham, Sir Francis, secretary of state, i, 532, 535; urged to send ammunition to the fleet engaged with the Armada, 537.
Walter, Herbert, justiciar, orders the arrest of Longbeard, i, 71.
Walton, Colonel, ii, 360, 363.
Walworth, William, contributes to a loan to the king, i, 202; carries a letter from the City to the king, 206; appointed joint-treasurer of Parliamentary grant, 214; displaced, 215; favours the Duke of Lancaster, *id.*; subscribes to fund for winning back the nobility to the City, 217; kills Wat Tyler, 219; knighted, 220.
Walwyn, Humphry, grocer, his school at Colwall, co. Hereford, i, 353.
Warbeck or Warboys, Perkin, conspiracy of, i, 331–333; hanged at Tyburn, 334.
Ward, John, M.P. for the City, ii, 628; iii, 4; his coach stopped by soldiers on their way through the City, 16.
—— Sir Patience, mayor, ii, 419; presents addresses to Charles II for a parliament, 475; receives the thanks of the City, *id.*; convicted of perjury, 493; M.P. for the City, 538; again stands for the City but is unsuccessful, 553.
—— Thomas, his poem touching the origin of the Fire of London, ii, 419.
Warde, John, elected mayor, i, 327.
Wardle, Colonel, M.P. for Okehampton, charges the Duke of

INDEX. 561

York with scandalous conduct, iii, 270; the Freedom of the City voted to, *id.*
Wardmotes, Act of Common Council for regulating elections at (1692), ii, 566.
Wark Castle, attacked by Scots, i, 372.
Warne, John, burnt, i, 474.
Warner, John, alderman, sent commissioner to the parliamentary army, ii, 248; elected mayor, 267.
Warren, Sir Ralph, i, 395, 438.
Warwick, Ambrose, Earl of, commander of the garrison at Havre, *temp.* Elizabeth, i, 491.
—— Edward, Earl of, committed to the Tower, i, 328; impersonated by Lambert Simnel, *id.*; charged with a conspiracy to seize the Tower, 333; executed on Tower Hill, 334.
—— Guy, Earl of, i, 137.
—— John, Earl of. *See* Northumberland, Duke of.
—— Richard, Earl of, enters the City with Richard, Duke of York, i, 290; leaves Calais for London, 294; drawn into an affray at Westminster, 295; returns to Calais, *id.*; joins his father at Bloreheath, 296; attainted, *id.*; returns to England and marches to London, 298, 299; admitted into the City, 305; his disgust at the marriage of Edward IV, 309; flees to France, 310; returns and restores Henry VI, 311, 312; killed at Barnet, 314.
—— Robert, Earl of, ii, 200.
—— Thomas, Earl of, i, 234, 235; arrested, 244.
Water, City supply of, i, 416; ii, 18-24. *See also* New River, Tyburn, &c.
Water-bailiff of the City, dispute with the Crown touching office of, i, 406.

Waterloo, battle of, iii, 290.
Watling Street, i, 5, 11.
Watson, William, plots against James I, ii, 6.
Watts, Sir John, ii, 66.
Waynflete, William de, bishop of Winchester, chancellor, i, 293.
Weavers of London, their quarrel with the Goldsmiths, i, 154; Committee of Arrears at hall of, ii, 216; Fairfax seizes treasury at hall of, 295; offer to raise a regiment in support of the Crown, iii, 53; disapprove of a remonstrance of the livery, 93.
Wedmore, treaty of, i, 11.
Weld, Sir Humphrey, mayor, ii, 46, 48.
—— Sir John, restored to the office of town clerk, ii, 382.
Welles, John, mayor, i, 275.
—— Lord, i, 289.
Wellesley, Sir Arthur, afterwards Duke of Wellington, signs the convention of Cintra, iii, 269; ordered home, *id.*; an annuity to, opposed by the City, 274; presented with the freedom of the City and a sword of honour, 276; a gold box voted for victory at Salamanca, 286; entertained at the Guildhall, 288; becomes prime minister, 327; receives the thanks of the City for the Catholic Emancipation Bill, *id.*; resigns, 331; endeavours to form a ministry on resignation of Lord Grey, 342, 343; abstains from voting against the Reform Bill, 343.
Wengrave, John de, mayor, opposes City ordinances of 1319, i, 142.
West, Francis, Lieutenant Colonel, appointed lieutenant of the Tower, ii, 215, 279.
Westley, Robert, mayor, knighted, iii, 50.
Westminster, foundation of abbey by Seberht, i, 9; dedication of

OO

the same, 29; riots at, ii, 150, 152, 192, 254.

Westmoreland, Charles, Earl of, insurrection of, i, 515.

Weymouth, lord, ordered by the king to make enquiries touching the nature of a remonstrance, iii, 94–96.

Wheble, John, arrested for printing parliamentary debates, iii, 108; discharged by Wilkes, *id.*

Whetstone, Thomas, committed to Fleet prison, i, 468.

Whig, origin of the name, ii, 460.

White, Sir Thomas merchant taylor, founder of St. John's College, Oxford, and of schools at Reading and Bristol, i. 353; elected mayor, 459; particulars of, 459 n.; defends himself before the Star Chamber, 466.

White Friars of London, their house suppressed, i, 398.

Whitelock, Sir Bulstrode, warns the Common Council of Monk's intention to restore the king, ii, 357.

Whitington, Richard, subscribes to a fund for winning back the nobility to the City, i, 217; appointed mayor by Richard II, 244; ordered to make valuation of property in the City, 251; return of rental of, 252; elected mayor for the third time, *id.*; his benefactions. 253; gives a library to the Grey Friars, 402.

Whitmore, Sir George, alderman, imprisoned in Crosby House, ii, 173; refuses to pay parliamentary tax for maintenance of the army, 181.

Whitworth, Lord, ambassador to France, leaves Paris, iii, 251.

Wilkes, John, M.P. for Aylesbury, criticises the king's speech, iii, 71; supported by Beckford, *id.*; No. 45 of his *North Briton*, 73–75;

committed to the Tower, 74; discharged, *id.*; recovers damages for seizure of papers, *id.*; his *Essay on Woman*, 77; expelled the House, 78; sentence of outlawry pronounced against, *id.*; communicates with the Duke of Grafton, 80; elected M.P. for Middlesex, 81; committed to the king's bench, *id.*; judgment on his outlawry postponed, 83; sentence pronounced in respect of his publishing the *North Briton* and *Essay on Woman*, *id.*; elected alderman of Farringdon Without, 84; counsel's opinion as to his being admitted alderman, 85; again expelled the House, 86; re-elected four times for Middlesex, *id.*; obtains his liberty, 100; admitted alderman, *id.*; attacks Trecothick for backing press warrants, 106; discharges printers arrested for printing parliamentary debates, *id.*; refuses three times to obey order to appear at the bar of the House of Commons, 118; elected sheriff, 120; his conduct during his shrievalty, 122–124; quarrels with his friends, 124; Horne's letter congratulating him on his election, *id.*; receives offer of support from *Junius*, 125; his reply, 126; at loggerheads with Sawbridge and Townshend, 128; gift of plate to, *id.*; returned at the head of the poll for the mayoralty, but rejected by the aldermen, 132-134; his supporters raise a riot at Guildhall, 134; the drafting of the remonstrance of the livery (1773) ascribed to, 136; again claims his seat as member for Middlesex, 137; again stands for the mayoralty, 140, 141; elected mayor, 143; again returned M.P. for Middlesex, and allowed to take his seat, 144; reaches his zenith,

145; his dispute with the Court of Aldermen over an election, 146-149; his gentlemanly behaviour at Court, 152; his friendship with Dr. Johnson, 152 n., 164-165; his letter to Lord Hertford, 153, 154; vote of thanks of the livery to, 155; refuses to assist in the ceremony of proclaiming war with America, 158; supports Oliver's motion in the House re war with America, 161; expenses of his mayoralty, 161-163; becomes a candidate for the chamberlainship, 163; his answer to creditors, 164; motion in Common Council to grant an annuity to, negatived, *id.*; elected chamberlain, *id.*; his speech in the House against press warrants, 166; blames Kennet and Bull for their conduct during Gordon riots, 190.

Willes, chief justice, iii, 53.

William I, claims the crown, i, 30; his victory at Hastings, *id.*; marches to London, 31; sets fire to Southwark, 32; negotiates with the City, *id.*; the City submits, 33; his charters to London, 33-36; his strong government, 37; his death, 38.

William I, Prince of Orange, the citizens of London render assistance to, i, 505; assassinated, 529.

William II (Rufus), his accession, i, 38; his death, 39.

William, Prince of Orange, afterwards William III, entertained by the City, ii, 443; invited to England, 529; lands, 533; declaration in favour of, drawn up by the lords at the Guildhall, 535; City address to, 536; enters London, *id.*; summons a representative assembly, 537; asks the City for a loan, 538; proclaimed king, 539; coronation of, 540; entertained at Guildhall, 551; picture of, at Guildhall, defaced, 552; goes to Ireland, 558; returns, 561; goes to Holland, 562, 567; attends the lord mayor's banquet, 570; sets out for the continent, 571; returns, 573; City address to, on death of Queen, 587; City address to, on discovery of the Assassination plot, 599; reception of, by the City on return from Flanders, 604-606; City address to, on death of James II, 607; his death, 609.

William IV, accession of, iii, 328; his visit to the City postponed for fear of riot, 329-330.

Williams, Sir Richard, portion of suppressed priory of St. Helen, Bishopsgate, granted to, i, 401.

Willimot, Robert, alderman, knighted, iii, 50.

Wills, Edward, sheriff, knighted, ii, 598.

Wilson, Rowland, alderman, placed on the commission for the king's trial, ii, 301; member of council of state, 303.

Winchester, its early rivalry with London, i, 10; the same weights and measures used in, as in London, *id.*; the mint at, 16; Henry I elected king at, 39; supports Stephen, 46; becomes the head-quarters of the Empress Matilda, *id.*; Synod held at, 48; reduced by Queen Matilda, 52; destroyed by fire, 55; Richard I crowned at, 69.

—— Bishop of, question of his precedency at the Guildhall, i, 257.

—— Bishops of. *See* Beaufort; Blois; Gardiner; Stratford; Wykeham.

—— William Paulet, Marquis of, his mansion house on the site of the Augustinian Friars, i, 399.

Windsor, Sir William de, husband of Alice Perers, i, 208.

Wine, charter of Edward IV granting office of gauger of, i, 307-308;

abolition of coal and wine dues, iii, 349.
Winnington, Sir Francis, solicitor-general, his opinion on the question of the aldermanic veto, ii, 454.
Wiseman, Thomas, ii, 151.
Withers, Sir William, M.P. for the City, ii, 607, 622n, 628, 638; candidate for aldermanry, 640, 642, 644.
Wollaston, Sir John, a candidate for the mayoralty, ii, 169; accused of making a disturbance in the Common Hall, 316.
Wolman, Benedict, engaged in the Trumpington conspiracy, i, 248.
Wolsey, Cardinal, brings about marriage of Mary, sister of Henry VIII, with the King of France, i, 347; charges against the City by, 354; advises the City touching payment of subsidy, 355; mediates between the king and City, 358, 359; calls upon the livery companies to surrender their plate towards a loan to the king, 368; letter of thanks to the City from, 369; applies for another loan, 369, 370; his dispute with the Speaker, 371; his assistance again invited by the City, *id*; his disappointment at not being elected pope, 373; an "amicable loan" suggested by, 374–376; consulted by Court of Aldermen touching discharge of Wythypol, elected alderman, 377; presides at proceedings in the divorce case of Catherine of Aragon, 380; the fall of, 380. 381–382.
Wood, Matthew, mayor, endeavours to rid the streets of foreign seamen, iii, 297–299; his report to the Court of Aldermen of the riot in Spa Fields, 299–305; elected M.P. for the City, 309; attends Queen Caroline at Brandenburgh House, 318, 319.

Woodstock, Thomas of. *See* Gloucester, Thomas, Duke of.
Woodville, Elizabeth, widow of Sir John Grey, welcomed by the citizens, i, 307; married to Edward IV, 309; takes sanctuary at Westminster, 312, 320.
Wool, a new tax on, i, 172, 173; the king's monopoly of, 181.
Wooldridge, John Thomas, admitted alderman of Bridge Ward, iii, 149.
Woolfe, Sir Joseph, alderman of Broad Street Ward, ii, 640.
Worcester, battle of, ii, 341.
—— Bishop of. *See* Latimer.
—— John, Earl of, sent to the City to raise a loan, i, 308; beheaded, 312.
Wotton, Nicholas, elected mayor, i, 259.
Wren, Sir Christopher, appointed to make a survey of the City after the Fire, ii, 428; to prepare Westminster hall for trial of Sacheverell, 634.
Wright, Edmund, mayor, ii, 130, 145.
Wriothesley, Thomas, Lord, appointed chancellor, i, 408; City gift to, 409.
Wyatt, Sir Thomas, his rebellion, i, 461, 462, 464; lodged in the Tower and executed, 465; report of an attempt to extort confession from, 466.
Wycliffe, John, i, 221, 248.
Wykeham, William de, Bishop of Winchester, restored to his temporalities, i, 210.
Wythypol, Paul, merchant-taylor, his election as Alderman, i, 377–379; particulars of, 377n.; refuses to accept aldermanry and is committed to Newgate, 378; M.P. for the City, 381.

Yelverton, Sir Henry, attorney-general, ii, 88.

INDEX. 565

Yong, Thomas, saddler, convicted of perjury, i, 343.

Yonge, Sir George, secretary at war, his correspondence with the lord mayor touching removal of the Bank guard, iii, 217, 218.

York, City of, letter of sympathy from, after the Great Fire, ii, 420.

York, Archbishop of. *See* Nevill; Neville.

—— Edward, Duke of, his precedence at the Guildhall, i, 257, 258.

—— Frederick, Duke of, thanks the City for gift of clothing, &c., to the troops in Flanders, iii, 222–223; resigns his command, 223; accused of scandalous conduct, 270.

—— Sir John, sheriff, Earl of Warwick takes up his residence in house of, i, 435; meetings of the lords at his house, 436, 440; entertains Edward VI, 439.

York, Richard, Duke of, his rivalry with Duke of Somerset, i, 286, 287; denied entrance to the City, 287; swears allegiance to Henry VI in St. Paul's, 288; takes up quarters in the City, 290; nominated Protector, 291; the mayor and aldermen wait upon, *id.*; wins the battle of St. Alban's, *id.*; again nominated Protector on the king's relapse, *id.*; seeks refuge in Ireland, 296; attainted, *id.*; raises money in the City, 302; claims the crown, 303; killed at Wakefield, 304.

—— —— Duke of, son of Edward IV, lodged in the Tower, i, 320; impersonated by Perkin Warbeck, 331.

Ypre, John de, i, 209.

Zouche, Lord, his efforts to obtain Northampton's release, i, 230, 231.

ERRATA.

Vol. I.

Page 48, last line, for *them* read *him*.
—— 107, line 4, for *Fitz-Thomas* read *Fitz-Thedmar*.
—— 170, line 12, for *1339* read *1330*.
—— 183, line 4, for *Winchester* read *Winchelsea*.
—— 223, lines 9 and 22, for *Aldermancy* read *Aldermanry*.
—— 228, line 10, for *Roby* read *Raby*.
—— 249, line 12, for *1401* read *1414*.
—— 264, line 13, for *25,000* read *2,500*.
—— —— line 20, for *Pointoise* read *Pontoise*.
—— —— note 3, for *fo. 1,222* read *fo. 122*.
—— 293, note 3, for *fo. 288 b* read *fo. 292*.
—— 310, note 3, for *fo. 128* read *fo. 182*.
—— 323, marginal note, for *1433* read *1483*.
—— 339, line 13, for *25 Dec.* read *28 Dec.*
—— 365, lines 15, 16, for *of Euphues fame*, read *the Grammarian*.
—— 391, note 2, for *1825* read *1525*.
—— 443, line 18, for *1850* read *1550*.
—— 487, line 15, for *followed* read *preceded*.
—— —— note 3, for *Repertory 4* read *Repertory 14*.

Vol. II.

Page 220, marginal note, for *arms* read *army*.
—— 312, line 9, for *resolved* read *was moved*.
—— 398, line 21, for *begining* read *beginning*.
—— 401, line 25, for *latter* read *later*.
—— 485, note 1, for *27* read *87*.
—— 528 and 532, marginal notes, for *Charles* read *James*.

www.ingramcontent.com/pod-product-compliance
Lightning Source LLC
Chambersburg PA
CBHW031937290426
44108CB00011B/586